TRANSFORMING THE NATION

# Transforming The Nation

## Canada and Brian Mulroney

Edited by Raymond B. Blake

McGill-Queen's University Press
Montreal & Kingston · London · Ithaca

ISBN 978-0-7735-3214-4 (cloth)
ISBN 978-0-7735-3215-1 (paper)

Legal deposit third quarter 2007
Bibliothèque nationale du Québec

Printed in Canada on acid-free paper that is 100% ancient forest free (100% post-consumer recycled), processed chlorine free.

McGill-Queen's University Press acknowledges the support of the Canada Council for the Arts for our publishing program. We also acknowledge the financial support of the Government of Canada through the Book Publishing Industry Development Program (BPIDP) for our publishing activities.

---

**Library and Archives Canada Cataloguing in Publication**

Transforming the nation : Canada and Prime Minister Brian Mulroney / edited by Raymond B. Blake.

Includes bibliographical references and index.
ISBN 978-0-7735-3214-4 (bnd)
ISBN 978-0-7735-3215-1 (pbk)

1. Mulroney, Brian, 1939–. 2. Canada–Politics and government – 1984–1993. 3. Canada – History – 1963–. I. Blake, Raymond B. (Raymond Benjamin)

FC630.T73 2007 971.064'7 C2007-902376-2

---

Typeset in New Baskerville 10/12
by Infoscan Collette, Quebec City

*For Wanda*
*and our two sons,*
*Robert Alexander Benjamin Blake*
*and*
*Benedict David Anderson Blake,*
*who, we hope,*
*will always take an interest in our nation's affairs*

# Contents

# Contributors

FRANCES ABELE is a professor in the School of Public Administration at Carleton University. One of several leading northern researchers to participate in a newly announced research project on the social economy in the north, she is the author of numerous articles and co-author, with Caroline Dittburner and Katherine Graham, of *Soliloquy and Dialogue: The Evolution of Public Policy Discourse on Aboriginal Issues* (1996).

MICHAEL D. BEHIELS is a professor of Canadian history and the University Research Chair in Federalism and Constitutional Studies at the University of Ottawa. He is the author of several books, including *La Francophonie canadienne, renouveau constitutionel et gouvernance scolaire* (2005) and *The Meech Lake Primer: Conflicting Views of the 1987 Constitutional Accord* (1989).

RAYMOND B. BLAKE is a professor of history at the University of Regina and formerly the director of the Saskatchewan Institute of Public Policy. He has authored and edited several books, including *Canadians at Last: Canada Integrates Newfoundland as a Province* and *Social Fabric or Patchwork Quilt: The Development of Social Policy in Canada.* He has just completed a book on the history of family allowances in Canada.

P.E. BRYDEN is an associate professor in the History Department at the University of Victoria. She is the author of *Planners and Politicians: Liberal Politics and Social Policy, 1957–1968,* and is currently completing a book on Ontario's relations with Ottawa after the Second World War.

PAUL L.A.H. CHARTRAND is a professor in the College of Law at the University of Saskatchewan. A member of the Indigenous Bar Association of Canada, and "Indigenous Peoples' Counsel," he teaches, researches, and publishes primarily in the fields of Aboriginal law and policy. His public-service record includes serving as commissioner on the Royal Commission on Aboriginal Peoples and on Manitoba's Aboriginal Justice Implementation Commission, and as a founding director of the Aboriginal Healing Foundation.

GINA COSENTINO is a PHD candidate and instructor in the Department of Political Science at the University of Toronto. Her dissertation is a comparative study of the participation of Indigenous women in constitutional reform in Canada and New Zealand and at the United Nations. She is currently the special adviser to the president of the Métis National Council on International Issues and is assisting the efforts of the Global International Caucus related to the adoption of the United Nations Declaration on the Rights of Indigenous People.

JOHN C. CROSBIE is one of Canada's best-known public figures, having enjoyed success in municipal, provincial, and federal politics. He was first elected to the House of Commons in 1976 as the member for St John's West and served as minister of finance in the government of Joe Clark. He ran for the leadership of the Progressive Conservatives in 1984 and held several portfolios in the Mulroney government, including international trade. His autobiography, *No Holds Barred*, was published in 1997.

MICHAEL HART is the Simon Reisman Professor of Trade Policy in the Norman Paterson School of International Affairs and Distinguished Fellow of the Centre for Trade Policy and Law (CTPL) at Carleton University. He is a former official in Canada's Department of Foreign Affairs and International Trade, where he specialized in trade policy and trade negotiations, and he provided strategic advice in the negotiations leading to the Canada-U.S. Free Trade Agreement and the North American Free Trade Agreement. He is the author, editor, and co-editor of more than a dozen books and numerous articles and essays in books on international-trade issues.

L. IAN MACDONALD is a political columnist and broadcaster and editor of *Policy Options*, the magazine of the Institute for Research on Public Policy. He is the author of *From Bourassa to Bourassa: Wilderness to Restoration* and *Mulroney: The Making of the Prime Minister*, and co-author of the recent best-seller *Leo: A Life. The Autobiography of Leo Kolber* (2003). He was also a speech-writer for Prime Minister Brian Mulroney.

SEAN M. MALONEY served in Germany as the historian for the 4th Canadian Mechanized Brigade, the Canadian Army's contribution to NATO during the Cold War. He is the author of several books, including *Canada and UN*

*Peacekeeping: Cold War by Other Means 1945–1970* (2002), *Chances for Peace: The Canadians and UNPROFOR 1992–1995* (2002), *Enduring the Freedom: A Rogue Historian Visits Afghanistan* (2005), and the forthcoming *Operation KINETIC: The Canadians in Kosovo 1999–2000*. He currently teaches in the RMC War Studies Programme and is a senior research fellow at the Queen's Centre for International Relations.

JUDITH MAXWELL was the founding president of Canadian Policy Research Networks (CPRN) and is now a CPRN research fellow. In 1985 she was named chair of the Economic Council of Canada, a post she held until the council was disbanded in 1992. She has extensive experience in both public- and private-sector think tanks and has established a national reputation as an expert on social and economic policy choices and how they intersect within the Canadian experience. She is a member of the Order of Canada and a director of BCE Inc.

ELIZABETH MAY is the leader of the Green Party of Canada. Formerly the executive director of Sierra Club of Canada, she has been an environmental activist since she was a teenager. For a brief period, she was an environmental adviser to the federal minister of the environment in the Mulroney government, Tom McMillan, but she resigned when the department granted permits to the Saskatchewan government to build the Rafferty and Alameda dams.

NELSON MICHAUD is associate professor of political science and international relations and chair of the Groupe d'études, de recherche et de formation internationales (Gerfi) and of the Labboratoire d'études sur les politiques publiques et la mondialisation at the École nationale d'administration publique. He has published in several journals, including the *Canadian Journal of Political Science* and *International Journal*, and he co-edited with Kim Richard Nossal *Diplomatic Departures: The Conservative Era in Canadian Foreign Policy 1984–1993* (2001).

KIM RICHARD NOSSAL is a professor in and the head of the Department of Political Studies, Queen's University, Kingston, Ontario. He and Nelson Michaud have edited *Diplomatic Departures: The Conservative Era in Canadian Foreign Policy, 1984–1993* (2001).

IAN PEACH is the director of the Saskatchewan Institute of Public Policy at the University of Regina. He was the director of constitutional relations in the Department of Intergovernmental and Aboriginal Affairs and a senior policy adviser in the Cabinet Planning Unit of Executive Council with the government of Saskatchewan. He has been involved in numerous intergovernmental negotiations, including the Charlottetown Accord, the Social Union Framework Agreement, First Nation self-government agreements, and the Canada-Saskatchewan Northern Development Accord.

JAMES M. PITSULA is a professor of history at the University of Regina and the author of *As One Who Serves: The Making of the University of Regina*, published by McGill-Queen's University Press in 2006. He is currently working on a book about Regina and the First World War.

ANN PORTER is assistant professor in the Department of Political Science at York University. Her research interests are focused, from a comparative perspective, on Canadian welfare-state restructuring, income security, women and public policy, feminism, and political economy. She recently published *Gendered States: Women, Unemployment Insurance and the Political Economy of the Welfare State in Canada* (2003).

MICHAEL J. PRINCE is the Lansdowne Professor of Social Policy at the University of Victoria. He is one of Canada's leading scholars on social policy and has written numerous articles and books, including, with James Rice, *Changing Politics of Canadian Social Policy* (2000).

BOB RAE was the premier of Ontario between 1990 and 1995. He is now a partner at the Goodmans law firm in Toronto, chairman of the Institute for Research on Public Policy, and a fellow of the Forum of Federations. He consults widely on issues of public policy.

JAMES J. RICE is professor emeritus, School of Social Work, McMaster University. He is the co-author, with Michael Prince, of *Changing Politics of Canadian Social Policy* (2000).

J. FRANK STRAIN is professor and head of the Department of Economics and holder of the Edgar and Dorothy Davidson Chair in Canadian Studies at Mount Allison University. His research focuses on Canadian public policy, economic history, and the economics of growth and technological change.

CHRISTOPHER WADDELL is the associate director of Carleton University's School of Journalism and Communication in Ottawa and holds the school's Carty Chair in Business and Financial Journalism. He was the parliamentary bureau chief in Ottawa for CBC Television News, he has won two National Newspaper Awards for business reporting, and programs he supervised at CBC Television won six Gemini awards for television excellence.

ROBERT WARDHAUGH is an assistant professor of history at the University of Western Ontario. He is a political and regional historian of Canada whose research interests include federalism, federal-provincial relations, and the history of the prairie west. He is author of *Mackenzie King and the Prairie West* (2000).

# Acknowledgments

It was nearly a quarter-century ago that Brian Mulroney, promising change and a new approach to governing, became Canada's eighteenth prime minister. In the election of September 1984, Canadians had sent Mulroney and 210 other Progressive Conservatives to Ottawa, but few imagined that their nation would change so rapidly and so much under the new government. Soon, however, many Canadians began having second thoughts, both about Mulroney's policies and about the man himself; opposition to the government's agenda became widespread, and increasingly smaller numbers of people were prepared to embrace Mulroney as a great visionary or even a great leader. In fact, when he left office in early 1993, he was one of the most unpopular prime ministers in Canadian history, and his government's programs were of far less interest to the public than his style of governing and rumours of wrongdoing both by Mulroney himself and by those around him. Even books that offered no evidence of any corruption were eagerly bought and presumably read by Canadians. Only now are we starting to investigate the substantive issues of public policy during the Mulroney era.

This book began with a discussion with Len Husband during the meetings of the Canadian Historical Association in Halifax in 2003. He encouraged me to pursue the project and offered sage advice early on. Since then, I have benefited from the advice of Jack Granatstein and Michael Davis. At McGill-Queens University Press, Philip Cercone and Joan McGilvray have been extremely helpful and moved expeditiously on this project, while Curtis Fahey has proven himself yet again to be an excellent editor, helping to save all this volume's contributors from themselves with his meticulous editorial assistance. Aimée Belmore took valuable time from her studies to prepare an excellent index.

I wish to acknowledge the generous financial support of the Humanities Research Institute at the University of Regina, and especially Professor

Nicholas Ruddick, the institute's director. Marilyn Bickford of the History Department at Regina ably assisted with preparing the manuscript for submission. Of course, the people who eagerly accepted my invitation to participate in this project made the book possible and their contributions to the volume attests to the importance of studying and understanding Prime Minister Brian Mulroney and Canada from 1984 to 1993.

As is usually the case, a book always takes more time than one either suspects or hopes, even a book where other scholars are willing to share their research and their insights. I was most fortunate to have the love and support of a wonderful family, though, I suppose, if I had spent less time at the local skating rinks watching Robert and Ben playing hockey or outside in the freezing Saskatchewan winters protecting the net for the boys and their friends, especially Daniel, we might have had this book sooner. But, as those who are researching and studying the policies of Brian Mulroney know, distance from the period is not a bad thing.

Raymond Blake
University of Regina
February 2007

# Foreword

JUDITH MAXWELL

In the 1984 election campaign, Brian Mulroney established four objectives for his leadership: unity and national reconciliation, economic renewal, social justice, and constructive internationalism. Canadians voted enthusiastically for his promise of peace and prosperity that year, re-elected Mulroney and his government in 1988, and then threw them unceremoniously out of power in 1993. Such is the sobering fate of Canadian prime ministers, as Raymond Blake explains in his Introduction to this volume assessing the Mulroney era.

The authors in this volume were all themselves direct witnesses – as politicians, as scholars, as journalists, as citizens – and their stories make it clear that, while the context may differ from one decade to the next, Canadians can never escape the trade-offs and dilemmas imposed by their geo-political space. Since 1993, the country has been transformed by the combined pressures of globalization, technology, immigration, urbanization, and environmental constraints. Yet, thirteen years after Mulroney's formal departure from public affairs, he still has influence as an adviser to Prime Minister Stephen Harper.

It would be interesting to listen in on these conversations, if only because the policy challenges facing the Conservative government elected in January 2006 look remarkably similar. If the issues are the same, however, it is clear that the new Conservative Party will not always choose the same responses as Mulroney's Progressive Conservatives.

One of the singular achievements of the Mulroney government was the Canada-U.S. Free Trade Agreement. It opened the door to a rapid expansion of trade between the two countries, but it has not by any means made it easier for Canadians to live next door to their vibrant neighbour. Today's tensions arise from the U.S. plan to require passports for all border crossings, worries about the security of the border in a time of terrorism, and the perennial fight about U.S. trade barriers for Canadian softwood lumber.

Mulroney grappled with softwood lumber without much success. The Harper government has reached an agreement with the Americans but critics argue that the deal is unlikely to bring an end to the U.S. industry's resistance to Canadian imports.

A second Mulroney breakthrough was the introduction of the Goods and Services Tax (GST) to replace the old, inefficient Manufacturers' Sales Tax. The GST is regarded by tax economists as the most efficient way to levy taxes and it generates a lot of revenue. But Stephen Harper, an economist himself, has made a break with his mentor. He was quick to fulfil his promise to reduce the tax from 7 to 6 per cent. This goes against the advice of all the experts, like the C.D. Howe Institute and the Institute for Competitiveness and Productivity, who argue that Canada should make greater use of the GST in order to make room for more cuts in business and personal income taxes. It seems that no one but economists and tax collectors likes the GST. It is as hard to sell politically today as it was in the 1980s.

Mulroney and Harper seem to be more aligned on the question of childcare. Mulroney abandoned his promise to expand the system. Harper has cancelled the recent federal-provincial agreements to build a more comprehensive system, and plans to pass the responsibility over to employers and unions. This transfer to the private sector is reminiscent of the Mulroney government's decision to get out of social housing and make room for the private sector – which steadfastly refused to become involved in such an unprofitable enterprise, leading directly to the housing crisis in many cities today.

Early in 2006, Mulroney was honoured for his Green Plan – the first national commitment to reduce Canada's excessive use of resources and clean up the environment. While subsequent Liberal governments grappled with the issue, they did not make much progress. Harper has scrapped the Green Plan and announced that Canada cannot meet its Kyoto commitments to reduce greenhouse-gas emissions. And the country now waits to see whether this Conservative government can bite the environmental bullet. Will Canadians someday honour Stephen Harper as a green prime minister?

The Mulroney government was the first to challenge the post-war consensus on the role of the state. It focused primarily on the relationship of the state to the economy. The big decisions were to privatize crown corporations and to introduce "new public management" ideas to the federal public service. The Conservative finance minister also worked hard to build national awareness of the need to put the government's fiscal house in order. The Mulroney approach raised many alarms at the time, but it looks modest in retrospect as we consider the major cuts in spending and taxes and the changes in regulatory systems introduced by the Liberals and by provincial governments in the 1990s. Harper seems destined to continue realigning government, as he redirects spending to the defence budget and cuts back on supports for civil society.

Mulroney also invested an enormous amount of his own time and political capital in building a renewed national consensus. He came close, but not close enough. Harper has started off with high hopes as well – planning to make incremental changes in the Senate and promising the provinces that he will correct the so-called "fiscal imbalance." But he, too, has run into heavy weather on national reconciliation. The provinces are deeply divided on proposed changes to equalization, and Finance Minister Jim Flaherty is now trying to shift the focus away from "fiscal imbalance." So the prospects are not good for a better working relationship with the provinces.

One of the messages in this book is just how difficult it is to govern this country. The structural changes in the economy, in society, and in world politics have diminished the federal government's power base. Decision making has to take account of vigorous markets, independent-minded provinces, international partners, and a much more informed, diverse, and ornery citizenry.

It seems that it will take a lot to convince this more educated and pluralistic citizenry that they can trust anyone to provide the kind of leadership they are seeking. The voters threw the Mulroney government unceremoniously out of office in 1993. By 2006, they were deeply distrustful of the Liberals, so they gave the new Conservative Party under Stephen Harper a grudging minority.

All the more reason to invest a bit of time with the authors contributing to this book – to revisit the battles of the past, to reconsider the trade-offs that were made and the promises kept and broken. Whether you are an aspiring politician or an engaged Canadian, you can rely on the distinguished authors in this book to offer an informative guide to public policy in Canada.

TRANSFORMING THE NATION

# Introduction

RAYMOND B. BLAKE

The Mulroney era does not yield easily to simple analysis. As a politician, Brian Mulroney rode a wave of immense popular support in 1984 to the largest number of seats ever given to a prime minister in Canadian history. He was the first prime minister in thirty-five years to win re-election with consecutive majorities, and the first Conservative leader to do so in more than a century. And his was a busy government that moved Canada in a new direction. His decisions on a variety of public-policy issues, ranging from free trade with the United States to social-security reform and Canada's north, represented a break with the past. He was severely criticized for many of his policies and new initiatives, but much of the legislation he put in place was not only embraced but also expanded upon by the Liberal government that succeeded him in Ottawa. Furthermore, the Liberals won three consecutive majority governments by following the direction that he had largely established. Yet Mulroney left office with the lowest approval rating of any Canadian prime minister. In the first election following his departure from Canadian politics, his Progressive Conservatives were utterly ruined. They managed to hold only 2 of the 211 seats that Mulroney had won in September 1984. Still, Mulroney transformed Canada. The nation was quite a different place for his years at the helm.

Brian Mulroney presided over one of the most turbulent and challenging eras in Canada's history. He governed at a time of considerable change and uncertainty – a period that, according to some, witnessed a revolution in Canadian society, politics, and attitudes.[1] As the events after 1993 have shown, however, there was no revolution in politics, or, if there was, it was short-lived, since Canadians were quite content to live in a virtual one-party state for the following decade with hardly a complaint. Even so, the Mulroney era was, indeed, a period of uncertainty and change if not of revolution. Mulroney and his government contributed to that uncertainty in their desire to be transformative. In many ways, the final decades of the

Brian Mulroney addresses the House of Commons for the last time as prime minister in February 1993. Library and Archives Canada 12-896-26, negative number e007140479.

twentieth century in Canada were not unlike those of the late nineteenth. It was a time when Canadians saw profound change in their own country. They were not accustomed to such change and they certainly were not comfortable with it. Strong protest movements, not witnessed for nearly a century, emerged on the national stage. Language and minority issues came to the fore just as they had at the end of the nineteenth century. Aboriginal militancy reached a level not seen since the days of Louis Riel. Regional discontent threatened the very fabric of the nation. The west again became the region of greatest disaffection, even if it was Quebec that renewed its threat of separation.

Moreover, Canada was mired in a prolonged recession. The industrial heartland in central Canada struggled as a large number of factories closed. The traditional resource economies were threatened. The fish disappeared from the waters off the east and west coasts. Commodity prices for much of the resource sector collapsed, and farmers worried about their survival. The period saw the dismantling of the National Policy, put in place more than a century ago, as Canada turned to free trade with the United States for the first time since the 1860s. Universality in social programs came to an end, and many publicly owned corporations, such as Air Canada, were sold to private investors. The CBC and a number of other cultural symbols endured deep and lasting cuts. There were massive reductions in the federal public service, and forty-six government programs and agencies were abolished, including the Economic Council of Canada and the Social Council of Canada. The federal government devolved powers to the provinces and promised self-government to Aboriginal peoples; both these policies unsettled many Canadians accustomed to a strong central government in Ottawa. Internationally, the heating up of the Cold War put additional stress on Canada's military and defence capacity, which had had been reduced considerably during the Trudeau years. The period also witnessed the collapse of the Soviet Union and the crumbling of communism. Canada had its first experience with international terrorism when an Air India flight was blown out of the sky after departing Vancouver. Canadians became uncertain of who they were and where they were heading as a nation. The country was in a foul mood, and many wondered if Canada would survive. At the end of the 1980s, for instance, nearly 50 per cent of Canadians did not think that their country would stay together long enough to see the new millennium in 2000.

That anxiety was just starting to become apparent in the federal election campaign in the fall of 1984, when most Canadians got their first real look at Mulroney. They liked what they saw. He was a refreshing change from the unpopular and tired Trudeau Liberals, then led by the lacklustre John Turner, who, though no Trudeauite, continued to be dogged by Trudeau's patronage appointments. The Progressive Conservatives campaigned in 1984 on the promise of change, and Canadians responded enthusiastically to that pledge. The once-mighty Liberals were reduced to forty seats, thirty-one of which were in Ontario and Quebec, and some commentators were even predicting the total demise of the Liberal Party in Canada – as had occurred in England.

Mulroney came to office believing that Canada was not living up to its potential and that his overwhelming support at the polls represented a clear mandate for change, not only in public policies but in the whole approach to governing Canada. He had achieved the rare feat of wining 50 per cent of the popular vote in the 1984 election, and it was clear in that campaign that he loved every minute of it, as Christopher Waddell shows in his contribution to this book. Mulroney held his Conservatives together throughout the race – never an easy feat for a party so long accustomed to the opposition benches in Parliament. In fact, winning the campaign was perhaps the easiest task for him in 1984. Governing Canada at any time is wrought with challenges, but it was especially difficult in 1984, when Mulroney and his new government were faced with a huge deficit, a regionally fractious country, and discontent across the land.

Mulroney soon became the lightning rod for much of the discontent, and often with good reason. By 1984, Canadians had become used to large government and relative prosperity. During the Liberal era, which began with Mackenzie King's election in 1935 and continued, with two interruptions, until 1984 (the interruptions, under Progressive Conservatives John Diefenbaker and especially Joe Clark, were brief), Canadians had come to believe that the main responsibility of their government "was to take care of our every need ... the unsigned but valid social contract we all took for granted at birth."[2] All of the national political parties subscribed to this philosophy. By the early 1980s, however, big government was coming under attack everywhere. Although he did not slay government – far from it, actually – Mulroney spoke the rhetoric of the New Right, talked about new directions, and promised dramatic change. In the end, while he did not always deliver as promised, he did alter the Canadian mindset. Under Prime Minister Mulroney, Canadians begin to think about issues in ways that they had not previously. But, in doing so, many of them grew uneasy.

What, then, were Mulroney's policy goals as prime minister? He had outlined four broad objectives during the 1984 election campaign, ones that he reiterated in the Conservatives' first throne speech on 5 November 1984: unity and national reconciliation, economic renewal, social justice, and constructive internationalism. Governor General Jeanne Sauvé noted in the throne speech that "for the first time in many years all regions of the country are represented in the national government." That represented a "magnificent opportunity," she said, "to build a renewed national consensus." By February 1993, when Mulroney announced that he was stepping down as prime minister and leader of the Conservatives, Canadians might have been hard pressed to give his government high marks in any of these policy areas.

With the failure of the Meech Lake Constitutional Accord in 1991, the rejection of the Charlottetown Accord in 1992, the rise of the Reform Party as the new voice of western disaffection, and the emergence of the separatist Bloc Québécois among disaffected Quebec Tories in the House of Commons, one could hardly applaud Mulroney and his government for reconciling the nation, though he did come close on three separate occasions. This, in itself, is a remarkable achievement, though, as the chapters by Ian Peach and Michael Behiels in this book show, there is still considerable debate about the quality of Mulroney's leadership on the subject of constitutional reform. The important question here, however, is whether the failure to achieve harmonious intergovernmental relations stemmed from Conservative policies or from structural factors. Acrimony has been commonplace in federal-provincial relations almost since Confederation. For his part, Mulroney adopted a traditional approach to dealings with the provinces; the ending of the National Energy Program and the offering of the Atlantic Accord to address western and eastern grievances, for instance, came as the result not of intergovernmental negotiations but of federal unilateralism, even if both regions readily and happily accepted the new federal initiatives. Furthermore, while Mulroney was able to secure (at least for a time) unanimity among the provinces on constitutional matters, as he did so he had to juggle a variety of other competing issues that often upset the intergovernmental apple cart. Many western Conservatives had been disappointed with Mulroney's support of francophone minority-language rights while he was leader of the opposition. It was Mulroney's decision to award a CF-18 aircraft fighter contract to Montreal rather than to Winnipeg-based Bristol-Aerospace in 1986, however, that confirmed for the west that its interests would always be secondary to those of Quebec. At the same time, even as Mulroney and the provinces were considering constitutional matters, Ontario, British Columbia, and Quebec were fighting with Ottawa over how best to resolve the problem of U.S. duties on softwood lumber. Mulroney discovered, as all other prime ministers have, that managing intergovernmental relations is an extraordinary balancing act where almost every issue is interconnected and no single one can be resolved without bringing others into play. Regional interests do matter in Canada and often make disagreement between Ottawa and the provinces inevitable. Mulroney showed us in the end that the deal brokering of executive federalism is no longer an option in Canada, and, as with Trudeau a decade earlier, his attempts to bring national reconciliation left the country further divided.

As for the economy, there has been much misconception about the philosophical underpinnings of Mulroney's policies in this area. Despite the numerous claims that Mulroney lived by the "ethic" of Margaret Thatcher and Ronald Reagan,[3] he had little interest in joining the Reagan and Thatcher revolutions even if he used some of the same rhetoric. He was committed to the principles of fairness and equity that governments in Canada had embraced since the Second World War. Mulroney believed that the state had an important role to play in Canada. His objective was to strike the proper balance between the state and the private sector so that both could perform their obligations effectively and efficiently. This was made difficult, however, by the debt-servicing costs that the Conservatives inherited from the Trudeau Liberals. By the end of its mandate, as Frank Strain shows below, the Mulroney government had, at least, achieved a primary budget surplus, and the size of the deficit was one-third of that inherited from the Trudeau years. Yet the national debt had ballooned to $423 billion by 1993, and the deficit was $34 billion – the amount required to service the national debt – in fiscal year 1992–93. Mulroney, then, failed to deliver on debt reduction and private-sector-inspired growth during his term even if he helped set the stage for subsequent strong economic growth in Canada after he left office. Strain argues that Mulroney's policies helped to make the dream of debt control possible for those that succeeded him. Still, Mulroney's commitment to fighting inflation through a monetary policy of high interest rates remains a questionable approach, even if he was responsible for the dramatic drop in the prime rate from 17.25 per cent in the early 1980s to a modest 8 per cent in 1993. In 1984, when the Conservatives formed the government, the national unemployment rate was 11.2 per cent. Though it dropped sharply to 7.5 per cent in 1989, it climbed back to above 11 per cent in the severe recession that hit just before Conservative rule came to an end.

Mulroney assured Canadians on the day he resigned that the difficult economic period had passed and the proverbial economic house was in order. Canadians, he said, should enjoy strong economic growth and prosperity for the rest of the 1990s and beyond. He was right on that score, but in 1993 most Canadians focused their attention on other fiscal matters, such as the hated Goods and Services Tax (GST), which the Liberals vowed to remove but never did. (Incidentally, the revenue generated by the GST contributed significantly to the government of Canada's ability to eliminate its deficits.) Despite the Liberals' criticisms of Mulroney's policies, they did not abandon many of his micro-economic initiatives. Indeed, the fruits of many of the Conservative policies were realized only after the Liberals were returned to power.

On the issue of social justice, Canadians again were hard pressed in 1993 to give the Mulroney government a high grade. It had abandoned its promise of a national day-care program, it had reduced transfers for social assistance to the provinces, it had attempted to partially de-index old age pensions and family allowances, it had pared unemployment-insurance benefits, and it had ended universality in family allowances. But, as various chapters in this book (particularly Frank Strain's) show, both income inequality and poverty declined in relative and absolute terms while Mulroney was prime minister, and Mulroney's social policies proved – in retrospect – to be kinder and gentler than those implemented by his successors, a point emphasized by Michael Prince and James Rice below. Mulroney cannot take full credit for the social-policy reform that occurred in this period, since the process had in fact begun in the Trudeau era, when the government introduced selectivity into a number of social programs. The Liberals, however, refused to tamper with universality in any of the programs that benefited the middle class, even though Trudeau and his officials knew since the late 1960s that universal programs such as family allowances had lost their effectiveness. It was Mulroney who implemented the major reforms that were long overdue, and nearly all of them were subsequently embraced enthusiastically – and even extended – by the Chrétien Liberals after 1993.

The social-policy regime under Mulroney moved from a more or less cooperative style in intergovernmental relations to one marked by a climate of contested and coercive federalism in which the federal government, often unilaterally, "off-loaded" programs to the provinces and withdrew support for provincial initiatives in health and social services. Even so, federal social spending increased more in real terms under the Mulroney Conservatives than it did under the Chrétien Liberals, who were more fixated on the deficit and the debt than the Conservatives. The increases under Mulroney were slower than those in the last term of the Trudeau Liberals, but, as a share of federal program spending, social expenditures increased slightly during the Mulroney era. Given the cuts made by Paul Martin after 1993, some of the social policies of the Mulroney era now appear less harsh, and others more progressive, than they did at the time. Constructing social policy in the Mulroney years was more complex and multilayered and textured than was often appreciated, since he held office at a time of shifting policy regimes in welfare states around the globe. Within the politics of fiscal restraint, Mulroney and his Conservatives pursued "a strategy of containment rather than neo-conservative dismantlement." Some might even be tempted to call him a "Red Tory" in light of the changes that came during the Liberal period that followed.

In international affairs and trade policy, Mulroney enjoyed considerably more success. There is no doubt that his policies here marked important points of departure from the Trudeau era. As Nelson Michaud and Kim Richard Nossal argue in their contribution, in the area of foreign policy, the Mulroney government set itself apart as one of the most activist governments in Canadian history. Mulroney's trade and economic policies were revolutionary, the prime example being, of course, free trade with the United States. Through the Free Trade Agreement (FTA), Mulroney – as Trudeau had done through the Charter of Rights and Freedoms – committed future governments to his policies and programs. However, this achievement – for good or ill, depending on one's perspective – has been eclipsed by issues of personality, as Canadians have heaped scorn on Mulroney's relationship first with President Ronald Reagan and then with President George Bush, Sr. Most Canadians still cannot forget the spectacle of Brian and Mila Mulroney singing *When Irish Eyes Are Smiling* with Ronald and Nancy Reagan at the Shamrock Summit in Quebec City in March 1985. In a nation where anti-Americanism has always played well, it was an image that disturbed many Canadians at the time and continues to "stick in their craw" some twenty years later.

All the same, Mulroney's record on foreign policy is substantial. Despite being portrayed as steadfastly pro-American, Mulroney refused to join with the United States on the Strategic Defense Initiative, or the "Star Wars" program, as it was popularly known. He opposed U.S. extraterritoriality in relation to Cuba and quarrelled with the Americans over Arctic sovereignty and acid rain. Moreover, during his term in office, Mulroney broke with the Liberal tradition and opened up the policy process on foreign affairs to the public at large as he attempted to re-establish Canada's presence on the international stage. He changed the tenor and substance of Canadian-American relations, transformed Canada's relationship with *la francophonie*, and made human rights an important issue (during the Ethiopian crisis, for instance, Mulroney involved Canada in partnerships with key non-governmental agencies and established special funding for famine relief). He often stood alone among the major international leaders in the fight against apartheid in South Africa – that was one of his most important accomplishments internationally. He also criticized China for its massacre of protestors in Tiananmen Square in June 1989 and questioned the principle of national sovereignty when leaders of nation-states committed unspeakable atrocities against their own people. All things considered, many of Mulroney's accomplishments in foreign policy, particularly those relating to good governance and human rights, provided the foundation for Lloyd Axworthy's "human security" agenda in the first Chrétien government. Here again, Mulroney's policy choices have proven enduring.

There were other achievements. Mulroney became prime minister as Canada evolved into a rights-conscious society, as a separatist-based nationalism escalated in Quebec, as the demands of women's groups entered virtually every aspect of government public policy, and as Aboriginal activism increased substantially. Gina Cosentino and Paul L.A.H. Chartrand claim that Mulroney inherited "a legacy of frustration" among a number of groups. During the Mulroney era, Aboriginal concerns were most obvious to Canadians at the time of the negotiation of the Charlottetown Accord and during the armed stand-off at Oka, but, in a larger sense, Mulroney understood the interconnectedness of Aboriginal land claims and self-government. Though many issues remain outstanding for Canada's Aboriginal peoples, it cannot be denied that Aboriginal politics and Aboriginal issues gained national attention during the Mulroney era. On this front, his efforts at national statecraft demonstrated conclusively that, in Canada, legitimate governance must allow space for Aboriginal self-government.

The Mulroney years brought significant – even historic – breakthroughs and steady progress for the north, ranging from the negotiation of new treaties, particularly the signing of the Nunavut Agreement, to a new approach to economic development and territorial participation in executive federalism. Under Mulroney's leadership, the government of Canada provided redress to Japanese Canadians for their internment and evacuation during the Second World War, and committed Canada to routing out those who committed Nazi war crimes. He made considerable progress with visible minorities, supporting linguistic constitutional equality for minorities across Canada and appointing the first Métis as lieutenant governor in Manitoba and the first person of colour as lieutenant governor in Ontario.

Still, Canadians were not impressed. It was a peculiar period in Canadian history, and well-known Canadian pollster Michael Adams noted in 1993 that "Canadians are in the mood to blame the weatherman for the weather." Linda Dyer of Baseline Market Research in Fredericton told the Ottawa *Citizen* that "Mulroney was despised because he brought [major changes] into Canada." Her research also found, she said, that "towards the end, people were blaming Mulroney if they put on mismatched socks in the morning."[4] The volatility of the time may have been best reflected in the changing attitude people had towards the Meech Lake Accord. It was welcomed when Mulroney and the premiers first announced it, and, in a rare moment of unanimity in Canadian politics, all of the party leaders in the House of Commons gave the constitutional pact their approval. Initially, the Canadian public supported it as well, but when the opponents of Meech raised objections, many Canadians changed their minds.

When Mulroney announced his resignation on 25 February 1993, after more than eight years as prime minister, he was reflective and philosophical but not contrite. Remarkably, the fact that a Gallup Poll had found that only 11 per cent of Canadians approved of his performance in the year before his departure[5] seems to have invigorated him. "It will now be up to history to place a definitive judgment on our efforts and our legacy."[6] A prime minister who was once the most popular politician in Canada now resorted to the mantra that he had to govern during a period of tumultuous change. His government, he said, never "side-stepped the most controversial questions of our time," and his "every effort was devoted to our common dream of a better, more united and more prosperous Canada ... I did not always succeed, but I always tried to do what would be right for Canada in the long-term – not what could be politically popular in the short term."[7] In this there was a large measure of truth. Mulroney had promised Canadians fundamental change, and he had delivered. His policy choices, whether one supported them or not, committed Canada to a new direction.

Most of the leading newspaper editorialists in Canada agreed that Mulroney had brought profound and fundamental change to Canada. The Montreal *Gazette*, for example, noted that "one does not usually expect a fundamentally practical politician to spend his energy and political capital on efforts that may not bear final fruit for a generation. But that is what Mulroney did. All honour to him."[8] The Ottawa *Citizen* was equally charitable, capturing the sentiments of many Canadians when it noted in 1993 that "Mulroney will go down in history as the prime minister who won the minds of Canadians but could never lay claim to their hearts."[9] Even the

New York *Times* editorialized that "regardless of who wins the next election, he has launched his nation in a promising new direction." Such praise must have pleased Mulroney, but he likely took greater comfort in the fact that Canadians had given him two solid majority governments, one on the divisive issue of free trade with the United States that had been the nemesis of several prime ministers. He was the first prime minister since John A. Macdonald to persuade all of the premiers to sign a constitutional accord, and he was able to do it three times – twice with Meech Lake and once with Charlottetown – though, in the end, it was all for naught as each constitutional accord failed. Mulroney was also the first prime minister to get Canada and the U.S. government to agree to a free-trade deal, a goal that had been pursued by such prime ministers as Macdonald, Laurier, and King (even Trudeau had considered sectoral free trade with the United States). Yet, on the other side of the ledger, the *Citizen* said that Mulroney offered Canadians " too much pragmatism and too little principle." It also pointed to "the character issue."[10] He was the one who was prepared "to roll the dice during the Meech Lake crisis" and to abandon the principle of universality in social programs. He also broke his promises on childcare and job training as part of the adjustment of the free-trade agreement, and his rewarding of political friends over the years – in stark contrast to his criticism of Liberal patronage during his memorable bout with Liberal leader John Turner in 1984 – angered many Canadians. For some, it was all too much.

Catherine Ford of the Calgary *Herald* captured the attitude that many Canadians had towards Prime Minister Mulroney. "History will probably treat Brian Mulroney well," she said, but the Canadian people will "find some kindness in their hearts [for him] ... just as soon as the polar ice caps melts." Ford went on to compare Mulroney to Dickens's Jacob Marley, noting that "the chain that Mulroney forged will be long and heavy. It will clank as he tries to drag its weight to wherever it is that former prime ministers go."[11] The clanking of that chain was heard in the fall of 2005 when Peter C. Newman published *The Secret Mulroney Tapes: Unguarded Confessions of a Prime Minister*, based on excerpts from hours of taped interviews, just in time for the Christmas season. Newman's best-seller was without significant analysis and context, but it did give Canadians a rare glimpse into the thoughts of a prime minister – there had been nothing like it since Mackenzie King's private diaries had been made available some years after his death. And, for many, what they saw reminded them why Mulroney had been so unpopular at the end of his term as prime minister. While the CBC quickly produced a two-hour documentary based on the tapes, Mulroney sued Newman over the book's publication. He accused Newman of a "breach of confidence" for not using the tapes for a scholarly biography, thereby violating, Mulroney claimed, the terms of his agreement with Newman. He also demanded that Newman transfer all the tapes and other "confidential" materials to the National Archives of Canada and that any income that he earned from the tapes be given to charity. The suit was settled in mid-2006, but no details were released.[12]

Without question, some Canadians are still annoyed by Mulroney's image, by his patronage appointments, and by the persistent rumours of his fondness for fine living. Perceptions are hard to shake, and the perception some Canadians have of Prime Minister Mulroney may be one reason why he has not received the credit he is due for his policy initiatives. Moreover, as Bob Rae notes below, Mulroney's image has been further sullied by developments after he left public office. When word leaked to the press in 1995 that the RCMP were investigating Mulroney for alleged corruption over certain business dealings with German-born businessmen Karl-Heinz Schreiber over the purchase of new airliners for Air Canada from Airbus Industrie, most Canadians did not particularly care.[13] The allegations just confirmed what many had suspected about Mulroney and his government. Neither did they pay much attention when Mulroney dropped his libel case against the Canadian government after he received a hand-delivered letter of apology from RCMP Commissioner Giuliano Zaccardelli telling him that the investigation was over and there was no evidence of wrongdoing. The government was forced to pay Mulroney's legal costs. Journalist Stevie Cameron's attempt to prove that Mulroney was "on the take" blew up in her face when it was discovered that she had been an RCMP informant. But then it came to light that Mulroney was paid $300,000 in cash as a retainer from Schreiber over an eighteen-month period beginning shortly after he stepped down as prime minister in 1993. Here, once again, was the taint of corruption that had always seemed to cling to the Mulroney government. The *Globe and Mail* concluded that Mulroney had not been guilty of anything "but perhaps poor judgement."[14] Yet Canadians were left shaking their heads.

As controversial now as when he held office, Mulroney continues to arouse strong feelings. Indeed, the only emotion that Mulroney fails to provoke in Canadians is indifference. When he was awarded the title of "Canada's Greenest Prime Minister" in April 2006 by *Corporate Knights*, a small independent environment magazine, Canadians, it seems, had forgotten that he had launched major initiatives on acid rain, climate control, and the ozone layer, as Elizabeth May points out in her contribution to this volume. In accepting his award, Mulroney remarked, "I want to tell you, when you've been where I've been, this is a hell of a ringing endorsement." It should be noted that Mulroney is greeted warmly by Canadians whenever he makes any public appearance. Even so, Canadians still argue about his impact on their nation and about his legacy.

Yet, for all the emotions that Prime Minister Mulroney elicits among Canadians, this book focuses not on personality but on the more important and substantive matter of policy. The contributors were selected either because of their expertise on aspects of Canadian politics, society, public policy, and history or because they participated directly in key events of the Mulroney era. Among the latter group, John Crosbie ran for the Conservative Party leadership in 1983 and lost to Mulroney, though he served in his cabinet until 1993; Bob Rae was a federal MP and later premier of Ontario and a candidate for the leadership of the Liberal Party of Canada; L. Ian Macdonald was a journalist who became a speechwriter for Mulroney; and Elizabeth May, a well-known environmental activist (and now the leader of the Green Party), served as an adviser to one of Mulroney's ministers. None of the contributors to this volume was given any instructions except the subject on which he or she was to write. Together, they present a variety of views and offer different interpretations of the legacy of Prime Minister Mulroney.

Each essay in this book was written to stand alone as well as contribute to our collective understanding of the complex world of Canadian public policy during the Mulroney era. Overall, I believe, the contributions highlight that there were both significant policy successes and significant policy failures during Mulroney's tenure. As for the failures, it cannot be disputed that Mulroney and his government did not achieve all that he and Canadians had hoped for in 1984. Still, his policy record will stand as one of the most ambitious, important, and, yes, controversial, of all of Canada's prime ministers. He saw a Canada that he believed needed change and a new direction, and he was more prepared than any of his predecessors to confront the problems that he was certain had to be addressed to make the country a better place. It is true that both his policies and his approach alienated many Canadians at times, but he was able, twice, to convince enough Canadians that his policies were better and more appealing than those offered by his opponents. In the end, the legacy of Brian Mulroney is twofold: one, he succeeded in changing Canada in many ways; and two, his successors – including not only the new Conservative government of Stephen Harper but also the Liberals, New Democrats, and Bloc Québécois – embraced many of his policies. He is clearly one of the most significant and important prime ministers Canada has ever had.

## NOTES

1 See, Peter C. Newman, *The Canadian Revolution 1985–1995: From Deference to Defiance* (Toronto: Viking 1995).

2 *Maclean's*, 15 February 1993.

3 See, for example, Robert Chodos, Rae Murphy, and Eric Hamovitch, *Selling Out: Four Years of Mulroney Government* (Toronto: James Lorimer 1988), xiii.

4 Ottawa *Citizen*, 25 February 1993.

5 Robert Everett, "Parliament and Politics," in David Leyton-Brown, *Canadian Annual Review of Politics and Public Affairs 1992* (Toronto: University of Toronto Press 1998), 40.
6 Quoted in Vancouver *Province*, 25 February 1993.
7 The text of prime minister's statement when he announced his resignation was reprinted in most major newspapers across Canada. See, for example, Montreal *Gazette*, 25 February 1993.
8 Ibid.
9 Ottawa *Citizen*, 25 February 1993.
10 Ibid.
11 Calgary *Herald*, 25 February 1993.
12 See Victoria *Times Colonist*, 12 June 2006.
13 *The Economist*, 11 January 1997.
14 *Globe and Mail*, 10 November 2003. See also William Kaplan, *A Secret Trial: Brian Mulroney, Stevie Cameron, and the Public Trust* (Toronto: University of Toronto Press 2004).

# 1

# Policy and Partisanship on the Campaign Trail: Mulroney Works His Wonder, Twice

CHRISTOPHER WADDELL

Brian Mulroney was a born campaigner. He liked meeting, charming, and talking to people. He loved recounting stories, especially political stories, to any audience. A campaign gave Mulroney a daily jolt of high-voltage adrenalin that he translated into the energy to work long hours from the moment the campaign began until its end. Those who worked most closely with him – the team that flew with him across Canada on two national election campaigns – describe him as having a killer instinct on the campaign trail. He had both extraordinarily good political instincts and the ability to pinpoint and exploit weaknesses in his opponents, fuelled by an overwhelming desire to win.

Day after day, he maintained a punishing pace, supported by his wife, Mila, who never left his side. Up each day in time to digest the morning newspapers and listen to radio newscasts, he then threw himself into a torrent of campaigning that included plant tours and "main-streeting," visits to farms, schools, and senior citizens' homes, lunchtime addresses to community groups, and, to cap it all, centre-stage speeches at highly partisan evening rallies of party supporters who gathered to hear him roast the Liberals and New Democrats. Then the campaign would often pack up and head to the airport, flying at night and usually arriving at hotels after midnight for a few hours' sleep before Mulroney would be up and doing it all again in another community. There was no rest, not even when flying at the end of the day, since that time was used for conducting strategy sessions with advisers, reviewing the day's events, and looking ahead to tomorrow.

If he wasn't in the air, though, it was standard practice for Mulroney to announce at just about 9:58 P.M. that it was time to go to bed. In fact, he wasn't going to bed at all and everyone knew it. He still had hours of networking to do. He was heading off to watch the television news, which, because he didn't want journalists to think he was influenced by the things

Brian Mulroney campaigning in Wolsley, Saskatchewan, during the 1988 federal election. Photographer Bill McCarthy. Library and Archives Canada 88-C-5151-30, negative number e007140472.

they said about him, he always claimed he never saw. When the news ended, he would move to the telephone, spending hours talking to friends and calling those who were participants in the stories he had seen, to offer his views and trade information. He could be critical or supportive of the participants in the TV stories, depending on what they had said, but, with everyone, he absorbed all the facts, gossip, and impressions that were conveyed to him over the phone, assessing what impact they would have on him and how they would alter voters' perceptions, and then applying this knowledge to the campaign. There would be a pause in the nightly round of calls when his old Toronto friend Sam Wakim phoned just before midnight to read Mulroney the headlines from the next morning's *Globe and Mail.* Mulroney was more intensely focused on the game of politics and campaigning than any of his advisers. It was a full-time addiction that ran wild when the campaign was under way. He was on top of absolutely everything that was happening both to his Progressive Conservatives (PCs) and to the other parties, and he had an opinion about every bit of it.

The ease with which Jean Chrétien won three straight majority governments between 1993 and 2000 made back-to-back electoral victories seem commonplace. Yet the two straight PC majorities won by Brian Mulroney in 1984 and 1988 were an extraordinary accomplishment, on several counts. His first win in 1984 produced the largest number of seats – 211 of 282 – won by a single party in the House of Commons in any Canadian election. John Diefenbaker in 1958 was the only other party leader since Confederation who had received the support of an absolute majority of voters. No one has done that since Mulroney in 1984. He broke the more than half-century stranglehold the Liberal Party had on Quebec by winning fifty eight of that province's seventy-five seats. The Liberals in Quebec have never recovered. Four years later, Mulroney did even better, winning sixty-two seats in Quebec and becoming the first PC leader that Quebec voters supported overwhelmingly in two straight elections.

Yet, despite his electoral victories, it is his failures that many Canadians remember: the political and public rejection of the Meech Lake and Charlottetown constitutional agreements; the overwhelming antagonism he faced from Canadians during his last years in office when his approval rating declined almost to single digits; and the 1993 collapse of the Progressive Conservative Party in the first election after his departure. A decade after Brian Mulroney left politics, the public's antipathy showed no sign of diminishing.

In 1983, seven years after Mulroney had tried and failed to win the party leadership in his political debut, he wrested the prize from Joe Clark. Pierre Trudeau, the then prime minister, was facing growing public dissatisfaction with his government's performance as Canadians struggled with high inflation and economic stagnation, record interest rates, and a war with western Canada over the Liberal government's National Energy Program. It was assumed that Trudeau would leave before the next election, which had to be held by 1985 at the latest. Mulroney vaulted his party almost immediately into first place in public-opinion polls, an achievement that reflected Canadians' desire for an alternative and their view of the new Conservative leader as an acceptable option (Clark had not been so fortunate, for he was never able to overcome the legacy of bungling that ended his nine-month minority government in 1979). However, the leadership race had been difficult and left the Progressive Conservative Party divided. It was a split that Mulroney knew would undermine his first election campaign unless addressed, and so he turned to this problem first. He had spent years as a labour lawyer in Quebec and excelled at finding common ground between bitter opponents. The fact that he counted both union leaders and powerful managers among his friends was proof of his exceptional skill at bringing people together – a skill he now applied to healing the post-leadership convention rifts in his party.

Mulroney passionately believed that the PCs could beat the Liberals, who had been in power for almost all of the twentieth century, only if all factions within the party put aside their differences and worked together. He concentrated on ensuring that happened in preparation for an expected election, possibly in 1984. One way to do that was to give jobs in the opposition leader's office to Tories who had worked for the candidates he had defeated. They became part of the team, advising and working for the new leader. Mulroney wanted everyone in the party to know what was going on in his office, rather than having to rely on rumours and whispers for their information. That was one way to minimize internal dissention as he found his feet as a political party leader, having never been elected or held any political office prior to becoming leader of the opposition.

Doing everything by consensus was the way to keep together the coalition that Mulroney assembled under the PC banner. The team combined the Quebec organization of both Conservative and sovereignist friends and supporters he had built over two decades; the Ontario Tories and the Big Blue Machine that had been responsible for William Davis's thirteen years as Ontario's premier and largely supported Joe Clark in 1983; and western Canadian Tories, some of whom opposed bilingualism and represented a wing of the party far to the right of Ontario's Red Tories. These groups had little in common beyond being perpetually out of power federally, and had no natural or obvious links between them. By giving everyone a role, Mulroney turned them into a strong campaign machine that convincingly won two elections. Simultaneously, he reserved a central place for himself and a small group that oversaw the headquarters and leader's tour operations. That meant striking a deal with the Big Blue Machine which handed its members day-to-day control of campaign headquarters. He recognized the organizational and managerial skill that the Ontario PCs had perfected through four decades in power and wanted this experience working for him.

Once amalgamated, these previously competing groups within the party then designed campaigns in both 1984 and 1988 that played to Mulroney's strengths. They focused on television, integrating a message about the specific policy or issue they had selected each day. The strategists knew that, in television, the eye always triumphs over the ear. Featuring Mulroney with good pictures or backdrops that related to the daily theme of his speech would deliver a message more effectively and powerfully than just audio and video clips from his speech. So each campaign day was carefully planned in advance and orchestrated to play to the media. It would begin with a morning event such as a plant tour that would provide television with interesting visuals to support the issue of the day. Mulroney's message on that policy issue would usually be delivered at a lunchtime speech to a non-partisan audience such as a service club. The luncheon would provide the sound bites for the television news story and, more important for the campaign, images of an audience listening attentively. The objective was to have television reporters package stories for the supper-hour and nighttime newscasts (this was in the era before all-news channels) by using pictures that regularly portrayed Mulroney as a strong and decisive leader with a thoughtful message for voters.

In the evenings, Mulroney would usually deliver a highly partisan, enthusiastic speech which was in obvious contrast to the more low-key policy and campaign-platform orientation of his daytime activities. Those partisan speeches frequently took place after television reporters had filed their stories for that evening. At the end of the day or perhaps even the next morning, headquarters staff in Ottawa and the small team on the plane with Mulroney would rehash the coverage they had received as well as that of their competitors, then decide how and if to react or alter their plans for the coming day. They had the luxury of taking comprehensive stock of their position in the media every twenty-four hours, and it was nothing like the frenetic, hourly repositioning that has become necessary in today's political campaigns.

Creating jobs was the central policy issue of both Mulroney campaigns, but his principal message in 1984 was very different from that in 1988. Mulroney's first election came in the midst of economic turmoil. In that summer, interest rates for five-year residential mortgages, for instance, averaged about 14 per cent; they had been as high as 19 per cent two years earlier, and since 1980 had been only momentarily below 13 per cent. From 1980 to 1982, inflation exceeded 10 per cent and fell below 5 per cent by 1984 only as the economy slipped into recession. Unemployment remained stubbornly above 11 per cent from 1982 through 1984. In that environment, Mulroney's cry of "jobs, jobs, jobs" was the rallying point for his campaign. Economic change was essential, he argued, and that meant such things as abandoning the National Energy Program, dismantling the Foreign Investment Review Agency, and renegotiating a deal on offshore oil and natural gas with the Atlantic provinces. Economic policy was the central and most important of the four themes Mulroney developed during that first campaign; the others were social policy, foreign affairs, and federal-provincial relations. They were selected to highlight how Mulroney and the PCs would change things from the previous four years of Trudeau's Liberal government. Creating jobs was central to each element of the platform, whether it was a foreign policy that concentrated on expanding trade, an economic policy that aimed at a reduction of the federal deficit to lower interest rates and help return the economy to growth, or a social policy that envisaged programs to help young people find work. Prior to the election, the party completed, but did not release, a study which concluded that its economic policies would create 800,000 new jobs in Canada. This fell slightly short of the one million new jobs the campaign team hoped they could promote, since they believed that such a round number would more easily stick in the minds of voters.[1] While Mulroney predicted at podiums from coast to coast how many jobs his government would create, he refused to specify what it would all cost. His political instincts told him to avoid that minefield, for whatever numbers he quoted would likely be thrown back at him at every stop. Instead, he sidestepped the issue by saying that such detailed calculations depended on economic variables he could not forecast.

It was the English-language debate in 1984 that galvanized Mulroney, giving him the opening he sought to go on the verbal offensive against the new Liberal leader, John Turner. Referring to the last-minute Trudeau patronage appointments that Turner insisted he could not undo, Mulroney, reprising the most memorable clash in the debate, went on the attack everywhere he travelled over the next week –Roberval, Quebec, Hamilton, Ontario, Bathurst, New Brunswick, and Sydney, Nova Scotia – in French and English: "'I had no option,' Mulroney would cry, mocking Turner and throwing up his hands. 'The devil made me do it.' He repeated this over and over."[2] He made an equally passionate and strident argument on a different theme, directed at Quebec audiences in Chicoutimi, Jonquière, Roberval, and Quebec City, in the week after the leaders' debates: "All day long he stressed the theme that 'democracy requires alternation,' that Quebeckers were not prisoners of a single party. Quebeckers, he said, were not 'the hostages of André Ouellette.' It was a guaranteed applause line in Roberval, in the Parti Québécois heartland of Lac St-Jean, as it was everywhere else."[3]

Four years later it was a different world, for then Mulroney and the Conservatives were the government and they had to defend themselves against Liberal and New Democratic Party (NDP) attacks on their record, which included a series of scandals and a failure to live up to the patronage standard they had set for themselves in 1984. Instead of directly debating those issues with the other parties, the Conservatives chose as the centrepiece of their campaign the nebulous theme of managing the changes taking place in the country's economy. Mulroney tried to put a human face on all this as he told an audience in Montague, Prince Edward Island, that "'this campaign is about choices, it's about challenges and it's about change. And most of all it's about you and me and our kids and our communities.'"[4] It was a tough sell in the campaign's early days.

Central to all his speeches in the opening weeks of the forty-seven-day campaign in 1988 were references to the econometric model developed by the Economic Council of Canada. It projected the creation of 250,000 jobs in the first decade after free trade began with the United States. On his first day campaigning in 1988, he toured a machine shop outside Toronto and drew attention to the 100,000 new jobs that the Economic Council predicted Ontario would gain under free trade. "'This is a powerful stimulus to the impressive economy of Ontario,' Mulroney said, sounding curiously formal for someone speaking to workers on a shop floor. 'We have done much to create a climate in which Ontario's economy can grow stronger.'"[5] He then made an argument that he would return to regularly over the next forty-five days, noting that the free trade deal "'may not be perfect but the option is tearing it up. For those who say they're going to tear it up, I ask you to ask them what they're going to do after they've torn it up,' adding that "'a policy of tearing up a sovereign treaty in 1988 is not good enough as a fundamental policy for the people and workers of Canada.'"[6] Linked to the Economic Council's projections was the broader message that the only way to ensure future prosperity would be to re-elect a PC government. As he put it, "'most Canadians are better off than they were four years ago. More of them are working and working in a steadily growing and expanding economy.'"[7] It was a message that was fine-tuned for each audience. For example, he told New Brunswickers that "'the free-trade agreement allows this region the opportunity to restore the historic natural patterns of trade and commerce which Canadian tariff policy destroyed and has ever since denied.'"[8]

It did not take long, though, for Mulroney to realize that econometrics wouldn't be enough to persuade Canadians to back free trade. Right from the start, Liberal leader John Turner and NDP leader Edward Broadbent fuelled concerns about the potential threat, particularly to social programs, posed by the harmonization of the Canadian and United States economies that might occur under free trade. "'Canadians know that you can trade goods and services with any country without buying its values or selling your own,'" Mulroney told an audience of three hundred at a lunch organized by the Toronto-Parkdale Rotary Club in mid-October, a message he would repeat endlessly. Then he challenged the other party leaders. "'We believe that freer trade is absolutely essential to sustaining economic growth and prosperity for Canada,'" he continued, adding that "'they would have you believe that you can have more by trading less: more government programs, more benefits, more services on less trade, less growth, less new wealth.'"[9] The campaign team constantly adjusted Mulroney's message to anticipate the concerns of each group he met on the campaign trail. Speaking to senior citizens in Summerside, Prince Edward Island, he pledged, "'In the future Canada will be doing more, not less for all of you. As long as I am Prime Minster of Canada, social benefits – especially those for the elderly – will be improved, not diminished by the government, which is committed to social justice and fairness for all Canadians,'" then, to ensure that everyone had the sound bite, repeating the remarks in French for the benefit of radio and television reporters.[10]

The campaign's focus on the need to manage change and on the benefits awaiting Canada under free trade did not mean that Mulroney's speeches ignored his other prized policy accomplishment, the Meech Lake Accord. It was an important element of every Quebec campaign stop, but Mulroney also drew attention to it regularly in the rest of Canada. Announcing early in the campaign in Charlottetown that Ottawa would provide $190,000 the following year to help celebrate the 125th anniversary of the 1864 Charlottetown conference, which had led to Confederation, he immodestly proclaimed about the Meech Lake Accord, "'I am convinced, absolutely convinced, the Fathers of Confederation would have been proud of what we have accomplished.'" Then, going even further, he added that the federal-provincial agreement was "'just as the Fathers of Confederation would have wanted.'"[11]

No matter what the audience, there was a standard approach to Mulroney's appearances in both 1984 and 1988. "Mulroney was to look like a leader and a statesman at all times: no footballs, no funny hats, no potentially embarrassing situations. No risks. No disruptions of the basic message."[12] That meant no unscripted or spontaneous meetings with reporters and no off-the-cuff remarks. Even a casual comment in a media scrum could derail all the planning that had been done to get a certain issue and policy message on the nightly newscasts. The Conservatives choreographed the early days of Mulroney's 1988 campaign to an extreme as the press was kept behind barriers. Reporters soon began complaining and reporting that he was campaigning inside a bubble too inaccessible to provide them with enough material for their stories. They realized that they were mere bit players in a script written by PC headquarters and they did not like it.

No detail was too small for Mulroney's media campaign advisers. For instance, in both 1984 and 1988, the Conservatives leased an aircraft for the leader's tour that was slightly larger than those of their competitors. Their Boeing 727 had two separate cabins so Mulroney and his team had private space at the front of the plane physically removed and protected from the eyes and ears of the reporters travelling with the leader on the tour. Just as important, the aircraft had two exits: one at the front was for the leader and campaign organization and another at the rear was for journalists on the tour. That allowed Mulroney to avoid mingling with the media as everyone boarded and disembarked, sometimes several times a day.[13]

The campaign team demanded that everything be in order because there was no guarantee the Conservatives would win either election. The spring 1984 leadership campaign that chose John Turner to replace Pierre

Trudeau gave the Liberals a sharp boost in public-opinion polls, after the Conservatives had led in public opinion for much of the previous year. A 54–32 Tory lead in March became a Liberal lead of 46–40 by April.[14] A late June post-convention Gallup poll showed the Liberals, with Turner as their new leader, in front 49–38 and helped persuade the new prime minister that he should call the election even with a year left in the Liberal government's mandate.

Although he did not show it, Mulroney was scared by the sudden and dramatic fall in the polls. Having lost the leadership in 1976, he had spent seven long years organizing and campaigning to win it in 1983. Just as he seemed headed for the Prime Minister's Office, the sharp reversal in the polls suddenly meant that he might end up as the latest in a string of Conservative leadership failures, just another politician unable to unseat the Liberals. While he worried privately that everything was collapsing, Mulroney carried on with planning for a general election.

The previous year, after winning the PC leadership, Mulroney had won a by-election in Central Nova. It was his first electoral victory and he entered the House of Commons in the fall as leader of the opposition. Then, in the spring of 1984, he slipped out of the national political spotlight while it was focused on the Liberal leadership, to prepare for an election. Yet, even if he was off the media's radar screen, he was extremely busy visiting the smaller towns across the country. It was a strategy that worked well for him and the party. The national media focused on the Liberal leadership campaign, but the regional and local media covered Mulroney.[15] It was a brutal schedule. He visited sixty communities and covered almost 50,000 kilometres in the air and on the ground, meeting people far from the media spotlight but generating volumes of local news coverage. More important, he and his team were rehearsing their act for the coming election.

At the same time, a handpicked team began planning how their campaign would unfold once the election was called. Ontario Senator Norman Atkins, along with other Big Blue Machine Ontario Tories, directed the campaign from the party's Ottawa headquarters. They put the pieces together. "'The key is the people on the [leader's] plane and the relationship they have with the leader and the confidence the leader has in the whole process; the ability to put together the physical elements of the tour; the right kind of a plane, the right buses. All of that, while it may look overdone, is very, very important to the success of the tour. It isn't by gosh and by golly,'" explained Atkins.[16] Neither Atkins nor party pollster Allan Gregg was close to Mulroney or belonged to his legendary networks of friends and acquaintances. However, Mulroney respected their skill and experience and the quality of their work and advice. Like most politicians, Mulroney believed that he knew the system better than anyone else and could be his own campaign manager. But he was also wise enough to know that he could not do that and be leader. So he handed day-to-day responsibility to professionals and followed their counsel.

Still, the leader plays a central role and Mulroney's character was perfectly suited to handle the ups and downs of campaigns and campaigning. As his successor Kim Campbell noted, Mulroney always exuded confidence and the sense that nothing that was happening, no matter how bad, was unanticipated. He saw his job as part consensus builder and part party cheerleader, preserving calm with soothing words, a phone call timed at the right moment to let someone know that he was thinking about him and that he was thankful for his efforts, or a pat on the back. No matter what setbacks might hit his campaign, or later his government, Mulroney acted to ensure that those around him were neither distracted nor disillusioned. He never let down his guard and displayed his true thoughts. "Were we at 20 per cent in the polls? That's about where he expected we would be at this point in the mandate," Campbell wrote in describing Mulroney's virtuoso performances at weekly Progressive Conservative caucus meetings. This unruffled approach was also a staple of his campaigning. "He communicated an attitude of unwavering confidence that he knew exactly what had to be done to put us in a position where we would win the next election."[17]

Mulroney always reacted with similar calmness to bad news and this approach generally served him well. It preserved party unity and unwavering caucus loyalty throughout campaigns and even as public support for Mulroney plummeted in the final years of his government. That had been his approach in private life and he followed it religiously while in office. Facing his caucus after the release of the post-Liberal convention Gallup poll in late June 1984 that showed the Tories trailing, Mulroney, despite his private doubts and concerns, "assured them the polls were just a blip and sent every caucus member copies of the laudatory clippings from the local press [covering his tour of the regions]. His soothing words calmed the alarmist mood."[18] He had a similar message to reporters asking about the same poll. "It meant nothing, he insisted, because it followed on the heels of the Liberal convention. 'Hang on to your hat,' he warned, 'you're going to see a campaign like you haven't seen in twenty-five years.'"[19]

Four years later, speaking to supporters after polls showed a sharp drop in Conservative support following Mulroney's poor performance against John Turner in the 1988 televised leaders' English-language debate, he once again was a master at being unflustered. "'Polls change every day,'" he told them. "'Polls are snapshots of the day before yesterday.'" And as for himself, he added, he had just begun to fight. "'I am going to fight and fight hard and I am going to win.'"[20]

Yet the public confidence he projected masked a constant worry that overconfidence might undermine his campaign's efforts. In the early days of the 1988 campaign, he revealed his anxieties only to those in his inner circle. The Liberal campaign was going poorly, handicapped by dissent that led to a fumbled attempt to dump leader John Turner in mid-campaign and a suggestion by NDP leader Edward Broadbent that Canada would be better off if the Liberal Party disappeared. But the NDP failed to benefit from the Liberal disarray and its campaign wasn't generating any great gains either. Though the Conservatives were cruising to re-election, Mulroney could not and would not relax even for a moment. When asked to comment on Broadbent's call for the death of the Liberals, Mulroney displayed his cautious instinct about the unscripted dynamics of elections. "'I think it is a little premature to predict the demise of the Liberal party,' he replied. 'They have a tendency to come back and bite you. They might even bite Mr. Broadbent. He should be careful.'"[21]

Inside the campaign, Mulroney regularly told those close to him that, while they thought they were winning, they could well be wrong. "Never underestimate the Liberals" was his constant admonition, no matter how well things seemed to be going. "Look at this campaign as a campaign with an 800-pound gorilla at the door that can jump on us at any moment." "Don't be complacent," he would often say, "for you don't realize what is going on and how quickly it can change."

His skill at standing back and analysing a set of circumstances even when he was a participant in them came from his negotiating experience as a lawyer. And, when he found an opening, such as John Turner's patronage appointments upon taking office in 1984, Mulroney would exploit it for all it was worth. John Sawatsky has written that "Mulroney recognized a gift-horse political issue and immediately jumped on the offensive. He accused the Liberals of having 'dishonoured the system' and vowed 'it shall never, never happen again under a Conservative government.' The campaign, Mulroney insisted, was about change and Turner had now shown himself to be part of the old gang. The government, he declared, had grown old and needed to be thrown out. The reporters who watched him could tell he was striking a chord with the public."[22]

He also had an exceptional ability to assess his opponents and predict how the dynamics of an election would play out in the campaign, as he demonstrated in the weeks before calling the vote in 1988. Journalist Graham Fraser recounts that, at a meeting with senior advisers shortly before the election was called, Mulroney predicted what he thought would happen. "'Well somewhere along the road, maybe during the debate, Turner is going to say something that will have a dramatic impact,' he said. 'This is because he is starting from so far back, there are such low expectations of him and the media will be looking for something to inject excitement into the race. All these things are going to be exaggerated and combined beyond their importance.'"[23]

In the 1988 English-language debate, Turner's passionate assault against free trade as a threat to the country set the 1988 campaign alive in a single evening, and put Mulroney and the Conservatives on the defensive. They were left scrambling to counter the effective Liberal attack. It was precisely the opposite of their 1984 confrontation when Mulroney, first in the French debate, clearly demonstrated to Quebecers that he was one of them while Turner was not and, then in the English debate, exploited the patronage issue skilfully to emerge as the clear winner again. But, when Turner scored surprisingly well in the 1988 debate, it only seemed to invigorate Mulroney and the Conservatives campaign team. The prime minister and Tory organizers immediately put together five of the biggest rallies of the campaign, even in unfriendly territory like southern Ontario. Gerald Caplan has noted that the "PM campaigned tirelessly, putting the heat on Turner, precisely on Turner's points of weakness. Even as Mulroney's reputation was being bruised by press coverage and polls in the wake of the debate, Conservative workers were being given a lift and the press could not find the slightest indication that the Tories were coming apart."[24] Placed on the defensive by the outcome of the debates yet able to sense what was happening and how he needed to change, Mulroney relied on his greatest skill as a campaigner, his ability to counterpunch with precision. Under attack from his opponents, he instinctively knew how and where to retaliate to score the maximum points while limiting the damage to himself.

Mulroney's effectiveness in counterpunching was rooted in three great strengths: his enormous energy, his genuine love of politics, and his ability to act on good advice. During a campaign, he was indefatigable – invigorated by the whole experience, from the camaraderie of the small group supporting him on the leader's plane to the adulation of cheering party supporters at rallies. Every move he made during those times was overwhelmingly political and often shaped by advice from his campaign team. He consulted broadly and indiscriminately. If it was a good idea, it did not matter where it originated. A long- time friend's ideas were given no more weight than those of a professional adviser. All that mattered to him was the quality of the idea. If it were sound, he would seize it and use it.

His love for the back and forth of campaigning, complete with counterpunching, made the initial phases of the 1988 election frustrating. His team had designed a front-runner's campaign in which he was to appear careful, cautious, and prime ministerial. They had also chosen a theme: the Conservatives' ability to "manage change." Mulroney gritted his teeth and stuck to the script even though everyone knew that sooner or later the free-trade agreement his government had negotiated with the United States would become the dominant issue for all parties. Michel Gratton, who left journalism from 1984 to 1987 to work as Mulroney's press secretary, described the early weeks of that campaign: "Mulroney prided himself on being one of the best on-the-stump campaigners in the country, and he was probably right. To run a campaign where he let his opponents take daily pot shots, without returning the first, was sheer torture to him. In the early days of the 1988 campaign, he was feeling rather miserable in his protective bubble, and would often complain aloud to his entourage, 'they want me to shut up, I shut up.' That meant of course that he thought the whole thing was utterly ridiculous. And that he would be far more effective doing what did best: swinging back instead of dancing away from the blows."[25]

His weak performance in the debates gave Mulroney the chance to swing back. While it took the Conservative campaign team time to devise a strategy to respond to the sudden rise in support for John Turner and the Liberals, Mulroney grabbed centre stage. Doubts had been growing within the Conservative team about free trade. Some on the campaign suggested that Mulroney should offer to put free trade to a referendum. That might diffuse the anti-free trade sentiment among voters, they argued, and make it easier for Mulroney to get re-elected.

The issue came to a head at a 2:00 A.M. meeting that Mulroney called in his suite at Toronto's Royal York hotel the day following the English-language debate. One of those in attendance described Mulroney as "white with I don't know if it was anger, determination, a mixture of both, or what," but the message delivered to the core campaign group from the plane was blunt. In Mulroney's mind, the gloves were off. No more managing change. That was history. This campaign would be about free trade and he told his staff that he did not want to hear about referendums ever again. If he were going to be defeated, he would be defeated for solid reasons. From now on, the campaign would centre on defending his free-trade agreement vigorously and unconditionally. The existing advertising campaign would be junked and replaced by new ads. Until they could be designed, written, produced, and distributed, everything would fall on Mulroney's shoulders. He would be the sole voice of the campaign and the Conservatives' fate would rest on how successful he was. The next morning, off he went. According to Conservative strategist Harry Near, Mulroney "'literally carried the campaign on his back for four or five days.'"[26]

Members of the campaign team saw a Mulroney who worked incessantly and tirelessly to ensure that people didn't cut and run on him, that they didn't lose faith, that they didn't panic or become despondent while the campaign team devised a response to Turner and the Liberals. Mulroney rewrote a speech and delivered it in Toronto, accusing Liberals and New Democrats of frightening voters by implying that a free-trade deal would undermine everything from old age pensions to supply management for farm products to social programs and Canadian culture. "'At its worst, the tactics of Mr. Turner and Mr. Broadbent are shameful and dishonest,' he said. 'At the least they are an attempt to hide the fact that they offer Canadians not realistic alternatives, no plan of their own to sustain and expand the economic momentum we have built these past four years. It is a classic negative politics – if you shout loud enough and long enough about what you are against, perhaps people won't notice there is nothing you are for.'"[27] In the twenty-five days remaining in the campaign, every one of Mulroney's speeches aggressively attacked the anti-free-trade position of John Turner and the Liberals, with some time also devoted to Edward Broadbent and the NDP.

Whether he was following orders from headquarters or redesigning campaign strategy himself, Mulroney always had difficulty with being told by others that he had made a mistake. He would immediately become aggressively defensive if a brave but unfortunate soul on the team suggested that he had done something wrong. He hated confrontation and hated even more to be the target of criticism. Anyone who dared tell him bluntly that he had said or done the wrong thing faced an immediate and withering counterattack. He took such comments as personal affronts and would often respond in kind, challenging the credentials of the person who dared say he was wrong. It was a response that highlighted his stubbornness and desire to remain in control, but his team learned to circumvent that response and still get what they wanted. For instance, the *Globe and Mail* reported an incident early in the 1988 campaign involving a Mulroney interview on ATV's supper hour newscast in Halifax: "Mr. Mulroney was asked whether a re-elected Conservative government would change any social programs or attempt to reduce benefits, as in the reduction of inflation protection for old-age pensions in May 1985. A national uproar forced the Tories into an embarrassing retreat on that idea a month after it was announced in the May budget. 'I can't answer a question like that, because to answer it would be to dignify it,' Mr. Mulroney responded. 'I have no intention of doing anything such as the kind you suggested,'" he told interviewer Steve Murphy.[28] Always looking for mistakes or hidden meanings in Mulroney's comments, reporters on the Conservative leader's tour thought that he might have left the door open to cutting social programs after he was re-elected. The campaign team on the plane had the same concern and a worried tour director John Tory went to Mulroney to tell him that a clarification was required. Mulroney was annoyed. His standard response to such advice was to revert to his legal training and analyse the issue through the eyes of a lawyer. He wanted a transcript to study his words. Then he would parse them to prove conclusively that he was correct and that the person who had challenged his comments was wrong.

The campaign team was caught between the leader's intransigence and the prospect that the other parties would try to generate public outrage over the possibility that the Tories had a hidden agenda of cutting social programs. The last thing the Conservatives wanted to do while running their low-key campaign was to hand an issue to the Liberals and New Democrats, particularly one that combined social programs and the sense that Mulroney had a hidden agenda, which was the essence of the critique about free trade as well. The campaign team faced a choice. Their trump card was always Mila Mulroney. She could speak with her husband privately in a way no one else could, offer advice to him, and help make him more responsive to the team's concerns. However, she could not be used too often – she had to be kept as a last resort when all else had failed. Before taking the drastic step of requesting Mila's help, the team turned to Mulroney's press secretary, Marc Lortie, a public servant who had been seconded to the Prime Minister's Office since 1985. As a Quebecer, Lortie shared with Mulroney an enthusiasm for and encyclopedic knowledge of the province's political history and knew many of the same characters Mulroney had encountered in his thirty years in Quebec politics. That created a bond between the two that gave Lortie an opening.

Following the remark in Halifax about social programs, Tory called on Lortie, who went to Mulroney and told him that the "boys" in the back of the plane – the media – were confused by Mulroney's comment. Mulroney expressed surprise at this turn of events. Why are they confused, he asked? Well, came the reply, they got your social-programs message but are still confused about it. Ah well, Mulroney responded, that's different. No one told me they were confused. It was all clear to him and it should be equally clear to everyone else. Maybe some clarification was in order after all and he suggested that he could do it in a scrum at the rear of the plane when he next landed in Sydney, Nova Scotia. Both sides knew it was a game but citing confusion among the boys, as Mulroney called the media even though the days of an all-male press corps were long gone, became a way to avoid pushing Mulroney into a corner and triggering a confrontation with his staff over something the campaign team felt had not gone as planned. It gave Mulroney a chance to reconsider and propose a change of approach, while staying in charge.

Circumventing a confrontation with Mulroney by asking him to show mercy on confused reporters was a powerful strategy because Mulroney was obsessed with the media. Long before he became a candidate himself, Mulroney was a wonderful source for reporters covering Quebec politics. "Get to know and talk to Brian" became a standard word of advice that print, radio, and television journalists passed to each other whenever news organizations shuffled their Quebec political reporters in the 1960s and 1970s. He knew everyone, seemed to have his finger in everything, and loved to gossip and trade political rumours and stories. He trotted them out during long off-the-record conversations that always left reporters feeling that they had been given an insider's tour of what was really happening, complete with all the details. Over the years he had developed close relationships with many journalists. That made it all the more difficult when he entered politics and went from being the source for stories to being the subject of them.

He read, watched, and listened to everything that was reported, particularly about him. When reporters whom he considered friends, or whom he had helped in the past, wrote negative and critical stories about him, he took it extremely personally. In his view, they had betrayed him. For someone who valued loyalty above virtually everything else, this was unforgivable. Mulroney often concluded that such reporters were out to get him. To the day he finally left office, he was unable to accept that good reporters wrote critical stories as objective professionals, without malice.

As a result, he was preoccupied with what was said and written about him, and this trait undermined his effectiveness as a campaigner. He could rarely resist trying to correct the record whenever he thought something incorrect had been reported or written, regardless of the occasion. Of course, the correctness of the story was often in the eye of the beholder but Mulroney could not stand back and see that. Only very rarely could he let an opportunity slip away without responding. That was not just a campaign preoccupation but was a staple of his life as prime minister and it made his media handlers cringe. For example, in the midst of a forty-five-minute speech to provincial premiers at the dinner prior to a week of constitutional negotiations in Ottawa in June 1990, "Mulroney produced a well-thumbed copy of *Where I Stand,* his collection of speeches published in 1983. He wanted to correct [Newfoundland premier Clyde] Wells who had quoted from the book in some recent remarks. 'The trouble is Clyde, you read the wrong section of the book,' Mulroney said. 'You should read this part.' He wanted to show that he had always thought it was unconscionable that Quebec was still buying cheap power from Churchill Falls under a forty-year contract Newfoundland had signed in 1969. Wells said little, although he did challenge him on a couple of constitutional points."[29]

During his campaigns, Mulroney's daily speeches became his opportunity to do whatever correcting to media reports that he felt was needed. Sometimes in mid-speech or at the end of a prepared text that had already been distributed to the media, he would pause, remove his reading glasses for dramatic effect, and then launch into whatever was on his mind – an extemporaneous dissertation that could last for sentences or minutes and could take off in any direction at all. His voice would rise and fall, using intonation for emphasis, and, as he continued, he would often speak faster and faster, clearly caught up and enjoying whatever message he was delivering to correct the record. Reporters quickly learned that this was the time to listen closely and take notes because Mulroney's hyperbole would often crowd out facts. It all spelled trouble for his campaign team, if only because no one could predict where the performance would lead, but they had to be ready to respond as soon as it finished.

As an example, in the early days of the 1984 election campaign, Mulroney planned to announce that he would run in his home riding of Manicouguan in Quebec. This meant surrendering the Central Nova seat in Nova Scotia he had won in a 1983 by-election to get into the House of Commons after being chosen party leader. Returning to Central Nova to thank the voters for their support, he told them with characteristic embellishment, "'It's not every day that a Conservative walks away from a twenty-thousand vote majority.'"[30] His actual margin was 11,024; the figure of twenty thousand was a pollster's pre-election prediction.

If Mulroney didn't get off his chest what he wanted to say in a campaign speech on any given day, he would use scrums with the media to make his point about whatever was bothering him. His advisers would recommend that he walk steadily out of an event without stopping to respond to journalists, who, knowing that what he said off the cuff was always good copy, would do everything they could to bait him. Mulroney would promise his team not to stop but merely to slow down so he could hear what the reporters were asking. Nine times out of ten, though, he just could not resist. He would stop to answer because he had something to say. It was usually something he had not shared with anyone on the campaign team prior to responding. That forced sudden, unexpected adjustments in campaign plans to ensure that events and circumstances matched what the leader had said.

For instance, at one point during the 1988 campaign, Mulroney was in Montreal to deliver a major lunchtime speech. The campaign staff warned him just before he went to speak that John Crosbie had said something about bilingualism while campaigning in Newfoundland and Mulroney should be prepared for a question or two from reporters after his remarks. Instead, Mulroney threw out his prepared speech and delivered an extemporaneous address to an increasingly mystified audience about the importance of the French presence in Canada. In this case, he took pre-emptive action to correct the record before it had even come out.

Mulroney's obsession with the media and how it portrayed him affected his performance in another way. His successor as prime minister and PC leader, Kim Campbell, put her finger on it when commenting, "There was a studied quality to Brian Mulroney, specially in public, a sense that he was *playing* himself rather then *being* himself. The impression of not quite 'touching bottom' when you observed him generated enormous mistrust. Some of the hostility was obviously a residue from the scandals of the first mandate, and the remainder I thought was a natural result of being associated with contentious policies."[31]

Many of those closest to him during his campaigns agree. They all describe the private Mulroney as convivial and warm with a sense of fun and willingness to tease those around him. This was the person who built, and worked twenty-four hours a day to maintain, widespread networks of life-long friends. But on a podium or indeed in any kind of public forum, all that disappeared. In its place was too often almost a caricature of what a politician might be – overblown and subject to exaggeration, using large words for their apparent dramatic effect and, above all else, appearing packaged and unnatural. It was a short jump from that to the conclusion some Canadians reached that he wasn't always telling the truth. His opponents knew that this was Mulroney's weakness, as Liberal Senator Michael Kirby commented prior to the 1988 election: "'The real question is whether the Prime Minister can run a campaign where on the one hand he doesn't become excessively partisan and on the other doesn't create or perpetuate the impression that he doesn't tell the truth. His biggest single weakness with the Canadian public is that even when he is telling the truth, he frequently sounds like he isn't. That's partly because he has a tendency to exaggerate, partly because of the way he uses the media and partly, because earlier on, there's evidence that he didn't always tell the truth. And that's a very hard perception to shake.'"[32]

Mulroney was not the only politician who had distinct public and private personas. It was a character trait shared with his long-time Conservative rival Joe Clark. Both were products of the John Diefenbaker era of the Progressive Conservative Party and Canadian politics. Their sense of how a politician should act and appear in public – somewhat puffed-up and unnatural – seemed to come from their time spent watching Diefenbaker, even though, for both Mulroney and Clark, this style was completely at odds with their private personalities and undermined their political effectiveness.

Some people imagine that the persona Mulroney created for himself came from his belief that at all times he had to appear and act prime ministerial – a principle that, as some of those closest to him concede, only Mulroney fully understood, just as he was the only one who knew how it should be applied. For many Canadians, he often appeared too slick and to be trying too hard to be perfect. Not only was it an image that was contrary to his private personality, television amplified its shortcomings – which, in an era when campaigning had become dominated by television pictures, was so small problem. Cabinet minister John Crosbie described how the public viewed Mulroney in his last years in office: "'The problem,' as pollster Michael Adams put it, 'is that in the public mind, he does not have the qualities of consistency and sincerity.'" In the opinion of *Maclean's*, while warm and sensitive in person, on television his warmth appeared effusive and his sensitivity often seemed insincere.[33]

Such comments were a reaction to Mulroney's body language. The words he used in answering questions in interviews may have read well in a printed transcript but he never appeared comfortable or at ease delivering them in front of a camera. He seemed publicly far too conscious about how he looked and about what he said, and far too anxious to create a prime ministerial impression. Viewers interpreted that as a sign of someone who was packaged and performing, not real or natural, and hence telling, at best, versions or parts of the truth. Others were blunter, saying he had hidden agendas and calling him a liar. It all contributed to the public antagonism that in 1988 dogged Mulroney's efforts to persuade Canadians that free trade was the right course for the future. University of British Columbia political scientist Richard Johnston highlighted Mulroney's credibility problem in his study of voter attitudes in the 1988 campaign: "Half the respondents were asked to say whether they supported or opposed 'the deal negotiated by Canada' and the other half the deal 'negotiated by the Mulroney government.' Following the televised leaders debate, use of the Mulroney version reduced support for free trade by 14 points, compared to the Canada version. But thereafter support for the FTA grew, almost all of it among respondents given the Mulroney form of the question. In other words, patterns of support and opposition on the free trade issue were strongly related to attitudes towards Mulroney and his government."[34]

Mulroney won in 1988 with his passionate attacks on John Turner and the Liberals and an equally committed defence of the free-trade agreement and the Meech Lake Accord constitutional deal with the provinces, but it was all done within a totally scripted and packaged campaign. That approach reinforced the impression frequently left by his television appearances. Every campaign event was stage-managed to the most minute detail. Mulroney had to know before he entered a hall precisely how many steps he would walk to the podium and what direction he would take, what would happen on the way, whom he would meet, what he would say, and what would others say in response. Just before he would head into the hall to speak, he would ask one of his staff whether they had checked the podium. That was code for asking whether every detail had been personally checked by the staff member and was in order. Scripting each event was a way to limit the disruptions from the anti-free-trade hecklers who were at every stop in 1988. It was also a way to provide consistency in the television images that were so important in delivering Mulroney's message to voters. If the physical surroundings – the lighting, the stage, and the sound system – were not perfect and consistent from place to place, the television images would vary in quality, which would undermine his message. It was essential to showcase Mulroney in the way the campaign organization required, as part of its strategy to meld message and visuals from the leader into a television image that would encourage voters to support the leader and his party.

At each speech, Luc Lavoie, a former TVA television reporter who joined the Prime Minister's Office in 1988 and oversaw the staging of all campaign events for maximum television impact, stood at one side in front of the podium in Mulroney's line of sight. He would use hand signals to provide some feedback to the leader on how the crowd was responding in case Mulroney ran into any problems, and also to offer mid-speech advice. When events were not turning out exactly as planned, Mulroney would continue along but his performance under such circumstances always suffered. The unexpected threw him off his game. It upset him and those deemed responsible for the surprise would hear about it afterwards, although not directly from Mulroney. He would send others to deliver blunt messages when he felt that his performance and effectiveness had been compromised by sloppy preparation.

The standards he set for himself also underscored what Mulroney did and how he did it on the campaign trail. "Beyond electoralism, this had something to do with Mulroney's privately held hopes of winning over the intelligentsia – the nationalist intellectuals in Quebec and the red Tories in English-speaking Canada. 'His secret dream,' Lucien Bouchard once confided to a friend, 'is to have the approval of the intellectuals.'"[35] In Quebec, that meant bringing the province back into the constitution, something Mulroney almost achieved with the Meech Lake and Charlottetown accords, while, in English Canada, it meant more than just campaigning and winning. It meant running a government that was progressive as well as conservative: "His problems with the intellectual wing of the Conservative party, those people from somewhere between Queen's University and the United Church, arose from the fact that he was simply different from them. They were generally Protestant, high-minded and disapproving of displays of affluence. He was Catholic, upwardly mobile and with no reticence about living at the top of the hill. Where he came from[,] that was part of what it was all about."[36]

Trying to win the approval of the intellectuals also contributed to his different campaigning styles in French and English Canada. His campaign staff found that he was never comfortable campaigning in Toronto, or even just being there. Although he would never say it, Mulroney's body language would change to be more rigid and scripted in Toronto, as he consciously tried to appear prime ministerial but in the end just looked unnatural and packaged. In Quebec, though, Mulroney was a totally different person. He was relaxed, causal, completely unscripted, and always visibly enjoying himself. Mulroney is an emotional person and that was both his strength and weakness as a campaigner. He knew that he was loved in Quebec, where even his opponents had a soft spot for him since he was one of them. He spoke the French he learned in the streets of the province and was folksy and down to earth. Quebec was also his political home and the place where he combined his love of political trivia and history. His speeches were less formal, his events far from choreographed. Feeling at ease, he could handle whatever came along and still make his points to his audience. Quebec was also the place where Mulroney the storyteller was in his element. He would be campaigning somewhere in the province and be reminded about the former premier Maurice Duplessis, which would lead into a story about the first time Mulroney met Duplessis or the first time he took Diefenbaker to Quebec and insisted he meet so and so. That in turn would lead to a competition with whomever he was talking to, about who knew whom and when they met them, starting Mulroney off on a new story. He knew and was involved with all the players and the backroom operators in Quebec politics since the 1950s. His comfort in Quebec also came from the fact that he was completely in charge of the campaign there. He may have privately chafed on occasion under the direction of Ontario's Big Blue Machine when touring the rest of the country, although he never tried to circumvent that campaign structure and organization. In Quebec, he did not have to give such matters a second thought. He was the campaign and its director and he knew it.

As already noted, Mulroney's campaigning successes all came prior to the arrival of twenty-four-hour all-news television. His failures, Meech Lake and Charlottetown, were in the early days of CBC Newsworld but they were featured prominently and for hours on end on the new channel. In the decade and a half since Newsworld went on the air in 1989, it has been followed by equivalents from CTV, RadioCanada, and TVA, and, collectively, the way these stations operate has fundamentally altered election campaigning and political reporting in Canada. News channels need to capture and retain viewers to make money by selling advertising. When there is a major event, people come to the news channels to find out what is happening and get the latest developments. That sends audience levels sharply higher. When the event ends, viewers return to whatever they were doing and news-channel ratings fall back into a trough, waiting for the next big event. News channels quickly learned the importance to their success of finding a regular stream of big events or, if they could not be found, creating them, to keep audiences glued to their televisions. To help retain audiences, news channels began to banner their stories across the bottom of the television screen, telling viewers what the big story was and teasing them constantly by promoting major developments or something new on the story that was coming up next, usually right after a series of commercials. It's a trick that works and keeps viewers away from their remotes.

An election campaign is perfect material for such a news machine. The campaign goes on continuously for thirty-six days (forty-seven in the

1980s), from early in the morning to late at night, as it stretches across Canada. There is an endless stream of people who are only too willing to talk, debate, and comment to fill hours of air time, and it is now easier than ever before to move television pictures from anywhere in the country to a network's headquarters to be broadcast. Television cameras follow party leaders all day long, providing video of their speeches, daily scrums with reporters, and other such events.

In a campaign, all-news channels become national video wire services, broadcasting pictures and clips from one party leader, usually live or nearly live, that can be seen by everyone at the same time, including the other parties and leaders. This creates an irresistible urge for reporters to ask leaders for instant reaction to something another leader has just said, for comments on statements – the more outlandish the better – made by any party's candidates, and for a response to any event going on anywhere. That is fed into the news machine and replayed on air by the news channels all day long until another leader comments on the comments the news channel is broadcasting. The phone-in programs that are another cheap staple of all-news television pick up the subject and chew it over for hours, as do an endless series of experts and commentators invited to appear on various talk shows. Unlike the world in which Mulroney campaigned, when there were only end-of-the-day television deadlines for the six o'clock and ten o'clock news and then a chance to regroup for the next day, deadlines now come hourly or even instantly on both all-news channels and on the Internet as well. It is a frenetic pace compared to fifteen or twenty years ago and one that would challenge even a natural campaigner like Mulroney.

Michel Gratton's assessment provides some insight into whether Mulroney and his campaigning style could survive and be as successful today as it was in the 1980s. "In the end I have come to believe Brian Mulroney is very much like a chameleon. He adapts to his surroundings. He is, above all, a practical man rather than an intellectual one. He does what he thinks has to be done to survive."[37] Campaign team members argue that Mulroney's adaptability would make him as effective a campaigner today as in his heyday. Yet they also concede that it is not quite that simple. His effectiveness as a counterpuncher would be highlighted by all-news television, where he could score well. However, the fast pace of back-and-forth news coverage would make it impossible to have everything scripted to the final degree. That continual spontaneity would be a tough adjustment for him. It amplifies the possibility of making mistakes and appearing far from prime ministerial. Could his campaign team stay enough ahead of events to give him the degree of comfort about predictability that he clearly required to perform at his best in front of an audience, when there would also be constant demands from the media for comment, reaction, and sound bites all day long? If it could be done, it would likely wear out the campaign organization long before the end of the thirty-six-day campaign and would even test Mulroney's legendary campaign stamina.

Then there is the matter of his obsession with the media and what was being reported about him. Not only did Mulroney aggressively devour everything in the media every day, but, as already pointed out, he constantly wanted to correct the record whenever he perceived an injustice or thought an error had been reported about what he said, what he meant, or what his government or campaign was doing or had done. His opponents as well as the media were frequent subjects for his spontaneous responses and messages. For such a politician, all-news television channels would provide a constant stream of information that would feed his fixation with being misreported and offer a platform for him to respond. Yet, in that unscripted, rapid give-and-take, there would also be daily if not hourly potential to get into trouble by saying more than he should. It would require more continuous self-discipline than Mulroney usually exercised to walk past the reporters, listen to the questions, and keep going without stopping. In his day, reporters knew that they would strike it rich if he stopped so they would do everything they could to play to his weaknesses to get a comment from him. Stopping today would create more trouble than in his campaigns. Not only would his comments be instantly transmitted across the country but his scrums would inevitably highlight two of his shortcomings – his tendency to exaggerate when talking off the cuff and his apparent insincerity on television, which, as John Crosbie has noted, diffused Mulroney's warmth and made him appear phoney. It is also a medium that frequently punishes rather than rewards emotion and passion, raising doubts about how the emotional appeals Mulroney made from podiums across the country during the final three weeks of the 1988 campaign would translate through live television coverage to voters and viewers if they were available non-stop all day. As Gerald Caplan, Michael Kirby, and Hugh Segal describe those campaign days, "one theme would dominate Mulroney's presentations: The purpose of his life was to build a nation; of Turner's to tear up a treaty. Who do you want, he challenged audiences night after night, 'Brian the builder or John the Ripper!' And [then he would be] … back in his home province pleading emotionally for help. The Meech Lake Accord and free trade were essential to the future of Quebec, he said as he waved copies of both agreements over his head: Aidez-moi! Aidez-moi!"[38]

Mulroney was a product of the pre-television era of large political rallies when audiences came to hear partisan speeches laced with humour and digs at his opponents. In those days, listening to good speeches was an entertaining and informative way to pass an evening. Mulroney viewed his speeches and campaign rallies in that light. He was a performer anxious to entertain and impress the audience in the room, with barely a passing thought for how someone watching the same speech on television might respond. His goal was to win votes in the venue where he was speaking, not in living rooms miles away. The emotion he often displayed on stage, the inflexion in his voice and his verbal excesses, all played to the crowd before him, often with great effect. However, the same speech that captivated live audiences would leave a totally different and often more negative impression when watched on television. Gesticulating and yelling would be too hot for the screen. Even worse for a campaigner like Mulroney, the video clips taken from his speeches for news stories often made less sense than they did in the room where they were delivered, since they lacked the context of the entire speech and did not reflect the emotional highs and lows he would hit over the course of twenty or thirty minutes at the podium. They would likely "play" even less well today.

On the other hand, in any election campaign, a candidate responds to his or her opponents. No one campaigns in a vacuum and the public's response to any individual candidate is relative to the choices before the voters. That basic fact, combined with Mulroney's adaptability and his obvious strengths in other aspects of campaigning and organization, might offset somewhat the likelihood that all-news television would highlight his shortcomings while minimizing his strengths.

"'Brian just doesn't want to be Prime Minister,' his former friend Lucien Bouchard once observed [in the early 1980s]. 'He wants to live in history.'"[39] He does. He was the last of more than a century of Canadian politicians and campaigners who drew his strength and performed at his best before large, sometimes hostile crowds in the traditional role of a politician defending himself before the public and persuading them to vote for him. By 2006, those large public rallies had disappeared. No politician would now risk the unexpected that could occur when speaking to the public. Instead, campaigns are centred on leaders speaking to fifty to one hundred of the party faithful crammed into a room that could comfortably hold usually half that number. That looks better on television and looking good on television is now what really matters. While Mulroney and his campaign team skilfully used television for maximum advantage, television has transformed politics, the media, and campaigning to the point where, to survive today, Mulroney's style would have to change so fundamentally that his effectiveness would undoubtedly be severely compromised, if not completely undermined.

More than two decades after his first historic victory, and more than ten years after most Canadians outside Quebec were only too happy to see him go, there is little evidence that antagonism towards Mulroney has moderated at all, even though almost three-quarters of Canadians now support many of his legacies, such as free trade, The Liberal Party successfully exploited his image and the memories that went with it in campaign advertising in 2004 to try to frighten voters away from supporting the Conservatives. But the degree to which Brian Mulroney can still be used as a bogeyman ignores much of what he was all about. The best campaigners are those whose demeanour, message, and performance capture the public's attention, dominate a campaign, and persuade voters that his or her policies are the only ones right for the times and the future. Mulroney did that twice, despite the fact that, outside Quebec, support came increasingly not because he was loved but because of a grudging recognition by voters that he had the best grasp of what the country needed and could deliver it.

## NOTES

1 L. Ian Macdonald, *Mulroney: The Making of a Prime Minister* (Toronto: McClelland and Stewart 1985), 282.

2 Ibid., 293.

3 Ibid., 295.

4 Christopher Waddell, "Mulroney Takes Nothing for Granted on PEI Tour," *Globe and Mail*, 17 October 1988, A12.

5 Christopher Waddell, "Trade Pact Will Ensure Ontario Growth, PM Says," *Globe and Mail*, 4 October 1988, A9.

6 Ibid.

7 Christopher Waddell, "East Coast Needs Trade Deal, PM says," *Globe and Mail*, 14 October 1988, A10.

8 Ibid.

9 Christopher Waddell, "PC Leader Defends Economic Record," *Globe and Mail*, 13 October 1988, A12.

10 Waddell, "Mulroney Takes Nothing for Granted on PEI Tour."

11 Ibid.

12 Graham Fraser, *Playing for Keeps: The Making of the Prime Minister, 1988* (Toronto: McClelland and Stewart 1989), 182; and Waddell, "Mulroney Takes Nothing for Granted on PEI Tour."

13 Michel Gratton, *Still the Boss: A Candid Look at Brian Mulroney* (Scarborough, Ont.: Prentice-Hall Canada 1990), 62–3.

14 John Sawatsky, *Mulroney: The Politics of Ambition* (Toronto: MacFarlane, Walter and Ross 1991), 523.

15 Macdonald, *Mulroney: The Making of a Prime Minister*, 281.

16 Fraser, *Playing for Keeps*, 179.

17 Kim Campbell, *Time and Chance: The Political Memoirs of Canada's First Woman Prime Minister* (Toronto: Doubleday Canada 1996), 96.

18 Sawatsky, *Mulroney: The Politics of Ambition*, 524.
19 Ibid., 526.
20 Gerald Caplan, Michael Kirby, and Hugh Segal, *Election: The Issues, the Strategies, the Aftermath* (Scarborough, Ont.: Prentice-Hall Canada 1989), 169.
21 Waddell, "PC Leader Defends Economic Record."
22 Sawatsky, *Mulroney: The Politics of Ambition*, 527.
23 Fraser, *Playing for Keeps*, 185.
24 Caplan, Kirby, and Segal, *Election: The Issues, the Strategies, the Aftermath*, 224.
25 Fraser, *Playing for Keeps*, 301.
26 Ibid.
27 Ibid., 300.
28 Christopher Waddell, "Polluters Will Pay, Mulroney Promises," *Globe and Mail*, 15 October 1988, A9.
29 Andrew Cohen, *A Deal Undone: The Making and Breaking of the Meech Lake Accord* (Toronto: Douglas and McIntyre 1990), 235.
30 Sawatsky, *Mulroney: The Politics of Ambition*, 531.
31 Campbell, *Time and Chance*, 257.
32 Caplan, Kirby, and Segal, *Election: The Issues, the Strategies, the Aftermath*, 69.
33 John C. Crosbie, *No Holds Barred: My Life in Politics* (Toronto: McClelland and Stewart 1997), 453; Caplan, Kirby, and Segal, *Election: The Issues, the Strategies, the Aftermath*, 69.
34 G. Bruce Doern and Brian W. Tomlin, *Faith and Fear: The Free Trade Story* (Toronto: Stoddart Publishing 1991), 240.
35 Macdonald, *Mulroney: The Making of a Prime Minister*, 303.
36 Ibid.
37 Gratton, *Still the Boss*, 150.
38 Caplan, Kirby, and Segal, *Election: The Issues, the Strategies, the Aftermath*, 189.
39 Macdonald, *Mulroney: The Making of a Prime Minister*, 299.

## 2

# Debts Paid and Debts Owed: The Legacy of Mulroney's Economic Policies[1]

J. FRANK STRAIN

The legacy of Brian Mulroney and his government is a controversial and contested one. To some, Mulroney was a hero; to others, a villain. In the spirit of this divided legacy, the following evaluation of the Mulroney government's policies and their impact on the Canadian economy is likely to contain something to offend everyone. The landslide victory of the Progressive Conservatives in 1984 gave Prime Minister Brian Mulroney a strong mandate to offer Canadians a new approach to government. Clearly, there was demand for change, and not just in Canada. Dramatic change was in the air.

In 1979 the United Kingdom had elected a Conservative government, under the leadership of Margaret Thatcher, which immediately embarked on a radical program that included privatization and deregulation, tax cuts, and new labour legislation designed to reduce the power of trade unions, all of which placed emphasis on market discipline, including the introduction of market mechanisms into health and education. In 1981 the United States embarked on a similar program with the election of Ronald Reagan. Under the Republican president, tax reform received special emphasis. During the 1980 primary campaign, Reagan had promised a 30 per cent across-the-board tax cut and, once in power, he managed to overcome congressional resistance to implement tax cuts of about 23 per cent. Like Thatcher, Reagan rejected Keynesian economic ideas; he believed that his program of tax-rate reduction and a smaller role for government would spark a dramatic surge in private-sector activity and produce the new revenues needed to finance increased military spending and the "Star Wars" defence initiative. The theory that tax-rate cuts could generate tax-revenue increases was particularly attractive to politicians everywhere since it suggested that one could implement popular tax cuts without having to reduce government expenditures.

Brian Mulroney with Michael Wilson, who served as the minister of finance from September 1984 to May 1991. This photo was taken in the Prime Minister's Office in February 1991, shortly before Wilson became minister of industry, science, and technology and minister for international trade. Photographer Bill McCarthy. Library and Archives Canada 91-C-9239-15, negative number e007140475.

Despite the environment of radical economic and social change internationally and the support of a significant number of party members and elected MPs who wanted his new government to follow a more radical route, Prime Minister Mulroney chose not to do so. He certainly embraced the general goals of the Thatcher-Reagan revolutions to reduce the role of government and increase individual self-reliance. He also placed greater faith in the private sector's ability to generate economic prosperity than he did in Pierre Trudeau's vision of a government-managed "just society." However, Mulroney set himself apart from Thatcher and Reagan in adopting a middle-of-the-road approach to government policy in Canada.

The reasons for this are complex and difficult to disentangle. The personal influence of Brian Mulroney himself as leader of the government was certainly an important factor. Mulroney was not an ideologue driven by a personal neo-conservative agenda to be implemented at all costs. Instead, he was a master of negotiation, compromise, and reconciliation, and so his middle-of-the-road approach is not surprising given the importance he personally placed on conciliation in the exercise of leadership. Mulroney was also committed to the principles of fairness and equity, ideals that featured prominently in his first campaign and in most of the major policy pronouncements by his government. He believed that the state had an important role in society and that the objective of governance was to strike the right balance, with the state and the private sector knowing their respective roles and playing them effectively.

The woeful condition of Canada's public finances at the end of Liberal rule in 1984 was also an important factor. The Mulroney government inherited a large and growing public debt, and controlling the debt quickly became the primary focus of the Conservatives. The preoccupation with debt and deficits not only distracted the government from more radical policy approaches but also increased significantly the risks associated with any such changes. With the benefit of hindsight, we now know that the Reagan tax cuts did not generate the much-anticipated surge in private-sector activity or increases in tax revenues but, instead, resulted in large and growing U.S. government deficits. Fear of this outcome for Canada played an important role in budgetary policy under Mulroney.

The Mulroney government's economic-policy objectives were clearly laid out in its first budget in November 1985, and the government remained committed to these objectives through its two terms in office. Michael Wilson, who would remain finance minister through most of the Mulroney mandate, articulated the government's agenda as follows: "Our objective is to put in place a framework that will release the energies of Canadians to focus cooperatively and constructively on expanding the economic pie rather than on an increasingly divisive struggle for a static or shrinking one."[2] To accomplish this wide-ranging goal, the Mulroney government set four concrete objectives: "(1) We must put our fiscal house in order so that we can limit, and ultimately reverse, the massive build-up of public debt and the damaging impact this has on confidence and growth; (2) redefine government to promote growth and innovation; (3) adopt policies that foster higher investment, greater innovation, increased entrepreneurial competitiveness and a positive climate for the birth and growth of new enterprise; and (4) in doing the above, remain committed to fairness and assisting those in need."[3]

This commitment to fairness and assisting those in need was not merely a rhetorical move designed to make radical neo-conservative policies more palatable to the Canadian public. Unlike Thatcher and Reagan, Mulroney did not believe that poverty was largely a consequence of perverse incentives introduced by well-meaning but inappropriate government policies. Nor did he believe in the simplistic "trickle down" theory, which suggests that increases in income of the rich will, in the fullness of time, ultimately benefit the poor. Without doubt, the Conservative government did, in fact, believe that anti-poverty programs could be redesigned to help the poor more efficiently, but it did not believe that they could be cut substantially with no negative impact on poverty. Indeed, as I show below, both poverty and income inequality declined in Canada during the Mulroney era, a fact that may surprise and even dismay those on the left and on the extreme right.

The decline in income inequality in Canada during the Mulroney era can be attributed largely to tax increases implemented as part of the government's pursuit of its first objective: deficit and debt reduction. This legacy of deficit and debt left from the Trudeau era was certainly the most important challenge facing Mulroney when he assumed office in 1984. However, despite continuous attention, debt and debt relative to income continued to rise through both of Mulroney's terms in office. A fair and balanced assessment of economic policy during the Mulroney years must acknowledge the centrality of this struggle and the deep mark it left on the policies that the Conservative government pursued.

In large part because of the important work by Ron Kneebone and other economists, we have a fairly clear understanding of the challenges posed by debt and deficit reduction and the reasons why the struggle in Canada never actually resulted in reductions in debt relative to income (the debt-to-GDP ratio).[4] The debt problem for Canada emerged in the 1974–76 period, with 1975 being a particularly significant year. At that time, the government of Pierre Trudeau responded to a sluggish Canadian economy – resulting from the so-called oil-price shock triggered by the Organization of Petroleum Exporting Countries (OPEC) and from corporate tax cuts in the United States – by increasing government spending and reducing taxes substantially. The tax cuts included "a three percentage point cut in the personal income tax rate, an accelerated write-off on purchases of capital equipment, the introduction of a $1,000 deduction for dividend and interest incomes and for private pension plans, and the introduction of a home ownership savings plan."[5] On the expenditure side, the Trudeau government introduced measures that "more than doubled business subsidies and capital assistance, an increase equal to 6 percent of total federal spending in that year."[6] In combination, the tax cuts and expenditure increases represented the largest single fiscal policy initiative in the 1962–96 period. Unfortunately, these stimuli did not have the desired effect on economic activity and, like the Reagan tax cuts that followed in the 1980s, produced only a substantial deficit. By 1981, the Trudeau government realized its mistake and introduced the second most dramatic change in budgetary policy in the 1962–95 period. In the 1981 budget the Trudeau government established the National Energy Program, which added almost \$3 billion to federal revenue (a figure representing about 15 per cent of Ottawa's total revenue). But this attempt to constrain the deficit failed and, as a result, the Mulroney government was left with a "deficit mess" to clean up.

Economists, and all who follow government budgetary policy, now understand why the Mulroney government's attempt to eliminate deficits failed. Although those uninitiated in the mechanics of debt accumulation typically believe that deficits are a simple outcome of excessive government spending relative to taxation, this is not the case. A combination of high interest rates and low growth can work against any attempt to lower deficits and debt through tax increases and/or expenditure cuts. Economists typically call the difference between program expenditures and tax collections the primary deficit (that is, the interest payments on public debt are part of the deficit calculation but are excluded in the calculation of the primary deficit). A government can run a substantial primary surplus yet see its debt relative to GDP rise if interest payments on the public debt are large enough to offset any primary surplus.

Understanding the dynamics of debt is critical in appreciating the difficulties Mulroney faced throughout his mandate. Pierre Fortin and Fortin and Osberg provide a simple treatment of debt dynamics.[7] Their treatment is not controversial because, as they note, "economists of all political persuasions agree on the debt stability equation since it is based on established accounting identities."[8] Debt in any year ($D_t$) will equal the debt in the previous year ($D_{t-1}$) plus any primary deficit ($PB_t$) and the interest payments on the debt ($rD_{t-1}$). If interest payments ($rD_{t-1}$) are high enough, debt will rise even if program expenditures are less than taxes. Simple manipulation of this equation shows that the ratio of debt to GDP will evolve according to the equation $\Delta(D/GDP)_t = (r - g)\ D_{t-1} / GDP_t - PB_{t-1} / GDP_t$. Thus, if the rate of interest exceeds the rate of growth in the economy (g), the debt-to-GDP ratio will rise unless the primary budget surplus relative to income is large enough. Moreover, if the interest rate exceeds the rate of economic growth, the primary surplus needed to keep the debt-to-GDP ratio constant will grow as the size of debt grows.

The sustainability equation not only illustrates the difficulties associated with debt and deficit reduction but also clearly reveals why debt control is an imperative: continuous growth in debt results in continuous growth in interest payments to holders of the debt and a steady reduction in the amount of total government revenue which can be used to finance government programs. It is also possible that increases in borrowing will increase real interest rates as governments compete with the private sector for the savings created by society. If interest rates increase and government spending is concentrated on current consumption activities, the rate of economic growth will fall, resulting in lower future incomes.

When Mulroney assumed power in 1984, not only was the debt large but also interest rates were significantly higher than the rate of economic growth. As a consequence, reducing program expenditures and increasing taxes were not sufficient to halt the explosion in debt. The primary budget surplus had to be large enough to offset the interest charges on the public debt. Had the economy been performing well as a result of careful macroeconomic management and luck, interest rates might have fallen below the rate of growth and the Mulroney government would have seen debt decline even if it ran primary deficits with program expenditures exceeding tax collections. As it was, with interest rates exceeding the rate of growth, the Conservatives had to take the extremely unpopular measure of reducing government expenditures and increasing taxes to control the burgeoning debt.

This was the strategy laid down in the first Mulroney budget: to reduce the primary budget deficit through a combination of tax increases and program expenditure cuts, many of which were phased in over a three-year period. Subsequent budgets continued to increase taxes and reduce expenditures, and Kneebone and McKenzie have shown that the second largest fiscal contraction in the 1962–96 period occurred in 1986. They claim that the very tight fiscal stance "can be traced to the first Mulroney budget. The increase in revenue resulted from a number of tax increases, including a partial de-indexing of income taxes, the application of two income surtaxes, and the end of the home ownership savings plan that added $5 billion to a revenue base of $77 billion in 1986. On the spending side, the budget phased out the Petroleum Incentive Program, announced the sale of a number of Crown corporations, and substantially reduced grants and subsidies to business."[9]

The heavy reliance on tax increases was completely at odds with the ideas of the Thatcher-Reagan neo-conservative movement. So, too, was the introduction of surtaxes (and a minimum federal tax) targeting the more affluent members of society. De-indexation proved to be a powerful and, in many respects, hidden revenue-raising tool. On the other hand, deregulation in transportation, telecommunications, and financial services clearly followed the Thatcher/Reagan model, as did the privatization of crown corporations. During the Mulroney years, dozens of crown corporations were privatized, including Teleglobe, Air Canada, Canadair, and part of PetroCanada. In total, privatization reduced federal government employment by about 90,000. Privatization not only provided a one-time injection of cash but was also undertaken in the hope that it would increase efficiency and boost economic growth.

As Edward Carmichael has argued, "Mulroney ... [had] lost his appetite for tough deficit reduction measures" by 1987.[10] Despite its backing away from deficit reduction, however, the Mulroney government introduced important budgetary changes in its remaining years in office. The two most controversial measures were the replacement of a number of universal transfer programs and tax deductions with tax credits and policies that more effectively targeted the poor, and the introduction of the Goods and Services Tax (GST) to replace the existing Manufacturers' Sales Tax (MST). In both cases, the changes were designed to be revenue neutral since they were not intended to increase revenue or reduce total expenditures; neutrality was a political necessity given the controversy generated by the government's tampering with the Canadian social-welfare system and its replacement of an invisible tax with a highly visible one.

Most economists applauded sales-tax reform, however. They believed that the MST was a bad tax because it penalized some (consumers and producers of goods manufactured in Canada) and favoured others (consumers and producers of services and foreign-produced goods). Moreover, with a high tax rate, the MST had a larger distorting effect than a tax with a lower rate. On the other hand, the GST was deeply unpopular with Canadians since it made sales taxation highly visible. An interesting feature of the GST was the simultaneous introduction of the refundable GST tax credit into the personal income-tax system. The refundable credit returned much of the GST paid by the poor to assure that the tax was not extremely regressive.

Another important part of Mulroney's deficit-reduction strategy involved targeting transfers to provincial governments that had traditionally supported provincial activities in health and post-secondary education. In doing so, the new government followed the previous Trudeau regime in exploiting special features of the Established Program Financing (EPF) transfer. Originally introduced in 1977, the EPF replaced transfers in support of hospital and diagnostic-services insurance, Medicare, and post-secondary education. Designed to provide a block of funds independent of provincial expenditures, this transfer was made half in cash and half in tax points (the federal government reduced its tax rates, provinces increased theirs). The legislation covering the transfer provided for continuous growth in the size of the total transfer at about the rate of growth of GDP. In the early 1980s, the Trudeau government subjected the transfer to its 6-and-5 anti-inflation program, which had the effect of significantly reducing the size of the federal government cash transfer. Because nominal incomes were growing faster than 6 per cent, the tax portion of the transfer was growing faster than the total, thus reducing the growth of the federal cash transfer.[11]

In the late 1980s and early 1990s, the Mulroney government continued this policy of reducing the rate of growth in the total transfer. Indeed, in 1990 the total transfer was frozen, and the 1991 budget extended the freeze to 1994–95. This was an irresistible opportunity since the strategy reduced cash transfers to the provinces while still allowing the government to claim that it was not reducing transfers to the provinces. But, from the point of view of the provincial governments, transfers were being cut since they focused on the cash portion of the transfer, which was steadily falling from 50 per cent of the total transfer towards 0 per cent. In other words, the caps imposed on the growth in the total transfer effectively transferred part of the federal government deficit to the provincial governments and would, if maintained for a period of ten to fifteen years, completely eliminate federal government cash support for health and post-secondary education.

Still, despite significant debt- and deficit-fighting efforts, including "off-loading" some of the debt onto the provinces, the Mulroney government did not achieve its objective of stopping the growth of debt or improving the debt-to-GDP ratio. However, by the end of its mandate, the government had, at least, achieved a primary budget surplus, and the size of the deficit was one-third of that inherited from the Trudeau years.

Why did the Mulroney government fail to stop the growth of debt and improve the debt-to-GDP ratio? Low growth rates and high interest rates are a large part of the answer. As illustrated by the debt-stability equation, growth rates must exceed interest rates in order for debt reduction to occur. Such conditions did not exist during the Mulroney years. Of course, this begs the question of why the Conservatives were unable to reduce interest rates and generate growth, and it is to this question that we will now turn.

Mulroney inherited an environment of low economic growth. In part, this was due to cyclical factors. A deep recession in 1981–82 (and another in 1990–91) shrunk the economy and reduced investment in fixed capital. The recession was induced by the Bank of Canada (as was the recession of 1990–91), which was attempting to establish credibility in its fight against inflation. Throughout Mulroney's mandate, the fight against inflation restrained demand by keeping interest rates high and capital formation low. Nonetheless, the recovery from the 1981–82 recession allowed room for some economic expansion in the 1984–89 period until the Bank of Canada applied the brakes and induced another round of economic decline. In part, low growth was a consequence of a global slowdown in productivity growth.

Some may argue that Mulroney's failure to stimulate growth was not entirely his fault. The Conservatives had little control over global trends, and Mulroney had given the Bank of Canada relative autonomy to fight

Table 1 Average annual growth of total factor productivity, G-7 countries, 1960–73 and 1974–93

| Country | Period 1960–73 | Period 1974–93 |
|---|---|---|
| Canada | 2.0 | 0.3 |
| United States | 1.6 | 0.1 |
| Japan | 5.6 | 1.4 |
| Germany | 2.6 | 0.5 |
| France | 4.0 | 1.4 |
| Italy | 4.4 | 1.4 |
| United Kingdom | 2.5 | 1.2 |
| G-7 Average | 3.2 | 0.9 |

*Source*: Pierre Fortin and Elhanan Helpman, *Endogenous Innovation and Growth: Implications for Canada* (Ottawa: Industry Canada, occasional paper no. 10, August 1995).

inflation and had trusted the dominant theory of appropriate monetary policy at the time. In an environment of tight monetary policy and a worldwide productivity slowdown, the micro-economic policy measures introduced by the Mulroney government, which included privatization, deregulation, tax reform, and eventually the Free Trade Agreement, simply had little impact on economic growth. As illustrated in Table 1, Canada was not the only country to suffer from this phenomenon.

As mentioned previously, high interest rates were, in part, a result of the monetary policy being pursued by the Bank of Canada to fight inflation. Indeed, the Bank of Canada was remarkably aggressive in its fight against inflation, with Canadian real interest rates increasing from an average of 0.9 per cent in the 1961–81 period to an average of 7.5 per cent in the period from 1982 to 1993, with short-term interest rates increasing by 2.25 points more in Canada than in the United States.[12] Numerous critics of the Bank of Canada policy note that much of the build-up of debt in the 1980s and early 1990s was due to monetary policy's contribution to high interest rates and low economic growth, not to "excessive federal government spending."

Ultimately, however, a prime minister must assume responsibility for monetary policy since his government continuously works with the Bank of Canada in policy formation and has the ultimate power to dismiss the governor if it believes that bank policy is inappropriate. Mulroney did not attempt to change bank policy by encouraging a less vigilant fight against inflation (or even a fight similar in scale to that waged by our biggest trading partner, the United States), and he certainly did not attempt to remove John Crowe, the bank governor. In fact, Mulroney strongly supported the governor and shared his preoccupation with inflation. In July

1989 Mulroney told the *Financial Post* editorial board that "we will sustain the Governor of the Bank of Canada and his interest rate policy because the fundamental evil in the economy is inflation, and it must and will be dealt with."[13] In retrospect, this belief in the importance of achieving zero inflation at all costs may be the most significant failure of Brian Mulroney and his government. Even a slightly better economic performance would have made his fight against the deficit more successful and his micro-economic policy initiatives much more effective.

Inflation, Mulroney's views notwithstanding, is not a fundamental evil in and of itself. It is the consequences of inflation that really matter, in particular the consequences for: (1) productivity, or real income per person, which determines living standards; (2) employment, which allows each citizen to contribute to the society in which he or she lives; and (3) income distribution, which determines how a society shares the goods and services produced. As American economist Paul Krugman has noted, other economic outcomes, including the inflation rate, the exchange rate, the government deficit, the trade balance, and the size of government, are important only through their impact on income per capita, employment, and the distribution of income.[14] My examination of the economic legacy of the Mulroney government, therefore, must now address these three fundamentals.

In a special issue of the Institute for Research on Public Policy's main periodical, *Policy Options,* Tom Velk and Al Riggs examine a variety of economic-performance indicators and, on this basis, rank Brian Mulroney as the best prime minister, statistically, in Canadian history.[15] In another *Policy Options* paper, Michael Hart and Bill Dymond adopt a similar approach and reach similar conclusions.[16] In particular, Hart and Dymond conclude that "as time passes the Mulroney legacy looks more and more impressive. He inherited a country with a growing number of problems. He left the country with many of them resolved or on their way to resolution. His economic initiatives will prove particularly enduring and constructive." My evaluation is not as glowing.

The conclusions reached by Riggs and Velk and Hart and Dymond are based on two methodological choices. First, they use a variety of economic indicators, a decision that significantly reduces the weight given to the fundamental data on per- capita incomes, employment, and inequality. Secondly, they adopt a time-series approach, which involves evaluating Mulroney's performance relative to other prime ministers. No recognition is given to the fact that the global environment in which each prime minister worked differed significantly. As a consequence, we cannot determine whether good performance was due to government policy or to the broader global environment in which policy was formulated.

An alternative approach is adopted here. To begin with, the focus is restricted to productivity (approximated by income per capita), employment,

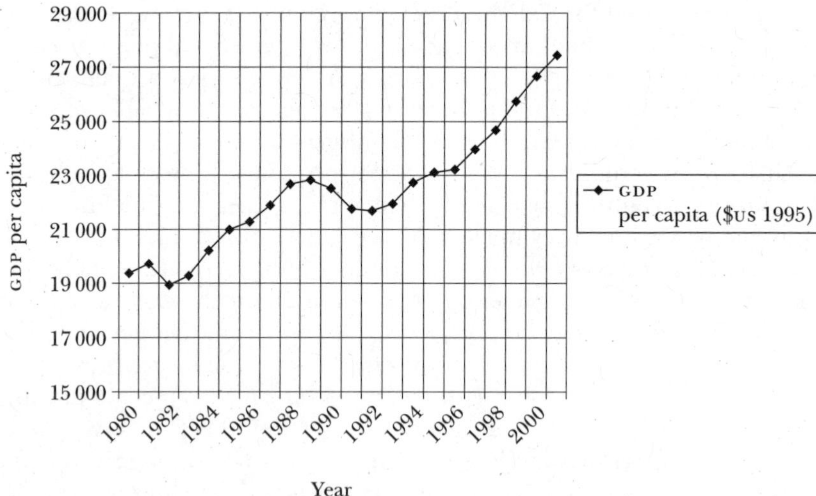


Figure 1 GDP per capita ($US 1995)

and inequality. This focus follows the work of Krugman, who argues that "for the economy, the important things – the things that affect the standards of living of large numbers of people – are productivity, income distribution, and unemployment."[17] Also, instead of adopting a time-series methodology, this evaluation uses a panel data set constructed by Andrew Sharpe and Lars Osberg for a paper released by the Centre for the Study of Living Standards.[18] The panel involved seven countries, including Canada, over the period from 1981 to 2001. The use of panel data holds the global environment constant but does not allow for the identification of the independent impact of governance since countries differ in ways that are not controlled for. Moreover, no attempt is made to incorporate persistence (the impact of past policies on current and future performance) or fixed and variable effects through use of econometric modelling techniques. Nonetheless, the comparisons provide some useful insights into the Mulroney years.

Figure 1 presents the time-series data on income per capita for Canada in the 1981–2001 period. The impact of the two major recessions is clearly evident, as is the period of recovery from 1984 through 1989. Figures 2 and 3 present the same data in a different way. In Figure 2, Canadian performance is compared to the performance of the United States, the United Kingdom, and Australia through a simple index. Canadian GDP per capita measured in 1995 U.S. dollars is divided by another country's GDP per capita measured in 1995 U.S. dollars and this ratio is then multiplied by 100. Note that, if Canadian real GDP per capita is equal to real GDP per capita in the other country, the index will equal 100. Moreover,

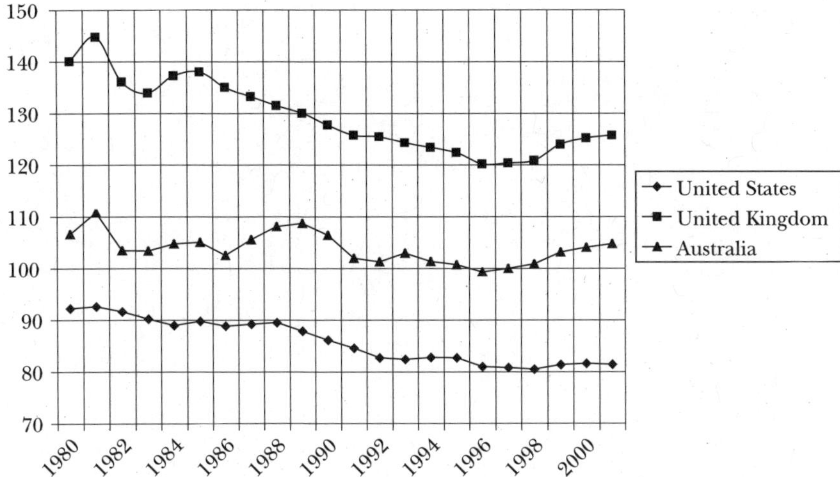


Figure 2 Relative GDP per capita

if the index grows over time, Canadian GDP per capita is growing relative to the other country; if the index is falling, Canadian real GDP per capita is declining. For example, in 1980 Canadian real GDP was about 90 per cent of that in the United States. By 1993, Canadian real GDP per capita had fallen to 82.5 per cent of that in the United States, a relative decline of almost 10 per cent. Indeed, real GDP per capita in Canada declined relative to all three countries during the Mulroney era.

Figure 3 repeats the exercise but with Sweden, Norway, and Germany as the control. Again, Canadian real GDP falls relative to all three countries, although the decline relative to Germany is small. In short, since the performance of the Mulroney government does not look good relative to these countries, a reconsideration of the rosy evaluations of Velk and Riggs and Hart and Dymond is in order (or, at the very least, least one should be sceptical of their conclusions).

A similar picture emerges when one looks at the employment rate. Figures 4, 5, and 6 present data on the employment rate (total employment divided by the fifteen- to sixty-five-year-old population) both in Canada alone and in Canada relative to the panel group of countries.

Figure 4 illustrates the significance of two Canadian recessions, especially that of 1990–91, for employment. Figure 5 shows that Canadian employment relative to population grew markedly slower than in the United States and that its employment rate fell relative to both the United Kingdom and Australia between 1987 and the end of the Mulroney regime. On the other hand, Figure 6 shows that the employment rate in Canada rose relative to that of Sweden, Norway, and Germany, but with a

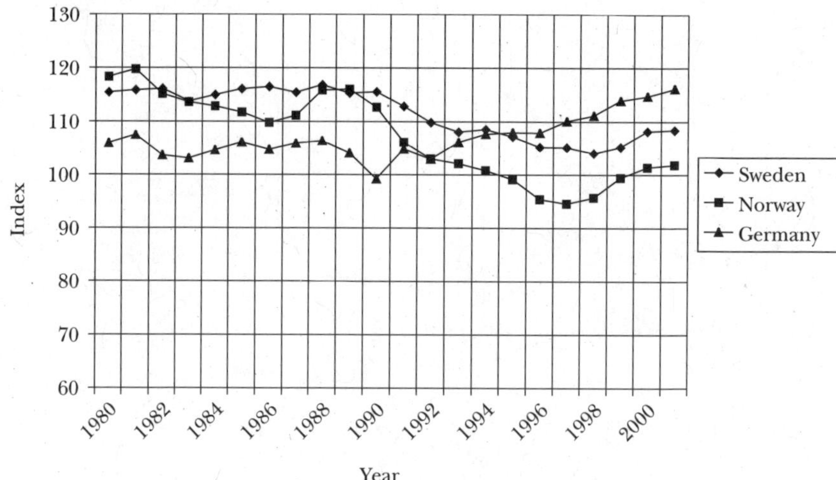


Figure 3 Relative per capita GDP

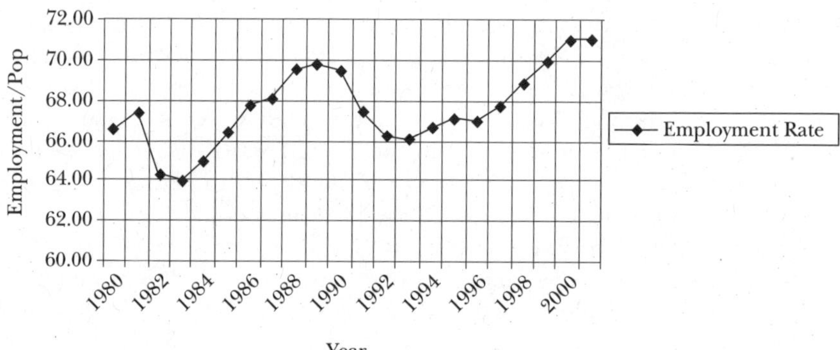


Figure 4 Employment rate

marked relative decline during the recession of 1990–91 and its aftermath. Thus, under Mulroney, Canada's employment performance was better than that of some countries and worse than that of others.

Figures 7 through 12 report data on inequality and poverty. Inequality is measured using a Gini coefficient, which always lies between 0 and 1. A value of 0 indicates that everyone has the same income and a value of 1 indicates that all income is in the hands of one person, with the rest of the society earning nothing. Thus, the Gini coefficient can be crudely interpreted as implying increased inequality when it is rising and reduced inequality when it is falling. Data on poverty rates are also presented to emphasize the outcomes for the poor. Poverty rates are defined as the

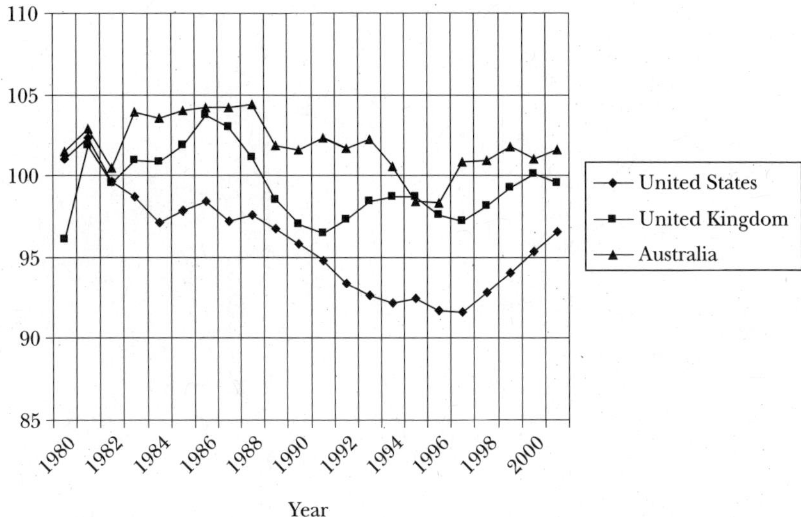


Figure 5 Relative employment rate

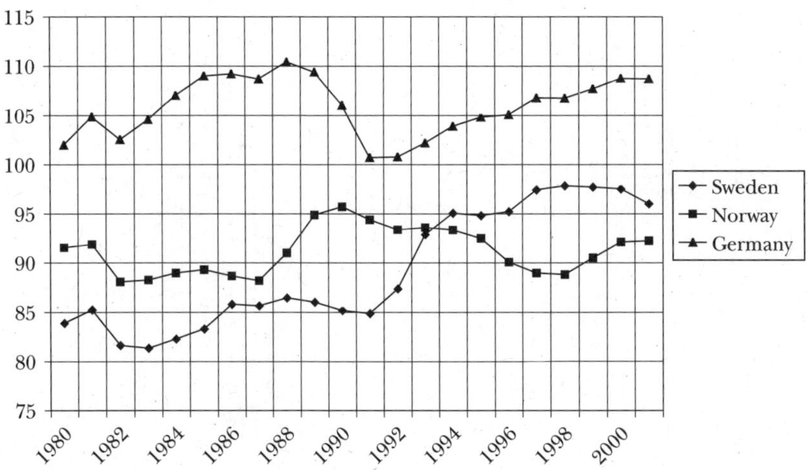


Figure 6 Relative employment rate

proportion of families with incomes less than 50 per cent of the median income. Family incomes are adjusted using an equivalence scale to make incomes across different family types comparable.

Both Figure 7, which reports income inequality, and Figure 8, which reports data on poverty in Canada, illustrate that incomes became more equally distributed and that poverty declined during the Mulroney period.

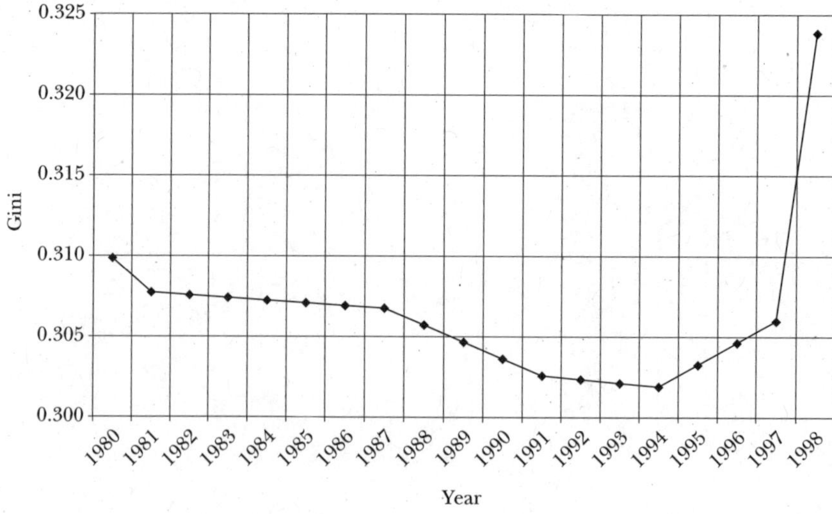


Figure 7 Income inequality in Canada

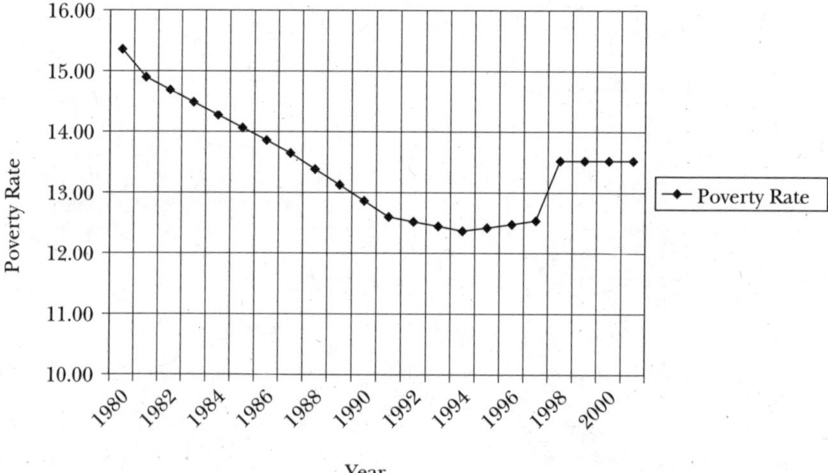


Figure 8 Poverty rate

Figures 9 through 12 provide a comparative perspective on the success of the Mulroney government in reducing both poverty and inequality. No matter what comparison is chosen, the data suggests that the government was remarkably successful in fulfilling its promise to fight the debt in an equitable way. Relative to most countries in the comparison group, Canadian society became more equal and had greater reductions in poverty.

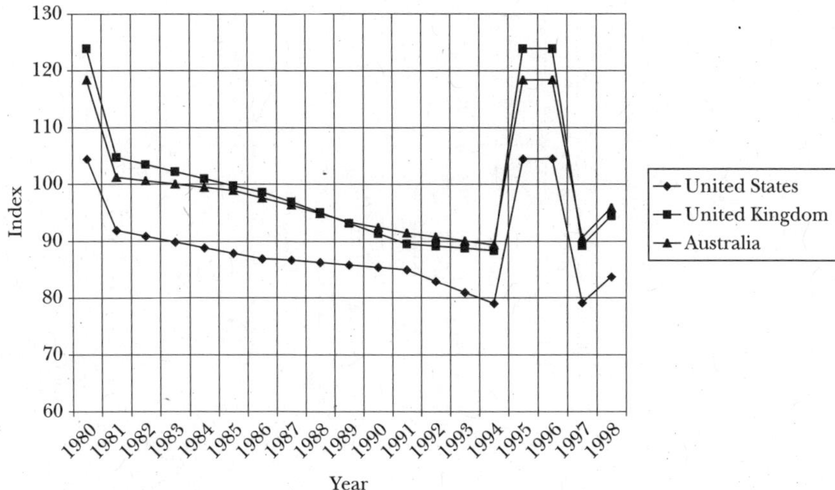


Figure 9 Relative income inequality

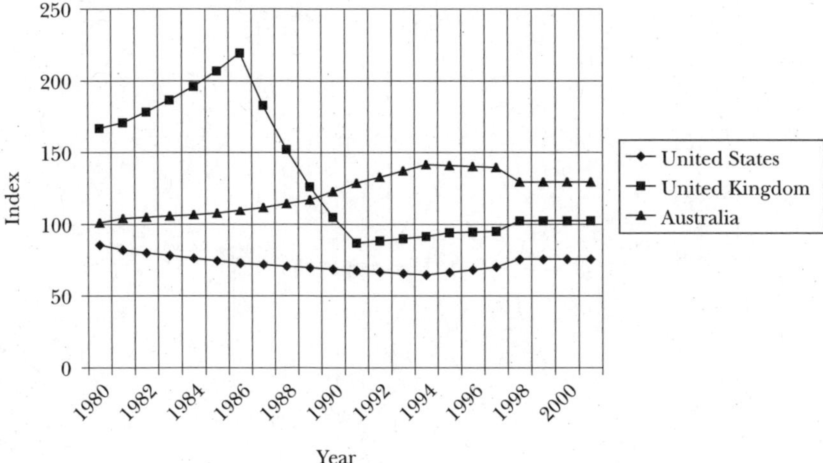


Figure 10 Relative poverty

This is not what most people would have expected to be an important part of the Mulroney legacy.

In summary, the Mulroney government consistently pursued its stated goals of debt reduction, economic growth, innovation, and fairness. The first, debt reduction, was never attained but the Mulroney government did manage to achieve a primary budget surplus towards the end of its second term. Poor macro-economic performance due to tight monetary policy

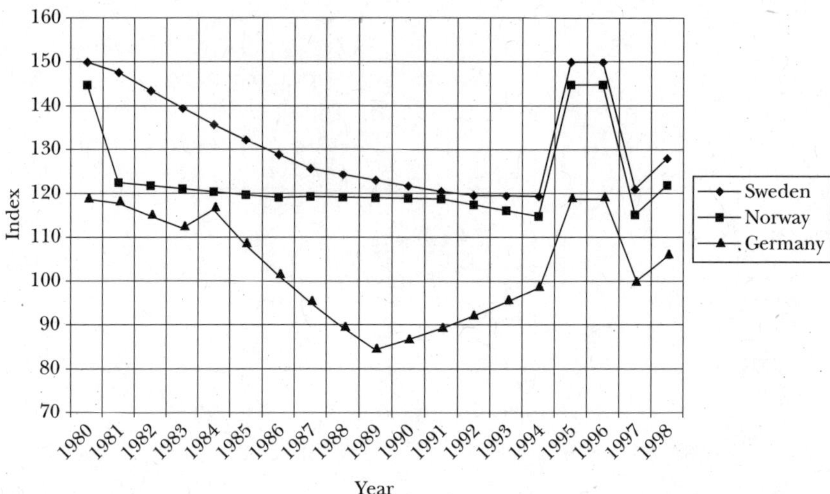


Figure 11 Relative income inequality

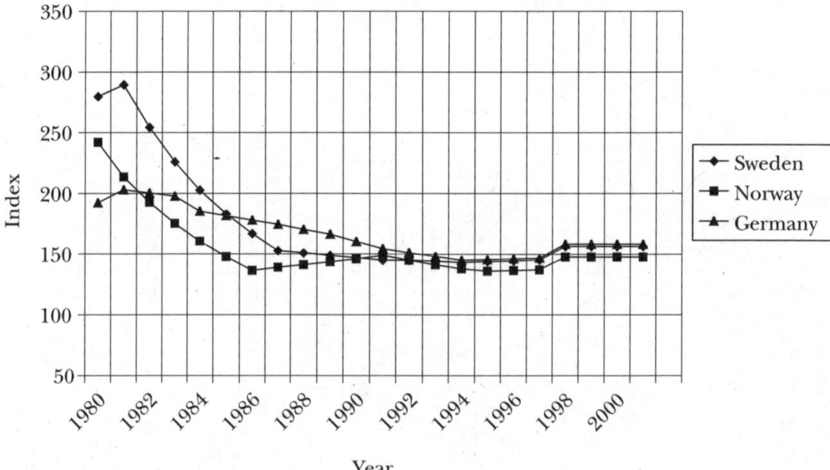


Figure 12 Relative poverty

was a critical factor in this failure and, when growth rates began to exceed interest rates in the late 1990s, the debt rapidly came under control and the debt-to-GDP ratio declined steadily. Thus, by creating a primary surplus, the Mulroney government left its successors in a position where the dream of debt control could be realized.

The other goals were not realized either. Growth of GDP per capita during the Mulroney years was slow by historical standards and weak relative to many other countries. For a government that placed so much emphasis on private-sector-led growth, this must have been a major disappointment. Again, monetary policy was a key factor in the poor performance; indeed, the decision to pursue a goal of zero inflation much more aggressively than the United States was, at least in retrospect, disastrous. Allan Greenspan, who set monetary policy in the United States, managed to reduce inflation significantly while simultaneously creating conditions conducive to a remarkable boom; John Crowe, his Canadian counterpart, did not. That macro-economic conditions improved markedly under the Liberal government that followed must have been particularly galling given that the Liberals, despite promises of change, did not abandon any of the micro-economic policy initiatives implemented in the Mulroney years and that the fruits of these Conservative policies were realized only when the Liberals were in power.

Of the four objectives, only the fourth – fairness – was truly realized. Income inequality and poverty declined in both absolute and relative terms. Simplistic characterizations of the Mulroney economic legacy as being pro-business and strongly pro-growth to the detriment of equality and the poor are clearly wrong.

Readers are left with the final task of evaluating the overall economic performance and legacy of Brian Mulroney. Those who put a significant weight on poverty and income distribution in their evaluation will have to consider the fact that Mulroney performed relatively well. Those who give equity concerns less weight will have to face the possibility that Mulroney and his government did not deliver on its promise of improving economic growth significantly.

## NOTES

1 I would like to acknowledge the research assistance provided by Michelle Langois, who carefully tracked down and compiled needed information in Canada while I was working on this chapter in the Peoples Republic of China. The helpful comments of Craig Brett and Owen Griffiths are also acknowledged.

2 Michael Wilson, "A New Direction for Canada: An Agenda for Economic Renewal," Department of Finance, 8 November 1985, 2.

3 Ibid., 2–3.

4 Ronald D. Kneebone and Kenneth J. McKenzie, "The Characteristics of Fiscal Policy in Canada," *Canadian Public Policy* 24(4) (1999): 483–501; Ronald D. Kneebone and John Leach, "The Accumulation of Debt in Canada," *Canadian Public Policy* 27(3) (2001): 297–312; and Ronald D. Kneebone and J. Chung, "Where Did the Debt Come from?" in Christopher Regan and William Watson, eds., *Is The Debt War Over? Dispatches from Canada's Fiscal Front Lines* (Montreal: Institute for Research on Public Policy 2004).

5 Kneebone and McKenzie, "The Characteristics of Fiscal Policy in Canada," 492.

6 Ibid., 493.
7 Pierre Fortin, "The Canadian Fiscal Problem: The Macroeconomic Connection," in Pierre Fortin and Lars Osberg, eds., *Unnecessary Debts* (Toronto: Lorimer 1996), 26–38; and ibid., Pierre Fortin and Lars Osberg, appendix A, "The Debt Stability Equation," 173–5.
8 Pierre Fortin and Lars Osberg, ibid., appendix A, 173.
9 Kneebone and McKenzie, "The Characteristics of Fiscal Policy in Canada," 493.
10 Edward Carmichael, "The Mulroney Government and the Deficit," in Andrew B. Gollner and Daniel Salee, eds., *Canada under Mulroney: An End of Term Report* (Montreal: Vehicule Press 1988), 233.
11 To illustrate, consider a simple example. Suppose that there is an initial total transfer of $1,000,000, $500,000 in cash and $500,000 in extra tax arising from a transfer of tax points. Now suppose that the economy grows by 10 per cent. If legislation increases the transfer at the rate of growth in the economy by 10 per cent, the total transfer will rise by $100,000. Tax collections by the provinces will also rise by 10 per cent ($50,000) and the federal cash transfer, which is equal to the difference between the total and the tax point, must rise by $50,000. But, if legislation caps the rate of growth in the total transfer to 5 per cent, the total transfer rises by $50,000. Provincial taxes still grow by $50,000, with 10 per cent growth, and thus the federal government does not provide any cash transfer.
12 Fortin, "The Canadian Fiscal Problem," 33–4.
13 *Financial Post,* weekly edition, 19 July 1989, 10.
14 Paul Krugman, *The Age of Diminished Expectations.* (Boston: MIT Press 1997).
15 Tom Velk and Al Riggs, "Brian Mulroney: The Man to Beat," Unpublished paper.
16 Michael Hart and Bill Dymond, "Six Steward's of Canada's Economy – History by the Numbers Favours Mulroney and Chrétien While Trudeau Leaves a Legacy of Deficits and Debt," *Policy Options,* June–July 2003.
17 Krugman, *The Age of Diminished Expectations,* 8.
18 Lars Osberg and Andrew Sharpe, "Human Well-being and Economic Well-being: What Are the Values Implicit in Current Indices?" *CSLS Research Report,* August 2003.

# 3

# Free Trade and Brian Mulroney's Economic Legacy

MICHAEL HART

In September 1984 Brian Mulroney succeeded in leading the Conservative Party of Sir John A. Macdonald, Sir Robert Borden, and John Diefenbaker to its largest electoral triumph ever, gaining 211 of the 282 seats in the House of Commons. In the year since his selection as party leader in place of the hapless Joe Clark, Mulroney had crafted a coalition of Ontario and Eastern Tories, Quebec nationalists, and western social and economic conservatives, and convinced Canadians that he was the man to replace the tired Liberals under their new leader, John Turner. Nine years later, having surrendered the leadership to Kim Campbell, he watched in dismay as Canadians turned against the Tories and reduced them to a corporal's guard of Jean Charest and Elsie Wayne. The coalition had imploded and reconstituted itself as Reform in the west, the Bloc Québécois in Quebec, and bickering remnants of Tories in Ontario and the Maritimes.

No other Canadian prime minister had ever seen his political fortunes reversed so quickly and completely. To be sure, it can be argued that in 1984 Mulroney had benefited from the end of Canadians' romance with Pierre Elliot Trudeau and that Kim Campbell bears some of the blame for the debacle of 1993. But the coalition that had triumphed in 1984 was very much one shaped by Brian Mulroney, and its subsequent implosion was equally the result of his inability to satisfy its disparate interests and hold it together. He had made a Faustian bargain in 1983–84 to build it, and by 1992–93 the devil had claimed his due.

From an electoral perspective, therefore, Brian Mulroney left a bittersweet legacy, the bitterness compounded by the visceral dislike he seemed to evoke among the chattering classes, and the sweetness easily forgotten by the Reformists, Blocistes, and Tories who had shared the fruits of victory in 1984 and again in 1988. The next ten years would prove just as disappointing, as the Conservatives' mutual recriminations helped to keep the pragmatic, transactional government of Jean Chrétien in power,

Prime Minister Mulroney signing the Canada-United States Free Trade Agreement, 2 January 1988. Photographer Bill McCarthy. Library and Archives Canada 88-c-03785-15, negative number e007140470.

a government that succeeded in astutely taking credit for many of the reforms introduced by Mulroney, and nowhere more so than in the realm of trade and economic policy.

The image of Mulroney projected by the media is of a savvy politician with few principles and ideas but a consummate practitioner of the art of the deal; they also like to portray him as too cozy with the Americans, too close to business barons, and too ready to help a crony. And, in some ways, Mulroney himself promoted this image. He loves deal making, is comfortable with Americans and business leaders, and maintains an extensive rolodex of friends and allies. He knows how to work a crowd, but the same folksy style tends to grate under the klieg lights of television. It is ironic that Jean Chrétien, one of the most vindictive politicians of his era, succeeded in projecting a media image as a regular guy, while Brian Mulroney, a loyal friend to hundreds of people, has been seen as a shallow showboat.

An even greater irony, however, is that the very same policies and values that steadily alienated Canadians over the course of Mulroney's two mandates may also prove the mainstay of his reputation as one of Canada's more successful prime ministers. As a recent survey of historians, economists, and public-policy specialists concluded, Mulroney ranks well ahead of Trudeau, Louis St Laurent, Jean Chrétien, and John Diefenbaker, and behind only Lester Pearson, as the most effective prime minister of the last fifty years. The survey also noted that, by the end of his second term, "he had used up his entire political capital, and left a country that was quite glad to see the end of him."[1] Mulroney used that capital to effect a revolution in the federal government's role in the economy. He came to office as an admirer of British Prime Minister Margaret Thatcher and U.S. President Ronald Reagan and their desire to trim the hectoring role of government in society to enhance the role of markets and to reward individual initiative. He left a country in which the default position had become the government if necessary, but not necessarily the government, and had cemented that position into a free-trade agreement with Canada's principal economic partner, the United States.

In the end, however, by trying to be both a man of principle and a master of brokerage politics, Mulroney satisfied Canadians on neither front. By the early 1990s, it seemed, they wanted him to compromise when he stood on principle, from free trade to the Goods and Services Tax (GST), and to stand on principle when he brokered compromises, particularly on the Meech Lake and Charlottetown constitutional accords. Still, like Trudeau, he left a legacy that would alter the nature of the country and could not easily be undone. Trudeau's proudest achievement was the Charter of Rights and Freedoms, Mulroney's the Canada-U.S. Free Trade Agreement (FTA). The one constitutionalized personal choice and equality, the other enshrined economic freedom and non-discrimination into Canada's international legal obligations. Both committed future governments to their policies and programs, Trudeau by empowering the courts, Mulroney by strengthening the role of international trade tribunals. Both proved controversial and far-reaching, reflecting fundamentally different conceptions of Canada as a country and Canadians as a people.[2]

## FREE TRADE CONSIDERED

When Brian Mulroney campaigned for the Conservative leadership in 1983, he dismissed talk of Canada-United States free trade. As a result, his critics have argued ever since that he lacked political legitimacy to negotiate the FTA, ignoring the fact that Canadians returned his government to power after the agreement was negotiated. In dismissing free trade in 1983, Mulroney was indulging a century-long Canadian political bugaboo. From the 1891 election through the 1983 Conservative leadership campaign, conventional wisdom had held that free trade with the United States was a political graveyard, as Sir Wilfrid Laurier had found out in both the 1891 and the 1911 elections. But, as Mulroney learned upon taking office in September 1984, perhaps the time had come to test that proposition, as had been advocated by a number of prominent Conservatives, including Michael Wilson and John Crosbie. More to the point, a number of other key Tory goals lent themselves to a decision to pursue a Canada-United States free-trade agreement, including a commitment to place Canada-U.S. relations on a less adversarial tone and a desire to allow markets to play a larger role in Canadian economic life.

The entry of free trade into the 1983 leadership campaign had not been a bizarre and isolated episode but a reflection of a growing debate in the country. The debate had emerged out of a budding appreciation of a number of relevant factors.[3] First, Canada's long-standing reliance on the export of raw materials as the mainstay of economic growth and development was being challenged at one end by a growing number of new, more competitive suppliers, particularly from developing countries, and at the other end by increasing extraction, upgrading, and distribution costs. Secondly, the Canadian economy was becoming both more diversified in its product mix and more focused on the lucrative and near U.S. market. Canadians had become engaged in much more than hewing wood and drawing water. Trade and related domestic economic policies suited to the needs of an export-oriented resource economy and a protected manufacturing sector needed to give way to policies more suited to a more advanced, diversified, and open economy. Thirdly, investment and growth in the non-resource sectors of the economy required that competitive firms could look beyond the confines of the Canadian market and count on secure access to at least one major world market. Experience over the previous twenty or more years had demonstrated that geography, business preference, consumer choice, and political reality all pointed to the United States as the obvious market to serve this need. Fourthly, the U.S. market, responding to increasing import pressure from lower cost offshore suppliers, was becoming a less certain market. Growing protectionist sentiment in political and business circles was finding expression in increasing resort to trade remedies and other, non-conventional forms of protection. Finally, Canada's post-war reliance on solving its export-market access problems through multilateral trade negotiations at the Geneva-based General Agreement on Tariffs and Trade (GATT) appeared increasingly remote from the most pressing Canadian priorities, particularly after the failure of the 1982 GATT ministerial meeting to launch a new round of negotiations.

Matters had changed. The Canadian economy of 1984 was vastly different from that of 1891, 1911, or even 1948. Political alignments were also different. The Canadian Manufacturers' Association, long the mainstay of central Canadian protectionism, was by 1984 a cautious voice favouring bilateral free trade. It was now economic conservatives who preferred market-based solutions, while liberals had become suspicious of potential curbs on government programs. Academic analysts had long considered the pros and cons of freer bilateral trade, with economists generally in favour and political scientists more dubious, but now think-tanks, lobby groups, and policy gurus were all lining up in support. Over the course of 1983–84, every major business conference included bilateral free trade on its agenda. Not every analyst saw bilateral free trade with the United States as the solution to all of Canada's economic problems, but they all acknowledged that bilateral free trade could not be ignored in considering the options. At the same time, free trade fit well with other, more market-oriented aspects of the more conservative tenor of society.

All of this churning and debate found its most detailed expression in the research and hearings of the Royal Commission on the Economic Union and Development Prospects for Canada chaired by former Liberal finance minister Donald Macdonald.[4] By the time the commission formally reported in September 1985, its central recommendation of a bilateral Canada-U.S. free-trade agreement had become an open secret, but the full expression of that recommendation and the volumes of its supporting research and analysis added to the credibility of the bilateral option.

The bureaucracy had been similarly engaged in exploring the options. Already in 1982–83, officials had engaged in a detailed review of Canada's trade policies.[5] While some officials advocated an interventionist and protectionist industrial policy, others had begun to consider once again the benefits of a comprehensive reciprocity agreement with the United States. The professional attachment to the multilateral gradualism of the GATT was being squeezed between those prepared to pursue a bilateral approach to achieving more open trade and stronger market disciplines, and those ready to reverse the achievements of the previous forty years by reintroducing interventionist policies. Multilateral gradualism was beginning to be characterized as dated and irrelevant, offering either too little or too much.

The review offered a solid, professional assessment of past Canadian trade policy but found it hard to come to grips with emerging challenges. Nevertheless, in the chapter devoted to Canada-U.S. relations, officials suggested a possible initiative: Canada and the United States could negotiate sectoral free-trade agreements to address the growing range of irritants between the two countries. This soon became the main focus of public discussion and spawned a modest project to explore its prospects. By the summer of 1984, however, the initiative had run out of steam, its well-intentioned but flawed approach underlining the need to think "outside the box" and consider a full-scale bilateral initiative as a necessary complement to multilateral orthodoxy.

## FREE TRADE IMPLEMENTED

Against this background, it is not surprising that the first two major documents that landed on Brian Mulroney's desk as prime minister summarized work that had been done by the bureaucracy over the course of the summer and captured the growing sentiment among business leaders, the senior mandarins, policy think-tanks, and academic analysts that Canada's economic circumstances were bleak and relations with the United States were in a parlous state. Both issues required immediate and high-level attention from the incoming government and both cried out for some new thinking.[6]

The documents, while written in the neutral tones of officials, suggested the direction that new thinking needed to take. In a document prepared by officials in the Department of Finance, Mulroney and his ministers saw the cumulative impact of years of deficit financing and government overreach. The solution was seen to lie in trimming government programs and fiscal reform. The general tenor of the document fit well with the political preferences of the new government and officials were asked to massage the document into the government's first major economic policy statement, *A New Direction for Canada,* delivered on 8 November 1984 by Finance Minister Michael Wilson.[7] Wilson indicated that the government wanted to inculcate a more entrepreneurial spirit in Canada by curbing government spending, reducing regulatory burdens, privatizing crown corporations, replacing the Manufacturers' Sales Tax (MST) with the GST, reducing business subsidies, and deregulating many sectors of the economy, particularly by dismantling the National Energy Program (NEP) and the Foreign Investment Review Agency (FIRA). During the government's first year in office, Deputy Prime Minister Erik Nielsen led a massive effort to discover the full extent of government programs, subsidies, and regulations and to map out specific proposals to address the government's desire to place Canada on a more competitive footing and to reduce the role of government in the economy.[8]

A complementary document prepared in the Department of External Affairs addressed the wider implications of refurbishing relations with the United States. Over the previous year, Mulroney, as well as some of his key advisers, had emphasized that alienating the United States on a range of files from defence to investment was a sure way to undermine Canadian economic development and other core Canadian interests. The document spelled out the challenges involved in meeting these expectations and suggested that, among the issues that needed to be tackled, was better and more secure access to the U.S. market. It evoked the same response as the Finance Department document: more of the same for broader public discussion.[9] Thus, by the end of their first four months in office, Mulroney and his colleagues had learned two important lessons: the bureaucracy had more to contribute than they initially thought and efforts to translate the promises made in the election campaign into effective programs and policies would require some tough political decisions. Free trade would be central to executing those decisions.

The process leading to the decision to negotiate, and the conduct of the negotiations, has been well told elsewhere and need not detain us here.[10] Suffice it to say that both entailed high doses of political drama, much uncertainty, many false starts, and astounding levels of hyperbole and cant, and culminated in a federal election that vindicated the government's policy. The immediate catalysts were the combined impact of business leaders looking for better ways to defuse and resolve trade and investment disputes with the United States, senior civil servants determined to find better ways to manage Canada-U.S. relations, and Mulroney and his ministers eager to change the tone of Canada's relations with the United States and to foster a more entrepreneurial economy. The most important element in the equation was not that trade would be free – although that obviously had important ramifications – but that it would be governed by a set of rules that would be equally binding on the U.S. and Canadian governments and contain procedures to ensure that these rules would actually be implemented. The price for meeting these objectives would, naturally, be to enhance and secure U.S. access to the Canadian market.

Brian Mulroney's contribution to these developments was twofold and critical: he appreciated early in his first mandate that the choices open to Canada were more limited than his critics would admit, and he had the courage and conviction to take the initial decision and see the issue through to its logical conclusion, despite setbacks and frustrations along the way and frequent counsel from all around him to abandon the project. By being gutsy, visionary, and steadfast, Mulroney effected a revolution in Canadian trade policy, changing the default approach from a cautious pragmatism grounded in safe and slow multilateralism to a bolder willingness to let markets work.

The embrace of free trade by the Liberals after 1993 should not blind us to the fact that they bitterly opposed it in the 1980s and had hinted at little more than a willingness to pursue incrementalism in the closing years of the Trudeau government. Mulroney's decision to go for bilateral free trade took courage and sticking with that decision required steady determination. Both were helped by a refreshing absence of that facile kind of anti-Americanism that has marred, and continues to mar, Canadian policy discussions from health care to foreign affairs. It was also facilitated by a clear recognition that the mild statism that had been a hallmark of postwar Liberalism had inculcated fatal barriers to Canada's further economic development.

At the same time, Mulroney was enough of a consensus politician to recognize that there are limits to change and thus some of Liberal Canada's sacred cows needed to be guarded from the full logic of free trade, including agricultural supply management and cultural protectionism. Other policy areas needed at least the cover of transitional fig leaves before facing the full effect of international competition, including foreign investment and financial services. Finally, U.S. reluctance to go as far as its own rhetoric sometimes suggests kept certain areas from the full application of free trade, such as government procurement. In all three cases, however, time would begin to erode some of these decisions. Supply management, for example, was placed under intense pressure by the Uruguay Round negotiations of GATT and its long-term survival is questionable in the face of further multilateral negotiations. Canadian foreign-investment policy, with the exception of a few residual areas, is now generally open to all investors. Following the decision that Canada's would be an open economy, the public-policy purposes served by some remaining areas of discrimination and protection became increasingly difficult to divine. This was as apparent under Jean Chrétien as it had been under Mulroney, but, without Mulroney's willingness to strike out on a new path, Canada's economy might still be burdened by some of the less inspired legacies of the Pearson-Trudeau years.

The agreement that resulted, while revolutionary in intent and psychology, was quite orthodox and straightforward in execution. It built on the well-trodden paths of the GATT, took a page or two out of the European experience in effecting a more integrated market, and cautiously assessed how far both governments were prepared to go in forging a new agreement. In negotiating the agreement, Mulroney and his cabinet sought three overriding objectives. The most important, if least publicized, was to effect *domestic economic reform* by eliminating, at least for trade with the United States, the last vestiges of Sir John A. Macdonald's National Policy and by constraining the more subtle new instruments of protection. By exposing the Canadian economy to greater international competition, while simultaneously improving access to the large U.S. market, Canadian firms would have an incentive to restructure and modernize and become more efficient, productive, and outward-looking. The most publicized objective was to provide a *bulwark against U.S. protectionism.* By gaining more secure and open access to the large, contiguous U.S. market, Canadian business would be able to plan and grow with greater confidence. Finally, the government wanted an improved and more *modern basis for managing the Canada-U.S. relationship*. Since 1948, the GATT had served this function but had increasingly proved inadequate. New and more enforceable rules, combined with more sophisticated institutional machinery, were needed to place the relationship on a more predictable and less confrontational footing.[11]

The agreement that entered into force on 1 January 1989 largely met these objectives. The main elements of the deal had been pursued by a team of officials headed by veteran negotiator Simon Reisman, with the final details hammered out by Mulroney's chief-of-staff, Derek Burney, based on direct instructions from the prime minister. The preamble and first chapter laid out the agreement's basic aims and objectives, providing the philosophical framework within which the whole document must be viewed. The heart of the agreement was set out in chapters 3 to 13 establishing a conventional free-trade agreement for trade in goods, eliminating various barriers to trade, including the tariff, and thus providing Canadian firms with open access to a combined market of three hundred million consumers. Where either side was not prepared to go as far as the other, provisions were made to continue negotiations, but within a new and more secure framework.

Chapters 14 to 17 made a cautious start on the so-called new issues of professional services, business travel, investment, and financial services. They froze the status quo and provided that any future laws and regulations should be based on the premise of fairness, extending equal treatment to each other's service providers, investors, and business travellers. Canada and the United States would remain free to set their own rules and priorities: investors and service providers would have to satisfy Canadian rules in Canada and American rules in the United States, but in each country they could count on being treated the same as their domestic competitors.

Chapters 18 and 19 set out rules for managing the trade and economic relationship. Chapter 18 took well-established GATT practice, committed it to a clear body of rules and procedures, and applied these to the enhanced and improved rules dealing with trade in goods as well as the new rules dealing with services, investment, and business travel. Chapter 19 addressed the thorny issues of trade remedies – anti-dumping and countervailing duties – with the United States for the first time recognizing that disputes between the two countries arising from dumped or subsidized goods are not a matter for the application of domestic law and unilateral decisions alone but should also be subject to bilateral dispute settlement. While both countries could continue to use their respective trade-remedy laws, they agreed to replace judicial review of domestic decisions by bilateral review. Canadians would sit on panels to determine whether U.S. laws were properly followed and whether any changes in U.S. laws were consistent with the GATT and the FTA.[12]

Within two years of the entry into force of the bilateral FTA, the prime minister and his colleagues were faced with a new free-trade challenge, this time from Mexico. Wounds that had only barely begun to heal in Canada were opened again as the United States and Mexico agreed to enter into their own bilateral free-trade negotiations.[13] Faced with the Hobson's choice of standing aside and letting the new negotiations erode what had been painfully achieved only a few years earlier or participating and thus reactivating the bruising debate of the FTA, the government decided to join the talks and use the opportunity to strengthen the FTA rules.[14] The 1993 result was an even more comprehensive trade agreement covering all of North America. One of its clauses hinted that the North American Free Trade Agreement (NAFTA), as the new agreement was called, might grow eventually into a Western hemisphere trading system.

Concurrently, negotiations continued in Geneva to conclude the largest, most ambitious, and most comprehensive global trade agreement ever attempted. In the closing days of 1993, after eight years of labour, the negotiators produced an agreement that was almost five hundred pages long. They added to this pact a long list of specific market-opening national commitments ranging from traditional tariff concessions to new commitments on agriculture, government procurement, services, and investment practices. Gaining the political support of the more than a hundred participating governments proved more difficult. The end of the Cold War and the waning of U.S. dominance complicated the political arithmetic of the negotiations and underlined the need for the emergence of a new equilibrium. A final push in the closing half of 1993 succeeded, however, in bringing the negotiations to a successful conclusion before the end of the year and the end of U.S. negotiating authority. Canada's active participation in the Uruguay Round negotiations underlined that its achievement of bilateral free trade with the United States, and then Mexico, in no way diminished its commitment to global regulation and liberalization.[15]

Both the North American and the Uruguay Round negotiations were largely concluded during Kim Campbell's brief tenure as prime minister and were implemented by the Liberal government of Jean Chrétien following the 1993 election. There was brief concern that the change in government might lead to a change in policy. After all, the Liberals had campaigned vigorously against the FTA during the 1988 election and had been critical of the NAFTA negotiations. In the event, despite an early flurry of words, Chrétien and his colleagues concluded that the changes effected by the free-trade revolution should not be undone. More to the point, Chrétien's government embraced the changes and pushed the free-trade revolution even further over the next decade, negotiating free-trade agreements with Israel, Jordan, Chile, Costa Rica, and Central America, and announcing a willingness to negotiate with any partner similarly inclined. Free trade had clearly become the default position. Brian Mulroney had successfully effected a revolution in Canadian thinking about the role trade should play in the Canadian economy and the extent to which it should be shaped by market forces and internationally agreed rules.

## EXPECTATIONS AND OUTCOMES

The results of this fundamental reorientation in Canadian attitudes met all expectations. Economists had long modelled the economic impact of free trade. To work, it would require firms to adjust, eliminating lines of business in which they did not believe they could be competitive and expanding lines of business in which they believed they could do well. As with all policy changes, small changes would require minor adjustments and lead to marginal results, while large changes would require substantial adjustment and presage major results. The changes required by the FTA were large enough to suggest major impacts. The effect of the agreement on the psychology of both business and government, however, went well beyond the simple contours of the agreement. It had a profoundly liberating effect. For most firms, even before the negotiations had successfully concluded, the decision to proceed had sent a critical message: the government was prepared to initiate and conclude an agreement that would encourage and underwrite its efforts to retool the Canadian economy from a domestic east-west to a North American north-south orientation. Business leaders saw it as a means to escape the narrow confines of the small and high-cost Canadian market for the heady possibilities of the large but highly competitive North American market and, from there, world markets.

For government, the agreement brought home the need to rethink the object and purpose of the modern regulatory state and bring it into line with the needs and opportunities available to a more competitive, more entrepreneurial, more open, and more market-oriented society. Again, some officials and their ministers found this a worrying prospect, but most accepted that the heavy involvement of government in society had been a mixed blessing and engaged the government in responsibilities and obligations for which private markets might be better suited or for which Canadians were not prepared to pay through their taxes. While perhaps not a direct outcome, the FTA negotiations were complemented by a subtle but important change in regulatory approach, from one focused largely on shaping economic outcomes to one more concerned with ensuring quality of life.

The political debate in Canada on the merits of the FTA was in many ways a debate on the merits of markets and of deepening global integration.[16] It indicated that the compromises that governments now had to forge differed significantly from those that had animated the trade negotiations of the 1950s through 1970s. Then the debate had been largely between import-competing (read manufacturing) and export-oriented (read agriculture and resource) producers. Echoes of old imperial sentiments and appeals to new economic nationalism added spice but were essentially secondary considerations. By the 1980s, however, Canadian producers were largely of one view. Even import-competing sectors accepted that there had to be significant restructuring if Canadians were going to compete in the global economy and that such restructuring could best take place within a framework of rules that allowed them to compete in a larger market, though this might come at the expense of more competition at home. The new opposition came from a coalition of populist groups worried about a range of issues – Canadian culture, health care, environmental protection, gender equality, and other largely non-economic concerns – believed to be threatened by a more open economy as well as by closer economic ties to the United States. The debate pitted a market-oriented internationalist vision against a government-centred nationalist one.

During the 1988 election, the claims and counter-claims on both sides of the divide at times attained an extravagance that transcended what was actually at stake and descended into the realm of the surreal. What made it particularly puzzling was that there seemed to be little appreciation on the part of opponents that, without a better set of rules and procedures, Canada's ability to promote and protect its interests in Washington would continue to deteriorate and likely lead to precisely the kinds of outcomes opponents most feared. A well-conceived and well-implemented trade agreement would do more to protect Canadian sovereignty and freedom of action than the continued drift toward a continentalism without rules in which the United States called all the shots. The nationalist alternative of a sturdy Canada going its own way and cocking its snoot at the United States was hardly more reassuring.

Of course, to some opponents, the better alternative to bilateral free trade was a revitalized multilateral system of rules. Mulroney and his ministers, however, were equally committed to negotiating a better-functioning GATT. Indeed, many of the professionals who contributed to the FTA and NAFTA negotiations also worked on the concurrent Uruguay Round of GATT negotiations and saw all three negotiations as individual parts of a single whole. The FTA would simply achieve more quickly and more thoroughly what was equally desirable at the multilateral level. There was also some scepticism about the ability of the Uruguay Round to deliver, given both the delays in launching negotiations and the difficulty of bringing them to a successful conclusion. Many sceptics, while not perhaps prepared to concur with Lester Thurow's catchy judgment in 1990 that the GATT was dead,[17] did not believe that the final result of the Uruguay Round would be as wide-ranging and professionally satisfying as it turned out to be. At a minimum, therefore, pursuing a bilateral agreement with the United States was an act of prudence. In the event, the final results of the Uruguay Round, as good as they proved, in no way matched the extent and depth of the commitments enshrined in the FTA and which convinced business to invest in a North American future.

The unitary nature of the Mulroney government's approach is demonstrated by the extent to which the FTA was firmly lodged within the structure and values of the multilateral GATT system. In all respects, the provisions dealing with trade in goods followed the contours of earlier free-trade area agreements negotiated under the auspices of GATT Article XXIV. The agreement also addressed issues that went well beyond a conventional free-trade agreement, including some that would normally be found in customs union or common-market agreements. Characterized as "new" trade issues, they were in reality the kinds of issues that need to be addressed as economic integration deepens and as the potential for cross-border commercial conflicts intensifies. Even for these, however, there was a scrupulous effort to try to negotiate rules that would fit into a GATT-plus mould and that were congruent with what would flow from the multilateral negotiations just getting under way.

## THE IMPACT OF THE FREE-TRADE AGREEMENT

Did this revolution pay dividends? The numbers are quite persuasive. In 1980 two-way bilateral trade in goods and services represented about 40 per cent of Canadian GDP. Two decades later, that figure had nearly doubled to reach about 75 per cent, valued at some Cdn$700 billion annually or $2 billion every day. Two-way flows of foreign direct investment (FDI) had similarly reached new highs: in the early 1980s, the value of annual two-way flows averaged under $10 billion. By 2000, they had reached $340 billion and reflected a much greater balance between U.S. and Canadian-origin flows. The products mix had also changed considerably, including a much higher level of value-added and finished products. To carry much of this trade, some eleven million trucks, or about thirty thousand per day, crossed the border in 2000; the Ambassador Bridge between Windsor and Detroit alone handled more than seven thousand trucks a day, or one every minute in each direction, twenty-four hours a day; about one hundred thousand passenger vehicles also crossed the Canada-U.S. border every day, in addition to millions of tons of freight carried by planes, railcars, ships, and pipelines. More than two hundred million individual crossings took place at the Canada-U.S. border, an average of more than half a million every day. Some fifteen million Canadians – out of a population of thirty-one million – travelled to the United States for visits of more than one day to conduct business, break up the long winter, visit friends and relatives, or otherwise pursue legitimate objectives, while slightly fewer Americans visited Canada for similar reasons.

The extent of cross-border integration had, by 2000, created a deep and rewarding, if asymmetrical, dependence by Canadians on the U.S. market. The U.S. market was taking more than 85 per cent of Canadians' exports of goods and services; U.S. firms supplied about 65 per cent of Canadian imports; U.S. exports to Canada constituted about 24 per cent of U.S. exports while imports from Canada constituted about 20 per cent of the U.S. import market. As a share of total U.S. economic activity and consumption, however, Canadian exports amounted to less than 3 per cent of U.S. consumption and Canadian imports a little over 2 per cent of U.S. production, compared to U.S. exports satisfying about 35 per cent of total Canadian demand and exports to the United States reflecting about 40 per cent of Canadian production.[18]

Not all economists are agreed that free trade was critical to these developments.[19] Recent economic analysis has tried to unravel the extent to which these emerging patterns flow from the broad impact of globalization, the magnetic effect of a red-hot U.S. economy, or the FTA/NAFTA. Such analysis, fascinating as it may be for economic modellers, poses questions to which there are at best speculative answers of only marginal interest to current policy issues. The extent of integration is clear. It has been largely market driven, and policy has played an important, facilitating role. Policy can continue to play an important facilitating role, but, except if there is a major redirection in policy, it is unlikely to change the basic direction of ever-deepening integration and its impact on steady improvement in the prosperity of Canadians.[20]

Similarly, some analysts express concern that Canada is not getting an appropriate "share" of global FDI and conclude that the FTA/NAFTA did not have the predicted investment effect. Such analysts are looking at the wrong evidence. Free trade did have a major investment effect, evident, for example, in the massive reorientation of the Canadian economy from an east-west to a north-south axis. It also helped to dispose Canadian investors to direct more of their savings towards foreign opportunities: in 1997 Canada crossed an historic divide from a net importer of capital to a net exporter, a position suggesting the emergence of a more mature economy. Whatever Canada's appropriate "share" of global FDI, the past two decades have seen Canadians become steadily more involved in global capital markets, both as investors and as hosts of foreign investments, taking advantage of growing specialization, expertise, and entrepreneurial confidence.[21]

Did the FTA improve the management of Canada-U.S. relations? Yes, to the extent that Canadian governments have been prepared to use the FTA's rules and procedures.[22] The existence of an international agreement does not mean there will not be conflict, only that there is a better basis for resolving conflict. The fact that there is a criminal code does not end crime, nor does the existence of courts stop civil litigation. Both the criminal code and the courts provide a more orderly, predictable, and just way of addressing conflict. They make it possible to bring a conflict to an end and resolve an issue. The same considerations hold true for international rules and procedures. A profound misreading of the FTA and the NAFTA led to many Canadian complaints about the rash of Canada-U.S. trade disputes in the late 1980s and early 1990s. But the existence of rules and procedures does not end disputes and, in fact, may increase the number of issues that need to be resolved on the basis of rules using formal procedures. John Holmes hit the nail on the head when he said, "What has been sought, after all, is not a formula for eliminating conflict but a more satisfactory process for resolving it, bearing in mind that the new agreement would probably multiply rather than diminish the number of conflicts."[23]

The agreement did at first seem to multiply disputes, as players on both sides of the border tested the will of the two governments to live by the new rules. Procedures under Chapter 19 dealing with anti-dumping and countervailing-duty cases proved particularly popular and have continued to engage parties in all three countries under the NAFTA. During the five years of the FTA, thirty-five cases were litigated, with a variety of results, some favouring Canadian parties, some American parties, but, as William Davey concludes in his study of all the FTA cases: "The dispute settlement mechanisms of the [FTA] have worked reasonably well, particularly the binational panel review process. The basic goal of trade dispute settlement … is to enforce the agreed-upon rules. By and large, these dispute settlement mechanisms have done that."[24] Chapter 19, which was much less than Canada had originally sought, proved a pleasant surprise in reducing the cross-border temperature in trade-remedy disputes, forcing administrators on both sides of the border to mind their "Ps and Qs" and reducing the capacity of U.S. legislators to pressure tribunals to favour the home team.

The more general dispute-settlement provisions of Chapter 18 of the FTA (20 of the NAFTA) have been used less frequently but as usefully. A variety of difficult issues, including salmon- and herring-landing requirements on Canada's west coast, the application of automotive rules of origin, and the continued right of Canada to maintain high tariffs to protect supply-managed agricultural goods, were all resolved with the help of high-quality panels and the procedures of the FTA or NAFTA. Additionally, the much-improved multilateral procedures under the World Trade Organization have been available since 1995 to help resolve conflicts. In all of these cases, the application of clear rules within a set of binding procedures to ensure the equality of standing of both parties greatly facilitated the management of relations between the two countries. Canada has not won all the cases, in large part because Canada's policies have not always been consistent with Canada's obligations. The purpose of dispute settlement is not to guarantee that Canada always wins but to ensure that issues are resolved on the basis of agreed rules and procedures rather than power politics.

Finally, the extent of active trade-remedy cases between Canada and the United States has steadily waned over the past fifteen years, largely as a result of the impact of deeper integration, as well as the disciplinary impact of Chapter 19. The extent of intra-corporate and other structural forms of commercial integration has virtually eliminated resort to trade remedies by firms in the manufacturing and industrial sectors. Residual problems, however, continue in the natural-resource and agricultural sectors. Many of these are related to different approaches to resource pricing, suggesting that an indirect approach to trade remedies – addressing the issues that give rise to complaints – may be more fruitful than further efforts to address the issue directly, as was central to the FTA negotiations. The softwood lumber case, long the outrider in dispute settlement, has, at least for a few years, been placed on the back burner, perhaps allowing the same forces that have reduced the appetite for litigation in other sectors to operate in this industry.

Polling done over the course of the past few years also indicates the extent to which Canadians have come to terms with bilateral trade liberalization and closer Canada-U.S. trade and economic ties. In August 2001, for example, Liberal pollster Michael Marzolini found that 85 per cent of Canadians supported closer trade and economic ties with the United States and 75 per cent would even support closer social and cultural connections.[25] Eighteen months later, he found that an astonishing 90 per cent of Canadians favoured closer economic ties and two out of three Canadians continued to support closer social and cultural ties. Marzolini noted, "These results are consistent with what we've seen over the past couple of years ... Canadians are interested in making the most of our close proximity to the United States."[26] Similarly, a June 2003 Ipsos-Reid poll indicated that 70 per cent of Canadians support the NAFTA, even though only 51 per cent believed it benefited Canada. *Globe and Mail* Ottawa bureau chief Shawn McCarthy concluded that "the poll suggests that Canadians are mostly content with the agreement and see closer integration in the North American economy as a positive trend for Canada." Liberal supporters were among the most supportive, at 77 per cent, followed by Conservatives at 75 per cent, but, even among New Democratic Party supporters, only 39 per cent said that the NAFTA had hurt Canada. Four out of five young people said that they were supporters of closer economic integration.[27]

## CONCLUSION

Brian Mulroney may not initially have considered a free-trade agreement with the United States as central to his economic policies, but it soon became the symbol for a whole series of reforms. He inherited a government in 1984 that was deeply in debt and had become convinced that government was central to resolving all of society's problems. He bequeathed a government to his successor that had significantly reduced barriers to economic growth and set the stage for the fiscal reforms needed to finish the job. While he was unable to tame the federal debt, a range of tax reforms helped to set the stage for the fiscal reforms pushed through by Jean Chrétien and Paul Martin. More important, however, Mulroney's commitment to freer trade released the economic forces needed to place Canada's further economic development on a more sustainable footing, and created a Canadian economy less reliant on the heavy hand of government direction. Complementary steps to curb spending, reduce regulatory burdens, privatize crown corporations, replace the MST with the GST, reduce business subsidies, eliminate the NEP, and refocus FIRA ensure that Mulroney's place in Canadian political history will steadily wax while the popular antipathy towards his reputation wanes.

## NOTES

1 L. Ian MacDonald, "The Best Prime Minister of the Last 50 Years – Pearson by a Landslide," *Policy Options* 24(6) (2003): 10.

2 This paper draws heavily on the research pursued in preparing Michael Hart, *A Trading Nation: Canadian Trade Policy from Colonialism to Globalization* (Vancouver: University of British Columbia Press 2002).

3 For a more detailed discussion of the rationale for a Canada-U.S. FTA, see ibid., chapter 12.

4 Royal Commission on the Economic Union and Development Prospects for Canada, *Final Report* (Ottawa: Supply and Services 1985). The commission report totalled 1,767 pages in three volumes. Its supporting research was published in seventy-one volumes, of which at least a dozen volumes were devoted to various aspects of bilateral free trade.

5 See Department of External Affairs, *A Review of Canadian Trade Policy* and *Canadian Trade Policy for the 1980s* (Ottawa: Supply and Services 1983).

6 Again, the research, hearings, and analysis of the Macdonald Commission provide an accurate guide to the concerns that preoccupied policy makers and lobby groups in the first half of the 1980s.

7 Department of Finance, *A New Direction for Canada: An Agenda for Economic Renewal* (Ottawa, 1984).

8 See, for example, "Services and Subsidies to Business: Giving with Both Hands,' 4 March 1984; "Natural Resources Program: From Crisis to Opportunity," September 1985; and "Agriculture," February, 1985 – Study Team Reports to the Task Force on Program Review (Ottawa: Supply and Services 1986).

9 See Department of External Affairs, *How to Enhance and Secure Market Access* (Ottawa, 1985).

10 See Michael Hart with Bill Dymond and Colin Robertson, *Decision at Midnight: Inside the Canada-US Free Trade Negotiations* (Vancouver: University of British Columbia Press 1994). Other accounts include G. Bruce Doern and Brian W.

Tomlin, *Faith and Fear: The Free Trade Story* (Toronto: Stoddart 1991), and Gordon Ritchie, *Wrestling with the Elephant: The Inside Story of the Canada-US Trade Wars* (Toronto: Macfarlane Walter and Ross 1997).

11 Expressions of these objectives can be found in various contemporary documents, a number of which the government collected and published as *Canadian Trade Negotiations: Introduction, Selected Documents, Further Readings* (Ottawa: Supply and Services 1986).

12 The best and most detailed analysis of the agreement and its antecedents can be found in Jon R. Johnson and Joel S. Schachter, *The Free Trade Agreement: A Comprehensive Guide* (Aurora, Ont.: Canada Law Book 1988). See also its sequel, Jon. R. Johnson, *The North American Free Trade Agreement: A Comprehensive Guide* (Aurora, Ont.: Canada Law Book 1994).

13 For a discussion of the issues that faced the government in 1990–91, see Michael Hart, *A North American Free Trade Agreement: The Strategic Implications for Canada* (Ottawa: Centre for Trade Policy and Law and Institute for Research on Public Policy 1990).

14 See Brian Tomlin and Max Cameron, *Negotiating* NAFTA*: How the Deal Was Done* (Ithaca, N.Y.: Cornell University Press 2000), and Frederick W. Mayer, *Interpreting* NAFTA*: The Science and Art of Political Analysis* (New York: Columbia University Press 1998), for two complementary academic accounts of the NAFTA negotiations.

15 For a discussion of Canada and the Uruguay Round, see Hart, *A Trading Nation,* chapter 14.

16 For discussions of globalization and Canadian trade policy, see Michael Hart, *What's Next: Canada, the Global Economy and the New Trade Policy* (Ottawa: Centre for Trade Policy and Law 1994); Hart, "The WTO and the Political Economy of Globalization," *Journal of World Trade* 31(5) (1997); and Hart and Bill Dymond, "Post-Modern Trade Policy: Reflections on the Challenges to Multilateral Trade Negotiations after Seattle," *Journal of World Trade,* 34(3) (2000).

17 See Lester Thurow, "GATT Is Dead," *Inside Guide,* February 1991, 27–30. The original speech was delivered at the annual Davos Leadership Forum in 1990.

18 See Department of Foreign Affairs and International Trade, NAFTA *at Ten: A Preliminary Report* (Ottawa: Supply and Services 2003), for a compilation of NAFTA trade and investment figures.

19 A good introduction to the range of conflicting opinions can be gleaned from the various contributions in L. Ian MacDonald, ed., *Free Trade: Risks and Rewards* (Montreal and Kingston: McGill-Queen's University Press 2000).

20 A review of recent literature assessing the economic impact of the FTA/NAFTA can be found in John Curtis, "What We Know about Integration So Far," *Art of the State II: Thinking North America: Prospects and Pathways,* Institute for Research on Public Policy, 2004.

21 For a detailed discussion of North American FDI flows, see Steven Globerman, "Assessing Recent Patterns of Foreign Direct Investment in Canada and the

United States," in Richard Harris, ed., *North American Linkages: Opportunities and Challenges for Canada* (Calgary: University of Calgary Press 2003).

22 Daniel Schwanen, while at the C.D. Howe Institute, provided the best continuous analysis of the trade impact of the FTA. In *Trading up: The Impact of Increased Continental Integration on Trade, Investment, and Jobs in Canada* (C.D. Howe Commentary no. 89, March 1997), his third report, he concludes that "the pattern of trade between the two countries has shifted roughly in the direction of pre-FTA expectations, and the competitive position of Canadian and US producers in each other's markets has improved relative to those in third countries in many sectors that were liberalized under free trade."

23 John Holmes, "The Disillusioning of the Relationship: Epitaph to a Decade," in Lansing Lamont and J. Duncan Edmonds, eds., *Friends So Different: Essays on Canada and the United States in the 1980s* (Ottawa: University of Ottawa Press 1989), 313–14.

24 William Davey, *Pine and Swine* (Ottawa: Centre for Trade Policy and Law 1996), 288–9.

25 Ottawa *Citizen,* 24 August 2001.

26 Terry Weber, "Canadians Seek Closer Ties with US, Poll Says," *Globe and Mail,* 25 March 2003, accessed at www.pollara.ca.new/Library/surveys/supportforcloserties.htm.

27 Shawn McCarthy, "Large Majority Backs Free Trade," *Globe and Mail,* 9 June 2003, accessed at www.theglobeandmail.com/servlet/ArticleNews/TPPrint/LAC/20030609/UPOLLN2/TPNational.

# 4

# Building or Severing the Bonds of Nationhood?: The Uncertain Legacy of Constitution Making in the Mulroney Years

IAN PEACH

Brian Mulroney's nine years as prime minister were ones of intense public debate over our constitution and our national identity, to the point where constitution making seemed to be as much a national pastime as hockey. Yet, at the end of that period, our constitutional text was no different and the threat of Quebec separation, which was the enemy Mulroney intended to defeat by entering the constitutional-reform battlefield, was stronger than when Mulroney became prime minister in 1984. Even eighteen years after the April day when Mulroney's constitutional odyssey began, one can argue with equal force either that that period of intense national debate built the bonds of nationhood, by increasing our understanding of what is required of a just multinational federation, or severed them, by exposing our divisions and undermining our sense of common purpose as a national polity.

One can reasonably debate Mulroney's intentions in reopening the constitution in the spring of 1987. Certainly, in the perception of most people in "English Canada,"[1] there was no external imperative demanding that the country once again engage in the arduous task of constitutional reform; indeed, polling across the country found significant popular support for the Charter of Rights and Freedoms in the existing constitution. Further, the separatist Parti Québécois government had been defeated by the Liberals in the December 1985 provincial election. Mulroney was, thus, often accused by his critics of being driven by an egotistical desire to secure for himself a place in history greater than that likely to be accorded to Pierre Trudeau as the prime minister who patriated the constitution and secured a constitutional Charter of Rights for Canada.

On the other hand, the Quebec Liberal government of Premier Robert Bourassa was by no means a supporter of the constitutional status quo. Leading up to the 1985 election, it made constitutional reform an important part of its platform, and this continued once it formed government.

Brian Mulroney with the premiers at Meech Lake, 3 April 1987.
Mulroney and Quebec Premier Robert Bourassa are in the centre of the picture.
Photograph Andy Clark. Library and Archives Canada 87-C-02803-29,
negative number E007140468.

The speech made by Quebec's minister of intergovernmental affairs, Gil Rémillard, at Mont-Gabriel, Quebec, in May 1986 is the best-known statement of the Quebec government's position at the time. Rémillard then stated:

> On 2 December 1985, the population of Quebec clearly gave us a mandate to carry out our electoral program, which sets out the main conditions that could lead Quebec to adhere to the *Constitution Act* of 1982.
>
> These conditions were:
>
> 1. Explicit recognition of Quebec as a distinct society;
> 2. Guarantee of increased powers in matters of immigration;
> 3. Limitation of the federal spending power;
> 4. Recognition of a right of veto;
> 5. Quebec's participation in appointing judges to the Supreme Court of Canada.[2]

Further, the other premiers supported Quebec in its desire to embark on constitutional-reform discussions. The communiqué for the August 1986 annual premiers' conference in Edmonton stated that "the Premiers unanimously agreed that their top constitutional priority is to embark immediately upon a federal-provincial process, using Quebec's five proposals as a basis for discussion, to bring about Quebec's full and active participation in the Canadian Federation."[3] It could be argued, therefore, that Mulroney was driven into launching constitutional discussions by an honourable desire to foster a more cooperative form of federalism than the one Canadians had seen in the Trudeau era.

Whatever his actual intentions, the tragic flaw that caused Brian Mulroney to fail to "bring Quebec into the constitution with honour and enthusiasm," and brought the country closer than ever before to a potentially fatal constitutional crisis, was an outmoded understanding of the political culture of the country he led. Since the modern political culture of Canada is both reflected in and influenced by the Constitution Act, 1982, it is to that document that one must first turn for a full understanding of the terms of the Canadian constitutional debate in the period between April 1987 and October 1992.

## THE CONSTITUTION ACT, 1982 AND CANADIAN POLITICAL CULTURE

As was the case in the Mulroney era, the period between 1978 and the patriation of the constitution in 1982 witnessed intense debate not just about the intricacies of constitutional drafting but about the principles and aspirations that guided Canada as a polity. The Constitution Act that Queen Elizabeth II signed in April 1982 was both the product of a national reflection on Canada's political culture and a source for the continued development of that political culture in a certain direction. There are two aspects of the Constitution Act, 1982, in particular, that reflect significant transformations in our understanding of the foundations of Canadian democracy and federalism. The adoption of the Canadian Charter of Rights and Freedoms and of a constitutional amending formula, based on the formal equality of the provinces, clearly declare one conception of the federation the victor over alternative conceptions that had been part of Canadian political debate in previous decades. Never before had our constitutional norms been so unequivocally stated.

Trudeau's proposal to enshrine a Charter of Rights in the constitution became the centre of a debate that took issues of constitutional law beyond the esoteric intergovernmental conflict over the division of powers and into deeper questions, which engaged the public interest in a serious manner, about what it meant to be a modern liberal democracy. Equity groups, in particular, played an important, and forceful, role in defining the substance of the Charter of Rights, through their advocacy in the parliamentary committee on the constitution in the winter of 1980–81. As Alan Cairns notes, "it had become their Charter by the end of the public

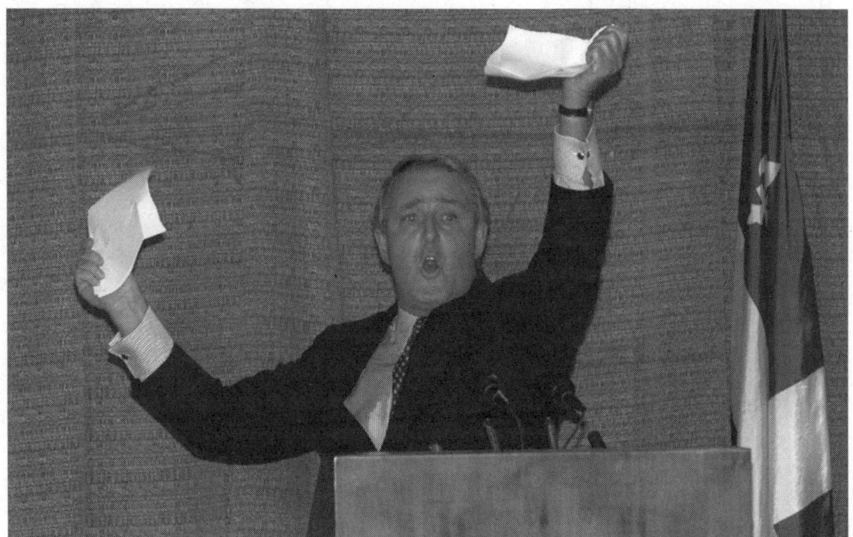

Prime Minister Brian Mulroney holds up a piece of paper he had torn during a speech in Sherbrooke, Quebec, during the Charlottetown referendum campaign to demonstrate that a "No" vote in the referendum would undo the thirty-one gains Quebec had made in the Charlottetown Agreement. Canadian Press / Fred Chartrand.

hearings."[4] As a consequence, the members of these groups, and those they represented, came to covet the sense of political empowerment that the debate over adoption of the Charter of Rights had given them. In turn, because equity groups saw the charter as a new front in their political battle for recognition and equality, they developed a strong attachment to the 1982 constitution as a statement of the fundamental human values that underlie Canada's existence as a liberal democracy.

This newfound connection to the constitution was not confined to an elite group of Ottawa-based social advocates, either. The Charter of Rights had a significant profile among the wider public, and Canadians in all provinces quickly developed a sense of attachment to the charter and the liberal-democratic values it reflected. With the patriation of the constitution and the entrenchment of the Charter of Rights, Canadians were able to conceive of their constitution as a culturally significant document, rather than a technical guide to the allocation of governmental authority. Citizens were now recognized as rights holders with a variegated identity that went beyond their identities as members of provincial communities. Canada could never again be a country governed by the elite-accommodation model of intergovernmental relations, since the powers of the federal and provincial governments were never again to play the central place in our political discourse that they had in the past. Instead, citizens now demanded, and played, a central role in the governance of the country. As Michael B. Stein notes, "elite structures and processes … are insufficient and incomplete by themselves for constitution-making in today's widely shared culture of popular sovereignty. Elite structures must somehow be combined with mechanisms of popular consultation, including referendums and interest group representations, in order to achieve long-term success and legitimacy."[5]

The other pronouncement that the Constitution Act, 1982 made about the politico-constitutional foundations of Canada was contained in the amending formula. This formula was built on the principle of formal equality of the provinces; no one province, not even Quebec, had a veto over proposed constitutional amendments. The question of whether the underlying theory of the federation was that of a new nation created out of British North American colonies, a compact of the provinces as the successors to pre-Confederation governance arrangements, or a compact of two founding peoples had been a live debate since Confederation. The amending formula that was entrenched in the constitution effectively chose a victor in this debate; the victor chosen, equality of the provinces, reflected the development of a Canadian national identity, and Canadian nationalism, since the 1960s. The view that all provinces in the federation were, and must remain, equal under the constitution had developed a particularly strong following in the west, where the favouring of historic "national" communities in our constitutional arrangements seemed at minimum irrelevant and, more frequently, unjust. The principle of equality of the provinces enshrined in the amending formula was, thus, more than a decision about how Canada ought to amend its constitution; it reflected, and secured the dominance of, a deep-seated notion in Canadian society that special status for Quebec was illegitimate and that all provinces should have equal powers within the federation. The dominance of the principle was further secured by the Supreme Court of Canada, when it decided that Quebec did not have a veto over constitutional amendments, even by convention.[6] The theory of Canadian federalism as a compact between two founding peoples was relegated to history in 1982, and Mulroney's effort to resurrect it five years later would meet with stiff, and ultimately insurmountable, opposition within English Canada.

Unfortunately for the success of their constitutional project, Mulroney and his fellow first ministers failed to understand how deeply attached Canadians had become to both the Charter of Rights and the principle of the equality of the provinces in the five years between the patriation of the constitution and their meeting at Meech Lake, Quebec. As Cairns has argued, "Meech Lake foundered for many reasons, but the central causes clearly included its conflict with two powerful equality norms given constitutional reinforcement by the 1982 Constitution Act, the equality of provinces stimulated by the amending formula and the equality of citizen rights expressed in the Charter."[7]

Mulroney, as prime minister of the country and the leader of a government with strong representation from Atlantic and western Canada as well as Quebec, is particularly open to criticism for failing to recognize this fact, and the attendant need to engage English Canada in a process of reconciling its conception of the federation with Quebec's "five conditions." He also failed to understand that the level of citizen engagement in the making of the constitution, particularly through the participation of citizens' and advocacy groups in the parliamentary committee on the constitution in the winter of 1980–81, set a new standard for democratic participation in Canadian constitutional discourse. Instead, he and the other first ministers reverted to a traditional, comfortable, but outmoded process of intergovernmental brokering to negotiate quickly a constitutional amendment that would respond to Quebec's five conditions. In so doing, they advocated a constitutional arrangement that was widely seen as both providing special status for Quebec and damaging the Charter of Rights. They also brought themselves directly into conflict with their citizens on matters of both procedural legitimacy and constitutional substance.[8]

## THE MEECH LAKE ACCORD AND ITS CRITICS

The Constitution Amendment, 1987[9] was born in a day-and-a-half first ministers' conference at Meech Lake in April 1987, with the constitutional text being written in the Langevin Block in Ottawa over the course of a long day and night that June. It was designed to respond directly to Quebec's five conditions, as outlined by Gil Rémillard at Mont-Gabriel the previous spring. The first ministers' willingness to put their own credibility at risk by agreeing to the accord in a closed-door meeting, rapidly converting their agreement into constitutional text, and then refusing to alter it in response to public debate, except in the case of "egregious errors,"[10] demonstrated the depth of their faith in the deference of Canadians and in the processes of intergovernmental accommodation.

As events would prove, the first ministers were clearly wrong about Canadians' level of deference, and the closed-door nature of their decision making locked them into an extended and bitter clash with the public. Since public involvement in constitutional debates had become part of the constitutional-reform process in 1980 and 1981, the lack of opportunity for citizen engagement in the formal decision making at Meech Lake in 1987 simply served to undermine the faith of the public in political leaders and in the ability of those leaders to build a national consensus. As Stein notes, "it was the unusually narrow, secretive and elitist style of negotiations adopted with that Accord that led to a strong political, academic and public critique of executive and summit federalism as the major structure for negotiating constitutional agreements after 1987."[11] Senator Lowell Murray, the federal minister of state for federal-provincial relations, likely summed up all that the public saw as wrong with intergovernmental politics when he told the special joint committee of the Senate and the House of Commons on the 1987 constitutional accord (the Tremblay-Speyer committee) that the Meech Lake Accord was a "seamless web" which could not be changed.[12]

Not only was the process by which this accord had been arrived at illegitimate, the substance of the accord itself was at odds with the conception of the federation that had achieved dominance in English Canada with the patriation of the constitution. The main object of criticism was the interpretive provision that was to become section 2 of the constitution, commonly known as the "distinct society" clause. This one provision simultaneously launched an assault on both of the constitutional principles Canadians held dear – their equality as citizens with constitutional rights under the Charter and the equality of the provinces. This clause stated that "the Constitution of Canada shall be interpreted in a manner consistent with ... (b) the recognition that Quebec constitutes within Canada a distinct society ... The role of the legislature and Government of Quebec to preserve and promote the distinct identity of Quebec ... is affirmed."[13] While all provisions of the Meech Lake agreement came under attack,[14] it was the potential for the distinct society clause to affect the interpretation of the Charter as it applied in Quebec and to create an asymmetrical division of powers, in which Quebec would have a greater scope of authority than other provinces, that formed the core substantive criticism of the accord. At the same time, the public's distrust of its political leaders and its suspicions about the interpretation of the accord were reinforced by the inconsistency of the messages being given to the public by governments; in French, among Quebecers, Mulroney and Quebec Premier Robert Bourassa claimed that the accord was going to create a powerful form of asymmetrical federalism, while in English, in the rest of the country, Mulroney and the other premiers claimed that the accord would create no substantive change to the constitution. It did not take long for these contradictory messages to be noted.

The image of "eleven white men in suits negotiating behind closed doors," to quote a phrase often used at the time, and the potential for the deal so negotiated to undermine English Canada's sense of national identity, grounded in highly symbolic ways in the Charter of Rights, made general acceptance of the accord unlikely.[15] Mulroney's leadership in the negotiations further undermined the accord's acceptability, since he had already embarrassed more nationalistic Canadians by singing "When Irish Eyes Are Smiling" with U.S. President Ronald Reagan and then infuriated them by launching the negotiation of a Canada-U.S. Free Trade Agreement, which, in their eyes, would have a damaging effect on Canada's economic sovereignty.

Criticism of Meech Lake started out small, centred in the academic community, but began to grow quickly once the iconic figure of Pierre Trudeau returned to the public spotlight to oppose the accord. The battle between Trudeau's liberal-democratic philosophy and Mulroney's tory emphasis on elite accommodation, which too often came down to a simple battle between Quebec and English Canada, would provide the subtext for the public debate over the acceptability of the accord. Ultimately, the Canadian majority proved to be strongly attached to the Trudeau vision of the country. Without any deliberative process having been put in place to try to reconcile the conflicting views by building legitimacy for Quebec's vision of the constitution (or to temper Quebec's demands by building legitimacy for the majority vision), the only option seemingly available to the majority was to seek the Meech Lake Accord's defeat.

One other factor that apparently had not been anticipated in April 1987, though it well could have been, and that proved critical to the success of the campaign to defeat the Meech Lake Accord was the election of new governments in three provinces. On 13 October 1987 Frank McKenna's Liberals defeated the Progressive Conservative government of Richard Hatfield in New Brunswick, winning every seat in the legislature.[16] Then, on 26 April 1988, Gary Filmon's Progressive Conservatives defeated the New Democratic Party (NDP) government of Howard Pawley after the Pawley government lost a vote on a non-confidence motion.[17] One of the most notable aspects of this election is that, while the Progressive Conservatives were elected in enough ridings to form a minority government, the Manitoba Liberals under leader Sharon Carstairs, one of Canada's strongest advocates for the Trudeau vision of the constitution, went from one seat in the legislature to twenty. Finally, on 20 April 1989 the Liberal Party in Newfoundland, under Clyde Wells, defeated the Progressive Conservative government of Tom Rideout (who had succeeded Brian Peckford upon Peckford's retirement).[18] These elections brought three premiers who had not signed the Meech Lake Accord, and indeed opposed it, onto the national political stage at a time when Mulroney was trying to secure the unanimous provincial consent necessary to make the agreement law. In the end, these three provinces would play pivotal roles in both the eleventh-hour attempts to save the Meech Lake Accord and its ultimate defeat.

## THE END OF THE MEECH LAKE ACCORD

By 1990, time was running out on the Meech Lake Accord[19] and the criticism of both the process for negotiating the agreement and its substance had become so strong that its failure seemed likely. Acceptance of the accord became that much more difficult in December 1988, when the government of Quebec used the constitution's "notwithstanding clause" to override the Supreme Court of Canada's decision against Quebec's language legislation.[20] This was viewed by many in English Canada as proof of the illiberal nature of Quebec nationalism, which Meech Lake was seen as giving sanction to, and served to intensify opposition to the accord. Filmon, having introduced a resolution into the Manitoba Legislative Assembly to approve the accord on 16 December 1988, withdrew it on 19 December, the day after the government of Quebec's use of the notwithstanding clause.[21] Both McKenna and Filmon also recognized the strength of the criticism of first ministers for the way the accord had been negotiated; in response, they set up committees to undertake public hearings on the accord in their provinces, McKenna on 18 May 1988 and Filmon on 6 April 1989.[22] Meanwhile, Wells was rapidly becoming a national hero in English Canada for what was seen as his principled opposition to the accord and his commitment to a vision of equality for all Canadians. He also won support from those opposed to the lack of public input into the accord for his commitment to holding a referendum on the accord in Newfoundland. To make way for further public debate within Newfoundland and Labrador, the Newfoundland legislature voted to rescind its approval of the accord on 6 April 1990.[23]

In the midst of these events, Mulroney was attempting to use the already-discredited processes of executive federalism and his skills as a negotiator to rescue the accord. The first ministers met three times in 1989 to discuss both economic issues and the Meech Lake Accord and, in November 1989, Mulroney sent Senator Murray on the first of two cross-country missions to consult with the provinces on ways to salvage the agreement.[24] It had become clear, however, that the accord would not receive the approval of all the provinces without amendments; the problem was that Quebec was not prepared to accept any such amendments.

New Brunswick Premier Frank McKenna initiated the final phase of the effort to save the Meech Lake Accord on 21 March 1990 when he introduced a "companion resolution," designed to supplement rather than amend the agreement, into the New Brunswick Legislative Assembly.[25] McKenna indicated at that time that New Brunswick's adoption of the Meech Lake Accord was conditional upon some progress towards adoption of the companion resolution by other legislatures and Parliament.[26] Unfortunately, the companion resolution would have done little to address the substantive criticisms of the effect of the accord on the Charter of Rights and the equality of Canadians, though it did seek to allay concerns about process by making public hearings mandatory in all provinces and the House of Commons prior to the adoption of a resolution to amend the constitution.

Mulroney quickly seized on the possibility of the companion resolution as a strategy to save the accord, setting up a special committee of the House of Commons to study the matter (the Charest committee) on 27 March.[27] In keeping with the belated realization that public involvement was essential to secure the legitimacy of any effort at national constitution making, the Charest committee organized public hearings into the companion resolution, a number of which were held in provincial and territorial capitals. In its report of 17 May 1990, the Charest committee supported the New Brunswick companion resolution but, in taking account of the concerns of the Manitoba and Newfoundland governments and of Canadians elsewhere, it went further and sought to address some of the more fundamental criticisms of the language of the Meech Lake Accord itself. With regard to concerns about interpretation of the Charter, for example, the Charest committee recommended that "First Ministers affirm in a Companion Resolution that the operation of the fundamental characteristic clause, recognizing the linguistic duality/distinct society, in no way impairs the effectiveness of the Charter of Rights. As an interpretive clause it works with the Charter and does not override the rights and freedoms contained in it. Similarly, the Companion Resolution should affirm that the clauses providing roles for Parliament and the provincial legislatures do not accord legislative powers."[28] The committee also suggested that minority-language rights be included on the agenda of the annual first ministers' conferences on the constitution and that Aboriginal peoples and Canada's multicultural heritage be recognized in the body of the constitution.[29] The recognition of these two "fundamental elements of Canada," in the words of the committee report, would have tempered the theory of two founding peoples that was contained in the original accord.

As well, the complaints of Aboriginal peoples and the territorial governments about their exclusion from both the Meech Lake process and the substance of the accord were attracting public sympathy that was further undermining the legitimacy of the agreement. The Charest committee attempted to tackle these concerns by recommending that the constitution be amended to allow the territories to become provinces through unilateral federal action, that the territorial governments be invited to any first ministers' conferences with an agenda item that directly affected them, and that the constitution provide for a separate process of constitutional conferences on Aboriginal issues.[30] These recommendations responded directly to the arguments made by the territorial governments and the national Aboriginal leaders in their testimony before the committee. Further, to address the west's chief concern with the Meech Lake Accord, that future Senate reform to create a "Triple-E" (equal, elected, and effective) Senate would be impossible under the accord's amending formula, the committee suggested that the unanimity formula be replaced by some sort of regional-approval formula if Senate reform was not achieved within three years.[31] A Triple-E Senate, of course, would further entrench the concept of the equality of the provinces in the country's political structure and, as such, was completely inconsistent with the conceptual thrust of the Meech Lake Accord.

Altogether, the Charest committee's recommendations would have significantly reduced the focus on Quebec's agenda in the Meech Lake Accord, and in some cases altered the accord itself, in response to the most serious criticisms of the document in English Canada. The effect of the Charest committee's recommendations on the accord, however, led to a number of defections of Quebec MPs from the Progressive Conservative caucus. These defectors, initially sitting as independents, would subsequently form the Bloc Québécois, under the leadership of Mulroney's former environment minister, Lucien Bouchard.

With the time for saving the Meech Lake Accord rapidly running out, Mulroney sent Lowell Murray on a second tour of the provincial capitals on 20–22 May 1990.[32] Although Murray's recommendation to the prime minister was to avoid another first ministers' conference, Mulroney called a conference for 3 June, in a final, desperate attempt to rescue the accord. This week of hard intergovernmental bargaining nearly paid off, since the first ministers were able to reach an agreement on 9 June. Subsequently, on 11 June, Wells announced that there would be a free vote on the accord in the Newfoundland Legislative Assembly on 22 June, rather than a provincial referendum, and, on 15 June, the New Brunswick legislature ratified the accord.[33] The opposition that effectively sounded the death knell for the Meech Lake Accord, however, appeared in Manitoba. There, on 12 June, Elijah Harper, an Aboriginal member of the Legislative Assembly, refused to give his consent to discuss a motion that would provide for the initiation of public hearings on the accord.[34] While Filmon introduced a motion to ratify the accord in the Legislative Assembly on 20 June, the assembly adjourned from 22 June until June 26, in accordance with its standing orders.[35] Seeing that there was no prospect of the accord being ratified in Manitoba before the 23 June deadline, Wells also proposed, on 22 June, that the Newfoundland Legislative Assembly be adjourned for an indeterminate period of time, thereby ensuring the failure of the agreement.[36]

## LIFE AFTER MEECH LAKE

In the aftermath of the failure of the Meech Lake Accord came a flurry of activity in both Quebec and English Canada. In Quebec, Robert Bourassa seemed to flirt with the idea of Quebec sovereignty as the Meech Lake Accord increasingly looked doomed over the course of the spring of 1990. He established two special committees to look into the future of Quebec.

While the Quebec Liberal Party's constitutional committee was working on its report, *A Quebec Free to Choose* (the Allaire report), which was released on 28 January 1991, the Quebec National Assembly established the Commission on the Political and Constitutional Future of Quebec (the Bélanger-Campeau Commission), which reported on 27 March 1991. Both of these reports recommended either the radical restructuring of federalism, to create in effect "sovereignty-association" (to use the term from the 1980 Quebec referendum),[37] or outright sovereignty. Bourassa, reflecting the recommendation of the Bélanger-Campeau Commission, stated that he would no longer negotiate with English Canada but would, instead, await acceptable offers. The deadline he established for offers was 26 October 1992, the day on which Quebec would hold a referendum either on renewed federalism, if an acceptable offer were presented to Quebec, or sovereignty. This was most famously described as the strategy to "put the knife to the throat of English Canada."

Bourassa's approach and the deadline he set generated a flurry of activity in the rest of Canada too. Unlike in 1987, though, this activity sought to engage citizens in the act of constitutional reform. The governments of Yukon, Prince Edward Island, Ontario, Alberta, New Brunswick, British Columbia, and Manitoba all set up commissions or task forces on the future of Canada in the latter half of 1990.[38] The other four jurisdictions in English Canada, the Northwest Territories, Nova Scotia, Saskatchewan, and Newfoundland, followed suit in 1991.[39] Each of these bodies included some form of citizen engagement as part of their process, whether through public hearings, the receipt of briefs, or roundtable discussions.

Mulroney, too, seemed to understand the importance of engaging citizens in democratic debate if, this time, Canada was to achieve an accommodation of the divergent visions of the country and its constitution. First, he announced the creation of the Citizens' Forum on Canada's Future (the Spicer Commission) on 1 November 1990 and, in the words of the forum's report, "sent it on a mission to listen to the people to find out what kind of country they wanted for themselves and their children."[40] The Spicer Commission was a radical departure from the closed-door executive federalism of the Meech Lake negotiation process.

In its eight months, the Spicer Commission sought to get Canadians talking to one another about the critical issues that faced their country at the time and, in so doing, improve the quality of civic dialogue by reducing distrust.[41] To do this, it utilized an incredible variety of means for citizen input, including a toll-free telephone "Idea Line," group discussions (focused through kits that included questions for discussion by the groups), letters and briefs, and seven "Electronic Town Meetings," which linked participants from across the country.[42] Through these processes, approximately four hundred thousand Canadians participated in the

Citizens' Forum, while another three hundred thousand elementary and secondary students participated in a separate Students' Forum.[43] As the commission's report noted, "the group discussions attracted everybody. They drew some lobbyists and special pleaders, of course ... But mainly the process encouraged the spontaneous and the unorganized – all the 'unofficial' or 'unrepresentative' people."[44] While others may argue that the Spicer Commission's impact on public dialogue in the period leading up to the Charlottetown Accord can be overstated, it is at least to some extent true that the Citizens' Forum on Canada's Future revitalized the art of consulting citizens on the fundamental issues that affect the country.

In the end, as the Spicer Commission's report stated, "the cry heard most often, a cry from the heart, demanded more effective involvement of ordinary Canadians in running the country. Their anger and frustration show[ed] and it is dangerous."[45] The commission provided Canadians with their first formal opportunity since the defeat of the Meech Lake Accord to articulate this key lesson of that accord's defeat, and Canadians made their attitude clear. It also allowed Canadians to articulate their anger with, and distrust of, Mulroney. In the words of Keith Spicer:

> Concerning the Prime Minister, I consider that our consensual editing of Part II [of the Commission Report] does not adequately echo the anger directed at him, and that Part III does not fully assess why it exists and what it means. I think our text assumes a little too much that all criticism comes with the territory; and it too readily treats the prime minister as "just another politician" among many who deserve criticism.
>
> The top person is of course always a lightning rod. And it is true that Canadians show little regard for opposition leaders, or many provincial ones either.
>
> But people wielding great power must be held responsible for how they wield it. And I think that, from most citizens' viewpoint, our report lets the PM off too lightly. At least for now, there is fury in the land against the prime minister. And although I happen to respect him much more than many, I have to say that I think our consensual editing understates the discontent with him.[46]

The Citizens' Forum also provided people with an opportunity to make clear the extent of their attachment to the values that are given constitutional significance by the Constitution Act, 1982, in particular, the equality of both individuals and provinces. As its report stated:

> The concept of equality applies both to individuals and to their provinces, territories and regions. The equality of individual citizens is a concept that has gained considerable currency in Canada since the Charter of Rights and Freedoms came into effect. Participants strongly disapprove of government policies which seem to promote

the rights of groups over individuals, or seem to limit the rights of individuals, especially in comparison with citizens in other Canadian jurisdictions. Similarly … the Canadians who spoke to the Forum will not countenance apparent inequality among provinces or "special privileges" for one or more provinces.[47]

The report emphasized, though, that this attitude did not represent a refusal to acknowledge Quebec's distinctiveness but was, instead, a reflection of a lack of knowledge that the provinces were not perfectly equal in the constitution, as well as a reaction to the idea that the Quebec *government* would obtain special powers that would create two different definitions of the rights of Canadians.[48] While the latter perspective inadequately recognizes the strength of Quebec's sense of nationhood, it does suggest that, even in the aftermath of an event as divisive as the defeat of the Meech Lake Accord, some room was left for finding common ground on the conflicting visions of the country that were at play. The Spicer Commission certainly believed this and, as an experiment, organized two exchanges between anglophones outside Quebec and francophone Quebecers. Its report noted: "The results were striking for both sets of participants … These exchanges clearly demonstrated, in our view, that the greater understanding that comes from personal contact between citizens of Quebec and of the rest of Canada can be enormously beneficial in creating a climate for dialogue and accommodation."[49]

The other issue that the Spicer Commission spoke clearly on was the place of Aboriginal peoples in Canadian society. In the aftermath of the stand-off between Mohawk Warriors and the Sureté du Québec at Oka, Quebec, in 1990 over a Mohawk land claim, as well as Aboriginal peoples' exclusion from the Meech Lake Accord negotiations, Canadians' sympathy for the desires of Aboriginal peoples to achieve self-government and have their rights respected had become impossible to ignore. The commission report was unequivocal about what the Citizens' Forum had heard:

Canadians want justice for the aboriginal peoples. On this, there is an astonishingly high degree of consensus – although also a potentially harmful ignorance of the realities of aboriginal peoples' aspirations … Forum participants stated a clear desire to see longstanding territorial and treaty claims resolved in the best moral, social, and economic interests of all Canadians. Further procrastination would serve only to increase the costs of settlements and exacerbate existing tensions between native and non-native communities. Further, such inaction would greatly damage Canada's international reputation.

In the interests of a more equitable Canada, Forum participants recognized the need for First Nations people to have greater control over decisions which affect their future … The concept of First Nations self-government serves to promote native dignity, respect, and economic independence. It is a key factor in the future determination of First Nations people as a distinct group and must be included in a review of confederation.[50]

This is likely the first time Aboriginal issues had been put so clearly on the constitutional agenda, and the description of the First Nations as a "distinct group" reflected a linkage between Quebec's agenda and the agenda of Aboriginal peoples that would persist throughout the constitutional discourse of 1991 and 1992.

Just after the Spicer Commission was established, Parliament also established the special joint committee of the Senate and the House of Commons on the process for amending the constitution of Canada (the Beaudoin-Edwards committee). This was to "consult broadly with Canadians and inquire into and report upon the process for amending the Constitution of Canada, including, where appropriate, proposals for amending one or more of the amending formulae, with particular reference to: i) the role of the Canadian public in the process; ii) the effectiveness of the existing process and formulae for securing constitutional amendments; and iii) alternatives to the current process and formulae."[51] Thus, the Beaudoin-Edwards committee was to serve the twin functions of engaging the public in constitutional-reform discussions and subjecting the process of constitutional reform itself, including the appropriate role of the public, to further scrutiny. The results of this committee would be fed into the process of arriving at "acceptable constitutional proposals" by Quebec's 26 October 1992 deadline.

To fulfil its mandate to consult Canadians, the Beaudoin-Edwards committee went to all twelve (at that time) provincial and territorial capitals and to Vancouver and Montreal, as well as holding public hearings in Ottawa. Witnesses, and ultimately the committee's June 1991 report, addressed all of the key issues of process that became the subject of such controversy during the debate over Meech Lake Accord, including changes to the constitution's amending formula, the principle of equality of the provinces, the role of the public in constitutional reform, and the role of Aboriginal peoples and territorial governments, who had been excluded from the Meech Lake negotiations. As one might expect, witnesses who came before the committee were sharply divided on the first two issues. Those who proposed amendments to the amending formula presented a wide variety of alternatives designed to make the constitution more or less easy to amend (with the unanimity formula proposed in the Meech Lake Accord at the extreme end of the scale). The different formulae proposed put a premium either on the principle of equality of the provinces or on the creation of a Quebec veto (whether it was to be for Quebec alone, through regional vetoes, or through unanimity).[52] Ultimately, the committee recommended regional vetoes over an extensive range of items, though a unanimity formula was retained for some items. [53] The committee was also careful to recognize that amendments to the amending formula could be adopted only as part of a substantial package of constitutional reforms including, "for instance," Senate reform.[54]

On the roles of Aboriginal peoples and the territories, the Beaudoin-Edwards committee broke with the content of the Meech Lake Accord, choosing instead to align itself with the weight of post-Meech Lake public opinion on these issues. With respect to Aboriginal peoples, the committee recommended that any amendment to the constitution that directly affected Aboriginal peoples require their consent, that representatives of Aboriginal peoples be invited to participate in all future constitutional conferences, and that there be biennial constitutional conferences on the rights of Aboriginal peoples.[55] On the role of the territories, the committee recommended that the extension of existing province boundaries into the territories require the consent of the territorial legislatures and that the creation of new provinces from the territories require *only* the consent of the legislature of the territory concerned and the Parliament of Canada.[56] The committee also recommended that territorial governments be invited to participate in all future constitutional conferences. These recommendations demonstrate how effective the lobbying by Aboriginal peoples and territorial governments to secure a place in the processes of constitutional reform (including, in the case of the territories, litigation by the Yukon premier challenging the Meech Lake Accord[57]) had been.

A substantial portion of the Beaudoin-Edwards committee's report was devoted to the role of the public in constitutional reform, with separate chapters devoted to referendums, constituent assemblies, and public hearings. The report tended to be relatively conservative on the matter of the public's role in constitutional reform. While it recommended that Parliament pass legislation to make a referendum an optional part of a future constitutional-reform process (and that, for an amendment to succeed, any referendum generate a national majority and a majority in each of the four regions in favour ), the report reflected significant criticism from the committee's witnesses on the utility of referendums as a constitutional-amendment procedure and a substantial degree of caution about their implications for parliamentary government and minorities.[58]

The committee's report also noted that, as a means of initiating constitutional-amendment proposals, constituent assemblies had "acquired something of a hold on the Canadian political imagination during the 12 months since the Meech Lake amendments failed to achieve ratification."[59] Yet, in spite of this, the report expressed a significant level of scepticism about constituent assemblies, as well as concern about the means by which participation of a representative group of Canadians in an assembly could be assured. This reflected an ongoing discussion within the committee about the possibility of constructing an assembly that was broadly representative of the Canadian population, when individuals carry a variety of identities simultaneously and sociological identities do not define individuals' opinions.[60] Thus, in the end, the committee came down in favour of mandatory public hearings on proposed constitutional amendments.[61]

While the committee did not recommend the use of constituent assemblies as a constitutional-reform mechanism, this was not the end of the debate. The NDP members of the committee filed a minority report advocating that a constituent assembly be appointed, on the basis of sociological representation, as part of the process of developing Canada's "acceptable offer" to Quebec. As this minority report noted, "158 witnesses supported the principle of a constituent assembly, while only twenty-three opposed the principle. Recent polls show that a significant majority of Canadians support this proposal. And a number of provincial Premiers, from across the country and the political spectrum … have recognized the necessity of such a process."[62] The idea of a constituent assembly, in fact, reappeared as part of the federal government's process to obtain input on its constitutional reform proposals as 1991 came to an end.

## THE 1991 FEDERAL PROPOSALS AND CITIZEN ENGAGEMENT IN CONSTITUTION MAKING

With the reports of the Spicer Commission and the Beaudoin-Edwards committee both being made public in the summer of 1991, the first phase of Mulroney's post-Meech Lake exercise in public engagement concluded. In contrast to the way in which the Meech Lake Accord was negotiated, though, substantive constitutional proposals would be subject to a second phase of citizen input before being put to legislatures. This second phase of public engagement, focused on a package of constitutional reforms that could form an "acceptable offer" to Quebec, began with the public release of the federal government's constitutional-reform proposals, entitled *Shaping Canada's Future Together*, on 21 September 1991. These proposals sought to respond not only to the Quebec agenda that had been addressed in the Meech Lake Accord but also to the concerns of the west, Atlantic Canada, Aboriginal peoples, the territories, and any number of other constituencies. The proposals dealt with institutional reform, the division of powers, Aboriginal self-government, amendments to the Charter of Rights, interprovincial trade and commerce, and intergovernmental relations, and they were immediately referred to the special joint committee of the Senate and the House of Commons on a "renewed" Canada (originally known as the Castonguay-Dobbie committee and, after Senator Claude

Castonguay's resignation from the body, the Beaudoin-Dobbie committee), which had been established in June 1991.

In keeping with the federal government's post-Meech Lake strategy of maximizing public involvement in developing a package of constitutional amendments, the Beaudoin-Dobbie committee held public hearings across the country. Initially, the committee was to go beyond provincial and territorial capitals and major cities by breaking into subcommittees and travelling to smaller locations. This mode of outreach was used in Prince Edward Island and Manitoba in the autumn of 1991, but the effort, and the committee itself, fell apart in Manitoba when one of the subcommittees arrived at a Manitoba town to discover there were no citizens there to engage with. When the committee reassembled that night in Brandon, Manitoba, it became clear to the committee members that there were severe problems with the management of the committee's public outreach and that the executive director of the committee, who was an associate of committee co-chair Dorothy Dobbie, was largely responsible for the committee's problems.

The most radical, and effective, form of citizen engagement that occurred in this period came about by accident, as a consequence of the then Castonguay-Dobbie committee's breakdown in Manitoba and the threats of the opposition members of the committee to resign if substantial changes were not made to its staff and processes. The negotiations to keep the committee afloat took several weeks, leaving the committee with too little time to undertake the extensive outreach to smaller communities that was originally intended. Instead, as a way to break the impasse that had developed over whether Dorothy Dobbie would resign as committee co-chair, the NDP proposed that the government hold a series of constitutional conferences in which randomly selected members of the public would participate, along with government officials, members of the committee, and representatives of interest groups. This was a return, in some way, to the idea of a constituent assembly that the NDP had proposed in its Beaudoin-Edwards minority report. Had the Castonguay-Dobbie committee not faltered, however, this experiment in direct public involvement in constitutional debate would never have been tried.

The six "Renewal of Canada" conferences[63] succeeded in restoring the credibility of the federal government's public-consultation process after the damage of the Castonguay-Dobbie committee's self-destruction and, through extensive media coverage, brought constitutional discussions into the public domain. More important, though, they gave members of the public a direct role in developing a constitutional-reform package, and one that had a great deal of influence on the Beaudoin-Dobbie committee's deliberations. The conferences also generated some unexpected results. For example, at the conference on the division of powers, which was held in Halifax on 17–19 January 1992, a strong consensus emerged in favour of asymmetrical federalism, while at the conference on the economic union, which was held in Montreal on 31 January–2 February 1992, the intended discussion of the economic union was almost completely replaced by a discussion of the government of Ontario's proposal for a "social charter," which the conference ultimately supported.[64]

By bringing people with a variety of backgrounds and opinions together for six weekends over the course of several weeks in forums in which they had a chance to discuss issues directly with one another, rather than simply presenting their views individually to a parliamentary committee, these conferences were also able to create a consensus among ordinary Canadians. A model of effective, deliberative public engagement, they demonstrated that Canadians were capable of undertaking the discussions and finding the compromises among competing interests that were necessary for renewing Canada, if a forum was created that allowed such a process to occur.

In spite of the impressive volume of direct citizen input into the Beaudoin-Dobbie committee's deliberations, writing a report that built a consensus out of an honest reflection on what the committee had heard from the public was a difficult task. Each party was sensitive to the desires of its natural constituencies to see the report reflect its views, a sensitivity that was, occasionally, reflected in the text.[65] As well, the committee was sometimes subject to manipulation by individuals within the political parties who were not part of it and were seeking to manipulate its process for partisan gain, and even by the committee staff.[66] Nonetheless, the lead committee members for the three political parties represented on the committee, and their chief advisers, all had a strong enough working relationship with one another, and a sufficient understanding of the importance of producing a consensus that would move national-unity discussions forward, that for the most part they were able to resist this manipulation.[67]

The Beaudoin-Dobbie report dealt with the same wide range of issues as the September 1991 federal proposals had. It also attempted to respond to some of English Canada's most serious criticisms of the Meech Lake Accord. The report unequivocally supported the recognition of an Aboriginal right to self-government and recommended that governments commit to negotiating self-government agreements.[68] It also replaced the controversial words of the Meech Lake Accord on "opting-out" – which would have allowed a province that opted out of a national shared-cost program to be compensated if it ran a program that was "compatible with" the national objectives – with a requirement that the provincial program "meet" the objectives of the national program.[69] On institutional-reform issues, it provided for a deadlock-breaking mechanism for Supreme Court appointments, to take account of concerns that the Meech Lake Accord would allow the court to become a pawn in a federal-provincial conflict,[70] and recommended an elected, effective, and more equitable (though not equal) Senate.[71]

The most controversial issue in the Meech Lake Accord, of course, was the meaning and implications of the "distinct society" clause. Here, the Beaudoin-Dobbie report sought to address the key bases for criticism by radically restructuring both the placement and the content of provisions to recognize Quebec's distinctiveness and by adding references to other key characteristics of Canada to the constitution. The report recommended that the distinct society clause, which the Meech Lake Accord would have placed in section 2 of the constitution, be replaced with a "Canada clause" setting out a variety of characteristics of Canada.[72] Since the Canada clause was a "declaration" rather than a clause per se, which is clearly meant to be interpretive in effect, its significance for the interpretation of the rest of the constitution was unclear. The interpretive equivalent to the Meech Lake distinct society clause would, instead, have been placed within the Charter of Rights and, as such, would have required the Charter to be interpreted in a manner consistent with the preservation and promotion of Quebec as a distinct society.[73] The Canada clause contained nothing equivalent to the Meech Lake Accord's reference to the role of the legislature and government of Quebec to preserve and promote Quebec's distinct society, and it would have clarified the meaning of the term "distinct society" by stating that it included a French-speaking majority, a unique culture, and a civil law tradition. It also would have balanced the distinct society reference with a reference to interpreting the Charter in a manner consistent with the vitality and development of the language and culture of francophone and anglophone linguistic-minority communities (unlike the Meech Lake Accord, which spoke only of the existence of anglophone and francophone Canadians, not linguistic communities). While these recommendations were designed to eliminate the key criticisms of the Meech Lake Accord's distinct society clause among people in English Canada, the report's changes to the accord were significant enough that, on 11 March 1992, the Quebec National Assembly voted overwhelmingly to reject it.[74]

## TOWARDS THE SHOWDOWN: INTERGOVERNMENTAL NEGOTIATIONS AND REFERENDUM

With the release of the Beaudoin-Dobbie report at the end of February 1992, public consultations at the federal level came to an end. There remained a question, however, about what process would be used to go from public consultations to constitutional amendment. Since the Quebec government had made clear its position that it was awaiting "offers" from English Canada and would not negotiate, Mulroney initially intended to present a federal constitutional resolution to Parliament and seek popular support for the resolution through a national referendum, thereby avoiding intergovernmental negotiations (from which Quebec would be absent) entirely.[75] This plan, reminiscent of Pierre Trudeau's 1980 threat to take a constitutional package to Britain unilaterally, was stopped by Ontario Premier Bob Rae, who insisted that not only the provinces but representatives of Aboriginal peoples be involved in developing the constitutional package.[76] As a result, the "Multilateral Meetings on the Constitution" (MMC) among federal, provincial, and territorial ministers responsible for constitutional affairs and representatives of four national Aboriginal organizations were born in March 1992.

These meetings confronted several pitfalls. First, intergovernmental negotiations had been discredited by the Meech Lake Accord, and it was unlikely Canadians would be willing to be shut out of further involvement in developing a constitutional-reform package. While Joe Clark and the other ministers were committed to creating transparency in the process of constitutional making, and gave daily briefings to the press on the progress of the negotiations, public mistrust of what was going on behind the closed doors of the intergovernmental meeting rooms quickly developed. Secondly, Mulroney never really abandoned his faith in his initial plan, or his mistrust of the English Canadian provinces and the public.[77] It is likely he assumed that the MMC process would fail and he would then be able to revert to his original strategy of providing a unilateral offer to Quebec that the other provinces would be forced to support. Thirdly, while these intergovernmental negotiations were the most extensive in history, including as they did the territorial governments and four national Aboriginal organizations as full partners, one critical partner, Quebec, refused to attend. This led to a combination of guesswork and bilateral conversations between the various governments at the table and Quebec, which often resulted in conflicting messages about what Quebec would agree to being presented by different delegations. The federal delegation, in particular, seemed schizophrenic at times; it was often unclear whether the federal government was at the table to represent the national interest or as a surrogate for Quebec's interests.

All three of these pitfalls combined over the course of the summer and fall of 1992 to separate the politicians from the public and undermine the trust that governments had invested so much in building between 1990 and the spring of 1992. The MMC process was long and difficult but ultimately succeeded; Joe Clark was able to announce, on 7 July 1992, that an agreement had been reached between himself, the provincial and territorial premiers (except Quebec Premier Bourassa), and the leaders of the four national Aboriginal organizations represented at the MMC negotiations. By then, Mulroney had left for that year's summit of the Organization for Economic Co-operation and Development (OECD) in Europe, likely still believing that the MMC process would end in a failure, and his enthusiasm for the 7 July agreement was notably absent when he was interviewed in Europe about Clark's success. Both Mulroney's distrust of the MMC process and the problems attendant on Quebec's absence from the negotiations became apparent in the days following. While other ministers and first ministers believed that the 7 July agreement would be acceptable to both Quebec and the other provinces, Mulroney was convinced that Quebec would reject it and tried to undo the deal.[78] In English Canada, this renewed suspicion that, to Mulroney at least, the public consultations that had gone before and the so-called "Canada Round" of constitutional negotiations were nothing more than a charade to resurrect the failed Meech Lake Accord.[79]

The public trust in governments that had been built up through public engagement, and that Joe Clark had tried to retain during the MMC process through the daily briefings, disappeared entirely when Mulroney invited the provincial premiers – but not the territorial premiers and the national Aboriginal leaders who had been part of the MMC negotiations – to a "First Ministers' lunch" on 4 August. It seemed to observers as though Mulroney had learned nothing from the aftermath of the Meech Lake negotiations about the importance English Canada attached to both Aboriginal issues and an open process. As the 7 July agreement was changed to accommodate Bourassa's demands in closed-door negotiations between 4 and 28 August 1992, the public's discomfort with intergovernmental negotiations, fed by memories of exclusion from the creation of the Meech Lake Accord, led to a deep suspicion about the Charlottetown Accord, as the new document became known. This concern caught Mulroney and the other first ministers in a bind; it made a national referendum on the Charlottetown Accord a necessity, despite the limitations of referendums as vehicles for democratic discourse, but it simultaneously made approval of the constitutional-reform package negotiated by the first ministers more difficult.

Public suspicion manifested itself most clearly in the demand of some citizens to see the legal text of the Charlottetown Accord, which did not yet exist in August and September 1992. Because of the controversy surrounding the interpretation of the Meech Lake Accord, many Canadians were unwilling to take the assurances of their political leaders about the meaning of the Charlottetown Accord at face value. They were deeply concerned that they would be asked to vote on an accord that would prove different from the legal text of the constitutional amendment put to the provincial legislatures and Parliament.[80]

There were some grounds for suspicion about the entire process of first ministers' negotiations and legal-text drafting. The Charlottetown Accord became less of a balanced accommodation of interests than the 7 July agreement had been and instead sought to benefit Quebec more clearly, for the sake of making the Quebec referendum easier for the federalists to win, without considering the effect of these actions on opinion in English Canada. The most famous example of the damage that this dynamic could do came in British Columbia, where Premier Michael Harcourt was quickly labelled "Premier Bonehead" for agreeing to a deal that would have provided Quebec (and British Columbia) with more seats in the House of Commons, as well as a guarantee to Quebec of 25 per cent of the seats in the House of Commons in perpetuity, to secure Bourassa's agreement to creating an equal Senate. Similarly, some officials involved in the legal drafting process sought to interpret the first ministers' agreement in a way that was as generous to Quebec as possible and limited the gains made by other parties to the agreement. Occasionally, this seemed to amount, in the view of some of the other drafters, to a renegotiation of the Charlottetown Accord itself. The secrecy that surrounded the negotiations in August and September 1992, and the lack of attention paid in those negotiations to the strength of English Canada's commitment to the Charter of Rights and Aboriginal issues, again exposed the extent to which Mulroney failed to understand the political dynamics of constitution making in Canada.

Mulroney further demonstrated his lack of understanding of the country he led in the 1992 referendum campaign. The Charlottetown Accord would have been a "hard "sell" regardless, but Mulroney's histrionics during that campaign – such as ripping up a copy of the Charlottetown Accord and stating that a vote against the accord would destroy Canada – made public approval of the agreement that much more difficult to achieve. In contrast, Clyde Wells, a hero in English Canada for his principled opposition to the Meech Lake Accord, recognized the damage that his support for the Charlottetown Accord might do to his reputation as a man of principle. Thus, his approach to the 1992 referendum campaign focused on the honour of a fair compromise. Wells's basic message was that, while the Charlottetown Accord was not what he would have created himself, it reflected an honourable compromise and respected the "three equalities" that make Canada function – equality of individuals, equality of provinces, and equality of peoples. While cause-and-effect relationships are always difficult to determine, it seems reasonable to theorize that the personal credibility Wells brought to the 1992 referendum campaign and his careful, even humble, message during its course helped encourage a majority of Newfoundlanders and Labradorians to vote "Yes" to the Charlottetown Accord.

If the supporters of the Charlottetown Accord were not up against enough challenges during the referendum campaign, Pierre Trudeau once again renewed his fight against Brian Mulroney to protect his vision of the constitution and the country. In a speech at Maison Egg Roll in Montreal on the night of 1 October 1992, Trudeau called the Charlottetown Accord "a big mess."[81] His views gave legitimacy to Canadians' distrust of Mulroney's vision of the country and their fear that the accord would leave them with a constitution they did not want, increasing still further the challenge that the "Yes" side in the 1992 referendum faced. It was a challenge the supporters of the Charlottetown Accord could not meet and, on the night of 26 October 1992, the accord was defeated, not only by a majority of the voters across the country but by a majority in each of six provinces, including Quebec.[82] Brian Mulroney's seven-year effort to secure the Quebec government's assent to the constitution of Canada had ended in failure. His party would be swept from power a year later.

## AFTERMATH: CANADA AND MULRONEY'S UNCERTAIN CONSTITUTIONAL LEGACY

The defeat of the Charlottetown Accord and the subsequent defeat of the Mulroney government may have ended constitutional-reform efforts in Canada for a time, but they did not end the national-unity debate. A Parti Québécois government was elected in Quebec in 1994, and it initiated a Quebec referendum on sovereignty, which was held on 29 November 1995. This referendum sparked an extensive debate in Canada on whether, and under what circumstances, Quebec could separate, and on what could be done, short of constitutional reform, to renew the federation. The fallout from this debate, and the incredibly narrow victory of those opposed to Quebec sovereignty,[83] included the *Quebec Secession Reference* to the Supreme Court,[84] the "Calgary Declaration" signed by the prime minister and the premiers of all provinces and territories except Quebec, legislation limiting the circumstances in which the federal government would introduce a resolution into the House of Commons to approve constitutional-amendment proposals,[85] and the federal Clarity Act.[86]

Despite all of this activity both during and after the Mulroney era, Canada looks largely the same as it did when Mulroney was elected in 1984. The constitution has not changed significantly since 1982, Quebec has a federalist government (in fact, one that is more avowedly federalist than the Bourassa government) once again, as it did in 1985, and the idea of constitutional reform does not have a significant place in the political consciousness of Canadians. Yet, there are differences, and it is not clear whether those differences are positive or negative.

The depth and intensity of discussions about constitutional issues and national unity between 1978 and 1996 probably made Canadians the most articulate populace in the world on matters of constitutional theory. Those discussions also made the different interests and conceptions of the country that have gone into building Canada far clearer to far more people than they had ever been previously. As noted at the outset of this chapter, it is uncertain whether the country is stronger or weaker as a result. What is certain, however, is that the Mulroney era brought Canadians' faith in their politicians and in the processes of political debate within a parliamentary democracy to a low ebb and that our governments today are even more fractious and uncooperative than they were at the start of the Mulroney era. Thus, the effect of this period on Canadian governance is, at best, mixed.

If he is judged solely on the basis of whether he achieved what he set out to do through constitutional reform, Brian Mulroney can only be deemed a failure. Before coming to a conclusion, though, one should ask how much of the failure to amend the constitution rests with Mulroney and whether his mistakes were preventable. Did Brian Mulroney actually suffer the fate, shared by all tragic heroes, of succumbing to the consequences of his own flaws?

Certainly, other political leaders of the period must share the blame for misunderstanding Canada's post-1982 political culture. It was the premiers, after all, and not the prime minister who issued the 1986 "Edmonton Declaration" calling for the accommodation of Quebec to be a top political priority for the country. This reflects a structural weakness of annual premiers' conferences, which traditionally cannot bear dissent; Bourassa exploited this dynamic in 1986. As well, the premiers had the capacity to refuse to agree to the Meech Lake Accord until proper public consultation had been undertaken or to agree to it subject to the results of such consultation; Clyde Wells used this approach when he agreed to the companion resolution in June 1990. Further, Bourassa must accept some of the blame for not preparing the Quebec public for the likely prospect that the Quebec sign law would be declared unconstitutional by the Supreme Court of Canada, as it had been by the lower courts in Quebec. By doing nothing to lead Quebec public opinion towards an acceptance of the Supreme Court's decision and, instead, allowing the Parti Québécois to dictate the terms of public debate in Quebec, Bourassa raised fears in English Canada about the potential for the Meech Lake Accord to justify illiberal political decisions in Quebec and left Gary Filmon's government, in particular, in a politically untenable position.

None of this, though, changes the fact that the instigator of the Meech Lake negotiations was Brian Mulroney and that the way in which the accord was arrived at, quickly and behind closed doors, reflects his preferred style of bargaining, learned in labour negotiations. As well, Mulroney, as prime minister, had a greater responsibility than any other first minister for carefully considering how to balance the competing interests of Quebec and English Canada so that the constitution would secure the maximum amount of legitimacy with the public all across the country; in this he clearly failed. Thus, Mulroney must carry most of the blame for both the procedural and substantive problems with the Meech Lake Accord. As well, since these problems were, at heart, rooted in Mulroney's misunderstanding of Canada's changed political culture, rather than in any malicious desire to destroy the country, the analogy to the literary tradition of the tragic flaw seems appropriate.

Similarly, Mulroney cannot carry all of the blame for the failure of the Charlottetown Accord. There can be little doubt that Robert Bourassa's decision not to participate in constitutional negotiations after the defeat of the Meech Lake Accord, while tactically sound within the context of the domestic politics of Quebec, was a serious strategic error on his part. The uncertainty about what would be acceptable to Quebec and the force that developed in the other provinces behind the 7 July agreement made it much more difficult than it otherwise would have been for Bourassa to achieve a constitutional proposal he could take into a referendum campaign with confidence. In addition, Bourassa's rhetoric between the summer of 1990 and the summer of 1992, constructed for a domestic audience within Quebec, made it difficult for him to support any "offer" coming from English Canada. If he had supported the 7 July agreement unequivocally, this may have been enough to convince "soft nationalist" Quebecers to support the accord. Yet Bourassa felt bound by his previous statements to be only lukewarm in his backing of the agreement of 7 July and to seek more from the other first ministers. His fixation with responding to his domestic audience in language that would reinforce its view of him as a true nationalist created a dilemma from which he could not escape.

That said, however, Mulroney cannot avoid blame for the failure of the Charlottetown Accord, either. His lack of support for the 7 July agreement created suspicion in English Canada about both the process and the results of the first ministers' meetings. As well, the strength of his support for Bourassa's position, and his use of his position as prime minister to direct the first ministers' discussions in a way that would make the Charlottetown Accord more beneficial to Quebec than the 7 July agreement, was a key factor in making the substance of the Charlottetown Accord less acceptable to English Canada. And, finally, Mulroney's approach to the referendum campaign was, at a minimum, unconvincing in its hyperbole and likely generated a visceral negative reaction within English Canada. Each of these failures, like his failures during the Meech Lake saga, were an expression of Mulroney's personal shortcomings. In fact, the contrast between the extensive public engagement, and even the careful transparency of the MMC process, and the final, secretive first ministers' negotiations demonstrated the distance between Mulroney and the political culture of English Canada, at least, more than any previous events had.

If Canada is as united today as it was in 1984, it is so in spite of, not because of, Brian Mulroney. While he did not go so far as to rend the bonds of nationhood, neither did he build them. Ultimately, he succumbed to a failure that was both preventable and a reflection of his own weaknesses. His legacy, then, is one of failure and defeat, the fate of all tragic heroes.

## NOTES

1 There is no ideal term that one can use to refer to the provinces and territories that make up Canada outside Quebec. "English Canada" was the term that had long been used but, in the face of criticism that it failed to reflect the linguistic and cultural diversity of the provinces and territories outside Quebec, it was generally replaced in the 1990s with the term "Rest of Canada" or the acronym "ROC." This term, however, is equally problematic, since it treats all of Canada outside Quebec as a single socio-political entity. I have chosen to return to the older term "English Canada," in spite of its descriptive limitations, as the best term of a bad lot.

2 Peter M. Leslie, *Rebuilding the Relationship: Quebec and Its Confederation Partners* (Kingston, Ont.: Institute of Intergovernmental Relations 1987), 42.

3 Mollie Dunsmuir, "Constitutional Activity from Patriation to Charlottetown (1980–1992)," Library of Parliament Backgrounder BP406, November 1995.

4 Alan C. Cairns, "Constitutional Theory in the Post-Meech Era: Citizenship as an Emergent Constitutional Category," in Janet Ajzenstat, ed., *Canadian Constitutionalism: 1791–1991* (Ottawa: Canadian Study of Parliament Group 1992), 32.

5 Michael B. Stein, "Tensions in the Canadian Constitutional Process: Elite Negotiations, Referendums and Interest Group Consultations, 1980–1992," in Ronald L. Watts and Douglas M. Brown, eds., *Canada: The State of the Federation 1993* (Kingston, Ont.: Institute of Intergovernmental Relations, 1993), 96.

6 *Reference re Amendment of the Canadian Constitution*, [1982] 2 S.C.R. 793 (commonly known as the Quebec Veto Reference).

7 Cairns, "Constitutional Theory in the Post-Meech Era," 30.

8 See Ian Peach, "The Death of Deference: National Policy-Making in the Aftermath of the Meech Lake and Charlottetown Accords," *SIPP Public Policy Paper #26* (Regina: Saskatchewan Institute of Public Policy 2004).

9 The formal name for the Meech Lake Accord.

10 See *The Report of the Special Joint Committee of the Senate and the House of Commons on the 1987 Constitutional Accord* (Ottawa: House of Commons 1987), 131–2. As noted by Dunsmuir in "Constitutional Activity from Patriation to

Charlottetown," once the government of Quebec passed a resolution adopting the Meech Lake Accord, it became virtually impossible to change the document even in the face of "egregious errors." Indeed, not providing territorial governments the right to recommend members of territorial bars for appointment as Supreme Court of Canada justices, when each province was given that privilege, was one such egregious error with few negative implications for the provinces. Mulroney's refusal to change the accord to correct this fairly small and technical error in drafting must be seen as a missed opportunity for him to demonstrate, in a way that would have little if any substantive effect on the accord, that the federal government was prepared to respond to public input.

11 Stein, "Tensions in the Canadian Constitutional Process," 106.

12 Ibid., 132.

13 Constitution Amendment, 1987, s. 1.

14 For example, the provisions for the appointment of senators were criticized for doing nothing to create a "Triple-E" (equal, elected, and effective) Senate, a demand of the West, while, it was said, the changes to the amending formula would make future Senate reform virtually impossible. Criticism was also levelled at the proposed procedure for appointing judges to the Supreme Court of Canada, which, it was claimed, would make it impossible for the federal government to appoint judges in the face of an uncooperative province that refused to submit any acceptable names (such as Quebec under a future separatist government); the provisions to provide compensation to a province that did not participate in a national shared-cost program but that carried on an initiative compatible with national objectives were criticized on the grounds that they would create a "patchwork quilt" of social policy and access to services in Canada; and, finally, critics said that the amendments to the amending formula, by creating a much longer list of items that required the unanimous support of the provinces, would make future constitutional reform impossible and preclude the eventual evolution of the territories into provinces. Further, the Accord as a whole and the negotiation process that led up to it were attacked for completely ignoring the demands of Aboriginal peoples for self-government. This last criticism took on special force because the Meech Lake Accord was successfully, and quickly, negotiated in response to Quebec's constitutional demands on 30 April 1987, little over a month after the failure of the last of three constitutional conferences on Aboriginal issues, held on 26 and 27 March 1987, to make any progress on Aboriginal peoples' demands for self-government.

15 Peach, "The Death of Deference," 3.

16 "Frank McKenna," Wikipedia (http://en.wikipedia.org/wiki/Frank-McKenna), accessed 17 January 2005.

17 "Gary Filmon," Wikipedia (http://en.wikipedia.org/wiki/Gary-Filmon), accessed 17 January 2005.

18 "Liberal Resurgence on the Rock," CBC Archives (http://archives.cbc.ca/IDC-1-73-928-5476/politics-economy/elections-newfoundland/clip4), accessed 17 January 2005.

19 The deadline for all of the provinces to approve the accord was 23 June 1990, the third anniversary of the passage in the Quebec National Assembly of a motion approving the amendment of the constitution. Unanimous approval of the accord within three years was required because of the constitution's amending formula; while some provisions of the accord required unanimous consent, a formula for which there is no deadline, others required approval within three years by 2/3 of the provinces representing 50 per cent of the population. Since the Meech Lake Accord was a package, and had to be approved as a package to be acceptable to Quebec, all of it had to be approved unanimously within the three-year time frame.

20 Constitution Act, 1982, s. 33. This provision allows a legislature to declare that a law inconsistent with ss. 2 or 7 to 15 of the Charter of Rights will have effect, notwithstanding this inconsistency, for a period of five years, after which the declaration must be renewed or the law changed.

21 Library of Parliament, "The Constitution since Patriation: Chronology" (http://www.parl.gc.ca/information/about/related/Federal/ConstPat.asp?Language=F&srt=ASC), accessed 17 January 2005.

22 Ibid.

23 Ibid.

24 Ibid.

25 Ibid.

26 *Report of the Special Committee to Study the Proposed Companion Resolution to the Meech Lake Accord* (hereafter the Charest report) (Ottawa: House of Commons 1990), 1.

27 Library of Parliament, "The Constitution since Patriation: Chronology."

28 Charest report, 9.

29 Ibid., 11.

30 Ibid., 11–12.

31 Ibid., 11.

32 Library of Parliament, "The Constitution Since Patriation: Chronology."

33 Ibid.

34 Ibid.

35 Ibid.

36 Ibid. One odd event in these final days was Lowell Murray's announcement, on 22 June, that if Newfoundland ratified the accord, the federal government would ask the Supreme Court to rule that the deadline could be moved to 23 September 1990, the third anniversary of Saskatchewan's ratification of the accord. It not clear how the Supreme Court could have been convinced to do this, since the amending formula is clear on the deadline. Further, colleagues who attended briefings by senior federal officials in the last days of the accord have suggested that there was a conscious effort on the part of the federal government to blame Wells for the accord's failure. That Murray would provide extra time for Manitoba, but not for Newfoundland, enraged Wells, as did the

federal government's efforts to cast the entire blame for the failure of the accord on Wells and ignore the role that the Manitoba Legislature played.

37 The Allaire report recommended that the Quebec government present a proposal for political and constitutional reform to the government of Canada, while the Bélanger-Campeau report recommended that the National Assembly prepare to assess any offers for a new constitutional partnership from the government of Canada and the other provinces while simultaneously preparing to hold a referendum on Quebec sovereignty in either June or October 1992. See Constitutional Committee of the Quebec Liberal Party, *A Québec Free to Choose* (Montreal: Quebec Liberal Party 1991), 47; *Report of the Commission on the Political and Constitutional Future of Quebec* (Quebec: National Assembly 1991), 79–82.

38 James Ross Hurley, "The Canadian Constitutional Debate" (http://www.uni.ca/cancon–background.html), accessed 17 January 2005; Library of Parliament, "The Constitution since Patriation: Chronology."

39 Hurley, *The Canadian Constitutional Debate.*

40 Citizens' Forum on Canada's Future, *Report to the People and Government of Canada* (Ottawa: Minister of Supply and Services Canada 1991), 15.

41 Ibid., 16.

42 Ibid., 17–22.

43 Ibid., 16.

44 Ibid., 27.

45 Ibid., 29.

46 Ibid., 6–7.

47 Ibid., 99.

48 Ibid., 123, 54–5.

49 Ibid., 57.

50 Ibid., 126–7.

51 *The Report of the Special Joint Committee of the Senate and the House of Commons on the Process for Amending the Constitution* (hereafter Beaudoin-Edwards report), (Ottawa: Senate and House of Commons, 1991), vii.

52 See ibid., chapter III.

53 Ibid., 26–7. The items that the committee recommended remain subject to unanimity were the use of the English and the French language, the proprietary rights of the provinces, and the offices of the queen, governor general, and lieutenant dovernors, as well as any changes to those provisions themselves. The committee also recommended that amendments that could be made through bilateral agreement or unilaterally under the existing amending formula not be changed. It is worth noting that Lynn Hunter, the only British Columbia MP on the committee, attached an addendum to the report in which she recommended that British Columbia be recognized as a region for the purposes of the amending formula. Following the negotiation of the Victoria formula in 1971, the issue of whether Canada is composed of four or five regions bedevilled, in western Canada at least, any discussion of a regional veto. It was

resolved only by the federal government's 1996 constitutional-amendment legislation, which effectively created five regional vetoes. This legislation, of course, did not amend the constitution and was not subject to the same level of public or intergovernmental consultation as an actual constitutional amendment. See n.84.

54 Ibid., 67.

55 Ibid., 17. The matters that directly affected Aboriginal peoples were ss. 91(24) of the Constitution Act, 1867 and ss. 25, 35, and 35.1 of the Constitution Act, 1982.

56 Ibid., 19. The committee did note, however, that the creation of a new province could change the "equilibrium within the federation" and necessitate a review of the amending formula.

57 *Penikett* v. *Canada* (1987) 43 D.L.R. (4th) 324; (1987) 45 D.L.R. (4th) 108 (C.A.); leave to appeal to the Supreme Court of Canada refused [1988] 1 S.C.R. xii.

58 Beaudoin-Edwards report, chapter IV.

59 Ibid., 43.

60 Indeed, while the committee's report was being drafted, the author and one of the committee members had a discussion of several hours' duration about how a constituent assembly, considering the variety of identies that individuals bear simultaneously, could legitimately answer the important question of "who represents me?"

61 See, for example, Beaudoin Edwards report, 55. Interestingly, the committee also recommended that the length of time for ratification of constitutional amendments by Parliament and legislatures be shortened from three years to two, and that it apply to all amendments, as a result of the much more extensive consultation that, the committee argued, should occur before the ratification process began. See Beaudoin-Edwards report, 31.

62 Ibid., 74. Of the premiers, likely the strongest and most committed advocate of a constituent assembly in the aftermath of the failure of the Meech Lake Accord was Newfoundland Premier Clyde Wells.

63 Five conferences, held in various locations across the country, were organized by various organizations on behalf of the federal government and one, on Aboriginal issues, was organized jointly by the federal government and the national Aboriginal organizations, as part of a parallel-consultation process among Aboriginal peoples. This last conference took place after the Beaudoin-Dobbie committee reported but before the intergovernmental negotiations that were to lead to the Charlottetown Accord began in earnest.

64 Peach," The Death of Deference," 8.

65 See, for example, the discussion of entrenching property rights in the constitution in *The Report of the Special Joint Committee on a Renewed Canada* (hereafter Beaudoin-Dobbie report) (Ottawa: Senate and House of Commons 1992), 34–5.

66 In the final days of drafting the report, in the midst of difficult negotiations to resolve potential conflicts among the positions of the committee members and

ensure that the report was unanimous, portions of the text that had been removed by agreement of the three parties' lead committee members had an odd tendency to reappear when the next draft of the report was printed, and text that had been inserted by agreement of those committee members had an equally odd tendency to remain absent. Since these mysterious occurrences seemed to correlate with the views of the committee's constitutional advisers, the author felt it necessary, at the end of one long and tense evening, to remind the committee's principal constitutional adviser that opinions of committee officials were of no relevance when they conflicted with an agreement that had been worked out among the committee members.

67 The committee did, however, make recommendations in favour of devolving powers to the provinces, as a way of responding to Quebec's agenda, that were subsequently criticized for not reflecting what the committee heard. See Susan Delacourt, *United We Fall: The Crisis of Democracy in Canada* (Toronto: Viking Press 1993), 139.

68 Beaudoin-Dobbie report, 28–9, 108.

69 Ibid., 83.

70 Ibid., 60. The concern was that, if a province produced a list of candidates, all of whom were known to be unacceptable to the federal government, the court could have been left with vacancies for an extended period of time.

71 Ibid., 40–58.

72 Ibid., 24.

73 Ibid., 26–7.

74 Delacourt, *United We Fall*, 445.

75 Ibid, 43–4.

76 Indeed, while what was then the Castonguay-Dobbie committee was in a state of suspended animation, awaiting the outcome of negotiations to save the constitutional-reform process, some officials within the federal NDP had developed a plan which they came to refer to as the "Runnymeade Strategy," after the place at which the barons forced the King of England to sign the Magna Carta in 1215. Under this strategy, the three NDP governments in Canada would spearhead provincial-territorial negotiations on a constitutional-reform package acceptable to the provinces and territories and force the federal government to sign on to it. When the Beaudoin-Dobbie committee went back to work, the Runnymeade Strategy was shelved, but its creation reflects the unassailable position of the provinces in constitutional reform since the establishment of the amending formula in 1982.

77 Delacourt, *United We Fall*, 44.

78 Ibid., 53. Interestingly, Bourassa's response to the 7 July agreement was noncommittal, rather than clearly opposed.

79 This view increasingly came to be shared by some premiers, such as Ontario's Bob Rae and British Columbia's Michael Harcourt. See, for example, Delacourt, *United We Fall*, 169.

80 One colleague of the author's who was also involved in drafting the legal text has told the story of her uncle, who threatened to vote "No" in the referendum if he did not see the legal text beforehand. According to this story, once the legal text was released, she asked him if he had read the legal text; his response was that he had no interest in reading all the legal language. This story is an excellent reflection of the breakdown in trust between politicians and the public between 1987 and 1992 and the public's suspicion that Mulroney wanted to prevent them from making an informed choice with their referendum vote.

81 Delacourt, *United We Fall*, 452. Preston Manning is also often remembered as playing an important part in the defeat of the Charlottetown Accord, by calling it "the Mulroney deal" in television advertisements. Yet one study found that, other things being equal, awareness of his opposition to the accord boosted the "Yes" vote. See Richard Johnston, André Blais, Elisabeth Gidengil, and Neil Nevitte, "The People and the Charlottetown Accord," in Watts and Brown, eds., *Canada: The State of the Federation 1993*, 34.

82 Ontario (by 0.2 per cent); New Brunswick, Prince Edward Island, and Newfoundland voted in favour of the accord, while British Columbia, Alberta, Saskatchewan, Manitoba, Quebec, and Nova Scotia voted against.

83 The results were 50.6 per cent "No" and 49.4 per cent "Yes," a spread of 1.2 per cent.

84 *Reference re Secession of Quebec*, [1998] 2 S.C.R. 217.

85 An Act Respecting Constitutional Amendments, S.C. 1996, c. 1.

86 Clarity Act, S.C. 2000, c. 26.

# 5

# Out of the Blue: The Mulroney Legacy in Foreign Policy

NELSON MICHAUD AND KIM RICHARD NOSSAL

An observer of Canadian politics in September 1984 would have been hard-pressed to predict that one of the most durable legacies of the new Progressive Conservative government of Brian Mulroney would be in the area of foreign policy. After all, in his year as leader of the opposition, Mulroney's foreign-policy pronouncements had been simplistic and naive, amounting to little more than an often-tiresome repetition of a few themes unambiguously intended to woo votes. There was not much evidence in September 1984 that, over the next nine years, the Mulroney government would make a number of important decisions in foreign policy, taking the country in new and very different policy directions, breaking with a number of traditions of Canadian statecraft, and embracing policy positions that, from the perspective of September 1984, were radical departures. In this chapter, we argue that the Mulroney legacy in foreign policy came "out of the blue" – in at least two senses. First, it was out of the blue in the sense that it was unforeseen and unexpected. But it was also out of the blue in the sense that Mulroney's foreign policies in his nine years in power transcended the simplistic foreign-policy prescriptions of the "Blue Tories" of that era. As we will show in this chapter, the prime minister – aided by a prominent "Red Tory," Joe Clark, as his secretary of state for external affairs – ranks as one of the most activist prime ministers in foreign policy in the twentieth century.

To be sure, it did not look that way in 1984. In his fifteen months as leader of the opposition, from June 1983 to September 1984, Mulroney's foreign policy had an exceedingly "Blue" hue. For his External Affairs critic, he chose Sinclair Stevens, one of the most right-wing members of the Progressive Conservative Party. Mulroney's own foreign-policy pronouncements consisted of a limited number of themes that, in the context of the politics of the time, would place him on the right: strong support for the global policies of the United States and the administration of

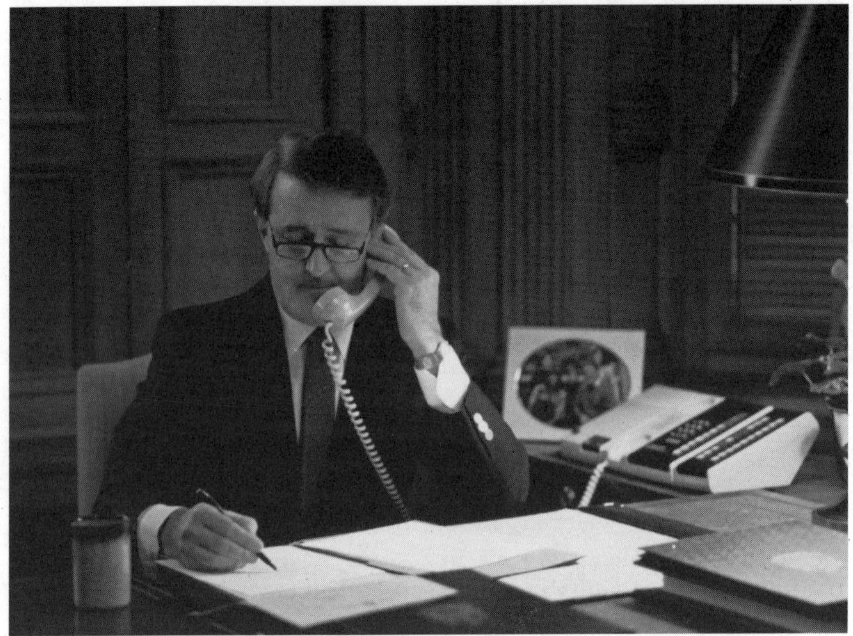

Prime Minister Mulroney promised Canadians that he would improve relations between Canada and the United States. Here, Mulroney has a telephone conversation with U.S. President Ronald Reagan. Photographer Andy Clark. Library and Archives Canada 87-C-03788-7, negative number e007140471.

President Ronald Reagan, strong support for an increase in defence spending, and strong opposition to the Soviet Union.

Much of Mulroney's foreign-policy critique in this period in opposition was focused on the Liberal government of Pierre Elliott Trudeau. In particular, Mulroney was highly critical of those Trudeau government policies that had led to a sharp increase in tensions between Canada and the United States, particularly since Ronald Reagan's election as president in November 1980. On numerous policy issues, ranging from energy policy to environmental policy to global politics, Canadian policy diverged from that of the Reagan administration, and the relationship between the two leaders had developed a testiness that was by 1983 barely concealed.[1] As opposition leader, Mulroney articulated a largely unidimensional critique of the Trudeau approach: a Progressive Conservative government, Mulroney promised, would embrace a "special relationship" with the United States. Both the substance and the tenor of the Canadian-American relationship would change; Mulroney promised to "refurbish" the relationship, as he put it on numerous occasions, by introducing a "new era of civility."[2] A refurbished relationship was crucial, Mulroney argued, for the health of the Canadian economy.

In order to secure this new relationship, Mulroney promised that Canada would be less critical of American global policy; the government in Ottawa would give the United States "the benefit of the doubt." Secondly, Mulroney promised that, under a Conservative government, Canada would be a better ally by spending more on defence. As he argued in a speech given in June 1983, Canada was "a first-class nation" and "first class means going first class in pay to our men and women who serve this country here and overseas, in training, in weapons, and equipment and deployment capacity. That is the way a Conservative government is going to go – first class in conventional defences."[3] In short, Mulroney promised that Canada would be a "better ally, a super ally" of what he inevitably characterized as Canada's "four traditional allies" – the United States, Britain, France, and Israel (even though Canada has never had an alliance with Israel, Mulroney, during his time in opposition, always added that country to his list of Canada's "traditional allies" in an apparent belief that it would woo Jewish voters to the Conservatives).

Guided by this singular goal of being a "super ally," the foreign-policy pronouncements of the Conservatives while in opposition consisted largely of aligning Canada with the United States on global issues. Thus, for example, after Soviet fighters shot down Korean Air Lines flight 007 in the early hours of 1 September 1983, Trudeau characterized the shootdown as an accident. Mulroney, by contrast, followed the harsher line out of Washington and called it an act of cold-blooded murder. When the United States invaded Grenada in October 1983 following a military coup, the Conservatives criticized the Trudeau government for refusing to support the action, noting that Washington's failure to consult with the Canadian government prior to the invasion was an indication that Canada had become an "untrustworthy" member of the Western alliance.[4] Mulroney was also prone to criticize the Soviet Union: to an international convention of Estonians in Toronto in July 1984, Mulroney denounced the Soviet Union as a "slave" state. He reminded his audience that another Canadian Conservative, John G. Diefenbaker, prime minister from 1957 to 1963, had criticized the Soviet Union at the United Nations so harshly that the Soviet premier, Nikita Khrushchev, had banged his shoe on his desk in protest; Mulroney promised that he would do no less than Diefenbaker in the cause of Eastern Europeans.[5] While Mulroney was merely repeating a durable Conservative myth (for Diefenbaker was in fact at home in Saskatchewan when Khrushchev banged his shoe in protest against a comment made by a Filipino speaker), it nicely reflected the Manichean perspective that characterized the Conservative approach to global policy in the year before the September 1984 elections.[6]

Prime Minister Mulroney became a leading critic of apartheid in South Africa and broke with Margaret Thatcher and Ronald Reagan on the issue of sanctions against that country. After his release from nearly three decades in prison, Nelson Mandela visited Canada in July 1990. Photographer Bill McCarthy. Library and Archives Canada 90-c-8143-30, negative number e007140478.

Once in power, however, Brian Mulroney and the Progressive Conservatives took a different tack. First, the new prime minister set the tone for his foreign policy by his choices of foreign-policy appointments, all of which were from the moderate or progressive wing of the Conservative Party. Joe Clark, whom Mulroney had replaced as party leader in 1983, was appointed the secretary of state for external affairs (as Canada's foreign minister was called before 1993). Douglas Roche was made ambassador for disarmament. David Macdonald, who had served as a minister in Clark's government in 1979–80, was appointed to oversee famine- relief efforts. Flora MacDonald, who had been Clark's External Affairs minister, was made minister of employment and immigration. James Kelleher, another moderate, was appointed as minister of international trade. Monique Vézina was appointed as minister of state for external relations. Roy McMurtry, who had been a Conservative minister in the Ontario government, was sent as high commissioner to London. From the large pool of Conservative backbenchers who had been elected in September, Mulroney chose Thomas Hockin, an academic whose specialty was in Canadian foreign policy, to co-chair a special parliamentary committee charged with reviewing Canada's foreign relations, and William Winegard, a former president of the University of Guelph, to chair the House of Commons standing committee on external affairs and international trade. Mulroney also made a number of other appointments that had the effect of consolidating the moderate line in foreign policy. He retained Allan Gotlieb, a senior civil servant, as ambassador in Washington. And, in a surprise move, Mulroney asked Stephen Lewis, a former leader of the Ontario New Democratic Party, to be Canada's permanent representative at the United Nations. The party's "Blue Tories" had to content themselves with other portfolios: Sinclair Stevens was appointed as minister of regional industrial expansion; Robert Coates was given National Defence; and Pat Crofton, a former navy commander from British Columbia, was appointed as chair of the standing committee on defence. Moreover, within two years, two of these right-wing voices on foreign policy would be gone. Coates was forced to resign in February 1985 for visiting a strip club while inspecting Canadian forces in Germany, and Stevens was forced to resign over a conflict of interest involving one of his companies.

Secondly, over nine years in power, Mulroney pursued a course in foreign policy that was markedly different from the one that might have been expected given his party's views while in opposition. While the range of foreign-policy departures under the Mulroney Conservatives was considerable,[7] our purpose here is not to write a history of the Mulroney government's foreign policy. Rather, by looking at particular case studies, we suggest that the most significant legacies of Mulroney's foreign policy lie in four areas: the opening up of the policy process; the improvement in Canadian-American relations; the transformation of relations with la Francophonie; and the development of new definitions of state sovereignty that had a transformative effect on the pursuit of human rights.

## THE ETHIOPIAN FAMINE AND THE POLICY PROCESS

One of the first foreign-policy crises the Mulroney government faced was the famine in Ethiopia, which appeared on the political agenda in October

1984, scarcely a month after the government had been sworn in.[8] The response of the new government to this crisis was, however, not at all in keeping with the impression that Mulroney had left during his year in opposition. On the contrary, this response revealed some of the initial impulses of the Conservative approach that would be manifested in many (though by no means all) other foreign-policy areas.

Needless to say, the Ethiopian famine itself did not suddenly appear: the Food and Agriculture Organization (FAO) had been issuing urgent appeals to the international community since the early 1980s for assistance to combat the famine in Ethiopia that had been aggravated by a massive and prolonged drought and the collapse of the country into civil war. But the response had been negligible: in 1983 the Trudeau government, for example, had considered and then rejected a proposal from the minister of agriculture for a $20-million emergency-relief scheme on the grounds that the situation was not sufficiently grave.[9] But, when video images of the famine were broadcast on television around the world in October 1984, these had a powerful effect on many countries. In Canada, they prompted what the *Globe and Mail* termed "a sudden outpouring of emotion and money."[10] Offers of assistance came from individuals, groups, and institutions from across Canada – "a quite remarkable demonstration of interest by ordinary Canadians," as Joe Clark, the secretary of state for external affairs, put it later.[11]

The response of the Mulroney government represented a number of shifts in policy. First, instead of turning to the Department of External Affairs or the Canadian International Development Agency (CIDA) to organize and coordinate the Canadian contribution to famine relief, Mulroney created a new layer of political administration. David MacDonald was appointed as Canadian emergency co-ordinator/African famine to organize the Canadian contribution to the Ethiopian relief effort, and given resources to establish an office separate from the line departments.

Secondly, Mulroney established a special financial facility for famine relief: by the middle of November, a Special Fund for Africa, amounting initially to $50 million, had been created. But this was a relief fund with a difference: in an effort both to reflect the number of Canadians donating to the relief effort and to encourage public participation, the government pledged that it would match donations from Canadians citizens dollar for dollar up to $15 million. That initial pledge turned out not to be enough. As large numbers of Canadians organized fund-raising activities over the winter of 1984–85, the government was prompted to contribute nearly $36 million in matching funds.

Thirdly, the government brought non-governmental organizations (NGOs) more closely into the process of organizing the relief effort. While the Canadian government had for a number of years allocated funds to

NGOs as a means of implementing its development-assistance policies, in the Ethiopian relief effort, MacDonald was charged with integrating the NGOs into the process of making program-allocation decisions. To orchestrate the relief effort, an umbrella coalition, Africa Emergency Aid, was created; MacDonald and a CIDA representative had seats on this group's board, but the NGO community held a majority. As David R. Morrison notes, this arrangement "broke new ground."[12] Finally, as the worst aspects of the crisis passed and donations fell, MacDonald sought to bolster the commitment of Canadians to the longer-term concern for African development by holding a series of community meetings across the country. Entitled Forum Africa, these meetings culminated in a National Forum Africa held in Ottawa in February 1986. The government also broke new ground by involving ordinary members of Parliament in the work of the relief operation. In particular, the standing committee on external affairs and national defence held hearings on the famine relief effort in April 1985, recommending that MacDonald's tenure be extended for an additional year and that the government continue making matching funds available.

The legacy of this initial foreign-policy episode was significant. First, it reflected the willingness of the Conservative government to try to open up the policy process by establishing what were termed "partnerships" with a broader public. It is no coincidence that the key players in this process were Clark and MacDonald, for the government's approach to Ethiopia was in part an echo of what Clark's government had sought to do in the case of the Vietnamese boat people during its brief tenure in 1979, when it encouraged the public to become personally involved in sponsoring refugees from Indochina.[13] Secondly, the Conservative response to the Ethiopian crisis in 1984–85 and the coordinating activities of MacDonald not only laid the groundwork for increased involvement of NGOs in policy making and policy implementation but, as important, had a profound effect on many parliamentarians who had been participants in the process. One in particular, William Winegard, chair of the House of Commons standing committee on external affairs and international trade, would be galvanized to try to reform Canada's development-assistance programs. Finally, this episode served to entrench the idea of an expanded role for Canadians citizens in the making of foreign policy, an idea that would be central to the process of reviewing foreign policy that began to unfold in 1985.

## CANADIAN-AMERICAN RELATIONS

Given the persistent criticism by the opposition Conservatives that the Liberal government of Pierre Elliott Trudeau had mishandled Canadian-American relations in the early 1980s, it was not surprising that the first priority of the new Conservative government in 1984 was to make good on Mulroney's promise to "refurbish" the relationship with the United States. One of the major changes in that relationship introduced by the Mulroney Conservatives – and one of Mulroney's major legacies – was the successful negotiation of the Free Trade Agreement (FTA) with the United States and then the successful trilateralization of free trade to include Mexico in the North American Free Trade Agreement (NAFTA) that came into force shortly after the end of the Mulroney era. While in opposition, Mulroney had rejected the idea a free-trade agreement with the United States, arguing that that issue had been decided in the 1911 election and promising that "we'll have none of it."[14] Once in power, however, Mulroney changed his mind, and in 1985 he began the process of negotiating a comprehensive trade agreement with the United States, discussed by Michael Hart earlier in this book.

Another major change was a conscious attempt to develop a closer relationship between the president and the prime minister as a means of dealing with some of the major irritants in the bilateral relationship. To that end, Mulroney worked hard to establish close personal relationships with both Ronald Reagan and his successor, George H.W. Bush. Indeed, the "Shamrock Summit" in Quebec City on St Patrick's Day, 1985, was designed to put in place an institutional mechanism for the regular exchange of views between Canada and the United States at the highest political level. Throughout the Mulroney period, this regularized summit, usually held in March or April, became a fixed part of the annual prime ministerial and presidential calendars – until Jean Chrétien abandoned it when the Liberals regained office in 1993. However, contact was not limited to these formal occasions; Mulroney regularly called Reagan on the phone. Moreover, during the Bush administration, Mulroney would frequently visit the president, since both leaders developed a close personal friendship that transcended their political relationship, and one that lasted well after both leaders retired from public life. While some elements of that closer relationship, such as Brian and Mila Mulroney and Ronald and Nancy Reagan singing *When Irish Eyes Are Smiling* together at the first summit meeting held in Quebec City in March 1985, were widely criticized in English-speaking Canada, there can be little doubt that during the Mulroney years the Canadian prime minister enjoyed a level of access and influence at the White House that had not been seen in the Trudeau era (and would not again be seen until the Conservative government of Stephen Harper came to power in 2006).

This is not to suggest that there were no conflicts in Canadian-American relations during Mulroney's time in power. On the contrary, the relationship continued to be marked by bilateral disputes and differences over policy. Trade disputes proliferated, despite the free-trade negotiations that were under way. There was conflict over American extraterritoriality on

Cuba, American unilateralism towards international institutions, American policy in Central America, and American challenges to Canadian sovereignty in the Arctic. And acid rain was as important a source of conflict during most of the Mulroney years as it had been during Trudeau's final term of office.

However, what marks the Mulroney approach in this sphere of foreign policy from the approaches of the Liberal prime ministers who both preceded and succeeded him is how conflicts in the relationship tended to be managed during the Conservative era. Policy disagreements with Washington were always conducted with the recognition that, while some aspects of the hugely complex Canadian-American relationship were relatively unaffected by changes in government policy, other aspects were quite fragile and easy to damage. Moreover, relations were conducted with the shadow of the future in mind: how conflicts are played out today shape responses to future disagreements.

A good example of this was the Conservative government's decision on the Strategic Defense Initiative (SDI), or, as it was colloquially known, "Star Wars,"[15] an American plan to develop a space-based defence shield against ballistic-missile attack. In March 1985 the Reagan administration invited all U.S. allies to participate in an SDI research program in the hope of increasing the program's international and domestic legitimacy. Although many expected that Mulroney would join SDI, given his promise that Canada would be a better ally and would give the United States the benefit of the doubt in global policy, in fact the government decided against participation. While Mulroney himself was in favour of SDI, and particularly the employment possibilities it offered, there was considerable opposition to Star Wars, not only among the Canadian public but also within the ranks of the Conservative backbench. A parliamentary committee that was reviewing Canadian foreign policy – the special joint committee on Canada's international relations – held public hearings across Canada in the summer of 1985. Although the governing Conservatives controlled the committee, an all-party consensus emerged that the committee should recommend to cabinet that Canada not participate in this scheme. Mulroney accepted the committee's advice: on 7 September 1985 the government informed the United States that it was not going to participate. But the Canadian refusal to lend legitimacy to SDI was delivered in such a way as to avoid offence: the Canadian government openly declared that SDI research was "prudent," and, in a barely disguised bid for economic benefits, it noted that Canadian firms and institutions could participate if they wished. What was widely called the "polite no" on Star Wars underscored the desire of the Conservatives to minimize friction between Ottawa and Washington.

Likewise, although Mulroney was intent on "refurbishing" the relationship, he was quite comfortable opposing the United States when he believed that Canadian interests demanded it. For example, Mulroney, like all prime ministers before (and since), opposed the use of extraterritoriality by the United States government in its policy towards Cuba. For years, Canadian governments had grumbled about the efforts of the United States to extend its jurisdiction extraterritorially as a means of forcing its friends and allies to join with it in sanctioning "enemy" countries such as Cuba. Historically, the response of the government in Ottawa to the attempts of the U.S. government to apply such legislation as the Trading with the Enemy Act to those outside the United States was an ad hoc protest to Washington and an attempt to secure an exemption. The Conservative government was the first to try to turn the tables on Washington's extraterritorial practices by adopting legislation, the Foreign Extraterritoriality Measures Act (FEMA) of 1985, that would make it illegal for anyone on Canadian soil – including Americans – to comply with American extraterritorial legislation.

Mulroney also proved to be a good negotiator in defence of Canadian interests. For example, in 1985 the Conservative government responded forcefully to what it saw as an American infringement on Canadian sovereignty in the Arctic when the U.S. Coast Guard sent one of its icebreakers, the *Polar Sea*, through the Northwest Passage. Mulroney adopted a number of measures designed to reaffirm the Canadian claims to sovereign "ownership" of those Arctic waters that the United States government argued were an international strait. But Mulroney went further and sought to remove the thorny and highly political issue of Arctic sovereignty from the Canadian-American agenda. He was able to extract a major concession from the United States government on this issue, almost entirely as a consequence of his personal relationship with Ronald Reagan.[16]

On some issues, however, no amount of goodwill or diplomacy could overcome entrenched conflicts of interest between Canada and the United States. The conflict over acid rain, which had contributed to the tension in the relationship in the early 1980s, persisted well into the Conservative era. Mulroney did manage to secure from Reagan an admission that had eluded Trudeau – that acid rain was a problem that needed to be addressed. But in the 1980s the "legislative geography" in the Congress made any resolution of the issue virtually impossible: too many members of Congress in both the House of Representatives and the Senate came from states where there was little or no interest in amending the Clean Air Act of 1970 in ways that would be necessary to reduce emissions of sulphur dioxide and nitrous oxide in the United States. As a result, the Mulroney government grew as frustrated as the Liberal government had become – to the point that the Conservatives adopted the strategy, first used by the Liberals, of distributing propaganda to American tourists visiting Canada reminding them of their country's responsibility for environmental damage in Canada. Eventually the issue of acid rain was resolved (in the sense that it was removed from the Canadian-American agenda of irritants) during Mulroney's time in office, but this had more to do with shifts in American politics than with Conservative diplomacy.[17]

## LA FRANCOPHONIE: INSTITUTIONALIZING THE FRANCOPHONE SUMMIT

One of the most important foreign-affairs legacies was Mulroney's initiative to put in place a francophone summit similar to the Commonwealth Heads of Government meeting. Prior to Mulroney's prime ministership, efforts to create a francophone summit had always been frustrated by the lack of interest on the part of the French government in establishing a French-speaking equivalent to the Commonwealth, as well as by the quarrels in Canada over what the proper role of the provinces – particularly Quebec – should be on the international stage. The Quiet Revolution had given rise to a willingness on the part of the Quebec government to assert an international role for the province, an attitude that intensified after the election of the Parti Québécois (PQ) under René Lévesque in 1976. By contrast, the central government in Ottawa under Prime Minister Trudeau articulated a highly centralized vision of Canadian federalism that sought to keep the role of the provincial governments on the international stage as limited as possible. Quarrels over the international role of the provinces were most acute in the case of Quebec under PQ governments, since the PQ had every interest in demonstrating to the Quebec electorate that it was capable of operating on the world stage, while Ottawa, by contrast, had every interest in denying the government in Quebec City the legitimacy that a robust international role would provide. Thus, when the French president, François Mitterrand, finally agreed to a suggestion by Trudeau for a summit of la Francophonie, it was not surprising that the Parti Québécois government mounted an intensive lobbying effort to be included in the francophone summit as a full partner. Fearful of getting enmeshed in a domestic Canadian quarrel, Mitterrand eventually withdrew the idea.

When Mulroney became prime minister in September 1984, he worked with both Parti Québécois and Liberal governments in Quebec to establish an international institution in which Canada's francophone provinces would play a permanent and legitimate role. He negotiated agreements with the governments in Paris and Quebec City on the terms and conditions of provincial participation in the new francophone summit. The agreement with the Parti Québécois government was signed in October 1985, by Mulroney and newly sworn-in Premier Pierre-Marc Johnson, who had just succeeded Lévesque, but it was implemented by the new Liberal government of Robert Bourassa which had been brought to office in the Quebec election of November 1985. The agreement with Paris granted membership in the francophone summit to Quebec and New Brunswick; the agreement between Ottawa and those provinces was that their premiers could attend the summit but make interventions only on those matters that fell under provincial jurisdiction.

The first summit was held in February 1986, when forty-one heads of government from countries with a French connection gathered in Paris; Bourassa and Richard Hatfield, premier of New Brunswick, attended as virtually equal participants with Mulroney.[18] The second summit was hosted by Quebec itself, institutionalizing the Conférence des chefs d'État et de gouvernement ayant en commun l'usage de français (Summit of Heads of State and Government having the Use of French in Common).

## HUMAN RIGHTS AND GOOD GOVERNANCE

In the year that he spent as leader of the opposition in 1983–84, Mulroney was not overly concerned with human rights, except where the issue could be used to demonstrate the evils of the Soviet Union. This lack of attention is ironic, for the promotion of human rights and good governance became one of the central features of Canadian foreign policy during Mulroney's time in power.

Apartheid in South Africa had not been on the agenda in 1983–84, but, as in the case of the Ethiopian famine, the Mulroney government confronted the issue soon after it took office as violence was renewed on a significant scale in South Africa. The prime minister's response to apartheid was visceral: he openly advocated sanctions against South Africa and even bruited the possibility of cutting off all diplomatic relations with the apartheid regime. Moreover, although he had promised to be a "better ally," Mulroney in fact adopted a confrontational approach to the two leaders who were most opposed to sanctions against South Africa, Margaret Thatcher and Ronald Reagan. At the 1985 Commonwealth Heads of Government meeting, for example, he joined forces with other leaders against Thatcher; at the G-7 he found himself pretty much alone. And at the United Nations, Mulroney's commitment to a policy of total sanctions if the South African government did not abandon apartheid evoked an emotional response by other leaders: one delegate told the Canadian ambassador that he never thought he would live to see the day that a Western white leader would stand up against apartheid as Mulroney had done.[19] Moreover, he must have been the only Western leader to express his view that he "understood" why the African National Congress embraced violence as a means to bring apartheid to an end.[20]

The issue of apartheid was not the only example of Mulroney's human-rights activism and innovation. One measure of the Conservative government's commitment to international human rights was its response to the Beijing massacre of 4 June 1989. With Mulroney's approval, Clark took the lead in fashioning the Canadian response, delivering an angry denunciation that even opposition MPs acknowledged was the harshest statement on human rights ever made by a Canadian government.[21] The massacre had a profound impact on Hong Kong, which was due to return to Chinese sovereignty in 1997; confidence in the territory sank and large numbers of Hong Kong people sought to emigrate, with Canada as a prime destination. The Tiananmen crackdown catalysed the Mulroney government to pursue an explicit policy of confidence building in the territory, including an intensification of links and an unprecedented five-day visit by Mulroney himself to Hong Kong.[22]

By the fall of 1991, the government had explicitly embraced human rights and good governance as a "cornerstone of our foreign policy," as Mulroney put it in October.[23] Moreover, aid conditionality became part of its human-rights policy. Both Mulroney and his new secretary of state for external affairs, Barbara McDougall, who had been appointed to succeed Joe Clark in April 1991, enunciated a policy that linked aid allocation to performance on human rights and good governance. For his part, Mulroney took his human-rights message to the Commonwealth summit in Harare in October and the francophone summit in Paris in November.

Yet another measure of the government's commitment to human rights was its response to the Dili massacre of 12 November 1991, when Indonesian security forces opened fire on mourners at a funeral in the capital of East Timor. As in the case of the Beijing massacre, the Mulroney government followed harsh denunciations of Indonesia with concrete sanctions.[24]

## RETHINKING STATE SOVEREIGNTY

The explicit embrace of good governance as a priority highlights another key change in foreign policy embraced by the Mulroney government: a rethinking of that pillar of the Westphalian international system – the notion of national sovereignty. For the promotion of good governance implies a willingness to embrace what Deon Geldenhuys has termed "political engagement"[25] – including outright intervention in the internal affairs of sovereign states.

The Canadian response to the outbreak of war in the Balkans in the early 1990s illustrated an important new dimension of international relations in the immediate post-Cold War era: more and more conflicts are erupting within the borders of a given country while the wars between two countries are declining. How should the international community react to such developments? How can countries intervene in such conflicts where sovereignty is at stake? The stance taken by the Mulroney government moved Canada from a traditional peacekeeping role to a more interventionist position.

As early as November 1990, Mulroney was making the argument for a bending of the rules of sovereignty in cases of humanitarian need. "The conventions of national sovereignty," Mulroney told a meeting of the Conference on Security and Co-operation in Europe, "are becoming too narrow a base from which to resolve the broadening global and regional problems."[26] A year later, he reiterated his belief in humanitarian intervention: "Some Security Council members have opposed intervention in Yugoslavia, where many innocent people have been dying, on the grounds of national sovereignty. Quite frankly such invocation of the principles of national sovereignty are [sic] ... out of date."[27] This theme would continue to be pressed until the end of the Conservative era. In May 1993 Barbara McDougall, the secretary of state for external affairs, argued: "We have to reconsider the UN's traditional definition of state sovereignty. I believe that states can no longer argue sovereignty as a licence for internal repression, when the absolutes of that sovereignty shield conflicts that could eventually become international in scope ... National sovereignty should offer no comfort to repressors, and no protection to those guilty of breaches of the common moral codes enshrined in the Universal Declaration of Human Rights."[28]

Canada had enunciated such a position when it joined the Organization of American States (OAS) in 1989. Earlier, Canada's reluctance to join the OAS had been in part due to its difficult position between Latin American countries and its powerful neighbour, the United States. With a view to sending out a clear message of independence from both sides, Canada succeeded, as it had done with the North Atlantic Treaty Organization, in having the OAS's charter include some "Canadian principles." In this case, the principles were that "the protection of democracy" would be a primary objective pursued by Canada.[29] The first instance when Canada evoked such a provision was to justify intervention in the Haiti crisis.[30]

But the Conservative government also embraced a conception of state sovereignty that represented a more fundamental change in traditional Canadian practice. For example, the Mulroney government was the first Canadian government to endorse, openly and unambiguously, independence for Ukraine in 1991. As noted above, because of the threat posed to the Canadian state by separatism in Quebec, governments in Ottawa had always been careful to avoid encouraging the idea of the disintegration of a federal state. Indeed, so committed had Canadian governments been to the integrity of federal states that Trudeau had been moved to deny the very existence of the breakaway state of Biafra during the Nigerian civil war, responding to a reporter's question about Canadian policy towards Biafra with a curt "Where's Biafra?" Moreover, a succession of Canadian governments had spent decades denying the efforts of Ukrainian Canadians to press for the independence of their homeland. But in the fall of 1991, Mulroney openly supported the move for Ukrainian independence, claiming that Canada would offer formal diplomatic recognition if Ukrainians voted to separate.[31]

Closely linked to the Mulroney government's rethinking of state sovereignty was a shift in the Canadian approach to the use of force during this period. Canada's participation in the U.S.-led coalition that used force to evict Iraqi troops from Kuwait in January and February 1991 represented a significant foreign-policy departure by the Conservatives, for it was the first time since the Korean War of 1950–53 that a Canadian government had gone to war. The process by which the Mulroney government committed itself to the use of force to reverse the Iraqi invasion of Kuwait of August 1990 was a slow one. Nonetheless, it reflected an enthusiasm on the part of Prime Minister Mulroney about the possibilities of what President George H.W. Bush called the "new world order" ushered in by the unprecedented level of cooperation between the United States and the Soviet Union in the immediate aftermath of the invasion.[32]

The principle that force can and should be used for certain political purposes would also lead Mulroney to approve peacekeeping missions in both the former Yugoslavia and Somalia. In the autumn of 1991 Mulroney was the first Western leader to call for active intervention by the United Nations in the growing civil war in Yugoslavia. Subsequently, in December 1992, he told an audience at Harvard University, that the UN should impose peace on Bosnia using force if it were necessary and that Canada would heartily support such an operation. Likewise, when he toured Europe in May 1993 just before retiring as prime minister, he expressed the view that force should be used in Yugoslavia "should the courageous peacekeeping attempts by UN forces fail."[33] The Conservatives also joined the American initiative in a forceful rescue mission to Somalia in December 1992, contributing over 1,200 soldiers to the Unified Task Force (UNITAF).

## CONCLUSION

In 1993, at the end of the Progressive Conservative era, Arthur Andrew, a former Canadian diplomat, argued that the main legacy of Brian Mulroney's government was that it had contributed the final blow in the "fall" of Canada as a middle power.[34] Yet, fourteen years on, it could be argued that, in international affairs, Mulroney left a longer and stronger legacy than Andrew would have us believe. Michael Hart's chapter on the

FTA and Sean Maloney's chapter on defence demonstrate the enduring legacies of the Mulroney government in those two international-policy spheres. In foreign policy proper, the record was similar. For example, the human-rights agenda that was embraced by Mulroney in 1984–85 over South Africa, and expanded to include the good- governance policy of the early 1990s, was, as Jennifer Ross has compellingly argued,[35] the real foundation of the concept of human security promoted by Lloyd Axworthy, the minister of foreign affairs from 1996 to 2000 in the Liberal government of Jean Chrétien. Likewise, the institutionalization of the francophone summit after 1986 was such that this international institution was able to withstand the return of bellicosity in the Ottawa-Quebec relationship in the mid-1990s. The increased cooperation between the government and NGOs in the area of development assistance introduced by the Conservatives in 1984 quickly became entrenched and has been standard practice since.

In some areas of foreign policy, however, the legacies left by Brian Mulroney have been less enduring. For example, the increased involvement of Parliament in the foreign-policy process in the 1980s was largely abandoned in the 1990s as the Chrétien government sought to bypass MPs in favour of more intense engagement with the NGO community. Likewise, in the area of Canadian-American relations, Mulroney's legacies have been largely distorted by the politics of succession. Mulroney devoted considerable energy to the creation of good and close personal relations with Ronald Reagan and George H.W. Bush, and he was not shy about his successes in this area. But he was ultimately caught in that most durable of Canadian political dynamics: the truism that Canadians appear to grow uncomfortable if the relationship between their prime minister and the American president gets too cosy – or too frosty – and will tend to punish prime ministers who deviate from a middling road.[36] During the 1993 election campaign, Jean Chrétien made much of the overly cosy relations between the Conservatives and the White House, promising to maintain a proper distance from the Americans. (Ironically, Chrétien was to develop a close and cordial relationship with President Bill Clinton but kept the relationship as much out of the public eye as he could).

Yet Chrétien's efforts to create some distance between his policies towards the United States and those of his predecessor meant that one of the most important of Mulroney's initiatives – the institution of an annual summit meeting between the president and the prime minister – was sacrificed. The disappearance of this institution for managing the relationship at the highest level would exacerbate the tensions between Chrétien and President George W. Bush between 2001 and 2003, triggering not only a political debate about Canada's place in the world[37] but also some of the same political dynamics that had been evident in 1984 when the Mulroney era in Canadian foreign policy began.

## NOTES

1 See Stephen Clarkson, *Canada and the Reagan Challenge: Crisis and Adjustment, 1981–85*, rev. ed. (Toronto: James Lorimer, 1985); Adam Bromke and Kim Richard Nossal, "Tensions in Canada's Foreign Policy," *Foreign Affairs* 62 (winter 1983–84): 335–53.

2 David Taras, "Brian Mulroney's Foreign Policy: Something for Everyone," *The Round Table* 293 (1985): 39.

3 Brian Mulroney, "Canada and the World" (mimeo, 10 June 1983), 2–3.

4 Canada, Parliament, House of Commons, *Debates*, 25 October 1983.

5 Taras, "Brian Mulroney's Foreign Policy," 40.

6 For other parallels between Diefenbaker and Mulroney, see Nelson Michaud, "Canadian Defence Policies: A Framework for Analysis," *British Journal of Canadian Studies* 13(1) (1998): 112–13.

7 For a full elaboration of this argument, see Nelson Michaud and Kim Richard Nossal, *Diplomatic Departures: The Conservative Era in Canadian Foreign Policy, 1984–1993* (Vancouver: University of British Columbia Press 2001).

8 The best account of the Ethiopian crisis is David R. Morrison, *Aid and Ebb Tide: A History of* CIDA *and Canadian Development Assistance* (Waterloo, Ont.: Wilfrid Laurier University Press 1998), 234–5.

9 *Sunday Star*, 4 November 1984, cited in ibid., 234.

10 *Globe and Mail*, 6 November 1984, cited in ibid.

11 Cited in Maureen Appel Molot and Brian W. Tomlin, "The Conservative Agenda," in Molot and Tomlin, eds., *Canada among Nations, 1985: The Conservative Agenda* (Toronto: James Lorimer 1986), 9.

12 Morrison, *Aid and Ebb Tide*, 235.

13 Howard Adelman, *Canada and the Indochinese Refugees* (Regina, Sask.: Weigl Educational 1982); Gerry Dirks, "World Refugees: The Canadian Response," *Behind the Headlines* 45 (May/June 1988): 1–18.

14 As Mulroney told a group of delegates to the leadership convention, "that's why free trade was decided on in an election in 1911 ... It affects Canadian sovereignty, and we'll have none of it, not during leadership campaigns, nor at any other times." Quoted in Lawrence Martin, *Pledge of Allegiance: The Americanization of Canada in the Mulroney Years* (Toronto: McClelland and Stewart 1993), 44. On another occasion, he told reporters that Canada "could not survive with a policy of unfettered free trade." Quoted in John Herd Thompson and Stephen J. Randall, *Canada and the United States: Ambivalent Allies* (Montreal and Kingston: McGill-Queen's University Press 1994), 286.

15 On SDI, see Norrin Ripsman, "Big Eyes and Empty Pockets: The Two Phases of Conservative Defence Policy," in Michaud and Nossal, eds., *Diplomatic Departures*; Adam Bromke and Kim Richard Nossal, "A Turning Point in Canada-United States Relations," *Foreign Affairs* 66 (fall 1987): 150–69; and Joel Sokolsky, "Changing Strategies, Technologies and Organization: The Continuing Debate

on NORAD and the Strategic Defense Initiative," *Canadian Journal of Political Science* 19 (December 1986): 751–74.

16 For accounts of how Mulroney convinced Reagan to order the Joint Chiefs of Staff, the Department of Defense, and the Department of State to abandon their hard-line opposition to Canadian claims to Arctic sovereignty, see Rob Huebert, "A Northern Foreign Policy: The Politics of Ad Hocery," in Michaud and Nossal, *Diplomatic Departures*; Christopher Kirkey, "Smoothing Troubled Waters: The 1998 Canada-United States Arctic Co-operation Agreement," *International Journal* 50 (1995): 405–8; and Franklyn Griffiths, ed., *Politics of the Northwest Passage* (Montreal and Kingston: McGill-Queen's University Press, 1987).

17 The United States introduced amendments to the Clean Air Act and signed an air- quality agreement with Canada after George Mitchell of Maine, a strong advocate of acid-rain controls, became Senate majority leader, replacing Robert Byrd, of the coal-producing state of West Virginia, and when an air-quality agreement was signed with Mexico, which altered opinions in the House of Representatives. See Don Munton and Geoffrey Castle, "Reducing Acid Rain, 1980s," in Don Munton and John Kirton, eds., *Canadian Foreign Policy: Selected Cases* (Scarborough, Ont.: Prentice Hall Canada 1992), 367–81.

18 See John Kirton, "Shaping the Global Order: Canada and the Francophone and Commonwealth Summits of 1987," *Behind the Headlines* 44 (June 1987).

19 Linda Freeman, *The Ambiguous Champion: Canada and South Africa in the Trudeau and Mulroney Years* (Toronto: University of Toronto Press 1997), 4.

20 *Globe and Mail*, 31 January 1987; Kim Richard Nossal, *Rain Dancing: Sanctions in Canadian and Australian Foreign Policy* (Toronto: University of Toronto Press 1994), 96.

21 Nossal, *Rain Dancing*, 172–3; Jeremy Paltiel, "Rude Awakening: Canada and China following Tiananmen," in Maureen Appel Molot and Fen Osler Hampson, eds., *Canada among Nations, 1989: The Challenge of Change* (Ottawa: Carleton University Press 1989), 43–58.

22 On Mulroney's Hong Kong policy, see Kim Richard Nossal, "Playing the International Card? The View from Australia, Canada, and the United States," in Gerard A. Postiglione and James T.H. Tang, eds., *Hong Kong's Reunion with China: The Global Dimensions* (Armonk, N.Y.: M.E. Sharpe 1997), 79–101.

23 *Globe and Mail*, 17 October 1991.

24 Nossal, *Rain Dancing*, 50–1.

25 Deon Geldenhuys, *Foreign Political Engagement: Remaking States in the Post-Cold War World* (London: Macmillan 1998).

26 Cited in Leonard J. Cohen and Alexander Moens, "Learning the Lessons of UNPROFOR: Peacekeeping in the Former Yugoslavia," *Canadian Foreign Policy* 6 (winter 1999): 87.

27 Ibid., 86.

28 Cited in Tom Keating and Nicholas Gammer, "The 'New Look' in Canada's Foreign Policy," *International Journal* 48 (autumn 1993): 727.

29 Canada, Department of External Affairs and International Trade, Press Release 191, 5 October 1993.

30 Nelson Michaud and Louis Bélanger, "La stratégie institutionnelle du Canada: vers une australisation?" *Études internationales* 30(2) (1999): 383–7.

31 Kim Richard Nossal, "The Politics of Circumspection: Canadian Policy towards the Soviet Union, 1985–1991," *International Journal of Canadian Studies* 9 (spring 1994): 27–45.

32 Kim Richard Nossal, "Quantum Leaping: The Gulf Debate in Australia and Canada," in Michael McKinley, ed., *The Gulf War: Critical Perspectives* (Sydney: Allen and Unwin 1994), 48–71; Martin Rudner, "Canada, the Gulf Crisis and Collective Security," in Fen Osler Hampson and Christopher J. Maule, eds., *Canada among Nations, 1990–91: After the Cold War* (Ottawa: Carleton University Press 1991); Harald von Riekhoff, "Canada and Collective Security," in David B. Dewitt and David Leyton-Brown, eds., *Canada's International Security Policy* (Scarborough, Ont.: Prentice Hall Canada 1995), 240–6.

33 Kim Richard Nossal, *The Politics of Canadian Foreign Policy*, 3rd ed. (Scarborough, Ont.: Prentice Hall Canada 1997), 183.

34 Arthur Andrew, *The Rise and Fall of a Middle Power: Canadian Diplomacy from King to Mulroney* (Toronto: James Lorimer 1993).

35 Jennifer Ross, "Is Canada's Human Security Policy Really the 'Axworthy' Doctrine?" *Canadian Foreign Policy* 8(2) (winter 2001): 75–93.

36 Consider the fate of the Liberals in 1957, the Conservatives in 1963, the Liberals in 1984, and the Conservatives in 1993: in each case, the government in power was accused by the opposition of being too friendly (1957 and 1993) – or too unfriendly (1963 and 1984) – towards the United States.

37 For example, Andrew Cohen, *While Canada Slept: How We Lost Our Place in the World* (Toronto: McClelland and Stewart 2003); Jennifer Welsh, *At Home in the World: Canada's Global Vision for the 21st Century* (Toronto: HarperCollins 2004).

# 6

# Better Late Than Never: Defence during the Mulroney Years

SEAN M. MALONEY

The Mulroney government held office as Canada and the rest of the international community struggled to deal with the transition from the end of the Cold War to the emergence of a "World Order Era" in the 1990s, a period of tremendous change that, even ten years later, we are still trying to understand. Two things can hamper any examination of Canadian defence and national-security policy during those years. First, the defence records on the period available to the public are minimal, and, as the Somalia affair amply demonstrated, those that do exist are suspect in that senior mandarins have manipulated them. Indeed, one public-affairs officer who was involved in the nuclear-submarine acquisition project during the 1980s told the author that he personally destroyed several filing cabinets full of documents not just for reasons of security but "so that historians like you can just keep on guessing and wasting your time." Moreover, several people involved in the policy process have informed me that, in many cases, two sets of records were kept: one for the archives without marginalia, and another for internal discussion with marginalia.[1] The second, and more important, factor that can hinder an examination of defence and security policy in the Mulroney years relates to perception. It is difficult for most observers to study the events of the 1980s within the Cold War context that prevailed at that time, and, in fact, it is generally easier to dismiss defence policy during the Mulroney years as irrelevant. We know how it all ended: with a whimper and not a bang. This tends to cloud the fact that we did not know at the time that the global situation would change so dramatically and so quickly. Canadian policy makers in the 1980s could not have known that the Cold War would end when it did.

The conventional wisdom is that Canada's last Cold War White Paper, released three years after the Mulroney government's accession to power and seven years after the rest of the North Atlantic Treaty Organization

Prime Minister Brian Mulroney and other officials were on hand at CFB Ottawa on 19 March 1991 to welcome home Canadian soldiers who were serving in the Persian Gulf. Canadian Press / Chuck Mitchell.

(NATO) had started to rebuild its forces after the 1970s to confront a revitalized Soviet threat, was fortuitously late. The Cold War ended before Canada spent piles of money on equipment programs that were supposedly not needed for the new world order and so Canadians could reap what the media commentators referred to as the "peace dividend." It is therefore tempting to focus on the dramatic early stabilization campaigns of the 1990s. However, the reality was that the 1980s were exceedingly dangerous times. Did Canada in fact play a constructive role or was it irrelevant during the endgame of the Cold War struggle and the transition to the new world order?

The full span of the Mulroney years, particularly with regard to defence issues, is rich and textured. There are numerous nuanced aspects that, when combined with the larger, broader issues and themes, give us at least a starting point to try to understand what was accomplished by the Mulroney government – and what was not – during this period of great transition.

## CANADA AND THE WORLD OF THE EARLY 1980S

By 1980, the combined effects of post-Vietnam and post-Iran American psychological and economic malaise were being exploited by Soviet-led and Soviet-inspired activities around the globe, activities that had the goal of expanding Moscow's brand of communist totalitarian ideology and power. Eastern Europe remained under Soviet domination despite the Solidarity movement's abortive attempts to refashion the Polish political system. A massive upgrade in conventional forces was in progress for Warsaw Pact armies facing weakened NATO forces in West Germany, while the destabilizing SS-20 MRBM systems[2] were being deployed with the intention of intimidating NATO member states. Vast sums of rubles were poured into the development of more and more strategic nuclear weapons for the armoury of Soviet Long Range Air Forces and Strategic Rocket Forces, renewing the already existing threat to North America. In Africa, Central America, the Caribbean, and Asia, a resurgence in Soviet intelligence and economic and military support for regimes in those regions continued unabated. Provocative military activity conducted by Soviet forces threatened the sea lanes with even more intimidation. The delusions of a thaw in the Cold War were shattered by the overt and brutally conducted Soviet military intervention into Afghanistan in 1979.[3] Indeed, briefings to the minister of national defence in the late 1970s reminded the government that "arms control negotiations and the process of détente tended to obscure the fundamentally competitive relationship between the superpowers and encouraged optimistic public expectations regarding the future of relations with the Soviet Union, expectations which proved to be unwarranted."[4]

Canada's response to all of this was muddled, at best. The interregnum of Prime Minister Joe Clark, lasting from June 1979 to March 1980, was unable to alter seriously the tone or direction of the decade-old policies established by the government of Pierre Elliott Trudeau. Indeed, from March 1980 to September 1984, it was business as usual. The last public statement of Canadian defence policy, *Defence in the 70s*, had been released in 1971 and no attempt was made to adjust it throughout the 1970s. The fundamental premise of that document, in concert with related material from the Department of External Affairs, was that Canada was a pseudo neutral in the ongoing drama of the Cold War.[5] Canada would continue to adhere publicly to the long-standing Cold War structures like NATO,

North American Air Defence (NORAD), and the United Nations, but this would be done with a minimalism that bordered on negligence.

Canada's hard-won influence, based on a nearly twenty-year policy of committing salient and effective military forces to NATO and dramatic international engagement through UN missions in the Third World designed to stave off Soviet influence,[6] was frittered away. The new policy consisted of catering to patently corrupt African dictators or those embracing unproductive socialist policies, hectoring Canada's purported allies on arms-control issues, spending aid monies with near-indiscriminate abandon through the Canadian International Development Agency (CIDA), and moving towards an almost isolationist retrenchment in the Canada-U.S. relationship. Trudeau was committed to making Canada, as some paraphrased it, the largest of the small instead of the smallest of the large. Some documents, specifically CIDA policy statements, went as far to suggest that Canada was a post-colonial Third World country.[7]

It is fair to assert that the primary problem overshadowing everything during those years was the possibility of a war which would involve the mass use of nuclear weapons. To this end, the Trudeau government succumbed to its fears and bent in the direction of surrender rather than what it viewed as probable suicide. It refused to accept that there was a third option available – defence, deterrence, and defiance in the face of blatant Soviet intimidation – and so would not consider the possibility that improvement in NATO's conventional forces would be a stabilizing factor. Trudeau's arms-control officials were utterly horrified by NATO's intermediate nuclear-force improvement plans, which were designed to counter the destabilizing Soviet SS-20s. Sincerely believing that Canada was some kind of impartial neutral, a peacekeeper of sorts, in a Cold War that they viewed not as a battle between freedom versus totalitarianism but solely as a competition between morally equivalent superpowers, they had skewed policy in that direction. Pierre Trudeau's earnest 1983 "Peace Initiative" merely punctuated this state of affairs.[8]

The only discernable policy in support of the Western alliance in the Cold War was the acceptance of Air Launched Cruise Missile (ALCM) testing in northern Canada. The ALCM and its ground-launched brother, the GLCM, used the same satellite-mapping guidance system (known as TERCOM, which gave the cruise missiles greater accuracy and made them harder to detect by ground radar). By supporting ALCM testing, the Trudeau government tacitly endorsed the project of modernizing the NATO theatre nuclear force. The move was, however, tactical, intended to gain an influence "card" with the Reagan administration. The Trudeau "Peace Initiative" demonstrated the folly of such a naive, piecemeal approach.[9]

On the defence side, the deterioration of Canada's conventional and nuclear forces progressed. Cosmetic changes, like the replacement of three hundred-plus Centurion main battle tanks with 118 rented West German Leopards, were implemented after tough bureaucratic infighting and pressure from West Germany, but the replacement of Maritime Command's obsolete 1950s anti-submarine vessels was a pipe dream. Granted, a New Fighter Aircraft program was launched and the aging Argus Maritime Patrol Aircraft were replaced with the CP-140 Auroras, but both were essentially sold as a way of maintaining Canadian sovereignty rather than as a contribution to Western defence. Canada's regular and reserve conventional ground forces were not reconstituted in depth to accommodate NATO's shift to Flexible Response, so the forces that did exist had no back-up and could not be sustained.

In terms of defence and national security, Canada under the Trudeau government was a liability to any effort to counter Soviet-led or Soviet-inspired communist influence or expansion. Its younger members (both elected and unelected), schooled in 1960s leftist rhetoric, and its selectively pliant older hands, steeped in obsolete strategies and frightened of nuclear extinction, were philosophically disabled when it came to understanding the nature of the threat, let alone developing a means to deal with it. Canada was, by the early 1980s, a powerless victim waiting to be victimized, not the global player it had once been, defending its values and security from a forward posture. Could things change with the new government that came to power in 1984?

When Brian Mulroney's Progressive Conservatives formed government, Canada was already five years behind the rest of the free nations in a number of respects. In the face of the Soviet resurgence of the 1970s, the newly elected British and American governments accelerated a variety of programs designed to respond to Soviet moves. The United States under Ronald Reagan developed and implemented a strategy designed specifically to attack the basis of Soviet power from a number of vantage points. Essentially, these strategies dealt with eight areas: the conduct of economic warfare; the projection of information warfare behind the Iron Curtain; the bolstering of NATO's conventional and nuclear forces to revitalize the alliance's resolve; the support of anti-communist efforts in Central America, Africa, and particularly Afghanistan; the development of missile-defence programs under the aegis of the Strategic Defense Initiative (SDI, or what the media quickly dubbed the "Star Wars" program); the modernization and improvement of strategic nuclear forces; and the strengthening of ideological unity among America's faltering allies.[10] The British followed suit, for the most part. Though they were somewhat pre-occupied with the Falklands War in 1982 and tended to be more focused on NATO Europe than other areas, they played a significant role in Afghanistan.[11]

In Canada, the five lost years in matters of defence, when combined with the decade-long neglect of the military in the 1970s, were potentially crippling to any attempt to alter course and have Canada once again play a significant role in the collective effort to confront the Soviet Union's violent ideology and expansionist efforts. There first had to be a philosophical basis for action, and from that a policy.

When the Clark government was in power in 1979–80, it produced a Green Paper on foreign policy. This document, entitled *Canada in a Changing World*, was ultimately designed to replace the Trudeau-era *Foreign Policy for Canadians.* Unlike the Trudeau-era document, *Canada in a Changing World* did not shy away from identifying the Soviet Union as a problem for the West (and therefore Canada), specifically with regard to the massive conventional imbalance of forces, the achievement of strategic nuclear parity by the Soviets, and the increase of their power-projection capabilities. Regions where the Soviets were leading or otherwise inspiring and supporting efforts detrimental to Western interests were also identified: the Middle East and particularly the Persian Gulf, eastern Asia, sub-Saharan Africa, the Caribbean, and Central America. And the emergence of international terrorism was highlighted, for the first time in a public Canadian policy document.[12] As an interpretation of the world scene, *Canada in a Changing World* was very different from *Foreign Policy for Canadians*, and arguably more honest. For one thing, it used blunt language instead of anodyne phrases, such as the Trudeau document's "harmonious natural environment."

The Trudeau government physically destroyed the print run of *Canada in a Changing World* once it took power again in 1980. Canadians were not permitted access to it, presumably for their own good. Officially, the only copy was read into Hansard.[13] Yet *Canada and a Changing World* formed the basis for the first Mulroney statement on foreign policy, released rapidly in 1985. Called *Competitiveness and Security*, it employed a language and tone almost identical to that of *Canada in a Changing World.* There were charts depicting NATO-Warsaw Pact force comparisons, where the Warsaw Pact had a "distinct edge" in conventional and theatre nuclear forces; the document discussed the fact that the Soviets had achieved parity in strategic nuclear weapons, and that NATO had to "maintain credible defences and preserve a balance of forces" to ensure that the existing peace held. The main problem was Europe, where the Soviet Union was "a formidable, conventionally and nuclear armed adversary," and indeed "the most direct threat to Canadian security [was] derived from both the Soviet Union's military capabilities and antipathy to Canadian values." Outside Europe, the main problem areas were Afghanistan, Poland, the SS-20 deployment, and human-rights violations in Warsaw Pact countries. Indeed, "Soviet behaviour was inimical to our interests" and there could be no neutrality for Canada: "We are determined to uphold and defend our ideals of freedom and democracy ... the need to defend ourselves is real." Notably, international terrorism was examined as a threat to Canadian interests. This was all very different from the Trudeau-era foreign policy.[14] *Competitiveness and Security* established several priorities: 1) sovereignty and surveillance; 2) NATO Europe, "which remains the most critical military region in the world"; 3) arms control; 4) the United Nations; and 5) regional conflicts.

## THE 1987 DEFENCE WHITE PAPER

There were three themes that drove Canadian defence policy under the Mulroney government. One was sovereignty. Without an effective contribution to continental defence, Canada was a protectorate of the United States. Being able to engage the United States as a partner in this field would have positive benefits in other areas while, at the same time, real threats from outside sources could be countered. Also, Canada had to become once again, in the eyes of the Americans and NATO, a willing partner and trusted ally. Canada had to be reliable, and Canada had to be included. The only means to achieve this end was to shoulder a fair share of the burden, something that was noticeably lacking during the Trudeau years. Finally, the Canadian government had to re-establish credibility with the neglected armed forces: it was immoral to commit them to missions like the Canadian Air-Sea Transportable (CAST) Brigade Group in support of NATO without adequate resources.[15]

With the Green Paper, sovereignty, and international credibility as the philosophical basis for action, the Mulroney government set out in 1985 to produce a Defence White Paper, the first since 1971. The initial move involved contracting Canadian defence analyst Nick Stetham to produce a framework document. This proceeded rapidly and was completed in three months. When exposed to the Defence and External Affairs bureaucracies, however, endless redrafts were demanded, so much so that the framework was no longer recognizable. An additional problem was the turbulence generated by rapid ministerial turnover in the Department of National Defence (DND) portfolio. From 1983 to 1986, no less than five men held the position: Jean Jacques Blais, Robert Coates, Joe Clark, Erik Neilsen, and Perrin Beatty. Each change necessitated more modifications to the draft documents and more delays.[16] Perrin Beatty eventually took the reigns and apparently told those involved in the process to get on with it and that he "didn't want the elephant to give birth to a mouse."[17]

Two groups were set up to sort out this mess, both working in the assistant deputy minister's (policy) section of National Defence Headquarters. Robert Fowler was brought over from the Privy Council Office to become ADM (policy) and Dr Kenneth Calder was assigned to assist him. They handled senior staff discussions. The Planning Guidance Team, which consisted of Colonel Bill Weston, Colonel Sean Henry, and Captain

(Navy) Jan Drent, collected data and answered the technical questions.[18] One component of the process involved consulting sessions, the importance of which was absolutely critical given the tenor of the times. First, it was essential to the Mulroney government that Canadian people have access to the process and that a variety of views be aired: they did not want a continuation of the secretive Liberal approach that had failed to keep Canadians involved and informed.[19]

But an open, transparent approach posed challenges. The Soviets viewed NATO theatre nuclear-force modernization and conventional-force improvements with some alarm: it was in their best interest that NATO nations in Europe remain weak, divided, and subject to coercion. The decision taken by the Reagan administration to revitalize America's strategic nuclear capability to keep ahead of the Soviet Union was seen the same way. In addition, the Strategic Defense Initiative drove the Soviets into a frenzy since the program might offset its newly acquired strategic nuclear parity and theatre nuclear dominance. As a result, the Soviet Union and its allies conducted a covert campaign to propagandize and influence the public debate in Western countries. What was collectively referred to as the "peace movement" was subtly directed and financially supported by Soviet proxies to achieve Soviet aims.[20] Using the West's open democracy against itself was ironic, to say the least, but in keeping with the Soviet Union's modus operandi established sixty years previously.

It was in this context that the Mulroney government's public consultations directed significant attention towards nuclear issues, particularly SDI. Those involved in the Canadian White Paper process had access to intelligence which confirmed that the Soviets would attempt to influence the process in Canada. Consequently, a position called the director of public policy (DPP) was created under Fowler. The DPP's job was to coordinate the government's response to the "peace movement" at the grass-roots, tactical level in order to ensure that the public consultations were not unduly subjected to manipulation from the outside via proxies.[21] For example, a retired Canadian general and former NORAD officer, Leonard Johnson, belonged to a group known as Generals for Peace; the East German Stasi funded it.[22]

It was not only SDI that would be of concern. In the long policy process, a proposal was made to acquire twelve nuclear-powered attack submarines for Canada's maritime forces. The "peace movement" would likely disseminate all sorts of misinformation equating nuclear-powered submarines (SSN) with nuclear ballistic missile-equipped submarines (SSBN). Apparently, even the secretary of state for external affairs, Joe Clark, did not understand the difference between SSN and SSBN submarines.[23] The fear that Canadian SSNs might be fitted to fire Tomahawk cruise missiles (of which there was a nuclear-equipped version) drove many bureaucrats crazy, as they tried to explain the technical differences between battlefield and strategic nuclear weapons and their respective places in the NATO strategy that Canada had agreed to long ago and the necessity of a flexible "fitted for but not with" policy.[24]

Internally, the neutrality argument was quickly dispensed with. Neutrality was simply too expensive a way for Canada to defend itself, besides being impractical on other grounds. Moreover, a neutral Canada would not only wield little or no influence but would also betray its most basic values. A National Defence analysis stated that "the Canadian people would regard the notion [of neutrality] as incompatible with the deep ideological and political affinity which the vast majority of Canadians have for Western values and associations."[25]

The broad outlines of the new policy were aired and eventually consolidated into *Challenge and Commitment: A Defence Policy for Canada*, which was released in 1987. Unlike its 1970s predecessor document (and, incidentally, its successor document under the Chrétien government in 1994), the 1987 White Paper took pains to lay out the nature and scope of the Soviet threat. Essentially, it drew attention to the same threats highlighted by NATO in the late 1970s and early 1980s: crushing conventional superiority, nuclear modernization, and aggressive behaviour.[26]

The White Paper identified three main areas of change: maintenance of strategic deterrence, credible conventional defence, and protection of Canadian sovereignty.[27] It portrayed NATO and NORAD as the key arms of collective defence and emphasized that Canada should participate in both with modernized and effective military forces. Deterring Soviet strategic action, specifically strategic nuclear attack, was absolutely critical and best done by protecting the West's strategic capabilities and by deterring Soviet-bloc adventurism in Europe.[28]

All-Canadian continental defence forces were to be upgraded (maritime patrol aircraft, fighters, surveillance capabilities), and the Arctic was identified as an important operating theatre since the Soviets were increasing their submarine presence there. Canadian naval forces would be modernized with SSNs and some twenty-four Canadian patrol frigates equipped for "Three Ocean" operations: Pacific, Atlantic, and Arctic. CF-18s would have Forward Operating Locations in the Arctic to confront Soviet air operations.[29]

In Europe, the Trudeau-era commitment of the CAST brigade to Norway was ended after Exercise BRAVE LION in 1986 demonstrated Canada's inability to deploy and then support the force.[30] Instead, the CAST brigade was re-equipped and committed to NATO's Central Region in West Germany and, alongside an improved, upgraded, and reinforced 4 Canadian Mechanized Brigade Group, would form 1st Canadian Division, situated in Lahr, West Germany. A battalion-sized unit remained committed to

North Norway as part of a new NATO Composite Force.[31] More CF-18 squadrons were committed to Central Region and 1 Air Division was reformed to replace 1 Canadian Air Group. These commitments, which were implemented by 1988, gave Canada and NATO salient and effective conventional forces as part of the collective-deterrent effort in Europe, something that was of key importance since the achievement by the Soviets of strategic parity and theatre nuclear superiority made the use of conventional forces more likely in a crisis.[32] The reserve forces would finally be improved so that there was a mobilization capability in the event of conventional war in Europe: this was also part of strategic deterrence. In effect, the neglect of the Trudeau era was to be reversed, in all areas and in one fell swoop, and the Alliance's confidence in Canada restored.

Mulroney successfully employed personal diplomacy. Elements within the U.S. Navy opposed the transfer of SSN technology to Canada. On the surface, the rather patronizing argument against such action was the concern that, if Canada messed up and the safety of a nuclear submarine was compromised, it would reflect badly on the American program. The reality was that there were U.S. Navy issues related to sovereignty involved, particularly the Northwest Passage, and precedents could be set that would affect the navy's freedom of movement elsewhere in the world. Discussions with President Ronald Reagan, Secretary of Defense Caspar Weinberger, Minister of National Defence Perrin Beatty, and the prime minister reversed the objections within U.S. Navy circles and even led Reagan to agree to positive discussions on the Northwest Passage issue.[33]

The most significant obstacle in the formation and implementation of Canadian defence policy during this time, however, was the animosity between the prime minister and his cabinet appointee, Joe Clark. This personality clash coloured several aspects of the process. Mulroney favoured refurbishing damaged Canada-U.S. relations; Clark wanted more distance. Mulroney was sceptical about what the United Nations could accomplish during the Cold War; Clark championed the UN as a tool for peace. Indeed, Clark asked his staff to create a list of the top ten points of disagreement between Canada and the United States so that he could use them publicly at every turn to interfere with Mulroney's policy implementation.[34] In fact, the "soft power" agenda of Lloyd Axworthy under the Chrétien government had some precedent in the policies pursued by Clark at External Affairs in the 1980s.

The main points of contention vis-à-vis the 1987 White Paper in this context were the nuclear-submarine acquisition program and SDI. As noted earlier, Clark did not understand the difference between SSN and SSBN types of submarines. He expressed concern that Canada would lose its allegedly "hard won" position at the UN if it acquired nuclear weapons. Even after being reminded that Canada still had access to nuclear weapons in the form of AIR-2A Genie air-to-air nuclear rockets for its CF-101 Voo Doo interceptors (though they were due to come out of service soon), and that it had had access to a plethora of nuclear weapons during the peak period of its influence with the UN in the 1960s, Clark was undeterred.[35] Though this did not alone torpedo Canada's nuclear-submarine program, it caused an inordinate amount of effort to be expended defending the nuclear-submarine program both internally and externally. It also generated confusion and uncertainty in certain American camps, particularly the submarine community. Clark's behaviour was much in line with the Trudeau-era view of the world: Canada was a neutral in the Cold War. The vast potential spin-off economic benefits for Canada, like the revitalization of the country's nuclear industry, let alone the capacity to deal with North American security issues related to increased Soviet submarine intrusion in Canadian waters and NATO forward security, were apparently unimportant to Clark and those surrounding him.[36]

The Strategic Defense Initiative posed another set of complex problems that were subject to Clark's interference. In the context of Canadian defence policy, space defence was closely linked to the air defence of North America: as one participant put it, air defence was the walls, space defence was the roof. The two were symbiotic. At this time, the revitalization of air defence under NORAD was being pursued through a planning process called SDA 2000. To get the full political, economic, and military benefit for Canada, it behooved the Mulroney government to participate in both space defence and air defence. Since the Americans viewed the two as connected, why should Canada not do so as well?[37]

Clark, along with some of his staffers, and assorted holdovers from the Trudeau era, were adverse to revitalized connections with a Reagan-led United States and SDI was on his list of sticking points; the situation was also aggravated by arms-control proponents in External Affairs who feared that SDI would result in "destabilization" of the Anti-Ballistic Missile (ABM) Treaty, a canard also thrown up by the so-called peace movement and, not incidentally since this was still the Cold War, the Soviet Union. The Mulroney government chose to compromise: Canada would not offer cash or forces for SDI, but Canadian industry would be encouraged to participate. The Americans, after a Clark speech, misunderstood this and took it as a slap in the face, which prompted the Mulroney government to embark on a time-consuming effort in damage control.[38]

Little was said in the 1987 White Paper with regard to Canadian peacekeeping activities. During the first decades of the Cold War, Canada used UN and non-UN peacekeeping missions as part of Cold War containment activities in the Third World to forestall Soviet influence and for crisis management as a Western surrogate force.[39] The Trudeau government, which was not a fan of UN peacekeeping, was reluctantly dragged into several

Middle East UN peacekeeping operations and forced to reinforce Canada's position on the island of Cyprus in 1974. By the Mulroney era, some of these missions were still in place: Canada had an infantry battalion in UNIFICYP in Cyprus; a logistics battalion served with UNDOF on the Golan Heights; and there were Canadian observers with UNTOS in Jerusalem. Though peacekeeping as a Cold War tool had declined to the point where it served merely to maintain the status quo, the Mulroney government did commit to the non-UN Multinational Force and Observers, which essentially replaced UNEF II in the Sinai Operation CALUMET to monitor compliance by Israel and Egypt with the historic Camp David Accords in 1986. Canada's contribution , however, was limited to a portion of a utility and tactical helicopter squadron which was not continuously deployed.[40]

Why, exactly, Canada remained committed to Middle East peacekeeping in the 1980s is open to speculation, for it was a stagnant environment after the Camp David Accords were implemented. Most of the action was in Lebanon, but Canadian troops serving with UNIFIL there had left by 1979 when the conflict heated up, which left the country's military in comparatively low-risk areas with little or no activity. It is highly probable that Clark's personal interest in the region (dating from his time as prime minister) was a significant factor, combined with the perpetual Canadian "Peacekeeping Myth" that Canada contributes to UN peacekeeping because Canada allegedly invented it and the UN asks us to do so.[41]

Elsewhere, Canada deployed a signals regiment and military observers with the United Nations Iran-Iraq Military Observer Group (UNIIMOG), which was established in 1988 at the conclusion of the eight-year Iran-Iraq War and was designed to monitor the disengagement of forces and handle confidence building. The Canadian objectives in contributing forces were to facilitate normalization of relations with Iran, to act as a Western surrogate or representative in the region, and to assist in stabilizing the vital oil-rich region on which NATO countries and Japan were dependent.[42]

## FIGHTING THE COLD WAR: CANADIAN COVERT ACTIVITIES

Mulroney also reversed the pseudo-neutral posture adopted by the Trudeau government when it came to covert activities. Canada already had a robust signals-intelligence capacity by the 1980s, including stations in Bermuda, West Germany, and the Arctic as well as on both Canadian coasts. Though some older stations were closed in 1986, the equipment utilized by the Canadian Forces SIGINT units and the DND-administered Communications Security Establishment (CSE) was improved. The most important site from a strategic perspective remained CFS Alert, in the high Canadian Arctic. Its purpose was to provide strategic intelligence and warning for Soviet preparations for nuclear attack. Personal linkages with the American National Security Agency and the British Government Communications Headquarters, which had atrophied in the 1970s, were renewed and strengthened. During the Mulroney era, more overseas deployments by CSE-SIGINT personnel to operating sites were undertaken than in years previous.[43] Similarly, underwater surveillance systems, specifically SOSUS, were improved.[44]

Canada also operated a technical-intelligence collection program, which was expanded during the Mulroney years. This was an opportunistic, low-key program, which gathered small items like torpedoes or other Soviet-bloc munitions, aircraft engines, manuals, and operating information.[45] On some occasions, Canadian Forces transport aircraft moved the material from Soviet client states in the Third World, and on at least one occasion a plane was prepared to land in a Warsaw Pact nation (with the concurrence of factions in that nation) to do a collection. In many cases, there was friction between External Affairs and National Defence on risk/benefit analysis of the missions.[46]

The Soviets' aggressive behaviour on the high seas, through units of their dramatically expanded blue-water fleet, prompted Canadian activity for two reasons. First, the Soviets could not be allowed or seen to be allowed to dominate the oceans and sea lanes. Secondly, intelligence had to be gathered and updated to keep track of the changes in the Soviets' global maritime posture. Soviet SIGINT-gathering trawlers, called "tattletales," frequently "fished" off Canada. On a number of occasions, these ships also interfered with Canadian army exercises at CFB Gagetown, New Brunswick, by intercepting, jamming, and manipulating communications.[47] Canadian naval activities were stepped up during the 1980s to gather intelligence on Soviet naval and air capabilities, while Air Command fighters regularly intercepted and observed Soviet bomber activity on the peripheries of NORAD.

One significant operation was conducted in 1986. Canada joined an American exercise which involved two carrier battle groups (USS *Vinson* and USS *Ranger*) and a surface-action group (USS *New Jersey*). Aggressive Soviet air activity in the Pacific, specifically strategic bomber "runs" towards "targets" in California, Alaska, and Hawaii, prompted reciprocal manœuvring. Three Canadian destroyers, an operational-support ship, and several Aurora patrol aircraft joined in. American carrier-based aircraft overflew Soviet bases in the Kamchatka peninsula, while the battle groups entered Soviet-dominated waters in the Sea of Japan and the Sea of Okhosk. The Canadian ships were involved in signals-intelligence collection designed to monitor the Soviet response to the aggressive movements of the American forces. Canada's participation was in part designed to highlight the fact that Canada was a Pacific nation had interests there and that the Cold War was conducted in that region as well as the Atlantic.[48]

The Mulroney government also facilitated, in a limited but useful fashion, non-lethal support for groups fighting communist expansion in the Third World. Afghan *mujihadeen* groups generally were "handled" by Pakistan's Inter-Services Intelligence organization, with some loose coordination by the Central Intelligence Agency (CIA). A variety of Canadian intelligence resources were provided as part of the effort to assist the *mujihadeen* campaign. Some seriously wounded *mujihadeen* were airlifted to Canada for specialized medical treatment. An American-coordinated non-lethal aid program was permitted by the Canadian government to operate from Toronto: American transport aircraft (both civilian and unmarked) used Toronto International Airport as an air head to move the material to Pakistan. On one occasion, a Canadian citizen was sent into Afghanistan to collect evidence of Soviet chemical weapons use. He was seriously wounded and had to be evacuated.[49]

There does not appear to have been any similar support for American efforts in Central America. Canada maintained development aid to Nicaragua, El Salvador, and Honduras through CIDA and played a role in the El Salvador peace process.[50] Although not a Cold War operation per se, the quiet marshalling and deployment of a Canadian joint task force to intervene in Haiti in 1988 was a significant departure for Canadian defence policy. Non-combatant evacuation operations (NEOs) had been conducted before by the Canadian Forces, usually in permissive environments. When Haiti exploded into political violence in December 1987, the estimated 1,200 Canadian citizens there, mostly missionaries, were in harm's way. A naval task group, with army helicopters and an infantry battalion, embarked from Halifax, and an Air Command Hercules and Buffalo transport aircraft deployed to the Caribbean. Operation BANDIT, as it was known, was the first non-UN, non-NATO expeditionary operation by Canada since 1963. However, it was compromised by the media before it could get into position to do its job and the Haitian government of Jean-Claude Duvalier government threatened retaliation against Canadians if any intervention was attempted. Eventually, political pressure brought to bear by Canada, the United States, and France alleviated the situation. Still, BANDIT served as a warning to National Defence that there were serious deficiencies in critical areas, including the strategic command and control system, joint doctrine and training, and special operations forces.[51] This early wake-up call would yield positive benefits by 1990 when Canada was confronted simultaneously with a serious domestic disturbance and a war in the Persian Gulf.

## THE CHICKEN AND THE EGG: THE 1989 BUDGET AND THE END OF THE COLD WAR

Barely two years passed before a number of events invalidated many of the premises of the 1987 White Paper as a basis for Canadian defence policy. The first was the recognition by the Mulroney government that, owing to fiscal realities, it would have to slash spending across the board. The second was the recognition by the Soviet leadership that the Reagan strategy had succeeded: the Soviet communist system was bankrupt and would be unable to continue to compete strategically with the West.

Canada's economy, burdened as it was with massive debt incurred during the Trudeau era, was not performing as expected. Did the cuts made to the government fiscal program have to cut as deep as they did in the defence area? This remains open to question. According to one perspective, Joe Clark and Michael Wilson were instrumental in forcing more cuts onto the armed forces than were necessary so that they could achieve a number of personal and party-oriented political objectives vis-à-vis the prime minister and Perrin Beatty.[52] It was clear, for example, that the jewel in the crown of the 1987 defence program, SSN acquisition, would have to go. Almost all equipment programs initiated in response to the 1987 White Paper were either cut outright or placed in limbo. Some would carry on: the maritime forces would eventually get twelve of the twenty four planned Canadian patrol frigates, but the land forces would not get a new main battle tank or a mechanized infantry combat vehicle.

On the international front, Mikhail Gorbachev conceded that the Soviet Union could not continue without imploding. Soviet aid to overseas operations in Central America, Africa, and Asia was frozen and then slowly withdrawn. Gorbachev gave the Soviet commander one year to win the war in Afghanistan, and when that proved impossible, plans were made for a phased withdrawal under UN oversight. In time, even the Berlin Wall and the Iron Curtain were breached.

This gave Joe Clark and those supporting him in External Affairs an opportunity to commit to nearly every UN operation involved in the disengagement of communism from Third World proxy fights and to laud, prematurely, every step as the dawn of a new UN era. In rapid succession, the Canadian Forces were committed to the UNTAG mission in Namibia and UNAVEM in Angola; ONUSAL (El Salvador) and ONUCA (Nicaragua) in Central America; ONUMOZ in Mozambique; and eventually UNTAC in Cambodia. Canada also committed combat engineers to the UN mission that was trying to sort out the post-Soviet situation in Afghanistan. In most cases, these missions involved unarmed Canadian observers, transport aircraft, and helicopter units for periods of limited duration.[53] Arms-control efforts in Europe, particularly negotiations for a Conventional Forces in

Europe treaty, were stepped up, as was Canadian involvement in the Conference for Security and Co-operation in Europe (CSCE, later the Organization for Security and Co-operation in Europe, or OSCE). The Canadian Forces committed personnel to observation and verification missions throughout the late 1980s and early 1990s, a not insignificant contribution during a confusing and potentially dangerous time.[54]

Against this background, there were serious discussions in Canada about the withdrawal of Canada's land and air commitment to NATO's Central Region. The prime champion for this was Robert Fowler, who had made the same suggestion during the 1987 White Paper process. Canada's ambassador to NATO, Gordon Smith, viewed such a move as disastrous to Canada's ability to retain influence in NATO and in the emerging new Europe. The Soviets had not withdrawn anything from their Warsaw Pact forces in Eastern Europe and there was no consensus that they would any time soon. In these circumstances, the withdrawal of Canadian forces would send the wrong signal during a period of extreme turbulence.[55] The issue moved to the back-burner. In the meantime, politicized analysis inside National Defence "confirming" the fiscal "need" to withdraw the forces was prepared for future use.[56]

## A YEAR OF PERIL: NATIVE INSURRECTION AND WAR IN THE PERSIAN GULF

The shift from the Cold War era was marked for Canada by organized and armed violence employed by what political scientists call "non-state actors" and directed against legitimate governance structures. In three instances, the Mulroney government was confronted with an unanticipated insurgency conducted by some of Canada's Aboriginal peoples, which in effect became a prototype of the sorts of problems that nations would face throughout the 1990s.

The first instance revolved around NATO low-level flight training, which was conducted from CFB Goose Bay in Labrador. In 1988 Innu from the Sheshatshit reserve became involved in a land-claims dispute with the crown. Between September and October 1988, there were ten protests at the base; in some cases, protesters camped out at the end of the runways and even entered the flight line and were within "touching distance" of aircraft from West Germany and the Netherlands. In time, the Canadian Peace Alliance (CPA) joined the protest.[57] Infiltrated and led by communists, the CPA was a collection of groups determined to neutralize Canada.[58] Clearly, the objective of the Innu-CPA alliance was to disrupt NATO low-level flight training and embarrass Canada. For the Innu, the publicity could be used to further their land-claims activities, while the CPA (and, naturally, the Soviets) benefited from the trouble caused between NATO partners over security at the base and the operational impact of not being able to train properly for the European deterrent mission.[59] Consequently, the Canadian Forces mounted Operation UNIQUE, which deployed a military police platoon, helicopters, and an infantry company to back up the defence force at CFB Goose Bay. From 1989 until 1995, Operation UNIQUE was an annual affair when the NATO training season was under way, ensuring that non-lethal force was used to prevent interference with base activities.[60]

In early 1990 internal tensions in the Akwasasne reserve near Cornwall, Ontario, escalated into arson, violence, and murder. In what media outlets called "the Mohawk civil war," pro-and anti-gambling elements overlapping with other factions shot it out with each other. Aboriginal militants from elsewhere deployed into the area, which exacerbated the situation. Operation FEATHER was mounted as an operation in aid of the civil power to support Canadian federal agencies in the region. A mechanized battalion, plus engineers, was moved to Cornwall and prepared to enter the reserve to quell the violence, while, on the other side of the border, the New York State government took similar measures. Faced with the threat of intervention, the insurgents melted back into the population or to training camps in northern New York. Six months later, a land dispute between municipal authorities and the Khanesatake Mohawk band in Quebec escalated into violence; an inept police raid further exacerbated the situation and armed insurgents fresh from the Akwasasne confrontation arrived to support the local Aboriginal effort. Another reserve, Kahnawake, blockaded the approaches to southern Montreal. The Mulroney government, after receiving a request from the government of Premier Robert Bourassa of Quebec under the "Aid of Civil Power" provisions, part of the National Defence Act, deployed a mechanized brigade. For several months, the stand-off between the Operation SALON forces and the Aboriginal insurgents continued, and it nearly exploded when local residents tried to force their way through the security forces to get at the Mohawks. After the employment of a variety of ad hoc psychological operations, the Canadian Forces were able to wear down the insurgents and bring about a peaceful end to the crisis.[61]

There were strategic ramifications to both Operation FEATHER and Operation SALON. First, the commitment of 5 Mechanized Brigade meant that NATO had to be informed since 5 Brigade was the other half of 1st Canadian Division committed to Europe as part of NATO's Strategic Reserve. Just because the Berlin Wall was down did not mean that trouble could not boil over again: there were still 300,000 Soviet troops stationed in eastern Germany, and, as the attempted coup by communist hardliners against Soviet President Mikhail Gorbachev in August 1991 demonstrated, the situation in Moscow was unstable.[62]

Intelligence assessments following the Oka crisis indicated, that if the violence had escalated further, the Mulroney government could have been faced with a countrywide insurgency. Nearly every important east-west strategic transport artery between New Brunswick and British Columbia had a reserve located adjacent to it. A coordinated effort on the part of the insurgents could have shut Canada down in critical areas and there would not have been enough troops to respond effectively. The means by which Operation SALON was conducted, combined with associated political negotiations, ensured that this scenario did not come to pass. Yet, even as it was, the situation nearly spun out of control again in February 1991 as the Warrior Society reorganized and re-equipped at Akwasasne and Kahnawake for round two. "Oka II: The Sequel" was prevented using a variety of non-military means.[63]

One policy result of the Oka affair was that the Canadian Forces were directed to cease non-lethal internal-security training and become the force of last resort. Police organizations were henceforth to be the lead agency for dealing with Aboriginal insurgency.[64] Operations UNIQUE, FEATHER, and SALON had indicated that the existing policy on the use of military forces in these instances was reactively ad hoc, likely because of the political dangers involved in setting out in print any firmly established defence policy statement relating to Aboriginal insurgency.

Operation SALON occurred simultaneously with Iraq's invasion of Kuwait in August 1990. The Mulroney government was confronted with both a potentially lethal domestic crisis and a major international crisis at the same time, each requiring a military response. This was a situation not faced by any other prime minister since 1945. In the case of the Gulf, several concurrent policy issues came to the fore: the invasion was a test of the efficacy of the United Nations to deal with crises in the post-Cold War era, something of great interest to those in External Affairs championing the role of the UN; Canada's response would be a significant indicator to the international community of how it wanted to proceed vis-à-vis its relationship with the United States; and how Canada handled the use of military force in this crisis would have long-term implications for its international credibility.

There were other important issues. By the 1970s, Canada had dispensed with an expeditionary capability for the armed forces. It had no strategic-lift vessels or aircraft. The Cold War posture committed mechanized forces forward and in position, with limited and small UN peacekeeping deployments constituting the expeditionary forces. One reason for the elimination of the CAST commitment was the inability to deploy forces strategically, with Operation BANDIT in 1988 highlighting problems of staff and command and control.[65] Now, in 1990, Canada was confronted with a complex, joint, interagency domestic operation and simultaneously had to deploy to a theatre of operations in a volatile region of the world. Should the Mulroney government have been able to anticipate the structural requirements of such a shift this early on? Probably not. In any case, ad hoc measures taken by the Canadian Forces' leadership produced the Joint Staff, a "temporary" measure, to deal with the two crises. The Joint Staff, or "J-Staff," exists today, albeit in a different form, and is integral to Canada's expeditionary capacity.

By and large, the Mulroney government followed the UN Security Council's lead in the Persian Gulf crisis. In August, Canada committed a three-ship naval task group to join the multinational force enforcing sanctions against the Saddam Hussein regime. The Joint Staff developed several contingency plans for expanded operations in the Gulf in addition to Operation FRICTION. These included the deployment of CF-18 fighters, augmentation of the naval task group, airlift for Pan-Arab forces in the Gulf, logistical support to coalition forces in the Gulf, and the deployment of ground combat forces.[66] In September, Operation SCIMITAR deposited two CF-18 squadrons in Bahrain. The public debate over expanded Canadian involvement was, it is fair to say, mishandled by the Mulroney government. The split between Clark and Mulroney aggravated this situation, with Clark and his External Affairs supporters insisting that, if Canada conducted combat operations in the Gulf, it would somehow "damage" its reputation in the world and adversely affect its influence within UN circles. Mulroney backed off: the CF-18s were deployed in a "defensive" role to protect the ships, not to bomb Iraq or support ground operations in Kuwait. This risk-averse posture may have placated the Clark faction, but it had ramifications.

The Canadian Forces were then working on a plan, called BROADSWORD, to deploy an augmented 4 Canadian Mechanized Brigade from Germany to the Gulf. The BROADSWORD exercise was a case study of process gone wrong, as numerous entities inside National Defence that were opposed to a ground-force option attempted to ensure that the force would never deploy. They were assisted, inadvertently, by those who thought they could piggyback the lost army-equipment programs of the 1980s onto the "we can't go without" list.[67] As the costs ballooned, casualty analysis using outdated models was used to spook the political leadership. National Defence's policy officials echoed the Clark faction's assertion that there would be a loss of Canadian influence in the UN if Canada fought in the Gulf. The Mulroney government rejected BROADSWORD, in part out of fear of casualties and the chimera of domestic political backlash that was waved in front of its nose by the politically motivated.[68]

In any event, the chief of defence staff (CDS), General John de Chastelain, "advised Cabinet not to commit land forces for reasons of Canada's inability to deploy and sustain these forces as well as the unlikelihood these forces will fight under Canadian command."[69] As the record demonstrates, this was a fig leaf to protect the government since Canada always historically operated as part of a coalition, some forces were indeed capable of deployment to the Gulf (like the Canadian Airborne Regiment Battle Group), and the ability to deploy did exist if the requests to access the Integrated Logistics system with the Americans were made in a timely fashion.[70]

Canada's involvement in the Gulf War of 1990–91 was not auspicious. It amounted to a "coat-holding" exercise: naval forces far from the front protecting logistics forces far from the front which were in turn protected by fighters against an air threat that was negligible. It was not a salient contribution to the coalition. While Canada's allies fought and died to liberate Kuwait from a vicious totalitarian state and stabilize the Gulf region, Canada held back. It was not the Mulroney government's finest hour. What did the Clark faction gain from opposing combat in the Gulf? Canada deployed an engineer regiment to Kuwait as part of UNIKOM to clean up the mess long after the fighting had stopped. Did Canada achieve its sought-after increase in UN influence? The advisability of using the United Nations as the primary expression of Canadian identity and security instead of the Canada-U.S. or America-Britain-Canada-Australia (ABCA) relationship remains open to debate, given the failure of the UN as an institution by 1995 and in light of who handled global stabilization after that.[71]

## 1991–93: NEW DEFENCE PRIORITIES IN A NEW WORLD ORDER

The fiscal situation coupled with the events of 1990 produced a running battle to redefine defence policy without reverting to another formal White Paper process. For example, in August 1990 the priority for defence commitments as established by the minister included the protection of Canadian sovereignty; the collective defence of North America, including aerospace and maritime defence; peacekeeping; and collective defence in Europe.[72] By the summer of 1991, there had been substantial changes and clarifications in these commitments. The primary problem was that Canada had to "adapt to a new and unstable era" while adhering to the government's "commitment to reducing Canada's accumulated national debt."[73] Indeed, the Mulroney government had a new defence policy with new priorities, including defence, sovereignty, and civil responsibilities in Canada; collective-defence arrangements through NATO, among them the continental defence partnership with the United States; and international peace and security through stability and peacekeeping operations, arms-control verification, and humanitarian assistance.

In terms of force structure, the policy reduced the size of the Canadian Forces from 84,000 to 76,000; the reserve force was supposed to be increased from 44,000 to 65,000; Canadian bases in Germany would close; and Canadian infrastructure would be significantly reduced. In practical terms, Canada would lose one of its four brigade groups, only twelve of the planned twenty-four new frigates would be built, obsolete ships and equipment would be retired, and everything else would be frozen in place.[74] From this policy flowed the decision by the Mulroney government to withdraw the battalion committed to the UNFICYP peacekeeping mission in Cyprus, which Canada had been a part of since its inception in 1964.[75]

These changes had several important aspects. First, there was the matter of pulling out forces from Germany and ending the nearly half century of close cooperation with Europe's economic powerhouse. There were those who were determined to get Canadians out of Europe and thereby fulfil the long-standing (1969) dream of the Trudeau government. But there were others, like Canada's ambassador to NATO, Gordon Smith, who realized that a complete pullout would significantly reduce Canada's influence. Some compromise was sought. This took the form of maintaining a battalion group on one of two remaining air heads and then closing the other and withdrawing the rest of the brigade to Canada. Called the Stationed Task Force (STF) concept, it fell prey to a combination of interservice rivalry and isolationists who demanded a "peace dividend." In the end, the orders were given to pull out Canadian forces by 1993.[76] In retrospect, this was a bad decision. It reduced Canadian influence, particularly with Germany, whose key officials shifted Canada to the bottom of their appointment lists. It eliminated Canada's forward-logistics and rest centre on the other side of the globe. It forced Canada to resupply its forward-based forces, which were considerable throughout the 1990s, from Long Point, Quebec. And, as was seen in the Kosovo war, the decision made it necessary for Canada to use "alternate service delivery" means such as vessels like the GTS *Katie*, which were unreliable and costly not only in dollars but in pride and prestige.

Moreover, a series of operations involving Canadian forces conducted in 1991 immediately after the Gulf War, when examined carefully, pointed in the direction of a new paradigm. The unwillingness of the United Nations Security Council to agree to expanded operations versus the Saddam Hussein regime in Iraq proper meant that some form of containment system had to be found to ensure that Iraq would not continue to threaten the Persian Gulf region. This threat took two principal forms. First, the Hussein regime retained weapons of mass destruction and the means to deliver them against a nuclear-armed Israel. Secondly, Hussein retained a substantial ground and air force. The West could not keep ground and air forces of a substantial size in the region continuously on account of the cost involved. Therefore, for the rapid reinforcement of Kuwait in the event of a crisis, the Americans established a REFORGER-like system.[77] The Hussein regime was also to be proscribed from acquiring a variety of military and non-military equipment.[78]

The containment mechanisms put in place involved Canadian forces. The American-led Multinational Interception Force (MIF) handled the enforcement of sanctions on the sea. Canada deployed a frigate or a destroyer in rotation, sometimes in the Red Sea but usually in the Indian Ocean, Straits of Hormuz, or Persian Gulf. It also contributed observers and planned to send an infantry battalion to serve with UNIKOM. The latter remains a misunderstood organization: it was not a peacekeeping force, even though it looked like one. It was in fact a trip-wire, a surveillance exercise intended to provide legitimacy to the American reinforcement operation if Hussein's forces menaced Kuwait. Finally, the American-led air operations designed to enforce the no-fly zone, Operation SOUTHERN WATCH, the aerial component of Operation PROVIDE COMFORT and its replacement, NORTHERN WATCH, included Canadian AWACS personnel.[79]

An important piece of the strategy to contain the Hussein regime, which also had a Canadian contribution, was Operation PROVIDE COMFORT. This was the prototype armed humanitarian-intervention operation. With its three light infantry brigades, PROVIDE COMFORT was designed to protect the Kurds from Hussein's retaliation and to enable the development of a base from which covert efforts to subvert the Hussein regime could be mounted. The humanitarian component stabilized the situation for the civilian population so that anti-Hussein resistance could flourish. Canada's contribution, Operation ASSIST, consisted of a medical unit from Lahr, Germany, and C-130 transport aircraft.[80] Finally, there was Operation FORUM, Canada's contribution to the United Nations Special Commission, better known as UNSCOM. Canadian intelligence personnel and DND experts on weapons of mass destruction made a significant contribution to UNSCOM's quest to rid the Hussein regime of its nuclear, biological, and chemical programs. When combined, Canada's contributions to all of these missions revealed the Mulroney government's view of the Persian Gulf as a region of Canadian interest equal to that of any other during this time.[81]

Canada's Gulf commitments, however, did not supercede its interest in the new Europe. The communist empire of Yugoslavia seethed with the same sorts of problems the Soviet Union (now Russia) was experiencing as the victims of past territorial conquests decided they were not interested in continuing their relationship with the centre. Slovenia withdrew from Belgrade's control in a ten-day war in July 1991, prompting the deployment of a peace-observation force sponsored by the European Community but led by the OSCE. The caveat, insisted upon by the belligerents, was that the European Community Monitor Mission (ECMM) contain observers from the United States and/or Canada since they did not trust the Europeans. The Mulroney government leapt at the opportunity, as did the bureaucracy, which had been stung by the loss of influence when the pullout of Canada's NATO forces was announced.[82]

The observers for Operation BOLSTER were mostly from the units that were withdrawing from Canadian bases in Germany. While they were preparing to deploy, Croatia exploded into war as the Franjo Tudjman government declared independence and the Krajinan Serbs, backed by Belgrade, rose to resist. The Europeans were unable to produce a Western European Union (WEU) peacekeeping force, let alone a stabilization force, and the CSCE was unequipped to do so; eventually, diplomatic efforts produced the Vance Plan, which essentially called for little more than a peacekeeping mission in a region where there was no peace to keep. The United Nations was the only other option, so the matter went to New York. This was the origin of the United Nations Protection Force (UNPROFOR). The Mulroney government, led by External Affairs and National Defence, realized that contributing Canadian forces to UNPROFOR would solve a myriad problems. Not only would it demonstrate Canada's continued interest and commitment to European security, it could reverse the damage caused by pulling out of NATO's Central Region. Still another consideration was that the newly freed Eastern European countries would face serious problems if the situation in the collapsing Yugoslavia got out of control and spilled over.[83]

A 4 Canadian Mechanized Brigade reconnaissance team sent to Croatia reported that the planned UNPROFOR mission was not really like Cyprus peacekeeping, no matter what officials in New York thought. They recommended that the Canadian contingent be prepared for combat in the former Yugoslavia and be equipped accordingly. Inside National Defence, there was some scepticism by those who thought they "knew" peacekeeping, but the force commanders won out and the Mulroney government approved the deployment of a mechanized infantry battalion to Croatia (Operation HARMONY). The UNPROFOR mission was very different from the Cyprus model (in its post-1974 incarnation) in that the UN force was responsible for protecting civilians in several enclaves, disarming auxiliary and paramilitary groups, and patrolling active zones of confrontation.[84]

Then Bosnia exploded. Since the Canadian battalion assigned to UNPROFOR was the only fully equipped unit, a request was made by the force commander for it to move from Croatia to Sarajevo to secure the air head at Sarajevo International Airport. After nearly coming to blows with belligerent forces on the drive south, the Canadian battalion eventually secured the airport and escorted aid convoys through belligerent-held sections of Sarajevo. Canadian snipers engaged those targeting UN forces, while Canadian commanders were given access to the firepower of an American aircraft carrier stationed in the Adriatic. There was no precedence for this type of operation: the Mulroney government had landed right in the middle of something that had never really been doctrinally defined. In time, the Bosnia mission coalesced as Operation CAVILIER or UNPROFOR II. Then a Canadian logistics battalion was added, and something resembling a brigade headquarters. Essentially, Canadian diplomats and the CDS could now assert in European circles that 4 Canadian Mechanized Brigade had never really left Europe: it merely redeployed to the former Yugoslavia. Claims that Canada contributed to UNPROFOR because of Mila Mulroney's Serbian background are greatly exaggerated.[85] Canada remained in the Balkans until 2004.

By the fall of 1992, it was becoming evident within National Defence Headquarters and ultimately in the Mulroney government that "peacekeeping" in the Cold War sense no longer existed. Yes, some Canadian units deployed overseas wore blue helmets and painted their vehicles white, but the types of missions now undertaken did not correspond to the ones conducted in the 1970s or 1980s. For example, Iraq did not agree to UNIKOM's presence. In Croatia, "the long term aims of the pace process were unclear," while in Sarajevo "there was no ceasefire" and with "a new form of peacekeeping, protective peacekeeping, [the peacekeeping] criteria could not fit." Consequently, a review of "stability, peacekeeping and humanitarian activities" was initiated between the Privy Council Office and DND.[86] Though recognized by the 1991 defence policy, the new "stability operations" continued to be confusingly called "peacekeeping" by the media and defence commentators alike. Analysis concluded, accurately for the time, that the role of the UN in the post-Cold War world had dramatically changed and that there "was a willingness to discuss preventative deployments and talk of peace enforcement units." The world was characterized by "complex internal multi-party conflicts" and "the line between peacekeeping and enforcement is becoming more difficult to discern."[87]

For Canada, there would be essentially four priority areas: the former Soviet Union, the former Yugoslavia, Iraq, and Somalia. What role should the Canadian Forces play in each area, and to what extent should Canada deploy its decreasing number of units? In effect, the DND analysts came up with four models for force employment:[88]

- *Cyprus*: This model represents a situation in which a force is put in place to monitor an existing agreement.
- *Cambodia*: The model is taken to represent a situation in which a major civic- action-type program is required to create a semblance of order.
- *Yugoslavia/Somalia*: This model represents a situation in which a force intervenes to facilitate the delivery of humanitarian assistance and/or

impose a cease-fire or settlement. An agreement may or may not exist and the intervention may require a degree of force or coercion.
- *Persian Gulf*: At the high end of the spectrum is the Gulf War model in which a force is put in place to impose a settlement.

This and other analysis formed the basis for discussions on the future of peacekeeping policy between National Defence and the Privy Council Office that extended into 1993, particularly when the Mulroney government was formulating a response to United Nations Secretary General Boutros Boutros-Ghali's document *An Agenda for Peace.* It is fair to suggest that the theoretical foundations of how Canada responded to stabilizing the post-Cold War world were developed at this time and that the Mulroney government, by requesting a review of policy, stimulated the serious thinking that went into systematizing stabilization operations. In hindsight, the main error made at the time was placing too much emphasis on the UN and not enough on other structures, though the analysis of the day correctly pointed out that the embryonic European security structures were working at cross purposes with a NATO which could not make up its mind about what role it was to play in the new world order. Indeed, there was a pro-UN zeitgeist that had not yet been sullied by Rwanda and Somalia.[89]

The Mulroney government's interest in the deteriorating situation in Somalia throughout the summer of 1992 coincided with the initial Balkans deployments. A UN operation, UNOSOM, was supposed to observe conditions in the collapsed former Soviet client-state and there was some thought that a multinational airborne brigade with a Canadian battalion could be used to provide armed humanitarian assistance. The Canadian Airborne Regiment was tapped as the unit for UNOSOM. As the equipment was being deployed, the mission changed. The situation as portrayed in the media (the first instance of what became known as the "CNN effect" whereby media-driven emotion overcomes reason) was so bad that the United States was considering deploying a non-UN force, UNITAF, to impose peace in Somalia so that aid could be delivered effectively before the job was handed over to a UN peacekeeping mission that would be called UNOSOM II. The prime minister approved a U.S. request that the Canadian force join UNITAF after direct telephone conversations with the American president.[90]

Militarily, Operation DELIVERANCE was successful in many respects, particularly in the Belet Huen area. Its strategic purpose, however, remains obscure and was never as well defined as Canada's role in the Balkans or in the Persian Gulf. Unfortunately, disciplinary problems within the Airborne Regiment and investigations surrounding the murder of a local by regiment members sparked what would become Canada's equivalent to Mai Lai and Watergate rolled into one. The resultant Somalia Inquiry would eventually, long after the Mulroney government left office, have lasting and positive effects on the Canadian Forces and, to a much lesser extent, on the Department of National Defence, particularly in areas relating to planning, command and control, joint operations, and training.

The final legacy of Mulroney-era defence policy was the formal acceptance by the government that the Canadian Forces should have their own special operations forces. In 1992 the Royal Canadian Mounted Police was unable to fund effectively its counterterrorism unit, SERT. Cabinet-level discussions ensued and the prime minister fully endorsed the creation and funding of Joint Task Force 2 in the spring of 1993. If this decision had not been taken, it is unlikely that a successor Liberal government would have had the tools to provide a salient and effective military contribution to the "Al Qaeda War" after the events of 11 September 2001.[91]

## CONCLUSION

What are the best criteria to use to assess defence during the Mulroney years? The answer is that there are different criteria for the era of the Cold War and World Order Era.

For the first period, in terms of Canada and its relationship with the United States, its closest ally and trading partner, Canadian defence policy was a significant factor in repairing the damage that had been caused during the Trudeau years and in bolstering Canadian confidence and influence. On the international stage, any assessment needs to place Canada's defence policy against the backdrop of an important question: To what extent did Canada contribute to the end of the Cold War in the 1980s? If we accept that Reagan's strategy was instrumental in accelerating the end of communism, then we can reach the following conclusions on Canada's role:

- *Economic warfare*: Canada did not contribute to any measurable extent.
- *Information warfare*: Canada did little with the exception of Radio Canada International.
- *Europe*: Canada did start to upgrade its conventional-defence NATO forces, but the programs were cut short by the abrupt end of the Cold War. Still, those changes that were implemented had tactical and operational significance.
- *Anti-communism in the Third World*: Canada provided extremely limited support and only to the Afghan effort.
- *SDI*: Canada provided little support to this endeavour.
- *Strategic/theatre nuclear-force modernization*: Canada's role was limited to providing territory for ALCM testing and then only during the Trudeau era.
- *Ideological support and resolve*: Canada overtly sided with the United States after 1984 and supported American actions when not hobbled by the Clark-Mulroney antagonism.

There were, of course, mitigating circumstances, like the seven-year lag between American and British development of a strategy for the post-1980 world order, and Canada's formal recognition of it between 1985 and 1987. If the Mulroney defence policy had been fully implemented and if the Cold War had continued, Canadian defence programs would have had a significantly greater effect. Note also that it was not "Quiet Diplomacy," the United Nations, or disarmament exercises – the tools favoured by previous Canadian governments – that forced the Soviet Union to the negotiating table and produced the collapse of one of the most violent, dangerous totalitarian regimes in history. It was the willingness to stand up and be counted that was more important and, during the Mulroney years, that was what Canada did.

In the second period, that of the World Order Era, the impact of Canadian defence policy was greater. Though Canada's commitment to the First Gulf War was ambivalent, its contributions to the effort to contain the Hussein regime were extremely useful additions to the American-led campaign in the region, particularly through UNSCOM, the MIF sanctions operation, and Operation PROVIDE COMFORT. Handling domestic political violence while at the same time committing to an expeditionary force to the Persian Gulf would have been formidable undertakings for any Canadian government. The fact that there were no deaths at Oka after the initial killing of a Quebec policeman was a major achievement, while the decision to commit Canadian forces to the exploding Balkans crisis will ultimately prove to be Canada's most important action in the post-Cold War era: its contribution to containing the violence in the Bosnia and Croatia was a significant factor in ensuring the stability of the former Eastern bloc at a critical time in history. On the other hand, more needs to be done to examine the impact of Canada's actions in Somalia. There has been a tendency to focus on the domestic political impact of certain events rather than looking at the strategic ramifications of Canada's first serious involvement in Africa since the 1960s Congo exercise.

As with any overview of complex events, more research needs to be done on defence policy in the Mulroney era, and it is hoped that this chapter will stimulate others to dig deeper into what is a fascinating period in Canadian history.

## NOTES

1 Obviously, these second- and third-tier-level bureaucrats do not wish to be identified out of fear of retaliation; indeed, over fifteen years after these events, critics of individuals involved in the policy process have been subject to such retaliation. During the Somalia inquiry, researchers discovered that it was policy

at a high level of DND to attach "stick-ums" (which contained valuable insights) to documents instead of using the proper "minuting" format. These "stick-ums" were removed when the documents were requested under Access to Information.

2 A medium-range ballistic missile with a range of 1,000 km. to 2,750 km.

3 As detailed in Stephen S. Kaplan, *Diplomacy of Power: Soviet Armed Forces as a Political Instrument* (Washington D.C.: Brookings Institution 1981); Stephane Courtois et al., *The Black Book of Communism: Crimes, Terror, Repression* (Cambridge, Mass.: Harvard University Press 1999); Brian Crozier, *The Rise and Fall of the Soviet Empire* (Rocklin: Forum Publishing 1999); and Oleg Sarin and Lev Dvoretsky, *Alien Wars: The Soviet Union's Aggressions against the World, 1919 to 1989* (Novato, Calif.: Presidio 1996).

4 Directorate of History and Heritage, 80/225 file 40 (15 January 79), Briefing to Minister, "The Strategic Outlook and the International Setting."

5 Department of National Defence, *Defence in the 70s: White Paper on Defence* (Ottawa: Supply and Services 1971); and Department of External Affairs, *Foreign Policy for Canadians* (Ottawa: Supply and Services Canada 1970).

6 As described in Sean M. Maloney, *Canada and* UN *Peacekeeping: Cold War by Other Means* (St Catharines, Ont.: Vanwell Publishing 2002).

7 This is my interpretation of Ivan Head and Pierre Trudeau's depiction of events in *The Canadian Way: Shaping Canada's Foreign Policy, 1968–1984* (Toronto: McClelland and Stewart 1995).

8 The Trudeau government's obsession with disarmament during this period is described in Albert Legault and Michel Fortmann's *A Diplomacy of Hope: Canada and Disarmament 1945–1988* (Kingston: McGill-Queen's University Press 1992). See also J.L. Granatstein and Robert Bothwell, *Pirouette: Pierre Trudeau and Canadian Foreign Policy* (Toronto: University of Toronto Press 1990).

9 Confidential interviews; Beatty interview.

10 See Peter Schweizer, *Victory: The Reagan Administration's Secret Strategy That Hastened the Collapse of the Soviet Union* (New York: Atlantic Monthly Press 1994); and Peter Schweizer, *Reagan's War: The Epic Story of His Forty-Year Struggle and Final Triumph over Communism* (New York: Doubleday 2002).

11 William Jackson, *Britain's Defence Dilemma: An Inside View* (London: BT Batsford 1990), chapters 7–9; on Britain in Afghanistan, see Tom Carew, *Jihad! The Secret War in Afghanistan* (London: Mainstream Publishing 2000).

12 Interview with Brigadier-General Don Macnamara, Kingston, 26 May 2004.

13 Teleconference with Flora MacDonald, 25 May 2004. See also Canada, Parliament, House of Commons, *Debates*, 21 April 1980, 215.

14 *Competitiveness and Security: Direction for Canada's International Relations* (Ottawa: Supply and Services Canada 1985).

15 Telephone interview with Perrin Beatty, 11 June 2004.

16 Macnamara interview; telephone interview with Colonel Bill Weston, 27 May 2004; Beatty interview.

17 Access to Information, Department of National Defence [hereafter ATI DND] (5 September 1986), memo Fowler to DM, CDS, VCDS, "The White Paper Process: The Way Ahead."
18 Weston interview.
19 Interview with Hugh Segal, Kingston, 27 May 2004.
20 Maurice Tugwell sounded the alarm with his book *Peace with Freedom*, which exposed the Canadian "Peace Movement" as early as 1988. After the Cold War, details emerged that support his overall view. See, in particular, Christopher Andrew and Vasili Mitrokhin, *The Mitokhin Archive: The* KGB *in Europe and the West* (Toronto: Penguin Books 1999); and Chistopher Andrew and Oleg Gordievsky, KGB*: The Inside Story* (London: Hodder and Stoughan 1990). For a case study in how this sort of subversion worked and for an excellent overview of the Euromissile situation, see Jeffrey Herf, *War by Other Means: Soviet Power, West German Resistance, and the Battle of the Euromissiles* (New York: Free Press 1991).
21 Weston interview.
22 It is clear from Leonard Johnson's memoir *A General for Peace* (Toronto: James Lorimer 1987) that he was naive and easily manipulated. East German spymaster Markus Wolf discusses with some glee about how Generals for Peace was an effective vehicle for communist interests. See *Man without a Face: The Autobiography of Communism's Greatest Spymaster* (New York: Random House 1997), 244–7.
23 Weston interview.
24 Confidential interview.
25 ATI DND (July 1986), "Canadian Security and Defence Policy Choices."
26 Department of National Defence, *Challenge and Commitment: A Defence Policy for Canada* (Ottawa: DND 1987).
27 As usual, there were two other areas tacked onto the list of priorities: "peaceful settlement of international disputes" and "arms control." These were essentially "sops" to elements in External Affairs.
28 Department of National Defence, *Challenge and Commitment.*
29 Ibid.
30 ATI DND (5 December 1986), message BNATO to External Affairs, "Defence Policy Review: Consolidation of Canadian Commitment to Europe"; See also Sean M. Maloney, "Purple Haze: Joint Planning in the Canadian Forces from Mobile Command to J-Staff, 1975–1991 Part 1," *Army Doctrine and Training Bulletin*, 5(4).
31 ATI DND (5 April 89), memo to DL, "Visit to NDHA: NATO Composite Force (NCF) Planning Liaison Group (PLG)."
32 The details are found in Sean M. Maloney, *War without Battles: Canada's* NATO *Brigade in Germany 1951–1993* (St Catharines, Ont.: McGraw Hill Ryerson 1997), chapters 5 and 6.
33 Beatty interview.
34 Confidential interviews.
35 Confidential interviews.
36 Weston interview.

37 Ibid.
38 Weston interview; confidential interviews.
39 As detailed in Maloney, *Canada and* UN *Peacekeeping.*
40 M.R. Dabros, "The Multinational Force and Observers: A New Experience in Peacekeeping for Canada," *Canadian Defence Quarterly,* autumn 1986, 32–5. See also Manon Tessier and Michel Fortmann, "The Conservative Appoach to UN Peacekeeping," *Diplomatic Departures: The Conservative Era in Canadian Foeign Policy, 1984–93* (Vancouver: University of British Columbia Press 2001), 113–27.
41 As discussed in the author's *Canada and* UN *Peacekeeping.* Note that the first time that the "Great Canadian Peacekeeping Myth" was invoked was with the UNIFIL deployment in Lebanon in the late 1970s: the External Affairs bureaucracy used this argument to get the Trudeau government to commit to an operation that had no Canadian strategic rationale.
42 ATI DND (11 August 1988), "Briefing Note to the Minister: Op VAGABOND"; ATI DND (26 July 1988), "Advice to Minister: Peacekeeping-Iran-Iraq"; ATI DND (27 September 1990), "Memo DM and CDS to MND, "Extension of Mandate: INIIMOG"; See also Sean M. Maloney, *War with Iraq: Canada's Strategy in the Persian Gulf 1990–2002* (Kingston: QCIR 2003), 5.
43 See Mike Frost and Michel Gratton, *Spyworld: Inside the Canadian and American Intelligence Establishments* (Toronto: Doubleday Canada 1994). See also Jeffrey T. Richelson, *Foreign Intelligence Organizations* (Cambridge, Mass.: Ballinger Publishing 1988), chapter 3.
44 Beatty interview.
45 The Edmond Pope episode merely exposed the tip of the proverbial iceberg. See Edmond Pope and Tom Schactman, *Torpedoed* (New York: Little, Brown 2002), 88–92.
46 Confidential interviews.
47 The author was present on one such occasion. The Soviet AGI in question was boarded and "inspected" when it made the mistake of entering St John's harbour.
48 The American components of the operation are discussed in Gregory Vistica, *Fall from Glory: The Men Who Sank the US Navy* (New York: Simon and Shuster 1995), 214–16; I have relied on confidential interviews for the Canadian component.
49 Confidential interviews. See also George Crile, *Charlie Wilson's War: The Extraordinary Story of the Largest Covert Operation in History* (New York: Atlantic Monthly Press 2003), 408.
50 My thanks to my colleague Dr Hal Klepak for this information. For critical perspectives on Mulroney-era diplomacy in the region, see Peter McFarlane, *Northern Shadows: Canadians and Central America* (Toronto: Between the Lines Press 1989); and James Rochlin, *Discovering the Americas: The Evolution of Canadian Foreign Policy towards Latin America* (Vancouver: University of British Columbia Press 1994).
51 "Never Say Never: Canada and Non-Alliance Operations," *Army Doctrine and Training Bulletin* 2(2) (May 1999).

52 Segal interview.
53 See Sean M. Maloney, "In the Service of Forward Security: Peacekeeping, Stabilization, and the Canadian Way of War," in Bernd Horn, ed., *The Canadian Way of War* (forthcoming).
54 Telephone interview with Gordon Smith, 1 June 2004.
55 Ibid.
56 Maloney, *War without Battles*, 481–2.
57 ATI DND (8 March 1989), AIRCOM HQ, "Operation UNIQUE Operations Order 1."
58 Tugwell, *Peace with Freedom*, 109, 127–38.
59 ATI DND (15 Februry 1989), NDHQ to AIRCOM, "DCDS Operation Instruction: Security CFB Goose Bay"; (27 March 89) Aide Memoire for the Minister, "CFB Goose Bay: Update."
60 ATI DND (8 March 89), AIRCOM HQ, "Operation UNIQUE Operations Order 1"; (9 February 1990) memo DCDS to CDS, "Employment of the Militia-Operation UNIQUE."
61 Sean M. Maloney, "Domestic Operations: The Canadian Approach," *Parameters*, 27(3) (1997).
62 ATI DND (27 August 1990), message NDOC to AIG 1704, "Possible Threat to CF Personnel and Facilities"; (2 December 90) message NDHQ to FMC HQ, "State of Preparations: Further Native Unrest."
63 ATI DND (20 February 91), "Armed Forces Council: Summary Record."
64 The incidents at Ipperwash and Gustafsen Lake later in the 1990s followed this pattern: the armed forces provided limited support, while the OPP and RCMP were the respective lead agencies.
65 Maloney, "Purple Haze."
66 Sean M. Maloney, "Missed Opportunity: Operation BROADSWORD, 4 Brigade, and the Gulf War, 1990–1991," *Canadian Military History*, spring 1995.
67 Ibid.
68 Confidential interviews.
69 ATI DND (17 October 1990), "Armed Forces Council: Summary Record."
70 Maloney, "Missed Opportunity."
71 See Sean M. Maloney, "Memo to Canada: The World Has Changed," in David Rudd, ed., *The New Security Environment: Is the Canadian Military up to the Challenge?* (Toronto: CISS 2004).
72 ATI DND (11 December 1990), "Briefing to the DMMD Manning Conference."
73 ATI DND (17 September 1991), message NDHQ to CANFORGEN, "MND Message-Release of New Defence Policy."
74 ATI DND (1992), Briefing Package: "Canadian Defence in the 1990s."
75 Beatty interview.
76 Smith interview; see also Maloney, *War without Battles*, 483–4.
77 REFORGER, or "Return of Forces to Germany," was a system whereby equipment was kept in storage sites in West Germany and troops flown in to marry up with it in an emergency. The same system was established in Kuwait.

78 See Maloney, *War with Iraq.*
79 See Maloney, *War with Iraq.*
80 Ibid.
81 Ibid.
82 Smith interview. The ECMM story is told in Sean M. Maloney, *Operation* BOLSTER: *Canada and the European Community Monitor Mission in the Former Yugoslavia, 1991–1994* (Toronto: Canadian Institute of Strategic Studies 1998).
83 Smith interview. See also Sean M. Maloney and John Llambias, *Chances for Peace: Canadian Soldiers in the Balkans, An Oral History* (Toronto: Vanwell Publishing, 2002), chapter 1.
84 Maloney, *War without Battles,* chapter 7; Maloney and Llambias, *Chances for Peace,* chapter 1.
85 Smith interview; Segal interview; Maloney and Llambias, *Chances for Peace,* chapter 1.
86 ATI DND (1 October 1992), ADM(Pol), "Review of Defence Policy Governing Stability, Peacekeeping, and Humanitarian Activities."
87 Ibid.
88 Ibid.
89 Ibid; see also ATI DND (30 March 93), memo ADM(Pol and Comm) to DM and CDS, "PCO Meeting-Peacekeeping Operations," plus the supporting document "Meeting the Challenge of 1995: Canada and Peacekeeping-Points for the DM."
90 Charles S. Oliviero, "Operation DELIVERANCE: International Success or Domestic Failure?" *Canadian Military Journal* 2(2) (2001): 51–8.
91 Segal interview.

# 7

# Governing through Shifting Social-Policy Regimes: Brian Mulroney and Canada's Welfare State

MICHAEL J. PRINCE AND JAMES J. RICE

Between 1984 and 1993, when Brian Mulroney was prime minister of Canada, a deep shift in governing style and the substance of government took place. Canada's version of a welfare state moved from a policy regime that was rooted in a set of ideas influenced by Keynesian economics, and that focused on social justice, social rights, and financial-resource enhancements, towards a style intellectually based in "Reaganomics" and supply-side economics and concerned principally with the national debt and deficits, budgetary constraints, and economic stability. The social-policy regime also shifted from a more or less cooperative style in intergovernmental relations to one marked by a climate of contested and coercive federalism in which the federal government, often unilaterally, "off-loaded" programs and withdrew support from provincial initiatives in health and social services. One of the hallmarks of this new form of governing was a move away from consensus building through public input to an approach based on "stealth" to achieve policy objectives. These shifts reflect a distinctive and identifiable approach taken by the Conservative government in addressing social-policy ideas, issues, processes, and decisions.

Mulroney did not invent this shift in policy regimes; nor was this the way his government acted during its entire time in power. Rather, there was a sea change, at the time, in the ideas and interests shaping how governments thought about the role of the public domain. In the preceding fifty years, Canadians had come to believe that governments could help solve many of the social problems facing society. There was general support for the development of social programs to help families deal with the costs of raising children and to provide income protection for people who lost their jobs. Similarly, there was support for public health care and universal old age security for the elderly. But much of this thinking began to change in the 1970s, when people began to doubt government's ability to improve the well-being of the nation, to trust politicians less than

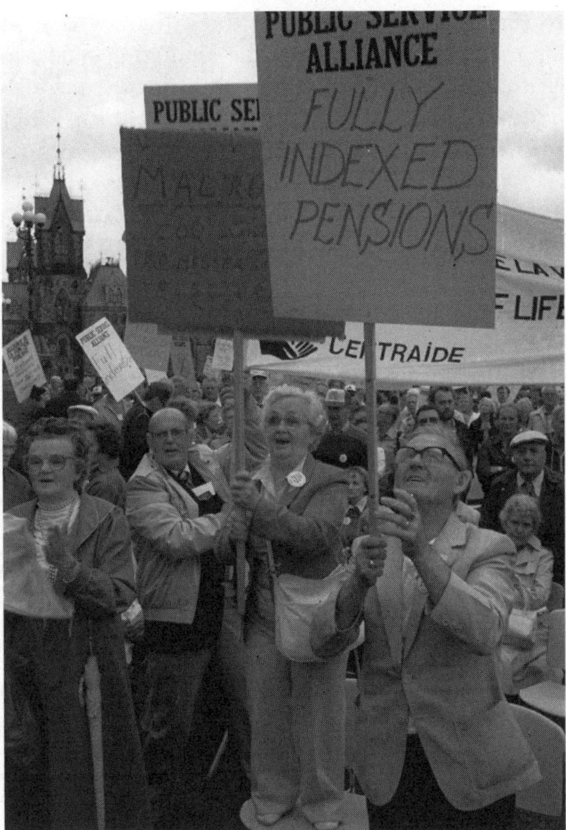


Seniors protesting on Parliament Hill in June 1985 after the Conservative government announced that it would begin partial de-indexation of some transfers to individuals. Photographer Wayne Cuddingham. Southam News, Ottawa *Citizen*, 85-3138R3. Reprinted with permission.

before, and to be much more cynical about government promises. These changes became part of Mulroney's legacy. Mulroney added to them, and they influenced his approach to policy. When he came to power in 1984, with a promise of maintaining social policies as a "scared trust," he had the largest parliamentary majority in Canadian history, but when he left office in defeat, he had a tattered party, and a tarnished reputation, and had begun the process of taking apart the social-welfare project in Canada.

This chapter focuses on the changes to social-policy processes and substance. It examines eight years of decision making that changed the face of Canadian social policy. During that time, there was a shift to a new policy agenda, a shift caught up with the changing beliefs about government and one that reflected a growing set of ideas, variously called neoliberal, neo-conservative, and New Right, within the social-policy world. We intend to show that Brian Mulroney went through a profound change in the way he governed. He assumed power having one set of preferred ideas on the content and process of social policy yet, nearly a decade later, left government operating with a different approach to social-policy making.

## COMING TO POWER: MULRONEY'S FIRST MANDATE

Mulroney began his first term as prime minister with his famous election promise of maintaining the "sacred trust" of universal income benefits for families with children and for seniors, specifically, the family allowance and old age security programs. This promise, and his rhetorical choice of phrase, reflected a long-standing pattern of support for the central role that social welfare played in the Canadian psyche. Mulroney wanted to reassure Canadians that his position on social welfare was not very different from the mainstream thinking epitomized by the Liberals. The "scared trust" promise was similar to the position taken in Trudeau's last major speech on social development, in which he pledged that Liberals would never abandon their long-time commitment to a compassionate social policy. In claiming that he would maintain the sacred trust implied in social programs, Mulroney reassured Canadians that there would be income security, national standards, and a societal recognition of the contingencies of childrearing and old age. This promise reflected his political need to let Canadians know that his government would not become radically conservative, unlike the administrations of Ronald Reagan or Margaret Thatcher, which had cut social programs and weakened the public health-care system.

However, a new, much more conservative agenda was shaping the social-policy world. Margaret Thatcher had confronted the labour-union movement in Britain by introducing legislation that limited the rights of workers and altered working conditions while increasing the influence of market forces. On this side of the Atlantic, Ronald Reagan introduced a bill limiting the amount of money governments could borrow to support welfare programs while at the same time lowering taxes on high-income earners. Welfare programs had their funding cut and were disassembled under the guise of market liberalism. In Canada, Mulroney was ideologically sympathetic to this new agenda, and he was seeking ways to alter the structure of the Canadian welfare system.

The pledge to keep the sacred trust became a shackle on Mulroney's policy aspirations and he used indirect means to achieve his policy objectives. He turned to dissuasion, program restriction, and expenditure freezes as a way of reshaping social programs and limiting the growth rate of social spending. With dissuasion, Mulroney tried to discourage people from thinking that government could solve all of their problems. The Mulroney Conservatives advocated greater self-reliance, extolling the virtues of charity and voluntarism and arguing for the acceptance of program cutbacks. In this way, the sense of government responsibility for human and social development narrowed psychologically. At the same time, Mulroney introduced policy changes that restricted the growth of programs. For example, he restricted the eligibility requirements and shortened the benefit period for unemployment insurance (UI). In general, program spending was constrained, frozen, or reduced in social housing, legal aid, health care, social assistance, and post–secondary education, among other areas.

During the first mandate, the Mulroney Conservatives oscillated between competing styles of government. On one hand, philosophically, many Conservatives wanted to move towards the pro-market liberalism of Thatcher and Reagan, while, on the other, politically, they needed to be seen as caring and compassionate. Their own party had Red Tories who supported the social agenda and business-oriented conservatives who wanted to "downsize" government. While Mulroney was committed to supporting the private sector and opposing the Ottawa-based bureaucracy and Trudeau-style centralism, he was eager to practise a new form of federal-provincial reconciliation. This led Mulroney's government to express its main policy preferences in rhetoric much milder than that of its fellow practitioners of the neo-conservative version of politics, policy making, and budgeting. Mulroney's first government tried fostering economic renewal by removing government obstacles to economic growth, cutting the federal deficit gradually, introducing better government-management programs, and reducing the size of the federal public sector.

From a social-policy perspective, the first Mulroney government focused on limiting the growth of social spending. Program spending restraint, including in the area social expenditures, became the cornerstone of the government's budgetary strategy. This restraint grew over Mulroney's first mandate, with ongoing reductions across a broad spectrum of social programs, client groups, and government departments. As part of this politics of restraint, the Conservatives pursued *a strategy of containment rather than neo-conservative dismantlement.* In an effort to contain government actives, Mulroney turned more and more often to incremental (that is, decremental) changes within the social-policy domain. He did this by changing the rates at which benefits were paid or the rates at which people paid taxes. Ken Battle, arguing that the 1985 federal budget ushered in a new style of changing policies and programs, has described this approach as government and social-policy reform by stealth.[1] Core elements of the Mulroney government's style led to policy changes through technical measures announced in budgets without a genuine process of public consultation or debate.

Governments have used stealth as a way to hide things from the public as long as there have been governments. Administrations do things they do not talk about. But social-policy analysts and critics depicted Mulroney as using stealth to make sweeping and far-reaching changes and cuts to social programs. He primarily used the Department of Finance as the prominent federal structure for achieving stealth in social-policy programs. Finance introduced changes to the tax rates, made cutbacks in intergovernmental fiscal transfers, and launched expenditure-restraint measures. Fundamental changes to federal social programs achieved by the stealth approach included the partial de–indexation of tax credits and brackets as well as certain transfers to individuals, cuts in federal social transfers to the provinces, changes in the financing of UI, and the "claw-back" of family allowance and old age security benefits. Using techniques and processes of stealth enabled Mulroney's government simultaneously to achieve social-policy reforms and budgetary management objectives while also making it difficult for the public to understand the actual reforms. Arcane and impenetrable language rationalized amendments to obscure legislation or regulations. Social-policy departments, Parliament, and the press played little if any meaningful role in explaining and scrutinizing the changes.

## THE SECOND MANDATE: 1988–93

In Mulroney's second mandate, methods of relatively moderate spending and program restraint expanded and escalated into a more intense restructuring of core elements of the social-security system. Restructuring meant downsizing government, privatizing crown corporations, reforming the tax system, downloading and devolving responsibilities onto provinces, and, most important for our purposes here, altering the social safety net.

Governments at both levels in Canada were increasingly adopting three additional forms of restraint: program retrenchment, program termination, and the privatization of programs. All relate to the downsizing of the state and the public service in absolute terms. Retrenchment is the withdrawal of resources from the base budget of an agency, policy, program, or activity. Under the termination approach, policies, programs, and staff are not simply cut back, they are cut out. Government cancels or eliminates public services. Privatization involves the "residualization" of public provisions, turning them over to families, communities at large, or private-sector firms and market forces. These three forms of restraint are the core vehicles used for dismantling the welfare state and facilitating the neo-conservative attack on social policy. Landmarks of this more fundamental restructuring, indicative of the shift in social-policy regimes, included ending the universality of family income and old age benefits, discontinuing direct federal government financing of the UI system, and unilaterally capping the Canada Assistance Plan (CAP).

Mulroney's dramatic restructuring of UI demonstrates, for instance, the power of changing ideas in the policy realm. Upon re-election in 1988, the Mulroney Conservatives implemented sweeping structural reforms to the UI program. By 1990, the federal government no long contributed to the UI account to pay for regionally extended benefits, extension benefits under job-creation projects and training programs, and fishermen's benefits. These changes meant that the program was now funded entirely by employer and employee premiums, ending a near fifty-year policy of tripartite funding of unemployment insurance in Canada. The premiums paid by employees and employers were raised in 1990, 1991, and 1992, by more than 30 per cent, to offset the $2.9 billion withdrawn by the federal government.

Deeper changes were made to UI as well. The Mulroney Conservatives increased the maximum qualifying period from fourteen to twenty weeks in some regions, reduced the maximum duration of benefits from forty-six to fifty weeks to a lower range of thirty-five to fifty weeks, and increased penalties for workers who quit their jobs voluntarily and for claimants and employers who defrauded the program. It must be stated that the Conservatives, nonetheless, improved benefits for maternity, sickness, and parental leave and restored coverage for workers over sixty-five to bring the UI program in line with judicial decisions and the Canadian Charter of Rights and Freedoms.

## FEDERAL SOCIAL EXPENDITURES: MULRONEY'S RECORD IN A WIDER CONTEXT

The basic structure and complexion of federal social spending changed over the two mandates. On the whole, there was a selective rather than a universal orientation in social budgeting and program development by the Conservatives. Preferred social-policy instruments of the Mulroney era included tax credits, the targeting of transfer payments, and the contracting–out of research and advice. As a share of federal social expenditures, transfers to other levels of government and payments to major social crown corporations, such as the CBC, declined, while selective transfers to persons increased. These trends were the result of a mix of factors: fiscal restraint and program reform designed to meet the needs of an aging population, an economic recession, and rising unemployment.

In Figure 1, we begin with the big picture by providing a thirty-year time span from 1973 to 2003. We then focus more tightly on the 1980–2003

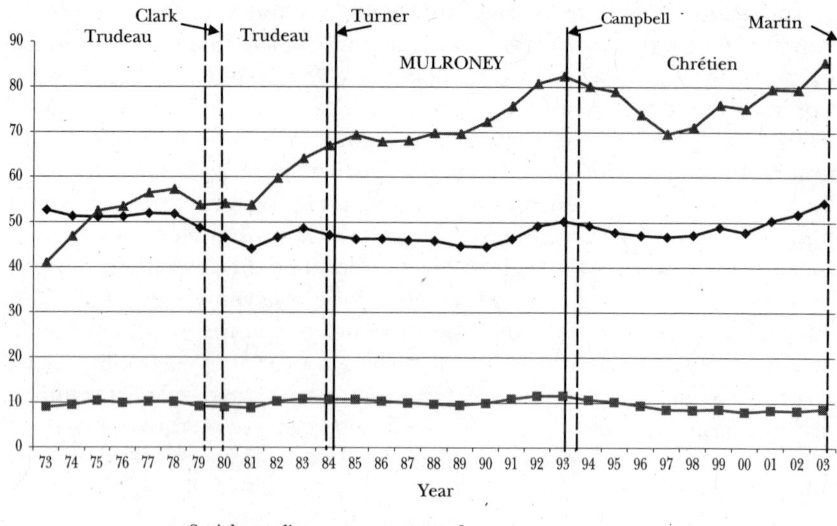


Figure 1 Federal social spending in context

period. We have used 1992 constant dollars to reflect the Mulroney period and factor out the effect of inflation on domestic purchasing power. As used here, federal social spending combines transfers to persons and transfers to governments. The transfers to persons include family and youth allowances, the child tax credit, employment insurance benefits, old age security payments, grants to Aboriginal persons and organizations, and the Goods and Services Tax (GST) credit. Transfers to governments cover a wide variety of areas, including post-secondary education, hospital insurance, Medicare, extended health care, the CAP, the Canada Health and Social Transfer (CHST), official-languages programs, special grants to universities, and grants to local governments.[2]

Federal social spending in Figure 1 reports on the *relative scale* of social expenditures, that is, as a share of total federal government expenditures and as a share of the overall Canadian economy. This information shows expenditures rising from $40 billion to $64 billion (in constant dollars) in the ten years prior to Mulroney, flattening out during his first term, and then rising during his second mandate. This trend took a deep dip with the election of Jean Chrétien's Liberals in 1993 and then began to rise again in the later 1990s and into the early 2000s.

When we examine social spending as a percentage of total expenditures, a different picture emerges. Social spending slowly declined as a percentage of total expenditure over the course of the Trudeau governments of 1968–79, then dipping and rising during his second period in office in the early 1980s. It slowly declined during the Mulroney era until the 1991 recession and then began rising again in the Chrétien period. As for social spending as a percentage of Gross Domestic Product (GDP), we see a slight wave effect, with expenditures rising slowly during the Trudeau years in the 1970s, declining through the brief period of Joe Clark as prime minister in 1979–80, and then rising at the outset of the Mulroney era and falling thereafter. Following Mulroney, the percentage slowly declined for the next eight years. Federal social spending rose in the early 1980s owing to the 1981–82 recession, peaking in 1983–84 at 12.3 per cent of GDP. Then, over the Mulroney years, it declined from 12.1 per cent in 1984–85 to 10.7 per cent in 1990–91, reflecting that social spending was growing slower than the Canadian economy. Federal social expenditures then rose as a share of GDP to 11.6 per cent in 1991–92 as a result of the recession of the early 1990s.

Table 1 provides rates of expenditure-change trends, from 1980 until 2003, that put Mulroney's budget record into perspective in terms of the *tempo* of social spending, that is, the rate of change (increases and decreases) over time, and therefore offer a rough measure of the *priority* of social spending relative to spending on other programs. Between 1980 and 1984, over the last Trudeau Liberal government, federal spending on social programs increased by 4.3 per cent. During the Mulroney era, the rate of growth was cut in half to 2.1 per cent. In fact, social spending by Ottawa decreased slightly in real terms from 1987–88 to 1990–91, reflecting the Conservatives' emphasis on expenditure restraint. In constant 1992 dollars, federal social spending grew modestly from $72.2 billion in 1984–85 to $73.4 billion in 1990–91, and afterwards, reflecting the impact of the recession on unemployment insurance and social assistance, jumped to $78.5 billion in 1991–92. The Chrétien government then cut back significantly, with social expenditures rising only 0.7 per cent over the next nine years.

As a share of federal program spending, social expenditures increased slightly over the Mulroney era. As a share of total budgetary expenditures (program spending plus public debt charges), with persistent deficits in the $30-billion range and a growing debt, social spending declined marginally. In relation to Canada's overall economic activity during the Liberal regime of 1980–84, the cumulative growth rate of total social expenditures grew faster than the GDP (118.4 compared to 99.2 per cent). Most of this increase was spent through direct transfers to people (130.9) rather than transfers to other levels of government (104.3). During the Conservative era, the total cumulative growth rate was 123.2 per cent, compared to GDP growth of 114.6 per cent. Again, the growth was greater in people (133.5) than in other levels of government (109.7). During both periods, social

Table 1 Rates of change in program spending, 1980–2003

| | *Average annual growth rates* | | | | *Cumulative growth rates (base year equal to 100)* | | | |
|---|---|---|---|---|---|---|---|---|
| | *1980–1983* | *1984–1993* | *1994–2003* | *1980–2003* | *1980–1983* | *1984–1993* | *1994–2003* | *1980–2003* |
| Real GDP* | -0.2 | 1.4 | 2.8 | 2.1 | 99.2 | 114.6 | 131.4 | 165.5 |
| Consumer Price Index | 7.2 | 3.5 | 1.8 | 3.6 | 131.9 | 141.2 | 119.9 | 233.4 |
| SOCIAL PROGRAMS | | | | | | | | |
| Transfers to persons | 7.0 | 2.9 | 0.4 | 2.5 | 130.9 | 133.5 | 104.4 | 178.8 |
| Transfers to other levels of government | 1.1 | 0.9 | 1.0 | 1.2 | 104.3 | 109.7 | 110.5 | 134.5 |
| Total social spending | 4.3 | 2.1 | 0.7 | 1.9 | 118.4 | 123.2 | 106.7 | 158.0 |
| OTHER PROGRAMS | | | | | | | | |
| Transfers to business | -7.1 | -10.1 | -0.2 | -5.2 | 74.6 | 34.4 | 98.0 | 27.9 |
| Other transfers | 1.7 | 1.1 | 0.2 | 1.1 | 107.2 | 112.0 | 102.5 | 130.2 |
| Defence | 2.5 | 0.3 | -1.6 | 0.2 | 110.4 | 103.2 | 85.2 | 104.0 |
| Total program spending | 2.3 | 1.1 | 0.5 | 1.2 | 109.5 | 111.6 | 105.1 | 133.3 |
| Debt charges | 7.6 | 2.8 | -3.4 | 1.6 | 133.8 | 132.2 | 70.6 | 147.2 |
| TOTAL EXPENDITURES | 3.2 | 1.5 | -0.3 | 1.3 | 113.4 | 115.8 | 96.8 | 135.5 |

* Real expenditures, constant 1992 dollars (1996 basket)

spending grew faster than spending on all other programs. Once the Liberals came back into power in 1993, spending on total social programs (106.7) dropped below the growth of GDP (131.4).

Table 2 focuses on changes in social spending by type of social programs: transfers to persons and transfers to other governments. The Mulroney government altered the structure of welfare in Canada: the universal family allowance program was terminated at the end of 1992; the universality of the old age security program was effectively abolished by 1991; and, as noted earlier, the federal government's direct contribution to financing the UI scheme was ended in 1991. Over the two Mulroney mandates, of all federal social programs, support to families was subject to the most significant restraint measures. The next most important changes were the indexation of health and post-secondary education transfer payments, which limited increases in these payments to the Gross National Product (GNP) less two percentage points. The indexation provision was lowered again after the 1988 election to the growth in GNP less three percentage points, and again in 1990, when the transfers were frozen until the end of 1994–95.

A number of important observations can be made on the basis of this budgetary analysis. First, overall social transfers to persons grew more on

Table 2 Spending by major social program, 1984–1993 and 1994–2003

| | 1984 | 1993 | 1994 | 2003 | 1984–1993 Absolute change | 1984–1993 Annual average | 1994–2003 Absolute change | 1994–2003 Annual average |
|---|---|---|---|---|---|---|---|---|
| | (Billions of constant dollars) | | | | ($) | (%) | ($) | % |
| Current transfers to persons | 27.4 | 51.6 | 50.2 | 62.8 | 24.2 | 6.5 | 12.6 | 2.3 |
| Family and youth allowances | 2.4 | 0.0 | 0.0 | 0.1 | –2.4 | –34.1 | 0.1 | 14.2 |
| Employment insurance benefits | 9.9 | 17.6 | 15.0 | 13.4 | 7.7 | 6.0 | –1.7 | –1.2 |
| Old age security payments | 11.0 | 19.5 | 20.2 | 26.9 | 8.5 | 5.9 | 6.8 | 2.9 |
| Grants to aboriginal persons/orgs | 1.0 | 2.9 | 3.0 | 5.0 | 1.9 | 11.3 | 1.9 | 5.1 |
| Goods and Services Tax credit | 0.0 | 2.7 | 2.8 | 3.3 | 2.7 | 0.01 | 0.4 | 1.4 |
| Other current transfers to persons | 3.1 | 3.7 | 3.8 | 6.1 | 0.6 | 1.7 | 2.2 | 4.7 |
| Current transfers to government | 20.9 | 32.3 | 31.5 | 41.8 | 11.4 | 4.5 | 10.2 | 2.9 |
| To provincial level | 20.7 | 32.0 | 30.9 | 41.5 | 11.2 | 4.4 | 10.5 | 3.0 |
| Provincial government subsector | 20.2 | 31.0 | 30.0 | 39.9 | 10.8 | 4.4 | 9.9 | 2.9 |
| Taxation agreements | 5.8 | 8.0 | 8.6 | 10.0 | 2.2 | 3.2 | 1.4 | 1.5 |
| Regional development | 0.2 | 0.1 | 0.1 | 0.0 | –0.1 | –5.8 | –0.1 | –19:4 |
| Other prov. Gov. subsector | 1.6 | 2.9 | 2.7 | 6.3 | 1.3 | 6.0 | 3.6 | 9.0 |
| Post-secondary education | 2.1 | 3.0 | 2.4 | 0.0 | 0.9 | 3.6 | –2.4 | n.a. |
| Health | 6.1 | 8.6 | 7.3 | 0.0 | 2.5 | 3.4 | –7.3 | n.a. |
| Canada Health and Social Transfer | 0.0 | 0.0 | 0.0 | 21.6 | n.a. | n.a. | 21.6 | n.a. |
| Canada Assistance Plan | 3.6 | 7.1 | 7.4 | 0.0 | 3.6 | 7.2 | –7.4 | n.a. |
| Territorial governments | 0.5 | 1.1 | 1.2 | 1.8 | 0.6 | 8.5 | 0.6 | 4.3 |
| Official languages | 0.3 | 0.1 | 0.3 | 0.2 | –0.1 | –6.9 | –0.1 | –3.8 |
| Universities subsector | 0.6 | 1.0 | 1.0 | 1.6 | 0.4 | 5.7 | 0.6 | 5.0 |
| To local level | 0.1 | 0.4 | 0.6 | 0.3 | 0.2 | 10.5 | –0.3 | –6.2 |
| Total social spending | 48.0 | 84.0 | 82.0 | 105.0 | 35.7 | 5.7 | 22.9 | 2.5 |

Note: Total social spending is the rounded sum of current transfers to persons and current transfers to governments.

an annual average in the Mulroney period than in the Chrétien years (6.5 per cent versus 2.3 per cent). This difference is most apparent in expenditures on unemployment benefits, old age security payments, and grants to Aboriginal persons and organizations. Secondly, a noteworthy counter-trend to this pattern is that spending on family and youth allowances was cut over the Mulroney years, both in absolute amounts and in percentage terms, while this area of spending expanded over the Chrétien period, especially in the later part of the period. Thirdly, with regard to transfers to other levels of government, the pattern, again, is that these transfers grew more in absolute dollar terms and on an annual average under Mulroney than under Chrétien (4.5 per cent versus 2.9 per cent). And, with respect to transfers to governments and agencies at the local or municipal level in Canada, such spending grew at a healthy average rate in the Mulroney years, while it actually shrunk in the Chrétien years (10.5 per cent versus –6.2 per cent).

In part, this decline in total social-spending growth, from the Mulroney to the Chrétien periods, reflects decisions made near the end of the second Mulroney government. And, in part, some of the growth rate in social spending in the later Mulroney years reflects automatic stabilization expenditures (unemployment insurance and social assistance) in response to the economic recession of the early 1990s. Still, much of the social-spending restraint over 1994–2003 was the result of decisions made by the Chrétien government.

The Chrétien Liberals, particularly in their first mandate, undertook a fundamental reconstruction of social programs. The federal role in the Canadian welfare state was itself transformed, as was the style of social policy making, to a politics of retrenchment and dismantling. The Liberal government continued the restructuring of social programs as part of expenditure restraint and deficit reduction. One year after taking power, the Liberals shocked policy watchers by terminating the Established Programs Financing (EPF) and the CAP. They replaced these with the much-reduced CHST. The introduction of this new funding mechanism resulted in deep absolute cuts in transfer programs to the provinces.

The introduction of the CHST, a striking and unilateral development in Canadian social-policy and fiscal federalism, continued a line of development begun with Trudeau's restraint of intergovernmental transfer formulae and continued by Mulroney's capping of the CAP. It was one more step in the process of responding to the new style of governing. Despite condemnations and disavowals of stealth tactics by senior Liberal ministers, the style continued under the Chrétien governments. By the late 1990s, many of the pillars of federal social policy had disappeared or diminished. Core Canadian beliefs about the nature of the social union had also substantially changed. After twenty years, we still have something that is recognizably a welfare state and a social union, but the content and architecture of the system is fundamentally different.

New program initiatives introduced by the Chrétien Liberals reflected the new policy regime of preferred ideas and program techniques. The National Children's Agenda targets benefits and invests in the human- and social-capital development of parents and their children. Changes to the Canada Pension Plan (CPP) were more conservative than the changes introduced by the Conservatives. Conditions for receiving disability and survivor benefits from the CPP changed from an average based on the last three years' maximum pensionable earning to an average of the last five years. Clearly, social-policy change does not necessarily flow along political party lines. It can also flow in the direction of the dominant ideas of the period.

## CONCLUSION

Our central analytical argument is that policy regime is a useful conceptual tool for understanding the approach and record of any prime minister and government, indeed, more useful perhaps than government mandates as indicators of policy outcomes. As we use the concept, a policy regime operates at the level of sectoral-policy making as compared to the macro level of the state or the micro level of specific programs.

Our contention is that the Mulroney years were characterized by a shift from one social policy regime to another, a shift for which Mulroney was only partly responsible, since external trends in the form of neo-conservative ideas and practices were also important. Table 3 summarizes the two social-policy regimes that together spanned the Mulroney years. These do not cleanly correspond to the two Mulroney governments (of 1984–88 and 1988–93) but rather blend and blur over the two mandates, with a shifting emphasis from the one regime of style and process to the other.

With the passage of time, we better appreciate that the practice of stealth in reforming and restraining social programs did not originate with the Mulroney governments, for the Trudeau Liberals were also artful practitioners of stealth and the Chrétien Liberals continued along the same path through the rest of the 1990s, despite some claims in 1993–94 that stealth would be ended. Even with the re-indexation of the personal income-tax system in 2000, elements of stealth live on in Ottawa and certainly across the provinces in welfare and workers' compensation systems.

We have focused on the social-policy behaviour of the Mulroney governments as revealed in their budgetary choices, outputs, and trends. In doing so, we employed expenditures as the indicator of government performance to determine the macro social- policy record of Mulroney and to compare his record to that of Liberal governments before and after. We recognize, of course, that a complete analysis would require consideration

Table 3 The shifting social-policy regimes of the Mulroney era

| *From* | *To* |
|---|---|
| Social welfare, citizenship perspective with rhetoric of sacred trusts and entitlements | Economic opportunity, selective programs, the value of incentives |
| Fiscal problem and need to restrain the growth rate of program spending and enhance and stabilize revenues | Fiscal crisis and need to retrench and restructure programs and benefits, and offer tax incentives |
| Fairly open and transparent consultative and development policy processes | Closed and stealth processes and methods |
| Consensual and cooperative approach to relations with provinces/territories and to interactions with societal organizations | More unilateral, coercive, and thus combative approach to relations |
| Relatively moderate to high level of trust and legitimacy in relations with other governments and sectors | Low levels of trust and legitimacy |

of tax and revenue data, regulatory activity, and public-sector employment trends. Nonetheless, expenditures are the central dynamic of governing and the visible expression of the welfare state, since spending is a quantifiable manifestation of government decision making.

Our analysis of budgetary outputs and trends yields the following observations. First, federal social spending grew in real terms at a slower rate under the Mulroney Conservatives than in the last term of the Trudeau Liberals, but, in turn, social spending increased notably more under the Mulroney Conservatives than under the Chrétien Liberals. The data in Table 2 show that average annual increases in federal social spending (measured in constant dollars) declined from the Mulroney to the Chrétien years. Total social-spending growth rates dropped by more than half from 1984–1993 to 1994–2003. Secondly, with the Chrétien years now part of our collective experience and perspectives, some elements of the Mulroney social-policy record appear less harsh than they did at the end of the Mulroney era in 1993. The most obvious example is Mulroney's treatment of transfer payments to the provinces for health, post-secondary education, and social assistance, which appears enlightened and generous compared to the Chrétien government's elimination of the EPF and the CAP and its introduction of the CHST. Thirdly, other elements of the Mulroney social-policy record appear in a more progressive light today than they did back then. An example is the reform of the CPP, especially in terms of disability benefits. In retrospect, the changes that the Mulroney Tories, in conjunction with the provinces, made to CPP/disability over the 1988–92 period represented the last phase of liberalization of benefits and eligibility.

In summary, social-policy making in the Mulroney years was more complex and multilayered and textured than often appreciated. It amounted to more than simply restructuring the welfare state; it entailed governing Canada at a time of shifting policy regimes in welfare states around the globe.

## NOTES

1 Gray Grattan, "Social Policy by Stealth," *Policy Options* 11(2) (1990): 26.

2 The unemployment insurance program (UI) became the employment insurance (EI) program in 1996. The Canada Health and Social Transfer was restructured in April 2004 and two separate transfers created in its place – the Canada Health Transfer (CHT) and the Canada Social Transfer (CST) – in order to increase transparency and accountability.

# 8

# Contained and Redefined: Women's Issues in the Mulroney Era

ANN PORTER

During the 1984 federal election campaign, the National Action Committee on the Status of Women (NAC) sponsored a leaders' debate on women's issues. All three party leaders participated. On this occasion and others in the campaign, Progressive Conservative leader Brian Mulroney acknowledged the importance of women's issues. However, by 1988, as the then leader of NAC, Judy Rebick, put it, "women's issues were on the back burner."[1] While women's groups had increasingly articulated concerns with respect not only to traditional "women's issues" but also to what were considered core agenda items of the Conservative government, they found a diminished willingness to accommodate these concerns as well as increased hostility to the voice of organized women. As Sylvia Bashevkin has noted, feminists were "on the defensive."[2] The events of the intervening years, and the place of women's issues by the end of the Mulroney mandate, are the subjects of this chapter.

I argue that there was an inevitable tension in approach between a women's movement increasingly concerned to go beyond equality of opportunity to address systemic discrimination and substantive inequalities, a goal that often required state intervention, and a Conservative government committed to an agenda based on reduced government intervention and giving greater weight to the free market.[3] Ultimately, women's issues were both subsumed by the larger ideological, economic, and social-policy agenda that was being put forward and redefined in important ways.

The late 1970s and early 1980s marked an unprecedented mobilization for women's equality. NAC had been founded in 1971–72 with the intent of lobbying for the implementation of the recommendations of the 1968 report of the Royal Commission on the Status of Women. A network of women's advisers had been created within the state, and women's service and advocacy groups were proliferating. This network was given added

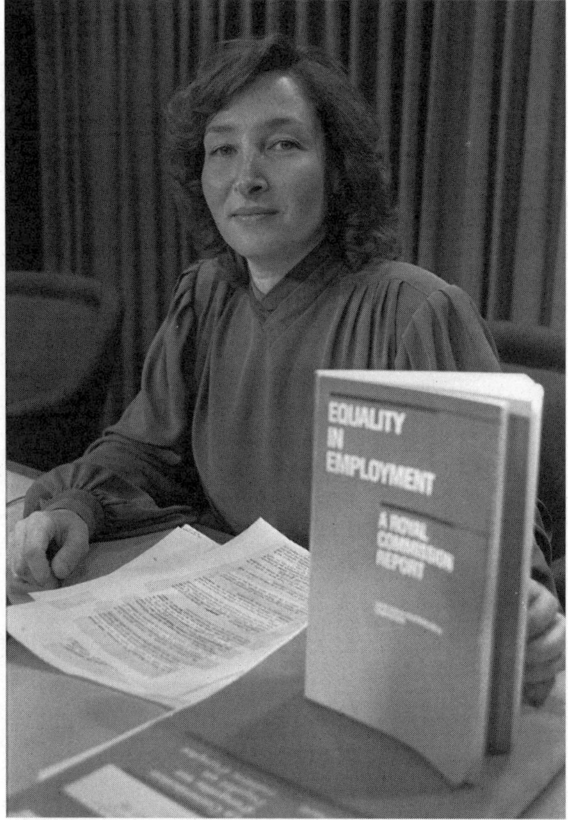


Justice Rosalie Abella is shown delivering her report on Equality in Employment in October 1984. Shortly after, the Conservatives implemented an Employment Equity Act. Canadian Press.

impetus when the Canadian Human Rights Commission was established in 1978. The growing participation of women in the labour force and the stronger representation of women's concerns within trade unions created additional pressure for governments to act on equity issues. The enactment of the Charter of Rights and Freedoms in 1982 and the coming into force of its equality provisions in 1985 both reflected the strength of women's organizing and provided a further important framework for advancing women's equality claims. Women's groups, and those concerned with such issues, had thus successfully opened up space on the state's agenda for a range of gender issues, including part-time work, employment equity, child care, maternity/parental leave, and abortion.

At the same time, however, the growing strength of the pro-market agenda that came to shape the contours of the period as a whole deeply affected not only the government's responses to this particular set of women's issues but also the opportunities available to women and the way they were to live their lives. The groundwork laid by the Mulroney government for what ultimately became in the 1990s a neo-liberal restructuring of the state had a major impact at ideological and concrete policy levels alike, and, in both areas, the impact was profoundly gendered. At an ideological level, the insistence that state involvement in the economy and social welfare needed to be reduced, that market forces should be relied on to a greater extent, that deficit reduction and increased international competitiveness should be priorities, and that individuals and households should assume greater responsibility for personal well-being had far-reaching implications for women's position in the household as well as the labour market. In terms of concrete policies, the Mulroney government's efforts to construct a new role for the state in both the national and continental economies, and its restructuring of a wide range of policy areas including trade, tax reform, and social and labour-market policy – as well as its efforts at constitutional renewal – similarly had profound implications for women's lives and equality issues.

To be sure, this period did witness a number of advances for women's equality and women's rights, advances that reflected both the strength of the women's movement as the Conservatives assumed power and the struggles taking place at the level of the courts as the equality provisions of the Charter of Rights came into force. Nevertheless, women's issues as a whole were subsumed by the larger questions at the top of the Mulroney agenda: free trade, deficit reduction, a reduced role for the state, and constitutional reform. This often meant not only that the latter issues were given a higher priority but also that such policies, as women's groups came increasingly to point out, tended to *deepen* structural inequalities and in many ways ran counter to efforts to address equity concerns. The Conservatives responded to equity-related pressures in part by greater gender neutrality in the language of government documents. At the same time, however, the Conservatives did not let this approach hinder the advancement of the economic, market-based agenda. Where the Conservatives did address issues of concern to women, such as childcare, they tended to do so in a manner that was compatible with a market-based approach and a reduced role for the state, often in the process redefining the issues in ways significantly different from how women's groups had been formulating them. In addition, the presence of a substantial contingent of social conservatives within the Conservative Party, and in later years the voice of the Reform Party, created further pressure to recast women's demands so as to make them more compatible with traditional views of the family and of women's role within it.

While the measures implemented in this period drew on the legacy left by earlier governments, the role that the Conservatives played in reconfiguring the relationship not only between the state and the market but also between the state and the family, between public and private in both these senses, cannot be underestimated. In addition, important developments occurred with respect to women's ability to articulate and put forward demands in the political arena. Indeed, the role of the Mulroney government in disempowering women as political actors is a further significant legacy of the period. In this sense, there was also, as Jane Jenson and Susan D. Phillips point out, a restructuring of citizens' relationship with the state, a process that had major implications for women's political voice.[4] All these changes had far-reaching ramifications for the status and position of women. In sum, the Mulroney era was significant in laying the basis for a new gender order that involved particular roles, ideological expectations, and material realities for women and that was compatible with the neo-liberal restructuring that was to take place over the subsequent decades.[5]

The first section of this chapter examines the context with respect to women's issues in the early 1980s. The next two sections, corresponding to Mulroney's two terms in power, consider how women's lives and women's issues came to be shaped by the unfolding of the market-based or neo-liberal agenda that was the hallmark of the Mulroney era. While changes of importance to women occurred in a wide range of areas, including abortion, family law, changes to women's status in the Indian Act, violence against women, and childcare and parental benefits, the most significant legacy of the Mulroney years for women was the way in which the far-reaching changes that occurred at an ideological level and in the overall economic and social policy framework came both to set the priorities and to shape and contain the approach to the range of issues on the agenda. The first term laid the groundwork for this shift in the policy paradigm. The second term witnessed the beginning of the implementation process. Both fundamentally redefined the nature of women's issues.

## THE CONTEXT OF THE EARLY 1980S: EQUALITY ISSUES AND THE CONSERVATIVES' ARRIVAL IN POWER

The women's organizations that mobilized following the report of the Royal Commission on the Status of Women had initially focused on such issues as formal juridical equality, family law, and equal pay. By the late 1970s, however, in the face of persistent inequalities, women's groups increasingly viewed it as important to go beyond this to consider how women's concentration within certain types of occupations and work structures meant that they were likely to be differentially affected by economic restructuring and by particular state policies, as well as how women's disadvantaged position in the workforce could be linked to their continued responsibility for childcare and other domestic tasks. The need to address the substantive inequalities that resulted from women's structural location within the home and in the workplace entailed the consideration of a range of measures including affirmative action in the workplace, improved childcare, and maternity-leave policies. It was the growing salience of these concerns that led women's groups to devote themselves to the task of ensuring that a strong definition of equality was entrenched in the Charter of Rights – one that would allow, for example, the establishment of affirmative-action programs and that might require looking at differences in the life patterns of men and women. It also provided the impetus for the establishment by the Liberals in the early 1980s of a number of task forces and commissions of inquiry addressing issues of concern to women. These included the Commission of Inquiry into Part-Time Work (the Wallace Commission), established in 1982; the Abella Commission, examining equality in employment, appointed in June 1983; and the Cooke Task Force on Child Care, appointed by the Liberals prior to the 1984 election.

It was in this context of considerable movement on women's issues that the Mulroney government was elected in 1984. Given Mulroney's approach as a conciliator interested in brokering a broad coalition, as well as the strength of the demands being put forward by women's organizations, it is not surprising perhaps that, before, during, and immediately after the election, some recognition of equity concerns appeared in the statements of the Conservative Party under his leadership. During the NAC-sponsored leader's debate on women's issues, for example, as we have seen, Mulroney stated his commitment to women's issues[6] to the extent that at least one commentator described his position as a "moderate feminist" one."[7] The Conservatives again indicated their commitment in their first throne speech after assuming power. Finance Minister Michael Wilson's November 1984 statement outlining the government's intentions for reform, *A New Direction for Canada: An Agenda for Economic Renewal*,[8] similarly appeared to give some consideration to equity concerns. References were made, for instance, to "equitable access to new job opportunities" for men and women,[9] and the statement noted that "barriers restricting full participation by natives, women, visible minorities and the disabled must be pulled down. These are the reasons why ... the government is committed to affirmative action."[10]

While the Conservative's early statements thus indicated an awareness of the importance of equity issues, what was even more clearly enunciated was the priority to be accorded to a sweeping ideological, economic, and social-policy shift based on reduced government intervention, increased individual responsibility for personal well-being, and the private sector's role as the "driving force of economic renewal in an increasingly competitive world marketplace." What was not clear was how equity concerns were to be reconciled with this new economic and ideological paradigm. Some indication was given by Mulroney during the 1984 leadership debate when he noted that "a better future for women will come when prosperity returns to Canada ... and women will share in the economic benefits of that new growth."[11] Considerable tension, however, clearly existed between an approach based on free markets and the hope that this would yield a kind of trickle-down benefit for women, on the one hand, and a women's movement where a more left-wing feminism was becoming more prominent and delving deeper into the causes of inequality through a focus on substantive inequalities and systemic discrimination, on the other. These tensions were made all the more acute by the presence in the Conservative Party of a fairly strong contingent of social conservatives opposed to legislation that would encourage mothers with young children to work outside the home. The result, despite early indications of a concern with consensus and national reconciliation, was an increasingly confrontational relationship between the women's movement and the Mulroney government.

## THE CONSERVATIVE'S FIRST TERM IN POWER: LAYING THE GROUNDWORK

Michael Wilson's 1984 economic statement indicated the government's intentions to undertake far-reaching economic- and social-policy reform. Economic priorities included deficit reduction, reduced state intervention in a range of areas, and increased international competitiveness. Social-policy restructuring goals included ending universality, targeting programs to those most in need, containing costs, and redesigning income-support programs in a way that would reduce disincentives to work and "facilitate labour market adjustments." The report of the Royal Commission on the Economic Union and Development Prospects for Canada (the Macdonald Commission), released in September 1985, further laid out a blueprint for a neo-liberal restructuring, proposing far-reaching changes in several areas – including social security, industrial and labour-market policy, equal pay, and federal-provincial relations – and calling for the negotiation of a comprehensive Canada-U.S. free-trade agreement.

These ideological and proposed policy shifts were extremely significant not only because they implied a new role for the state in the economy but also because they touched in important ways on activities and responsibilities within households and on the relationship between the public and private in a whole range of senses. In redefining the contours of paid work available to women, notions of individual and community responsibility for personal well-being, and the role of state support, they were critical in laying the groundwork for what was to become a new gender order compatible with the neo-liberal paradigm that was being advanced.

The significance for women of the changes taking place was well grasped by the women's movement of the time. Indeed, one of the distinctive features of this period was the emergence of a deeper understanding of what constituted issues of importance to women, as women's groups increasingly came to intervene not only on questions of the family, social policy, and the status of women but also with respect to the broader restructuring and neo-liberal shift that was occurring. Briefs and position papers, for example, were written on free trade, privatization, tax reform, unemployment insurance (UI), and various employment-related issues. The extension of women's concerns to incorporate such seemingly gender-neutral issues was not particularly welcomed by the government. Indeed, it has been noted that in 1986 NAC met on several occasions with the prime minister but that its "increasing efforts to expose the gendered consequences of supposedly gender-neutral policies [such as free trade, UI, and immigration] were strongly opposed by the government, which wanted it to stick to 'women's issues.'"[12]

I examine below the points of tension between the women's movement and the Mulroney government in its first term in power in a number of key areas: the Macdonald report, free trade and the economic agenda, income security, childcare and family/child benefits, and employment equity.

### *The Macdonald Report, Free Trade, and the Economic Agenda: A Women's Issue*

The release of the Macdonald Commission's report in 1985 became a focal point for women's groups, as well as labour and other "popular sector" groups anxious about the implications of a neo-liberal shift in government policies.[13] Thirty-four women's groups had made presentations to the Macdonald Commission hearings,[14] and NAC provided a written response to the final report. By then, free trade, the centrepiece of the commission's recommendations, had already become a major focus of interest for women. NAC had passed a resolution opposing free trade as early as its 1984 annual convention and it had sent representatives to the founding meeting of the Council of Canadians, where it emphasized that issues of Canadian sovereignty and free trade were also "women's issues."[15] The Canadian Advisory Council on the Status of Women (CACSW) had also raised concerns about the implications of a free-trade agreement for women as early as 1985.[16]

Following Mulroney's announcement that his government intended to pursue a free-trade agreement with the United States, women's groups played a central role in opposing the proposal. According to Jeffrey M. Ayres, the impetus for the development of an anti-free-trade coalition came from NAC and, indeed, the first anti-free-trade coalition meeting was held in NAC's Toronto office.[17] The free-trade campaign has been described as a "watershed" for the women's movement, since it was "the key mainstream economic issue" that moved women's groups beyond traditional "women's issues" and marked the moment when women came to have "a significant voice in national political/economic issues."[18] Through 1986 and 1987, NAC continued to be active in raising the free-trade issue and opposition to the agreement became a focal point for women's groups in the months before the 1988 election.

There clearly emerged in this period a concern about how the economic and labour-market policies being recommended by the Macdonald Commission and others could have a differential impact on men and women. NAC argued strongly that women were likely to be adversely affected by free trade both because of their concentration in vulnerable manufacturing sectors such as clothing and textiles and because the possibility of free trade in services threatened their employment possibilities as well as existing social programs of importance to them. Another issue was the possibility that Canadian labour and social legislation would be weakened through a downward harmonization with U.S. standards. Free trade was thus considered likely to have negative consequences for women in terms of jobs, employment legislation, and social services. Similar views were also expressed with respect to other aspects of the Macdonald agenda. Wage-control programs (such as legislation restricting wage increases to 6 and 5 per cent) could have a negative impact on women since "percentage increases on higher salaries are greater than on lower salaries."[19] It was feared that recommendations to scale back the UI program and reduce benefit rates would be "disproportionately hard on women," given that they tended to be in intermittent employment and at the lower end of the income scale.[20] It was thought that retraining or assistance that focused on "willingness to undertake adaptive behavior" (including a willingness to relocate) would be more difficult for married women than for men.

Yet another major concern was the overall ideological approach of both the Macdonald Commission and the new Conservative government, which emphasized reduced state involvement, greater individual responsibility for personal well-being, and increased reliance on the free market. It was pointed out that this approach implied, for example, that market competition could itself lead to a levelling of wage differences and that state intervention was therefore not necessary. Women's groups, in contrast, asserted that positive state programs, including affirmative-action measures, paid maternity leave, legislation providing equal pay for work of equal value, and access to good-quality daycare for women workers,[21] were absolutely essential in order to address effectively the problem of women's inequality.

A considerable polarization between women's groups and the Conservative Party thus quickly emerged. While women's groups had increasingly come to identify economic issues and systemic discrimination as key to understanding women's inequality, the Conservatives were introducing processes that would both threaten women's jobs and dismantle the state infrastructure needed to address equity concerns.

*Income Security*

The UI program had long been targeted as a Keynesian-style welfare-state program in need of overhaul. Extensive demographic, labour-market, and family work-life changes had been under way for some time, making issues of both income security and labour-market policy critical to women. When the Conservatives came to power in the early 1980s, women had been entering the labour force in growing numbers, although often in part-time and non-standard work categories.[22] A new approach to unemployment, the unemployed, and income security was central to the neo-liberal agenda. Restructuring had begun in the late 1970s under the Liberals, but the Conservatives, eager to move farther down the same road, soon indicated their intention to undertake reforms in this area and in July 1985 established a commission of inquiry on the subject (the Forget Commission).[23] The Forget Commission, like the Macdonald Commission, emphasized supply-side factors, including individual characteristics such as attitudes towards work and levels of skill or training and individual responsibility for personal well-being, and was concerned about social programs creating "long-run dependencies." Considerable emphasis was placed, therefore, not only on reducing costs but also on the disincentives to work thought to be found within the structures of income-security programs themselves. This could include, for example, benefit rates that were thought to be high enough to act as an incentive to stay at home rather than look for work. The Forget Commission recommended greatly restricting benefits and reducing overall benefit levels, particularly for those with short-term or intermittent work patterns.

Again, while the analysis was put in relatively gender-neutral terms, both the discussion and the policy recommendations had strong gender implications. NAC, CACSW, and other women's groups objected to the tenor of the discussions, which implied that women's labour-market behaviour – their entry or withdrawal from the labour force – was, itself, a cause of unemployment. They pointed out that the Forget recommendations would particularly disadvantage women who "tend to be more heavily represented among part-time and temporary workers and they are more likely to be working in marginal industries which frequently lay off workers." Similarly, a reduction in benefit levels to, for example, 50 per cent of previous income would make it difficult for those at the low end of the wage scale (a disproportionate number of whom were women) to make ends meet. In contrast, women's groups called for "a specific employment strategy based on the particular characteristics of women's employment and unemployment" and that would also include such things as improved maternity and parental benefits.[24]

### *Childcare and Family/Child Benefits*

Child and family-related benefits was another key area where the Conservatives moved quickly to develop their own policy responses and to begin the reform process. The May 1985 budget changed the family allowance program, paid universally to all mothers, along with old age security (OAS), from being fully to partially indexed. While protests about the de-indexing of OAS benefits led to the withdrawal of that particular proposal, the government did proceed with the partial de-indexing of family allowances.[25] The Child Tax Credit, directed at low-income families, was increased while the value of Child Care Expense Deduction (a tax exemption allowing a proportion of childcare expenses to be deducted from net income and therefore of greatest benefit to high income earners) was reduced.[26]

These changes raised a number of important issues for women. Overall, they aimed to limit social-policy expenditures, since, for example, the value of the family allowance eroded over time as inflation rose. The changes involved a shift from universality (the family allowance program) to the targeting of benefits to those most in need (via tax credits). In addition, there was a shift from *individual* entitlement to entitlement based on *family* income. Women's groups in the mid-1980s strongly opposed the partial de-indexing of the family allowance.[27] Family allowances had traditionally been seen as important in that they were paid universally to individual women regardless of family income and, in addition, offered some recognition of women's work as mothers. A key argument put forward was that the independent financial security of women was critical and that both the erosion of family allowances and targeting based on family income would erode women's individual entitlements.[28]

Childcare was dealt with as a separate issue. In the early 1980s childcare activists and women's organizations, as well as the Abella Commission and the Cooke Task Force, were strongly urging a national system of publicly funded, universally accessible childcare and the removal of daycare funding from the welfare-based Canada Assistance Plan (CAP). The Conservatives appointed their own special parliamentary committee on childcare in November 1985, which held hearings and released a report in 1987. In doing so, the Conservatives were able to refocus and redefine the childcare issue. The special committee argued that the funding of childcare through the CAP should be maintained (thus maintaining the link between welfare and child support for poor parents) and focused on the central role of families in childcare, parental choices, and market-based solutions. It recommended a complex combination of subsidies to not only non-profit but also commercial childcare centres, tax breaks to parents who purchased childcare, and the use of tax credits to support parents looking after their children at home.

In December 1987 Jake Epp, minister of health and welfare, announced the government's National Strategy on Child Care. As Epp described it, the key underpinning of the strategy was choice: "choice for those parents who wanted their children in childcare, choice for those parents who wanted their children in childcare spaces related to the industry where those parents worked, and choice for those parents who decided they wanted to stay at home with their children."[29] The result was a three-pronged strategy: one, an increase in the number of childcare spaces in non-profit and commercial facilities by 200,000; two, the doubling of the Child Care Expense Deduction (CCED) from $2,000 to $4,000 per year for children under six or with a disability and to $2,000 a year for children seven to fourteen; and, three, an increase in the refundable Child Care Tax Credit (CCTC) by $200 a year for children under six.[30] Shortly after the strategy was announced, the CCED and the CCTC changes were implemented. In December 1988 Bill C-144, providing for the creation of the 200,000 new childcare spaces, was introduced. Childcare activists and women's organizations strongly opposed this new measure, arguing that the increased role of both the for-profit, commercial sector and the tax system in ensuring childcare provision would make impossible the kind of universal, publicly funded childcare system long advocated. The bill died on the order paper once the 1988 federal election was called.

### *Employment Equity: Redefining the Issue within the Context of the Economic Agenda*

The Royal Commission on Equality in Employment, headed by Judge Rosalie Abella, issued its report in October 1984, shortly after the Conservatives came to power. In a climate where, as noted above, there was considerable momentum on women's issues and where positive measures to address employment discrimination had been on the agenda, the Mulroney government, particularly in light of its recent election promises, clearly felt compelled to carry through and implement some form of employment-equity legislation.[31] At the same time, however, the Conservatives were faced with a number of constraints. First, given the new government's emphasis on deregulation and privatization, it was felt that there should be only minimal constraints with respect to hiring and promotion decisions. As Michael Sabia states, "it was simply *not on* that the government was going to set up an enforcement agency; a separate, identifiable, employment equity enforcement agency … because we weren't going to have a government which, at the time, was trying very hard to send deregulatory signals to the business community … now say we're going to set up a new bureaucratic agency and tell you how to run your businesses."[32] Secondly, there was some opposition from social conservatives within the Conservative Party, who did not wish to see legislation that, in their view, would encourage women to work outside the home.[33] Finally, in many ways, Abella's recommendations contrasted sharply with those of the Macdonald Commission, the major report laying out a blueprint for market-based restructuring that was released in 1985. Whereas the Macdonald Commission discussed only measures to improve the status of women within the context of a free-market economy, the Abella report suggested that "massive policy intervention" was necessary to address women's inequality.[34] While Abella recommended tackling the problem of wage discrimination by both encouraging women to move into higher-paid jobs traditionally held by men and increasing the pay of women's jobs (the notion behind equal pay for work of equal value), the Macdonald Commission was prepared to accept only the former – essentially an equality-of-opportunity approach involving minimal regulation.

The Conservatives did carry through and implement a new Employment Equity Act in 1986. Following Abella's recommendations, the act was designed to address the inequalities in employment faced by four target groups: women, the disabled, Aboriginal people, and visible minorities. It required employers to produce an annual report showing target group members' participation rates, occupational distribution, salary range, and so on and indicating goals and timetables to improve the position of those groups. The legislation covered those in the public service as well as federally regulated employers with one hundred or more employees.[35] In addition, a Federal Contractors Program was introduced, to be applied to companies with over one hundred employees placing bids on government contracts over $200,000. Such companies were required to have employment-equity plans available for on-site inspection by Canadian Employment Insurance Commission (CEIC) officials.

Overall, then, what had happened to women's issues by the end of the Conservative's first term in power? While initially there had been some acknowledgement of the importance of equity issues, the major priority of the Conservatives in their first term was clearly to lay the groundwork for a sweeping ideological, economic, and social restructuring which in many ways ran counter to equity concerns. The emphasis on deregulation, free markets, and reduced state expenditures, for example, left little room for positive state programs or the regulatory measures necessary for making advances with respect to equality. Indeed, at an ideological level, the emphasis on free markets and individual responsibility signalled an important move away from the very *notion* of substantive inequalities. At a concrete policy level, in many areas the divisions were too deep at this point for the government to implement far-reaching reforms, yet the first term was nevertheless critical in preparing the way for changes that were subsequently introduced. Mechanisms for a free-trade deal had been put in place. In the area of social policy and income security, important steps had been taken in the shift from universality to the targeting of benefits, an increased emphasis on family-based benefits, and the notion that UI needed to be restructured in such a fashion that would make it more difficult for those working short-term or part time to qualify. All this had important implications for the position of women in the home as well as in the labour force. Where policies of concern to women *were* introduced, such as in the areas of childcare and employment equity, this occurred in a way that substantially redefined both the issues and the solutions. In particular, market- or family-based solutions to childcare were put forward, and employment-equity measures were minimized in order not to interfere with the larger emphasis on deregulation and free markets. In other words, the beginning of a somewhat contradictory new gender order was being established: one where increasing numbers of women were working in the paid labour force, but where, at the same time, income security was less available, private solutions were being put forward, and the family was still being upheld as the centre in which caring and other activities were to take place. Finally, as the organized women's movement began opposing these changes in a more vocal manner, the stage was set for the discrediting of such groups as "special interests" and for the reductions in their funding that would occur in the second term.

## THE CONSERVATIVE'S SECOND TERM IN POWER: WOMEN'S ISSUES MARGINALIZED

The Conservatives emerged from the November 1988 election in a much stronger position to proceed with both their economic- and social-policy agendas. Following the election, the Canada-U.S. Free Trade Agreement (FTA) was implemented and sweeping social-policy restructuring along the lines being suggested by the major business think-tanks and by the federal government commissions of the mid-1980s began. In the initial part of the second term, some reference was made to women's issues and equity concerns. In the throne speech in early April 1989, the government noted its intention to pursue a number of initiatives that were of interest to women and designed to promote "equality of opportunity." These included the creation of a Task Force on Barriers to Employment and Promotion of Women in the Public Service, a continued commitment to a national childcare program, initiatives "to reduce violence in the family and the abuse of children," a royal commission to inquire into "the implications of new reproductive technologies for Canadian society," and consideration of the route to follow given the Supreme Court of Canada's 1988 ruling that provisions for abortion found in the Criminal Code violated the Charter of Rights.[36] In 1991 the government, responding to a petition from a range of groups for the establishment of a royal commission on violence against women, announced that it would appoint "a blue ribbon panel of concerned Canadian men and women to inquire into the serious problem of violence against women in our society."[37] What continued to come through most strongly, however, was the goal of building a "strong economy" through international competitiveness, the priority given to debt reduction and trade liberalization, and the intention to develop a "comprehensive human resource strategy" for the 1990s that would complement the direction of macro-economic policies. Equity concerns, then, remained limited and defined by the larger economic and social agenda that was being put forward. Overall, relations between the Conservative government and women's groups became increasingly acrimonious in this period, and the Mulroney government appeared much less willing to "broker a deal" or accommodate a diversity of voices.

Key issues of Mulroney's second term that are examined below are the economic agenda, income security and family and child benefits, constitutional debates, women's political voice and rights, equality, and the Charter of Rights.

### *A Market-based Economic Agenda: A Continuing Women's Issue*

The Conservative government's priorities in both economic and social policy areas were clearly enunciated in a series of second-term budgets. Again, what is striking is the interconnection between policies in a wide range of areas, including economic, social, and labour-market policy, policies with respect to children and the family, and policies bearing upon the structure of the government itself. This reconfiguration of public and private and of state, market, and family was of profound significance to women. The April 1989 budget, unlike the throne speech earlier that month, contained no specific references to equity concerns. Rather, the message forcefully delivered was the need to take strong action to address the high level of debt. Finance Minister Michael Wilson announced extensive expenditure-reduction measures, including a decrease in program spending of $2.5 billion a year.[38] This affected a host of programs from defence spending to subsidies for VIA Rail, transfers for social programs (Established Program Financing), and federal government financing for the UI program. A reduction in planned expenditures was announced in the areas of both childcare and family allowances, and restraint measures also began to affect funding for women's groups and programs.

In the 1990 budget Michael Wilson announced a two-year expenditure-control program affecting virtually all spheres of government, and this was extended with both the 1991 and 1992 budgets.[39] In all these budgets, the government's economic priorities were reasserted: putting "the government's financial house in order," fostering a "dynamic innovative and competitive private sector,"[40] setting out a "clear, achievable inflation target,"[41] increasing international competitiveness, and "streamlining government."[42] Major initiatives included extensive privatization; replacement of the Manufacturers' Sales Tax with the Goods and Services Tax (GST); reform of government management, including through wage-restraint measures; elimination of a range of government agencies and commissions; and continued reduction of expenditures, including "grants and contributions to businesses, interest groups and individuals."[43] Funding cuts to women's organizations continued with the budgets of the early 1990s. The 1990 budget entailed major expenditure reductions to women's centres, feminist organizations, and women's magazines.[44] In 1992 funding for the Court Challenges Program, which provided support for groups such as the Women's Legal Education and Action Fund (LEAF) to intervene in Charter of Rights equality cases, was cut;[45] and the government announced that it would not honour retroactive pay settlements to women in the public service[46] and that the saving generated from a $7-billion spending cut would be used to reduce taxes.[47] While the government did indicate its intention in the 1992 budget to increase assistance to Canadian families (for example, in the area of child benefits), this and other new initiatives were to be paid for by "reducing and reallocating expenditures, not by increasing the burden of borrowing and taxing."[48] Unlike earlier statements, no mention was made of equity concerns. On the whole, then, within the key documents setting the government's priorities, equity slowly faded from the discourse, to be replaced by a discourse that emphasized reducing the size of government, balancing the budget, and encouraging private-sector initiatives.

Women's groups, both on their own and as part of coalitions such as the Pro-Canada Network (renamed the Action Canada Network in 1991), remained active in opposing this new policy paradigm. According to Ayres, NAC "spearheaded the campaign" to highlight the budget cuts to social services, education, and crown corporations.[49] It organized anti-budget strategy meetings and encouraged a "riding the rails" cross-country Via Rail protest. It produced briefs and pamphlets on privatization, the GST, and other tax-reform proposals,[50] arguing that the direction of Conservative policy was harmful to women.

By 1991, NAC, in keeping with the government's focus on international competitiveness and trade agreements, was increasingly shifting its focus to incorporate an understanding of the global situation and the need to establish international networks. NAC, along with other women's and labour groups, was concerned about the possible gender implications of the North-American-wide free-trade agreement (NAFTA) that was under consideration by the early 1990s.[51] Women from Canada, the United States, and Mexico, for example, drew attention to the possible consequences of continental-wide economic integration for women's paid and unpaid labour, and argued that rights to education, health care, food, nutrition, housing, and so on be guaranteed in any trilateral agreement.[52] Women further warned how gender, race, and class interacted in ways that would make women of colour particularly vulnerable under continental free trade.[53] The possible impact of NAFTA or other international agreements on social programs, the public sector, national sovereignty, and equity goals also became a subject of concern. Marjorie Cohen, for example, argued that the creation of a global economic market with minimal controls over international finance and investment would make it more difficult to institute the economic and social policy initiatives that had traditionally been important for equality-seeking groups.[54]

### *Income Security and Labour-Market Changes*

Linked to new developments in economic policy were sweeping changes to labour-market strategy. Extensive economic restructuring had been taking place, in part as the FTA came into effect. In addition, the early 1990s were years of deep recession, with the growth of both unemployment and unstable working conditions, and, for women, employment growth continued to be disproportionately in part-time, contingent work categories. Labour-market policies in this period were critical for women in that, rather than addressing the new forms of inequalities that were developing, they served to further deepen them. This occurred in a number of ways. First, the public sector had been an important source of employment for women, not only because of the large number of jobs involved but also because, at times, the state had played an important role as a model in setting equity and wage guidelines. The emphasis on "streamlining" government and on wage restraint, therefore, had a major impact on women's employment. The 1988 Task Force on Barriers to Women in Public Service had been created to increase women's representation at all levels within the bureaucracy, but it had to operate within a climate of downsizing and restraint. This necessarily limited any attempts to promote women's employment or address equity issues.[55] The limitations on redressing inequalities in an environment of restraint were evident even when directives came from the courts. A statement from the 1992 budget is telling in this regard: "We are ... taking action to manage future spending pressures in a fiscally responsible way. The government is prepared to act when necessary to counter the serious fiscal effects that may come from legal challenges to government programs. For example, while the government will continue to implement equal pay for work of equal value, it will not make any further retroactive payments for the period prior to November 1, 1990."[56]

Secondly, more general labour-market policies also served to deepen inequalities. While changes to UI had been too controversial to implement in the first term, extensive reform measures were introduced soon after the 1988 election. Bill C-21, introduced in June 1989, increased the difficulty of qualifying for UI benefits and reduced the maximum length of time benefits could be collected.[57] The major rationale for these changes was expenditure reduction and removing the disincentives to work, both to be achieved largely by limiting benefits for seasonal and short-term workers or those with intermittent work histories. Most significantly for women, these changes constituted an initial step towards a type of two-tiered benefit system where greater income security would be available to those who already had stable full-year, full-time employment (but were temporarily laid off) while those with intermittent work histories would have a harder time qualifying.

Women's organizations, which actively participated in the extensive hearings on the proposed changes, expressed much concern not only about the new benefit levels and qualifying requirements but also about a proposed amendment that would increase the penalty for those who quit voluntarily, refused a suitable job offer, or were fired for misconduct. It was feared that women forced to leave jobs because of sexual harassment or to look after family members would have difficulty qualifying for benefits. Bill C-21 was passed in 1990 with little alteration. Further UI changes, including reducing the benefit rate (from 60 to 57 per cent) and completely disqualifying anyone who quit voluntarily, refused a suitable job offer, or were fired for misconduct, were announced in 1993.

While the consequences of labour-market policy restructuring were felt more strongly with the Liberals' reforms of the mid-1990s, the direction of change was clearly laid out under the Conservatives; rather than lessening inequalities, the measures introduced increased the polarization between those with access to good jobs *and* state- provided income-security benefits and those with access to neither. Given women's domestic responsibilities, work histories, and job locations, they tended to be in the latter categories. The consequence of the Conservatives' UI changes, combined with other forms of labour-market restructuring, was a dramatic drop in the proportion of unemployed people receiving UI income security. In 1989, prior to the changes, the ratio of UI regular beneficiaries to unemployed was 85 per cent for men and 82 per cent for women. By 1993, this had dropped to 67 per cent for men and 63 per cent for women.[58] This new labour-market strategy, then, resulted in an economy where it became more difficult for people to leave low paying, dead-end, stressful, or exploitative work situations, with those in non-unionized workplaces (the situation of many women) being particularly at risk. The move to increased international competition and globalization joined with the new labour-market strategy to help form a low-wage industrial environment – one where women played a particular, marginalized role and which promoted the notion that unemployment is the result of individual choices and actions.

### *Family and Child Benefits*

The Conservative government also continued apace with extensive reforms in the area of child and family benefits, as much more definitive steps were taken towards the goals of ending universality, targeting those most in need, and reducing expenditures. In terms of childcare, the 1989 budget, in keeping with the strategy announced in 1987, allocated $2.3 billion over seven years to increased tax assistance for families, as well as $100 million to support "special initiatives to improve child care services." However, the government also announced that, "because of the fiscal situation," it would no longer proceed with the creation of the 200,000 additional childcare spaces that had been promised in 1987.[59] In addition, the budget further reduced the value of family allowances, as well OAS, by introducing tax "claw-backs" (high-income earners were to repay benefits at a rate of 15 per cent of individual net income exceeding $50,000).[60] In 1991 the government announced a further review of policies in relation to the family. Finally, the 1992 budget announced a number of child-related measures. The family allowance program was eliminated entirely. The Child Care Expense Deduction was increased to $5,000 per child. A new Child Tax Benefit, targeted towards lower- and middle-income families, was introduced to replace both the former family allowance and the Child Tax Credit program.[61] In addition, in 1992 the "Brighter Futures Program" and the "Child Development Initiative" were announced, each focused on developing initiatives for children at risk.

With these changes, the Tories fundamentally reoriented the nature of benefits to children and families. A goal that had been on the agenda for more than a decade – establishing a national childcare strategy and substantially increasing the number of childcare spaces – was effectively eliminated. The changes entailed a shift away from a universal program (family allowance) to one targeted to low-income families with parents in the labour force (child tax benefits). It was based on *family* income rather than *individual* entitlement.[62] Also, as women commentators pointed out, in this period there was a movement away from the framing of policy in terms of women's equality and entitlement towards an approach that emphasized "child poverty" and "child development" – a movement that, as Wendy McKeen has argued, contributed to "writing women out of the poverty problem" and further reduced the opportunities for feminists to make claims on behalf of women.[63]

### *Women in the Political Arena: Constitutional Debates and Women's Political Voice*

A further issue of concern to women in the Mulroney era was the question of political representation and political voice. Two aspects of this issue are examined here: women's participation in constitutional discussions, and the changing role, more generally, of women's groups in the political process.

When the 1987 Meech Lake constitutional proposals were put forward, women's organizations had just begun to go beyond traditional "women's issues" to examine the implications of a broad range of policies for women. In this climate, the women's movement focused its attention on three features of the proposed constitutional amendments. First, it was feared that the decentralization implied in the proposed accord would have implications for economic and social policy, making it impossible, for example, to implement a new national social program in areas such as daycare. Secondly, feminists in English Canada (although not in Quebec) were concerned about whether the entrenchment of "special status" for Quebec would jeopardize the equality rights that had been won. Finally, objections were raised to the closed-door, elite-driven process through which the accord had been reached and which effectively excluded the voice of women and the disadvantaged.[64]

These concerns were raised anew with the complex set of proposals that were brought forward in the fall of 1991 and eventually became the Charlottetown Accord. This second set of constitutional proposals addressed a wider range of issues, including not only the place of Quebec in Confederation but also Aboriginal self-determination, Senate reform, shared-cost programs, and the economic union. Alexandra Dobrowolski argues that feminist activism had an impact on the constitutional-reform process in that the new "Canada Round" contained far more extensive public hearings than had occurred in the Meech Lake negotiations.[65] NAC, for example, was successful in insisting on strong representation of women at the five constitutional congresses organized by the federal government prior to the negotiation of the final proposals. Significantly, however, women's groups were excluded from the most important forum in which the final proposals were hammered out.[66]

NAC became a key player in the constitutional debate, urging a "no" vote in the referendum on the Charlettetown Accord held in October

1992. In general, constitutional issues were seen as issues of concern to women because of their implications not only for political representation but also for equality rights and for the maintenance of social-welfare programs. NAC feared that the clause giving provinces the right to opt out of new shared-cost programs would decentralize power and make the implementation of equitable national standards difficult. It was thought that the "Canada Clause" listing some seven items constituting "fundamental Canadian values" would set up a hierarchy of rights where equality rights ranked lower than some others. Drawing on the position developed by the Native Women's Association of Canada (NWAC), NAC noted the lack of guarantees for Aboriginal women. Essentially, NAC developed a "three nations" position incorporating a kind of asymmetrical federalism which recognized Quebec's right to have "different powers" from those of the other provinces as well as the Aboriginal right to self-government.[67] It argued that Senate reform should include a provision for the representation of women. This view allowed for special status for both Quebec and the First Nations and for a strong federal government with the power to implement national social programs across the entire country.

On the one hand, then, the extent of women's involvement in the political arena, including both the range of issues and the forums in which they participated, appeared to have expanded. On the other hand, despite (or perhaps because of) women's increased visibility on a variety of national political and economic issues, one of the most significant developments of the Mulroney era was an effort to limit the effectiveness of women's organizations.[68] Key in this regard were the funding cuts to women's organizations in 1989 and 1990. According to Bashevkin, in the mid-1980s NAC relied on the federal government for about two-thirds of its annual budget, but that funding was reduced by about half in this period.[69] Certainly, the reduction in state funding had a major impact on a range of women's centres and organizations. At the same time, a group of women opposed to feminism, Realistic Equal Active for Life (REAL WOMEN), received state funding.[70] In 1989 Conservatives also refused to meet with representatives of NAC at the annual lobby on Parliament Hill. Thus, there was not only a reduction in state funding but a shift in support away from equality-seeking groups towards those committed to traditional family values.[71]

While there was a strong feeling that women's groups were losing funding as a result of their vocal opposition to the Mulroney government,[72] a more complex series of changes was also altering the nature of interest-group representation and advocacy. From the mid-1980s, the Department of Finance had assumed an increased role in the making of social policy. The restructuring of social-security programs through technical changes, often to tax programs and announced as part of the federal budget, that came to be referred to as "social policy by stealth"[73] had an impact on women's ability to influence the policy agenda. Criticisms were made regarding the difficulty of understanding the changes that were taking place, the lack of transparency and accountability, and the shift away from existing processes through which policy was formulated – a shift that involved a reduced role for interest groups, including women's groups.[74] Though the period was characterized by an increased presence of interest groups at the level of hearings and formal consultations, they appeared to have little influence over the key decisions that were made.[75] As Jenson and Phillips suggest, fundamental changes were occurring in many aspects of political representation and accountability, and these changes contributed to a broad restructuring of citizens' relationship with the state. The increased emphasis on the individual and individual responsibility for "life's hardships" was also reflected in the institutions of representation, where intermediary organizations, representing collective interests, were no longer to be actively supported by the state and where a "marketization" of representation was occurring.[76]

*Rights, Equality, and the Constitution*

While the Conservative government was emphasizing market forces and narrowing the scope of state activity in ways that called into question the very notion of systemic discrimination, the courts were increasingly broadening the concept of equality and accepting substantive-equality arguments. The Abella Commission had taken important first steps in this respect, emphasizing "equality of results" and arguing that "sometimes equality means treating people the same, despite their differences, and sometimes it means treating them as equals by accommodating their differences." The Boyer committee, established by the Conservatives to review the legislative changes necessary with the 1985 coming into force of the Charter of Right's equality provisions, adopted what it described as a "broad and generous" approach to equality. It too, for example, incorporated the notion that providing greater equality for women entailed accommodating their differences with respect to childbearing and childrearing responsibilities.[77]

By the Mulroney government's second term in power, the judicial system had become an increasingly important institution with respect to women's equality issues as the Charter of Rights necessitated a review of existing legislation and opened up the possibility of challenges to legislation on equity grounds. Thus, for example, in 1985 changes were introduced to remove the discriminatory provisions of the Indian Act, which had resulted in many native women losing their legal status under the act.[78] In January 1988 the Supreme Court struck down existing restrictions with respect to abortion, arguing that the abortion provisions, found in section

251 of the Criminal Code, violated women's rights to "life, liberty and security of the person" because of lack of access and delays in the operation of the system.[79] Again, this was a landmark decision for those who had argued for a woman's right to choose. (While in November 1989 the Conservative government had attempted to introduce a new abortion law, both the Conservative caucus and Parliament itself were deeply divided over the issue and the bill died with a tied vote in Senate.[80]) A Charter of Rights challenge was also key in the area of parental benefits. In June 1988 the court accepted the argument that the denial of benefits to a father, Shalom Schachter, who wished to share the fifteen-week "maternity" benefits available to his wife, contravened the charter, noting that the roots of this discrimination were in the sexual stereotyping of the roles of father and mother. In response to this ruling, the Conservative government instituted a ten-week parental-leave benefit, to be made available to either the mother or the father, in addition to the fifteen weeks already available to the mother. Key Supreme Court decisions in 1989 (*Andrews* and *Turpin*) reinforced a contextual approach to equality and marked a turn away from a formal model of equality in which "likes are treated alike" and "unlikes are treated unalike" to an approach that included an examination of the social context.[81]

## CONCLUSION

The Mulroney era left a significant mark with respect to women's issues in Canada. In this period, some advances were certainly made with respect to gender equity. Employment-equity legislation was implemented, parental-leave provisions were put in place, and much in the way of discriminatory clauses within legislation was removed. These changes, however, largely reflected the coming into effect of the Charter of Right's equality provisions, as well as the strength of the forces in the late 1970s and early 1980s pushing for equality measures, the necessity to deal with items that were already on the agenda when the Conservatives came to power, and Mulroney's own brokerage, consensus-building style that, at least in the first term, compelled him to address some of the equity issues that were then being discussed.

The overriding legacy of this period, however, was the implementation of sweeping ideological, economic, and social-policy changes based on a paradigm emphasizing free-market forces, reduced government intervention, and a dramatic decrease in state expenditures. The tension between addressing equity concerns (often through state intervention) and an overall economic agenda focused on reducing state involvement was clearly reconciled in favour of the latter. As the Mulroney government entered its second term, equity concerns occupied less and less space, women's groups became marginalized, and the discourse on equity slowly faded from view. Indeed, one of the most important implications for women, as for all disadvantaged groups, was how the emphasis on market forces and individual responsibility undermined the very notion of systemic discrimination or structural inequalities. This was a major reversal of the arguments that women and others had been making over the previous twenty-five years, and its significance for equity goals cannot be underestimated. In addition, the funding cuts to women's groups and women's centres, the labelling of advocacy groups as "special interests," and the increased support for groups promoting more traditional notions of family all served to marginalize even further the voice of women in the national political arena.

The emphasis on reduced state involvement, deficit reduction, and free-market forces not only had an impact at an ideological level but also came to shape women's lives in wide-ranging ways in both the home and the labour force. It laid the groundwork for restructuring the relationship between public and private, between the state and market, and between state and family .While these changes may have opened up opportunities for some women, overall, they have meant a further step towards a gender order characterized by the growing insecurity of employment and income, where there is greater reliance on individuals and the family for personal well-being and where polarization and inequality remain a part of everyday life. It has presented new challenges for women's efforts to advance an equity agenda.

## NOTES

1 Judy Rebick, "Unity in Diversity: The Women's Movement in Canada," *Social Policy,* summer 1992, 54.

2 Sylvia Bashevkin, *Women on the Defensive: Living through Conservative Times* (Toronto: University of Toronto Press 1998).

3 On this tension, see also Annis May Timpson, *Driven Apart: Women's Employment Equality and Child Care in Canadian Public Policy* (Vancouver: University of British Columbia Press 2001); Judy Fudge, "From Segregation to Privatization: Equality, the Law and Women Public Servants, 1908–2001," in Brenda Cossman and Judy Fudge, eds., *Privatization, Law and the Challenge to Feminism* (Toronto: University of Toronto Press 2002).

4 Jane Jenson and Susan D. Phillips, "Regime Shift: New Citizenship Practices in Canada," *International Journal of Canadian Studies* 14 (fall 1996).

5 On the new gender order: R.W. Connell, *Gender and Power: Society, the Person and Sexual Politics* (Cambridge, U.K.: Polity Press 1987). In the Canadian context, see Judy Fudge and Brenda Cossman, "Introduction: Privatization, Law and the Challenge to Feminism," in Cossman and Fudge, eds., *Privatization, Law and the Challenge to Feminism*; Janine Brodie, "Canadian Women, Changing State Forms and Public Policy," in Janine Brodie, ed., *Women and Canadian Public Policy*

(Toronto: Harcourt Brace 1996); Ann Porter, *Gendered States: Women, Unemployment Insurance and the Political Economy of the Welfare State in Canada, 1945–1997* (Toronto: University of Toronto Press 2003).

6 Mulroney promised, for example, to negotiate with the provinces "to see that the transition houses and rape crisis centres receive the support that they need." See John Cruickshank et al., "Issue of Trust Left Hanging after Debate," *Globe and Mail,* 16 August 1984.

7 Lisa Young, *Feminists and Party Politics* (Vancouver: University of British Columbia Press 2000), 166.

8 Canada, Department of Finance, *A New Direction for Canada: An Agenda for Economic Renewal,* presented by the Honourable Michael H. Wilson, Minister of Finance, 8 November 1984.

9 Ibid, 44.

10 Ibid, 69–70.

11 John Cruickshank et al,, "Issue of Trust Left Hanging after Debate."

12 Jill Vickers, Pauline Rankin, and Christine Appelle, *Politics as if Women Mattered: A Political Analysis of the National Action Committee on the Status of Women* (Toronto: University of Toronto Press 1993), 223.

13 Canada, Royal Commission on the Economic Union and Development Prospects for Canada (Macdonald Commission), report (Ottawa 1985). For the views of popular-sector groups, see Daniel Drache and Duncan Cameron, *The Other Macdonald Report* (Toronto: James Lorimer 1985).

14 Jeffrey M. Ayres, *Defying Conventional Wisdom: Political Movements and Popular Contention against North American Free Trade* (Toronto: University of Toronto Press 1998), 40.

15 Ibid. See also Sylvia Bashevkin, "Free Trade and Canadian Feminism: The Case of the National Action Committee on the Status of Women," *Canadian Public Policy,* 15(4) (1989): 366

16 It subsequently commissioned three background papers assessing the possible impact of free trade for women.

17 Ayres, *Defying Conventional Wisdom,* 42–3.

18 Martha MacDonald, "Economic Restructuring and Gender in Canada: Feminist Policy Initiatives," *World Development,* 23(11): 2008. See also Sylvia Bashevkin, "Free Trade and Canadian Feminism."

19 National Action Committee on the Status of Women, "The Persistence of Inequality," in Drache and Cameron, eds., *The Other Macdonald Report.* See also Cohen, "The Macdonald Commission Report," National Action Committee on the Status of Women, 1985, 7.

20 Cohen, "The Macdonald Commission Report," 9.

21 NAC, "The Persistence of Inequality"; Cohen, "The Macdonald Commission Report"; Margot Trevelyn, "Women's Equality," in CUPE*: The Facts: Rebutting the Macdonald Report,* 8(2) (1986).

22 Leah F. Vosko, *Temporary Work: The Gendered Rise of a Precarious Employment Relationship* (Toronto: University of Toronto Press 2000).

23 Canada, *Report of the Commission of Inquiry on Unemployment Insurance* (Forget Commission) (Ottawa: Ministry of Supply and Services Canada 1986).
24 NAC, "The Problem is Jobs ... Not Unemployment Insurance," brief to the Commission of Inquiry on Unemployment Insurance, January 1986; CACSW, "Brief Presented to the Commission of Inquiry on Unemployment Insurance," prepared by Monica Townson (Ottawa: January 1986).
25 Dennis Guest, *The Emergence of Social Security in Canada*, 3rd ed. (Vancouver: University of British Columbia Press 1997); Allan Moscovitch Prince, "'Slowing the Steamroller': The Federal Conservatives, the Social Sector and Child Benefits Reform," in Katherine A. Graham, ed., *How Ottawa Spends, 1990–91* (Ottawa: Carleton University Press 1990).
26 Guest, *The Emergence of Social Security in Canada*, 221.
27 McKeen notes that 50,000 people responded to NAC's call to write and send petitions to the government: Wendy McKeen, *Money in Their Own Name: The Feminist Voice in the Poverty Debate in Canada, 1970–1995* (Toronto: University of Toronto Press 2004), 77.
28 Ibid., chapter 5.
29 Canada, Parliament, House of Commons, *Debates*, 19 December 1988, 298.
30 The strategy also called for the creation of a research and special-projects fund (the Child Care Initiatives Fund).
31 Timpson, *Driven Apart*, chapter 7, provides an excellent discussion of the Mulroney government's response to the Royal Commission on Equality in Employment. Timpson also notes Employment and Immigration Minister Flora Macdonald's commitment to the issue.
32 Quoted in ibid., 133.
33 Sandra Burt, "The Changing Patterns of Public Policy," in S. Burt, L. Code, and L. Dorney, eds., *Changing Patterns: Women in Canada*, 2nd ed. (Toronto: McClelland and Stewart 1993), 226.
34 Trevelyn, "Women's Equality."
35 Yasmeen Abu-Laban and Christina Gabriel, *Selling Diversity: Immigration, Multiculturalism, Employment Equity and Globalization* (Peterborough, Ont.: Broadview Press 2002), 138–40; Timpson, *Driven Apart*, 131–2.
36 Canada, Parliament, House of Commons, Speech from the Throne, *Debates*, 3 April 1989, 1–5.
37 Ibid., 5. In 1992 five national women's groups – NAC, the Disabled Women's Network (DAWN), the Congress of Black Women, the Canadian Association of Sexual Assault Centres, and the National Organization of Immigrant and Visible Minority Women – withdrew their support for the panel. Andrea Levan, "Violence against Women," in Brodie, ed., *Women and Canadian Public Policy*, 341.
38 Canada, Department of Finance, "The Budget Speech," the Honourable Michael H. Wilson, Minister of Finance, 27 April 1989.
39 Canada, Department of Finance, *The Budget*, the Honourable Michael H. Wilson, Minister of Finance, 20 February 1990, 3; Canada, Department of Finance, *The Budget*, the Honourable Michael H. Wilson, Minister of Finance, 1991; Minister

of Finance Don Mazankowski, Canada, Parliament, House of Commons, *Debates*, 25 February 1992.

40 Canada, Department of Finance, *The Budget*, 1990, 4.

41 Canada, Department of Finance, *The Budget*, 1991.

42 Minister of Finance Don Mazankowski, House of Commons, *Debates*, 25 February 1992, 7602.

43 Canada, Department of Finance, *The Budget*, 1991, 8.

44 Susan D. Phillips, "How Ottawa Blends: Shifting Government Relationships with Interest Groups," in Frances Abele, ed., *How Ottawa Spends, 1991–92* (Ottawa: Carleton University Press 1991), 201; Leslie Pal, *Interests of State: The Politics of Language, Multiculturalism, and Feminism in Canada* (Montreal and Kingston: McGill-Queen's University Press 1993); Bashevkin, *Women on the Defensive*, 124; Jenson and Phillips, "Regime Shift: New Citizenship Practices in Canada."

45 Bashevkin, *Women on the Defensive*, 126. The Court Challenges program was re-established by the Liberal government in 1994 and eliminated again by Stephen Harper's Conservative government in September 2006.

46 *Action Now. Newsletter from the National Action Committee on the Status of Women*, 2(4) (1992).

47 Minister of Finance Don Mazankowski, House of Commons, *Debates*, 25 February 1992, 7595.

48 Ibid., 7595.

49 Ayres, *Defying Conventional Wisdom*, 119.

50 See, for example, NAC, "Why the Goods and Services Tax Will be Harmful to Women: A Brief to the House of Commons Standing Committee on Finance" (1989); NAC, "Women Want Fair Taxes: Alternatives to the GST" (1990); NAC, "Federal Budget Consultation with Minister of Finance, Michael Wilson," prepared by Marjorie Cohen (1990); NAC, "Draft Notes for Presentation to the Standing Committee on Finance on Bills C-20 and C-32 (budget) (1991).

51 Marjorie Cohen, "What's Wrong with Free Trade with Mexico," *Feminist Action*, 5(3) (1991).

52 This group was known as the First Trinational Working Women's Conference on Free Trade and Continental Integration. Christina Gabriel and Laura Macdonald, "NAFTA and Economic Restructuring: Some Gender and Race Implications," in Isabella Bakker, ed., *Rethinking Restructuring: Gender and Change in Canada* (Toronto: University of Toronto Press 1996), 165.

53 Gabriel and Macdonald, "NAFTA and Economic Restructuring."

54 Marjorie Griffin Cohen, "New International Trade Agreements: Their Reactionary Role in Creating Markets and Retarding Social Welfare," in Isabella Bakker, ed., *Rethinking Restructuring*.

55 Timpson, *Driven Apart*, 166; Fudge, "From Segregation to Privatization," 108–9.

56 Canada, Parliament, House of Commons, *Debates*, 25 February 1992.

57 "Success in the Works": Canada, Parliament, House of Commons, *Debates*, 6 June 1989, 2674; ibid., 11 April 1989, 317. I have discussed the implications of UI changes for women more extensively in Ann Porter, *Gendered States*.

58 Porter, *Gendered States*, 208.

59 Canada, Department of Finance, "The Budget Speech," 27 April 1989; fiscal plan, 24.

60 Ibid., 10.

61 Timpson, *Driven Apart*, 168–9; Katherine Teghtsoonian, "Who Pays for Caring for Children? Public Policy and the Devaluation of Women's Work," in Susan B. Boyd, ed., *Challenging the Public/Private Divide: Feminism, Law and Public Policy* (Toronto: University of Toronto Press 1997); Guest, *The Emergence of Social Security in Canada*; McKeen, *Money in Their Own Name*.

62 McKeen, *Money in Their Own Name*.

63 Ibid., 97, 102.

64 Bashevkin, *Women on the Defensive*,125.

65 Alexandra Dobrowolsky, *The Politics of Pragmatism: Women, Representation and Constitutionalism in Canada* (Don Mills, Ont.: Oxford University Press 2000), 119.

66 Rebick, "Unity in Diversity"; Dobrowolsky, *The Politics of Pragmatism*.

67 Rebick, "Unity in Diversity"; Vickers et al., *Politics as if Women Mattered*, 277.

68 Bashevkin, *Women on the Defensive*, 92, 124.

69 Ibid, 124.

70 Pal, *Interests of State*, 113–17; Burt, "The Changing Patterns of Public Policy," 226.

71 On REAL's persistent lobbying for funds, see Pal, *Interests of State*, 140–7.

72 Bashevkin, *Women on the Defensive*.

73 Michael J. Prince, "From Health and Welfare to Stealth and Farewell: Federal Social Policy, 1980–2000,"in Leslie A. Pal, *How Ottawa Spends 1999–2000* (Don Mills, Ont.: Oxford University Press 1999).

74 McKeen, *Money in Their Own Name*.

75 Keith Banting, "Social Policy," in Leslie Pal and Brian Tomlin, eds., *Border Crossings: The Internationalization of Canadian Public Policy* (Don Mills, Ont.: Oxford University Press 1996).

76 Jenson and Phillips, "Regime Shift: New Citizenship Practices in Canada," 120.

77 Canada, *Equality for All: Report of the Parliamentary Committee on Equality Rights* (Boyer committee) (Ottawa, 1985), 5.

78 Sally Weaver, "First Nations Women and Government Policy, 1970–92: Discrimination and Conflict,"in Burt, Code, and Dorney, eds., *Changing Patterns*, 115–24.

79 Jane Jenson, "Competing Representations: The Politics of Abortion in Canada," in Caroline Andrew and Sandra Rodgers, eds., *Women and the Canadian State* (Montreal and Kingston: McGill-Queen's University Press 1997); Heather MacIvor, *Women and Politics in Canada* (Peterborough, Ont.: Broadview Press 1996), 180.

80 MacIvor, *Women and Politics in Canada*, 364–5.

81 Diana Majury, "Women's (In)Equality before and after the *Charter*," in Radha Jhappan, ed., *Women's Legal Strategies in Canada* (Toronto: University of Toronto Press 2002).

# 9

# Brian Mulroney and Intergovernmental Relations: The Limits of Collaborative Federalism[1]

P.E. BRYDEN

When Brian Mulroney took office in 1984, he did so with the professed goal of achieving "national reconciliation" between the provinces and Ottawa. His concerns about the recent tenor of federal-provincial relations were well founded, since, across the country, polling data indicated "a strong desire to reduce the wrangling."[2] His arrival at 24 Sussex Drive thus heralded what many hoped was the beginning of a period of fruitful cooperation and much-needed healing. When he left office in 1993, however, it seemed that few of the differences had been reconciled; in fact, even more points of conflict had emerged. Mulroney's goal of consensus building and cooperation had given way to "a new culture of confrontation and tribalism,"[3] and an angry public responded by returning only two federal Conservatives to the House of Commons in the federal election of 25 October 1993. Certainly, Mulroney fell short of achieving his goals, however overly optimistic they may have been. But was he unsuccessful in securing the degree of intergovernmental harmony that he sought because of the policies he pursued or because of structural impediments deeply rooted in the Canadian political system? Prime ministers both before Mulroney and after have all struggled in varying degrees to secure a working federal system; the failure of one so committed to the goal, and one so well placed to achieve it, may suggest that securing intergovernmental harmony in any kind of meaningful way is essentially impossible in Canada.

From the outset, Brian Mulroney was clear on how he would approach federal-provincial relations, and what he expected to achieve in that arena. In many significant ways, the approach undertaken during Pierre Trudeau's final term in office dictated what the Conservative strategy would *not* be. Increasingly prepared to act unilaterally, and "proclaiming a new concern with building closer and more direct ties with Canadian citizens" which circumvented interaction with provincial governments,[4] the Trudeau

Brian Peckford, premier of Newfoundland and Labrador, and Prime Minister Mulroney signed a Statement of Principles on 18 July 1988 with four oil companies for the development of the offshore Hibernia oilfield, ending a decade-long feud between the province and Ottawa. Photographer Bill McCarthy. Library and Archives Canada 88-c-05201-9A, negative number e007140467.

strategy was characterized by confrontation. In contrast, Mulroney argued on the hustings that "the Canadian federation is not a test of strength between different governments."[5] The first step towards a new philosophy of federal-provincial relations was to establish an environment of cooperation, which Mulroney's background as a labour negotiator put him in a good position to achieve. Ultimately, however, he recognized that the building of a national consensus had to "be reflected in the fundamental law of our land, for it is obvious that constitutional agreement is incomplete so long as Quebec is not part of an accord."[6] Federal-provincial cooperation would be the vehicle through which constitutional reform was to be secured, and that constitutional change would then entrench, as much as possible, the basis of intergovernmental bonhomie. Mulroney's vision of federal-provincial relations was of a perfect, if closed, universe.

It all seemed so possible in the first year of Mulroney's administration. The new prime minister's first meetings with his provincial counterparts were positive, and, with seemingly little effort, long-standing complaints from the regions were addressed. First, the Atlantic Accord between Ottawa and Newfoundland, described as the "apogee of Mulroney's cooperative federalism,"[7] secured the province's right to revenue from offshore oil reserves and had a "jubilant" Premier Brian Peckford claiming that Newfoundlanders had never come as "close to achieving economic and social equality" as they did with this agreement.[8] The following month saw the beginning of the end of the much-reviled National Energy Program, as the Mulroney government entered into the Western Accord with British Columbia, Alberta, and Saskatchewan. In eliminating a series of federal taxes in the oil and gas field, the agreement confirmed the principle, advanced by the oil producers, that taxes should be levied on profit rather than revenue and thus marked another important rejection of Trudeau's efforts to "restructure the basic relationships of power … between Ottawa and the provinces."[9] The general sense of harmony and accommodation continued at full first ministers' conferences. Mulroney used his first short lunch meeting with all the premiers in November 1984 "to play his overture for a new era of federal-provincial relations," following it up with a slightly longer meeting on the economy in February.[10] Although brief and carefully planned to avoid potentially divisive issues, the Regina meeting was nothing less than "astonishing. Ears accustomed to acrimonious exchanges suddenly heard protestations of good faith and mutual praise." Even Quebec's Premier René Lévesque claimed that there was "reason for hope" on the intergovernmental front.[11]

Honeymoons are an expected part of settling into the chore of government; that Mulroney did not immediately experience the wrath of any one or several provinces should come as no surprise. There seemed to be a more fundamental realignment of the intergovernmental relationship, however, than would be implied simply by early goodwill on the part of first ministers still assessing the intentions of a new prime minister. In committing his government to collaborative federalism, Mulroney promised that he "would be guided by the principle of respect for provincial authority." That cooperative model would function "at the highest level, namely with 11 leaders themselves working together in an appropriate institutional framework advising as to the options envisaged and the directions to take."[12] Mulroney was determined, therefore, to harness the palpable spirit of cooperation among the premiers in the early days of his administration towards the achievement of clearly articulated policy goals.

The intergovernmental reconciliation that Mulroney sought would underscore two key sets of policy initiatives. First, it would provide the environment for "economic consensus building [whereby] government would act as a guide, mediator and catalyst" for largely private-sector economic growth.[13] Intergovernmental cooperation would not be used to solve the economic problems confronting Canada so much as it would provide the backdrop that would make it possible for private enterprise to flourish. Where real multilateral cooperation would be necessary was on the second front of the reconciliation strategy, the amendment to the constitution necessary to secure Quebec's signature on the document. Although the new spirit of collaboration embraced both the economy and the constitution, it was not clear until into the second year of Mulroney's mandate how provincial participation in the two policy areas was expected to differ.

The initial first ministers' conference on the economy, held in Regina, had been a great success, "firmly embedding the perception that this government was willing to listen to the provinces."[14] Yet at least one observer noted that the actual outcomes of the conference were modest: while "the media sang the hymns of praise for intergovernmental peace and a new era of co-operation [it is] co-operation to do what? That remains a mystery."[15] The real test of how the two levels of government would interact with Mulroney in power took shape around an issue that was raised only quietly at the Regina conference. Following "encouragement" from the premiers, Mulroney told the press following the conference that he would "take the [free trade] process ahead ... with President [Ronald] Reagan, but with prudence."[16] Although there were only whispers of regional disagreement over pursuing a free-trade deal with the United States audible in Regina, the western provinces would obviously have a different position on the issue than that of Ontario. Its leading provincial proponent, Alberta's Peter Lougheed, managed an economy based largely on the export of raw or semi-processed materials; in contrast, Ontario's more sceptical Frank Miller had a manufacturing economy to protect against the enormous processing capabilities of the United States.[17] Mulroney's commitment to governing through collaboration, combined with clear regional differences on what was destined to become the most important economic initiative of his administration, produced a volatile and ultimately untenable combination.

Long an opponent of Mulroney's version of accommodation politics, which he regarded as benefiting the west over Ontario, new Ontario Liberal Premier David Peterson launched the first attack on free trade.[18] According to a provincial study, "as many as 281,000 manufacturing jobs in Ontario ... could be endangered by a free trade agreement with the United States."[19] On the eve of a first ministers' conference in Halifax to discuss, among other things, the Canadian approach to the upcoming bilateral trade negotiation, Peterson used the study's data to press for a greater provincial role around the bargaining table. He told reporters that "he was concerned that there has not been enough study or national consensus on some of the thornier by-products of any move to lower trade barriers," and then later argued that provincial premiers "must be intensely involved in the decisions that affect the people we represent – not just told about those decisions after they are made."[20] Peterson was thus the first to question openly Mulroney's commitment to consultation within the context of economic renewal, one of the two key areas in which the prime minister had anticipated harvesting the fruits of "reconciliation." Firing his salvos at a conference that heard fairly vociferous provincial complaints about federal cuts in transfer payments, Peterson might be expected to garner support from his colleagues for his stance on free trade.[21]

Despite the accusations that were bandied about at the first ministers' conference, the participants were able to reach an agreement of sorts on how to proceed on the issue of free trade. Mulroney agreed to "the principle of full provincial participation" in the trade talks, which Peterson interpreted to mean that "the negotiating team will take instructions from the first ministers."[22] But his was not the only interpretation of the contentious "principle" included in the final communiqué, and the prime minister himself remained silent on what was meant. Clearly, however, the Mulroney strategy should not have been underestimated, since the outcome of the conference seemed to be precisely what the federal government representatives had been hoping for: Ottawa had shown "that it was capable of acting resolutely and not backing down in the face of opposition," as it was forced to do on the transfer-payment issue, and it was able to "emphasize the fact that it was offering leadership while the provinces were only concerned with defending their narrow interests."[23] Consultation on the economy, Mulroney was in the process of making clear, would not extend to equal partnerships, nor would it involve a wholesale emptying of the federal treasury.

The intergovernmental debate over free trade, and what was rapidly becoming the deal's bilateral negotiation, established the Mulroney government's approach to economic issues. Provincial premiers would not be participants in international trade talks, but they would be kept informed about the progress of those negotiations. A Continuing Committee on Trade Negotiations (CCTN) was established, composed of senior provincial and territorial finance officials who would meet monthly with Canada's chief trade negotiator, Simon Reisman. This, combined with the regular meetings between Mulroney and his provincial counterparts, provided the opportunity for provincial input on the content and strategies of the free-trade deal. By the time an agreement was finally hammered out, there had been eighteen meetings between Reisman and the CCTN, and six first ministers' meetings dealing with the issue.[24] In addition, there had been more informal occasions when the premiers had been given access to information on the progress of the talks.[25] To be sure, it was a far cry from the intergovernmental collaboration that many had anticipated when Mulroney first took office, and the ousting of several provincial Conservative regimes after 1984 suggested "how dramatically the federal-provincial climate has changed."[26] But, if the provincial premiers were not the full participants in the economic dialogue that some had expected, there was still clearly room for consultation, even if it did often seem after the fact.

The initial progress of the free-trade negotiations, as well as the events of the first two years of Mulroney's mandate, served to crystallize two aspects of his approach to intergovernmental financial relations. Guided by a commitment to the ideal that it was the federal government's responsibility to achieve national economic renewal, Mulroney approached his relationship with the provincial premiers as the first among equals, consulting when possible and acting unilaterally when necessary. The early western and Atlantic accords, for example, were federal offers, made in the wake of failed negotiations under the former prime ministers but not as a result of consultation between Mulroney and the relevant provincial premiers. That each accord was received so enthusiastically shrouded the fact that they were both, essentially, unilateral federal decisions. The longer the Mulroney government remained in office, the more of these sorts of economic decisions there would be, and the greater effect they would have on other areas of intergovernmental negotiation.

The decision to establish the Atlantic Canada Opportunities Agency (ACOA) was characteristic of the Mulroney approach to financial matters in that there were elements of consultation combined with a fairly strong unilateralism. Announced in the 1986 throne speech as a way of alleviating the chronic underdevelopment of the Atlantic provinces, any provincial input would be received after the agency was established. Although Mulroney claimed that the development strategy would not be "made-in-Ottawa" like similar plans implemented by his predecessors, ACOA "was clearly aimed at shoring up Conservative votes in a region where support for the party had eroded badly."[27] Moreover, although decisions over how the more than $1 billion was to be distributed in the region rested with its Moncton-based board of directors, the federal minister responsible for ACOA "may exercise powers and perform duties and functions that affect economic opportunity and development in Atlantic Canada."[28] Still, once the agency was in place, Prince Edward Island Premier Joe Ghiz was hopeful that "it will be a federal agency with significant provincial input. The agency will operate in Atlantic Canada, by Atlantic Canadians and for Atlantic Canadians."[29] While it did little to challenge what one commentator has called the "feudal federalism" in operation in Atlantic Canada, ACOA at least promised to provide a degree of coordination at the national level that had not previously existed.[30]

In intergovernmental negotiations over the equalization program, Mulroney's government also made some effort in the direction of consultation, but the final decisions, when it came to spending money out of the federal treasury, came from Ottawa. As probably the single most important fiscal issue concerning both levels of government, the equalization program had been redistributing tax dollars from the "have" provinces to the "have-nots" since 1957. It was renegotiated every five years. Each debate was characterized by calls for a reconsideration of the equalization formula, and 1986 was no different. Federal Finance Minister Michael Wilson was sent "back to the drawing board" after his provincial counterparts rejected his first offer, arguing that the $175 million that was offered to enhance the program was insufficient to meet the needs of the six poorest provinces.[31] Upon return to the drawing board, however, the federal government found even less money than it had anticipated: Mulroney told premiers in November that "for the foreseeable future, the federal Government's room to maneuver will be seriously limited – a direct result of interest payments on the national debt." By December, Wilson had come to the conclusion that the cupboard was virtually empty, and he "stunned his provincial counterparts ... when he withdrew half of a $175 million payment the poorer provinces thought they would be getting [the] next year."[32] Once again, the federal government demonstrated that intergovernmental consultation could go only so far; on economic issues, Ottawa would have the final say.

As Mulroney moved into his second mandate, the depth of the financial woes of the federal government became even clearer, and the effects of economic decisions began to be felt in other important areas of intergovernmental contact. In the second Mulroney government, one commentator noted, "incremental fiscal transfer changes made for budgetary reasons have driven social policy outcomes, and exacerbated any efforts to overhaul social programs that have been in place for decades."[33] Governments at both levels began to recognize the seriousness of their deficit problems towards the end of the 1980s, but all were loath to attack the problem until it worsened in the following decade.[34] The federal government, at least, was able to "off-load" some of its financial commitments onto the provinces as a way of addressing its deficit. Not surprisingly, the decisions to limit federal transfers to the provinces through the Canada Assistance Plan (CAP), Medicare, post-secondary education, and other social services were not ones likely to elicit provincial enthusiasm; they were seen as "decisions made unilaterally by the federal government [which will] ... change the nature of the federation."[35]

In an effort to shore up its finances, the Mulroney government made a number of cuts to existing transfers to the provinces. Of all the reductions, the most "destructive to the integrity of federal-provincial fiscal relations" was "the cap on CAP."[36] Ottawa's unilateral decision to limit its contribution to the Canada Assistance Plan to a 5 per cent annual increase for the "have" provinces of British Columbia, Alberta, and Ontario had more broad-reaching implications than some of Mulroney's other unilateral fiscal decisions. By targeting Ontario's growing welfare lists, at a cost to the province of $400 million in 1990–91, the year the cap was introduced, and $1.2 billion and $1.7 billion in the two fiscal years following, the federal government risked – and earned – the ire of the single largest source of fiscal redistribution in the country.[37] Ontario's New Democratic Party (NDP) Premier Bob Rae made clear at the first ministers' meeting of March 1992 that, unless Ontario was restored the right to claim a full 50 per cent of its CAP costs from the federal government, the province's support of the equalization system would be compromised.[38] As Mulroney's second mandate began to wind down then, first ministers' meetings on the deteriorating economy were characterized by some combination of "provincial 'bitching'" that Mulroney warned he "would not tolerate" and the absence of any specific agreements to provide intergovernmental solutions.[39]

Federal-provincial cooperation on issues that had clear and immediate effects on the federal budget was less likely under Mulroney the more dire the deficit situation became. That this unilateralism had serious effects on the delivery of social services in the provinces served to drive home the significance of Ottawa's "dis-spending power" as much as its "spending power."[40] But, while the Mulroney government seemed to move away from its initial commitment to collaborative federalism on issues affecting the economy, as it was clear would happen when the two levels of government considered the question of how free-trade discussions with the United States would proceed, it did not diverge too far from what had become the norm in the intergovernmental relationship in the post-war years. While face-to-face meetings of first ministers had always been one of the ways in which intergovernmental finances had been worked out, it was not until the 1960s that they had become common. If one thing could be said to characterize these meetings, it was that they provided an opportunity for bickering: they were annual, ritualized, anticipated occasions for intergovernmental disagreement. However unseemly it appeared, agreements continued to be made and the system of federal-provincial fiscal relations continued to function in much the same way as it always had.

Mulroney's approach to the provinces when money was at stake seemed to recognize not only the primacy of the federal government but also the need for opportunities for disagreement. Both of these elements of the Mulroney approach were first made apparent during the negotiations over free trade: in the end, the federal representatives proceeded as the sole negotiators for Canada, but talks had not broken down nor were the provinces kept out of the loop because one province – Ontario – had been especially vocal in its criticism of the federal approach. Dissension was expected and was perhaps a welcome part of the process. In a country as diverse as Canada, disagreement can either be part of the process or can occur outside the formal process, but there is no chance of eliminating disagreement entirely. On questions of the economy, Mulroney's approach to intergovernmental relations seemed to recognize this need to disagree. In fact, after the staggering harmony of his first meeting with the premiers, there were numerous occasions for vitriol over issues as varied as military contracts, social policy, and softwood lumber.

Consensus had been the theme of Mulroney's first throne speech, in which he promised that, through national cooperation, great things, including economic renewal, could be achieved. But as his two mandates unfolded, it became increasingly clear that the economy could be managed without the benefit of cooperation. First free trade, then economizing on equalization payments, then limits on social spending had all been undertaken with declining levels of provincial support or even provincial consultation. While the success of Mulroney's economic management may be questioned, particularly when judged by his administrations' ability to control the deficit, it was certainly clear that he was able to make financial decisions without the degree of intergovernmental cooperation his early pronouncements had indicated was desirable. The high hopes of 1984 were replaced, remarkably quickly, with a fairly traditional approach to federal-provincial relations characterized by regular meetings, frequent acrimony and bickering, and considerable national control of the key economic levers.

Steamrolling ahead unilaterally on the constitution, however, was definitely not a possibility, as Pierre Trudeau had discovered in 1980.[41] Although achieving an agreement that would bring Quebec back into the constitutional family was secondary to Mulroney's goal of securing economic security, it required considerably more intergovernmental finesse and, ultimately, had a much greater effect on the future of federal-provincial relations in Canada than did negotiations with the provinces over finances. The key difference between the two types of intergovernmental negotiations was the degree of dissent that was possible while still achieving progress on the policy issue. Provincial opposition to various economic decisions did not preclude agreement or, in some cases, the federal government proceeding regardless; when the constitution was under discussion, however, there was no opportunity for disagreement and therefore not only did discussions have to proceed with extreme caution, but the ramifications for failure were much more serious.

Despite having been elected at least in part because he was seen to be able to address the "Quebec problem," Brian Mulroney moved slowly and carefully in the direction of constitutional renewal. René Lévesque's Parti Québecois government, wooed into a sense that all might be possible under the federal leadership of Brian Mulroney, issued a twenty-two-point list of conditions for Quebec's return to the constitutional table. It was an overpowering, and ultimately unmanageable, list.[42] The election of Liberal Robert Bourassa in early December 1985, however, created a more positive environment for achieving constitutional reform than had been the case with the Péquistes in power. With a federal government in place that "was prepared to accept at least some of the fundamental assumptions about the distinctive character of Quebec," the electoral victory of a federalist party in Quebec marked the achievement of the second of the two conditions necessary to begin serious constitutional renewal.[43] Ontario's Premier David Peterson signalled that big changes were possible with a return to the "federalism of the sixties," when the alliance between the two central provinces was at its strongest. Peterson predicted that the 1980s would see "a new era of harmony between Quebec and Ontario and with the federal government as well."[44] The partnership of the earlier generation had produced the beginning of mega-constitutional renewal with the opening of the Confederation of Tomorrow Conference; surely, a similar alliance between Ontario and Quebec could announce the beginning of the end of mega-constitutional politics by stimulating a final round of intergovernmental cooperation.[45] The prime minister quickly took the opportunity to underline the need to commence discussions on the constitution as soon as possible.[46]

The point of opening up the constitutional kettle of fish was to introduce amendments to the Constitution Act, 1982 that would address Quebec's concerns and make it possible for that province to sign onto the document. It was thus the "Quebec round," and the Quebec government was the first to make a tangible move in the direction of achieving constitutional reform. At an academic conference in Mont-Gabriel in May 1986, provincial intergovernmental affairs minister Gil Rémillard, architect of the Quebec Liberal Party's earlier blueprint on the constitution, *Mastering Our Future,* and a former adviser to Mulroney on the constitution, made public Quebec's five proposals for change and the minimum demand for Quebec's participation in the process. The tone was conciliatory, and the proposals both familiar and modest: Quebec's distinctiveness must be recognized, it required increased power over immigration and the appointment of Supreme Court justices, the federal spending power needed to be limited, and Quebec called for a constitutional veto over amendments that affected its interests. The conference participants, consisting mainly of academics and intergovernmental professionals, responded positively to the proposals. The "genie [was] out of the bottle."[47]

In some important ways, the federal strategy on the constitution and the Quebec strategy were remarkably similar. And, equally important, the federal strategy was in marked contrast to its approach in other areas of intergovernmental relations. Under the leadership of Senator Lowell Murray, who had a strong personal commitment to bringing Quebec back into the constitution, and secretary to the cabinet for federal-provincial relations Norman Spector, an informal federal strategy began to take shape. With the ultimate goal of securing unanimous provincial consent on Quebec's place in the federation – a hitherto impossible level of agreement – Murray and Spector sought to limit the agenda, delay formal negotiations until success was guaranteed, generalize Quebec's demands in order to maintain the principle of equality of the provinces, and ensure that Ottawa played the role of broker between competing provincial interests, and not of participant in the negotiating process, until the very end.[48] Of paramount importance was the need for unanimity, and Mulroney's government was prepared to go to great lengths to achieve it.

Quebec's strategy paralleled that of the federal government, and therefore perhaps increased its chances of success. Like Mulroney, Bourassa sought to limit the agenda, reducing the Parti Québécois demands from twenty-two to five. When other provinces made moves toward adding their own constitutional demands to the list, Mulroney quickly reminded them that "the only realistic way to proceed is first to bring Quebec back into the fold, and to undertake a more extensive revision of the Constitution at a later stage."[49] Like the federal government, Bourassa also sought to stall formal negotiations until informal discussions had cleared the way: his advance team of Jean-Claude Rivest, André Tremblay, and Diane Whilhemy had already travelled to each of the provincial capitals in June and July "selling Quebec's five conditions for signing the Constitution." This was followed by "some high-powered lobbying" on the part of the Quebec premier prior to a meeting with his provincial counterparts in Edmonton in August.[50] Also in keeping with the federal strategy, participants at the Mont-Gabriel conference had agreed to broaden the demand for a Quebec veto to all provinces, which essentially meant increasing the number of issues already included in the constitution that required the unanimous consent of the provinces to amend. Thus, Quebec would not be seen to be getting special favours.[51]

Early responses from the provinces were mixed. While everyone seemed to be in agreement that it was desirable to get Quebec's signature on the constitution, premiers across the country expressed reservations about all of Quebec's proposals except that dealing with Supreme Court appointments.[52]

But the cumulative effect of private meetings with Quebec officials and with Premier Bourassa served to lay the groundwork for the Edmonton Declaration. It stated: "The premiers unanimously agreed their top constitutional priority is to embark immediately upon a federal-provincial process, using Quebec's five proposals as a basis for discussion, to bring about Quebec's full and active participation in the Canadian federation. There was a consensus among the premiers that then they will pursue further constitutional discussion on matters raised by some provinces, which will include, amongst other items, Senate reform, fisheries, property rights, etc."[53] The stage was set.

Mulroney remained cautious. As difficult as it might be to achieve "national reconciliation" between Ottawa and ten provinces, the process of maintaining a functioning intergovernmental relationship was made all the more difficult the more policy areas there were under discussion simultaneously. Although Mulroney had made clear his commitment to amending the Constitution Act, 1982, its appearance on the table at the same time that free-trade negotiations were unfolding made for a difficult balancing act. Mulroney's inability to follow his first incredibly harmonious federal-provincial conference with more of the same meant that most intergovernmental issues would continue to be dealt with in a confrontational manner. In 1986 the constitution was still largely untarnished by argument – at least during Mulroney's tenure – and still held out the promise of achieving that elusive harmony. Yet, as it turned out, the result of the Herculean effort to secure the necessary unanimity on the constitutional amendments was that competing interests had to find new areas in which they could be balanced. In the early stages of multilateral intergovernmental negotiations, that meant that other policy areas were affected by the impending constitutional discussions; later, the party system itself provided an outlet for differences masked by the façade of federal-provincial harmony over the constitution.

In the months after Bourassa's team had made clear Quebec's constitutional agenda, Canadian free-trade negotiator Simon Reisman continued to try to crack the American refusal to deal in concrete proposals while simultaneously juggling the vociferous demands of the provinces to be included in some capacity. Normal trade discussions – outside the media circus surrounding Reisman's negotiations with his American counterpart Peter Murphy – took on new significance as provincial premiers flexed the muscles they seemed suddenly to have as a result of the anticipated constitutional talks.[54] On the question of softwood-lumber duties, a perennial point of conflict between Canadian and American producers, disagreement quickly broke out between various provinces and between the two levels of government. In response to a protectionist U.S. duty, Canada first sought to increase the domestic stumpage fees and then, when that strategy failed, Mulroney and Trade Minister Pat Carney attempted to broker a negotiated settlement. Pandering to American protectionism irritated Ontario's David Peterson, who argued that the issue should be adjudicated through the General Agreement on Tariffs and Trade (GATT); Bourassa and British Columbia's Premier Bill Vander Zalm, representing provinces considerably more affected by the American duties than Ontario, both supported any and all efforts on the part of the federal government to resolve the issue as quickly as possible. A deal was finally brokered, but Ontario increased its criticisms of the ongoing free-trade negotiations as a result.[55] Similarly, the federal government's controversial decision to award a CF-18 contract to Montreal rather than to Winnipeg served to increase Manitoba's Howard Pawley's criticism of any constitutional accord, and precipitated a growing sense in the west that other constitutional issues were more important than those Quebec had raised.[56] In the third year of his mandate, Mulroney was discovering the multiple balances that needed to be maintained in intergovernmental relations. With one area requiring unanimity, the federal-provincial cooperation he had so wanted to secure in all policy spheres ended up being sacrificed in the interests of governing.

But the constitution remained Mulroney's baby, much as it had been Trudeau's before; its amendment had become something of the Holy Grail of Canadian politics since the 1960s. Criticized for letting Quebec dictate the terms of constitutional renewal, and wary of being accused of favouring one provinces over the others, Mulroney offered a federal response to the Rémillard proposals, but he had become "guardedly pessimistic about the chances of a Quebec deal."[57] As the premiers gathered at Meech Lake on 30 April 1987 to commence formal discussions with Mulroney about the constitution, there was little that suggested the meeting would be successful. As little as two weeks earlier, the prime minister had publicly mused over "whether it would be better to close the books and wait for a more favourable moment"; and, on the eve of the conference, some officials put the chances of success at no better than 50–50.[58] And yet, miraculously, ten hours of negotiating and "nation-building" later, the first ministers emerged with a "historic pact." As Mulroney stated, "Today has been a good day for Canada. Today's discussions have been marked by generosity and flexibility and, above all, the political will to find agreement in the spirit of compromise that characterizes the Canadian people."[59]

The inconceivable, in seemed, had happened. Under the watchful eye and keen negotiating skills of Brian Mulroney, ten willing provincial premiers had hammered out an agreement on the constitution. The fact that the Meech Lake Accord failed to win ratification in all the provincial capitals by the deadline three years later tends to overshadow the tremendous achievement of the original agreement. The early response to the agreement attests both to its uniqueness in the field of intergovernmental constitutional negotiation and to its popularity. Advisers to the premiers, who had been present but not been privy to the discussions on that fateful day at Meech Lake, were "in a mild state of shock" at the "apparent ease" with which the negotiators "discovered an untapped capacity to put aside regional differences and focus on the things they had in common."[60] Although the next step – translating an agreement in principle into constitutional language – was somewhat more difficult than the first, following, as it did, Trudeau's "impassioned polemic" against the agreement and some second-guessing on the part of a number of premiers, a final formal agreement was still eked out in the early hours of 3 June 1987.[61] Even end-of-term evaluations of Mulroney's first administration found that the Meech Lake Accord epitomized the achievement of "national reconciliation."[62]

Yet the deal unravelled. Despite the good intentions, the careful preparatory work, the cautious strategy pursued through close to three years of edging around the issue, and the last push that saw Mulroney doing "his job in a marvellous, marvellous way that was appreciated by everyone,"[63] the Meech Lake Accord still failed. Brokering the deal was perhaps Mulroney's finest moment, and the most important showcase for his remarkable negotiating skills. According to one of the prime minister's advisers, "Brian did what he has always done when he wants to cut a deal: he locked the big guys in one room where no one else could hear them, and threw out everybody else, so no one wasted any time posturing."[64] Securing the agreement of ten provincial premiers and the federal government had never before happened, and likely never will again, because not only was the Meech Lake agreement the apex of executive federalism, it was also its swan song.

Managing the intergovernmental relationship in Canada requires an extraordinary balancing act. On the one hand, there are so many contentious issues being considered at any particular point that it is impossible to deal with each in an entirely independent manner. Mulroney discovered this as free trade affected constitutional negotiations and equalization affected the trade deal. His pre-political negotiating career had allowed him the luxury of, essentially, hammering out deals in the antiseptic environment of the closed room. In the real world – or the fantasy world, if you prefer – of politics, that kind of controlled environment was not possible. A variety of other factors also affect intergovernmental outcomes, beyond those structural contaminants caused by the interconnectedness of policy areas. Mulroney soon discovered with Meech Lake that the "posturing" that had been eliminated from the negotiating room itself could manifest itself in many different voices in the years leading up to ratification. First came Trudeau's broadside against the accord, but this was soon followed by new governments in the provinces expressing reluctance to ratify the deal, calls from special-interest groups that their constitutional concerns be addressed in the accord, and ultimately a cacophony of voices attacking the very closed-door negotiations that had made the deal possible in the first place. Intergovernmental agreements could never be made entirely in a vacuum, but the failure of the Meech Lake Accord seemed to seal the fate of executive federalism entirely. Now the already messy field of federal-provincial relations must be conducted in the even messier environment of the public court.

After Meech's failure, Mulroney attempted to revise his strategy to contend with the new realities. Quebec's determination to hold a referendum on its role in Confederation forced another, almost immediate round of constitutional talks in the wake of the heartbreaking failure of Meech Lake. The earlier strategy was stripped of all the features that had drawn criticism. The new approach would not be dictated by Quebec, would not be conducted behind closed doors, and would leave no one out. Thus, for a year, from the September 1991 release of its own twenty-eight-point constitutional proposal to the October 1992 national referendum on what became known as the Charlottetown Accord, the federal government attempted to chart a new course through the stormy waters of federal-provincial relations. First, a joint Senate-House of Commons committee was established which reported in February 1992. Simultaneously, a series of cross-Canada investigations into the constitution were taking place, and premiers from all provinces were making clear their particular constitutional wish lists. The only group conspicuously absent from the constitutional cauldron was Quebec, where Premier Bourassa had made clear he was not interested in negotiating until the rest of the country was prepared to make an offer.

The first ministers – including Bourassa – finally met in Charlottetown in August 1992. The accord to which they added their signatures would be considered by all Canadians in a national referendum; the age of executive federalism was definitely over. In its wake, however, was a complex process that produced an unwieldy document purporting to have something for everyone. The Charlottetown Accord included a "Canada clause" with a comment on Quebec's distinctiveness as well as nods to multiculturalism, gender equity, and Aboriginal rights; a social charter that addressed health care, collective bargaining, child welfare, the environment, and a slew of other issues; means for securing Senate and other institutional reforms; and, in case anything was missing, it committed everyone to more negotiations in the future over areas not addressed by the accord. No wonder the public rejected the document, for, in offering something to everyone, it also ensured that there was something for everyone to dislike.[65] The rejection of the Charlottetown Accord was a sorry end to Mulroney's promise of "national reconciliation" made eight years earlier.

A number of factors combined to make the Mulroney record on intergovernmental relations less impressive than it appeared was possible in the first few year of his mandate. Two structural realities proved more difficult for this administration to manage than they had been for federal governments more comfortable with confrontation. First, the Canadian federal system has produced a complex interconnectedness between national and provincial governments that precludes dealing with issues independently. Secondly, the extent of regional diversity in Canada makes policy disagreement impossible to avoid. The particular style that Mulroney brought to the intergovernmental table was honed in labour negotiations and was best suited to brokering deal at the first ministers' level. While this style produced immediate goodwill in the early months of government, it was not particularly well suited to managing the intergovernmental conflict that was bound to occur. In focusing on one area where his own negotiating skills could be best employed – constitutional amendment – and where disagreement was forbidden, Mulroney virtually guaranteed that conflict would erupt in other parts of the federal system. We see this in the events leading to the failure to ratify the Meech Lake Accord, as well as in the many-sided Charlottetown Accord, and in the emergence of new political parties like the Bloc Québécois and Reform. The result of the failure of the Mulroney approach has been an end not only to the deal brokering of executive federalism but also, at least for the foreseeable future, of mega-constitutional politics. The price of unanimity is too high; now, we content ourselves with non-constitutional change rather than engaging in a full-scale constitutional overhaul.[66] While Mulroney's handling of federal-provincial affairs may not have been particularly successful, the lessons learned from his inability to establish harmony have perhaps been the most important lessons of Canadian political history in the twentieth century. Our current leaders would do well to learn from him.

## NOTES

1 The author would like to thank April Clyburne-Sherin for able and timely assistance with the research for this project, and the Social Sciences and Humanities Research Council for partial funding.

2 Richard Simeon, "National Reconciliation: The Mulroney Government and Federalism," in Andrew Gollner and Daniel Salée, eds., *Canada under Mulroney: An End-of-Term Report* (Montréal: Véhicule Press 1988), 27.

3 Jeffrey Simpson, "Tories Failed Their Own Test," *Globe and Mail*, 23 October 1993.

4 Kenneth McRoberts, "Unilateralism, Bilateralism and Multilateralism: Approaches to Canadian Federalism," in *Intergovernmental Relations* Richard Simeon, research coordinator (Toronto: University of Toronto Press 1985), 97.

5 Quoted in Donald C. Wallace, "Ottawa and the Provinces," in R.B. Byers, ed., *Canadian Annual Review of Politics and Public Affairs, 1984* (Toronto: University of Toronto Press 1987), 37.
6 Canada, Parliament, House of Commons, *Debates*, 5 November 1984 (Speech from the Throne), 6.
7 David Milne, *Tug of War: Ottawa and the Provinces under Trudeau and Mulroney* (Toronto: James Lorimer 1986), 99.
8 *Globe and Mail*, 11 February 1985.
9 G. Bruce Doern and Glen Toner, *The Politics of Energy: The Development and Implementation of the* NEP (Toronto: Methuen 1985), 478–9.
10 *Globe and Mail*, 14 February 1985.
11 Jeffrey Simpson, "Voices in Harmony," *Globe and Mail*, 16 February 1985, and ibid., 15 February 1985.
12 Mulroney campaign speech, Sept-Îles, 6 August 1984, quoted in Richard Simeon and Ian Robinson, *State, Society, and the Development of Canadian Federalism* (Toronto: University of Toronto Press 1990), 301.
13 House of Commons, *Debates*, 5 November 1984 (Speech from the Throne), 6.
14 Donald C. Wallace, "Ottawa and the Provinces," in R.B. Byers, ed., *Canadian Annual Review of Politics and Public Affairs, 1985* (Toronto: University of Toronto Press 1988), 55.
15 Jack McArthur, Toronto *Star*, 19 February 1985, quoted in Donald C. Wallace, "Ottawa and the Provinces," in Byers, ed., *Canadian Annual Review of Politics and Public Affairs, 1985*, 57.
16 "Mulroney to Pursue Talks on Freer Trade," *Globe and Mail*, 16 February 1985.
17 Jeffrey Simpson, "Mr. Lougheed's View," *Globe and Mail*, 19 February 1985.
18 See "Tories' Free Trade Bad for Ontario: Peterson," *Globe and Mail*, 27 March 1985; "Peterson Says Energy Accord Can Cost Ontario 55,000 Jobs," *Globe and Mail*, 29 March 1985; "Peterson to Monitor Gas-price Deal," *Globe and Mail*, 3 November 1985.
19 "281,000 Ontario Jobs Vulnerable to Free Trade, Study Says," *Globe and Mail*, 26 November 1985.
20 Ibid.; and "Ontario Proposes Provincial Role in Negotiations on Trade with US," *Globe and Mail*, 29 November 1985.
21 "Federal Cuts Threaten to Spoil Tory Honeymoon," *Globe and Mail*, 27 November 1985.
22 "Premiers Win Voice in Trade Talks," *Globe and Mail*, 30 November 1985.
23 Wallace, "Ottawa and the Provinces," in Byers, ed., *Canadian Annual Review of Politics and Public Affairs, 1985*, 62.
24 Michael Hart, *A Trading Nation: Canadian Trade Policy from Colonialism to Globalization* (Vancouver: University of British Columbia Press 2002), 376, 384.
25 Christopher Waddell, "Canadian Envoy to Brief Premiers on Protectionist Mood in Congress," *Globe and Mail*, 18 November 1986.
26 Mary Janigan, "Backlash in the Provinces," *Maclean's*, 8 September 1986.
27 Chris Wood, "Toward a New Atlantic Strategy," *Maclean's*, 27 October 1986.

28 Bill C-103, quoted in Agar Adamson, "Atlantic Canada: The Tories Help Those Who Help Themselves," in Gollner and Salée, eds., *Canada under Mulroney*, 81.
29 Wood, "Toward a New Atlantic Strategy."
30 Adamson, "Atlantic Canada," 85.
31 Matthew Fisher, "Finance Ministers Disagree over Equalization Payments," *Globe and Mail*, 1 November 1986. The recipient provinces for the 1982–87 period were the four Atlantic provinces, Manitoba, and Quebec.
32 John Cruikshank and Christopher Waddell, "No More Cash Available, Mulroney Tells Premiers," *Globe and Mail*, 21 November 1986; Bruce Little, "Ottawa Cuts Payments to Poorer Provinces," *Globe and Mail*, 13 December 1986.
33 Douglas M. Brown, "Overview," in Douglas M. Brown and Janet Hiebert, eds., *Canada: The State of the Federation, 1994* (Kingston, Ont.: Institute of Intergovernmental Relations 1994), 9.
34 See Janice Mackinnon, *Minding the Public Purse: The Fiscal Crisis, Political Trade-Offs and Canada's Future* (Montreal and Kingston: McGill-Queen's University Press 2003).
35 Terrance Hunsley, "Constitutional Change and National Social Programs," in Douglas M. Brown, ed., *Canada: The State of the Federation, 1991* (Kingston, Ont.: Institute of Intergovernmental Relations 1991), 118.
36 Thomas J. Courchene, "Canada's Social Policy Deficit: Implications for Fiscal Federalism," in Keith G. Banting, Douglas M. Brown, and Thomas J. Courchene, eds., *The Future of Fiscal Federalism* (Kingston, Ont.: Institute of Intergovernmental Relations 1994), 101.
37 Thomas J. Courchene with Colin R. Telmer, *From Heartland to North American Region State: The Social, Fiscal and Federal Evolution of Ontario* (Toronto: Centre for Public Management, University of Toronto 1998), 78, 166; Paul A. R. Hobson, "Current Issues in Federal-Provincial Fiscal Relations," in Ronald L. Watts and Douglas M. Brown, eds., *Canada: The State of the Federation, 1993* (Kingston, Ont.: Institution of Intergovernmental Relations 1993), 184–5.
38 Courchene, "Canada's Social Policy Deficit,"101.
39 Brian Bergman, "No Quick Fixes," *Maclean's*, 30 December 1991.
40 Richard Simeon, "The Political Context for Renegotiating Fiscal Federalism," in Banting, Brown, and Courchene, eds., *The Future of Fiscal Federalism*, 141, 146.
41 Roy Romanow, John Whyte, and Howard Leeson, *Canada Notwithstanding: The Making of the Constitution, 1976–1982* (Toronto: Carswell 1984), 106–87.
42 Patrick Monahan, *Meech Lake: The Inside Story* (Toronto: University of Toronto Press 1991), 42–3.
43 Richard Simeon, "Meech Lake and Shifting Conceptions of Canadian Federalism," *Canadian Public Policy*, vol. 14 supplement, September 1988, S8–S9.
44 Robert Sheppard, "Peterson Invokes Robarts-Johnson Alliance," *Globe and Mail*, 4 December 1985.
45 P.E. Bryden, "The Ontario-Quebec Axis: Postwar Strategies in Intergovernmental Negotiations," in Edgar-André Montigny and Lori Chambers, eds., *Ontario since*

*Confederation: A Reader* (Toronto: University of Toronto Press 2000), 390–402. Peter Russell has coined the term mega-constitutional politics to refer to the tendency since the 1960s to attempt a complete constitutional overhaul rather than piecemeal amendments. See *Constitutional Odyssey: Can Canadians Become a Sovereign People?* 2nd ed. (Toronto: University of Toronto Press 1993).

46 Graham Fraser, "PM, Bourassa Intent on Constitution Talks," *Globe and Mail*, 14 December 1985.

47 Monahan, *Meech Lake*, 446, 56–8.

48 Ibid., 50–3. A participant on Ontario's constitutional team, Monahan proposes these five elements of the federal strategy, not on the basis of anything expressly articulated, but after considering the content of numerous policy papers, correspondence, and private conversations.

49 Quoted in Paul Gessell, "A Secret Proposal," *Maclean's*, 28 July 1986.

50 Bertrand Marotte, "Quebec Ready for Another Go …," *Globe and Mail*, 9 August 1986.

51 Monahan, *Meech Lake*, 57–8.

52 "Provinces Criticize Quebec's Demands," *Globe and Mail*, 7 July 1986.

53 John Cruikshank, Matthew Fisher, and Ross Howard, "Premiers Set for Discussions on Quebec and Constitution," *Globe and Mail*, 13 August 1986.

54 Hart, *A Trading Nation*, 378–9.

55 Donald C. Wallace, "Ottawa and the Provinces," in R.B. Byers, ed., *Canadian Annual Review of Politics and Public Affairs, 1986* (Toronto: University of Toronto Press 1990), 56. See also the following articles in the *Globe and Mail*: "Ottawa Demands US Revoke Lumber Duty and Stop Inquiry," 1 November 1986; "Ontario Opposes Lumber Deal," 22 November 1986; "BC Ready to Act Alone to Stop Tariff," 26 November 1986; "Accord Reached over Softwood, BC Chief Says," 10 December 1986; and "Ontario Fires off Broadside at US Trade Protectionism," 12 December 1986.

56 Wallace, "Ottawa and the Provinces," *Canadian Annual Review 1986*, 67; Monahan, *Meech Lake*, 64.

57 "PM Faces Balancing Act on Quebec Issue," *Globe and Mail*, 22 September 1986; Jeffrey Simpson, "Proposal for Quebec," *Globe and Mail*, 17 April 1987.

58 Graham Fraser, "Outlook Unsettled for Talks on Constitution," *Globe and Mail*, 30 April 1987.

59 "Premiers Approve Quebec Demands," *Globe and Mail*, 1 May 1987.

60 Monahan, *Meech Lake*, 98–9.

61 "Quebeckers Disagree with Trudeau," *Globe and Mail*, 29 May 1987; "Text's Dry Phrasing Can't Convey Long Years of Work and Passion," *Globe and Mail*, 4 June 1987; "Accord Welcomes back Quebec," *Globe and Mail*, 4 June 1987.

62 See Simeon, "National Reconciliation," 32–9 and Roger Gibbons, "National Reconciliation and the Canadian West: Political Management in the Mulroney Era," in Gollner and Salée, eds., *Canada under Mulroney*, 92–4.

63 Anthony Wilson-Smith, "Breakthrough," in *Maclean's*, 11 May 1987.

64 Ibid.

65 Michael Howlett, "Ottawa and the Provinces," in David Leyton-Brown, ed., *Canadian Annual Review of Politics and Public Affairs, 1992* (Toronto: University of Toronto Press 1998), 59–70.

66 See Harvey Lazar, "Non-Constitutional Renewal: Toward a New Equilibrium in the Federation," in Harvey Lazar, ed., *Canada: The State of the Federation 1997* (Kingston, Ont.: Institute of Intergovernmental Relations 1998), 3–35, as well as the other articles in the volume.

# 10

# Brian Mulroney and the West

ROBERT WARDHAUGH

When Brian Mulroney won the leadership of the Progressive Conservative Party in June 1983, he realized the opportunity to cripple the Liberal juggernaut that had dominated national politics since Pierre Trudeau's appearance on the political scene almost fifteen years earlier. The Liberals were a lame-duck party with a lacklustre leader in John Turner, and the winds of political change were swirling fiercely all around. But nowhere was the atmosphere more charged than in the west. With the brief exception of the Joe Clark interlude in 1979–80, western Canadians had generally rejected participation in national government since 1972. The region had also emphatically rejected Liberal policies. The sense of western alienation had long been felt most strongly in Alberta, where the province had given every seat to the Progressive Conservatives (PCs) in the elections of 1972, 1974, and 1980. That sentiment, however, had become shared across the region.

Western Canadians were tired of confronting national governments dominated by central Canada and, more specifically, by Quebec Liberal MPs. While the west had long harboured deeply rooted regional anger and frustration, during the late 1970s and early 1980s there emerged an "even more emphatic regional consensus" – parliamentary institutions were inherently flawed, they did not and could not provide western Canadians with adequate or even fair representation in the national government, and, as a consequence, national policies would inevitably fail to reflect western Canadian interests and aspirations. The result was a period of political debate in the region "charged with the rhetoric of institutional reform as western Canadians promoted the virtues of Senate reform, electoral reform, party reform, enhanced provincial powers and even separatism."[1]

In April 1984 polls across the four western provinces indicated that the Conservatives held 58 per cent of popular support, while the Liberals held 25 per cent and the New Democrats 15 per cent.[2] The legendary name

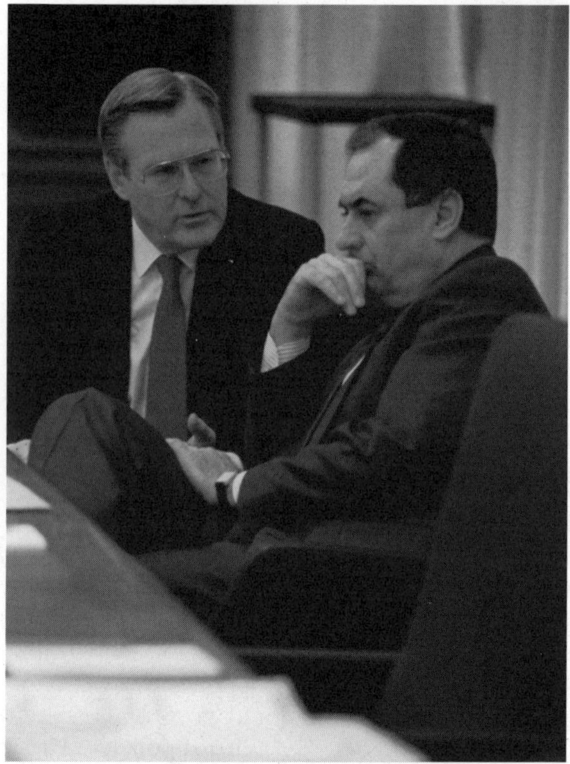

Michael Wilson, minister of finance, and Don Mazankowski, one of the thirteen ministers in the cabinet from western Canada. Mulroney appointed Mazankowski deputy prime minister and government house leader in 1986, and "Maz," as he was commonly known, became one of the most powerful ministers in the government. Library and Archives Canada 91-C-9150-28.

of John Diefenbaker (despite his poor reputation as a prime minister elsewhere across the nation) still carried impressive weight, particularly on the rural prairies. By the time of Trudeau's exit from politics, the region was Tory blue. Trudeau's focus on Quebec's place in Canada, his policies of official bilingualism, his focus on the constitution and French-English relations, and his arrogance and dismissal of western alienation led to an atmosphere in which young boys sported ball caps decorated with a noose and the warning: "Trudeau Come West." No policy, however, stuck in the craw of westerners more than the National Energy Program (NEP). The

Table 1 Party Seat allocation in the west: Elections of 1968, 1972, 1974, 1979, and 1980

| | *Liberal* | *Progressive Conservative* | *NDP* | *Independent* |
|---|---|---|---|---|
| 1968 ELECTION | | | | |
| Alberta | 4 | 15 | 0 | 0 |
| British Columbia | 16 | 0 | 7 | 0 |
| Manitoba | 5 | 5 | 3 | 0 |
| Saskatchewan | 2 | 5 | 6 | 0 |
| 1972 ELECTION | | | | |
| Alberta | 0 | 19 | 0 | 0 |
| British Columbia | 4 | 8 | 11 | 0 |
| Manitoba | 2 | 8 | 3 | 0 |
| Saskatchewan | 1 | 7 | 5 | 0 |
| 1974 ELECTION | | | | |
| Alberta | 0 | 19 | 0 | 0 |
| British Columbia | 8 | 13 | 2 | 0 |
| Manitoba | 2 | 9 | 2 | 0 |
| Saskatchewan | 3 | 8 | 2 | 0 |
| 1979 ELECTION | | | | |
| Alberta | 0 | 21 | 0 | 0 |
| British Columbia | 1 | 19 | 8 | 0 |
| Manitoba | 2 | 7 | 5 | 0 |
| Saskatchewan | 0 | 10 | 4 | 0 |
| 1980 ELECTION | | | | |
| Alberta | 0 | 21 | 0 | 0 |
| British Columbia | 0 | 16 | 11 | 0 |
| Manitoba | 2 | 5 | 7 | 0 |
| Saskatchewan | 0 | 7 | 7 | 0 |

*Source*: Library of Parliament

NEP, designed to force western energy reserves into the central Canadian market in order to keep the rising prices of oil and gas down, was bitterly viewed in the region as a resource grab of western wealth. "In the years of the Trudeau government," Roger Gibbins points out, "the Conservative party became the primary vehicle for western Canadian political discontent ...To an important extent, the Conservative party had been captured by its western arm; it had become a western Canadian party as much as a national party."[3]

But, unlike John Diefenbaker and Joe Clark, the new Tory leader did not hail from the west. Brian Mulroney was undoubtedly a Quebecer. He was of Irish Catholic descent, but his connections were in the province; he was a student of Quebec politics, and his goals for the nation were based on finally constructing a powerful and enduring Quebec base of support for the Conservative Party.[4] "From his boyhood fascination with the Duplessis regime," one biographer observes, "Mulroney has been immersed in a distinct political culture that is alien to most English Canadians."[5] Regardless, his selection as Progressive Conservative leader was generally met by optimism from Tories across the west. Most of the western heavyweights in the party had supported Clark at the convention, but there was a general sense that Mulroney was also committed to finally giving western Canadians an equal stake in Confederation. The new leader confirmed this commitment by immediately seeking to assure the influential Conservatives in the west that they would indeed play prominent roles in any new government.[6]

The Tory faithful in the west, however, were a bit taken aback in March 1984 over Mulroney's support for the francophone minority in Manitoba, not to mention his castigation of the province's Conservative MPs for supporting the stance against "forced bilingualism." The New Democratic Party (NDP) government of Premier Howard Pawley was attempting to address perceived historic wrongs to the French minority in Manitoba through legislation, when the PC opposition, led by Gary Filmon, forced prorogation of the House. To make matters worse, several of Mulroney's own MPs in the province were supporting the provincial Tories. Mulroney was quoted in an interview as telling "these guys that it's my way or the way out." He was shocked by the attitudes held in Manitoba: "That's what being an opposition party for too long does to you, you tend to confuse prejudice and politics. Bilingualism is the goddamn law of the land. We are either for it or against it, and as long as I'm the leader we are for it!"[7]

By mid-summer 1984, Brian Mulroney and the Progressive Conservative Party were poised for an election call. The party held a two-day policy meeting for the seventy-five-member western caucus (fifty-two MPs and twenty-three candidates) in Prince Albert, Saskatchewan (the home constituency of former prime ministers John Diefenbaker and Mackenzie King), but it was difficult to keep the members focused on anything but the expected election call. Although he had been criticized for failing to outline specific policy positions as opposition leader, Mulroney used the Prince Albert gathering to announce a series of policy changes of particular interest to western Canada. He promised to overhaul the NEP; to scrap the Liberal government's controversial Petroleum Incentive Program (grants paid to oil companies on a sliding scale, based on the location of their drill sites and their degree of Canadian ownership); to offer tax incentives designed to make it more attractive financially for Canadian companies to find and exploit new energy sources; to introduce a new "Canadian share" program encouraging Canadian investors – whether public or private – to invest in the energy sector; to abolish capital gains taxes on farm sales, as long as the property remained in agricultural use; and to remove the 9 per

Table 2 Party seat allocation in the west: 1984 federal election

| | *Liberal* | *Progressive Conservative* | *NDP* | *Independent* |
|---|---|---|---|---|
| Alberta | 0 | 21 | 0 | 0 |
| British Columbia | 1 | 19 | 8 | 0 |
| Manitoba | 1 | 9 | 4 | 0 |
| Saskatchewan | 0 | 9 | 5 | 0 |

*Source*: Library of Parliament

cent federal sales tax on farm fuel. More emphatically, Mulroney promised "a new era" in relations between Ottawa and the west, as well as programs that would result in 200,000 immediate jobs.[8] By July 1984, the west was extremely friendly to Mulroney and the Tories. The PCs held fifty-two seats compared to two for the Liberals and twenty-four for the New Democrats.[9]

"It is difficult," Gibbons claims, "to exaggerate the impact of the 1984 election on the political landscape of western Canada."[10] The Progressive Conservative wave swept through the four western provinces, with the party winning all twenty-one seats in Alberta and thirty-seven of the fifty-six seats in the other three provinces.

The support was rewarded with significant regional representation in the cabinet; western Canada went from having a single representative to having thirteen members.[11] From Alberta, Joe Clark was appointed as minister of external affairs, Don Mazankowski took over his former portfolio from 1979–80 as transport minister, and Harvie Andre became the minister of supply and services; from Manitoba, Jake Epp was given the portfolio of national health and welfare, Jack Murta became the minister of state for multiculturalism, Duff Roblin became government leader in the Senate, and Charles Mayer was given responsibility for the Wheat Board; from Saskatchewan, Ray Hnatyshyn became justice minister and Bill McKnight became government house leader; from British Columbia, Pat Carney from took over the energy department, while John Fraser was given fisheries and oceans, and Tom Siddon became minister of science and technology.

According to Charlotte Gray, Mulroney and his government had little choice but to repay the region for its support and "the new government set about remedying western grievances." This agenda consisted of several measures. Two symbols of the Trudeau era – the NEP and the Foreign Investment Review Agency (FIRA) – were dismantled. Freight rates were reduced and the transportation industry was deregulated. Emergency support in the amount of over $1 billion was granted to farmers from 1985 to 1988.[12] Gray notes that both Mazankowski and McKnight had long been planning fundamental changes in the way that the federal government dealt with the four western provinces: "They didn't just want more money for their region. Their goal was to grab for the West the same kind of clout in the inner circles of the bureaucracy that Quebec has. They were determined to make the West part of the power structure."[13]

In the election of 1984 western Canadians may have helped elect a federal government in which the region enjoyed impressive representation, yet, at the same time and perhaps inevitably, the region lost proportionate influence within the Conservative Party. Winning office (as Diefenbaker discovered) was one thing; holding it was another. To remain in power, the Mulroney Conservatives would have to woo Quebec, court Ontario, and pay some attention to the Maritimes. Anti-French feelings were strong in the west, and Trudeau's policies had only deepened the sentiment. Westerners already felt that central Canada was given far too much prominence in national affairs and that their region was always watching hopelessly from the outside. The west feared that, once in office, the Tories would redirect their focus to the real bases of power. "Bluntly put," Gibbins writes, "western Canadians won a government but lost a party."[14]

Still, Conservative MPs from across the west controlled some of the most important posts of the new Mulroney government, the best example being (the newly promoted) Deputy Prime Minister Don Mazankowski and Minister of External Affairs Joe Clark. With the abandonment of the much-maligned NEP, as outlined by the Western Accord of April 1985, the long decade of energy conflict seemed to be ending. Prairie farmers were pleased with the financial relief they were receiving from Ottawa in the face of drought and depressed world grain prices. Prime Minister Mulroney focused on improving the state of intergovernmental relations, a gesture much appreciated by the western premiers. The Conservative premier of Saskatchewan, Grant Devine, emerged as a staunch supporter of Mulroney.[15] Alberta Premier Peter Lougheed also offered his support. After the gathering of the first ministers in Regina in February (at which point a decision was made to meet annually), Lougheed noted that "the mood is very positive toward the new Government. There's a belief that the Prime Minister will treat the West equitably." The premier did go on to note that the support was tenuous. There were "some very strong feelings below the surface in Alberta that could flare up," if expectations were dashed.[16] Still, as Gibbins claims, "there is little doubt that the Mulroney government was initially well-received in western Canada, and that there was broad regional support for the policy course being pursued by the Conservative government. At least with respect to western Canada, the national government was delivering on the policy front."[17] And the prime minister was pleased. He was particularly proud of dismantling the NEP and of the number of westerners in cabinet: "For the first time in twenty-five years," Mulroney noted, "Western Canada is now very much a part of the decision-making process in Ottawa ... Western power is back in existence."[18]

One year into its first term, however, western attitudes towards the Mulroney government began to "shift uncomfortably." Westerners expected the same level of attention as the region had received from "Dief the Chief." They were prepared to give the Mulroney Tories the chance to show their mettle but expectations were high, perhaps impossibly high for a federal government that had to satisfy divergent interests from across the nation. If the government faltered, western patience would prove fleeting at best. The elimination of the NEP, particularly the hated Petroleum Gas Revenue Tax (PGRT), was viewed as an obvious move rather than an indication of a west-friendly government. According to the Canada West Foundation, "cessation of an unprecedented injury is a rather negative and limited kind of 'benefit.'"[19] In addition, according to Gray, "those western Canadians who had looked forward to a return of real Conservative values (less bilingualism and more law and order) discovered to their disgust that their party had gone soft on social issues."[20]

The "shift" was also occurring in part because of the traditional perception that, once elected, the prime minister was taking the west (and its support) for granted and instead turning his attentions to central Canada and the issue of Quebec's place in the nation. There was resentment, an article in *Maclean's* indicated in September 1985, over the fact that Mulroney had made only three brief visits to the region in the past year. There was also anger over Ottawa's slow response to calls for a comprehensive federal program to cushion farmers from financial failures and over the federal refusal to adopt a red-meat stabilization plan to help struggling beef producers.[21] International grain prices had collapsed along with farm income. The good news for the Tories in the polls was that the government, for the most part, retained its support in the west. An Angus Reid survey showed the Tories leading the Liberals by 52 per cent to 15 per cent on the prairies and 40 per cent to 28 per cent in British Columbia.[22]

But in October 1986 the west "exploded with rage." The Mulroney government announced that a billion-dollar maintenance contract for the CF-18 aircraft fighter used by the Canadian Forces would go to Montreal-based Canadair, although Winnipeg-based Bristol Aerospace had made a technically superior and cheaper bid. The CF-18 decision was vigorously attacked in the media across the region. According to Peter McCormick and David Elton, it paralleled the hated National Energy Program: "In both cases a national party made the hard-headed decision on the basis that to any government Central Canadian seats are life and death, but western Canadian seats are a luxury...The economic well-being of the West must be sacrificed to the political needs of Central Canada."[23] Not only was the contract worth a great deal, but it represented the actual and symbolic basis for the Manitoban and indeed western Canadian aerospace industry. Politically, it appeared that the prime minister's "obsession with Quebec" had "blinded him hopelessly" to the needs and sensibilities of other regions.[24] The lesson seemed clear: despite all the talk about the west's influence in cabinet, when it came to a critical decision, the region would still lose to central Canadian interests: "All through the Trudeau years, we were told that we just weren't using it [government] properly. If we would only smarten up and vote for the party in power, we would discover that Ottawa's inclination to walk all over us stopped. Ottawa would become sweet, reasonable and beneficent. Well, now we've done that. In fact, practically the whole West is on the government's side of the house. And for six months or so, it looked as though the proposition might be true. We are now discovering that it is not. However we vote, we are still walked on."[25]

To make matters worse, the CF-18 decision was followed up by a British Columbia report that examined the distribution of federal spending. It argued that the province had 11.3 per cent of the national population but received only 5 per cent of federal money. Quebec, on the other hand, with 26 per cent of the population, received 24 per cent of the money, while Ontario, with 34 per cent of the population, received 55 per cent. Meanwhile, Alberta, Saskatchewan, and Manitoba all received less than half their due.[26] The report indicated that even vociferous western cabinet ministers like Harvie Andre or Don Mazankowski could not resist the practices of decades of federal procurement practices entrenched in Ottawa.

Near the mid-point of Mulroney's first term in office, "the bloom was coming off the new Tory rose." Gibbins blames this on the fact that Ottawa's political management did not match its public-policy management. It was argued that the prime minister's preoccupation with Quebec and his party's fortunes in that province made him little different from his Liberal predecessors.[27] According to Jeffrey Simpson, however, it was more a matter of the government landing "four-square in the unwinnable game of meeting exaggerated expectations." Following the CF-18 fiasco, the Mulroney government tried to make amends to the west by awarding other contracts, responding generously to farmers' demands, and moving towards a Western Diversification Policy. But it was now too late for Ottawa to change course. Though the policy of assisting first this company or region, then another, brought no discernible political benefits to the government, the game would have to continue because of the fear of potential losses. The Mulroney government, as a result, was "trapped in the vortex of escalating expectations and diminishing gratitude."[28]

The dilemma led to crisis in both cabinet and caucus. Don Mazankowski, for example, found himself pitted against Finance Minister Michael Wilson over offering more incentives to the west, such as the restoration of oil-depletion allowances.[29] The same dynamics were at work in the weeks before an election in Saskatchewan, which saw Ottawa promise $1 billion to farmers to help boost the fortunes of Premier Grant Devine.[30]

After defending the record of the government in the west for two years, Alberta PC rebel David Kilgour delivered an ultimatum to the party caucus: either the government made good on its promises to the west or he would cross the floor and sit as an independent. In April 1987 Kilgour was advised not to attend national and Alberta caucus meetings; he was fired from his job as parliamentary secretary to the then transport minister, John Crosbie.[31] The popularity of the Mulroney government plummeted in the west but it was still collapsing even more rapidly across the rest of the nation.[32]

Regional arguments for institutional reform, meanwhile, were revived and the federal government now came under increasing pressure for Senate reform. The creation of Preston Manning's Reform Party in 1987 provided a vehicle for this push and in particular the calls for Triple-E Senate reform. More emphatically, however, formed by disgruntled Conservatives and other neo-conservatives from across the region (but most specifically Alberta), the Reform Party threatened to "burrow into the soft underbelly of Conservative electoral support in the West." As Alvin Finkel points out, "though the party wrapped itself in the cloak of western populism, its founders were four wealthy Westerners who believed the Conservative Party was moving too slowly to reduce the role of government in the economy."[33] With the honeymoon over, "it seemed the defeat of the Liberals and the election of a new Conservative government had not dramatically improved the West's fortunes within the national political arena." Even with so many western MPs in the cabinet and on the government side of the House, it was not enough to "ensure a fair shake for the West." According to Gibbins, "the West seemed to be retreating to a mood of sullen alienation as the national Conservative government drifted more and more into Quebec's orbit."[34]

Not all the signs were discouraging for the government. Mulroney's efforts to restrain and reduce federal expenditures and to promote both deregulation and privatization found a receptive audience among the majority of western Canadians. In late 1987 the region welcomed the federal government's establishment of the Western Diversification Office (WDO), with a head office in Edmonton and regional offices in each of the four western provinces. The WDO had its own minister, Bill McKnight from Saskatchewan, as well as a deputy minister, Saskatoon-born Bruce Rawson, who had been a senior official in both the Alberta and the Ottawa governments. It was given $312 million for the 1988–89 fiscal year with which to promote new economic activity in the region; this money constituted the first instalment on the government's August 1987 promise of $1.2 billion over five years to help diversify the western Canadian economy and "co-ordinate, support, and encourage the creation of enterprises" in the four western provinces.[35] In the first nineteen months of operation, the department funded 873 projects (about 20 per cent of all applications) to the tune of $488.5 million.[36] According to Gray, however, the significance of the program lay not in its ability to give away money but rather in the pressure that the department applied to the Ottawa system: "Its officials, exuding the same high moral purpose that characterized Ottawa's bilingualism zealots in the early 1970s, moved in on the established departments. They elbowed their way into discussions on defence, procurement, and research and development contracts. Turf battles erupted."[37] And the "combination of powerful ministers and pushy bureaucrats bore fruit." McKnight announced in July 1988 that federal procurement in western Canada would increase by $600 million over the next four years.[38] But pundits claimed that the WDO was of more symbolic than real value to the region. "The financial impact is miniscule," the *Globe and Mail* noted, "but the political stakes are high for Brian Mulroney and the four western premiers who must show they are getting some action from Ottawa." The plan paled beside "Ottawa's recent attentiveness to the West," including the previous year's $1-billion special grain payment, early abolition of special energy taxes worth $1.2 billion, federal petroleum drilling incentives worth about $350 million annually, and a new national park for British Columbia worth $106 million.

On another front, the 1987 Meech Lake constitutional initiative did not strengthen western Canadian support for the Mulroney government, but it did gain the support of provincial premiers in the region. It also created an atmosphere of national conciliation that some called the "spirit" of Meech Lake. "This is widely taken to mean a constructive tolerance in the family of confederation," the *Globe and Mail* declared, "a symbol of the flexibility and accommodation that are the bricks and mortar of nation-building." The "spirit," however, was almost immediately banished when an Alberta MLA was scolded for asking a question in French in the legislature.[39]

According to Gibbins, Meech Lake was clearly directed at the constitutional aspirations of Quebec, but, at the same time, by universalizing Quebec's long-standing demand for a distinctive if not necessarily special constitutional status, the accord strengthened the position of all provincial governments in the country. For example, western premiers came away from the 1987 constitutional negotiations with the prospect of control over Senate and Supreme Court appointments, greater control over immigration policy, and greater flexibility with respect to future federal government programs: "While the accord did nothing to strengthen the intrastate representation of western Canadians within the institutions of the national government, it did provide additional inter-state protection from those institutions by strengthening the role of provincial governments within the Canadian federal system."[40]

Through the Meech Lake Accord, Prime Minister Mulroney successfully forged an impressive alliance between provincialists in the west and nationalists in Quebec. The effectiveness of this coalition was demonstrated by Quebec Premier Robert Bourassa's April 1988 tour of western Canada. Bourassa's visit came on the heels of the Supreme Court's affirmation of minority-language rights in Saskatchewan, and more directly in the wake of the province's decision to nullify those rights legislatively while, at the same time, providing enhanced services and limited translation of government statutes for the province's francophone minority. In statements to the press following meetings with both Saskatchewan Premier Grant Devine and Alberta Premier Don Getty, and to the dismay of francophone groups within the two provinces, Bourassa took the opportunity to support the policy adopted by the Saskatchewan government.[41] Mulroney, meanwhile, was "treading judiciously" by neither attacking nor embracing the Saskatchewan decision.[42]

It was generally agreed that the first three years of Brian Mulroney's federal government represented a marked change over the record of the Trudeau Liberals in western Canada. Several of the region's major grievances were addressed and the west appeared finally to be exerting some real power and influence in the nation's capital. Yet there were some unmitigated disasters, such as the CF-18 debacle, the "tainted tuna" scandal (in which a western cabinet minister, John Fraser, was hung out to dry for maladministration in the Department of Fisheries and Oceans), the Tory waffling on de-indexing pensions, the failure of the Canadian economy everywhere but Toronto, and the Bob Coates, Michel Gravel, André Bissonette, and Sinclair Stevens affairs (in which federal cabinet ministers were compelled to resign under somewhat unsavoury circumstances), which were all still fresh in the mind of the electorate. Stalwart Tories were also aware that no governing federal party in the nation's history had ever fallen to 22 per cent popularity, the level reached by the Mulroney government in 1987.

But party fortunes would turn around during the course of 1987. The government's record, only recently viewed as an "unmanageable burden," was transformed into "a solid and popular agenda"; the scandal-plagued PCs began "scoring one success after another." They overhauled the tax system, deregulated the financial sector, held a free vote on capital punishment, introduced a $5.2-billion daycare program, produced regional-development initiatives for the west and the Maritimes, hammered out the Meech Lake Constitutional Accord and – most important – achieved a historic free- trade agreement with the United States. The Tories' record on the economy began to pay dividends. Tax reform, including income tax and sales tax changes, along with an overhaul of the Broadcasting Act and deregulation of the pharmaceutical and transportation industries, were popular policy initiatives. Fifteen crown corporations were fully or partially sold off, including de Haviland, Canadair, Teleglobe Canada, and Air Canada, and the unloved symbol of energy policy, the integrated petroleum company Petro-Canada, was readied for partial privatization, which occurred in 1991. Unemployment, interest, and inflation levels, along with the federal deficit, were all lower than when the Tories took office. The Conservatives rebounded in the opinion polls. These polls also demonstrated that, once again, the Tories were "pulling away from the pack" in the west, where free trade enjoyed widespread support.[43]

The issue of free trade was remarkably successful at uniting the region behind Mulroney. "There is no question," Gibbons claimed, "that the Mulroney government's free trade initiative enjoys broad though by no means universal public support across the West and...it has enjoyed the enthusiastic, almost jingoistic support of provincial governments." The west may have supported free trade not primarily for economic reasons but rather for ideological ones: "Free trade in this sense is supported because it promotes a deregulated, market-based economy, one close to the ideological hearts of small-c conservative governments now ensconced across the West." Another reason was an extremely strong "widespread regional mythology" in favour of lower tariffs, stemming back to the days of the National Policy. Virtually all western provincial governments from the 1880s to the 1970s had railed against national tariff policy and most favoured free trade. Hostility to the tariff as an actual burden on regional development and a symbol of central Canadian bias had motivated both prairie protests for equal treatment and British Columbian demands for better terms in Confederation. In addition, free trade was seen as a way of preventing Ottawa from intervening in the national and continental economies to the detriment of western Canadian interests.[44]

Mulroney was well aware that the Free Trade Agreement (FTA) would be popular in the west. He viewed past "National" policies as schemes that penalized the region and under which the west had always lost. He viewed the recent NEP in the same light. "When I had to make the decision about free trade," Mulroney indicated, "one of the major things that I thought it would correct would be a historical injustice...I don't think anybody set out with any malice to devise a straitjacket for Western Canada, but one originated." Don Braid and Sydney Sharpe claim that, unlike Trudeau, Mulroney was genuinely concerned with the west and he hoped that one day westerners would realize that he had their best interests at heart.[45]

The FTA would help the Progressive Conservatives make gains in the region but signs across the western provinces contained mixed messages. In the spring of 1988 an upsurge by the provincial Liberals led by Sharon Carstairs denied the PCs a majority government in a Manitoba provincial election that had defeated an NDP administration deemed too weak in dealing with Ottawa. Political pundits agreed that the results were meant to send a message to the Mulroney government. The ghosts of the CF-18 decision still haunted Winnipeg but opposition to the Meech Lake Accord was also growing. Premier Gary Filmon bolstered his own popularity and that of his minority government when he reversed his support of Meech Lake, citing Quebec's defence of Bill 101 – language legislation restricting the use of English in the province – as the justification. In March, Deborah Grey won the Beaver River by-election in east-central Alberta for the upstart Reform Party. As Edmonton MP David Kilgour pointed out, "anyone who dismisses the Reform Party win as a by-election quirk should recall that in the 1921 general election, following an equally decisive rout in a Medicine Hat by-election, the new Progressive party won fully 39 of western Canada's then 57 seats." The Reform Party's message of "the West wants in" was attracting considerable support across the region. "The more we hear about regional fairness," the *Alberta Report* announced, "the more elusive the concept appears to become."[46]

On the eve of the 1988 election, using the Meech Lake Accord and the FTA as the planks, and with the west and Quebec as the twin pillars of support, Brian Mulroney had built a political alliance that was "reminiscent of the Mackenzie King Liberal alliances in the past."[47] In addition, by the end of the first Mulroney mandate, the national per-capita average of regional industrial spending was $213 but for westerners the figure was $224. The percentage of Canadian International Development Agency contracts with Alberta alone had jumped from 1 per cent to 9 per cent between 1984 and 1988.[48] "We have achieved fundamental structural change," Mazankowski boasted.[49] But, according to David Bercuson, this "uneasy coalition" between Quebec and the west was highly dangerous for the Progressive Conservatives because there were few shared assumptions and many competing interests. In essence, "westerners deeply resent Quebec's power."[50] Mackenzie King may have built an alliance based on support from Quebec and the west, but ultimately he learned that he could not hold both bases and he was forced to make a choice. He chose Quebec.[51]

In the summer of 1988, the passage of Bill C-72, a bill to "fulfill the bilingualization of Canada in general and the Canadian government in particular," infuriated the west and demonstrated the instability of Mulroney's bases of power. In western eyes, the bill's passage resulted from MPs of all parties being harangued into support under the threat of damaging national unity.[52] Mulroney threatened not to sign the nomination papers of government members who refused to vote for the bill. The prime minister fired Manitoba Tory Dan McKenzie as parliamentary secretary to the minister responsible for veterans' affairs; Mulroney indicated that the MP was stripped of his responsibilities because he voted against the bill. The next day the prime minister announced that McKenzie would be replaced by Quebec Conservative MP Charles Hamelin, who had previously threatened to quit the party and join the Parti Québécois if Tory backbenchers who opposed the legislation were successful in blocking it.[53] By 1988, many westerners viewed bilingualism as "an ill-conceived pipe-dream, concocted by central-Canadian politicians to appease the francophone vote and implemented by a self-serving bureaucracy."[54] An Angus Reid poll in the autumn of 1988 indicated that 60 per cent of all English-speaking Canadians felt that the Mulroney government had "done too much for Quebec." That figure rose to 71 per cent on the prairies and in British Columbia.[55]

By the fall of 1988, the influence of Don Mazankowski reached its zenith and Mulroney hoped that his presence could at least rein in Alberta's anger. As a result of a pre-election cabinet mini-shuffle, the "minister of everything" added the agriculture portfolio to a growing list of responsibilities that included deputy prime minister, government house leader, president of the Privy Council, and minister in charge of privatization. Much of the restoration of Tory popularity was linked to the rise of Mazankowski: "He runs interference for the prime minister in the House, douses uprisings in the huge and potentially fractious Tory caucus, and is the *de facto* minister responsible for the West." In the wake of the CF-18 travesty, the Meech Lake Accord, and the new Official Languages Act, it seemed to be only Mazankowski's stature as the number-two man in Ottawa that kept many western Conservatives from bolting the Progressive Conservatives for the Reform Party en masse.

The federal election of November 1988 gave the Conservatives 43 per cent of the popular vote while the Liberals received 32 per cent and the NDP 20 per cent.[56] In terms of seats, the Progressive Conservatives won a comfortable majority, with 169 seats; the Liberals won 83, and the NDP 43. The west gave Mulroney 44 out of 83 constituencies (11 in BC, 22 in Alberta, 4 in Saskatchewan, and 7 in Manitoba). Western support for Mulroney may have slipped in 1988, but the Reform Party still failed to make a major breakthrough in the federal election: Preston Manning's Reform Party failed to win a single seat. That said, the party did attract more than 15 per cent of Alberta votes and ran second in nine of the twenty-six Alberta ridings. According to Kilgour, the issue of free trade saved the Tories in the 1988 election because western Conservatives who were tempted to vote Reform grudgingly supported the PCs in order to save the deal. "Next time," predicted Kilgour, "we won't have the advantage of a mega-issue."[57]

In June 1989 *Saturday Night* magazine announced that "Westerners have more power in Ottawa today than at any other time in our history." According to Charlotte Gray, they had an "arm lock" on the big-spending departments. "They have their own shock troops within the bureaucracy – officials at the western diversification department. Best of all, they have as their generalissimo the guy responsible for the day-to-day running of the government – Deputy Prime Minister Don Mazankowski from Alberta."[58] In the thirty-nine-member cabinet announced by Mulroney in January 1989, ten ministers were westerners. "Mazankowski's boys" had achieved a grip on nearly all the government's discretionary spending: "Central Canadians may be in charge of economic policy (Ontario's Michael Wilson at Finance; Robert de Cotret at the Treasury Board), but westerners run departments like defence, regional industrial expansion, energy, agriculture, western diversification, science and technology."[59] The "western shift" was apparently even evident in the details. According to Gray, powerful westerners, such as Bill McKnight, Harvie Andre, and Charlie Mayer, proudly displayed photographs of John Diefenbaker on their walls: "Ten years ago, Liberal insiders ate at the baronial Chateau Laurier on the east side of Parliament Hill. Members of Trudeau's staff and cabinet sipped French wines in its dimly lit Canadian Grill, the faded gentility of which breathes the old money hauteur of Westmount or Rosedale. But brightly lit Hy's [Steak House], one block west of the Hill, is the venue for today's power lunchers."[60] Mazankowski was quoted as saying, "'This government has done more for the West than any other government since Confederation. We've reversed the trend. The West is getting its share today.'"[61]

External Affairs Minister Joe Clark was more restrained in his regionalism but he was equally as optimistic about the west's influence in the Mulroney government. For Clark, the west had spent too much time and energy aggressively and angrily asserting its sense of regional injustice from the periphery: "Instead of fighting a rearguard action to defend our regional interests, we have the chance to exert real and enduring national leadership." Western members of cabinet and caucus, as far as Clark was concerned, had a choice: "Do we act as insiders trying to shape national institutions, or do we act as outsiders, treating national goals as inherently hostile to our own?"[62]

But following the November 1988 election, the Tories again commenced a steady decline in popularity. By the spring of 1989, Mulroney's party reached 22 per cent, equalling the record low set in 1987 for a governing party. And the Tory free fall was not over. By April, the government's popularity had dropped to 15 per cent. Even more ominous, the unpopularity was being felt in the Conservative strongholds of Quebec and Alberta. Seventy-six per cent of all those polled by Gallup in July indicated dissatisfaction with Mulroney's personal performance; of the three national leaders, Mulroney received the support of only 14 per cent.[63]

Demands for Senate reform which would, it was hoped, provide the western provinces with a stronger voice at the centre – were now reaching a fever pitch in the region. In February 1989 a bill was introduced into the Alberta legislature that would allow the province's voters to elect the next Senate nominee. This was in conflict with section 25 of the Meech Lake Accord, according to which provincial governments would be able to submit a list of proposed names to fill Senate vacancies. The prime minister chose to abide by the "spirit" of Meech Lake and follow its selection procedure, even though he was not obligated do so until the accord was ratified. Mulroney did make it clear, however, that he expected provinces to submit a list of at least five names. Premier Getty of Alberta intended to submit only the name of the election winner. Regardless, the eventual election result (Stan Waters of the Reform Party) was initially ignored by the prime minister.[64]

In April, Mulroney made his first tour of Alberta since the 1988 election. He repeated his promises for public hearings on Senate reform options, followed by a policy for reform, and then a first ministers' conference to discuss the issue. There was a catch, however. None of this would happen unless the Meech Lake Accord was ratified. But opposition to the accord was growing in the west owing to the belief that it would actually kill the region's single essential constitutional goal: the Triple-E Senate. Although the western premiers tried desperately to convince the populace that ratification of the agreement would lead to Senate reform, opponents noted that a single province would be able to veto any plan put forward. Because Quebec and Ontario would only lose by having the west receive more Senate seats, it was widely believed across the region that Senate reform remained a pipe dream.

Moreover, some of the policies of the Mulroney government were becoming increasingly unpopular. The Goods and Services Tax (GST) along with the Meech Lake Accord were rapidly losing support in the west. According to Braid and Sharpe, even Don Mazankowski was now "puzzled and confused." He was convinced that his government was a "true friend of the West" but now "found himself in the strange spot of defending a prime minister almost as unpopular with westerners as Pierre Trudeau was ten years earlier. In a way this is even worse; westerners respected Trudeau through their hatred, but they have little regard for Brian Mulroney, whom they brand with contemptuous insults – liar, cheat, hypocrite." According to Mazankowski, on the one hand, westerners wanted federal spending to make up for many years of neglect; on the other, they insisted that the government cut waste and reduce the deficit: "We get mixed signals. We started out in 1984 in an attempt to scale down government spending. We were clobbered. There was a sense that just as the West was about to get its due, you guys are going to cut back. And we did. We went through that, and came out with the GST, and now we're hammered with the charge that we're spending too much money. As politicians we're somewhat exasperated ... It's not getting any easier."[65]

In the spring of 1990, Tory renegades David Kilgour and Alex Kindy were suspended from the Alberta caucus for voting against the GST. Political analysts predicted that the Reform Party (which now had twice as much support in Alberta as the Conservatives) would rout the entire

Alberta Tory caucus in the next election. According to Stephen Harper, policy adviser to the Reform Party, "even putting myself in the Tories' place, I can see no plausible recovery strategy. Their constitutional strategy is out the window. The fiscal situation is worsening. We've just entered a recession. Their one claim to superiority over the Liberals and NDP, their ability to manage the economy, has been blown out of the water."[66]

In 1988 the PCs had had a plethora of popular policies that were capped off by the free-trade deal, all of which allowed the party to rebound from its mid-term lows. With a recession setting in, such a comeback seemed highly unlikely in the early 1990s. To make matters worse, a prevailing mood of disaffection and cynicism towards Ottawa was evident not only in the west but across the nation. This mood also translated into a general contempt for the current stock of politicians. "To judge by the opinion polls," the *Alberta Report* noted, "westerners are as disgusted by the Tories today as they were by the Liberals in the early 1980s." Polls indicated that 87 per cent of western voters disapproved of the Mulroney government. A steady stream of Tory workers were pouring into the Reform Party, and the Tory dynasty in the west was on the verge of collapse.[67]

The Reform Party was confident that the anti-federal sentiment indicated that voters were ready to accept the western-based organization as a legitimate and viable alternative. "The Tories failed to see there was a desire in the West for systematic changes," Reform leader Preston Manning observed. "They assumed simply eliminating the worst Liberal policies was sufficient to discharge their responsibilities to the West."[68] Kilgour predicted that "the Conservatives will lose every western seat in the next election. Mulroney's policies will wipe them out for a generation to come."[69]

The failure of the Meech Lake Accord came as a further blow to the Mulroney government. Alberta Premier Don Getty proclaimed that the death of the accord killed the dream of Senate reform. "Mr. Mulroney will turn Ottawa's attention ever more to satisfying the needs of Quebec," the *Alberta Report* claimed. "The West's economic and constitutional agenda, chiefly Senate reform, will be ignored … Mr. Mulroney will ignore the West's needs."[70] The tension was mounting between those who wanted Ottawa to be more responsive to the west's needs by reforming federal institutions and those who wanted to increase provincial power and independence while stripping Ottawa of its powers, thus making the west immune to federal heavy-handedness.

By September 1990, with the failure of Meech Lake, Brian Mulroney was being harangued in the western press for falling prey to "Liberal patronage habits" and filling Senate vacancies with Tories. The move dismayed advocates of a Triple-E Senate, despite Mulroney's obvious need to begin loading the Senate, then dominated by Liberals, with Conservatives in order to force through the enabling law for the GST as well as unemployment-insurance legislation. Mulroney further shocked advocates of Senate reform by threatening to use section 26 of the constitution to appoint up to eight additional senators in order to outnumber the Liberals in the upper house for the first time in forty-nine years. According to Ted Morton, the threat, whether real or illusory, "demonstrated Mulroney's contempt for the West." The region viewed Mulroney's "Senate wrangling" as "stemming from his alignment with the agenda of Quebec, which vehemently opposes any reform that gives the other regions a greater voice in Ottawa."[71]

The major dilemma facing Mulroney's Progressive Conservative Party by 1990 was the realignment on the political right. A Tory government was in power in Ottawa, yet two parties led by disgruntled Conservatives were emerging and both were taking shape in Mulroney's supposed strongholds. Coinciding with the plummet in PC fortunes was the rise of the Reform Party in the west and the birth of the Bloc Québécois. Preston Manning had nearly defeated Joe Clark in his Alberta riding in the 1988 election and Lucien Bouchard betrayed Brian Mulroney in May 1990 by leaving the federal party over the impending demise of Meech Lake and then seeking to steal Quebec as the Tory base of support and deliver it to the nationalists. Western alienation was also increasing as a result of the the weak group of prairie provincial premiers then in office. Gone were the days of Peter Lougheed, Allan Blakeney, and Sterling Lyon, premiers who built reputations speaking for the west on the national stage. In post-Meech Canada, after the "spirit" of national conciliation had apparently failed, the west was left with three much weaker premiers representing an increasingly angry region. The new wave of western alienation, aggravated by the lack of a strong western voice at the provincial level, manifested itself in rising support for the Reform Party. Saskatchewan's premier, Grant Devine, seemed to recognize the void in western leadership. With the death of Meech, he emphasized the need to develop a western agenda and a united western front, and in July 1990 he convened a meeting of the four western premiers in Lloydminister.[72]

Most western Conservatives placed the blame for the miserable Tory fortunes in the region on Mulroney's preoccupation with Quebec. Indeed, by the early 1990s, western alienation was most often taking the form of a powerful and bitter anti-Quebec bias. In 1984 Mulroney had won the temporary loyalty of French-Canadian nationalists by promising a new constitutional deal. Now, with Meech Lake's failure, the Bloc Québécois had been formed and Mulroney, in going after the old Liberal constituency in Quebec, lost his rapport with the west. It was argued that the most powerful Tory ministers from the west, such as Mazankowski and Clark, had lost their regional edge by being in national politics for so long. Clark became increasingly unpopular, even in his home province of Alberta, owing to his opposition to Triple-E Senate reform. It was speculated that neither would face the electorate again. According to Bercuson, no Tory seats in Alberta were safe in the next election. "It's an end-road," Alex Kindy claimed in the *Alberta Report*. "Mulroney has antagonized both the electorate and the last Conservatives in Canada."[73] Braid and Sharpe were more sympathetic to the Mulroney government. "The old western feeling that all the federal goodies go to Ontario and Quebec" is difficult to dispel. Despite significant federal spending in the region, they argued, the roots of western alienation and scepticism run so deeply that the region was not prepared to believe anything can change: "Western grievance, so deeply rooted in history, doesn't turn its head easily to the present."[74]

Throughout 1991 the antagonism between the Alberta and Quebec wings of the Tory caucus threatened to divide a government and party already in dire trouble. The release of Jean Allaire's report, *A Quebec Free to Choose*, followed by the report of the Belanger-Campeau Commission, *The Political and Constitutional Future of Quebec*, only increased the divide. The notion of a leadership change for the beleaguered party was openly bantered about. In the west, Mulroney's obsession with Quebec was now viewed as more obvious than that of the region's nemesis, Pierre Elliot Trudeau. "Mulroney is clearly a lame duck when it comes to representing English-Canada's interests," Ted Morton wrote. "It's time for the Conservatives to sharpen their knives. Historically, they've been good at dumping bungling leaders. But so far, it's been easterners knifing westerners – Diefenbaker and Clark. Maybe it's time for westerners to get into the act. It may give them one slim hope to save their own skin."[75]

Early in April 1991, the Alberta Progressive Conservative Party severed all ties with its federal counterpart. The provincial party was then free to throw its support behind the Reform Party. On 21 April 1991 Mulroney shuffled his cabinet in an attempt to give even more prominence to western MPs. Clark was moved from External Affairs to become the minister responsible for constitutional affairs, and he would also chair a new cabinet committee on Canadian unity and constitutional negotiations. Mazankowski remained deputy prime minister but was also named the first minister of finance from the west in almost sixty years years. The region now held ten of thirty-nine cabinet posts (it previously held ten but in a cabinet of thirty-seven). Harvie Andre was named government house leader, Kim Cambell was given the influential justice portfolio, Bill McKnight was given agriculture, and Jake Epp retained the energy post. All of this, according to the Toronto pundits, indicated that the west was virtually running the government.[76] The following day, Mulroney, Clark, and Mazankowski set off on a trip to Alberta (it was the prime minister's fourth trip to Calgary in a year). The objective was to woo former Tory faithful back from the Reform Party.

According to the *Alberta Report*, Mulroney "recited some western Canadian history, made direct appeals to regional sensibilities and borrowed a few policies from the more popular Reformers." He attacked the Reform Party's decision not to run candidates in Quebec, warning against a general retreat "into our respective solitudes," and blamed Reform for the rise of the Bloc Québécois. "It is sad to see that both are preparing for a break-up and, in doing so," the Prime Minister noted, "that both are hindering the chances for reconciliation."[77] He also promised movement on the issue of Senate reform, but not Triple-E reform: "In short, Mr. Mulroney did his best to present himself as a champion of western interests."[78] Before the week was out, however, the Tories suffered a setback. A Gallup poll showed them with 15 per cent support on the prairies, well behind the Reform Party at 43 per cent. Stephen Harper expressed surprise that Mulroney would even be focusing on Alberta because the battle between Conservatives and Reformers was over. "If you look at it in terms of us and them," Harper argued, "the front lines are no longer in this province but in B.C. and Saskatchewan and Ontario."[79]

The national policy conference of the federal Progressive Conservatives in August 1991 highlighted "a party at war with itself." The policy booklet contained a program that demonstrated the seemingly irreconcilable differences within the party. Resolutions varied from Red Tory notions to capture the moderate Conservatives to right-of-centre initiatives designed to appeal to the Reform Party. But the most glaring division lay between the west and Quebec. Resolutions from some western ridings condemned official bilingualism and called for equal constitutional powers for all provinces while some Quebec ridings demanded recognition of the province as a distinct society with a right to self-determination, along with veto power over all future constitutional amendments.[80] The defeat of Grant Devine's PC government in Saskatchewan in October 1991 by Roy Romanow's NDP was simply another sign of the general malaise facing the Tories in the west.

The rejection of the Charlottetown Accord in the referendum of October 1992 delivered a further blow to the Mulroney government. During the referendum campaign, it became clear that British Columbia and Alberta were strongly opposed to the agreement, and, by voting day, the "No" forces were in the ascendancy in Manitoba and Saskatchewan as well. With the defeat of the accord across the country, Mulroney's nationalistic dream of healing the wounds of the constitutional wars and bringing his home province of Quebec into the constitution were dashed. He had bet everything on this gamble and lost. Brian Mulroney retired prior to the 1993 federal election but the results brought this loss home. Even the choice of a westerner, the prominent cabinet minister Kim Campbell from British Columbia, did not make a dent on western alienation. The PCs won a

Table 3 Party seat allocation in the west: 1993 election

| | *Liberal* | *Progressive Conservative* | *NDP* | *Reform* |
|---|---|---|---|---|
| Alberta | 4 | 0 | 0 | 22 |
| British Columbia | 6 | 0 | 2 | 24 |
| Manitoba | 12 | 0 | 1 | 1 |
| Saskatchewan | 5 | 0 | 5 | 4 |

*Source*: Library of Parliament

staggering total of only two seats, neither of which was in the west. In western Canada the Reform Party won fifty-one of eighty-five seats.

## CONCLUSION

When examining the legacy of Prime Minister Brian Mulroney, one would be hard-pressed not to argue that his relationship with the west was a dismal failure. As Braid and Sharpe point out, "after a tentative embrace in 1984 and 1985, most westerners now think of Mulroney as the blind date they're sorry they accepted."[81] Why did this love affair turn so sour so quickly? By the end of the Mulroney years, the Canadian west was an even more small-c conservative region than it had been in 1984. Yet, in the federal election of 1993, the Mulroney Conservatives were utterly and completely decimated across the region. How could this happen?

The increasingly right-of-centre west rejected the Mulroney "vision" and embraced that of Preston Manning and the Reform Party for several reasons. Over the course of a decade, the west had shifted to the ideological right more rapidly than Brian Mulroney (who was, in reality, a Red Tory) or, for that matter, the majority of the Progressive Conservative Party. The government was increasingly criticized by its western caucus (most notably that vociferous but numerous cabal from Alberta) for not being socially conservative enough. While its economic policies from free trade to privatization and deregulation were lauded, its social policies (or lack thereof) were seen to be too soft and liberal. In addition, its handling of taxation (most notably the GST) and the deficit were viewed as continuations of typical Liberal government-interventionist tactics.

At the same time, it became increasingly apparent to the majority of westerners that Brian Mulroney was preoccupied with Quebec and there was little chance of this changing. "Ultimately, all Canadian leaders fall back to the populous fortress of Central Canada if they intend to survive," Braid and Sharpe claim. "And Brian Mulroney certainly means to survive."[82] But Mulroney was not merely following a pragmatic course by seeking to maintain his Quebec support. One of the major criticisms aimed at

Diefenbaker (and the major reason for the praise he received in the west) was that he was preoccupied with his home region. Canadian politics are fundamentally regional; individual politicians are inevitably so as well. Every politician, no matter his or her attempts to rise above localism, has roots somewhere. For Brian Mulroney, these roots were in Quebec and his resulting vision was of a bilingual and bicultural Canada that was prepared to do everything possible to accommodate Quebec. He could never understand or accept that other parts of Canada did not see the nation in the same light. "They don't understand that we are all hostages of our environment and prisoners of our childhood," he was quoted as saying in 1984 in response to the position taken on the language controversy by the Manitoba Conservative Party. "I don't see the history of Canada in the same way as somebody from the north of Manitoba. They have lived in a different historical current than mine. So I can understand very well some of the reactions I witness in western Canada. I understand – but I cannot share them because I witness them with a totally different appreciation."[83]

From the instant of Mulroney's election victory in 1984, it became apparent that the key to Conservative Party strategy was Quebec. Mulroney was in a unique position to establish the Tories in Quebec on a firm base,[84] and his attempts at constitutional reform placed him in the undisputed role as Quebec's champion. In truth, he was much closer to Trudeau's vision of a Canadian identity than Tory leaders of the past. His refusal to deal effectively with the west's demands for Senate reform only made this charge stick even more.

The accusation that Ottawa was obsessed with Quebec was not new and certainly the Mulroney government, or even the Trudeau government for that matter, was not the first to be tarred with it.[85] "Western mistrust of Ottawa is built into Canadian history and the national system," Braid and Sharpe note: "History can't change, and until the system does, the West will likely follow its old pattern of taking from the federal government with one hand and smacking it contemptuously with the other ... westerners believe the country isn't fair. Until it is, they will scold and fume at Ottawa and generally make pests of themselves. This is what colonials do best, and westerners are very good at it. History has taught them well."[86] In this sense, then, some of the criticism aimed at Mulroney's governments was clearly unfair and inevitable: "Mulroney's personality and Quebec identity boil vigorously in fevered western minds to form a potent political poison. When the prime minister talks about regional equality, westerners hear blarney; when he does a favour for his riding, they think they see the real prime minister."[87] By the end of the Mulroney years, the Conservative Party had been almost completely eclipsed in western Canada by the Reform Party. Through this new vehicle, the west would seek not only to remake the Progressive Conservative Party but to forge a new path, once again, for the region in Confederation.

## NOTES

1 Roger Gibbins, "National Reconciliation and the Canadian West: Political Management in the Mulroney Era," in Andrew B. Gollner and Daniel Salée, eds., *Canada under Mulroney: An End-of-Term Report* (Montreal: Vehicule Press 1988), 88–9.
2 *Alberta Report,* 9 July 1984.
3 Gibbins, "National Reconciliation and the Canadian West," 97.
4 David Bercuson, J.L. Granatstein, and W.R. Young, *Sacred Trust: Brian Mulroney and the Conservative Party in Power* (Toronto: Doubleday 1986), 1–5.
5 Rae Murphy, Robert Chodos, and Nick Auf der Maur, *Brian Mulroney: The Boy from Bai-Comeau* (Toronto: James Lorimer 1984), 1.
6 John Sawatsky, *Mulroney: The Politics of Ambition* (Toronto: Macfarlane Walter and Ross 1991), 494.
7 Sawatsky, *Mulroney: The Politics of Ambition,* 514–15.
8 *Alberta Report,* 20 April 1987.
9 *Maclean's,* 16 July 1984.
10 Roger Gibbins, "National Reconciliation and the Canadian West," 88–9.
11 In addition, three western senators had served as ministers of state in the last Trudeau government.
12 *Saturday Night,* June 1989.
13 Ibid.
14 Gibbins, "National Reconciliation and the Canadian West," 97.
15 Ibid., 90.
16 *Globe and Mail,* 19 February 1985.
17 Gibbins, "National Reconciliation and the Canadian West," 90–1.
18 As quoted in Claire Hoy, *Friends in High Places* (Toronto: Key Porter Books 1987), 88–9.
19 As quoted in *Saturday Night,* June 1989.
20 Ibid.
21 *Macelan's,* 9 September 1985.
22 *Alberta Report,* 3 February 1986.
23 As quoted in *Saturday Night,* June 1989.
24 *Alberta Report,* 19 September 1988.
25 *Alberta Report,* 4 August 1986.
26 *Alberta Report,* 20 April 1987.
27 Gibbins, "National Reconciliation and the Canadian West," 91.
28 *Globe and Mail,* 23 April 1987.
29 These were eliminated when the Trudeau government introduced its schemes for grants for exploration in frontier areas. Their restoration had become a symbolic issue in Alberta.
30 *Globe and Mail,* 11 February 1987.
31 *Alberta Report,* 20 April 1987.
32 Gibbins, "National Reconciliation and the Canadian West," 91.

33 Alvin Finkel, *Our Lives: Canada after 1945* (Toronto: James Lorimer 1997), 291.
34 Gibbins, "National Reconciliation and the Canadian West," 91–2.
35 Ibid., 90; *Saturday Night,* June 1989.
36 *Saturday Night,* June 1989.
37 Ibid.
38 The same month, McKnight announced that a Calgary heavy-machinery manufacturer had won a $420-million contract for 820 northern-terrain vehicles for the Canadian Forces. In September, Defence Minister Perrin Beatty announced that a significant portion of the work on a new $1.3-billion communications system for the armed forces would be done in western Canada. *Saturday Night,* June 1989.
39 *Globe and Mail,* 3 July 1987.
40 Gibbins, "National Reconciliation and the Canadian West," 92.
41 Ibid., 92–3.
42 *Globe and Mail,* 13 April 1988.
43 *Alberta Report,* 28 December 1987.
44 Gibbins, "National Reconciliation and the Canadian West," 94–5.
45 Don Braid and Sydney Sharpe, *Breakup: Why the West Feels Left out of Canada* (Toronto: Key Porter Books 1990), 86–7.
46 *Alberta Report,* 1 May 1989.
47 Gibbins, "National Reconciliation and the Canadian West," 98.
48 *Saturday Night,* June 1989.
49 As quoted in ibid.
50 Ibid.
51 See Robert Wardhaugh, *Mackenzie King and the Prairie West* (Toronto: University of Toronto Press 2000).
52 *Alberta Report,* 25 July 1988.
53 *Alberta Report,* 18 July 1988.
54 Ibid.
55 *Alberta Report,* 19 September 1988.
56 Finkel, *Our Lives: Canada after 1945*, 315.
57 *Alberta Report,* 19 June 1989.
58 *Saturday Night,* June 1989.
59 Ibid.
60 Ibid.
61 As quoted in ibid.
62 As quoted in ibid.
63 *Alberta Report,* 1 October 1990.
64 After some delay, Mulroney appointed Waters following private talks with Getty during the Meech Lake negotiations in June 1990.
65 Braid and Sharpe, *Breakup,* 10–12.
66 *Alberta Report,* 1 October 1990.
67 *Alberta Report,* 6 August 1990.

68 Ibid.
69 Ibid.
70 *Alberta Report,* 9 July 1990.
71 *Alberta Report,* 10 September 1990.
72 *Globe and Mail,* 24 July 1990.
73 *Alberta Report,* 6 August 1990.
74 Braid and Sharpe, *Breakup,* 13.
75 *Alberta Report,* 18 February 1991.
76 *Alberta Report,* 6 May 1991.
77 Ibid.
78 *Alberta Report,* 20 May 1991.
79 *Alberta Report,* 6 May 1991.
80 *Alberta Report,* 5 August 1991.
81 Braid and Sharpe, *Breakup,* 75–6.
82 Ibid., 76.
83 As quoted in Sawatsky, *The Politics of Ambition,* 515.
84 Bercuson, Granastein, and Young, *Sacred Trust,* 77.
85 See Wardhaugh, *Mackenzie King and the Prairie West.*
86 Braid and Sharpe, *Breakup,* 14.
87 Ibid., 79.

11

# Mulroney and a Nationalist Quebec: Key to Political Realignment in Canada?

MICHAEL D. BEHIELS

From the moment Brian Mulroney became leader of the Progressive Conservative Party in 1983, he was determined to create a political realignment in Canadian politics. He was obsessed with obliterating the Liberal Party as Canada's "Government Party" much in the same way that Wilfrid Laurier had destroyed the long-standing dominance of the Macdonald-Cartier Tory/Blue party in the watershed election of 1896. Mulroney was confident that he could use Québécois nationalist and secessionist movements to transform Quebec into the bastion of his Progressive Conservative Party. With the support of Conservative parties and governments from the Atlantic provinces, Ontario, and the west, Mulroney believed that a disciplined Progressive Conservative Party would become, after two or perhaps three successful elections, the new "government party" of Canada. Laurier's legacy would be laid to rest and Mulroney's would begin.

Since joining the Conservative Party in the mid-1950s, Mulroney had been an ardent Red Tory and a John Diefenbaker Canadian nationalist who proudly promoted "One Canada" and an interventionist federal government. Mulroney applauded, supported, and then agonized over Diefenbaker's determined but ultimately unsuccessful attempt to rebuild the Conservative Party's long-vanished base in Quebec.[1] Once Trudeau reestablished the Liberal party's dominance over Quebec from 1968 to1979, with his policy of official bilingualism and a tough stance on separatism, Mulroney knew that a divided Conservative Party – torn over the issue of "two nations" – could not achieve power let alone fulfil Diefenbaker's dream of a momentous political realignment in Canada.

On the question of Quebec and its place in Confederation, Mulroney, an inordinately ambitious and well-connected Quebec businessman and politician, became a supporter of Trudeau's vision of Canada and national unity. This ideological shift, as well as his high-rolling aggressive campaign, contributed to his defeat in the 1976 Conservative Party leadership race.[2]

Premier Robert Bourassa and Prime Minister Mulroney congratulate each other on 3 June 1987 during the Meech Lake Accord meetings. Photographer Andy Clark. Library and Archives Canada 87-C-02985-12A, negative number 007140469.

After he witnessed the political dominance of the Parti Québécois (PQ) following its election in November 1976, the clash of Canadian and Québécois nationalisms during the 1980 referendum on secession, and Trudeau's attainment of the Constitution Act, 1982 with its popular yet controversial Canadian Charter of Rights and Freedoms, Mulroney altered his political strategy and tactics. He came to understand the potent political force of Québécois nationalism, the ideological driving force behind Quebec's ongoing economic, social, cultural, linguistic, and political "Quiet Revolutions" since the 1950s.[3] Once he decided to seek the party leadership again in the early 1980s, his political strategy and tactics were heavily influenced by Quebec's impassioned nationalist environment. The re-emergence in Quebec of nationalistic discourse leading up to and during the 1984 federal election provided Mulroney with the illusive key required to make a breakthrough. That key was the Constitution Act, 1982, with its charter, that Trudeau had put into place following more than a decade of divisive mega-constitutional politics. For nationalist and class reasons, Quebec's political and intellectual circles would not or could not give their consent to the Constitution Act, 1982. Having broken ties with the francophone and Acadian minority communities outside Quebec in the 1960s, they rejected the charter's section 23 – education rights for Canada's official-language minorities – because it eroded exclusive provincial control over education.[4] Led by Claude Morin, they concocted a powerful and disturbing myth whereby the Québécois "people" had been betrayed by Canadian politicians during the "night of the long knives."[5]

Leading Québécois nationalist politicians, journalists, and academics, exemplified best by Lucien Bouchard, convinced Mulroney that the key to winning the hearts and minds – and the political support – of *les Québécois* was to remove or override the offending clauses of Constitution Act, 1982 and its charter so that these would conform to the modern constitutional vision of the Québécois francophone majority. Québécois nationalists and separatists of all stripes had been striving since the 1960s to achieve their far more radical and comprehensive conception of political realignment. They were determined to transform the long-established reality of pan-Canadian cultural and linguistic duality – French Canada and British Canada – into a new conception of territorial duality of Quebec and Canada, reconfigured into a decentralized confederation of two equal nation-states. The challenge for Mulroney, who was seeking a more modest form of political realignment, was to make this Québécois nationalist territorial conception of an equal Quebec/Canada duality co-exist with the conception of the equality of the provinces already entrenched in the Constitution Act, 1982, as exemplified in the general amending formula of 7/50, whereby seven provinces comprising 50 per cent of the population and Parliament can alter most provisions of the constitution.

Convinced that the road to Canada's political realignment came via Quebec's signature on an amended Constitution Act, 1982, Mulroney opened mega-constitutional negotiations with Premier Robert Bourassa's Liberal government, re-elected to office in 1985, thanks in part to his five-point constitutional agenda. Between 1986 and 1992, Canadians witnessed not one but two destabilizing rounds of mega-constitutional politics. The Quebec round, quickly transformed into the provincial round, culminated in the Meech Lake Constitutional Accord of 30 April 1987. When the accord failed to be ratified within the three-year deadline, a second, more comprehensive constitutional-reform package, dubbed the Charlottetown Consensus Report, was negotiated by Joe Clark, the premiers, and four national Aboriginal organizations, but this deal was rejected by Canadians in their first ever national constitutional referendum on 26 October 1992. Mulroney's and Bourassa's failed attempts to achieve their respective political realignments via mega-constitutional politics ended both of their political careers. What Prime Minister Mulroney had conceived as a straightforward process of displacing the Liberal Party as Canada's governing party had a much different outcome from the one he had intended, encompassing both the rise of new parties in the west and Quebec and the virtual destruction of the Conservative Party. The purpose of this chapter is to explain this remarkable turn of events.

## CANADA, QUEBEC, AND THE CONSTITUTIONAL CONUNDRUM

The process of political realignment in Canada began imperceptibly when Joe Clark's Progressive Conservative Party defeated Trudeau's Liberals in the election of 22 May 1979, winning a minority government of 136 seats. The Liberal Party retained 114 seats, 67 in its bastion of Quebec. Clearly, Clark had failed to make the necessary breakthrough in Quebec. His misguided sympathies with the constitutional aspirations of Quebec's old and new nationalists had not been rewarded.

Prior to the election, Clark's public disagreement with his chief Quebec lieutenant, Roch La Salle, over the issue of self-determination for Quebec and his belated rejection of "special constitutional status" for the province ensured that few Québécois nationalists of any political stripe would work or vote for Tory candidates. (He appointed Arthur Tremblay, a well-known Québécois neo-nationalist, to the Senate to advise him on a constitutional policy for Quebec.[6]) Nor did his constant vacillating on constitutional reform – premised on his conception of Canada as a "community of communities" – endear him to the vast majority of Canadians. Yet Clark's promise of greater decentralization assured his short-lived government of the momentary support of Tory provincial governments, especially in the west, and, in the election of 1979 his commitment to "downsizing" government, deregulating the economy, and providing tax breaks to middle-class homeowners more than doubled Tory seats in Ontario – from twenty-five in 1974 to fifty-seven in 1979.[7] Clark would not get the opportunity to take advantage of the political realignment that was under way in Ontario and the west, however, as his government was defeated after only 259 days in office.[8] Lacking what Jeffrey Simpson called the "discipline of power," the Progressive Conservative government's "brave new era" was over before it began; in the national election of 18 February 1980, Clark's Conservative Party retained only 103 seats – a loss of thirty-three – with a dismal one seat from Quebec, and Trudeau's Liberals were returned to office with 44 per cent of the vote and 146 seats, once again the bulk of them from Quebec.[9] With only two Liberal seats in the west, Canada no longer had a truly national party, and a regionally divided country headed into a Quebec referendum on secession and a divisive political struggle over constitutional renewal. Both developments widened old and new cleavages, thereby contributing to the underlying pressures for political realignment.

To the dismay and chagrin of the national and provincial Conservative parties and the Parti Québécois, the Liberal Party had regained office under the leadership of a chastened yet reinvigorated and formidable Pierre Elliott Trudeau. As promised repeatedly in the 1979 campaign but played down in 1980, Trudeau fully intended to settle the national-unity crisis. He began by defeating the Québécois separatists in the 20 May 1980 referendum by a resounding margin of twenty percentage points, sixty to forty.[10] True to his word, Trudeau announced in the House of Commons on 21 May 1980 his government's decision to proceed unilaterally with a constitutional resolution to patriate the British North America Act, 1867 with an amending formula and a Charter of Rights. Following negotiations and a failed September 1980 constitutional conference with the premiers, lengthy public hearings on a constitutional resolution before a joint committee of the Senate and the House that garnered strong public support for the charter, three provincial court rulings – one against the resolution – followed by a reference to the Supreme Court of Canada (which ruled that the resolution was legal but politically unconstitutional) and several appeals to the British crown, courts, and Parliament, Trudeau achieved his goal. On 5 November 1981 Trudeau and all the premiers except René Lévesque approved an amended constitutional package.[11]

## MULRONEY, QUEBEC, AND THE CONSTITUTIONAL IMPERATIVE

The PQ government's decision to reject the Constitution Act, 1982 provided the Conservative Party with a political opening it had been seeking for nearly two decades. But it would be Brian Mulroney, not Joe Clark, who would take advantage of the situation when he began his second run at the leadership of the Conservative Party in March 1983. This time, he astutely avoided all the pitfalls and mistakes of his first attempt in 1976. Mulroney and his coterie of Quebec advisers and supporters appealed to neo-conservatives – called neo-liberals in Quebec – by emphasizing his corporate experience with the Iron Ore Company of Canada. But his trump card in his drive to replace Clark was his argument that only he could bring nationalistic francophone Quebecers into the Progressive Conservative Party. He repeatedly declared that, by winning enough seats in Quebec, a Mulroney-led Progressive Conservative Party would achieve a majority in the next federal election. Unlike Clark in 1980, he was determined not to write off the 102 constituencies in the country where francophones and Acadians constituted more than 10 per cent of the voters. He reminded Conservatives that the 1980 election in Quebec had been a tragicomedy. "We lost our deposits in fifty-six seats, we finished third in forty-one seats, behind the NDP in thirty-nine seats, and behind the Rhinoceros Party in two."[12]

The national Liberal Party's monopoly over Quebec had to be broken at all costs if an ambitious Mulroney hoped to become prime minister.

Mulroney and his Quebec team, Michel Cogger, Peter White, Jean Bazin, Bernard Roy, and Rodrique Pageau, built a political base in Quebec by obtaining public endorsements from well-known Liberals like Paul Desrochers and PQ supporters like Lucien Bouchard; gaining control of the provincial Conservative Party executive; creating nearly forty riding organizations where they did not exist; and increasing the party membership, which in 1983 stood at a dismal 10,000. Mulroney, who supported Trudeau's Constitution Act, 1982 and the Charter of Rights, denounced Clark's constitutional proposal for full financial compensation to any province opting out of shared-cost programs under provincial jurisdiction.[13] The amending formula could not be altered without unanimous consent, and, Mulroney argued, if it was altered it would end up putting federal funds at the service of the PQ's drive to dismantle Canada.[14] Thanks to a spirited and determined leadership campaign which he carried into the Conservative leadership convention in mid-June 1983 at the Ottawa Civic Centre, Mulroney narrowly defeated Joe Clark on the fourth ballot. He did so in large measure by garnering the votes of 60 per cent of the 726 registered Quebec delegates and nearly 70 per cent of John Crosbie's votes when he was knocked out after the third ballot.[15]

The year 1984 was a tumultuous one on the national political scene. It began with Prime Minister Trudeau abruptly announcing his resignation on 29 February, after a walk in a blinding snowstorm. John Turner, returning from his sojourn in the private sector, defeated Jean Chrétien for the leadership of the Liberal Party in a bitter struggle and assumed the office of prime minister. His stint in office was brief. Badly misjudging a momentary surge in the polls for the Liberals, Turner called a fateful snap election for 4 September. Mulroney and his strategists were ecstatic with both developments. They preferred to face Turner rather than Chrétien, especially in the battle for the hearts and minds of Québécois. Mulroney's perception of the country's problems and the Conservative Party's socio-economic policies corresponded closely with those of a Turner-led Liberal Party, and this levelled the playing field in Ontario and the west. More important, from the Quebec angle, Turner appeared distinctly uncomfortable with minority-language issues, both inside and outside Quebec, and he displayed little or no rapport with his Quebec caucus and constituency militants, many of whom remained profoundly loyal to Trudeau and Chrétien.[16]

Mulroney, realizing that the Liberal Party remained deeply divided between its Turner and Chrétien wings, set out to exploit these divisions in order to destroy the Liberal bastion in Quebec. With the assistance and financial support of long-standing friends in Quebec's legal and business circles, he applied the same approach that had won him the leadership – this time "pour transformer leur 'parti de Blokes' en machine capable d'arracher le Quebec à la tutelle liberale."[17] The central element of his strategy was to attract high-profile local candidates, be they members of the provincial Liberal Party, the moribund Union Nationale Party, or a Parti Québécois in the midst of self-destructing. When Robert Bourassa freed Liberal Party militants to work for whom they wished in the election, Mulroney was delighted since many of them decided to work for or run as Tory candidates. Another effective tactic was to identify the Conservative Party almost exclusively with Brian Mulroney – a Quebec-born Conservative chief who confronted a Bay Street Liberal leader out of touch with the aspirations of Québécois. By providing the Quebec wing of the Progressive Conservative Party with a well-funded political organization and well-known local candidates of various political stripes, and by shrewdly identifying the party with Quebec's francophone majority, Mulroney was convinced that he could break the long-standing Liberal stranglehold over that province.[18]

From the moment Mulroney entered federal politics in 1976, he had consistently portrayed himself as an ardent supporter of a bilingual and multicultural Canada. He was opposed to the theory of "two nations" entrenched via a constitutional special status for Quebec because, in his view, it threatened national unity. In fact, on this issue his vision of the country was similar to Trudeau's. Following his maiden speech in the House on 13 September 1983, Mulroney agreed to support Trudeau's proposal for an all-party resolution on full restoration of Franco-Manitobans' constitutional language rights. Section 23 of the Manitoba Act, 1870, mandating official bilingualism in the legislature and courts of Manitoba, was abolished by the Manitoba legislature in 1890. Nearly a century later, the Supreme Court of Canada ruled that section 23 language rights must be restored.[19] Mulroney's speech on the issue was a superb performance, one that set him apart from his rival, John Turner, who waffled. While Mulroney's position did not go down well in many western Tory ridings, it put him on the side of the angels among Canada's francophone and Acadian communities, including most Québécois.

In the public imagination, it appeared that Mulroney had taken on the mantle of the defender of the linguistic minorities, that he belonged to the Trudeau school on the issue of Quebec's place in the federation and the need for official bilingualism in Ottawa and certain provinces like New Brunswick and Manitoba. And yet, by the time the summer 1984 federal election was under way, Mulroney was already shifting dramatically his constitutional position. The reason was simple. He was convinced that, for struggling Progressive Conservative candidates – lagging far behind the Liberals in the polls – to defeat incumbent Liberals, they would have to be able to win the hearts and minds of Québécois conditional federalists, Liberal neo-nationalists, and disillusioned PQ supporters. If they failed, Mulroney would not make the breakthrough in Quebec that he had promised Conservatives, a prerequisite to becoming prime minister with a majority Tory government. He did not relish the thought of repeating Joe Clark's humiliating experience of 1979.[20]

Appealing to Québécois nationalists of all stripes, especially the intellectuals and journalists who influenced public opinion, was not going to be easy task for a well-known partisan Tory federalist like Mulroney. Always the superb opportunist, he decided that the most effective way to signal his dramatic shift on the constitutional question was to convince a long-time friend and PQ militant, Lucien Bouchard, to join his Quebec Conservative team. Dismayed at the collapse of the Parti Québécois and the imminent departure of René Lévesque, Lucien Bouchard agreed to join the Tory campaign as a speechwriter. In undertaking his version of what Lévesque dubbed the federalist "beau risqué," Bouchard most assuredly had his own Québécois nationalist agenda. Indeed, he succeeded in convincing Mulroney that the Constitution Act, 1982, with its Canadian Charter of Rights and Freedoms, was a catastrophic and humiliating imposition on the Québécois people. It needed to be revamped if the Québécois political, intellectual, and economic classes were going to be reconciled to Canada. Choosing his words carefully, Mulroney began to make statements to the effect that a Conservative government, given the appropriate political climate and the strong likelihood of a positive outcome, would reopen constitutional negotiations with Quebec. He proposed to redress what the Quebec elite considered the unacceptable outcome of Trudeau's constitution and charter, especially the loss of Quebec's "traditional" constitutional veto.[21]

Clearly, Mulroney believed that the political risks of altering his constitutional position could be managed. His confidence was based on the fact that, as prime minister, he would be negotiating not with a separatist PQ government but with a Liberal government headed by his old friend, Robert Bourassa, who he was certain would be eminently reasonable in his constitutional demands. Indeed, it was no secret that Bourassa favoured a Mulroney government. Twenty per cent of provincial Liberal riding associations, and about half of the Liberal rank and file, were supporting and, in some cases, working for Conservative candidates.[22] A Mulroney-Bourassa alliance was being forged in the political trenches of Quebec, an unusual alliance that would have an incalculable and far-reaching impact on Quebec and Canadian politics. The alliance would play a central role in Mulroney's quest for a comprehensive and enduring political realignment at the national level, one that had eluded every Conservative prime minister since Robert Borden.

Urged to be more explicit by his Quebec team, Mulroney opted to make a major policy announcement on the constitution – based on a revised text prepared by Bouchard – during his nomination meeting in Sept-Îles in northern Quebec on 6 August 1984.[23] In a forceful and passionate speech full of codes easily understood by all Québécois nationalists and secessionists, Mulroney promised to do whatever he had to in order to "convince the National Assembly of Quebec to give its consent to the new constitution with honour and dignity."[24] Mulroney's forthright appeal to Québécois nationalists proved highly effective. Many Québécois nationalists, including a large number of PQ, Liberal, and former Union Nationale supporters, threw their support behind, and eventually voted for, relatively unknown Conservative candidates. They had come to perceive that Mulroney and not Turner was the appropriate successor to former prime minister Trudeau. Like Trudeau, Mulroney came across as one of their own, a sympathetic and reliable defender of the francophone cause in the Canadian federal system.[25]

The Conservatives were rewarded beyond their wildest dreams. In Quebec, Mulroney successfully convinced a majority of Québécois that it was essential for them to be part of what was going to be a majority Conservative government. In the election of 4 September 1984, the Progressive Conservative Party defeated the Liberal government of John Turner in a landslide victory, one that surpassed even that of Diefenbaker in 1958. With 50 per cent of the vote, the Tories garnered 211 of 282 seats. They swept 67 seats in Ontario, up from 38 in 1980, but the most dramatic and crucial breakthrough came in Quebec. Mulroney and his Quebec campaign team, overcoming the drawbacks posed by a slate of inexperienced candidates, delivered a stunning blow to the Quebec wing of the national Liberal Party by winning 58 of the province's 75 ridings. The once impenetrable Liberal bastion of Quebec was in tatters, reduced to a rump of 17 MPs, most of them representing English-speaking ridings in the Montreal and Hull regions.[26] And yet a far more daunting challenge lay ahead. Could Mulroney, his advisers, and MPs consolidate their breakthrough or would the Quebec Tories suffer the same dismal fate experienced by Diefenbaker's Quebec MPs in the 1962 and 1963 elections?

## FORGING THE MULRONEY-BOURASSA ALLIANCE

The Mulroney government's accession to power in Ottawa accelerated the political transition in Quebec. Prime Minister Mulroney's challenge was how best to forge an alliance with the soon-to-be Liberal premier of his home province. First, he would do whatever he could to help his friend and potential ally on the major issues of the economy and the constitution, Robert Bourassa, to become premier once again. Bourassa, overcoming the machinations of Trudeau and the national Liberal Party, had been elected as Liberal leader in October 1983. Eager to get into the fray, Bourassa felt compelled by the summer of 1985 to seek a seat in the National Assembly. To the surprise of most pundits, he chose to contest a by-election in the Montreal south shore riding of Bertrand, a veritable "Fortress PQ." He won by a whopping margin of 57 to 37 per cent. His confidence restored, Bourassa was convinced that the premier's job was his for the taking.[27]

Bourassa's easy victory reaffirmed and widened the divisions in Lévesque's demoralized Parti Québécois. Hoping to outmanœuvre Bourassa on the constitutional question, Lévesque welcomed Mulroney's election promise in 1984 to undertake constitutional negotiations with the Quebec government. He announced his government's intention to seek a constitutional accord with Ottawa if and when Mulroney became prime minister. Initially agreeing with the militants that the PQ should remain committed to independence, Lévesque then questioned the tactic of turning the next provincial election into a vote on sovereignty-association. At the PQ's convention, backed by a three-to-two margin among the delegates, Lévesque declared that the party would not fight the next election on sovereignty. This decision accelerated the internecine warfare between the orthodox camp, represented by Pierre-Marc Johnson, the justice minister, and the hardliners or revisionists, led by the finance minister, Jacques Parizeau. By the end of the year, nearly a dozen backbenchers and cabinet ministers had resigned from the caucus and the cabinet. Parizeau himself resigned from the National Assembly and did what he could do to undermine Johnson's leadership of the PQ.

Clearly, Mulroney and Bourassa held the upper hand. Yet the prime minister had to finesse the situation until Bourassa was premier. Indicating that he had no intention of undertaking constitutional negotiations before the next provincial election, Mulroney met Lévesque late in 1984 to ferret out his constitutional bottom line and to make his own position clear to francophone Quebecers. Prior to the meeting, Lévesque indicated that he felt that restoring Quebec's constitutional veto was an absurdity – he had given up the veto in the April 1981 accord with seven premiers. Mulroney retorted that he considered the veto indispensable for the protection of Quebec's distinct character in the federation.[28]

In May 1985 Lévesque released a *Draft Agreement on the Constitution: Proposals by the Government of Quebec*. The document set out a comprehensive list of constitutional demands: the recognition of Quebec as a distinct society; the primacy of the Quebec Charter over the Canadian Charter of Rights and Freedoms; Quebec's exclusive jurisdiction over language matters; full financial compensation for opting out of any amendment; the return of Quebec's traditional veto over all constitutional changes; a severe curtailment of federal spending powers; the elimination of Ottawa's powers of reservation of disallowance; and full control over immigration, communications, economic and manpower policy, and marriage and divorce laws. In return, the National Assembly would ratify the Constitution Act, 1982.

Lévesque's constitutional bottom line read like a vast shopping list of Québécois nationalists' ever-expanding demands. For a leader running out of time, Lévesque had little option but to hold his fractured party together as he contemplated almost certain defeat in the rapidly approaching election. Using the most recent terminology of Québécois nationalists, Mulroney declared that Quebec was "distinct" and then met with Lévesque in June 1985 to discuss the PQ's radical demands. Considering them to be a starting point for negotiations, he asked that Lévesque speak to the other premiers about his demands and promised that his government "would never do anything to diminish the rights of a minority anywhere."

In the interim, Bourassa's Liberal Party made public its own five constitutional conditions for signing the Constitution Act, 1982. Hammered out by Gil Rémillard, a law professor, the five conditions were somewhat less radical but no less far-reaching than those of the PQ. The two crucial demands were constitutional recognition of Quebec as a distinct society in a preamble applying to the entire constitution and the restoration of Quebec's de facto veto over amendments to federal institutions or the creation of new provinces. The three other conditions were: limitation of federal spending power; Quebec's participation in the appointment of judges to the Supreme Court of Canada; and increased powers over immigration.[29] There was nothing in the Liberal package that Mulroney publicly disagreed with, a sure sign that he had been allowed to vet the proposals. The emerging Mulroney-Bourassa alliance would not have to wait in the wings much longer. Surprising everyone, including members of his entourage, cabinet, and caucus, Lévesque submitted his resignation on 20 June, the day after receiving lavish praise in the National Assembly on the twenty-fifth anniversary of his election in 1960. Undoubtedly facing almost certain defeat in the upcoming election, Lévesque preferred to leave on his own terms rather than face a much-rumoured putsch. He left office convinced that he had done his utmost for his party and for his beloved Québécois people since 1968. No doubt, he hoped that his successor, Pierre-Marc Johnson, would be better able to carry out the "beau risque" constitutional strategy with Ottawa and consequently be in a stronger position to face Bourassa in the forthcoming election thanks to his appeal to moderate nationalists of all political stripes.[30]

Mulroney was not about to shore up Johnson by negotiating a constitutional deal with the PQ government. But, in the interim, another snag emerged. Mulroney and Bourassa learned that a few old-line, Union Nationale Tories were planning to set up a provincial Conservative Party, something that Mulroney had always championed. During a hurried meeting in January 1985, Bourassa convinced Mulroney that the attempt had to be stopped cold. The prime minister obliged, since neither he nor Bourassa wanted a provincial Conservative Party stealing Liberal votes and seats and thereby ensuring a PQ win. Mulroney would reopen constitutional negotiations to gain Quebec's signature on the Constitution Act, 1982 only once a federalist party was in power in Quebec.[31]

Shortly after Johnson dropped the writ for an election on 2 December 1985, Mulroney enhanced his growing popularity among francophone Quebecers, especially the middle-class elites. He announced, in the presence of the premier, a federal-provincial agreement that allowed the Quebec government to participate as a full member of la Francophonie, a French-language commonwealth whose creation had been delayed by the French government until Quebec could be made a full partner. Lucien Bouchard had a heavy hand in the process, since Mulroney had appointed him Canada's ambassador to France in return for his joining the Conservative election campaign. Of course, Bourassa was pleased because he was confident that, as Quebec's new premier, he would preside over the Quebec delegation at the inaugural Paris conference in February 1986.[32]

As most political analysts and pundits had predicted, Lévesque's and Johnson's decision to abandon the Parti Québécois commitment to sovereignty-association destroyed its *raison d'être.* Despite Johnson's perceived competence and popularity among the voters, the PQ's chances of re-election were marginal. The political door was opened wide for Robert Bourassa to reassume the office of premier after an absence of nearly a decade. He and his new team of younger, nationalistic Liberals ran a highly effective campaign promoting economic renewal based on Quebec's immense water and hydro-electric resources, social peace on the language issue, and a promise to regain Quebec's constitutional veto along with special status within the federation. On 2 December 1985 the Parti Québécois was routed. With 56 per cent of the vote, Bourassa's Liberal Party won 99 seats (Bourassa lost his seat on Montreal's South Shore but would win easily in a Saint-Laurent by-election on 20 January 1986). The PQ and its new leader, Johnson, with 38 per cent of the vote, barely managed to hold on to 23 seats while 19 of 29 cabinet ministers, including heavyweights like Bernand Landry and Pauline Marois, were defeated. Parizeau waited offstage to pick of the remnants of the disaster and keep a close watch on the emerging Mulroney-Bourassa alliance.[33]

## THE ALLIANCE PAYS OFF: THE MEECH LAKE ACCORD

The Mulroney-Bourassa alliance, forged during their respective leadership and election campaigns, produced one of the most unusual constitutional deals in Canadian history. Following a late January 1986 meeting, Mulroney and Bourassa stated publicly that fulfilling the constitutional aspirations of Quebec was the top priority of both governments. They set up teams of trusted advisers, ministers, and senior mandarins.[34] By March 1986, Quebec's intergovernmental affairs minister, Gil Rémillard, announced that the Canadian Charter of Rights would be given precedence over the Quebec Charter. The National Assembly would no longer invoke the "notwithstanding clause" to override sections 2 and 7–15 of the charter. At a conference at Mont-Gabriel, Quebec, on 9 May 1986 – organized by the Institute of Intergovernmental Relations at Queen's University – Gil Rémillard reiterated Quebec's five conditions for signing the 1982 constitution. There was one crucial alteration to the initial conditions laid out in the Liberal Party's platform *Maîtriser l'avenir.* Symbolic recognition of Quebec as a distinct society in the preamble to the constitution no longer sufficed. Recognition had to be explicit and legally meaningful.[35] How this was to be done was eventually spelt out in the Meech Lake Constitutional Accord. The "distinct society" clause, to achieve Quebec's long-term constitutional and political objectives, would function as a powerful interpretive clause applying to the entire Canadian constitution. In other words, Quebec could use the Supreme Court to reshape the federation in its interests. Rémillard concluded his remarks by warning Canadians that "Quebec nationalism is not dead, far from it. It is thriving more than ever but in a different form. It is no longer synonymous with isolationism or xenophobia but rather with excellence."[36]

The drive for a constitutional accord with Quebec was on in earnest. Mulroney and Bourassa, eager to dispose of the constitutional question in a pragmatic and rapid manner, met on 4 June 1986 to discuss Quebec's five demands. Mulroney, without formally endorsing the five demands, indicated that he was receptive to Bourassa's constitutional initiative. He encouraged Bourassa to convince the premiers, before their annual meeting in Edmonton in mid-August 1986, to give Quebec's constitutional demands serious consideration. Rémillard was dispatched to all the provincial capitals to convince his counterparts to accept Quebec's constitutional agenda. Quebec would not proceed until it had the assurance of provincial support since some aspects of its package required the application of the unanimity amending formula. Bourassa was well aware that failure would rekindle the fires of Québécois nationalism and secessionism.

Mulroney wrote the nine premiers before their August meeting urging them to look favourably upon Quebec's demands. His and Bourassa's efforts were partially successful. At the conclusion of their August 1986 meeting, the premiers issued a vaguely worded "Edmonton Declaration" in which they agreed to hold constitutional discussions based on Quebec's demands in order to facilitate "Quebec's full and active participation in the Canadian federation." Nonetheless, most of the premiers remained reluctant to become involved in another round of mega-constitutional politics so soon after their bruising experiences of 1980–81. Their constituents were far more interested in economic development, trade, jobs, and taxation matters than in the constitution. If they were going to reopen constitutional negotiations, many of the premiers and their constituents had priorities of their own, including Senate reform and the entrenchment of property rights. Brian Peckford insisted on greater control over the Grand Bank fisheries.[37]

Getting the premiers to the constitutional table required considerably more political arm-twisting. Taking on the role of advocate for Bourassa and backed initially by Premier David Peterson of Ontario, Mulroney undertook to meet the premiers one-on-one to convince them of the importance of finding the appropriate formula for accepting Bourassa's constitutional demands. During the first ministers' conference on the economy held in Vancouver in November 1986, Mulroney convinced the premiers that they should give Quebec's five demands priority over their own constitutional shopping lists. Yet the premiers remained wary of undertaking any formal constitutional negotiations unless there was something in the process for them. Concerned that the process was stalling, Mulroney dispatched his trusted minister of federal-provincial relations, Senator Lowell Murray, to carry out bilateral talks with his provincial counterparts to see how the circle could be squared. Murray, like his boss Joe Clark, had voted against the Constitution Act, 1982 because the province of Quebec was not a signatory. A staunch advocate of special status and a constitutional veto for Quebec, Murray was one of the initial supporters of Rémillard's conditions and would be a steadfast protagonist of the Meech Lake Accord. Roger Tassé and Senator Arthur Tremblay kept Bourassa's people informed of the sensitive negotiations and so ensuring that the Ottawa-Quebec alliance never wavered.[38]

Following up on Senator Murray's advance work, Mulroney launched an intense lobbying blitzkrieg that culminated in the Meech Lake Accord. Already in considerable political difficulty in Quebec, Mulroney had urgently required the political credit that would accompany the constitutional reconciliation of the province. But how was he able to forge the deal, one he was not convinced was possible? The agreement emerged as a result of the negotiating strategy proposed by Senator Murray and his deputy, Norman Spector, and adopted by Mulroney. The prime minister, rather than putting a single constitutional demand for the Canadian government on the table, played the role of broker between his ally, Premier Bourassa, and nine reluctant premiers. On 30 April, Mulroney convened an informal first ministers' meeting at Willson House, located on Meech Lake in the Gatineau Park. With no officials in the room and facing the unrelenting pressure tactics of Mulroney, the nine premiers, one at a time, eventually agreed to Bourassa's five demands on condition that four of Bourassa's provisions – the distinct society interpretive clause was reserved for Quebec – be available to them. As one perceptive journalist demonstrates in his account, [39] the premiers hijacked the Quebec round at Meech Lake and transformed both the process and the final accord into a provincial round. The ambiguous accord married asymmetrical federalism for Quebec in the distinct society clause with the nine other premiers' determination to obtain recognition of the equality of the provinces in the clauses pertaining to the limitation of Ottawa's spending power, an amending formula giving provinces a veto over national institutions and the creation of new provinces, bilateral immigration agreements, appointments to the Supreme Court and the Senate, and annual first ministers' conferences. Much to Mulroney's and Bourassa's surprise and ultimate dismay, the premiers' hijacking of the deal set in motion an uncontrollable political chain reaction which contributed to the eventual demise of the Meech Lake Accord three years later.

Throughout the trials and tribulations of the accord, the Mulroney-Bourassa alliance held firm. Mulroney had come to embrace Bourassa's vision of a distinct constitutional role for Quebec in an increasingly decentralized, asymmetrical, binational federation called Quebec-Canada. The traditional pan-Canadian dualism of French Canada and British Canada was dead. It had to be transformed constitutionally into a binational federation comprising two territorially defined national states: a francophone national state represented primarily by an officially unilingual state of Quebec, and an officially bilingual and multicultural national state represented by Canada, the provinces, and territories. Furthermore, both leaders were driven by their respective political agendas. Mulroney was convinced that his Conservative Party should and would replace the Liberal Party as Canada's long-standing governing party by winning big in Quebec. Bourassa wanted to overcome the humiliation of his defeat at the hands of René Lévesque's Parti Québécois in 1976 by associating himself, the Quebec Liberal Party, and the Quebec government with the resolution of the impasse over the Constitution Act, 1982 and the Charter of Rights and Freedoms through the entrenchment of a territorial conception of dualism, Quebec-Canada, in the constitution.

The Bourassa government ratified the Meech Lake Accord on 24 June 1987, despite strong denunciations by the leader and members of the PQ and the Québécois "chattering classes." In doing so, the premier kick-started the three-year ratification process. Convinced that the accord offered francophone Quebecers far too little too late, Parizeau declared that a PQ government led by him would use the accord's distinct society clause to advance the cause of independence.[40] Outside Quebec, there was initially little indication that the accord would encounter widespread opposition since all political leaders appeared to be onside. Polls indicated that the general public was in favour of the deal while groups committed to the defence of the Charter of Rights remained dormant or disorganized. The leader of the official opposition, John Turner, pressured by Raymond Garneau, a Québécois nationalist and leader of the Quebec wing of the Liberal Party, immediately committed himself and his caucus to the accord despite the fact that the concept of Quebec as a distinct society had been rejected at the November 1986 policy convention. Turner was convinced that supporting the accord was essential in order to reverse the political realignment under way in Quebec.[41]

Little did Turner realize that his impromptu decision momentarily accelerated the realignment and eventually contributed to his early political demise. Indeed, he foolishly refused to heed a major warning sign. On 27 May 1987, in the Toronto *Star* and *La Presse*, Pierre Elliott Trudeau declared that the accord, if ratified, would render the Canadian state so impotent that it was destined, "given the dynamics of power, to be governed eventually by eunuchs." [42] A great many prominent Liberals, including Donald Johnson, Jean Chrétien, Marc Lalonde, and Michael Kirby, realized that the future of their party and their vision of Canada were under siege. They waged a relentless and ultimately successful campaign against the accord and the Mulroney-Bourassa alliance.[43]

Aiding and abetting the emerging opposition to the accord was a fundamental disagreement between Mulroney and Bourassa over how to interpret and then sell the distinct society clause to Canadians in general and more specifically to francophone Quebecers. Outside Quebec, Mulroney, his closest advisers, and his government proclaimed immediately and repeatedly that the recognition of Quebec as a distinct society was purely symbolic and did not grant Quebec any additional powers. In contrast, Bourassa, feeling triumphant, argued that the distinct society clause confirmed Quebec's exclusive control over all language matters, including those pertaining to education. "We must acknowledge," he declared in the National Assembly, "that in the distinct society clause we are getting a major gain that is not limited to the purely symbolic, since the country's entire Constitution ... including the Charter of Rights, will be interpreted and applied in the light of the article on the distinct society. This directly involves the exercise of legislative power, and will allow us to consolidate our gains and make even greater advances."[44] In 1982 Bourassa proclaimed that, under the unacceptable Constitution Act, 1982 which recognized the constitution as the supreme law of Canada, the federal government was henceforth "constitutionally required to use all means necessary to enforce respect of [Canada's] territorial integrity."[45] Bourassa then made a blatantly unfounded assertion to the effect that the Meech Lake Accord's distinct society clause recaptured Quebec's right to national self-determination, a right that it had lost with the Constitution Act, 1982.[46] In time, Bourassa's highly exaggerated interpretation of the distinct society clause lost him credibility among nationalist academics and journalists in Quebec while setting off a political firestorm throughout Canada, one that sealed the fate of his cherished accord.

With all three national parties formally adopting the Meech Lake Accord for a second time in June 1988, the issue was effectively eliminated from the national political agenda during the heated "free-trade election" of that fall. While John Turner won the television debate on free trade, he lost the election once the Tory attack ads demolished his character. Turner did manage to increase the number of Liberal seats from forty to eighty-three, with gains in Ontario and British Columbia, but the party suffered a further decline in Quebec, obtaining an all-time low of twelve seats.[47] Bitter and humiliated over his treatment by Robert Bourassa and the Quebec Liberal Party, Turner lashed out at Bourassa for resorting to section 33 of the Charter of Rights, the "notwithstanding clause," to ensure that Bill 178 (requiring the use of the French language for commercial purposes) was immune from a court challenge. It was painfully clear to Turner that that a majority of the new Liberal caucus, now based in Ontario, was strongly opposed to the Meech Lake Accord. Unwilling to alter his stance on the accord and seeing the writing on the wall, Turner had no option but to step down. In early May 1989 he instructed the Liberal Party to organize a leadership convention to choose his successor. His erratic political career was over.[48] The barely concealed rift among the rank and file of the party erupted into the open as Jean Chrétien and Paul Martin, to name only two, launched their respective leadership campaigns by taking opposite stances on the Meech Lake Accord.

The crisis in the national Liberal caucus and party emboldened an increasing majority of Canadians to question both the process and the substance of the Meech Lake Accord. It also prompted several political commentators to argue that the process of political realignment – initiated by Mulroney's 1984 election, and consolidated via the Bourassa-Mulroney Meech Lake Accord and the 1988 Free Trade Agreement – was all but irreversible. The national Liberal Party, encouraged by provincial party leaders opposed to the Meech Lake Accord – Sharon Carstairs in Manitoba and premiers Frank McKenna of New Brunswick and Clyde Wells of Newfoundland – and its rank and file from coast to coast, appeared to be turning its back on the increasingly nationalistic francophone Quebec electorate and concentrating on rebuilding its political fortunes in Ontario. This analysis was confirmed, in part, by the inordinately influential role exercised by Quebec's sixty-two Tories in the Mulroney caucus and cabinet following the election. In the minds of francophone Quebecers, Mulroney's Conservative party had replaced the Liberal Party as their preferred political vehicle for defending and promoting their national interests within Confederation.

This was a remarkable development, one that Joe Clark could only dream of before his short-lived minority government, owing to his lack of support in Quebec, went down to defeat at the hands of the Trudeau Liberals.[49]

## THE UNRAVELLING OF THE MEECH LAKE ACCORD, 1988–90

The Quebec political realignment precipitated by the Mulroney-Bourassa alliance on the constitution and the Free Trade Agreement invariably fostered political reaction and political realignment in the rest of the country. Given the fundamental disagreement over the substance of the Meech Lake Accord – reflected in Mulroney's and Bourassa's divergent political strategies to sell it – the three-year ratification period gave its opponents plenty of time to organize at the provincial level. Encouraged by Trudeau's blunt criticism of the accord in September 1987 and the retirement or defeat of premiers in New Brunswick, Manitoba, and Newfoundland, a wide range of "charter groups," Aboriginal organizations, and Preston Manning's fledgling right-wing populist Reform Party in western Canada went to political war against the accord. What ensued was one of the most tumultuous and divisive periods in the history of Canada's political and constitutional development.

The first serious political setback for the Meech Lake Accord occurred in New Brunswick. It was fuelled, in part, by a rapidly growing and increasingly powerful Acadian community and its nationalistic leaders, who felt betrayed by Prime Minister Mulroney's and Premier Bourassa's determination to entrench a territorial conception of dualism, Quebec-Canada, in the constitution. While favourable to the distinct society clause, Acadian leaders insisted on two amendments. It was essential to include in the accord a constitutional obligation for Ottawa to defend and promote the francophone minority communities as well as the entrenchment of New Brunswick's Bill 88, An Act Recognizing the Equality of the Two Official Linguistic Communities in New Brunswick.[50] Conversely, the accord was denounced by right-wing Conservatives – those opposed to any and all forms of official bilingualism or the recognition of Quebec as a distinct society – as a sell-out to Québécois nationalists and separatists. A young, brash, and relatively inexperienced leader of the New Brunswick Liberal Party, Frank McKenna, used the outcries against the accord to launch his political career. Before a special parliamentary joint committee in late August 1987, McKenna declared that substantive amendments – pertaining to the charter, linguistic minorities, spending powers, Senate reform, the Supreme Court, and fisheries – would have to be made to the accord before he would ask the New Brunswick Legislative Assembly to proceed with ratification.[51] The strategy paid off. McKenna's Liberals soundly defeated the seventeen-year administration of Premier Richard Hatfield on 13 October 1987, winning all fifty-eight seats.

For nearly two years, McKenna used grass-roots opposition to the Meech Lake Accord to ward off the incessant campaign by the Mulroney government – led by Senator Lowell Murray – and Premier Bourassa to have his government ratify an unamended accord. McKenna, guarding his leverage, established a committee of the legislature to hear testimony on the accord and to submit a report in the fall of 1989. As expected, the vast majority of those intervening before this committee criticized various aspects of the accord and demanded that it be substantially amended or rejected. Yet many New Brunswickers feared that their premier would cave in to the immense pressure to ratify. McKenna was called upon repeatedly to deny stories of either a provincial cabal against Ottawa or a sweetheart deal with Quebec.[52] Buoyed by the emergence of two other anti-accord premiers – Gary Filmon of Manitoba and Clyde Wells of Newfoundland – McKenna momentarily strengthen his resolve in 1989.[53]

Hard-core political opposition to the accord surfaced among all three parties in Manitoba. The New Democratic Party (NDP) government, led by premier Howard Pawley, a reluctant supporter of the accord, procrastinated. On 8 March 1988 Pawley's shaky government was brought down by a vote of non-confidence triggered by an angry backbencher. The defeat of the NDP in a surprise election on 26 April 1988 produced a minority Progressive Conservative government, with twenty-five of fifty-seven seats, led by Premier Gary Filmon. The Manitoba Liberal Party, led by the feisty and inveterate pro-Trudeau, "anti-Meecher" Sharon Carstairs, emerged from obscurity to form the official opposition in the legislature. She predicted the imminent death of the Meech Lake Accord. Meanwhile, Premier Filmon, still loyal to Mulroney, promised in the throne speech to ratify the accord at the first opportune moment.[54] Considering that over half the Tory caucus was opposed to the accord, particularly the distinct society clause, Filmon's challenge would prove far more difficult than he and Mulroney ever imagined. Sensing the need to recuperate ground lost to the Liberal Party, Gary Doer, Manitoba's new NDP leader, announced within days of the federal election of 21 November 1988 that his party was committed to killing the accord. The combination of free trade and the Meech Lake Accord, he argued, would destroy the political and constitutional integrity of the country.[55]

Pressured by Mulroney and Bourassa, on 16 December 1988 Filmon introduced the accord into the Manitoba legislature and spoke passionately in its favour as a powerful embodiment of a renewed phase of cooperative federalism.[56] And yet a delighted Mulroney had no time to rejoice. His alliance with Bourassa was challenged by a Supreme Court ruling on

15 December 1988 striking down the commercial-signage provisions of Quebec's Bill 101 (the provisions mandated the use of the French language exclusively). The decision called for the restoration of bilingual commercial signage with prominence given to French throughout Quebec.[57] On 18 December, Premier Bourassa, pressured by ardent nationalists in his government – Claude Ryan threatened to resign – and vociferous public demonstrations in support of Bill 101, introduced Bill 178. This controversial bill, which clearly violated the letter and spirit of the Supreme Court's ruling, authorized a bizarre and discriminatory outside-inside approach to commercial signage. All outdoor commercial signs had to be exclusively French while indoor signage could be bilingual as long as French was given priority and predominance. The government invoked the charter's "notwithstanding clause" to prevent any legal challenges to Bill 178. Bourassa foolishly maintained that, if the Meech Lake Accord had been ratified, he would not have had to take this step. Mulroney, pleading privately with Bourassa to refrain from using the "notwithstanding clause," understood immediately that the Meech Lake Accord was on life support. But, fearing that his alliance with the premier was in jeopardy, he kept his public criticism to a bare minimum, thereby fuelling fears that he was a weak defender of the Charter of Rights. Bourassa had opted to preserve the stability of his government and the unity of his party even if his actions meant endangering his cherished accord. Most emphatically, Quebec's interests, not Ottawa's, came first. Facing Jacques Parizeau, a hard-line secessionist at the head of the Parti Québécois, and an angry English-speaking community, nevertheless, Bourassa's government was re-elected on 9 August 1989 with 50 per cent of the vote and 92 of 125 seats. He had a renewed mandate to push for the ratification of an unaltered accord because, in the words of Lowell Murray, it was a seamless web.[58]

On 19 December, Filmon shocked Mulroney, Bourassa, and the entire nation by withdrawing the accord from the Manitoba legislature. He justified his action by stating that Bourassa's Bill 178 was a "national tragedy" and a harbinger of worse things to come since the Quebec government might use the Meech Lake Accord to achieve constitutional special status. Early in 1989, Premier Filmon urged Mulroney to refer the distinct society clause to the Supreme Court for a ruling, but the prime minister, fearful of the reaction in Quebec, demurred.[59] Hearings held by the Manitoba legislature's task force on Meech Lake that spring demonstrated the depth and breadth of public resentment over what was termed the Mulroney-Bourassa deal.[60] The task force's report, published in October 1989 and endorsed by all three party leaders, called for dramatic amendments to the accord. The Charter of Rights was deemed paramount. A "Canada clause," recognizing the distinct nature of Canada by virtue of its Aboriginal and ethno-cultural communities, encapsulated and constrained the

Quebec distinct society clause. The spending-power provision and the extension of a veto to all provinces over national institutions and the creation of new provinces were dropped. Premier Filmon had lost all manœuvring room.[61]

The Mulroney-Bourassa alliance also faced a major political setback in Atlantic Canada. Premier Peckford of Newfoundland, an unabashed supporter of the Mulroney government and decentralization of the federation, had pushed the controversial accord through the House of Assembly without public hearings. Hoping to prevent the Conservative Party's impending defeat, Peckford resigned in favour of Tom Rideout but to no avail. Promising to rescind the accord, Clyde Wells and the Liberal Party were swept into office in Newfoundland on 20 April 1989 on an anti-Meech ticket.[62] Premier Wells, the brilliant, articulate, and determined constitutional lawyer and Trudeauite, preached the gospel of the equality of the provinces and the need for an elected Senate. He criticized the interpretive nature of the distinct society clause because it granted the government and legislature of Quebec "special powers to protect and promote that status." Like Trudeau, Wells contended that this would enable Quebec to achieve constitutional special status, thereby endangering the federation.[63] Wells hired a talented and outspoken constitutional lawyer and close friend of Trudeau, Deborah Coyne, to advise him on his government's struggle to amend or defeat the accord.[64]

Over several months, Mulroney and his advisers opted to ignore Premier Wells and to isolate him by convincing McKenna and Filmon to ratify the accord. Working in tandem with Trudeau, who denounced the accord as a "bad deal" on 26 October, Wells, four days later, confirmed his decision to rescind the province's ratification of the accord if amendments were not forthcoming. During the first ministers' conference on the economy on 9 November 1989, Mulroney and Premier Peterson repeatedly urged Wells not to rescind ratification or hold a referendum. It proved to be a foolish strategy. A disgusted but determined Wells encouraged the Newfoundland House of Assembly to pass a private member's bill condemning the accord on 23 November 1989 and then had the assembly rescind its ratification of the accord on 6 April 1990. Bourassa proclaimed to the media that Wells "is an extremist." A visibly angry Lucien Bouchard, during a joint press conference with Gil Rémillard, declared that Canadians would have to choose between Quebec and Newfoundland. Wells, an unlikely national hero, was in the driver's seat, hell-bent on checkmating the Bourassa-Mulroney alliance. Canadians from coast to coast turned to him as the only politician capable of derailing the detested accord.[65]

Mulroney, Bourassa, and their advisers were frustrated and shaken. They were convinced they had set the stage for the ratification of an unamended accord. The internal and external pressure on McKenna began to pay dividends. The report of the New Brunswick select committee on the Meech Lake Constitutional Accord, released in October 1989, recommended a few substantial amendments but left the accord formally untouched. It embraced both the distinct society clause and the expansion of the veto and recommended the entrenchment of the Charter of Rights as a fundamental characteristic of Canada as well as an obligation by the federal government to preserve and *promote* both official languages. The amendments, set out in a "parallel accord," would be ratified at the same time as the Meech accord.[66] McKenna was ripe for the picking. Following extensive negotiations with Mulroney's constitutional advisers, the premier dropped the report's demand for a "parallel accord." On 20 March 1990 he introduced resolutions into the assembly calling for the ratification of an unamended Meech Lake Accord followed by the negotiation and ratification of a separate "companion accord" comprising a watered-down version of the select committee report's additional constitutional proposals.[67]

Two days later, desperate to legitimize the widely condemned and despised elitist Meech Lake Accord process and consume all the remaining time available to those seeking amendments, Mulroney created a special House of Commons committee to study McKenna's companion resolution. He named an unknown Quebec MP, Jean Charest, as its chairperson and requested a report by 18 May. Ten days later, Bourassa's government supported a Parti Québécois motion stating that Quebec reject all constitutional proposals including those of New Brunswick "which would constitute an amendment or modification susceptible to changing the content and the scope of the Meech Lake Accord."[68] Undeterred, an inexperienced, ambitious Charest plunged ahead, seemingly oblivious to the potentially explosive nature of the report that his impromptu committee was mandated to prepare. The Charest report, submitted to the House on 17 May 1990, called for the ratification of an unaltered Meech Lake Accord by 23 June and recommended a list of twenty-three additional constitutional amendments – providing, among other things, for recognition of Aboriginal peoples and Canada's multicultural heritage and setting the stage for Senate reform – that the first ministers might include in a "Companion Accord" to be negotiated and ratified at a later stage.[69]

This controversial, tactical report, even before its release, ignited a political firestorm in Quebec City and Ottawa, one that was intended to, but did not, derail the Mulroney-Bourassa alliance. Bourassa and Rémillard, pondering the probability of either the amendment of Meech or its demise, proffered dark warnings that the nation of Quebec would seek a fundamental restructuring of Quebec's association with the "Rest of Canada," one that respected its long history as a distinct society. Both reiterated that they would not accept a single amendment to the accord. Meanwhile, as polls revealed rapidly declining support for Mulroney's Conservative Party in Quebec, which now found itself nearly thirty percentage points behind the Liberals, rumours circulated that up to twenty-five Quebec Tory MPs would bolt the party. On 18 May Quebec Conservative MP François Gérin, claiming that Mulroney had broken his promise to francophone Quebecers, triggered the unravelling of Mulroney's Québécois nationalist coalition by resigning. He was soon joined by another Tory MP and a couple of disgruntled Liberals, supporters of Paul Martin, who backed Meech.[70]

Three days later, in the wake of his deliberately provocative telegram – referring to the Quebec people's right to self-determination – to the Parti Québécois on the tenth anniversary of the 1980 referendum, an ambitious Lucien Bouchard resigned from cabinet and the Conservative Party. His pretext was that Charest had ignored his input and his disastrous report proposed totally unacceptable amendments, ones that would destroy the essence of the Meech Lake Accord, the distinct society clause. The accord was a bare minimum because it "comprised a gesture of reparation ... toward Quebec, ostracized by the coup of Pierre Elliott Trudeau."[71] Opting for his beloved Quebec over Canada, Bouchard's long-time friendship with Mulroney and the latter's crucial link to the Québécois nationalist movement came to an abrupt end. Believing that it was all a dark plot, a betrayed and anguished Mulroney readily accepted Bouchard's resignation. Aware of the magnitude of what had transpired and the fact that they had lost all room to manœuvre, Bourassa and Rémillard used Bouchard's precipitous departure as a warning to Canadians of what would happen if the accord failed.[72]

Mulroney and Bourassa decided that they had no option but to forge ahead – "roll all the dice," as the prime minister later boasted. On 3 June 1990, a Sunday, Mulroney gathered the premiers for a dinner at the Museum of Civilization to prime them for negotiations on the basis of a Charest report embellished by other premiers' demands. Using the threat of another referendum on separatism and sensing that they could logroll the recalcitrant Filmon and Wells, Bourassa and Mulroney convinced the premiers to reconvene next day for a make-it-or-break-it constitutional conference in the National Conference Centre, Ottawa's old train station.[73] In the midst of a wild media-feeding frenzy, Mulroney kept the premiers around the negotiating table for the entire week, convinced that Filmon and Wells would succumb eventually to the pressure to accept a "pass it now, fix it later" approach to the Meech Lake Accord. The high-stakes political blackmail, constant verbal harassment, and occasional physical bullying tactics worked but only in part. It took the premiers four days to agree to ratify an unamended Meech. This occurred only because the premiers, Wells excluded, agreed to solicit an informal opinion letter from a group of constitutional experts on the significance of the distinct society clause and because Bourassa withdrew from the meeting on Thursday evening.

In his absence, the shell-shocked premiers relented. They reconvened to tackle the even more daunting task of determining the nature and scope of significant amendments destined for a separate constitutional package to be ratified after the Meech Lake Accord came into effect. By late Saturday evening, 9 June, a complicated and ambiguous agreement of sorts was reached. Its main elements were: the three hold-out provinces would do everything in their power to ratify Meech before the 23 June deadline; there would be three years to achieve an elected, more "equitable," and more effective Senate, failing which there would be automatic changes to seat distribution; a special House of Commons committee would be formed to fashion a "Canada clause" by September 1990; a non-binding legal opinion would be obtained from six constitutional experts clarifying the impact of the interpretive distinct society clause on the Charter of Rights; a series of constitutional conferences with Aboriginal organizations would be held; gender equality and official-language minority rights in the charter would be strengthened; and a review of the amending procedures would be undertaken. Totally exhausted, Mulroney and the premiers signed a highly questionable "Constitutional Agreement," one that had little chance of surviving the harsh scrutiny of the media and the accord's growing legions of determined critics. Indeed, Premier Wells's signature was conditional. Frustrated and distraught, yet determined not to betray his principles or his supporters, Wells agreed only to put the Meech Lake Accord to referendum or to submit it to the House of Assembly for a vote.[74]

Bourassa, well aware that Québécois nationalists and secessionists were displeased with the scope of the companion agreement, kept a low profile. McKenna proceeded as promised and the New Brunswick Legislature unanimously ratified the accord on 15 June. Meanwhile, Mulroney, Murray, and Spector worked overtime to keep up the full-court press on Filmon and Wells to ratify the accord. In addition, conscious of strong opposition from Ovide Mercredi's Assembly of First Nations (AFN), Mulroney dispatched a federal delegation to make Manitoba's Aboriginal leaders a six-point offer, which, however, was refused. Elijah Harper, an NDP Cree MLA, was instructed by Manitoba chiefs and AFN leaders to deny the Manitoba legislature the necessary unanimous consent to allow the procedural motions required to consider the Meech Lake Accord. Meanwhile, McKenna, Peterson, and Mulroney appeared before the members of the Newfoundland House of Assembly urging them to prevent a second Quebec referendum on secession by ratifying the accord. Elijah Harper informed Wells at noon, central time, on 22 June that debate in the Manitoba legislature on the accord would be adjourned at 12:30 without a vote. Wells, outraged at Mulroney's and Murray's ongoing attempts to manipulate the process despite their ignominious defeat in Manitoba, promptly moved to adjourn the Newfoundland legislature without a vote. Following three long years of acrimonious threats and counter-threats, the ill-fated Meech Lake Accord was finally put to rest.[75]

Mulroney and Bourassa faced a momentous decision. Should they persevere in their quest for Meech or should they turn to other more pressing matters?

## THE CANADA ROUND: THE MARRIAGE OF CONVENIENCE IMPLODES, 1990–92

The death of the Meech Lake Accord did not terminate mega-constitutional wrangling. Mulroney and Bourassa, surfing the rising tide of Québécois nationalism and secessionism, forged ahead with a more destabilizing series of constitutional negotiations that produced a highly controversial, comprehensive, yet incomplete constitutional agreement that was rejected by Canadians in a referendum held on 26 October 1992. The unsuccessful "Canada Round," as it was dubbed, severely challenged and then virtually demolished the Mulroney-Bourassa alliance, producing a remarkable but unintended national political realignment, one that altered inextricably the course of Canadian politics. This happened for two reasons: first, because Mulroney and Bourassa were determined to achieve their respective political agendas at almost any price; and secondly, because Québécois nationalist and secessionist critics of the accord proved to be far more skilful in "spinning" Meech's demise to their advantage. The accord – like the Conquest of 1759, the Rebellions of 1837–38, the 1980 referendum, and the Constitution Act, 1982 – was another humiliating defeat to be used effectively to advance the struggle for an independent Quebec. Quebec *nationalistes* blamed the accord's defeat on the Trudeau-inspired Canadian nationalists who rejected the Québécois conception of territorial duality, Quebec-Canada, in favour of their own unrealistic conception of pan-Canadian linguistic duality and cultural pluralism.[76]

Québécois nationalists' claims of victimization were never challenged by Canada's political leaders. On the contrary, their highly questionable interpretation of events was legitimized by some leading anti-Trudeau Canadian nationalists[77] and, more important, by the Mulroney-Bourassa alliance. Acutely conscious that the demise of Meech had fuelled the growing rift in the Quebec Liberal Party and caucus, a development that could lead to the Liberal government's defeat at the hands of Jacques Parizeau's hard-line Parti Québécois, Bourassa embraced a Québécois neo-nationalism based on a European Union style of sovereignty-association. In an emotionally charged speech in the National Assembly on 22 June, Bourassa offered a prophetic but ominous warning: "English Canada must understand that no matter what anyone says or does, Quebec is today and forever a distinct society, free and able to undertake its own destiny and development."[78] Quebec would achieve distinct society status de facto if not de jure. Parizeau, who had just urged all Québécois to circle the wagons against English Canada, was so impressed that he crossed the floor to shake the premier's hand. Determined to deal directly with Ottawa – nation to nation – in defending and promoting Quebec's interests, Bourassa informed Canadians on 23 June that he would not return to the constitutional bargaining table. If the Canadian government came forward with acceptable constitutional proposals, however, Bourassa just might agree to bilateral discussions on a new status for Quebec in the federation, one that reflected the Canada-Quebec territorial duality at the heart of the Meech Lake Accord.

Bourassa had two enormous challenges: one, keep his troubled government and party intact; two, with Mulroney's full endorsement and participation, enhance the Quebec government's bargaining power vis-à-vis the premiers and citizens in the "Rest of Canada" by harnessing the sharp increase in support for sovereignty-association among francophones. Determined to control and manipulate his caucus and party militants – a neo-liberal, extreme nationalist minority represented by Jean Allaire and Mario Dumont was threatening to bolt – Bourassa urged the constitutional committee of the Quebec Liberal Party, chaired by Allaire, to proceed with its mandate of analysing Quebec's constitutional options. On 4 September 1990, intent upon harnessing the rising tide of separatist sentiment to his and Mulroney's constitutional agenda, Bourassa had the National Assembly establish a commission to "examine and analyze the political and constitutional status of Quebec."[79] With representatives from provincial and federal parties, nationalist organizations, labour centrals, and business groups, the commission was granted a mandate to consult widely and make recommendations on the full range of constitutional options available to his government, including, if necessary, independence.[80]

The commission, dubbed Bélanger-Campeau after its co-chairs, Michel Bélanger, federalist president of the Quebec-based Banque Nationale, and Jean Campeau, secessionist chairman of the Caisse de Dépôt et Placement du Québec, was designed to create a sacred union, that is, to rally both Quebec parties and their supporters behind Bourassa's second attempt to obtain the substance of the Meech Lake Accord. Determined to outflank Parizeau and to increase Quebec's *rapport de force* with the "Rest of Canada," Bourassa appointed the highly popular Lucien Bouchard – recently crowned leader of the Bloc Québécois, the new separatist party at the federal level which Bourassa fully endorsed – as one of the most prominent members of the commission. Determined to achieve his goal at virtually any price, Bourassa pursued a hard-line strategy of putting "a knife to the throat" of Canada.[81] Yet, given the deteriorating state of his health owing to skin cancer, Bourassa quickly lost control of the commission to the extreme nationalists and secessionists who considered Bouchard their rightful leader. Québécois politicians, academics, journalists, and a wide range of organizations and citizens' groups – many of whom submitted briefs and/or gave testimony to the Bélanger-Campeau Commission – stoked the fires of secessionism by reinforcing over and over the potentially destructive myth that English Canada was to blame for the defeat of the accord and that francophone Quebecers had no choice but to opt for secession.[82] As was the intention, the commission's hearings legitimized the claim that Québécois were the victims of Confederation, thereby helping drive support for secession among francophone Quebecers to a all-time high of 64 per cent by November 1990.[83]

At the end of January 1991, the constitutional committee of the Quebec Liberal Party released its report, *A Quebec Free to Choose*. Intended to shock the "Rest of Canada" and undercut the PQ, the Allaire report, as it was known, called for a comprehensive political disengagement of Quebec from Canada while retaining important economic ties: that is, sovereignty-association, a concept heretofore the primary goal of the Parti Québécois. Once the "Rest of Canada" agreed with the report's recommendation for a transfer of powers to Quebec in twenty-two areas – a highly dubious assumption – a referendum would be held in the fall of 1992 to ratify the new arrangement. If the "Rest of Canada" refused to negotiate, the Allaire report endorsed the holding of a referendum on Quebec's secession from the federation. The Quebec Liberal Party, during its convention on 8–10 March 1991, endorsed the radical Allaire report. Bourassa, deploying his iron-fist in a velvet-glove approach, reminded Canadians that if the federation was not reformed to suit Quebec, he would have no option but to follow his party's constitutional policy. He did open the door to possible negotiations with the premiers if and when an acceptable offer was made to Quebec.[84]

The Bélanger-Campeau report, based on the same highly selective and questionable Québécois nationalist interpretations of Quebec's past, present, and future as those of the Allaire report, was submitted to the National Assembly on 28 March 1991. It proclaimed that "Quebecers are aware that they form a distinct national collectivity: the language of the majority of Quebecers and their culture, which are in a minority situation in Canada, are unique across the continent." Since Quebecers "have always expressed the need to be masters of their own destiny," it was imperative that they choose their constitutional future with "serenity."[85] The divided commissioners – unable to develop a consensus on either Bourassa's European Union style of a highly decentralized, binational, Canada-Quebec federation or Parizeau's call for outright secession with possible future ties with the "Rest of Canada" – recommended that the National Assembly adopt a two-track approach whereby all Quebecers would determine their political and constitutional future. Track one entailed passing a law authorizing a referendum on secession no later than 26 October 1992. Track two called for the creation, by legislation, of two special parliamentary commissions: one would "assess any offer of a new partnership of constitutional nature made by the Government of Canada," and possibly hold a referendum if the offer was deemed acceptable; the other, dear to Parizeau's heart, would evaluate the political complications and economic costs of secession.[86] Well aware that a CROP opinion poll, released in January 1991, revealed that 67 per cent of francophone Quebecers favoured some form of Quebec "sovereignty," and that an astonishing 54 per cent agreed with unilateral action, Bourassa decided to make his move. He did so despite the fact that the same poll clearly indicated that 65 per cent of Canadians outside Quebec rejected the granting of additional powers to Quebec in order to avoid secession.[87] Putting into action his "knife-to-the-throat" strategy, Bourassa authorized Bélanger-Campeau's two-track approach in his government's Referendum Bill 150, enacted by Quebec's National Assembly on 20 June 1991.[88] The highly contentious and ambiguously worded law – based on the disputed premise that, under international law, Quebec had the right to secede unilaterally from Canada within a year of a majority vote in a referendum *proposing* sovereignty – was criticized by Prime Minister Mulroney but never legally challenged.

Mulroney's role in this "do-anything-to-get-Meech" strategy was multifaceted. First, he had to buy time for Bourassa to build his *rapport de force* vis-à-vis the "Rest of Canada." This goal was accomplished in various ways. Responding to Canadians who condemned the elite-accommodation process of Meech Lake, Mulroney created, on 1 November 1990, the Citizens' Forum on Canada's Future, headed by the irascible and outspoken Keith Spicer. As observers predicted, the forum's function was largely that of a reverberating sounding board for thousands of Canadians to vent their political spleen against Mulroney for his determination to accommodate Bourassa's constitutional demands while ignoring the economy and social issues and imposing the hated Goods and Services Tax (GST). The forum's report of 27 June 1991 confirmed that ever-widening old and new cleavages and the constant wrangling over constitutional structures, jurisdictions, and status were destroying Canadian unity and the shared values and citizenship inherent in the Charter of Rights and Freedoms. Spicer, in his foreword to the report and at the press conference where the document was released, laid most of the blame for the crisis then confronting the country on a lack of visionary and courageous political leadership, especially from Prime Minister Mulroney.[89] In December 1990 Mulroney appointed a joint parliamentary committee on the "Process for Amending the Constitution of Canada," chaired by MP Jim Edwards and

Senator Gérald Beaudoin, The committee's report, released in June 1991, recommended that little could be done about the three-year time limit for ratification of amendments set out in the Constitution Act, 1982 and called for the adoption of a region-based amending formula, one that ensured a veto for Quebec. The report rejected widespread calls for a constituent assembly to democratize the constitutional-renewal process but did accept the need for public hearings and non-binding referendums.[90]

Mulroney's second challenge was to set the parameters for the constitutional offer that needed be made to Quebec if a second referendum on secession was to be avoided. To oversee the sensitive process, on 21 April 1991 the prime minister appointed Joe Clark as minister for constitutional affairs and chair of the cabinet committee on Canadian unity and constitutional negotiations. On 24 September 1991 the Mulroney government released a document, *Shaping Canada's Future Together*, comprising a pastiche of constitutional reforms drawn from the defunct Meech Lake Accord and the Companion Agreement. The twenty-eight proposals, none requiring unanimity, included: recognition of Quebec as a distinct society via an interpretative clause that applied only to the charter and not the entire constitution; a "Canada clause" defining the essence of what is was to be Canadian; additional powers to the provinces; the entrenchment of property rights; restrictions on the "notwithstanding clause"; the entrenchment of Aboriginal self-government within a decade; and the creation of an elected, equal, and partially equitable Senate.[91] Québécois nationalists rejected the proposals outright. While Parizeau rejected the proposal aimed at strengthening the Canadian economic union, Bourassa queried the absence of a veto for Quebec and called for clarifications.[92]

During a National Assembly debate with Parizeau on 9 November 1991, Bourassa confirmed that Ottawa's offer would have to be a great deal more enticing before his government would even contemplate constitutional negotiations. Bourassa, no doubt, was well aware that Quebec cabinet ministers and MPs refused to sell Mulroney's package in Quebec. Responding to Ottawa's decision to put in place a law authorizing a national referendum on constitutional proposals, on 27 November the National Assembly reaffirmed Quebecers' right to determine alone their constitutional future. Members passed a resolution calling on Ottawa to respect Bill 150's authorization of a referendum on Quebec's secession by refraining from holding a national referendum.[93]

The Mulroney-Clark proposals were put into the hands of a special joint committee on a "Renewed Canada" chaired by the Manitoba Conservative MP Dorothy Dobbie and Senator Gérald Beaudoin, the latter conscripted to rescue the committee from criticism and ridicule (a development that prompted Quebec Senator Claude Castonquay to resign in disgust).[94] In January 1992, doing an end run around the blundering committee and hoping to undermine the growing demand for a formal constituent assembly, Joe Clark's office organized a series of innovative regional thematic conferences on all aspects of the government's proposals.[95] This enlarged elite- accommodation process produced a wider understanding of, and some increase in support for, the government's proposals among English-speaking Canadians. There was virtually no input from highly nationalistic and secessionist Québécois organizations, citizens, and the media – all viewed the exercise as intended exclusively for the "Rest of Canada." More ominously, the conferences produced a major expansion in the nature and scope of the constitutional-reform agenda, including controversial demands for a social charter and entrenchment of the inherent right of self-determination of Aboriginal peoples. This unintended development ultimately derailed Mulroney's plan to fashion a limited package that was acceptable to Bourassa and Québécois federalists, conditional and non-conditional.[96]

The Beaudoin-Dobbie committee's report, released on 1 March 1992, set out Ottawa's radical vision for reshaping Canada's constitutional structure. It encompassed modified elements of the Meech Lake Accord: a circumscribed distinct society clause within an omnibus "Canada clause"; a veto limited to cultural and linguistic legislation and an entrenched Supreme Court with three justices from Quebec; and concurrent federal-provincial powers covering a range of jurisdictions. In addition, the report recommended the strengthening of the economic union, an elected and effective Senate based on four regions (not provincial equality), and the recognition of the Aboriginal peoples' inherent right of self-government with a veto over constitutional changes affecting them, as well as the inclusion of a limited number of social and economic rights in the charter.[97]

As expected, the report was denounced vehemently by Parizeau and Bouchard. Bourassa characterized the Beaudoin-Dobbie report's conception of federalism as "domineering" and centralist rather that "flexible" and decentralist. Clearly, it did not satisfy his criteria for an acceptable constitutional offer.[98] Signalling rising tension in Mulroney's cabinet was the fact that his minister of defence, Marcel Masse, also criticized the report. Yet it was Ontario Premier Bob Rae, backed by fellow NDP premiers in British Columbia and Saskatchewan, who altered the course of events. His steadfast refusal, made clear throughout his testimony to the joint committee, to let Ottawa alone determine the constitutional offer to Quebec compelled Mulroney to authorize Joe Clark to chair a series of multilateral meetings of the provincial and territorial ministers responsible for constitutional matters. On 12 March the continuing committee of ministers on the constitution (CCMC), again at the insistence of Rae, invited representatives of the four national Native organizations, except for the Native Women's Association of Canada, to join the negotiations.

Bourassa was visibly shocked and dismayed when he learned of the addition of Aboriginal representatives at the negotiating table during an interview with the CBC's *The Journal*. He agreed only to send observers, a decision he would later regret because he lost a great opportunity to influence directly the shape of the constitutional offer to Quebec.[99]

Clearly, Bourassa and Mulroney faced the risk of losing control of the complex mega-constitutional negotiating process at a crucial stage. How could they regain the upper hand? Observers maintained that Mulroney and Bourassa were gambling on the multilateral process failing. Mulroney could then step in and make Bourassa a unilateral federal offer, one that would allow the Quebec and Canadian governments to hold referendums, not on secession, but on a restructured constitutional relationship between Canada and Quebec.[100] Indeed, their high-stakes gambit appeared to be working when it became clear that the CCMC negotiations had quickly reached a serious impasse.

Ministers and Aboriginal representatives involved in the closed-door multilateral ministerial conferences, travelling back and forth across Canada, laboured in vain throughout April, May, and June to reach a consensus on both the substance and the scope of a comprehensive constitutional package, one that had to satisfy provincial and territorial leaders, Aboriginal representatives, and Premier Bourassa. They agreed on all five elements of the Meech Lake Accord, a revised omnibus "Canada clause," and the constitutional recognition of the Aboriginal peoples' right to self-government leading to a "third order" of government. But there was one major condition. In exchange for granting Quebec a veto over the reform of national institutions, Alberta's Premier Don Getty, with the backing of other premiers, demanded a Triple-E Senate. As with the Meech and Companion Resolution process, Senate reform emerged as an intractable deal breaker. Mulroney convened the premiers on 29 June for lunch at 24 Sussex and warned them to settle their differences on Senate reform or his government, upon his return from a G-7 summit in Munich, Germany, would recall Parliament on 15 July to discuss his government's unilateral set of constitutional proposals for Quebec. Working under extreme duress, the nine premiers came to an agreement once Ontario's NDP Premier Bob Rae accepted a watered-down version of the Triple-E Senate – elected, equal, but not very effective. Despite conflicting messages, they were given repeated assurances that Bourassa would go along with the complex deal on Senate reform if he got a veto for Quebec.[101]

Clark reconvened the multilateral ministerial conference in Ottawa on 6–7 July at the Lester B. Pearson Building to hammer out the details of its Final Status Report, which was to include all the items mentioned above plus an astonishingly radical restructuring of the Senate and its role in the federation. The new Senate would be composed of eight senators from each province and one from each territory. Senators could veto tax and natural-resources legislation with a simple majority, while it would take a 70 per cent vote to veto ordinary legislation. Legislation dealing with French language and culture required approval of a majority of the senators and a majority of the francophone senators.[102]

Somewhat shocked that Clark had accomplished the improbable, Mulroney and Bourassa were reluctant to endorse the Final Status Report. Mulroney knew that his government's future, his political future, and his legacy were all on the line. Both awaited the reaction in francophone Quebec – which was immediate and negative, especially on the Senate proposals.[103] Responding to the proposals on 9 July 1992, a cautious and conciliatory Bourassa indicated that he and his colleagues would study the report carefully before deciding what amendments might make its recommendations acceptable to Quebec. He warned that the distinct society clause needed to be strengthened by the recognition of Quebec as a sovereign nation and that Quebecers would have to be convinced of the benefits of the Triple-E Senate because under it the province would lose considerable power. Bourassa's ambivalence reflected that of francophone Quebecers.[104] A June CROP poll revealed that a majority remained attached to Canada and over 70 per cent supported the Charter of Rights. On the other hand, the Québécois "chattering classes" unanimously rejected the report's proposals as a dramatic watering down of Meech, especially concerning the distinct society clause. For them, Quebec did not get enough new powers to justify accepting the Triple-E Senate and Aboriginal self-government. Their outcry had its effect. Polls soon revealed that nearly 44 per cent rejected the package and 55.5 per cent of francophones supported a second referendum on sovereignty-association.[105] The Canadian and Aboriginal nationalisms expressed in the report had fuelled a counter-reaction from Québécois nationalists and secessionists.

Nonetheless, encouraged by Bourassa's conciliatory demeanour, eager to avoid a referendum on secession, and fearing that unilateral action would backfire, Mulroney invited him to meet informally with the premiers on 4 August at Harrington Lake, his summer residence, to discuss the possibility of reopening constitutional negotiations. During lunch, Bourassa convinced the premiers, yet again, to accept a strengthened distinct society clause that functioned as an interpretative clause applying to the entire constitution. As a quid pro quo, he agreed to meet them again on 10 August. At that meeting, he made it clear that the Triple-E Senate was unacceptable to Quebec and needed to be reconsidered. Once Mulroney, Clark, and the premiers concurred, Bourassa consented to participate in a full-scale, closed-door constitutional conference, including territorial leaders and Aboriginal representatives, in Ottawa on 18 August 1992.[106]

Throughout five tense days of negotiations centred on the Canada and distinct society clauses, the Senate, Aboriginal self-government, and the division of powers, the participants agreed on a complex, wide-ranging, ambiguous, and incomplete – twenty-five political accords remained to be negotiated – Charlottetown Consensus Report, named after Charlottetown, Prince Edward Island, where it would be formally signed on 28 August. The vast majority of the document's sixty clauses resembled those of the Status Report of 7 July except for those amendments required to get Bourassa on board. The latter won a partial victory on the interpretative omnibus "Canada clause" 2, which incorporated a distinct society clause 2(1)(c) as well as another clause (2[2]) authorizing the "legislature and Government of Quebec to preserve and promote the distinct society of Quebec." Bowing in part to pressure from francophone and Acadian community leaders, Bourassa agreed to a clause 2(1)(d) which stated that "Canadians and their government were committed to the vitality and development of official language minority communities." In return for accepting a drastic reduction of the number of Quebec senators from twenty-four to six, Bourassa obtained the right for Quebec to appoint its senators, eighteen additional seats in the House of Commons, and a guarantee in perpetuity that Quebec would have "no fewer than twenty-five percent of the members in the House of Commons." [107] Bourassa was unable to obtain any limitations on Aboriginal peoples' inherent right to self-government leading, in due course, to a "third order" of government in the federation, one that was immune from the Canadian Charter of Rights and Freedoms. On the division of powers, Bourassa obtained a degree of decentralization but not the radical restructuring of the federation called for in the Allaire report or his musings about a Canada-Quebec union modelled on the European Union.

The Charlottetown Consensus Report was submitted to Canadian voters for their approval or rejection in a nation-wide referendum set for 26 October 1992. In Quebec, the process was subject to the rules and regulations of the province's Referendum Law and regulations authorizing the establishment of only two committees, one for the NO side and one for the YES side, forcing anti-accord federalists like Trudeau and separatists like Parizeau into the same camp. In an emotional but rather defensive speech, Bourassa presented his case in favour of the accord in the National Assembly on 9 September. Portraying the accord as fulfilling only the minimum of Quebec's constitutional objectives, he focused on the gains: full control over the integration of immigrants; increased cultural and linguistic security via the distinct society clause working in tandem with section 1, the "reasonable limits" clause, and section 33, the "notwithstanding clause," of the Charter of Rights; appointment of Quebec's senators by the National Assembly; and strengthening of the Canadian common market, which would enhance Quebec's ability to play a greater role on the international stage.[108]

The reaction of francophone Quebecers to the Charlottetown deal was not what Mulroney or Bourassa expected or needed if they were to win the high-stakes, winner-takes-all referendum. Following the Quebec Liberal Party's ratification of the accord on 29 August, members of the youth wing and Jean Allaire left the party, setting the stage for the emergence of Mario Dumont's Action Démocratique du Québec. Bourassa and his YES campaign committee were put on the defensive when a late-August private cell-phone conversation between his leading constitutional advisers, Wilhelmy and Tremblay, was taped, transcribed, and then broadcast throughout Quebec on 16 September. During their candid chat, they concurred that Bourassa had caved in completely during the negotiations. Other briefing notes published in *L'Actualité* just before the vote inflicted more damage on the beleaguered YES campaign. These revelations confirmed what Parizeau and Bouchard repeatedly claimed during their increasingly successful NO campaign.[109]

Bourassa and Mulroney responded in two ways. First, they sowed fear by claiming that a YES vote was a vote for Canadian unity while a NO vote would bring the secession of Quebec. In English-speaking Canada, Mulroney, as he had done in the Meech Lake debate, claimed that a rejection of the Charlottetown deal would be interpreted by francophone Quebecers as a rejection of Quebec. Meanwhile, in Quebec, appealing to *nationalistes*, Mulroney warned that a rejection of the distinct society clause would reduce Québécois to the sorry state of Louisiana's assimilated Acadians – Cajuns. Both Mulroney and Bourassa also boasted that, with the Charlottetown Accord, Quebec had made the most significant constitutional gains since Confederation. To emphasize this rather questionable assertion, Mulroney ripped up a copy of the Charlottetown deal in front of the cameras, commenting that all Quebec's gains would be lost if the deal were rejected. He was widely ridiculed in the media for this tactic.[110]

Early September polls revealed the YES side leading in Quebec by ten percentage points, forty-nine to thirty-eight. But, by 2 October, the NO side had reversed the tide and was leading by fourteen points. There were two main reasons for this dramatic shift. No doubt, Bourassa and Mulroney's failure to convince Québécois nationalist federalists that Charlottetown represented a "Meech Plus" instead of a "Meech Minus" package prompted many of them to reconsider their support. In addition, Trudeau's two well-timed and highly effective interventions for the NO side accelerated the growing opposition to the deal. In an article published in *Maclean's* and *l'Actualité* in September, entitled "Quebec's Blackmail," Trudeau castigated Quebec's corrupt "blackmailing" political culture and fingered Premier Bourassa as the master blackmailer for his dangerous use of the threat of secession to obtain more powers for the province. Then, during his 1 October *Cité libre* dinner speech at the Maison Egg Roll Chinese restaurant in Montreal, Trudeau dissected the Charlottetown deal's contradictions, myths, and questionable principles, all of which, he said, threatened democracy, the Charter of Rights, and national unity by constructing an explosive hierarchy of conflicting collective and individual rights. He then pronounced the deal "a mess that deserves a big NO!"[111] Once again the sly fox had emerged from his lair to slay the beast of Québécois nationalism. In doing so, he helped defeat the Mulroney-Bourassa alliance's attempt to establish a decentralized, binational confederation, Quebec-Canada, via radical amendments to the Constitution Act, 1982 and the charter.

When the campaign concluded and the ballots were counted, the pollsters were proven correct. The complex and ambiguous Charlottetown deal, comprising an explosive cocktail of conflicting Canadian, Québécois, and Aboriginal nationalist dreams, was rejected by a respectable margin of nearly ten percentage points, 54.4 to 44.6. The Quebec results, 55.4 to 42.4, mirrored the national outcome.[112] Of course, one must realize that the NO side included some anglophone and "allophone" federalists as well as some francophone nationalists and all francophone separatists while the YES side consisted largely of francophone conditional federalists who supported Bourassa's illusory and unrealistic third option between Canadian federalism and outright secession.

## TORPEDOED BY QUÉBÉCOIS NATIONALISM: AN UNINTENDED POLITICAL REALIGNMENT

The Mulroney-Bourassa alliance paid the ultimate political price for opening, not once but twice, the constitutional Pandora's box. Their failed attempts at mega-constitutional politics, using Québécois nationalism and secessionism to entice the "Rest of Canada" onside, brought to a brutal end their respective quests for political realignment. Bourassa failed in his effort to redefine Canada's cultural and linguistic duality into a territorial, state-based duality of Quebec-Canada. Rather than applauding him for his valiant efforts, Québécois nationalists abandoned his Liberal Party and turned to the secessionist parties, Jacques Parizeau's Parti Québécois and Lucien Bouchard's Bloc Québécois, to achieve their dream of independence. Mulroney's dangerous dalliance with Québécois nationalism and secessionism cost him his jobs as prime minister and leader of the Conservative Party. More important, it ushered in a dramatic but unintended political realignment. His failure to entrench a special constitutional status for Quebec precipitated the wholesale destruction of the Progressive Conservative Party of Canada. Three sectional parties emerged from the political crash, one in western Canada, the second in Quebec, and a third comprising the remnants of the Red Tory wing of the party dispersed through Atlantic Canada and Ontario.

Preston Manning's Reform Party, created in November 1987, was rooted in the deep-seated political culture of western-Canadian alienation (which Alberta premier Peter Lougheed had earlier channeled to enhance the province's bargaining power with the Trudeau government over natural-resource control and taxation and to obtain the "Alberta" amending formula in the constitution). In 1984 the "new west" had backed Mulroney's Conservative government, believing that it would address western Canadians' desire for more say in the formulation and implementation of national policies and programs, especially those involving provincial jurisdictions. Despite their early disappointments, westerners were kept on board by the promise and delivery of free trade in the 1988 election. Yet Quebec's provincial and federal politicians continued their dominance over the national agenda and thereby thwarted the ambitions of western Canadian politicians, intellectuals, and businessmen.[113] The divisive and bitter political wrangling surrounding the Mulroney-Bourassa alliance's attempt to impose the Meech Lake and Charlottetown accords on the prosperous but politically weak "new west" handed Preston Manning the "perfect storm." He used the constitutional slugfest to consolidate the various western political forces seeking a national right-wing populist movement committed to the equality of provinces and the equality of citizens, and opposed to the constitutional protection and promotion of all "special interest" groups and their organizations. Reformers failed to obtain their cherished goal of a Triple-E Senate in the Charlottetown Accord. In return for an ineffective Senate, they had to accept a "Canada clause" that recognized the inherent right of Aboriginal peoples to self-government and the entrenchment of a territorial conception of a Quebec-Canada via a distinct society clause and the reaffirmation of a pan-Canadian conception of linguistic duality. Manning and his Reformers campaigned non-stop to ensure the defeat of a deal that, in their minds, was egregiously flawed.[114]

The political fallout in Quebec for Mulroney's nationalist Conservative Party was just as devastating. Six nationalistic Québécois MPs deserted the Conservative caucus before and after the demise of the Meech Lake Accord. The most dramatic departure, of course, was that of Lucien Bouchard. His charismatic appeal to fellow Québécois of all political stripes to create a powerful "rapport de force," a sacred union against the "Rest of Canada," accelerated the rise of support for the secessionist movement. The six, joined by one disgruntled nationalistic ex-Liberal, Jean Lapierre, rallied around Bouchard like moths to a candle. He responded by announcing, in his 25 July 1990 manifesto, the creation of the Bloc Québécois. The Bloc's primary *raison d'être* was to defend and promote the sovereignty of the Quebec people, the National Assembly, and the Quebec state.[115] With the financial backing of the provincial Liberal Party and Bourassa's encouragement, Bouchard found a Bloc candidate, Gilles Duceppe, to run in a Laurier-Sainte-Marie by-election the next month, a contest that Duceppe was to win handily. Several more Québécois Conservative MPs, sensing a devastating defeat for their party, started planning their move to the Bloc. The "fiery and dark, brooding and brilliant" political chameleon, Bouchard, rapidly became the most prominent hero of francophone nationalists and secessionists, surpassing Jacques Parizeau. He did not disappoint. He used his podium on the Bélanger-Campeau Commission, which he had obtained through Bourassa, to campaign successfully for the calling of a second referendum on sovereignty-association.[116]

Bouchard, advised by Jean-François Lisée, was cagey enough to leave Bourassa enough room to make one last attempt to obtain the essentials of Meech from the "Rest of Canada." If Bourassa failed a second time, then Bouchard could lead a coalition of nationalist and secessionist forces into a second referendum.[117] During the Bloc's founding convention in June 1991 in Sorel-Tracy, Bouchard set as its goal the winning of more seats in Quebec than either the Conservatives or the Liberals. When Bourassa agreed to a referendum on the Charlottetown deal, Bouchard quickly denounced the accord as a sell-out by his ally Bourassa and campaigned energetically, and successfully, for its defeat. Bouchard plunged into the 1993 federal election campaign at the head of a Bloc committed to sovereignty-association, with the organizational support and financial backing of Parizeau's Parti Québécois. A titanic struggle was under way over which of the two would control the Québécois secessionist movement in the 1990s.[118]

An exhausted, dejected, and humiliated Mulroney, forced to acknowledge the damaging polls, decided to step down as party leader in February 1993. He hoped that a new leader, someone not associated with the constitutional fiascos or the despised GST, would regenerate the beleaguered Conservative Party enough to undermine both Manning's western Reform Party and Bouchard's Bloc Québécois. The battle was between a virtually unknown young British Columbia cabinet minister, Kim Campbell, and Jean Charest, a bilingual Québécois closely associated with the Mulroney-Bourassa alliance. At a leadership convention, Tory delegates gave the nod by a slim majority to Campbell on the second ballot. The party rebounded in the polls vis-à-vis the Reform Party when a popular Campbell, imitating Ralph Klein, moved the party to the right on fiscal and monetary policy and crime while appealing to socially concerned Red Tories and cultural nationalists. Yet the polls exuded a false optimism. Campbell's and her party's fortunes plummeted dramatically as Lucien Bouchard and Preston Manning hammered the Conservatives in Quebec and the west, while, coming up the middle, Jean Chrétien – promising to refrain from constitutional negotiations and to rectify the problems of the deficit and the debt – picked up disillusioned Red Tories in Atlantic Canada, Ontario, and British Columbia.[119]

The election of 25 October 1993 was a political watershed. Chrétien's Liberal Party, with 41 per cent of the votes, took 177 seats, enough for a comfortable majority government. The Liberals won every seat in Ontario except one, turning the once mainly Conservative province into the new political bastion of the national Liberal Party. In Quebec, Chrétien's disorganized, old-fashioned party was limited to nineteen seats, better than expected but a sign of future troubles to come. The Liberals also garnered every seat except one in Atlantic Canada. Campbell's hapless Progressive Conservative Party, garnering a mere 16 per cent of the votes, was reduced to a humiliating two seats. It was the beginning of a difficult and protracted period that eventually led to the party's demise. Lucien Bouchard's Bloc Québécois, with 48 per cent of Quebec votes, won 54 seats, enough to take on the role of official opposition in the House of Commons. Preston Manning's fledgling Reform Party, with 18 per cent of the national vote, 26 per cent outside Quebec, sent 52 MPs to Ottawa, all from western Canada except one.[120] Canada had been carved up into three political fiefdoms, Quebec, Altantic Canada-Ontario, and the "new west."

Mulroney's dream of political realignment was displaced by other attempts at political restructuring as Manning's populist Reformers and Bouchard's Bloc Québécois continued to rearrange the Canadian political landscape over the next decade. That process had been set in motion by Mulroney's and Bourassa's unbridled determination to redraw the political map of Quebec and Canada, each using Québécois nationalism to that end. Their decision to pursue fundamental alterations to the Constitution Act, 1982 and the Charter of Rights and Freedoms destabilized Canadian politics, a dynamic that was accentuated by the struggle over, and eventual ratification of, the Free Trade Agreement. The resulting conflict between federal and provincial political elites, dependent upon traditional political cultures of deference, and a wide range of groups and a majority of citizens, all inspired by a democratic approach to constitutional renewal, culminated in the defeat of two mega-constitutional deals. More important, these dramatic failures had a profound, and perhaps even permanent, impact on Canadian politics and the federation. They generated an unforeseen and unintended political realignment that has thrown national politics into turmoil and weakened Ottawa while giving the Québécois secessionist movement a second opportunity to achieve its dream of a radical constitutional realignment through the creation of an independent Quebec state with an economic association with what remains of Canada.

## NOTES

1 John Sawatsky, *Mulroney: The Politics of Ambition* (Toronto: Macfarlane Walter and Ross 1991), 129–56.
2 Ibid., 289–314. Paradoxically, Diefenbaker turned against Mulroney during the leadership race. No doubt he misunderstood and distrusted a bilingual Mulroney's Irish, French-Canadian Catholic background and his success as a businessman.
3 Michael D. Behiels, *Prelude to Quebec's Quiet Revolution: Liberalism versus Neo-nationalism 1945–1960* (Montreal and Kingston: McGill-Queen's University Press 1985); Ramsay Cook, *Canada, Québec and the Uses of Nationalism*, 2nd ed. (Toronto: McClelland and Stewart 1995).
4 Michael D. Behiels, *Canada's Francophone Minority Communities: Constitutional Renewal and the Winning of School Governance* (Montreal and Kingston: McGill-Queen's University Press 2004).
5 Claude Morin, *Lendemains piégés: De la referendum au nuit de longs couteaux* (Montreal: Boréal, 1988).
6 Arthur Tremblay, *Meech Revisité. Chronique politique* (Montreal: Les Presses de l'Université du Québec), 135–50. Tremblay would serve Prime Minister Mulroney in the same capacity.
7 Frederick J. Fletcher and Donald C. Wallace, "Parliament and Politics," *Canadian Annual Review of Politics and Public Affairs 1979* (Toronto: University of Toronto Press 1981), 24–46.
8 Ibid., 56–9, 74–80.
9 David V.J. Bell and Donald C. Wallace, "Parliament and Politics," in *The Canadian Annual Review 1980* (Toronto: University of Toronto Press 1982), 6–17.
10 Ibid., 48–58.
11 Michael D. Behiels, "Pierre Elliott Trudeau's Legacy: The Canadian Charter of Rights and Freedoms," in Joseph Magnet et al., eds., *The Canadian Charter of Rights and Freedoms* (Toronto: Butterworths 2003), 154–8.
12 Cited in L. Ian MacDonald, *Mulroney: The Making of the Prime Minister* (Toronto: McClelland and Stewart 1985), 154.
13 Lawrence Martin, *The Antagonist: Lucien Bouchard and the Politics of Delusion* (Toronto: Penguin Books 1998), 84, 97.
14 Ibid., 164–75, 214–26.
15 Ibid., 7–21.
16 Robert J. Drummond, "Parliament and Politics," in *Canadian Annual Review 1984* (Toronto: University of Toronto Press 1987), 10–19.
17 Lysiane Gagnon, "Le Quebec et les Tories," *L'Actualité*, 8(4) (1983): 72–9; Gilles Lesages, "Le rêve de Brian Mulroney," *L'Actualite*, 8(4) (1983): 38–44.
18 Benoît Aubin, "La bataille du Québec," *L'Actualité*, 9(4) (1984): 68–74. A. Wilson-Smith, "The Tory Revival in Quebec," *Maclean's*, 9 April 1984, 14–15; "The Tories Assault a Liberal Bastion," ibid., 20 August 1984, 16–17; "The Tory Dawn in Quebec," ibid., 17 September 1984, 26–7.

19 MacDonald, *Mulroney*, 259–67, 272–4, 300–1; for an excellent analysis of this crucial struggle and Mulroney's input, consult Raymond Hébert, *Manitoba's French-Language Crisis: A Cautionary Tale* (Montreal and Kingston: McGill-Queen's University Press 2004), 127, 169.
20 MacDonald, *Mulroney*, 288–90.
21 Morin, *Lendemains piégés*, 305–14.
22 MacDonald, *Mulroney*, 299–300.
23 Lucien Bouchard, *À visage découvert* (Montreal: Boréal 1992), 143.
24 Morin, *Lendemains piégés*, 327, author's translation. See also MacDonald, *Mulroney*, 289. This remarkable statement was repeated during the French-language TV debate, which Mulroney won hands down. His performance had a profound impact throughout francophone Quebec.
25 Martin, *The Antagonist*, 98–105.
26 J.L. Findlay and D.N. Sprague, *The Structure of Canadian History*, 3rd ed. (Toronto: Prentice Hall 1989), 504, Table 14; Carol Goar, "The Conservatives' Mandate for Change," *Maclean's*, 17 September 1984, 12–20.
27 L. Ian MacDonald, *From Bourassa to Bourassa: Wilderness to Restoration* (Montreal and Kingston: McGill-Queen's University Press 2002), 233; Michel Vastel, *Bourassa* (Toronto: Macmillan Canada 1991), 82–3.
28 Donald C. Wallace, "Parti Québécois: A Party in Crisis," *Canadian Annual Review 1984* (Toronto: University of Toronto Press 1987), 39–49.
29 Gil Rémillard, "Under What Conditions Could Quebec Sign the Constitution Act of 1982?" in Michael D. Behiels, ed., *Quebec since 1945: Selected Readings* (Toronto: Copp Clark Pitman 1987), 209–20.
30 Donald C. Wallace, "Ottawa and the Provinces," *Canadian Annual Review 1985* (Toronto: University of Toronto Press 1988), 83–7.
31 MacDonald, *From Bourassa to Bourassa*, 235–6.
32 Ibid., 240–1.
33 Ibid., 242–3; René Durocher, "Quebec," *Canadian Annual Review 1985* (Toronto: University of Toronto Press 1988), 310–16.
34 Bourassa's team comprised Minister Gil Rémillard and his deputy minister, Diane Wilhelmy; André Tremblay, a constitutional specialist; Roch Bolduc, head of the Quebec civil service; and Jean-Claude Rivest, his alter ego. Mulroney's team was led by Senator Lowell Murray and his deputy minister, Norman Spector.
35 Gil Rémillard, "Unofficial English Language Text of the Speech to the 5 May, 1986 Mont-Gabriel Conference, 'Rebuilding the Relationship; Quebec and its Confederation Partners,'" in Peter M. Leslie, ed., *Canada: The State of the Federation 1986* (Kingston, Ont.: Institute of Intergovernmental Relations, Queen's University 1986), 97–104.
36 Ibid., 105.
37 Peter Leslie, "Rethinking Basic Relationships," in Leslie, ed., *Canada: The State of the Federation 1986*, 5–6.

38 Tremblay, *Meech Revisité,* 448–53; MacDonald, *From Bourassa to Bourassa,* 245–52; Vastel, *Bourassa,* 100–2.

39 Andrew Cohen, *A Deal Undone: The Making and Breaking of the Meech Lake Accord* (Vancouver/Toronto: Douglas and McIntyre 1990).

40 Consult *Le Québec et le Lac Meech: Un Dossier du Devoir* (Montreal: Guérin Littérature 1987).

41 Donald C. Wallace, "Ottawa and the Provinces," *Canadian Annual Review 1986* (Toronto: University of Toronto Press 1990), 76–7.

42 Pierre Elliott Trudeau, "Say Goodbye to the Dream of One Canada," Toronto *Star,* 27 May 1987, repr. in Donald Johnston, ed., *With a Bang, Not a Whimper: Pierre Trudeau Speaks out* (Toronto: Stoddart 1988), 8–22.

43 Donald Johnston, "A Dismembered Confederation of Fiefdoms?" Ottawa *Citizen,* 16 May 1987; his extensive brief to and testimony before the Senate committee of the whole on the Meech Lake Constitutional Accord, Canada, Parliament, *Debates of the Senate,* 23 March 1988, 2912–21; his testimony to the Legislative Assembly of Ontario, Select Committee on Constitutional Reform, 1987 Constitutional Accord, *Hansard Official Report of Debates,* 7 March 1988.

44 Quebec, *Journal des Débats,* 18 June 1987, 8708.

45 Cited in Vastel, *Bourassa,* 114–15.

46 *Journal des Débats,* 18 June 1987, 8709.

47 Findlay and Sprague, *The Structure of Canadian History,* 504, Table 14.

48 Greg Weston, "Turner Attacks Bourassa for Quebec Language Policy," Ottawa *Citizen,* 6 April 1989; Susan Delacourt, "Grits Bare Souls on Meech Lake," *Globe and Mail,* 17 April 1989, and "Race Is on as Turner Bows out," *Globe and Mail,* 4 May 1989; Paul-André Comeau, *Le Devoir,* 4 May 1989.

49 Gretta Chambers, "Federal Liberals Turn Backs on Quebec," Montreal *Gazette,* 18 May 1989; Michel Vastel, "Le leadership liberal se prepare sur le dos du Québec," *Le Devoir,* 19 June 1989; Richard Cleroux, "Quebec MPs Emerge as Surprise Powerhouse," *Globe and Mail,* 24 May 1989.

50 Behiels, *Canada's Francophone Minority Communities,* 260–2.

51 Frank McKenna, testimony before the Special Joint Committee of the Senate and the House of Commons on the 1987 Constitutional Accord, *Minutes of Proceedings and Evidence,* no.12, 25 August 1987, 5–19.

52 Michel Vastel, "McKenna veut son petit lac Meech," *Le Devoir,* 27 November 1987; Don Richardson, "Delaying Ratification of Meech Lake," Fredericton *Telegraph-Journal,* 17 February 1988; "Murray Confident N.B. Will Eventually Throw Its Support to Meech Lake Deal," Fredericton *Telegraph Journal,* 27 April 1988; Bernard Descoteaux, "Lac Meech: McKenna envoie paître Bourassa," *Le Devoir,* 18 March 1988; "Le Quebec et le Nouveau-Brunswick on fait la paix," *Le Devoir,* 23 August 1988.

53 McKenna Steadfast on Meech Lake," Ottawa *Citizen,* 13 January 1989; Susan Delacourt, "McKenna Questions Meech Lake Deadline," *Globe and Mail,* 13 January 1989; Roy MacGregor, "McKenna Wants Answers from Mulroney, Bourassa," Ottawa *Citizen,* 24 May 1989.

54 Don McGillivray, "Manitoba Catches Nation by Surprise," Ottawa *Citizen*, 25 April 1989; William Johnson, "Liberal Votes in Manitoba Kill Meech Deal," Montreal *Gazette*, 27 April 1989; "Filmon Gov't Makes Meech a Priority, Report Says," Ottawa *Citizen*, 21 July 1989.

55 Geoffrey York, "Will Kill Meech Lake, Manitoba NDP Warns," *Globe and Mail*, 23 November 1989; Michel Vastel, "Bourassa paiera cher son appui à Mulroney," *Le Devoir*, 18 December 1989.

56 Cohen, *A Deal Undone*, 194–5.

57 *Quebec* v. *Ford et al.* [1988] 2 S.C.R. 712.

58 MacDonald, *From Bourassa to Bourassa*, 294–9.

59 Geoffrey York and Benoît Aubin, "Manitoba Premier Ends Meech Debate," *Globe and Mail*, 20 December 1989; "Half Man. PCs Oppose Accord," Ottawa *Citizen*, 21 December 1989; Geoffrey York, "Filmon Urges Judicial Clarification of Accord's Distinct Society Clause," *Globe and Mail*, 12 January 1989.

60 Geoffrey York, "Meech Lake Accord Comes under Attack at Manitoba Hearing," *Globe and Mail*, 7 April 1989; "Opposition to Meech Dominates Hearing," *Globe and Mail*, 12 April 1989.

61 *Report of the Manitoba Task Force Report on Meech Lake*, Summary of Recommendations (Manitoba Legislative Assembly, 21 October 1989), 72–9.

62 Kevin Cox, "Newfoundland Liberals Win Majority," *Globe and Mail*, 21 April 1989; Hugh Winsor, "Newfoundland Liberals' Win Raises Alarms in Ottawa," *Globe and Mail*, 22 May 1989; Don McGillivray, "Federal Tories Blew Nfld. Election," Ottawa *Citizen*, 21 April 1989.

63 Michael Valpy, "Wells a New Star on Political Stage," *Globe and Mail*, 22 May 1989; Hugh Winsor and Kevin Cox, "Wells Pledges to Oppose Meech Lake Agreement," *Globe and Mail*, 22 May 1989.

64 Deborah Coyne, *Roll of the Dice* (Toronto: James Lorimer 1992), 7–24.

65 Ibid., 35–48, 68–79. Quote at 78.

66 New Brunswick, Select Committee on the 1987 Constitutional Accord, *Final Report on the Constitution Amendment 1987* (Fredericton, October 1989).

67 New Brunswick, *A Guide to New Brunswick's Companion Resolution to the 1987 Constitutional Accord* (Fredericton, March 1990).

68 Darrel R. Reid, "Chronology of Events, 1989–90," in Ronald L. Watts and Douglas M. Brown, eds., *Canada: The State of the Federation 1990* (Kingston, Ont.: Institute of Intergovernmental Relations, Queen's University 1990), 253.

69 Canada, Special Committee to Study the Proposed Companion Resolution to the Meech Lake Accord, *Report* (Ottawa, May 1990).

70 Martin, *The Antagonist*, 198–9.

71 Bouchard, *À visage découvert*, 320.

72 Ibid., 205–8; MacDonald, *From Bourassa to Bourassa*, 302–5.

73 MacDonald, *From Bourassa to Bourassa*, 306–7.

74 Patrick J. Monahan, *Meech Lake: The Inside Story* (Toronto: University of Toronto Press 1991), 210–37; Cohen, *A Deal Undone*, 233–56.

75 Cohen, *A Deal Undone*, 258–67.

76 Guy Laforest, *Trudeau et la fin d'un rêve canadien* (Montreal: Septentrion 1992), 149–71; Pierre Fournier, *A Meech Lake Post-Mortem: Is Quebec Sovereignty Inevitable?* (Montreal and Kingston: McGill-Queen's University Press 1991), 68–83.

77 Philip Resnick, *Toward a Canada-Quebec Union* (Montreal and Kingston: McGill-Queen's University Press 1991); Kenneth McRoberts, *Misconceiving Canada: The Struggle for National Unity* (Toronto: Oxford University Press 1997).

78 Cited in William Johnson, *A Canadian Myth: Quebec between Canada and Utopia* (Montreal: Robert Davies Publishing 1994), 249.

79 An Act to Establish the Commission on the Political and Constitutional Future of Quebec (Bill 90), s. 2.

80 Johnson, *A Canadian Myth*, 260–1.

81 MacDonald, *From Bourassa to Bourassa*, 322–3. The expression "a knife to the throat" was first used by a renowned Laval University political scientist, Léon Dion, during his testimony before the Bélanger-Campeau Commission.

82 Max Nemni, "Canada in Crisis and the Destructive Power of Myth," *Queen's Quarterly* 99(1) (1992): 222–39.

83 Kenneth McRoberts, *Quebec: Social Change and Political Crisis*, 3rd ed. (Toronto: Oxford University Press 1993), 449.

84 *A Quebec Free to Choose: Report of the Constitutional Committee of the Quebec Liberal Party for Submission to the 25th Convention* (Quebec Liberal Party, 28 January 1991). Called the Allaire report. Robert Bourassa, Interview on the Allaire report, *La Presse*, 2 February 1991.

85 Quebec, *Report of the Commission on the Political and Constitutional Future of Quebec*, 15. Called the Bélanger-Campeau Commission.

86 Ibid., 79–82.

87 CROP Public Opinion Poll, *L'Actualité*, January 1991.

88 An Act respecting the Process for Determining the Political and Constitutional Future of Quebec, s. 1.

89 Citizens' Forum on Canada's Future, *Report to the People and Government of Canada* (Ottawa: Ministry of Supply and Services Canada 1991), 10, 167–8.

90 Canada, *The Process for Amending the Constitution of Canada: The Report* (Ottawa: Queen's Printer, 20 June 1991).

91 Canada, *Shaping Canada's Future Together: Proposals* (Ottawa: Minister of Supply and Services 1991).

92 Bourassa cited in *Globe and Mail*, 27 September 1991.

93 Quebec, *National Assembly Debates*, 9 and 27 November 1991.

94 Robert Everett, "Parliament and Politics," in David Leyton-Brown, ed., *Canadian Annual Review of Politics and Public Affairs 1991* (Toronto: University of Toronto Press 1998), 26–9.

95 Canada, *Renewal of Canada Conferences: Compendium of Reports* (Ottawa: Privy Council Office, Constitutional Conferences Secretariat, March 1992).

96 David Milne, "Innovative Constitutional Processes: Renewal of Canada Conferences, January-March 1992," in Douglas Brown and Robert Young, eds.,

*Canada: The State of the Federation 1992* (Kingston, Ont.: Institute of Intergovernmental Relations, Queen's University 1992), 27–51.

97 Canada, Special Joint Committee of the Senate and of the House of Commons on a Renewed Canada, *A Renewed Canada*, in *Minutes of Proceedings and Evidence*, 66 (28 February 1992).

98 Robert Bourassa, "Conference de presse," *Le Devoir*, 4 March 1992; *Globe and Mail*, 4 March 1992.

99 Susan Delacourt, *United We Fall: The Crisis of Legitimacy in Canada* (Toronto: Viking 1993), 138–41.

100 Ibid., 147; See also Jean-François Lisée, *The Trickster: Robert Bourassa and the Quebecers, 1990–1992* (Toronto: James Lorimer 1994).

101 Delacourt, *United We Fall*, 141–66; Johnson, *A Canadian Myth*, 318–20.

102 Canada, Continuing Committee of Ministers on the Constitution, *Final Status Report of the Multilateral Meetings on the Constitution, July 16, 1992* (Ottawa: Government of Canada 1992).

103 Johnson, *A Canadian Myth*, 321–2.

104 Delacourt, *United We Fall*, 166–70.

105 CROP Poll, *L'Actualité*, June 1992) Léger et Léger poll, *Le Journal de Montréal*, July 1992.

106 Delacourt, *United We Fall*, 171–2.

107 *Consensus Report on the Constitution, Charlottetown, August 28, 1992, Final Text.* See also *Draft Legal Text, October 9, 1992*.

108 Quebec National Assembly, *Journal des Débats*, 9 September 1992.

109 Johnson, *A Canadian Myth*, 338–9.

110 Delacourt, *United We Fall*, 176–81.

111 Michael D. Behiels, "Who Speaks for Canada? Trudeau and the Constitutional Crisis," in Andrew Cohen and J. L. Granatstein, eds., *Trudeau's Shadow: The Life and Legacy of Pierre Elliott Trudeau* (Toronto: Random House Canada 1998), 343–8.

112 Robert Everett, "Parliament and Politics," in David Leyton-Brown, ed., *Canadian Annual Review of Politics and Public Affairs 1992* (Toronto: University of Toronto Press 1998), 26–7.

113 Trevor Harrison, *Of Passionate Intensity: Right-Wing Populism and the Reform Party of Canada* (Toronto: University of Toronto Press 1995), 81–104.

114 Ibid.,105–20, 131–8, 143–52, 164–77, 222–36.

115 Manon Cornellier, *The Bloc* (Toronto: James Lorimer 1995), 28–31.

116 Martin, *The Antagonist*, 211–13, 216–21.

117 Ibid., 228–40. Consult Lisée, *The Trickster.*

118 Cornellier, *The Bloc*, 53–68.

119 Harrison, *Of Passionate Intensity*, 239.

120 Ibid., 240–5; Cornellier, *The Bloc*, 84.

# 12

# Dream Catching Mulroney Style: Aboriginal Policy and Politics in the Era of Brian Mulroney

GINA COSENTINO AND PAUL L.A.H. CHARTRAND

This chapter reviews various factors and key events that shaped and defined federal Aboriginal[1] policy and Aboriginal-state relations during the administration of Prime Minister Brian Mulroney.[2] In so doing, it also considers the notable policy and political lessons and consequences that can be learned from the period. While there have been significant changes in Aboriginal policy, and in the federal government's relationship with Aboriginal people, over the last forty years, the Mulroney era produced some enduring legacies and lessons that have created challenges and opportunities for Aboriginal policy makers in the new millennium. Critics and supporters alike can agree that the Mulroney period was, in many important respects, both a turning point and a breaking point in Canadian Aboriginal policy and the Aboriginal-federal government relationship. The Mulroney era coincided with a time when Aboriginal-state relations had reached a critical juncture. Concerted social-movement activism, instances of protest and mass demonstration, and armed confrontation had shown both Canada and the world that meaningful and effective change in its relationship with Aboriginal peoples was urgent. In addition to the highly visible and emotive politics of mega-constitutional reform and the armed stand-off at Oka, there were also less visible developments both in the direction and outcomes of policy and at the level of public debate, as well as institutional and procedural changes.[3]

Prime Minister Mulroney's particular leadership style and his political and economic views are important for assessing Aboriginal policy, and will be considered here. However, his government inherited a particularly complex policy environment from the Trudeau Liberal administration.[4] This environment consisted, not only of institutional and policy constraints that arose from past judicial and legislative decisions, Aboriginal social-movement activism, and the process of constitutional reform, but also what one commentator has called "a legacy of frustration" resulting from the lack of

In this photo of 27 March 1987, Prime Minister Brian Mulroney is presented with a feather by Aboriginal elder Alex Skead before the start of the second day of the first ministers' conference on Aboriginal constitutional matters. Canadian Press / Greg Teckles.

tangible advancements under the previous administration towards the goals of Aboriginal people.[5] Adding to the frustration, according to the same commentator, was the lack of improvement in the living conditions of Aboriginal people in Canada and the obstacles that consistently thwarted attempts for meaningful and significant transformation in the Aboriginal-state relationship when discussions about real change took place.[6]

Our understanding of Aboriginal-state relations and Aboriginal policy under the Mulroney administration is based upon an appreciation of the relevant domestic and external policy environments, which in turn involve the interplay of various interests, ideas, and institutions. What is offered here is a cursory analysis of these environments and relationships. We provide some preliminary insights into the politically charged and distinctive Aboriginal-state relationship during the Mulroney era. In particular, against the backdrop of Mulroney's reform agenda, we assess Aboriginal policy in relation to constitutional reform, self-government and Aboriginal rights, public administration, and land claims, all the while recognizing that policy and politics are much more complex and difficult to evaluate than mere policy statements and goals.

## ABORIGINAL POLITICS AND THE CONSTITUTIONAL-REFORM EXPERIMENT

The 1982 constitutional amendments, which included specific provisions relating to Aboriginal peoples and their rights, can be seen as a high point in Canadian constitutional history and as a turning point for Aboriginal people in their quest to experience self-determination in a new constitutional order.[7] Ten years later, in 1992, however, the Aboriginal dream of pursuing self-determination through self-government was shaken with the unsuccessful attempt in the Charlottetown Accord to amend the constitution to recognize self-government as an inherent Aboriginal right. It has also been argued that the 1982 constitutional round, which culminated in the "patriation" of the Canadian constitution and an entrenched Charter of Rights and Freedoms, signaled the "end of a *Canadian* dream"[8] and ushered in an era of a deeply, and possibly permanently, divided Canada.

On the heels of Trudeau's dashed hopes for Canadian national unity sprang Brian Mulroney's particular dream for Canada. In his opening statement at the first ministers' conference (FMC) on the rights of Aboriginal peoples in 1985, Mulroney spoke of the importance of having "dreams to guide and sustain us."[9] For Mulroney, this meant, among other things, "building" and "rethinking" traditional Canadian institutions to make space for Aboriginal governments.[10] The process of constitutional reform coincided with mounting pressure by Aboriginal people and the public to restructure Aboriginal-government relations so as to have them better reflect the aspirations of Aboriginal people for self-determination.[11] Mulroney hoped to heal the constitutional and social fissures that had deepened since 1982, especially with respect to the constitutional status of Quebec and Aboriginal peoples.

The constitutional changes in 1982 acknowledged Aboriginal peoples as having a distinctive status and role with respect to constitutional change (section 35.1).[12] The inclusion of specific provisions dealing with Aboriginal and treaty rights (sections 25 and 35) and a guarantee of constitutional conferences with provincial, federal, and Aboriginal leaders to deal with Aboriginal issues, including clarifying the constitutional status and meaning of Aboriginal self-government in a series of FMCs (section 37), highlighted the special place of Aboriginal people and Aboriginal rights within the Canadian federation and in a vision of a just Canada.[13] Constitutional "dreaming," it seems, is believed to hold the possibility of transforming traditional Canadian institutions and renewing, rebuilding, and redefining Aboriginal-state relationships.[14] As a result, in Canada, it is not surprising that constitutional reform has been the setting against which much of the relationship between Aboriginal peoples and the federal government has developed. Constitutionalism, it is thought, not only represents past and present relationships but also embodies the hopes for a future based on substantive and meaningful change.[15]

The high politics of constitutional reform from 1985 to 1992 proved to be a distinctive period in the Mulroney era and in Canadian political history generally, as the Aboriginal-state relationship, land rights, self-government, federalism, citizenship, diplomacy, participatory and representative democracy, and national unity were magnified under the spotlight of domestic and international attention. In these years, some important gains were made at the level of policy ideas on self-government, political practice, and constitutional convention regarding Aboriginal consultation, participation, and process,[16] with significant consequences for both Aboriginal policy and the practice of Aboriginal affairs flowing from a range of factors and events. These consequences included the clarification of the meaning and scope of treaty rights and self-government powers that would have been gained with the successful resolution of the FMCs and the passing of the Charlottetown Accord, and the challenges to harmonious Aboriginal-state relations that stemmed from the Meech Lake Accord and the Oka crisis.

The successive attempts to secure national reconciliation through constitutional reform after 1982 grew increasingly complex, cacophonous, and conflict-ridden, especially given the "multi-stakeholder" interests represented at the negotiating table during the 1982 constitutional round. This was especially the case as the Mulroney government had to contend with the triple forces of a heightened rights-conscious society, escalating Québécois separatist-based nationalism, and the growing nationalism, political assertiveness, and social activism of Aboriginal peoples. The animated politics of mega-constitutional reform drew worldwide attention to Canada's tenuous political fault lines, especially the growing tensions between the federal and provincial governments and Aboriginal peoples.

A number of watershed moments in the history of Aboriginal-state relations occurred under the Mulroney administration, the implications of which were felt beyond his term in office. These included Mulroney's attempts at constitutional reform, the convening of constitutionally mandated FMCs to deal specifically with Aboriginal issues, the Oka crisis, and establishment of a royal commission soon after the Oka stand-off to examine Aboriginal rights and Aboriginal-state relations.

### *First Ministers Conferences, 1983–87, and the Meech Lake Accord, 1987–90*

A series of four FMCs on Aboriginal constitutional reform were held between 1983 and 1987.[17] The participants were Aboriginal political leaders and territorial, provincial, and federal ministers. Initially mandated to elaborate the meaning of the rights that received recognition in general terms in the Constitution Act, 1982, the conferences dealt in a general way with the main constitutional implications of recognizing and affirming the rights of the Aboriginal peoples. [18] That a constitutional guarantee was needed to deal with the matter of calling meetings between Aboriginal leaders and government representatives is indicative of the level of mistrust that plagued Aboriginal-state relations.

The dialogue that occurred at the FMCs quickly established "self-government and lands and resources" as primary areas of focus. By the end of the last FMC in 1987, however, it had become clear that the government leaders were not willing to lend their support to these issues. The FMCs thus ended with bitter disappointment and cynicism on the part of Aboriginal representatives,[19] and distrust between the two sides.

While the emphasis on brokering a consensus could, in part, account for the failure to secure agreement in these high-stakes and high-pressure forums, events that followed the final FMC in 1987 served to convince Aboriginal representatives that they had good reasons to distrust government leaders.[20] One month after the breakdown of the final conference, the prime minister and premiers met at Meech Lake to reach agreement on securing Quebec's place in the Canadian constitution. Aboriginal representatives were not invited to what was known as the "Quebec round" because it purported to deal only with that province's political grievances. Thus, the perception grew that Aboriginal rights had been left off the constitutional-reform agenda.[21] Although Aboriginal representatives did not oppose the recognition of Quebec as a distinct society, there were many who were opposed to what they viewed as the accord's silence regarding the distinct status of Aboriginal peoples.[22]

Moreover, the Meech Lake Accord showed Mulroney's capacity to reach a national agreement with the premiers, and this fact, viewed against the failure to do the same in the Aboriginal FMCs, quickly acquired a political and symbolic value in the dialogue on Aboriginal-state relations.[23] For many Aboriginal people, the closed-door decision-making process leading to the Meech Lake Accord represented a violation and betrayal of any goodwill generated in the Aboriginal-federal government relationship over the past twenty years. The political consequences became clear when two of the provinces that initially signed the agreement – New Brunswick and Manitoba – delayed ratifying it. [24] In June 1990, with the end of the three-year time limit for ratification of constitutional amendments rapidly approaching, the prime minister convened another constitutional conference with the premiers. This one lasted ten days and the result was that New Brunswick and Manitoba governments agreed to introduce Meech Lake resolutions into their legislatures as soon as possible, while all parties also undertook to resume constitutional conferences on Aboriginal issues.[25] Mulroney sent Senator Lowell Murray as his special envoy to urge

Aboriginal leaders in Manitoba to accept his new six-point plan for Aboriginal people, a plan that included a federal-provincial process to set the agenda for an FMC on Aboriginal issues, a commitment by the government of Canada to recognize Aboriginal peoples as a fundamental "characteristic" of Canadian society, the participation of Aboriginal peoples' representatives at any future FMC held to discuss the "recognition clause," an invitation to Aboriginal peoples' representatives to participate in all FMCs where matters being discussed directly affected them, the joint definition of treaty rights, and the establishment of a royal commission on native affairs.[26] The promises represented what Mulroney considered to be possible in respect to Aboriginal constitutional reform and participation of Aboriginal peoples in the process.

But they came too late. While New Brunswick ratified the Accord, Manitoba was a different story.There, Elijah Harper, an Oji-Cree MLA from Red Sucker Lake, became a symbol of Aboriginal peoples' insistence on their right to participate in national statecraft when he responded with a quiet "No" to the official request for the unanimous support required to introduce a resolution ratifying the Meech Lake Accord into the Manitoba Legislative Assembly. The result was that the legislature adjourned without ratifying the accord, following which Newfoundland rescinded its earlier ratification of the deal. The Meech Lake Accord was officially dead.

Harper's stance galvanized widespread Aboriginal opposition to the accord and overshadowed the support that the Métis National Council (MNC) gave it.[27] The MNC viewed nation-building as an exercise in compromise, and it concluded that, on balance, the accord ought to have been adopted, for afterwards, according to the promises of the prime minister, Aboriginal issues as well as other matters requiring constitutional attention, including Senate reform, would be tackled.[28] Yet, in retrospect, the majority of Aboriginal people opposed the Meech Lake Accord because they resented their exclusion from the constitutional-reform process, as well as a vision of Canada that made no room for them.[29]

Relations between Aboriginal peoples and the Canadian state reached a violent boiling point soon after the demise of the Meech Lake Accord when Mohawk occupied lands near Oka, Quebec, to protest against the commercial development of a golf course on sacred territory that belonged to them.[30] A seventy-eight-day armed confrontation between the Mohawk Warrior Society and the Canadian state – in the form first of the Quebec provincial police and later of the Canadian army – put Canada's relationship with Aboriginal peoples on the international map and sparked heated debate about Aboriginal rights across Canada.

While the Oka crisis was certainly a dark period in Canada's relationship with Aboriginal peoples, it also represented a turning point. Just after the crisis, in September 1990, Mulroney announced a new federal Aboriginal agenda. This agenda was premised on four key pillars: facilitating a new working relationship between the Canadian government and Aboriginal peoples so as to expedite land-claims settlements; improving the social and economic circumstances of Aboriginal peoples; renewing and reforming Aboriginal relations with government; and accommodating self-government within the constitutional framework.[31] Mulroney hoped to foster an effective new working arrangement based on the treaty relationship, Aboriginal rights, and the recognition in the Canadian constitution of the distinct status of Aboriginal peoples within the federation.[32]

### *Royal Commission on Aboriginal Peoples* (RCAP)

The promised Royal Commission on Aboriginal Peoples was established in August 1991.[33] Its mandate and membership were based entirely on the recommendations of Mulroney's special representative, the late and then retired chief justice of Canada, the Honourable Brian Dickson.[34] Set out under sixteen headings, the commission's mandate was to propose specific solutions to problems that had long plagued the relationship between Aboriginal peoples, Canadian governments, and Canadian society; indeed, this was the first commission in history charged with the task of addressing, in a comprehensive fashion, the entire scope and complexity of Aboriginal policy. The membership of the commission was chosen to reflect Canadian and Aboriginal diversity. Four commissioners represented status and non-status Indian, Métis, and Inuit peoples, and three other, non-Aboriginal representatives were from Quebec, Ontario, and western Canada.[35]

The commission held extensive public hearings across Canada, commissioned research reports, and consulted experts in a wide range of fields. One of issues that initially proved divisive was whether to have hearings without first publishing a set of tentative recommendations on the items set out in the commission's mandate. Some argued that offering such recommendations at the outset would serve to test public opinion and, by taking advantage of the relatively high level of support for Aboriginal issues that existed at the time, would allow the work of the commission to be completed quickly. In the end, the commission held hearings without first making recommendations.

In its initial round of hearings, the commission promised to consult on a set of tentative recommendations to be made following the initial round, but, by the time that its work was in fact completed, a new government had been elected and it announced that no new funds would be appropriated for what was then widely described by the press as Canada's most expensive royal commission ever, having cost some $58 million (which included a $12-million research project supplemented by an $8-million "community participation" program).[36] Notably, the commission published an analysis of the constitutional right of Aboriginal self-government that was said by participants to have influenced the decision to include recognition of this right in the Charlottetown Accord of 1992.[37]

RCAP's central recommendations focused on the idea of a "nation-to-nation" relationship with Aboriginal peoples, to be negotiated locally or regionally following an agreement on general negotiating principles reached at an FMC with national Aboriginal leaders. The new relationship also required a significant overhaul of the machinery of the federal government, and a new, legislated recognition of "nations" with whom Canada would negotiate "nation-to-nation" agreements or treaties. The Indian Act and the Department of Indian and Northern Affairs Canada would become obsolete, replaced with a Crown Treaty Office, an Aboriginal Relations cabinet committee, and newly negotiated treaty arrangements. A new federal policy would include executive and legislative recognition of all Aboriginal peoples accorded that distinction in the constitution.

The five-volume final report was published in November 1996.[38] If the commission had concluded its work earlier, it likely would have been positively received (if only rhetorically) by the government that created it. As it was, any thoughts that the new Chrétien Liberal government might welcome the recommendations of the commission were dashed by Minister of Indian Affairs Ron Irwin's quip that he could have bought a lot of houses for Indians with $58 million. Not only did the Liberals not provide the funds to enable the RCAP to publish the full body of its commissioned research work, but it also did not adopt the commission's recommendation to make the report available in university, college, and school libraries. The report and other accompanying publications were soon sold out and out-of-print.[39]

The Liberal response to the commission's report came in the form of a statement on Aboriginal policy in January 1998. The statement was silent on the basic recommendations, and it has been criticized for not offering Canadians a competing vision.[40] The fact that the statement was made by the minister for Indian affairs and not by the prime minister indicated the low priority that the Chrétien government accorded the RCAP's recommendations.

Notwithstanding the neglect of the Chrétien Liberal government, the commission's work has had an enduring significance for Canadian Aboriginal policy.[41] The comprehensive treatment of policy issues and the depth of analysis in the commissioned research work guarantee its continuing relevance. Some particular policy elements have received international attention and support. This includes United Nations "treaty bodies" which have criticized Canada for failure to implement the RCAP recommendations. These UN bodies have noted in particular the government's failure to abandon the policy of extinguishing Aboriginal rights in treaty negotiations and agreements, and to implement the commission's self-government recommendations as a domestic application of the right of self-determination.[42] If the main role of a policy commission is to change the way that the public and governments think about its subject matter, rather than cause short-term policy shifts, then perhaps, in the long run, Mulroney's commission might achieve its goals.

In the end, the RCAP inevitably set policy parameters for the succeeding Liberal government as to what would be seen by the Aboriginal community as legitimate proposals for change, especially given the extensive consultation with Aboriginal peoples that formed the basis of the recommendations of the final report. In this light, the 1995 Liberal government's decision to recognize the inherent right of Aboriginal self-government[43] reflects the high-water mark of political recognition that was achieved in the Charlottetown Accord under Mulroney's government.

### *Aboriginal Politics and the Charlottetown Accord*

In November 1990 the Canadian government announced the creation of the Citizens' Forum on Canada's Future, known as the Spicer commission after its chair, Keith Spicer, to ascertain the views and opinions of Canadians on the on the future of their country. Mulroney also created a special joint committee of the House of Commons and the Senate, the Beaudoin-Edwards committee, to examine constitutional- amendment processes. The reports that resulted from these initiatives shaped the federal government's 1991 constitutional-reform agenda, as outlined in a document called *Shaping Canada's Future Together.* This agenda included: constitutionally recognizing the fundamental characteristics of Canada, such as the distinctiveness of Quebec and Aboriginal peoples; and institutional reform, including changes to the Supreme Court of Canada, the Senate, the division of powers, and the economic union.[44]

The lessons learned from the failure of the 1987 Meech Lake Accord led to the opening up of the constitutional-reform process through public-consultation forums and a national referendum on the agreement that was ultimately reached. [45] The culmination of a set of meetings in Charlottetown, Prince Edward Island, the birthplace of Canada's original constitution in 1867, the Charlottetown Accord attempted to reconcile the interests of the various constitutional participants involved. While this accord was rejected in the ensuing referendum, the process created constitutional history nonetheless. Mulroney initially opposed Aboriginal peoples' participation in Charlottetown, and their eventual inclusion resulted from pressure exerted by premiers such as Joe Ghiz of Prince Edward Island and Bob Rae of Ontario. In the result, the unprecedented level of participation by

Aboriginal representatives in the Charlottetown negotiations arguably produced sweeping implications for the practice of politics and the representation of Aboriginal people in Canadian policy-making institutions.[46]

Had the Charlottetown Accord been successful, it would have constitutionally entrenched Aboriginal government as one of the three orders of governments in Canada as well as the recognition of an inherent right of self-government, while also providing for Aboriginal seats in the Senate. The accord also contained a separate agreement on the same matters with the Métis representatives, entitled the "Métis Nation Accord," reached between the prime minister, five provincial premiers, and the MNC. Moreover, as a testament to the innovative capacity for compromise inherent in federalism, the powers of federal-provincial governments would be restructured in a way to uphold Aboriginal or treaty rights, the fiduciary responsibility for Aboriginal peoples, and Aboriginal self-government rights.[47] The Charlottetown Accord, then, was groundbreaking with respect to process, participation, and content. Its provisions represent the standard against which all future advances will be measured, whether achieved through the judiciary or the executive or legislative branches. Moreover, as media coverage of the Charlottetown debates attest, Aboriginal issues were prominently featured in public discussion of the constitution, federalism, and Canadian society.[48]

However, the gains achieved in democraticizing the process were also the reason for its demise. In the end, despite provincial support, approval from all federal political parties except the Reform Party of Canada, business interests, and national Aboriginal organizations, the multiplicity of opinions on various elements of the accord frustrated Mulroney's attempt to broker a constitutional deal.[49] The reasons for the accord's failure lie in part in the difficulty involved in reaching consensus on a constitutional package that dealt with so many diverse and conflicting interests, ideas, and visions of equality, Canada, and citizenship. The constitutional package of the "Canada Round" was perhaps too complex for consensus to be captured by referendum. Ultimately, the extensive set of proposals in the accord was subjected to a simplistic "yes or no" public debate and referendum question. While four national Aboriginal organizations supported it officially, the Accord was not supported in the referendum by their constituencies. In particular it was rejected by First Nation people, although studies reveal regional variations in support among First Nations, Inuit and Métis.[50]

Various explanations have been offered for this result, including the fact that there had not been sufficient time for Aboriginal people to absorb the implications of the accord before the referendum, divisions in the different Aboriginal organizations between the rank and file and the leadership, and the role of the Native Women's Association of Canada, which raised questions about women's rights under Aboriginal self-government and objected to its exclusion from the constitutional discussions with government representatives.[51]

While Mulroney has been accused of making policy by stealth, that is, through closed-door decision making,[52] the degree of public participation and consultation with respect to the Charlottetown Accord undoubtedly opened up the constitutional-reform process. But this is a double-edged sword: it can enhance participatory democracy, but it can also make the operation of democracy difficult. Since Charlottetown created new constitutional conventions, and expectations, regarding process, negotiations with multilateral and multi-stakeholder interests who oftentimes have conflicting ideas regarding the constitution, democracy, citizenship, and equality have rendered Canadian federalism, Aboriginal-state relations, and governing more complex. Moreover, after two highly publicized and emotional attempts at constitutional reform within a relatively short period, such an objective is no longer seen as a viable way, at least in the foreseeable future, to mediate existing tensions between Aboriginal peoples, society, and federal and provincial governments.[53] The Liberal government that followed Mulroney was inclined towards non-constitutional approaches for addressing intergovernmental tensions and coordinating public policy on a range of issues with Aboriginal representatives.[54]

In the end, during the 1992 constitutional round, Mulroney had presented Canadians with an opportunity within which meaningful change could occur in Canadian federalism and Aboriginal-state relations. However, he was not able to recover from two rounds of mega-constitutional reform, which had exacerbated divisions between Quebec and the rest of Canada.[55] For this and other reasons, the 1993 federal election saw the Progressive Conservatives' representation reduced to only two seats, their worst performance since 1867 and a far cry from the 211 and 169 seats won in the 1984 and 1988 federal elections respectively.[56] It also saw the emergence of a House of Commons deeply fragmented on regional lines, with a separatist party from Quebec as the official opposition, a populist Reform Party dominant in the west, and a Liberal Party that owed its victory to its overwhelming strength in Ontario.[57]

## RETHINKING AND RESTRUCTURING GOVERNANCE: THE INFLUENCE OF THE NEO-LIBERAL EXPERIMENT ON ABORIGINAL PROGRAMS, ADMINISTRATION, AND FUNDING

In a broader global context, the politics of constitutional reform, Aboriginal-state relations, and federalism in Canada coincided with an ideological shift towards the same neo-liberalism then in the ascendant in many other

Western industrial nations.[58] Neo-liberal ideas permeated both the practices and the policies of the Mulroney government, embracing ideas such as fiscal conservatism, deficit reduction, smaller government, free-market enterprise, trade liberalization, private-sector management techniques in government operations, greater political accountability and transparency, meritocracy, individual self-reliance, and welfare-state retrenchment.[59] Given the interdependency of legal, constitutional, political, and economic issues, it is necessary to situate the Mulroney government's project of restructuring or reforming institutions within this larger neo-liberal context.[60]

The economic and political direction of the Mulroney government converged with that of Margaret Thatcher's Conservative government in Britain and Ronald Reagan's Republican administration in the United States.[61] In Canada, the 1985 Royal Commission on the Economic Union and Development Prospects for Canada, known as the Macdonald Commission, legitimated the neo-liberal agenda to such an extent that it still has currency today.[62] For Mulroney, the challenge of governing at this political, economic, ideological, and social juncture proved particularly significant in the area of Canadian Aboriginal policy and Aboriginal-state relations. Neo-liberal ideas regarding fiscal restraint and restructuring certainly had an impact on self-government policy, Aboriginal program and service delivery, Aboriginal economic-development policy, and Aboriginal-government networks and alliances.[63]

Mulroney's assumptions about the legitimate role of the state, the economic inefficiency of government versus the efficiency of the free market, and the need to apply private-sector managerial techniques to public administration can be linked to various changes his government initiated with respect to institutional, fiscal, and procedural relationships between the federal government and First Nations.[64] Restructuring extends beyond reducing funding for programs and transfers; it reduces and redefines government responsibility.[65] As will be seen below, fiscal restructuring, spending cutbacks, and reorganizing and "downsizing" departments to make them more efficient and, therefore, more cost-effective were important decisions that influenced many areas of Aboriginal policy.

## *The Nielsen Task Force, 1985*

In line with the priorities of restructuring, reducing the deficit, and eliminating inefficiencies in government spending and programs, the Nielsen Task Force on Program Review (the Nielsen Task Force) was one of the first initiatives of the Tory government. The aim of this task force, which consisted of private sector-consultants and government officials, was to review government spending and programs.[66] In the end, its recommendations were not acted upon; however, they did have important political repercussions. A leaked cabinet memo, which referred to the report of the Task Force as "The Buffalo Jump of the 1980s,"[67] indicated that deep cuts to the Department of Indian Affairs were planned.[68] Echoing the distrust and suspicion that the assimilationist 1969 White Paper on Indian policy had generated, the memo drew an intense – and negative – response from First Nations.[69] This episode cast a shadow on the motives of the newly elected Mulroney government, which continued to linger through both of his terms in office. Aboriginal relations with the federal government were certainly off to a shaky start.

*The Administration of Indian and Northern Affairs and Funding Arrangements*

Perhaps to contain the political fallout stemming from the "Buffalo Jump" memo, both Brian Mulroney and David Crombie, the minister of Indian affairs and northern development, renounced the proposed spending cuts and declared that current levels of funding programs and services for First Nations would be sustained.[70]Yet it has been observed that, even though spending increased in the Mulroney years, it did not account for inflationary and population growth.[71] Moreover, after 1987, the federal government was less attentive to the aspirations of First Nations with respect program spending.[72] In 1989 the Mulroney government was criticized again when it imposed a spending ceiling on status Indian post-secondary education as part of its fiscal-restraint agenda. [73] However, in an attempt to ease government relations with Indians and Inuit, programs for these groups were exempted from the expenditure reductions of 1991–92, and spending increases of 4.8 per cent over the year prior were planned.[74] This was an acknowledgment by the federal government that, given the depressed living conditions that continued to prevail among First Nations and Inuit people in Canada, the failure of the FMCs, and the subsequent exclusion of Aboriginal peoples and Aboriginal issues from the Meech Lake Accord, instituting a policy of fiscal restraint would do little to ameliorate the Aboriginal-federal government relationship.[75] It seems that the federal government's economic agenda of cutting costs collided with unforeseen or undervalued political costs in Aboriginal-state relations.[76]

In keeping with the spirit of the Mulroney government's ideas about the appropriate role of government, the Department of Indian Affairs and Northern Development (DIAND), now known as Indian and Northern Affairs Canada (INAC), continued a policy of downsizing its operations and devolving or transferring greater responsibility for program and service delivery, such as education, to First Nation people on reserves.[77] Correspondingly, Alternative Funding Arrangements (AFA) were created in 1986 to allow First Nations more decision-making and administrative control over funds and programs.[78] These initiatives were consistent with Mulroney's larger goal of diminishing welfare dependency and improving socio-economic conditions among First Nations. In his notes to the 1985 conference on Aboriginal Rights, he stated that "the answer lies in aboriginal peoples assuming more responsibility for their own affairs, setting their own priorities, determining their own programs."[79] As a result, INAC developed a five-year plan (1985–86 to 1990–91) to increase efficiency, a plan that consisted of devolution and downsizing initiatives.[80] By 1991, more than 77 per cent of program spending on Indian and Inuit affairs was managed by Aboriginal people themselves (nearly an 88 per cent increase from ten years earlier), and this went hand in hand with program-staff cutbacks of nearly 32 per cent.[81]

Under this new structure, AFA offered Aboriginal people some scope for greater decision making in the application of funds, the opportunity for multi-year planning, and a capacity to create community-based programs consistent with local priorities, along with less arduous program and financial-reporting requirements. However, bands were required to manage within the fixed funding limit for the entire multi-year period of the agreement. This arrangement can create problems when the agreed-on funding limits fall short of requirements.[82]

In addition to AFA, Flexible Transfer Payments (FTP) were added in 1989 to other funding arrangements as an alternative both to annual funding assistance, used for a particular purpose and subject to terms and conditions, and to AFA, which are multi-year agreements that offer more flexibility but also more risks for First Nations given their fixed budgets.[83] In the Mulroney period, particular changes in funding arrangements and the fiscal relationship revealed attempts to innovate and experiment with the parameters of self-government in the Indian Act in order to increase decision-making capacity at the band level while reducing the federal government's role in administering Indian affairs. Such changes included the "Kamloops Amendment" to Indian band taxation powers in section 83 of the Indian Act, and the creation of the Indian Taxation Advisory Board. [84]

These arrangements have been described as being consistent with the notion of devolution or the transfer of service delivery and some decision-making capacity to the community level, which can enhance community-based approaches to problem solving and decision making. Similarly, others insist that community-based governance solutions and program and service delivery were important signposts of change in Aboriginal policy and offer important opportunities for innovation and input among First Nations.[85] This can open up the possibility for First Nations and Inuit service delivery and program planning in economic development, education, health care and other social services, all of which can have important consequences for their well-being.

On the other hand, some commentators contend that what is described as the community and individual empowerment underlying administrative reforms such as devolution actually promote the assimilationist goals of past Aboriginal policy and is based upon a view of self-government that is restricted to self-management or limited autonomy.[86] These observers hold that the new approach did not provide for the sharing of real political or economic power, and that the ideal of promoting national reconciliation with Aboriginal peoples cannot occur through devolution and bureaucratized Aboriginal relations.

The Tory government's professed goals of enhancing self-government through devolution and self-sufficiency seemed to be at odds with federal spending cuts and curtailment of services. Given these changes in the fiscal relationship, government spending reduction required Indians and Inuit included within federal programs, "to establish priorities as government extended few resources to combat social and health issues. Changing educational benefits and shifting health responsibilities onto the bands were just two ways in which government action forced Indians to reallocate their meager resources."[87] This left unresolved questions about the meaning of self-government in the absence of an adequate fiscal base.[88] As the socio-economic evidence suggests, greater self-government has not yet translated into significantly improved living conditions for Indians and Inuit people…[89]

The idea of devolution is based upon the premise of productive and self-sufficient citizens who must be responsible for their own and their family's well-being. The government's role is reduced to assisting the local level, or individuals, to perform their devolved tasks.[90] The implications of devolution, especially with respect to maintaining national standards in services, programs, and the delivery of same have been effectively dealt with elsewhere.[91] Suffice it to say here that the Tory government's desire to reduce its role and, to an extent, shift responsibility and ministerial accountability for Indian and Inuit programs and services revealed certain inclinations or policy approaches, which leaned towards liberal individualism, devolution, and a market-driven response to Aboriginal issues. Much the same sort of mentality was evident in the Tory government's Aboriginal economic-development policy. To promote economic self-sufficiency, the Tories turned to market-based solutions, entrepreneurialism, and integration into the global capitalist political economy to aid Aboriginal business development, community economic planning and development, and employment-skills training.[92]

This approach may be seen as conflicting with the collective self-determination goals that were articulated by the representatives of the Aboriginal peoples in the FMCs. While the language of self-government was often linked to devolutionary policies, it is evident that that the actions of Mulroney's government can be more accurately described as Indian self-administration based on delegated authority within the established federal system.[93]

As a result, First Nation people and the national Aboriginal organizations were receiving mixed messages in this period regarding the sincerity of the federal government's intentions about working towards and implementing self-government. This contributed to, and exacerbated, feelings of mistrust of the federal government among some Aboriginal people and leaders, feelings that were carried over to the processes of constitutional reform and land-claim settlements.[94]

## EXPERIMENTS IN SELF-GOVERNMENT AND LAND CLAIMS

The politics of resolving land disputes, making treaties, and crafting and implementing self-government policy in the Mulroney period had its roots in judicial decisions, Aboriginal legal and political mobilization, and government policy and reports.[95] Aboriginal involvement in political activism and legal mobilization among Aboriginal organizations drew greater public and political attention to land and other Aboriginal rights. Issues relating to Indian land and governance were firmly placed on the policy agenda after the 1969 White Paper.[96] In addition, the 1973 landmark decision of the Supreme Court of Canada in *Calder*[97] and the passing of the Constitution Act, 1982 were influential in shaping both land-claims and self-government policy. Section 35 of the Constitution Act, 1982 explicitly recognizes and affirms "the existing Aboriginal and treaty rights" of Aboriginal peoples, which include rights resulting from comprehensive land claims.[98] In this regard, it should be noted parenthetically that the political and legal implications of the 1982 provisions should not be underestimated, given that only a decade earlier the federal Liberals had refused to acknowledge Aboriginal title.

Efforts to restructure Aboriginal-state relations moved to the centre of Mulroney's constitutional and legislative agendas as federal, provincial, and Aboriginal representatives worked towards accommodating[99] the demands of Aboriginal peoples to have their inherent right of self-government fully recognized, treaty promises fulfilled, and land disputes settled.[100] The recognition of Aboriginal and treaty rights, especially rights pertaining to land and self-government, proved particularly trying for Mulroney, given their high political volatility and potential for generating political violence.

In the first of the four FMCs, which occurred within the closing months of the Liberal government in 1983, section 35 of the Constitution Act 1982 was modified to include both existing and future land-claims settlements. Section 35 now entrenched several classes of Aboriginal and treaty rights, of which land-claims settlement rights were just one. While it was left to the government and Aboriginal leaders to further "identify and define" Aboriginal rights, Mulroney put self-government and land and treaty rights on the Canadian political map by making the connection between land and self-government issues more explicit.[101]

Perhaps one of the most enduring legacies of the Mulroney government in Aboriginal policy is the reaffirmation of the importance of land to self-government as a basis for renewal and negotiation with Aboriginal peoples, and the making of the decisions to tackle such issues beyond the scope of the Indian Act.[102] During the 1985 FMC, Mulroney expressly agreed to include land for the Métis people in his constitutional agenda, in response to a question by MNC leader Harry Daniels. In 1989 the minister of Indian affairs, Pierre H. Cadieux, outlined priorities for a "new relationship" based on the interconnection between land and self-government.[103]

### *The Coolican Taskforce, 1985, and the Aboriginal Comprehensive Claims Policy, 1986*

The 1973 *Calder* decision was a decisive factor in Aboriginal claims policy. It led to a policy reversal by the Liberal government, which announced that it was prepared to enter into negotiations with Indian and Inuit people to resolve disputes concerning "comprehensive claims" to Aboriginal title. Furthermore, the new policy direction included "specific claims" relating to breaches of treaty obligations.[104] The latter was a turning point given that, just four years earlier, the federal Liberals had wanted to abandon special programs and Indian status in the White Paper.[105] The main features of the policy included consultation in the management of residual crown lands, restricted subsurface rights, preferential wildlife harvesting rights, and cash compensation.[106]

The 1973 policy has been described as an "inflexible straitjacket" that stymied progress in reaching land-claims settlements. In this view, the policy was ambiguous and narrow in focus. A primary point of contention was the requirement to extinguish Aboriginal land rights. The policy also did not include self-government rights with land-claims settlements.[107] This clashed with the position of some First Nation representatives, who viewed the claims process as an opportunity to negotiate accords relating to economic, social, political, and cultural issues.[108]

A number of factors offered Mulroney the opportunity to reform land-claims policy. These included shifts in thinking about self-government and Aboriginal land rights and changes to the country's institutional framework, particularly section 35 of the 1982 constitution, which placed the extinguishment of Aboriginal and treaty rights through land claim-settlements beyond legislative reach.

In 1985 the Mulroney government demonstrated that it was willing to consider changes to federal government comprehensive-claims policy by subjecting it to a full-scale review. The Task Force to Review Comprehensive

Claims Policy, known as the Coolican Task Force, consulted First Nation representatives and offered a different approach to land-claims policy in its final report.[109] It recommended that land claims should not extinguish but affirm Aboriginal rights, that the process be reformed to expedite resolution and allow for the negotiation of self-government and co-management of lands and resources with the government, and that an independent monitoring body be created.[110] The report, entitled *Living Treaties, Lasting Agreements,* viewed land-claims settlements not as an end-point or final destination in Aboriginal-state relations but as a "living" relationship in which comprehensive-claims treaties settled immediate issues in the short term and also offered directions for dealing with other issues as they arose on an ongoing basis.[111]

The government responded with the 1986 Federal Comprehensive Land Claims Policy, [112] which did not follow Coolican and fell short of First Nations' expectations.[113] Under the policy, self-government agreements would not be included within land-claims agreements and the nature and scope of self-government institutions would be limited to band or community-level institutions established by delegated authority under statutes. Extinguishment of Aboriginal rights, which continues to be a feature of federal policy, notwithstanding official policy statements to the contrary, was continued under the guise of establishing legal certainty. The RCAP final report deals succinctly with the main problems in the new policy: "To the disappointment of Aboriginal groups and others who supported the Coolican report, the federal response offered an alternative to extinguishment of rights that was more illusory than real: self-government negotiations, if they resulted in an agreement, would receive no constitutional protection or independent monitoring authority. By and large, this remains the federal position with respect to comprehensive claims." [114]

Nonetheless, the Mulroney period saw resolution of some land disputes in northern Canada under the comprehensive land-claims policy. For example, in 1984 the Inuvialuit people reached an agreement with the federal government with respect to lands in the western Arctic. In 1993 the Inuit people of the eastern Arctic reached an agreement and the relevant legislation was passed in Parliament during the closing weeks of the Mulroney government to create Nunavut, a third territory. Other settlements include the 1992 Gwich'in Comprehensive Land Claim Agreement and the 1993 Sahtu Dene and Métis Comprehensive Land Claim Agreement. It may be noted that these agreements were reached in the territories and thus indirectly illustrate the difficulties of attempts to agree on the recognition and protection of the rights of Aboriginal peoples in areas where the provinces are also involved as parties.

Given that First Nations generally do not have the financial resources of their own to carry out the research to substantiate claims as mandated by the government claims process, federal funding is important for the ability of claimants to pursue a claim successfully. Between 1984 and 1993, federal government contributions to research and loans for specific claims decreased significantly while comprehensive-claims funding remained constant. Also, between 1990 and 1993, "major expenditures were provided to settle both comprehensive and specific claims" although research contributions were discontinued in 1990.[115]

Through the implementation of some self-government accords and the resolution of certain land claims, Mulroney's political project of restructuring the Aboriginal-federal government relationship was made visible. It appears that the prime minister appreciated the possible political implications associated with land-claims policy and a successful completion of his constitutional agenda.

### *The Non-Constitutional Route to Self-government: Community-based Self-government Policy*

The direction of First Nations self-government policy under Mulroney has been described as having its roots in some of the ideas underpinning the 1983 Report of the Special Committee of the House of Commons on Indian Self-Government, known as the Penner Report.[116] Among other things, that report saw self-government as a means to address the problem of Indian poverty and depressed living conditions through Indian-derived solutions, and it called as well for constitutional entrenchment of the principle of self-government. While the issue of securing Quebec's place in the federation was a major concern of federal and provincial governments at the time, the constitutional status of Aboriginal self-government and the need to reconcile land claims and self-government issues in the Northwest Territories was also on the negotiation agenda of the federal and provincial governments. Self-government as a policy issue had currency during the first Mulroney government in large part as a result of the FMCs on Aboriginal matters. Proposals for accommodating self-government ranged from constitutionally entrenching self-government subject to negotiation; committing governments to participate in negotiations aimed at reaching agreements; and passing federal and provincial legislation.[117] The FMCs of 1983–87 have been extensively and effectively dealt with elsewhere; the important point for our purposes is that the conferences were unable to achieve consensus on the issue of entrenching the right of Aboriginal self-government in the constitution.[118]

One of the non-constitutional initiatives undertaken by Mulroney's government for First Nations was community-based self-government.[119] The Indian Self-government Community Negotiation Program was launched by INAC during the 1985 FMC in the hope that agreements reached using a non-constitutional approach would muster support and goodwill in advance of the 1987 FMC.[120] This policy initiative showed that the federal government's preferred model of self-government for First Nations was limited to municipal-style government.[121] However, many Aboriginal people objected to a model of self-government that derived its authority from federal legislation. More consistent with the concept of inherent rights and the norms behind self-determination was a model that recognized the authority of Indian groups to legislate for themselves and that made that recognition effective in intergovernmental relations.[122] Furthermore, the complex application procedures for community-based self-government agreements, the reluctance of provinces to relinquish areas of legislative authority, and the difficulty of agreeing on funding parameters impeded the successful and timely realization of self-government initiatives.[123]

The Sechelt Indian Band in British Columbia reached an agreement with the provincial and federal governments under the policy. It was ratified in legislation passed by the province and Parliament in 1986.[124] The Sechelt Act, which was accompanied by multi-year funding, applied to all residents on Sechelt territory and, among other things, gave the Sechelt decision-making latitude as well as some powers that had previously been held by federal and provincial governments, included provisions for the role of the band in service delivery, recognized a fee simple title to land,[125] and provided the band with limited taxation powers and the capacity to construct roads, zone land, and grant access to and residence on their lands. The Sechelt agreement generated debate among many First Nations across Canada who argued for a model of self-government with some exclusive legislative authority, on the model of provincial legislative authority, as opposed to the limited autonomy of the municipal model.

Community-based self-government was consistent with the federal government's Self-government Funding Agreements (SGFAS) project in 1986, which were established to to secure funding arrangements in self-government negotiations as a five-year block intergovernmental transfer payment.[126] As a result, some argue that the federal government's self-government proposals offered the appearance of creating greater political and economic autonomy while simultaneously accomplishing cost cutting and other fiscal objectives. [127] Similarly, while this process for locally based self-government can offer greater political and economic autonomy for First Nations, it also can be seen as a "piecemeal approach" that stands in stark contrast to the idea of self-government envisioned in the Charlottetown Accord.[128] It is also one that perpetuates the historic policy of assimilation based upon the Indian Act and fails to make the constitutional recognition of the Indian, Métis, and Inuit peoples effective through executive and legislative recognition, as the RCAP later proposed in its "nation-to-nation" approach.[129]

Mulroney also introduced initiatives that marked the initial responses of the federal government to the claims and aspirations of the "non-status" Indians not recognized in federal legislation. Prominent among these were the establishment of the office of a federal "interlocutor" for Métis and non-status Indians; the appointment of a cabinet minister responsible for relations between government and the representatives of these groups; and the launching, with the cooperation of the western provinces, of tripartite non-constitutional negotiations on Aboriginal self-government involving Métis and off-reserve Aboriginal people.

## MULRONEY UNDER REVIEW: IMPLICATIONS FOR POLICY, PROCESS, AND PARTICIPATION

Mulroney's vision of Canada, democracy, and governance following the 1984 election was premised on, among other things, fiscal *restraint*, institutional, procedural, and program *reform*, *restructuring* of the economy, the federation, and the country's governing institutions, and national *reconciliation*. Aboriginal people saw Mulroney's resounding electoral achievement as a mixed blessing, given the Tory agenda of cost-cutting and deficit reduction.[130] Others, however, believed that his election opened a new window of opportunity on account of his reputation as a pragmatist, conciliator, and skilful broker of intergovernmental relations and divergent interests.[131]

A notable achievement in the Mulroney era was that, despite their relative lack of electoral importance as a result of their small population relative to the size of the Canadian population as a whole, Aboriginal peoples were able to capture the nation's attention during both constitutional-reform processes. The effect of this on process, participation, and representation cannot be understated.

The experience with constitutional reform under Mulroney also engendered new constitutional norms about the participatory and consultative dimensions of Aboriginal rights. These held far-reaching implications for consultation and participation of Aboriginal peoples in decision making, not only during times of mega-constitutional reform, as guaranteed by section 35.1 of the Constitution Act, 1982, but also as part of political decision making more generally across many fields of public policy, a status not afforded to any other non-government group in Canada. Aboriginal representation and participation in formulating policy is no longer considered a strange practice. Aboriginal people are seen as key actors, alongside provincial representatives, in decision-making processes that encompass many areas of public policy in addition to Aboriginal policy. Furthermore, during the negotiation of the Charlottetown Accord, Aboriginal organizations were treated as a de facto third level of government, thereby informally recognizing the inherent right of self-government.[132]

The federal Tories created an opportunity for a fundamental restructuring of both Aboriginal federal policy and Aboriginal relations, but Mulroney ultimately failed to sell his constitutional "dream" to Canada. As a result, litigation and the courts remain the most likely route to shape Canada's constitution, and as the means to resolve conflicts regarding land claims and governance rights and to mediate Aboriginal-state relations more generally. This is not the most desirable option, given the extensive fiscal resources required to pursue legal strategies and the uncertainty of legal outcomes. However, the need to generate greater political incentive for Canadian governments to act on implementing government and treaty rights – gains that would have been achieved through the Charlottetown Accord – has left the courts as the primary institution to develop the principles for Aboriginal policy and to mediate Aboriginal-state relations in the post-Mulroney period.[133] As a result, changes in Aboriginal policy remain slow and incremental – a more politically desirable and manageable route for government officials than RCAP's recommendations for fundamental restructuring.[134]

Mulroney's continuation of the process of devolving INAC's responsibilities to First Nation reserve communities also had important implications for First Nation autonomy, governance, and Aboriginal-state relations. His attempt to achieve greater self-government for First Nations while simultaneously trying to restrain the direct costs of government activities sent mixed messages, especially by reducing funding to Aboriginal organizations which depend on such funding to push forward with governance issues.[135] Nonetheless, despite the neo-liberal ideas underlying the government's approach, programs in funding arrangement, economic and business development, and community-based self-government, for instance, have allowed First Nations some scope in which to innovate in the areas of service and program delivery and to create community-directed and community-building solutions of their own.

Under Mulroney, also, the first hesitant steps were taken towards official recognition of the Indian and Métis people who fall outside the federal Indian Act, through the establishment of the federal Interlocutor's Office and the initiation of tripartite self-government negotiations involving provinces and Métis and off-reserve Indian groups. Today, these groups continue to await a definitive renunciation of the entrenched view that Métis people are not within the scope of federal legislative jurisdiction , as well as the passage of legislation to render concrete the 1982 constitution's recognition and affirmation of the rights of the non-recognized Indians and Métis.

## FROM "NO" TO "NO": A POSTSCRIPT

In 1969 Prime Minister Trudeau uttered his notorious "No" in answer to a question he had asked himself: Was it was right to honour and respect Indian treaties? Trudeau's resounding answer was based on his view of what his concept of a just society meant for Indian people, and specifically on his misguided view that the liberal notion of equality of citizens living within a democratic state was applicable to Aboriginal group rights.

Five years into the Mulroney Conservative government's mandate, Elijah Harper's "No!" in the Manitoba legislature was instrumental in defeating the Meech Lake Accord, for which he is widely remembered. Harper's "No!" was a whisper, but that whisper carried the reverberations of the intellectual and political progress that had been made in understanding and improving Aboriginal-state relations in Canada in the space of nearly a generation following Trudeau's 1969 remark. Harper's quiet "No" is a symbol of the quiet, yet unrelenting, determination of the Aboriginal peoples of Canada to refuse to legitimize a constitutional order that fails to include them as historic nations. It symbolizes the ascendancy, if not the triumph, of the claim of Aboriginal self-government, a concept that began to germinate during the Trudeau round of Aboriginal FMCs but that matured during the Mulroney era, notably in the 1985 FMC discussions, and that flowered in the provisions of full recognition in the Charlottetown Accord in 1992. By the time the Chrétien Liberals gained power in 1993, the idea of Aboriginal self-government had become so widely accepted that it was made part of federal policy in the 1995 policy statement that still guides treaty negotiations today.

The claim of Aboriginal self-government is based loosely upon the concept and the right of self-determination. It is a claim that challenges the legitimacy of the state that has come to govern Aboriginal peoples by dispossessing them of their homelands. This claim has dismantled the liberal notion of equality of citizens by dismantling the legitimacy of the polity that includes Aboriginal peoples as individual citizens. The triumph of the collective right of self-government will be complete when the standards that are used to assess this legitimacy are the ones that Canadians want to apply to themselves today: the principle of the consent of the governed, and the principle of self-determination.

This change has not come about by application of liberal, conservative, or neo-liberal ideas. It does not represent the triumph of one ideology over another. It is simply the result of the aggregated experience of government and Aboriginal representatives working together to resolve their differences and reconcile their competing interests. Out of this have emerged practical ideas for accommodating competing visions of the good society. This, perhaps, is the core of the legacy of the Mulroney government as far as Aboriginal peoples are concerned: his attempts and failures at national statecraft demonstrated conclusively that, in Canada, legitimate governance must include space for Aboriginal self-government. The inclusion of Aboriginal representatives as participants in national decision making was the organizing principle around which the Royal Commission on Aboriginal Peoples based its recommendations, and it is the same principle that legitimizes state action and Aboriginal policy alike. The experience of democratic participation is a dream catcher.

## NOTES

1 The term "Aboriginal" is used to refer to all the Aboriginal peoples of Canada, and the upper case is used where the word refers to the specific groups in Canada that are known as, and call themselves, "Aboriginal peoples," compared to the generic term used to refer to the origin or character of the people rather than their political designation. The constitution expressly recognizes and affirms the rights of the Aboriginal peoples of Canada. The Constitution Act, 1982 section 35(1) states: "The existing aboriginal and treaty rights of the aboriginal peoples of Canada are herby recognized and affirmed." Three peoples or categories of peoples are included in this provision: Indian, Inuit, and Métis (s. 35(2)). There are also several other constitutional provisions that refer to one or more of these Aboriginal peoples, and the appropriate terms will be explained in their context.

The historical use of various terms in reference to the Aboriginal peoples, recent changes and additions to the terminology in official documents, and differences between official and popular terminology have created an assortment of usages, and a fair degree of confusion in the literature. The following comments are useful to clarify the language that is used generally in this chapter.

The federal Parliament has unilaterally defined "Indians" in the Indian Act (Indian Act, RSC 1985, c. I–5.), and those persons have often been called "status Indians." They are, by the same statute, defined to comprise "bands" of Indians entitled to live on reserves set aside for their exclusive occupation. In recent years, the term "First Nations" has often replaced "bands," both in popular usage and in statutes, although this usage is also used more generally in popular language and literature in reference to various groups of "Indians." Since "status Indians" are those entitled to registration under the Indian Act, other Indians in Canada are sometimes called "non-status Indians" when that distinction is material. The Inuit are the Aboriginal people of the far north of Canada; they are not included in the terms of the Indian Act, but federal policy and administration deals with them in the Department of Indian and Northern Affairs (currently Indian and Northern Affairs Canada, or INAC). The Métis people had a prominent role in the history of western Canada, and are associated with the political leader Louis Riel and the Métis negotiations with Canada that gave birth to the province of Manitoba in 1870.

A number of factors have operated to make the meaning of the term "Métis" particularly elusive, whether in official or popular usage. In the last forty years or so, Métis and non-status Indians have often united in political organizations, and loose popular language has led to confusion between the two groups. Since the express inclusion of "the Métis people" in section 35, which recognizes the rights of the Aboriginal peoples of Canada, many persons and groups who are descended from various historic Aboriginal persons or societies across Canada have adopted the term "Métis" to designate themselves. Furthermore, many individuals descended from Indians, while not recognized officially as such in the federal statute, nevertheless wish to assert their personal descent from various Aboriginal people and so also identify themselves as "Métis." The Mulroney government dealt with four national organizations: the Assembly of First Nations, representing status Indians; the Inuit Tapirisat of Canada; and the Métis National Council, which had split off from the Native Council of Canada, a body that represented both Métis and non-status Indians, in 1983 prior to the first ministers' conference on Aboriginal constitutional reform under Prime Minister Trudeau.

See, generally, Paul L.A.H. Chartrand, "Terms of Division: Problems of 'Outside-Naming' for Aboriginal People in Canada," *Journal of Indigenous Studies/ La Revue des etudes indigenes* 2 (1991): 1–22. For a commentary on a case dealing with the constitutional meaning of Métis, see Chartrand, "The Hard Case of Defining the Mêtis People and Their Rights: A note on R. v. Powley," *Constitutional Forum* 12(3) (2003): 87.

2 This chapter will examine mainly, but not exclusively, status Indians or First Nations, the primary focus of federal Aboriginal policy. For a discussion on northern Aboriginal policy, see F. Abele and K.A. Graham, "Plus Que Ça Change … Northern and Native Policy," in K. Graham, ed., *How Ottawa Spends 1989–89: The Conservatives Heading into the Stretch* (Ottawa: Carleton University Press 1988), 113–38; Mark O. Dickerson, *Whose North? Political Change, Political Development and Self-government in the Northwest Territories* (Vancouver: University of British Columbia Press 1992); Frances Abele, "Conservative Northern Development Policy: A New Broom in an Old Bottleneck?" in Michael J. Prince, ed., *How Ottawa Spends 1986–87: Tracking the Tories* (Toronto: Methuen 1986); Frances Abele and Peter J. Usher, "A New Economic Development Policy for the North? The Impact of the Canada-U.S. Free Trade Agreement," October 1988 (Ottawa: Canadian Centre for Policy Alternatives), 1–46; Graham White with Kirk Cameron, *Northern Governments in Transition: Political and Constitutional Development in Yukon, Nunavut and the Western Arctic* (Montreal: Institute for Research on Public Policy 1995); Graham White with Jack Hicks, "Nunavut: Inuit Self-determination through a Land Claim and Public Government?" in Keith Brownsey and Michael Howlett, eds., *The Provincial State in Canada: Politics in the Provinces and Territories* (Peterborough, Ont.: Broadview Press 2001), 389–439.

3 Frances Abele, Katherine A. Graham, and Allan M. Maslove refer to the "hidden achievements" of Aboriginal policy as "quiet advances in Aboriginal policy" beyond the highly visible and well-documented politics of constitutional reform and the Oka crisis: "Negotiating Canada: Changes in Aboriginal Policy over the Last Thirty Years," in Leslie A. Pal, ed., *How Ottawa Spends 1999–2000: Shape Shifting: Canadian Governance Toward the 21st Century* (Don Mills, Ont.: Oxford University Press 1999), 266. The term "mega-constitutional politics" was coined by the distinguished political scientist Peter Russell. Russell argues that mega-constitutional politics represents more than debating specific constitutional proposals. It is about the debates regarding the identity and basic principles of a society, and, as a result, it tends to overshadow other public issues and sparks intense emotions. See Peter H. Russell, *Constitutional Odyssey: Can Canadians Be a Sovereign People?,* third edition (Toronto: University of Toronto Press 2004), 74–6, 314 n.8.

4 On this point, see Katherine Graham, "Indian Policy and the Tories: Cleaning up after the Buffalo Jump," in M. Prince, ed., *How Ottawa Spends 1987–99: Restraining the State* (Toronto: Methuen 1988), 237.

5 Ibid. Pierre Elliott Trudeau's Liberal Party governed from 1969 to 1984, with the brief exception of Joseph Clark's Conservative government from May to December 1979.

6 Graham, "Indian Policy and the Tories," 237 and 244.

7 James (Sákéj) Youngblood Henderson, "Postcolonial Ledger Drawing: Legal Reform," in Marie Battiste, ed., *Reclaiming Indigenous Voice and Vision* (Toronto: University of British Columbia Press 2000), 165–6. See n.13 below for the text of the constitutional provisions referring to Aboriginal people in the 1982 Constitution Act.

8 Guy Laforest, *Trudeau and the End of a Canadian Dream* (London, Ont.: McGill-Queen's University Press 1995), emphasis added. See also Kenneth McRoberts, *Misconceiving Canada: The Struggle for National Unity* (Toronto: Oxford University Press 1997).

9 Brian Mulroney, "Opening Statement at the First Ministers' Conference on the Rights of Aboriginal Peoples," 2–3 April 1985. Library and Archives Canada, http://www.collectionscanada.ca/primeministers/h4-4021-e.html (accessed 3 June 2004). See also Brian Mulroney, *CARC-Northern Perspectives,* 21(3) (1993), http://www.carc.org/pubs/v21no3/mulroney.htm.

10 Ibid.

11 Gina Cosentino, PHD thesis in progress, chapter 1. Examples of recent works on the significance of the right of self-determination for Aboriginal peoples include Royal Commission on Aboriginal Peoples (RCAP), *Canada's Fiduciary Obligations to Aboriginal Peoples in the Context of the Accession to Sovereignty by Québec,* vol. 1, S. James Anaya, Richard Falk, and Donat Pharand, *International Dimensions* (Ottawa: Canada Communication Group-Publishing, August 1995); Grand Council of the Crees, *Sovereign Injustice: Forcible Inclusion of the James Bay Cree Territory into a Sovereign Québec* (Nemaska, Eeyou Astchee, Canada: Grand Council of the

Crees 1995); S. James Anaya, *Indigenous Peoples in International Law,* 2nd ed. (Toronto: Oxford University Press 2004); Pekka Aikio and Martin Scheinin, eds., *Operationalizing the Right of Indigenous Peoples to Self-determination* (Turko, Finland: Aboriginal Akademi University. Institute for Human Rights 2000); M.J. Bryant, "Aboriginal Self-Determination: The Status of Canadian Aboriginal Peoples at International Law," *Saskatchewan Law Review* 56 (1992): 375.

12 Paul L.A.H. Chartrand, "Conclusion," in Chartrand, ed., *Who Are Canada's Aboriginal Peoples?: Recognition, Definition, and Jurisdiction* (Saskatoon: Purich Publishing 2002), 305. See also, for a detailed discussion of the constitutional rights of Aboriginal peoples, Peter W. Hogg, *Constitutional Law of Canada, Student Edition 2002* (Scarborough, Ont.: Carswell 2002), 622–3.

13 Constitution Act, 1982, being Schedule B of the Canada Act, 1982, (U.K.) 1982, c. 11; R.S.C. 1985, app. II, no. 44, as amplified by the Constitutional Amendment Proclamation, 1983, ss. 25, 35, 35.1, and 37.1. Section 25 of the Constitution Act, 1982 falls under the Charter of Rights and Freedoms:

25. The guarantee in this Charter of certain rights and freedoms shall not be construed so as to abrogate or derogate from any aboriginal, treaty or other rights or freedoms that pertain to the aboriginal peoples of Canada including
   (a) any rights or freedoms that have been recognized by the Royal Proclamation of October 7, 1763; and
   (b) any rights or freedoms that now exist by way of land claims agreements or may be so acquired.

Section 35 reads as follows:

(1) The existing aboriginal and treaty rights of the aboriginal peoples of Canada are hereby recognized and affirmed.
(2) In this Act, "aboriginal peoples of Canada" includes the Indians, Inuit and Métis peoples of Canada.
(3) For greater certainly, in subsection (1) "treaty rights" includes rights that now exist by way of land claims agreements or may be so acquired.
(4) Notwithstanding any other provision of this Act, the aboriginal and treaty rights referred to in subsection (1) are guaranteed equally to male and female persons.

Section 35.1:

The government of Canada and the provincial governments are committed to the principle that, before any amendment is made to Class 24 of section 91 of the "*Constitution Act, 1867,*" to section 25 of this Act or to this Part,
(a) a constitutional conference that includes in its agenda an item relating to the proposed amendment, composed of the Prime Minister of Canada and

the first ministers of the provinces, will be convened by the Prime Minister of Canada: and

(b) the Prime Minister of Canada will invite representatives of the aboriginal peoples of Canada to participate in the discussions that item.

Section 37 (part IV of the Constitution Act, 1982), reads:

(1) A constitutional conference composed of the Prime Minister of Canada and the first ministers of the provinces shall be convened by the Prime Minister of Canada within one year after this Part comes into force.

(2) The conference convened under subsection (1) shall have included in its agenda an item respecting constitutional matters that directly affect the aboriginal peoples of Canada, including the identification and definition of the rights of those peoples to be included in the Constitution of Canada, and the Prime Minister of Canada shall invite representatives of those peoples to participate in the discussions on that item.

(3) The Prime Minister of Canada shall invite elected representatives of the governments of the Yukon Territory and the Northwest Territories to participate in the discussions on any item on the agenda of the conference convened under subsection (1) that, in the opinion of the Prime Minister, directly affects the Yukon Territory and the Northwest Territories.

In 1983 Aboriginal and federal and provincial representatives agreed on several changes to the constitution. Among these changes are ss. 35.1 and 37.1, which relate to the consultation and participation of Aboriginal representatives with respect to constitutional amendment of s. 9124) of the 1867 Constitution Act, and ss. 25 and 35 of the 1982 Constitution Act. Section 91(24) of the 1867 Constitution Act gives the federal government legislative authority over "Indian, and Lands reserved for the Indians." The conference was held in March 1983, but no agreement was reached regarding the recognition and definition of the rights of Aboriginal peoples. Section 37 was repealed by the operation of s. 54 on 17 April 1983, but another series of conferences were held pursuant to a new provision added by the Constitution Amendment Proclamation, 1983, which was repealed on 18 April 1987 by operation of s. 54.1.

Section 37.1:

(1) In addition to the conference convened in March 1983, at least two constitutional conferences composed of the Prime Minister of Canada and the first ministers of the provinces shall be convened by the Prime Minister of Canada, the first within three years after April 17, 1982 and the second within five years after that date.

(2) Each conference convened under subsection (1) shall have included in its agenda constitutional matters that directly affect the aboriginal peoples of Canada, and the Prime Minister of Canada shall invite representatives of those peoples to participate in the discussions on those matters.

(3) The Prime Minister of Canada shall invite elected representatives of the governments of the Yukon Territory and the Northwest Territories to participate in the discussions on any item of the agenda of a conference convened under subsection (1) that, in the opinion of the Prime Minister, directly affects the Yukon Territory and the Northwest Territories.

Nothing in this section shall be construed so as to derogate from subsection 35(1).

See Paul L.A.H. Chartrand, "Aboriginal Self-Government" and "Conclusion," in Chartrand, ed., *Who Are Canada's Aboriginal Peoples?* 305. Constitution Act, 1867 (U.K.) 30431 Vict., c. 3; R.S.C. 1985, app. II, no. 5, s. 91(24). See Peter W. Hogg for a detailed discussion of the constitutional rights of Aboriginal peoples: *Constitutional Law of Canada*, 577–624. On the meaning of s. 25, see, for example, Thomas Isaac, *Aboriginal Law: Cases, Materials and Commentary*, 2nd ed. (Saskatoon: Purich Publishing 1999), 393–4. In the *Corbiere* case, *The Queen and Batchewana Band* v. *Corbiere* [1999] 3 CNLR 19, the Supreme Court of Canada declined to address the meaning of s. 25.

14 Gina Cosentino, "Treaty Federalism: Challenging Disciplinary Boundaries, Bridging Praxis, Theory, Research and Critical Pedagogy in Canadian Political Science," in C. Nelson and C. Nelson, eds., *Racism, Eh? A Critical Inter-Disciplinary Anthology of Race and Racism in Canada* (Toronto: Captus Press 2004), 135–52. See also RCAP, "Stage Four: Negotiation and Renewal," vol. 1 (Ottawa: Minister of Supply and Services Canada 1996), chapter 7; Poka Laenui (Hayden F. Burgess), "Processes of Decolonization," in Marie Battiste, ed., *Reclaiming Indigenous Voice and Vision* (Toronto: University of British Columbia Press 2000), and, in the same volume, James (Sákéj) Youngblood Henderson, "Postcolonial Ledger Drawing: Legal Reform," 165–7, for a discussion on dreaming and constitutional reform. For a brief discussion on how constitutional reform has and should reflect the needs, ideas, and visions of Aboriginal peoples in Canada, see: Patricia Monture-Okanee, "Seeking My Reflection: A Comment on Constitutional renovation," in D. Schneiderman, ed., *Conversations among Friends/entre amies: Proceedings of an Interdisciplinary Conference on Women and Constitutional Reform* (Edmonton: Centre for Constitutional Studies 1991), 28–33.

15 Alexandra Dobrowolsky, *The Politics of Pragmatism: Women, Representation, and Constitutionalism in Canada* (Don Mills, Ont.: Oxford University Press 2000), 2.

16 Roger Gibbins, "Constitutional Politics," in B.G. Bickerton and A.G. Gagnon, eds., *Canadian Politics*, 3rd ed. (Peterborough, Ont.: Broadview Press 1999), 272. On the process of constitutional reform in this period, see Leslie A. Pal and F. Leslie Seidle, "Constitutional Politics 1990–1992: The Paradox of

Participation," in Gene Swimmer, ed., *How Ottawa Spends, 1993–1994: A More Democratic Canada ...?* (Ottawa: Carleton University Press 1993), 143–202.

17 See ss. 37 and 37.1 at n.13 above.

18 For a detailed discussion and analysis of the first ministers' conferences, see the publications of the conferences by the Institute of Intergovernmental Relations at Queen's University, which include, among other works, three studies by David C. Hawkes: *The Search for Accommodation* (1987), *Negotiating Aboriginal Self-government: Developments Surrounding the 1985 First Ministers' Conference* (1985), and *Aboriginal Peoples and Constitutional Reform: What Have We learned?* (1989). See also a commentary published by the RCAP on the Aboriginal right of self-government and the commission's recommended criteria for dealing with the right of Aboriginal self-government and suggested options for constitutional amendments: *The Right of Aboriginal Self-government and the Constitution: A Commentary* (Ottawa: 13 February 1992). For a discussion of this document, see John Giokas, "Domestic Recognition in the United States and Canada," in Chartrand, ed., *Who Are Canada's Aboriginal Peoples?* 126–90.

19 Jim Sinclair, speaking for the MNC, offered a biting and eloquent rebuke in his closing statements at the last FMC in 1987 which has been put to music and is now an icon in the historical records of Aboriginal rights. See also M.E. Turpel and P.A. Monture, "Ode to Elijah: Reflections of Two First Nations Women on the Rekindling of Spirit at the Wake for the Meech Lake Accord," *Queen's Law Journal* 15(2) (1990): 345 at 349.

20 Chartrand, "Background," in Chartrand, ed., *Who Are Canada's Aboriginal Peoples?* 28–9.

21 For a discussion of the Meech Lake Accord, see: Alain Desruisseaux and Sarah Fortin, "Failed Reconciliation: The Meech Lake Accord (1987)," in J. Meisel, G. Rocher, and Arthur Silver, eds., *As I Recall, si je me souviens bien: Historical Perspectives* (Montreal: IRPP 1999). For an critique of the Meech Lake Accord and its impact on First Nations, see Tony Hall, "Closing an Incomplete Circle of Confederation: A Brief to the Joint Parliamentary Committee of the Federal Government on the 1987 Constitutional Accord," *Canadian Journal of Native Studies,* 6(2) (1986): 197–221. For analysis of Canada's involvement with constitutional reform including the 1982 charter and the Meech and Charlottetown accords and related events, see Kenneth McRoberts, *Misconceiving Canada.* For set of analyses and commentaries on the various round of constitutional reform, including the Meech Lake Accord: Alan C. Cairns, *Reconfigurations: Canadian Citizenship and Constitutional Change,* D.E. Williams, ed. (Toronto: McClelland and Stewart 1995), especially chapters 4, 6, 9, 10, 11, and 12; and Peter Russell, *Constitutional Odyssey.* See also Pauline Comeau and Aldo Santin, *The First Canadians: A Profile of Canada's Native People Today* (Toronto: James Lorimer 1995), 21–6.

22 RCAP, vol. 1, *Negotiation and Renewal,* chapter 7, "Looking Forward, Looking Back: Negotiation and Renewal," 209. See below at nn.29 and 30 for a references regarding the MNC's support of the Meech Lake Accord.

23 The mistrust was no doubt aided by the understanding that the Quebec Round had started before the demise of the Aboriginal FMCs in March 1987. See, generally, David C. Hawkes and Marina Devine, "Meech Lake and Elijah Harper: Native-State Relations in the 1990s," in F. Abele, ed., *How Ottawa Spends 1991–92: The Politics of Fragmentation* (Ottawa: Carleton University Press 1991), 33–62, 117. See also Pauline Comeau, *Elijah: No Ordinary Hero* (Toronto: Douglas and McIntyre 1993), 1.

24 Manitoba and New Brunswick had failed to ratify the accord in their legislatures within the three-year period. In Newfoundland, a newly elected premier rescinded the previous government's ratification.

25 The description of the conference and the six-point plan is contained in RCAP, vol. 1, *Negotiation and Renewal* (Canada: Minister of Supply and Services 1996), chapter 7, 202–16.

26 Ibid., 211–12.

27 At the time, the MNC was headed by W.Y. Dumont, the president of the Manitoba Métis Federation, and later lieutenant-governor of Manitoba, who had been prepared to accept Mulroney's promises on Aboriginal constitutional reform and participation.

28 See the presentation of W.Y. Dumont, president of Manitoba Métis Federation, on behalf of the MNC: Manitoba Public Hearings respecting the Constitutional Accord, 1987, 18 April 1989, in Paul L.A.H. Chartrand's personal files. To those who did not trust the prime minister, the MNC asked whether Aboriginal people could expect to get support for constitutional reform affecting them if the Meech Lake Accord collapsed. The MNC was not troubled by the recognition of Quebec as a distinct society, since it viewed s. 35 as already recognizing the distinct character of Aboriginal societies through the recognition of their special rights. See also Hawkes and Devine, "Meech Lake and Elijah Harper," 40–2.

29 The MNC, on the other hand, represented a people that had already negotiated the entry of Manitoba into Confederation in 1870 but that had nevertheless experienced the marginalization that followed large-scale immigration to the west. This experience suggested the need for a pragmatic approach which would seek a broad agreement that was likely to be politically acceptable, rather than a grand constitutional bargain that could then be ignored. The Métis are still in court asserting the constitutional invalidity of government actions following the 1870 Manitoba Act. On the legal history, see Paul L.A.H. Chartrand, *Manitoba's Métis Settlement Scheme of 1870* (Saskatoon: University of Saskatchewan Native Law Centre 1991) See also, by the same author, "Aboriginal Rights: The Dispossession of the Métis," *Osgoode Hall Law Journal* 29 (1991): 457–82.

30 See Desruisseaux and Fortin, "The Oka Crisis," 325–9; Georffrey York and Loreen Pindera, *People of the Pines: The Warriors and the Legacy of Oka* (Toronto: Little, Brown (Canada) 1991); "Materials relating to the History of the Land Dispute at Kanesatake," prepared for the Claims and Historical Research Centre, Comprehensive Claims Branch, Indian and Northern Affairs Canada (INAC)

(January 1991, revised November 1993); and *The Summer of 1990*, Fifth Report of the Standing Committee [of the House of Commons] on Aboriginal Affairs (May 1991).

31 Brian Mulroney, CARC–*North Perspectives.* See also, A. Fleras and J.L. Elliott, *The Nations within: Aboriginal-State Relations in Canada, the United States, and New Zealand* (Toronto: Oxford University Press 1992), 97.

32 Department of Indian Affairs and Northern Development (DIAND), "The Native Agenda," *Information* 33 (March 1991). Fleras and Elliott, *The Nations within,* 97.

33 The RCAP was created by federal order-in-council on 26 August 1991 (PC 1991–1597). Schedule 1 of the order-in-council lists the sixteen terms of reference for the commission. It must be disclosed that Paul Chartrand, one of the authors of this chapter, was one of the seven commissioners.

34 The chief justice was appointed in May 1991 and conducted extensive consultations on the mandate and membership of the commission. In its mandate, the commission was authorized to investigate the historical development of the relationship between Aboriginal peoples, Canadian society, and the Canadian government, to propose solutions to problems experienced by Aboriginal peoples, and to make recommendations on sixteen areas. See order-in-council, n.35. Prior to the RCAP, the Canadian Human Rights Commission issued a statement in 1990 that is consistent with RCAP's recommendations for fundamental reform in federal Aboriginal policy. Canadian Human Rights Commission, "A New Commitment: Statement of the Canadian Human Rights Commission on Federal Aboriginal Policy" (Ottawa: Canadian Human Rights Commission 1990), 21. For an introductory overview of Aboriginal issues and concerns at the national level during the Mulroney period, see *Unfinished Business: An Agenda for all Canadians in the 1990s,* Second Report of the Standing Committee on Aboriginal Affairs (March 1990), 20.

35 Although each commissioner served in his or her own capacity, the four Aboriginal members were undoubtedly appointed with the view that they would represent status Indians (co-chair George Erasmus), non-status Indians (Viola Robinson), Métis (Paul Chartrand), and Inuit (Mary Sillett). Mr Justice Rene Dusseault of the Quebec Court of Appeal was the co-chair. Mme Justice Bertha Wilson, now retired from the Supreme Court of Canada, and Alan Blakeney, former premier of Saskatchewan, rounded out the appointments. During the term of the commission's work, Blakeney resigned and was replaced by Peter Meekison, a university official and scholar from Alberta.

36 The work of the commission is explained in RCAP, vol. 5, *Renewal: A Twenty-Year Commitment* (Canada: Supply and Services 1996), app. C, 296–305.

37 RCAP, "The Right of Self-Government and the Constitution: A Commentary by the Royal Commission on Aboriginal Peoples" (Ottawa: RCAP 1992).

38 The commissioners completed work for the final report a year earlier, but publication was delayed for French translation, as required by law. The complete set of materials is housed in Library and Archives Canada, Ottawa.

39 A CD version of RCAP publications is available from Libraxus in Ottawa (www.libraxus.com/).

40 Alan C. Cairns, "The Constitutional Vision of the Royal Commission on Aboriginal Peoples," in *Citizens Plus: Aboriginal Peoples and the Canadian State* (Vancouver: University of British Columbia Press 2000), 116–60. The Liberal "response" focused heavily on the idea of "partnerships" with Aboriginal peoples. Incredibly, federal officials developed this partnership policy in isolation from their professed partners, with the exception of the Assembly of First Nations (AFN), which represents the Indian people for whom INAC is responsible. At the nationally publicized release of the federal policy statements, the excluded national leaders angrily denounced the failure of the Liberals to adopt the RCAP principle of "participation," which, they said, should underlie all federal policy making: policy should be conceived, designed, and implemented only with the effective participation of the ostensible beneficiaries of that policy, the Aboriginal peoples. See RCAP, vol. 1, *Looking Forward, Looking Back*, "Opening the Door," (Ottawa: Supply and Services 1996), xxiii–xxvii. See also Canada, *Gathering Strength – Canada's Aboriginal Action Plan* QS-6121–000–EE-A1 (Ottawa: Minister of Public Works and Government Services Canada 1997). The government's response was published in *Gathering Strength*, which refers to its 1995 policy of recognizing the right of self-government.

41 Mel Watkins, "Out of Commission: When Ottawa Decided to Ignore the Recommendations of the Royal Commission on Aboriginal Peoples," *This Magazine* 31 (July-August 1997): 11–12; Canadian News Facts: "[Ovide] Mercredi plans protest [re. government inaction on the RCAP report]," 31(4), 16 February 1997, 54; David Stack, "The Impact of RCAP on the Judiciary: Bringing Aboriginal Perspectives into the Courtroom,' *Saskatchewan Law Review* 62 (1999); "'Implement RCAP Report: UN,'" *Catholic New Times*, 23(2), 26 April 1999; Ted Moses, "The Right of Self-Determination and Its Significance to the Survival of Indigenous Peoples," in Aikio and Scheinin, *Operationalizing the Right of Indigenous Peoples to Self-Determination*, 155 at 170–7; James S. Frideres, "Royal Commission on Aboriginal Peoples: The Route to Self-government?" *Canadian Journal of Native Studies* 16 (1996); Catherine Bell, "Comment on Partners in Confederation: A Report on Self-government by the Royal Commission on Aboriginal Peoples," *University of British Columbia Law Review* 27 (1993); Kiera Ladner, "Negotiated Inferiority: The Royal Commission on Aboriginal People's Vision of a Renewed Relationship," *American Review of Canadian Studies* 31 (2001): 241–64; J. Borrows, "Domesticating Doctrines: Aboriginal Peoples after the Royal Commission," *McGill Law Journal* 46 (2001); Aboriginal Rights Coalition, *Blind Spots: An Examination of the Federal Government's Response to the Report of the Royal Commission on Aboriginal Peoples* (Ottawa: Aboriginal Rights Coalition 2001); Kerry Wilkins, "But We Need the Eggs: The Royal Commission, the Charter of Rights and the Inherent Right of Aboriginal Self-Government," *University of Toronto Law Journal* 49 (1999).

42 See Moses, "The Right of Self-Determination."

43 INAC, *Aboriginal Self-government: The Government of Canada's Approach to Implementation of the Inherent Right and the Negotiation of Aboriginal Self-government,* Federal Policy Guide (Ottawa: INAC 1995). In fact, it appears that the 1995 statement is the basis of current treaty negotiations, rather than the 1998 statement, *Gathering Strength.* See n.42.

44 Canada, *Shaping Canada's Future Together: Proposals* (Ottawa: Supply and Services Canada 1991). See also Desruisseaux and Fortin, "The Charlottetown Accord," in *As I Recall, si je me souviens bien,* 337–9; Peter Russell, *Constitutional Odyssey,* 171–73; and Citizens' Forum on Canada's Future, *Report to the People and Government of Canada* (Ottawa: Supply and Services 1991).

45 Mulroney created a traveling committee known as the Beaudoin-Dobbie committee to make its proposals known and assess public opinion on its constitutional proposals. In 1992 five public conferences were held to record the public's view on subjects such as the distribution of powers, Canadian identity and values, the economic union, and institutional reform. At the insistence of Aboriginal peoples, a sixth conference was held that dealt specifically with Aboriginal issues. See Desruisseaux and Fortin, "The Charlottetown Accord," 337–8; and Avigail Eisneberg, "Participation and Process," *The Network* 2(2) (1992): 1617. See also *Draft Legal Text, Charlottetown Accord,* 28 August 1992.

46 On the issue of Aboriginal participation in Canadian governance, see, generally, Paul L.A.H. Chartrand, "Aboriginal Self-government: Two Sides of Legitimacy," in Susan D. Phillips, ed., *How Ottawa Spends, 1993–1994: A More Democratic Canada ...?* (Ottawa, Carleton University Press, 1993) 231–256; and, by the same author, "Canada and the Aboriginal People: From Dominion to Condominium," in F. Leslie Sidle and David C. Docherty, eds., *Reforming Parliamentary Democracy* (London, Ont.: McGill-Queen's University Press 2003), 99–127. See also Hogg, *Constitutional Law of Canada,* 623–4.

47 Comeau and Santin, *The First Canadians,* 25. For a discussion on the innovative capacity of federalism, see Paul L.A.H. Chartrand, "The Aboriginal Peoples in Canada and Renewal of the Federation," in Karen Knop, Sylvia Ostry, Richard Simeon, and Katherine Swinton, eds., *Rethinking Federalism: Citizens, Markets, and Governments in a Changing World* (Vancouver: University of British Columbia Press, 1995), chapter 8; and Paul L.A.H. Chartrand, "Aboriginal Self-government: Towards a Vision of Canada as a North American Multinational Country," *Issues in the North* 2 (Winnipeg: Canadian Circumpolar Institute and Department of Native Studies, University of Manitoba, 1997): 81–6.

48 Vancouver *Sun,* 25 October 1991.

49 Roger Gibbins, "Constitutional Politics," 272–3; Cairns, "Aboriginal Canadians, Citizenship and the Constitution," 238–60. See also INAC, "Future of Self-government Proposals Determined This Month," *Transition* 5(10), October 1992, for support of the accord by the four national representative organizations (Assembly of First Nations, Native Council of Canada, the Métis National Council, and Inuit Tapirisat of Canada).

50 James Ross Hurley, "The Canadian Constitutional Debate: From the Death of the Meech Lake Accord of 1987 to the 1992 Referendum" (Government of Canada Privy Council Office, The Constitutional File and Unity File). http://www.pco-bcp.gc.ca/aia/default.asp?Language=E&Page=consfile&Sub=Theconstitutionaldebate. Russell L. Barsh, "Canada's Aboriginal Peoples: Social Integration or Disintegration? (see especially table 8) http://www.brandonu.ca/native/cjns/14.1/barsh.pdf.

51 In fact, propelled in part by their exclusion from the FMCs on Aboriginal rights in 1982–87, and from the Charlottetown process in 1992, the Native Women's Association of Canada (NWAC), launched an action against the federal government for not funding its participation in the FMCs, where only the national Aboriginal peoples' organizations had received funding and had been invited to participate, pursuant to the s.37 duty of the Prime Minister to invite representatives of the Aboriginal peoples. The federal government and representatives of the AFN did not concur with the NWAC. The decision of the Supreme Court of Canada in 1994 held that the federal government's decision not to provide equal funding and rights of participation to the NWAC in the constitutional discussions did not violate freedom of expression and sex equality under the Charter or existing treaty rights under s. 35. *Native Women's Association of Canada* v. *Canada*, [1995] 1 C.N.L.R 47, [1994] 3 S.C.R. 627, 24 C.R.R. (2d) 233, 173 N.R. 241, 119 D.L.R. (4th) 224, 84 F.T.R. 240 (S.C.C.). The four national organizations represented were the AFN, representing status Indians; the MNC, representing Métis; the Inuit Tapirisat of Canada (ITC), representing Inuit in the NWT, Labrador, and Quebec; and the Native Council of Canada (NCC), representing non-status Indians and some Métis. Lilianne Ernestine Krosenbrink-Gelissen outlines many differences between national Indigenous women's organizations such as the NWAC and what she terms "male-dominated Indigenous organizations": Lilianne Ernestine Krosenbrink-Gelissen, *Sexual Equality as an Indigenous Right: The Native's Women's Association of Canada and the Constitutional Process on Indigenous Matters, 1982–1987* (Saarbrücken, Germany: Verlag breitenback Publishers 1991), 89. Jo-Anne Fiske also makes a distinction between "male-dominated, federally funded national Indigenous associations" and national Indigenous organizations representing women: "The Womb Is to the Nation as the Heart Is to the Body: Enthnopolitical Discourses of the Canadian Indigenous Women's Movement," in Pat Armstrong and M. Patricia Connelly, eds., *Feminism, Political Economy and the State: Contested Terrain* (Toronto: Canadian Scholars' Press 1999), 293. The NWAC is an organization representing Aboriginal women (who choose to be represented by it) regardless of their status under the Indian Act.

52 Examples include the Meech Lake Accord and changes to social policy and the welfare state. For a discussion on the fundamental changes to social programs, spending, and the welfare state in the Mulroney era, and the "stealth" approach that the government took in implementing these changes, see Michael J. Prince,

"From Health and Welfare"; and Ken Battle and Sherri Torjman, "Federal Social Programs: Setting the Record Straight" (Ottawa: Caledonia Institute of Social Policy 1993), 1–18. For a discussion on the importance of a participatory process of constitutional development for Indian peoples, see Menno Boldt, *Surviving as Indians: The Challenge of Self-Government* (Toronto: University of Toronto Press 1993), 156–7. Boldt refers to the executive, closed-door decision-making style of the Mulroney government at page 157.

53 See Peter Russell, *Constitutional Odyssey*; and Roger Gibbins, "Constitutional Politics."

54 For a discussion on non-constitutional routes to policy formation that includes Aboriginal participation, such as the Social Union Framework Agreement (SUFA 1999) and the Health Accord of 2000, see Alain Noël, "Power and Purpose in Intergovernmental Relations" (IRPP, November 2001); Harvey Lazar, "Non-Constitutional Renewal: Toward a New Equilibrium in the Federation," in Harvey Lazar, ed., *Canada: The State of the Federation 1997: Non-Constitutional Renewal* (Kingston, Ont.: Institute of Intergovernmental Relations 1998). There are two points to be made regarding the entitlement of Aboriginal peoples' representatives to participate. First, Aboriginal representatives still have to fight to participate; there is no policy to include them in all intergovernmental meetings. Secondly, in respect to constitutional change, there may be a constitutional convention to include Aboriginal representatives in meetings on changes that affect their interests, beyond s. 35.1, but its scope is narrow . See Hogg, *Constitutional L aw of Canada*, 622–4; Chartrand, "Canada and the Aboriginal Peoples: From Dominion to Condominium," 116–17; and Norman Zlotkin, *Unfinished Business: Aboriginal Peoples and the 1983 Constitutional Conference*, Discussion Paper no. 15 (Kingston, Ont.: Institute of Intergovernmental Relations 1983).

55 See Alan Cairns, *Reconfigurations*; Peter Russell, *Constitutional Odyssey*; Kenneth McRoberts, *Misconceiving Canada*; and Guy Laforest, *Trudeau and the End of a Canadian Dream*.

56 A. Brian Tanguay, "Canada's Party System in the 1990s: Breakdown or Renewal?" *Canadian Politics*, 3rd ed. (Peterborough, Ont.: Broadview Press 1999), 338. Brian Mulroney resigned from politics in 1993 At the June 1993 Progressive Conservative Leadership convention, Kim Campbell was elected party leader and became Canada's first women prime minister. Campbell's Progressive Conservatives were succeeded by Jean Chrétien's Liberals in the October 1993 federal election.

57 See Gibbins, "Constitutional Politics"; McRoberts, *Misconceiving Canada*; and Tanguay, "Canada's Party System in the 1990s."

58 Much has been written about neo-liberalism in the Mulroney era, especially in the area of social policy. See Michael J. Prince, "From Health and Welfare to Stealth and Farewell: Federal Social Policy, 1980–2000." For an overview of the role of economic ideas in Canadian politics, see Neil Bradford, "Governing the

Canadian Economy: Ideas and Politics," in M. Whittington and G. Williams, eds., *Canadian Politics in the 21st Century*, 6th ed. (Toronto: Thomson Nelson 2004), 231–53. See also Allan M. Maslove, "Ottawa's New Agenda: The Issues and Constraints," in Allan M. Maslove, ed., *How Ottawa Spends 1984: The New Agenda* (Toronto: Methuen, 1984); G. Bruce Doern, Allan M. Maslove, and Michael J. Prince, *Public Budgeting in Canada: Politics, Economics and Management* (Ottawa: Carleton University Press 1988), chapter 1; and Donald J. Savoie, *Thatcher, Reagan, Mulroney: In Search of a New Bureaucracy* (Pittsburgh: University of Pittsburgh Press 1994). See also Martin Papillion and Gina Cosentino, *Lessons from Abroad: Toward a New Social Model for Canada's Aboriginal Peoples*, Canadian Policy Research Networks, Social Architecture Papers Research Report F/40, Family Network (April 2004), 1–41; Janine Brodie, "Canadian Women, Changing State Forms, and Public Policy," and "Isabella Bakker, "Deconstructing Macro-economics: Through a Feminist Lens," in Janine Brodie, ed., *Women and Canadian Public Policy* (Toronto: Harcourt Brace Canada 1996), 1–25 and 31–56. Fleras and Elliott argue that neo-liberal restructuring has hidden repercussions for disadvantaged groups and persons. See Fleras and Elliott, *The Nations within*, 49. For a discussion on the impact of the economic priorities of the Mulroney government on Aboriginal peoples, see Boldt, *Surviving as Indians*, 17 and 20.

59 Keynesian economic theory organized federal policy for nearly thirty years after the Second World War. Keynesianism allowed for a bigger role for the federal government (centralization), whereas neo-liberalism favoured decentralization and a greater role for the provinces – giving provinces less money but with fewer strings attached. This coincided with the constitutional- and economic-reform agenda of the 1980s and 1990s. See Robert M. Campbell, "Federalism and Economic Policy," in François Rocher and Miriam Smith, eds., *New Trends in Canadian Federalism* (Peterborough, Ont.: Broadview Press 1998), 187–210, especially 199–202; Neil Nevitte, *The Decline of Deference: Canadian Value Change in a Cross-National Perspective*; Jonan Butovsky, "The Salience of Post-materialism in Canadian Politics," *Canadian Review of Sociology and Anthropology*, 39(4) (2002): 471–85. For the role of neo-liberal ideas in the practice of governing in Canada, see Donald J. Savoie, *Governing from the Centre: The Concentration of Power in Canadian Politics* (Toronto: University of Toronto Press 1999). See also Douglas D. Purvis, *Report of the Policy Forum on the May 1985 Federal Budget*, Policy Forum Series 9 (Kingston, Ont.: John Deutsch Institute for the Study of Economic Policy, Queen's University, July 1985).

60 See Thomas J. Courchene, *Forever Amber: The Legacy of the 1980s for the Ongoing Constitutional Impasse*, Reflections Paper no. 6 (Kingston, Ont.: Institute of Intergovernmental Relations, Queen's University 1990); and Michael B. Stein, "Lessons for Post-Meech Lake Constitutional Negotiations: A Review of *Reflections*, Papers nos. 5, 6, and 7, *Canadian Public Policy* 17(4) (1991): 507–11.

61 Reg Whitaker, "Politics versus Administration: Politicians and Bureaucrats," in Whittingdon and Williams, ed., *Canadian Politics in the 21st Century*, 68. See also

Maureen Baker, "The Restructuring of the Canadian Welfare State: Ideology and Policy," Social Policy Research Centre (SPRC) Discussion Paper no. 77, June 1997; Prince, "From Health to Welfare," 166–72.

62 Neil Bradford, "Innovation by Commission: Policy Paradigms and the Canadian Political System," in Bickerton and Gagnon, eds., *Canadian Politics*, 557–8.

63 For an analysis of the administration and policy of Aboriginal economic development in Canada, see Mark R. Macdonald, "Re-Learning our ABCs? The New Governance of Aboriginal Economic Development in Canada," in L. Pal, ed., *How Ottawa Spends 2000–2001: Past Imperfect, Future Tense* (Don Mills, Ont.: Oxford University Press 2001), 161–84. For an analysis of northern Indigenous administrative changes, see Graham White, "Nunavut: Challenges and Opportunities of Creating a New Government," *Public Sector Management* 9(3) (1999): 4–9; and Graham White, "Nunavut and the Northwest Territories: Challenges of Public Service on the Northern Frontier," in Evert Lindquist, ed., *Government Restructuring and Career Public Service in Canada* (Toronto: Institute of Public Administration of Canada 2000), 112–47. For an outline of the goals of the Mulroney government in Aboriginal economic development, see Martin McAllister, "New Economic Development Strategy," INAC, *Transition*, 2(7) (1989). See also Prince, "From Health to Welfare," 166–76; and Campbell, "Federalism and Economic Policy," 199.

64 Whitaker, "Politics versus Administration," 68.

65 Prince, "From Health and Welfare," 173.

66 Whitaker, "Politics versus Administration," 68. See also Ian Greene, "Lessons Learned from Two Decades of Program Evaluation in Canada," http://www.yorku.ca/igreene/progeval.html (accessed 2 June 2004); and Fleras and Elliott, *The Nations within*, 49–50; Gilles Paquet, "Tetonic Changes in Canadian Governance," in Pal, ed., *How Ottawa Spends 1999–2000*, 90.

67 The Neilsen report was apparently referred to as "The Buffalo Jump of the 1980s" in a leaked memorandum to cabinet. The reference to the Buffalo Jump carried an obvious negative connation: buffalo were destroyed by leading them over cliffs. The memo harkened back to the widely repudiated 1969 White Paper and, as a result, cast serious suspicions over the motives of government in the minds of the public, and particularly among Indian people. Graham, "Indian Policy and the Tories," 248; and Abele, Graham, and Maslove, "Negotiating Canada," 267–8.

68 Graham, "Indian Policy and the Tories," 248; and Kathy Brock, "Aboriginal People: First Nations," in A.F. Johnson and A. Stitch, eds., *Canadian Public Policy: Globalization and Political Parties* (Toronto: Copp Clark 1997), 195.

69 Graham, "Indian Policy and the Tories," 248; and Brock, "Aboriginal People: First Nations," 195. In addition, Sally Weaver provides a seminal account and analysis of the politics surrounding the Trudeau government's 1969 White Paper. See Sally Weaver, *Making Canadian Indian policy: The Hidden Agenda 1969–70* (Toronto: University of Toronto Press 1981). See also DIAND, *Statement of the*

*Government of Canada on Indian Policy, 1969* [hereafter the White Paper] (Ottawa: Queen's Printer 1969).

70 Brock, "Aboriginal People: First Nations," 195.

71 Ibid. See also Hawkes and Devine, "Meech Lake and Elijah Harper," 47. The 1990 federal budget was one based on fiscal restraint through spending cuts. Indian Affairs indicated that many programs for Indians and Inuit were spared, such as health, education, social assistance, and comprehensive claims. See INAC, "Budget (Mostly) Spares Native Programs," *Transition*, special edition, Budget '90, March 1990.

72 Hawkes and Devine, "Meech Lake and Elijah Harper," 46.

73 Brock, "Aboriginal People: First Nations," 195. See Michael H. Wilson, Minster of Finance, *A New Direction for Canada: An Agenda for Economic Renewal* (Ottawa: Department of Finance 1984), 66–7. Able, Graham, and Maslove reveal that there was a substantial increase in the number of Aboriginal students in post-secondary educational institutions in that period: "Negotiating Canada," 269. See also Michael Prince, "From Health to Welfare," 166–8; and Reg Whitaker, "Politics versus Administration," for a discussion on Mulroney's attempts at cost containment through bureaucratic downsizing.

74 Brock, "Aboriginal People: First Nations," 195; Hawkes and Devine, "Meech Lake and Elijah Harper," 48.

75 See n.78. It should be noted that the Mulroney government continued to base its Aboriginal policy on the nineteenth-century recognition of "Indians" in the Indian Act, and dealt with the Inuit through its overall policy for the north.

76 Hawkes and Devine, "Meech Lake and Elijah Harper," 46.

77 Though devolution was introduced in 1956 with education transfers, it was accelerated in the 1970s and 1980s, a response to initiatives by the National Indian Brotherhood and the AFN. See INAC, *Performance Report for the Period Ending March 31, 1996, Improved Reporting to Parliament, Pilot Document* (Ottawa: Minister of Public Works and Government Services Canada 1996), 16. Devolution is also listed as one of the four pillars of the 1988 Northern Political and Economic Framework. See INAC, "Minister Outlines Northern Priorities," *Transition* 2 (11), November 1989.

78 Brock, "Aboriginal People: First Nations," 195; David C. Hawkes and Marina Devine, "Meech Lake and Elijah Harper: Native-State Relations in the 1990s," in Abele, ed., *How Ottawa Spends 1991–92*, 49; and Abele, Graham, and Maslove, "Negotiating Canada," 269.

79 Brian Mulroney, "Opening Statement at the First Ministers' Conference," 3.

80 Hawkes and Devine, "Meech Lake and Elijah Harper," 49.

81 Michael J. Prince, "Federal Expenditures and First Nations Experiences," in Susan D. Phillips, ed., *How Ottawa Spends 1994–95: Making Change* (Ottawa: Carleton University Press 1994), 263; and Devine and Hawkes, "Meech Lake and Elijah Harper," 49.

82 Prince, "Federal Expenditures and First Nations Experiences," 270; Graham, "Indian Policy and the Tories," 253; and Hawkes and Devine, "Meech Lake and Elijah Harper," 49–50.

83 For an analysis of the benefits and disadvantages of AFAS and FTPS, see Prince, "Federal Expenditures," 274–85. FTPS provide fixed annual payments for specific purposes and aim to simplify the administration of funding by allocating the payments on a formula-driven basis. See also, INAC, *Transition*, 2(10), October 1989.

84 Prince, "Federal Expenditures," 285. Even though the federal Indian Act was an imposed and restrictive piece of legislation, it does contain some structures of self-government. See, generally, Indian Act, R.S.C. 1985, c. 1–8, esp. ss. 74–86.

85 See Abele, Graham, and Maslove, "Negotiating Canada."

86 Fleras and Elliott, *Nations within.* See also Sally Weaver "A New Paradigm in Canadian Indian Policy for the 1990s," *Canadian Ethnic Studies* 22(3) (1991): 8–18.

87 See Boldt, *Surviving as Indians*, 15–18. See also James S. Frideres, *Aboriginal Peoples in Canada: Contemporary Conflicts*, 5th ed. (Scarborough, Ont.: Prentice Hall Allyn and Bacon Canada 1998), 292.

88 Prince, "Federal Expenditures,"289. See also RCAP, vol. 2, *Restructuring the Relations*, chapter 5, "Economic Development" (Canada: Supply and Services 1996).

89 Fleras and Elliott, *Nations within*, 16–21. See also Hawkes and Devine, "Meech Lake and Elijah Harper," 48. See also Frances Abele, "Urgent Need, Serious Opportunity: Towards a New Social Model for Canada's Aboriginal Peoples," Canadian Policy Research Network, April 2004; Russel Lawrence Barsh, "Canada's Aboriginal Peoples: Social Integration or Disintegration?" *Canadian Journal of Native Studies* 14(1) (1994): 1–46.

90 Paquet, "Tetonic Changes in Canadian Governance," 89–90.

91 See Comeau and Santin, *The First Canadians.*

92 Graham, "Indian Policy and the Tories," 256. For a case-study evaluation of Aboriginal Business Canada as an example of a "governance model" for First Nations economic development, see Mark R. Macdonald, "Re-Learning our ABCS." See also Canada, *The Canadian Aboriginal Economic Development Strategy* (Ottawa: INAC 1989).

93 Radha Jhappan, "The Federal-Provincial Power-grid and Aboriginal Self-government," in Rocher and Smith, eds., *New Trends in Canadian Federalism*, 179. It is interesting, also, to compare the similar interplay between concepts and policies relating to "self-determination" and "self-administration" in Australia, from the Whitlam Labour government's policy of self-determination in 1972 to the announcement, in 1996, of the present Howard coalition government's decision to opt for the language and policies of "empowerment" instead of "self-determination." The Howard government's statement reads in part: "The

Government prefers the term self-management or self-empowerment [to self-determination] believing that these terms are consistent with a situation in which Indigenous people exercise meaningful control over aspects of their affairs in active partnership and consultation with government." See Heather McRae, Garth Nettheim, Laura Beacroft, and Luke McNamara, *Indigenous Legal Issues: Commentary and Materials*, 3rd ed. (Sydney: Lawbook 2003), esp. 40–61, quotation at 60. A "paradigm" is a set of governing ideas that shape policy: problem definition, policy goals, policy instruments, policy outcomes, policy debates. For a theoretical discussion regarding policy paradigms and paradigmatic changes that uses Canadian Aboriginal policy as a case study, see Michael Howlett, "Policy Paradigms and Policy Change: Lessons from the Old and New Canadian Policies towards Aboriginal Peoples," *Policy Studies Journal*, 22(4) (1994): 631–49.

94 Hawkes and Devine, "Meech Lake and Elijah Harper," 46.

95 For a discussion on Aboriginal claims-settlement policy and institutions, see Peter Clancy, "The Politics and Administration of Aboriginal Claims Settlements," in M.W. Westmacott and H.P. Mellon, eds., *Public Administration and Policy: Governing in Challenging Times* (Scarborough, Ont.: Prentice Hall Allyn and Bacon Canada 1999), 53–72.

96 Ibid., 56–7.

97 The *Calder* decision recognized common law Aboriginal title and led the federal government to announce that it was prepared to enter into negotiations with Aboriginal peoples to resolve disputes concerning claims of Aboriginal title or breaches of treaty obligations. *Calder* v. *BC (A.G.)*, [1973] S.C.R. 313. There were also other cases that influenced federal government policy on comprehensive land claims, such as *Baker Lake* (1979), *Guerin* (1984), and *Sparrow* (1990). See also David W. Elliott, *Law and Aboriginal Peoples in Canada*, 4th ed. (Toronto: Captus Press 2000).

98 Clancy, "The Politics and Administration of Aboriginal Claims Settlements," 64. Comprehensive land claims apply to areas for which no treaty yet exists. Two processes for claims were established by the federal government in 1973: comprehensive and specific claims. The specific-claims process is designed to resolve claims for alleged crown failure to uphold treaty obligations and other unlawful crown action. See s. 35 at n.13 above.

99 Patricia Monture-Angus cautions that the idea of accommodation can be and has been tokenistic since, often, the proposed changes do not challenge "the overall structure": Patricia Monture-Angus, "Standing against Canadian Law: Naming Omissions of Race, Culture and Gender," in E. Comack et al., *Locating Law: Race/Class/Gender Connection* (Halifax: Fernwood Publishing 1999), 76–97 at 82.

100 The Hawthorn report in 1967 called for radical reform of the relationship between the governments of Canada and [Indigenous] Aboriginal peoples on the basis of "citizens-plus." The opposite was proposed in the 1969 federal Liberal's White Paper.

101 Clancy, "The Politics and Administration of Aboriginal Claims Settlements," 65.
102 Abele, Graham, and Maslove, "Negotiating Canada," 269.
103 This new relationship is based on improving consultation by creating procedural mechanisms to formalize and institutionalize dialogue between the federal government and First Nations (such as creating the Office of the Treaty Commissioner in Saskatchewan and establishing bilateral processes with the Federation of Saskatchewan Indian Nations) and by adopting a consensus-building approach to policy development, especially with respect to specific- and comprehensive land-claims processes. John Bray, "Minister's Priority: New Relationship with Indians," INAC, *Transition*, 2(1), October 1989.
104 For a review of comprehensive-claims policy, see RCAP, *Restructuring the Relationship*, 535–44. This chapter will not review specific claims policy. However, it should be noted that, following the events at Oka in the fall of 1990, "the federal government asked First Nation Chiefs to recommend ways to improve the claims process. Following consultations with their communities, the Chiefs Committee on Claims produced the First Nations Submission on Claims. It received the support of a special assembly of the *Assembly of First Nations* in December of that year. In July 1991, the federal government responded to the Chiefs' submission by creating the Indian Specific Claims Commission as a Commission of Inquiry." http://*www.indianclaims.ca*. See also RCAP, *Restructuring the Relationship*, 549–52, for the mandate of the commission and a review of specific claims initiatives from 1990 to 1995. For a review of the specific-claims process, see pages 544–8; Daniel J. Bellegarde, commissioner, "Notes for an Address by the Indian Claims Commission to the Aboriginal Law Conference of the Continuing Legal Education Society of British Columbia," Vancouver, 1 March 2002, http://www.indianclaims.ca/english/about/bellegardeeng.html.
105 Clancy, "The Politics and Administration of Aboriginal Claims Settlements," 56–7. See also RCAP, *Restructuring the Relations*, chapter 4, "Lands and Resources," 531.
106 "From Recommendations to Policy: Battling Inertia to Obtain a Land Claims Policy," *Northern Perspectives* 16(1) (1987): 12–15. See also DIAND, *In All Fairness: A Native Claims Policy* (Ottawa: DIAND 1981).
107 Hawkes and Devine, "Meech Lake and Elijah Harper," 51.
108 Fenge and Barnaby, "From Recommendations to Policy." See also AFN, "A Critique of Federal Government Land Claims Policy," in Frank Cassidy, ed., *Aboriginal Self-determination: Proceedings of a Conference held September 30–October 3, 1990* (Lantzville, B.C.: Oolichan Books and the Institute for Research on Public Policy 1990), 232–49.
109 The Task Force to Review Comprehensive Claims Policy, *Living Treaties: Lasting Agreements* (Ottawa: DIAND 1985).
110 RCAP, *Restructuring the Relationship*, 539–40; Fenge and Barnaby, "From Recommendations to Policy," 2. See also Frideres, *Aboriginal Peoples in Canada*, 82–5; and DIAND, *Living Treaties: Lasting Agreements*.

111 This anticipated the later approach of the RCAP on extinguishment policy: *Treaty Making in the Spirit of Co-existence: An Alternative to Extinguishment* (Ottawa: Supply and Services 1995).

112 Office of the Auditor General of Canada, 2001 Report, chapter 12, "Indian and Northern Affairs Canada – Comprehensive Land Claims, 1998," http://www.oag-bvg.go.ca/domino/reports.nsf/html/0112ce.html#ch12hd3h.

113 The Comprehensive Claims Coalition (CCC), a coalition of status Indian bands or First Nations engaged in comprehensive-claims negotiations, attempted to influence the contents of land-claims policy by advocating recommendations consistent with those in the Coolican report.

114 RCAP, *Restructuring the* Relationship, 540. For a list of published critiques of land-claims policy, see same volume, 704 at n.255.

115 Frideres, *Aboriginal Peoples in Canada,* 82.

116 Graham, "Indian Policy and the Tories," 251; Abele, Graham, and Maslove, "Negotiating Canada," 262. See Special Committee on Indian Self-government, *Indian Self-government in Canada* (Ottawa: Queen's Printer 1983). The Penner report was named after the chairperson of the standing committee on Indian affairs and northern development in 1982, Liberal MP Keith Penner. The standing committee argued that the federal government "take a radically different approach to its fiscal arrangements" with First Nations (264–5). The Penner report examined the federal government's financial and other relationships with First Nations. Though the report's focus is on status Indians, many of its recommendations and ideas are nonetheless generally applicable to other Aboriginal peoples. With respect to fiscal arrangements with First Nations, the Penner report concluded that the existing arrangements inhibited the development of Indian self-government. In general, federal fiscal arrangements denied Indian band and tribal councils control of the programs they administered; excluded Indian people from policy making; placed impossible accountability burdens on band councils that have assumed responsibility for program administration; and generated an exclusive federal administrative and monitoring arrangement. While many of the report's ideas related to the funding and fiscal arrangements between the federal government and First Nation band/tribal councils run through the Tory program of devolution and funding arrangements, the cost-cutting agenda seems to run counter to the report's recommendations given that First Nations were being forced to manage limited scarce resources – which decreases the possibility for innovation and decision making. For a critique of the Penner report, see Giokas, "Domestic Recognition in the United States and Canada," 164–70; and S.I. Pobihushchy, "A Perspective on the Indian Nations in Canada," *Canadian Journal of Native Studies* 6(1) (1986): 105–28. See also House of Commons, Special Committee on Indian Self-Government, *Indian Self-government in Canada, Report of the Special Committee* (Ottawa: Queen's Printer 1983).

117 Hawkes, "Search for Accommodation," 21–4. See also RCAP, *Restructuring the Relationship,* chapter 3, for a discussion on self-government proposals. See also Roger Gibbins and J. Rick Ponting, "Faces and Interfaces of Indian Self-government," *Canadian Journal of Native Studies* 6(1) (1986): 15–32. For a critique of the various federal government's proposals for self-government, see Menno Boldt and Anthony Long, "Aboriginal Self-government," *Policy Options,* November 1986, 33–7.

118 Abele and Graham, "Plus Que Ça Change," 117. See David C. Hawkes, "Aboriginal Peoples and Constitutional Reform: What Have We Learned?" in *Aboriginal Peoples and Constitutional Reform, Phase Three, Final Paper* (Kingston, Ont.: Queen's University, Institute of Intergovernmental Relations 1989); David C. Hawkes, "The Search for Accommodation," *Aboriginal Peoples and Constitutional Reform, Discussion Paper* (Kingston, Ont.: Queen's University, Institute of Intergovernmental Relations 1987); and David C. Hawkes, "Negotiating Aboriginal Self-government: Developments Surrounding the 1985 First Ministers' Conference," *Aboriginal Peoples and Constitutional Reform, Background Paper number 7* (Kingston, Ont.: Queen's University, Institute of Intergovernmental Relations 1985). See also Fleras and Elliott, *Nations within,* 63–71; Hawkes and Devine, "Meech Lake and Elijah Harper," 34–42.

119 Jhappan, "The Federal-Provincial Power-grid," 174.

120 Hawkes and Devine, "Meech Lake and Elijah Harper," 50.

121 For the legislative model, see DIAND, *Indian Self-government Community Negotiation* (Ottawa: Minister of Indian Affairs and Northern Development, May 1989); DIAND, *Policy Statement on Indian Self-government in Canada* (Ottawa: Minister of Indian Affairs 1985).

122 See Chartrand, "Aboriginal Self-Government: The Two Sides of Legitimacy," 231–56.

123 Jhappan, "The Federal-Provincial Power-grid," 174. Frideres discusses some of the reasons why more progress has not been achieved in community self-government: *Aboriginal Peoples in Canada,* 386–7. Boldt provides a critique of the Mulroney government's legislative approach and its policy of community-based self-government: *Surviving as Indians,* 90–1, 156–7. For the legislative model, see DIAND, *Indian Self-government Community Negotiation*; DIAND, *Policy Statement on Indian Self-government in Canada.*

124 Sechelt Indian Band Self-Government Act, S.C. 1986, c. 27. See also the companion British Columbia statute, the Sechelt Indian Government District Enabling Act, S.B.C. 1987, c. 16, proclaimed in force on 23 July 1987. See also, J.P. Taylor and G. Paget, "Federal/Provincial Responsibility and the Sechelt," in Hawkes, *Aboriginal Peoples and Government Responsibility,* chapter 8.

125 Fee-simple title to land allows one to be able to sell and buy land.

126 Graham, "Indian Policy and the Tories," 251.

127 Fleras and Elliott, *Nations within,* 52.

128 Jhappan, "The Federal-Provincial Power-grid," 179–80.

129 RCAP, *People to People, Nation to Nation: Highlights from the Report of the Royal Commission on Aboriginal Peoples* (Ottawa: Canada Communication Group 1996), chapter 5.

130 Graham, "Indian Policy and the Tories," 245.

131 Hawkes, "Negotiating Aboriginal Self-government," 19. See also Peter Aucoin, "Organizational Change in the Machinery of Canadian Government: From Rational Management to Brokerage Politics," *Canadian Journal of Political Science* 19(1): 3–28.

132 Hogg, *Constitutional Law of Canada,* 624.

133 Chartrand, "Background," in Chartrand, ed., *Who Are Canada's Aboriginal Peoples?* 36–7.

134 Ibid.

135 Abele and Graham, "Plus Que Ça Change," 131.

# 13

# Beyond the Blue Horizon: The Strength of Conservative Northern-Development Policy in the Mulroney Years[1]

FRANCES ABELE

For most of Canada, the real north[2] is out of sight, just over the horizon. You cannot see it from the CN Tower in Toronto, from the towers of the National Capital Region, or from most provincial capitals. The north is a vague, redolent, and pervasive symbol, not well understood as a region of the country with distinctive political, economic, and social circumstances. If any confirmation of the over-the-horizon problem is required, consider that none of the monographs dealing with the Mulroney governments even mentions the Progressive Conservatives' northern-development policies. Nor was the north a prominent element of the Mulroney government's self-presentation.[3] This is particularly surprising considering that the Mulroney years brought significant – even historic – breakthroughs and steady progress in key areas of federal northern policy.[4] Significant events include the signing of the Nunavut Agreement, a modern treaty that created two new territories and changed the map of Canada forever; the successful conclusion of modern treaty negotiations with Yukon First Nations, with consequent permanent changes to territorial governance; the elaboration and implementation of a new model of policy development resulting in a new approach to Aboriginal economic development; the establishment of new benchmarks for Aboriginal and territorial participation in executive federalism with negotiation of the Charlottetown Accord;[5] and alterations to the shape and scope of territorial government.

The Conservative government achieved more in northern policy than its official public program and overall ideological bent might have led the public to expect. Even after the fact, the Conservatives did not receive much credit for their northern breakthroughs, though these substantial achievements required imagination and a certain boldness. This chapter describes what the Tories achieved in the north, explains how some breakthroughs were made, and reflects upon why these breakthroughs have remained largely unknown and ignored.

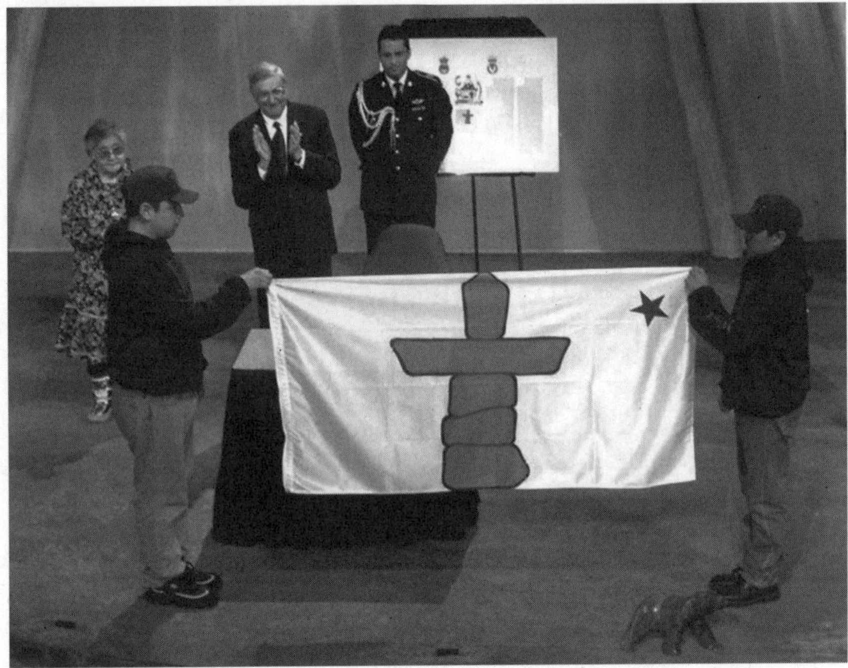

Two Inuit Junior Rangers unveil the new Nunavut flag as Governor General Romeo LeBlanc (centre) and Nunavut Commissioner Helen Mamayaok Maksagak (top left) look on during the inaugural event in Iqaluit, Nunavut, on 1 April 1999, when Nunavut officially became Canada's newest territory. The groundwork for the creation of Nunavut had been laid when the Mulroney government signed the Nunavut Agreement-in-Principle on 30 April 1990. Canadian Press / Kevin Frayer.

The analysis proceeds in four stages. First, it outlines the general context of the Conservative northern-development policy, by way of beginning an explanation of what was achieved and what was not resolved. Important factors include the policy legacy of the preceding Trudeau governments, the nature of federal institutions for northern policy development, and the major preoccupations of the Progressive Conservatives on their ascent to power. Secondly, there is a consideration of the tensions inherent in the Department of Indian Affairs and Northern Development[6] (DIAND), and the practical consequences of these tensions for public policy. This discussion is followed in a third section by a quick review of the major events in Conservative northern-development policy, in the areas of political development, economic development, health and social development, and the environment. The chapter concludes with an explanation of how so much was achieved with so little recognition, and offers some reflections on the broader importance of the changes the Mulroney Tories brought to the north.

## THE TEXTURE OF THE TIMES: CONSERVATIVE NORTHERN-DEVELOPMENT POLICY IN CONTEXT, AND THE LIBERAL LEGACY

In contrast to what was the case for the Diefenbaker, Pearson, and Trudeau governments, the Mulroney Conservatives evidently did not see the north as a major zone of economic opportunity – for example, as a hinterland region whose development might be of central importance to Canadian economic development (as did Diefenbaker) or as a secure source of energy resources in internationally perilous times (as did the Trudeau cabinets). For the first Mulroney government and during the election of the second, the Canada-United States Free Trade Agreement was the central economic plank, with the second being federal expenditure reduction and reorganization of federal responsibilities. With small populations and no concentrations of economic power, the northern territories would have seemed largely irrelevant in the larger trade discussions (although the trade deals were not irrelevant to the north),[7] and, in their necessary fiscal dependence on the federal government, the northern territories were an unlikely source of significant expenditure reduction.[8]

After the government's economic program, dealing with the prevailing constitutional distemper and regional entropy dominated. The Progressive Conservatives came to power in the aftermath of the patriation battles, with the large task of wooing Quebec back into the constitutional consensus. Moreover, two of three constitutionally required first ministers' conferences on Aboriginal matters remained to be held, in order to reach a consensus on the meaning of the "existing Aboriginal and treaty rights" (section 35 of the Constitution Act, 1982), which many parties to the decision to include this phrase in the constitution had considered to be incomplete.

The government's constitutional efforts eventually failed, with the defeat of, first, the Meech Lake Accord and, then, the Charlottetown Accord, but achieving these outcomes was to consume most of the nine years that the Conservatives enjoyed federal power. The third "task of reconciliation" left over from the long Liberal reign was defined by the Conservatives as a matter of "dealing the regions in," with the regions in need of attention defined as Atlantic Canada and "the west." No institutions such as the Western Diversification Office or the Atlantic Canada Opportunities Agency were created with the north in mind, although certainly it was part of the general approach of this government to attempt to knit each region into the federation, or at minimum avoid conflict.

If the attention of the prime minister and his cabinet were clearly not on the north, but elsewhere, it is still true that there was a basis among the politicians for some progress on northern matters. First, a significant number of cabinet ministers had northern experience and knowledge. Pat Carney and Mary Collins had both lived and worked in the Northwest Territories (NWT) during the 1970s, mainly consulting to the energy industry; Erik Nielsen grew up in Yukon; Brian Mulroney himself hailed from the northern Quebec resource frontier;[9] and Jake Epp had been minister of Indian affairs and northern development during the short-lived Joe Clark government, when Yukon was given responsible government. In addition, key ministers recruited advisers with significant northern knowledge.[10]

They came to power at a moment when a number of large historical processes affecting northern development were beginning to have a significant effect on institutions and political culture. In retrospect, it is clear that by far the most important factor was the adjustment to the regional balance of power brought about by the successes of Aboriginal peoples' political self-mobilization. The northern economic-development debates of the 1970s had mobilized and strengthened regional Aboriginal organizations, while also mobilizing the entire electorate in Yukon and the Northwest Territories. The ninth Legislative Assembly in the NWT, formed after the 1979 territorial election, registered the changes that had occurred. Ten years earlier, most of the members of the legislature (then called the Council) were appointed, not elected, and few were Aboriginal. In the mid-1970s, the move to an entirely elected legislature was completed, but the representatives were bitterly divided over northern-development issues along racial lines. By 1979, the ninth assembly had an Aboriginal leader (not yet called premier), an Aboriginal majority in cabinet, and, perhaps even more important, other Aboriginal and non-Aboriginal members who were all committed to working together towards a new constitution for the territory based upon some form of historic compromise across the NWT's main divisions. By 1984, when the Progressive Conservatives achieved power in Ottawa, the legislators of the NWT had formed the Constitutional Alliance, a device through which they would work on redesigning the shape of their government; they had held a plebiscite on division of the NWT which was answered in the affirmative; and they had put in place research- and consultation-driven processes to define new constitutions for a divided NWT.[11]

During the same period, the shape of government in Yukon had solidified. With its much smaller proportion of Aboriginal electors (20 per cent of territorial votes as opposed to about 65 per cent in the NWT), Yukon had seen the introduction of political parties in territorial elections[12] and in 1979 had achieved responsible government. These new institutions created the framework for the sometimes intense political conflicts that attended the negotiation of modern treaties and resolution of Yukon First Nations' land and other claims. In both territories, the institutional stage was set for the further transfer of increased powers of self-government from federal control.[13]

On the other hand, when the Conservatives came to power in 1984, most of the key issues for Aboriginal peoples themselves were yet to be resolved. Only one modern treaty had been concluded north of 60 degrees, negotiated by the Inuvialuit in the far northwest of the NWT just as the Liberals were leaving power. The land issue in the entire Yukon Territory and almost all of the Northwest Territories remained outstanding.[14] Negotiations with all of the major groups had been initiated, but were stalled at least partly for reasons arising from certain outmoded aspects of federal comprehensive-claims policy. There were two key sticking points. First was the bald federal requirement that Aboriginal signatories to the modern treaties "extinguish" all of their Aboriginal rights, in perpetuity; Aboriginal parties to the treaties saw these rather as a means of affirming and giving force to rights they would hold in perpetuity. A second sticking point was the firm federal refusal, since 1977, to negotiate political arrangements within the framework of what the federal side insisted was merely a *land* claim – essentially, a real estate deal. To the Aboriginal peoples who were negotiating what they understood to be a new relationship with Canada, it made no sense to separate "land" from the institutional arrangements under which they would be self-governing in stewardship of the land. In the mid-1980s, the impasses over the extinguishment clauses and over negotiated political arrangements appeared formidable. Yet the Progressive Conservatives were able to take decisive steps to move the process forward in each of these complicated areas.

A final aspect of the northern circumstances inherited from preceding Liberal governments was the federal role in the territorial economies. In this period, as now, development on all crown land in the territorial north was controlled by the federal Department of Indian Affairs and Northern Development, which set the pace, shape, and location of such development as well as the taxation regime governing it. The Liberals' National Energy Program (NEP) had supercharged the territorial economies, particularly in the Mackenzie Delta/Beaufort Sea area, and the 1983–85 construction of the Norman Wells oilfield expansion and pipeline brought the boom southward into the rest of the territory. In Yukon, NEP-stimulated exploration was important, although to a lesser extent. The prospect of such economic activity in the 1970s had led to the mobilization of Aboriginal political power and eventually to the transformation of territorial governing institutions. The existence of a non-renewable resource-development boom in the early 1980s, coupled with the (as yet flawed) federal commitment to negotiating comprehensive land-claims agreements with all of the Aboriginal collectivities in the territorial north, had another effect. It began to erode the old polarizations over development and to create new manœuvrability for government-led development plans. This was in large part the Liberal legacy.

The Conservatives began to wind the NEP down immediately after they were elected. They did this in fulfillment of their election promises in western Canada, just as the Liberals had launched it in fulfillment of their own promises, made for other ears. The cancellation of the NEP had an immediate, depressing economic impact in the north, particularly in the western NWT and Yukon, but it had a salutary effect as well. The development slowdown created a breathing space, a time in which northerners had an opportunity to reflect on what was happening, rather than devoting themselves to strenuous mobilization to have some effect on major decisions being taken elsewhere. At the same time, the NEP demonstrated the general vulnerability of the northern economies to federal purposes, shaped in other regions' interests. This ultimately strengthened demands in the two territories for the devolution of more control to the territorial level, and likely created a stronger incentive for cooperation among Aboriginal and non-Aboriginal territorial leaders.

## IN THE STRUCTURE OF THE SITUATION: BEING THE MINISTER OF NORTHERN DEVELOPMENT

Canada has had ministers of Indian affairs and northern development since the major reorganizations after the Glassco Commission (1966–67) created the so-named department. Built into the ministry is a contradictory mandate, as responsibility for development of the north has collided frequently with the minister's responsibilities to respect and support the "Indians" who frequently resisted externally directed economic development. As Simon McInnis observed in 1983,[15] just before the election of the first Mulroney government: "The dominant concern in northern development is resource exploration and exploitation as it benefits Canada as a whole. Northern-development policy in this regard is fairly coherent and consistent. However, the government has two other objectives: enhancing Northerners' lives and protecting the environment. The consequence is that these two objectives are simply irreconcilable with the interests of Canadians as a whole." McInnis goes on to speculate that "the growing maturity of northern political institutions and Ottawa's increased sensitivity to aboriginal concerns could bring about a reconciliation of northerners' and national goals." Such reconciliation can be seen to have begun during the Mulroney government's years, and to be continuing today – although not perhaps as McInnis might have envisioned it. While the environment continues to be poorly served – except for clean-ups – a considerable amount of the distance between the national interest in northern resource development and northerners' vision of their economic future has disappeared, with the solidification of northern political institutions and Ottawa's increasingly nuanced response to Aboriginal land and self-government rights.

Any minister of Indian affairs and northern development wrestles with the fundamental contradictions of the portfolio. It must be said as well that the "Indian affairs" portion of the portfolio draws almost all ministerial attention: First Nation citizens across Canada outnumber all territorial residents by a factor of at least ten, as they have for decades, and conditions on many First Nations reserves and in "peak" (national) Aboriginal association politics are often more dramatic and challenging than are territorial issues. The minister of Indian affairs and northern development is, almost all the time, compelled to be the minister of Indian affairs.

There are as well other structural problems for the minister of northern development. Although he or she is literally the "Minister of Everything" in the north, and so in the north both a target and potentially the source of major change, in fact in every area of major responsibility the minister of northern development must share power with at least one other, generally more powerful, minister. For each of the four ministers of northern development in the Mulroney years, progress in northern economic development required, minimally, the cooperation of the energy, industry, and environment ministers, as well as the ministers responsible for the Canadian Aboriginal Economic Development Strategy (CAEDS) and labourforce training. Similarly, progress in political development required that the entire cabinet be convinced, with particular attention from the purse-minders at Finance and the intergovernmental-relations managers in the Privy Council Office. Northern sovereignty and security necessarily engaged the ministers of external affairs and national defence as well.

It is in the structure of this situation that if the minister of northern development, already in a weak position, becomes a cabinet outsider, he will be powerless despite his heavy responsibilities. On the other hand, if the minister of northern development enjoys the esteem and support of his colleagues and especially the prime minister, a great deal can be achieved. It would appear that at least the three longer-serving ministers of Indian affairs and northern development in the Brian Mulroney governments found themselves in this latter, more favourable position, and that this situation accounts for the progress that was made in northern affairs despite its low priority in the overall government agenda. The ministers of Indian affairs and northern development in the Mulroney cabinets[16] included David Crombie (1984–86), William McKnight (1986–89), Pierre Cadieux (1989–90), and Tom Siddon (1990–93).

## THE TASKS OF THE TIME: WHAT WAS TO BE DONE, AND HOW?

Surprisingly to many, the first minister of Indian affairs and northern development appointed by Prime Minister Brian Mulroney was David

Crombie, a frankly Red Tory and populist who had been an extremely successful mayor of Toronto. His had not been self-evidently a career path that developed strong skills in Aboriginal-Canada relations or much knowledge of the sparsely populated northern territories. Crombie, however, approached the new post with enthusiasm, promising to open for fresh consideration the most challenging policy knots that had built up over a couple of decades of polarized politics.

Crombie's declared priorities were expressed very generally – the nurturing of community, the preservation of the environment, and the creation of wealth – and he proved to be adroit in political communication of these goals and in gaining the confidence of his constituency.[17] He also launched some consequential specific initiatives: a review of federal comprehensive-claims policy resulting in a public report prepared by independent consultant Murray Coolican, and an acceleration of the process of devolution (transferring "province-like" responsibilities from federal departments to territorial governments).

Like most ministers before and more after him, Crombie confronted large challenges in the Indian affairs aspect of his ministry. The largest crisis that he had to deal with arose from the Nielsen Task Force on Program Review, and the leaking of a cabinet memorandum that recommended radical and (in the eyes of most First Nations observers) retrograde changes to federal responsibilities in Indian affairs. Crombie repudiated the perspective presented in the memorandum, but the controversy over these proposals and Aboriginal peoples' frustration at the lack of progress at the 1985 first ministers' conference on Aboriginal matters threatened to dominate his agenda.[18]

While dealing with these fraught relations with First Nation leaders, Crombie also mandated a departmental reorganization that saw a different vision of the department's role gain ascendancy. The departmental *Annual Report* of 1986–87 explains: "In general terms, the department moved toward becoming an 'enabler' and an advocate for initiatives launched by native people themselves, rather than a controller and regulator of Indian issues."[19] The department also identified four "priority themes" in Indian affairs, namely, self-government, economic development, quality of community life, and protection of the special relationship between the federal government and the Native peoples of Canada. Four themes for northern policy were also identified: the transfer of provincial-type responsibilities to northern governments, the promotion of economic development, the settlement of land claims, and an affirmation of Arctic sovereignty.

Of these themes, two in particular engaged other, arguably more powerful ministries: External Affairs responded to the sovereignty question, while Energy and Industry (via the Ministry of State for Small Business and Tourism) led in the promotion of northern economic development.

Safeguarding recognition of Canada's Arctic sovereignty, particularly with respect to the United States, is a durable policy problem dating ultimately back to the formation of the country. In more recent times, the large U.S. military presence in the Arctic during and after the Second World War, and its refusal to recognize Canadian sovereignty over the Northwest Passage, demanded a strong response. There were lingering, though less tense, boundary issues too, particularly concerning the eastern boundary with Greenland (Denmark).[20] In 1986 External Affairs Minister Joe Clark reinforced the Canadian position considerably by asserting that Canada's borders were defined by straight "baselines," long lines of longitude drawn to the North Pole to enclose the entire Arctic Archipelago, including the disputed Northwest Passage.

The general area of improving the prosperity of Aboriginal peoples in Canada was the subject of a large national program, the Canadian Aboriginal Economic Development Strategy (CAEDS). Formallly a collaboration of DIAND and the Department of Industry (with the minister responsible being the minister of state for small business and tourism, Thomas Hockin), CAEDS can be seen as a second-generation program, succeeding the National Aboriginal Economic Development Strategy of the 1970s. It was a grant-making program mandated to subsidize the development of an Aboriginal business sector in northern Canada and in the rest of the country. Unlike the economic-development initiatives managed in DIAND for many years, CAEDS was "status blind" – available to Metis, Inuit, and First Nation entrepreneurs equally – and it was managed by appointed, largely Aboriginal, boards. This model for policy development and program delivery was relatively new and, ultimately, viable, being emulated under later Liberal governments in such areas as Aboriginal labour-force development and health-care administration. In northern Canada, CAEDS supported Aboriginal small businesses as they adapted to post-NEP economic circumstances. This measure, and the Progressive Conservatives' more stable and pro-business regulatory "stance," set the terms for northern economic development in the 1980s and early 1990s.

With respect to sovereignty and economic development, ministers of DIAND did not lead but rather followed. They dominated, at least until cabinet approval was required, in the areas of land-claim negotiations and political development. Successive Tory ministers were to advance these issues considerably.

After not quite two years in the portfolio, David Crombie was replaced by Saskatchewan Member of Parliament William McKnight. McKnight brought a strong interest in economic-development issues, a managerial approach, and a taciturn, pragmatic public style. In matters of substance, he proceeded in much the same way as Crombie.[21] Federal-territorial negotiations concerning the devolution of powers to the territorial level continued, as did comprehensive-claims negotiations. Under McKnight, as well, a long overdue restatement of federal purposes in the territorial north was developed. The *Northern Political and Economic Framework* affirmed the federal commitment to devolution, the early settlement of "land claims," support for deliberations about the future shape of territorial government to be led by northerners, federal territorial cooperation on economic development, improvement of the northern business climate by clarification of the federal role, and a more comprehensive approach to safeguarding northern sovereignty.[22] The policy framework outlined in this document consolidated rather than launched federal initiatives, but the consolidation was an important step towards the maintenance of a coherent federal approach to the broad process of political development proceeding on its own momentum in the territorial north.

In the period of preparation for the general election of 1988, William McKnight moved to more politically useful duties, with Pierre Cadieux replacing him in a caretaker role pending the outcome of the election. The new cabinet formed immediately after the Conservatives returned to power included a new minister of Indian affairs and northern development, Thomas Siddon. Hailing from British Columbia, Siddon was a cabinet veteran who had been minister of fisheries and oceans in the previous government. Understated and serious, Siddon began his term during what was again a period of serious crisis in federal relations with First Nations. The armed confrontation at the Kanestake Reserve at Oka in 1990, the subsequent resolution of the crisis and the appointment of a Royal Commission on Aboriginal Peoples, and the years of intense constitutional preoccupation attending the negotiations towards the Charlottetown Accord and the subsequent national referendum drew most public attention – and likely a good portion of ministerial time as well.

Once again, however, the north and federal northern policy was following a distinctive path, largely out of sight in southern Canada. Modern treaty negotiations began to bring results, with the federal government initialling three final agreements in principle (with the Council for Yukon Indians [CYI], the Dene-Métis in the Northwest Territories, and the Tungavik Federation of Nunavut, representing Inuit in the eastern NWT) in the conflict-ridden year of 1990. Of these, two were ultimately realized. The Dene-Metis agreement collapsed in 1989, leading to the fragmentation of the Aboriginal coalition that had supported it, and, subsequently, "regional" negotiations with smaller groups of Dene and Métis were begun. The other two agreements, with the CYI and the Inuit of the eastern NWT, are particularly noteworthy.

With respect to each of the successful negotiations, the parties found a way to mitigate the negative impact of the long-standing sore point of the federal "extinguishment" requirement, and in different ways each agreement responded to the enduring Aboriginal demand that land negotiations be accompanied by negotiations about the political regime under which the Aboriginal people concerned were to be governed. With these agreements, the federal government moved gently and (in the case of the Nunavut Agreement) not so gently away from the policy positions that had contributed to delay in modern treaty negotiations during the 1970s and 1980s.

The CYI Umbrella Final Agreement enables the negotiation by each Yukon First Nation of specific institutional arrangements with respect to a wide array of governing powers. These self-government agreements are still in the process of being negotiated, one by one. The Nunavut Agreement contained an even more direct contradiction of the traditional federal stance that political arrangements specific to a particular group of people in Canada would not be negotiated as part of a land settlement. It included a clause committing the federal government to division of the Northwest Territories to create two new territories. The new territory of Nunavut, established in 1999, would have a large Inuit majority and a variety of innovative governing arrangements – it would be indeed a public government but one that, for demographic reasons, would also be the prime political vehicle through which the Inuit of Nunavut would gain control of their collective future. Reportedly, Thomas Siddon, the last minister of northern development of the Mulroney years, saw the sense and the justice in the Inuit position, and in the midst of negotiations he agreed to the Nunavut provision in advance of having received formal cabinet approval to do so. He had the imagination and the weight in cabinet to take this final, decisive step, without which it is unlikely that the Nunavut Agreement could have been concluded. If this step was bold, it was also effective.

In a decade marked at the national level by dramatic reversals and high-stakes conflicts in constitutional and Aboriginal affairs, attended ultimately by frustration and failure, and by the creation of deep national divides over major economic programs such as the negotiation of the Canada-United States Free Trade Agreement, Conservative northern-development policy unfolded much as it should have. By 1993, when the Conservatives left power, their northern agenda had to a surprising degree been fulfilled. Indeed, in some respects it likely exceeded the estimations of achievable progress made by the first minister and his staff. By 1993, significant governing responsibilities had been transferred to the territorial governments, which had, by the 1990s, completed broad and deep public processes to envision their new constitutional futures. The terms of northern economic development had been solidified, and, with the launch of some large-ticket stimulative programs, the participation of northern Aboriginal peoples in economic development had been advanced. Modern treaties had been successfully concluded with two of three Aboriginal collectivities, and each of these significantly altered the structure of public government in Canada towards a more meaningful inclusion of Aboriginal peoples and traditions. Finally, the important symbolic step of asserting Canadian sovereignty in terms of "straight baselines" had been taken.

Probably the greatest issue left unresolved still lingers. In a non-renewable resource-based economy, successful promotion of non-renewable resource development, even with extensive involvement by Aboriginal workers, managers, and entrepreneurs, brings with it the prospect of high environmental costs. The Progressive Conservatives' Green Plan took the special circumstances of the Arctic into account, and even included a modest allotment of designated funding for that region.[23] But, as the Conservatives left power, they left behind a modest record in northern environmental protection, having to do with some efforts towards pollution clean-up, and an untried and complex set of regulatory and management boards. This cumbersome system remains, better than nothing but far from encouraging far-sighted and effective measures to safeguard the environment.[24]

## CONCLUSION

The Progressive Conservative northern-development strategy was not an unmitigated success. An imaginative, strong, and far-reaching strategy for stewardship of the northern environment was not developed, and federal and territorial regulatory arrangements grew complex without necessarily growing stronger. The Conservative northern agenda was, though, remarkably successful in other policy areas, advancing northern political and economic development *through* negotiation of modern treaties and public participation in constitutional change.

In retrospect, a number of sources of this success may be identified. First, the Conservatives inherited more "progress" in modern treaty negotiations than may have been apparent at the time. The agreement between the Inuvialuit and the government of Canada signed just as the Liberals were leaving power was the true breakthrough – the first comprehensive-claims agreement concluded in the territorial north. The effect of this agreement on other Aboriginal groups – and on federal negotiators – is hard to measure but should not be ignored.

Secondly, there was an important ideological balance in the Mulroney cabinets that is apparent when considered in contrast to subsequent changes in the parties of the right in Canada. In the Mulroney cabinets the "redder" Tories were strong, and some of them held ministries important to the north. They were committed to the promotion of wealth creation but were not shy of public expenditure and imaginative public programs to this end. Crombie, McKnight, and Siddon all pressed significant policy innovations forward, and, of these, Siddon stands out for his successful "beau risque" in accepting the Inuit demand that a commitment to division of the Northwest Territories be enshrined in their modern treaty.

Thirdly, the overall cabinet commitment to expenditure restraint and deficit reduction led to a readiness to transfer responsibilities away from the federal level to other organizations and governments. In Canada as a whole, this created general hardship and conflict with Aboriginal organizations and governments which saw, largely correctly, that the whole Tory program would lead to reduced resources for them and reduced services to Aboriginal peoples as a whole.[25] With respect to northern policy, however, the commitment to "off-loading" dovetailed nicely with territorial governments' interest in acquiring more powers and resources, and the evident federal commitment to advancing in this area created a strong incentive for Aboriginal and non-Aboriginal northerners to work together.

Lastly, it is possible that the very chaos and contention at the national level – so distracting and so damaging to the Conservative government – may have created the room for progress in the north. Fresh from the consequences of the confrontation at Kanesatake with sovereignty-claiming Mohawks, how could Siddon's cabinet colleagues reject the vigorous bid by Inuit to join Confederation, albeit on their own terms? Given the determined and effective national mobilization by First Nations against the radical measures envisioned by the Neilsen Task Force, how could ministerial colleagues not support new initiatives (such as CAEDS) designed to achieve the same ends but using the "carrot" of business subsidy and promotion rather than the razor of program expenditure cuts and the hammer of ideological retrenchment?

Surely the enduring legacy of the last Progressive Conservative government to hold power in Canada lies in its contribution to the development of northern political institutions, and institutions for self-determination across Canada as well. The public- government model as a choice for the realization of Aboriginal self-determination will have a fair test in the development of the government of Nunavut. But the superceding of the conceptual obstacles to negotiating forms of self-government as an aspect of treaty negotiations to resolve sovereignty and land-ownership issues was also necessary in the achievement of the agreement with Yukon Indians, and the same conceptual progress is evident in all of the agreements reached since, including the Nisga'a Treaty and the recently concluded Tli Cho Agreement in the NWT.

The policy reconsideration and the concrete steps that made the change to this new direction possible were not sole results of the actions of key ministers of Indian affairs, though these certainly helped. The major shift occurred as a result of the ability of large numbers of officials and leaders, Aboriginal and non-Aboriginal, in and out of the federal government, to reflect on the justice and the practicality of experience to date with the negotiation of modern treaties, and to locate solutions to specific problems. Some people had to change their minds. The new approach to treaty negotiation did not solve all of the outstanding problems, and it created some new ones. It is as if the Mulroney Progressive Conservatives were offered the opportunity to be midwife to this historic shift, and by and large they accepted the job. Perhaps strangely for the party of sovereignty-limiting trade agreements, deficit reduction, and program off-loading, its legacy in the north is a set of stronger, more resilient, and more democratic public institutions.

## CHRONOLOGY OF KEY EVENTS IN NORTHERN DEVELOPMENT 1984–94

1984 David Crombie appointed minister of Indian affairs and northern development.
1983 Release of the Penner report on Indian self-government.
1985 Bill C-31 eliminates gender discrimination from the Indian Act. Publication of *Living Treaties, Lasting Agreements*. Report of the Task Force to Review Comprehensive Claims Policy (Coolican report).
1986 Sechelt Indian Band Self-Government Act passed, establishing municipal-like self-government for this British Columbia band. No other bands seek similar arrangements.
1986 Revised federal policy on Aboriginal land claims released, following Coolican report.
William McKnight replaces Crombie as minister of Indian affairs and northern development.
Pierre Cadieux replaces William McKnight as minister of Indian affairs and northern development.
1988 "Free Trade election" returns the Conservatives to Ottawa (21 November).
1991 Tom Siddon appointed minister of Indian affairs and northern development.
1992 Nunavut Agreement signed.

## NOTES

1 I wish to acknowledge Katherine Graham, Peter Usher, and Gerald Wright for perceptive comments, and George Kinloch for so many good conversations and good ideas. Although I am not now and never have been a member of the Progressive Conservative Party or its successors, I did serve in an order-in-council appointment to the Eastern Board of the Canadian Aboriginal Economic Development Strategy during the years under analysis in this chapter.
2 Using any sensible demographic, geographic, social, and economic standards, "the north" includes the northern two-thirds of Canada – the territories and about half of every province except the three Maritime provinces. For this discussion, though, for reasons of space, my focus is entirely on federal policy in the territorial north.
3 In the four throne speeches of the Mulroney era, the north is mentioned only twice, and only once substantially, on 1 October 1986, when the government announced that it had drawn straight base lines around the Arctic islands and was taking some other measures to confirm Canada's sovereignty in the north. The second mention occurs in passing in the 13 May 1991 throne speech. In a

list of the government's guiding principles for constitutional change, an awkward sentence attempts to balance language, culture, region, and Aboriginal peoples: "that Quebec's unique character must be affirmed and that the particular interests of the West, the Atlantic provinces, Ontario, the North and aboriginal Canadians [sic] must be recognized, as well ..."

4 I have not been able to discover a single academic article on Conservative northern- development policy. In the related area of Aboriginal affairs, more scholarly work has been done. See the chapter by Gina Cosentino and Paul L.A.H. Chartrand in this volume, and Angus 1990 for a solid and concise discussion of the Mulroney governments' policy in Aboriginal affairs.

5 The Charlottetown Accord, which was, of course, defeated in a national referendum the same year, was certainly ground-breaking. It would have included constitutional recognition of the inherent right of self-government for Aboriginal peoples, a recognition that came in any event through jurisprudence a few years later. In the negotiation of the accord, leaders of four Aboriginal organizations, and of two territories, were full participants. Since the referendum rejected the resulting compromise, this unprecedented feat of elite accommodation had no immediate constitutional effect, but its effects lingered as a demonstration of what was conceivable.

6 Known today as Indian and Northern Affairs Canada (INAC).

7 See Noel Schacter, Jim Beebe, and Luigi Zanasi, *Globalization and the North: Impact of Trade Treaties on Canada's Northern Governments* (Ottawa: Canadian Centre for Policy Alternatives 2004): Frances Abele and Peter Usher, "The Danger to the North," *Policy Options* 11(1) (1990); and Abele and Usher, *A New Economic Development Policy for the North? The Impact of the Free Trade Agreement* (Ottawa: Canadian Centre for Policy Alternatives October 1988).

8 Per-capita public expenditures in the territorial north are very high, for reasons having to do with climate and a highly dispersed population. Since these are ineluctable facts, northern budgets are difficult to trim. Overall, the costs of territorial administration form a small portion of the federal budget. For these two reasons, they are seldom an attractive target, though, in the last two decades, some modest per-capita reductions have been realized.

9 Mulroney's speech opening the 1985 first ministers' conference on the rights of Aboriginal peoples spells out his awareness of the importance of Indigenous voters in his largely northern constituency of Manicouagan. See http://www.collectionscanada.ca/primeministers/h4–4021-e.html.

10 For example, the first minister of Indian affairs and northern development, David Crombie, hired as chief-of-staff Ron Doering, a former executive director of the Canadian Arctic Resources Committee, a non-governmental environmentalist organization focused on the north; Tom Hockin, minister of state for finance, small business and tourism, and science, hired Gerald Wright, who, as executive director of the Donner Canadian Foundation, had been central to the funding of several northern research and community-development initiatives.

Both Hockin and Wright, earlier in their careers, had written and taught on issues of northern sovereignty and security.

11 Gurston Dacks, *A Choice of Futures: Politics in the Canadian North* (Toronto: Methuen 1981; Frances Abele and M.O. Dickerson, "The 1982 Plebiscite on Division of the Northwest Territories: Regional Government and Federal Policy," *Canadian Public Policy*, March 1985, 1–15; Frances Abele, "Canadian Contradictions: Forty Years of Northern Political Development," *Arctic* 41(4) (1987): 310–20, repr. in Kenneth Coates and William R. Morrison, eds., *Interpreting Canada's North: Selected Readings* (Toronto: Copp Clark Pitman 1989); Mark O Dickerson, *Whose North?: Political Change, Political Development, and Self-Government in the Northwest Territories* (Vancouver: University of British Columbia Press 1992); Graham White and Kirk Cameron, *Northern Governments in Transition* (Montreal: Institute for Research on Public Policy 1995).

12 This is a step that has not yet been taken in either Nunavut or the post-division Northwest Territories.

13 Both territories were initially administered almost entirely from Ottawa and each territorial government had been "built" by transferring areas of governing responsibility from direct federal control, albeit at a different pace in each territory. In the 1980s key areas of what would be provincial jurisdiction elsewhere were exercised by federal departments in the territories. Gurston Dacks, *Devolution and Constitutional Development in the Canadian North* (Ottawa: Carleton University Press 1990).

14 Federal policy after 1973 was to negotiate new agreements with Aboriginal collectivities whose rights had not yet been the subject of concluded treaty negotiations. Originally referred to as "land claim agreements," these agreements came to be seen as true modern treaties over time. In the Northwest Territories, Treaty 11 had in fact been concluded in 1921, and it did cover most of the western part of the territory. But the negotiating process for Treaty 11 was shown to be illegitimate, and so the Dene who were parties to Treaty 11 joined the general move to negotiate new agreements.

15 Simon McInnis, "The Policy Consequences of Northern Development," in Michael M. Atkinson and Marsha Chandler, eds., *The Politics of Canadian Public Policy* (Toronto: University of Toronto Press 1983), 247. The internally contradictory mandate was nothing new: see Edgar J Dosman, *The National Interest: The Politics of Northern Development 1968–1975* (Toronto: McClelland and Stewart 1975).

16 Ministers of state for Indian affairs and northern development were Bernard Valcourt (1986–89), Kim Campbell (1989–90), Shirley Martin (1990–91), Monique Landry (1991–93), and Pierre Vincent (1993). Parliamentary secretaries: Grive Fretz, David Kilgour, Stan Schellenberger, James Stewart Edwards, Dorothy Dobbie, and Ross Reid.

17 Frances Abele, "Conservative Northern Development Policy: New Wine in an Old Bottleneck?" in Michael J. Prince, ed., *How Ottawa Spends 1986–87: Tracking*

*the Tories* (Toronto: Methuen 1986); and Gurston Dacks, *Devolution and Constitutional Development in the Canadian North.*

18 Katherine Graham, "Indian Policy and the Tories: Cleaning up after the Buffalo Jump," in Michael J. Prince, ed., *How Ottawa Spends 1987–88: Restraining the State* (Toronto: Methuen 1987).

19 Canada, Department of Indian Affairs and Northern Development, *Annual Report,* 1986–77, 8.

20 Edgar J. Dosman and Frances Abele, "Offshore Diplomacy in the Canadian Arctic: The Beaufort Sea and Lancaster Sound," *Journal of Canadian Studies* 16(3) (1981): 3–15; Edgar J. Dosman, ed., *The Arctic in Question* (Toronto: Oxford University Press 1976).

21 Typically, Indian affairs preoccupied this minister as well, since he led the department during the period that saw the failure of the third, and final, first minister's conference on Aboriginal matters and the subsequent Meech Lake Accord debacle.

22 Canada, Department of Indian Affairs and Northern Development, *A New Political and Economic Framework for the North, 1988*; Frances Abele and Katherine A. Graham, "Plus Que Ca Change ... Northern and Native Policy," in Katherine Graham, ed., *How Ottawa Spends 1988–89: The Conservatives Heading into the Stretch* (Ottawa: Carleton University Press 1988).

23 The Arctic received $100 million of a total $3 billion.The Green Plan, of course, was not financially "watered" by the Liberals who were elected in 1993, and so it withered. See Robert J. P. Gale, "Canada's Green Plan," in *Nationale Umweltpläne in Ausgewählten Industrieländern* [a study of the development of a national environmental plan, with expert submissions to the Enquete commission on "Protection of People and the Environment" for the Bundestag (German Parliament)] (Berlin: Springer-Verlag 1997), 97–120.

24 Since the issue of northern environmental protection and stewardship was sidelined during the Progressive Conservatives' time in power, it has received little discussion in this chapter.

25 Murray Angus, "... *And the last shall be first": Native Policy in an Era of Cutbacks* (Ottawa: Aboriginal Rights Coalition [Project North] 1990); Michael J. Prince, "The Mulroney Agenda: A Right Turn for Ottawa?" in Prince, ed., *How Ottawa Spends 1986–87*; Michael J. Prince, "Restraining the State: How Ottawa Shrinks," in Prince, ed., *How Ottawa Spends 1987–88*; Graham, "Heading in the Stretch," in Graham, ed., *How Ottawa Spends 1988–89.*

# 14

# The Mulroney Government and Canadian Cultural Policy

JAMES M. PITSULA

The Mulroney government is indelibly associated with the signing of the 1988 Canada-U.S. Free Trade Agreement (FTA) from which culture was, supposedly, exempt. In fact it was not. The final text gave the United States the right to retaliate "with measures of equivalent commercial effect, against actions by Canada in the cultural sphere that would have been prohibited by the FTA had cultural activities not been exempted."[1] Canada thereby conceded the legitimacy of American counter-measures to Canadian cultural protectionism. At a deeper level, culture could not possibly have been excluded from the free-trade deal. Culture, politics, and economics are so intertwined that a major change in one area cannot help but influence the other two.

Broadly considered, culture may be understood as "the order of life in which human beings construct meaning through practices of symbolic representation."[2] It is what people draw upon to make sense of the meaning of their existence: not only the books they read and the plays they attend, but also "the trip around the local supermarket aisles, or to the restaurant, the sports hall, the dance club or the garden centre, the conversation in the bar or on the street corner ... [all the] mundane practices that directly contribute to people's ongoing 'life-narratives.'"[3] As Bernard Ostry puts it:

> Culture, however we define it, is central to everything we do and think. It is what we do and the reason we do it, what we wish and why we imagine it, what we perceive and how we express it, how we live and in what manner we approach death. It is our environment and the patterns of our adaptation to it. It is the world we have created and are still creating; it is the way we see that world and the motives that urge us to change it. It is the way we know ourselves and each other; it is our web of personal relationships, it is the images and abstractions that allow us to live together in communities and nations. It is the element in which we live.[4]

From left, Kiefer Sutherland, Marcel Masse, Anne Claire Poirier, Colin Low, and Donald Sutherland accept an Oscar in 1989 at the Academy Awards as an honorary award for the National Film Board of Canada. Canadian Press / Associated Press / Lennox McClendon.

Viewed in this light, the cultural dimension of life (that is, the realm of "existentially significant" meaning)[5] cannot be separated from the economic (the "practices by which humans produce, exchange, and consume material goods") or the political ("practices by which power is concentrated, distributed and deployed in societies").[6] People do not turn from "doing the political" or "doing the economic" to "doing the cultural."[7] This is especially true in consumer-oriented societies where culture is increasingly commodified. Advertisers do not just pitch products; they offer visions "of how life may be lived, references to shared notions of identity, appeals to self-image, pictures of 'ideal' human relations, versions of human fulfillment, happiness and so on."[8] Similarly, cultural context shapes political discourse, as in the case of the debate on the Meech Lake Accord, when television images of Ontarians stomping on the Quebec flag and French-only signs in Quebec inflamed the national-unity crisis.

The intersection of economics, politics, and culture is a central theme of the literature on globalization, a term that is just as hard to define as is "culture." Cultural studies and communication scholar John Tomlinson describes globalization as "complex connectivity," by which he means "the rapidly developing and ever-densening network of interconnections and interdependences that characterize modern social life."[9] Since the United States is currently the dominant economic, military, and cultural power in the world, it lies at the heart of globalization. The FTA, therefore, may be construed as a vehicle for American-led globalization to project itself more deeply and comprehensively into Canada. It follows that the literature on the relationship between globalization and culture provides a theoretical framework to interpret the cultural policies of the Mulroney government.

A central question is how globalization influences culture, that is, "how it affects people's sense of identity, the experience of place and of the relation of the self in relation to place, how it impacts on shared understandings, values, desires, myths, hopes and fears that have developed around locally situated life."[10] Is globalization westernization or, more specifically, Americanization by another name?[11] Is it leading to "the emergence of one single culture embracing everyone on earth and replacing the diversity of cultural systems that have flourished up to now"?[12] The answers to such questions must remain in the realm of speculation since no one knows with certainty how the future will unfold. American Marxist media expert Herbert Schiller argues that a capitalist monoculture is spreading throughout the world. Capitalism is not only extending its reach through the global political economy but also determining global culture "in the distribution of commercialized media products containing the ethos and values of corporate capitalism and consumerism."[13] The selling of the product and the selling of the culture (understood as "the social production of existentially significant meaning") go hand in hand, each reinforcing the other. Sinclair Stevens, a minister in the Mulroney government who was involved in dispute over the American takeover of a Canadian publishing company, had practical experience of this phenomenon. After he lost the battle, he said: "I came to the conclusion that it's the way Americans market their whole society to the world. If you control print, video and movies, you in effect get to show the world what good culture is all about: the clothes they want to wear, the food they want to eat. It's a tremendous marketing tool for your whole way of life."[14] All the same, Schiller's account seems too schematic. The "capitalist monoculture" he speaks of can also have the effect of energizing local cultures by providing them with a market niche, thereby enhancing their ability to survive and flourish.

The sale of U.S. cultural products in foreign markets netted a trade surplus in 1989 of $U.S.8 billion, the third-largest sectoral surplus after the food and aerospace industries.[15] Of the 250 all-time top-grossing movies around the world, only four are not American: *The Fully Monty* (United Kingdom), *Life Is Beautiful* (Italy), and *Spirited Away* and *Howl's Moving Castle* (Japan).[16] In 1993 the U.S. film industry generated a $4-billion surplus, with foreign markets accounting for a growing percentage of Hollywood revenues. The major studios received 65 per cent of earnings from the U.S. market in 1986, as compared with 53.2 per cent in 1991. In absolute numbers, total revenues from foreign markets increased from $6.7 billion in 1986 to $13.4 billion in 1991.[17] No country (other than the United States itself) is more dominated by American cultural products than Canada. On a per-capita basis we are "the largest cultural-sector importer in the world."[18] According to a Department of Communications report, 76 per cent of books sold in Canada in 1987 were imported, 97 per cent of screen time in movie theatres was devoted to imported films, 89 per cent of earnings in the sound-recording industry flowed to 12 foreign-controlled firms, and 90 per cent of dramatic television presentations were non-Canadian.[19] Even Brian Mulroney, who generally favoured close ties with the United States, found these statistics worrisome. He asked President Ronald Reagan, "What if the Russians had 97 per cent of the screen time in the United States and Hollywood had 3 per cent? Wouldn't you at least try to react?"[20] Reagan was impressed, but not enough to soften his opposition to cultural protectionism.

Globalization theorists ponder the question: What makes U.S. culture so attractive to the rest of the world? No one is forcing Canadians to watch American television programs or movies; they do so of their own accord. The need to respect consumer choice lies behind Mordecai Richler's dig: "Nationalists are lobbying for the imposition of Canadian content quotas in our bookshops and theatres ... In a word, largely second-rate writers are demanding from Ottawa what talent has denied them, an audience."[21] While Richler has a point, it is also true that U.S. cultural industries enjoy undoubted advantages of economies of scale. The average budget for a movie production by the Hollywood major studios in 1994 was about $U.S.35 million. The comparable Canadian figures were $CDN.2.1 million for feature films and $3.3 million for television movies.[22] The cost of making a U.S. film can be amortized over a larger market, since the American audience is ten times the size of the Canadian. This means that more money is available to fill the airwaves and Internet channels with advertisements for the latest not-to-be missed blockbuster, or, as Schiller bluntly puts it, to inundate the media with "homogenized North Atlantic cultural slop."[23] Canadians can counter their competitive disadvantage by producing films, videos, and other cultural products with the American audience in mind, but this is a self-defeating strategy if the objective is to reflect and develop Canadian culture.

The global appeal of American cultural products is not based solely on economic factors, as important as they may be. French political economist Serge Latouche suggests that a deeper process is at work, which he characterizes as the "drive towards planetary uniformity" and the "world-wide standardization of lifestyles."[24] This includes not only the spread of the English language and consumer capitalism but also "styles of dress, eating habits, architectural and musical forms, the adoption of an urban lifestyle based around industrial production, a pattern of experience dominated by the mass media, a set of philosophical ideas, and a range of cultural values and attitudes – about personal liberty, gender and sexuality, human rights, the political process, religion, scientific and technological rationality and so on."[25] As a cultural phenomenon (cultural in the sense of a "response to the problem of being"[26]), the "American dream" is based to a considerable extent on Enlightenment values: liberty, equality, democracy, and the free market. These are powerful ideas and their appeal should not be underestimated, but it is not clear that they are becoming globally ubiquitous.

Resistance to globalization and the "new international order"[27] persists throughout the world. As sociologist Anthony Smith points out, national cultures remain obstinately particular, drawing upon deep feelings of collective identity, shared memories, and a sense of common destiny. These attachments are often based on "the community's ethno-history," the subjective "core" on which national identities can be constructed.[28] Canada, given its bilingual and multicultural heritage, lacks such a unified subjective core, which makes it more vulnerable to American-style globalization. George Grant concluded forty years ago in *Lament for a Nation* that Canadians were no longer essentially different from Americans (in the cultural sense as defined in this chapter). He opposed the Canada-U.S. Free Trade Agreement, not because he thought anything could be done "to prevent the eventual annihilation of Canadian, or Quebec uniqueness," but because "rootedness was good and it was noble to bear witness to it, even in a doomed cause."[29]

Most cultural nationalists deny that the cause is doomed. At least since the 1951 Massey Commission (Royal Commission on National Development in the Arts, Letters and Sciences), culture has been recognized "as a legitimate concern of government, and as such, one that require[s] serious attention, coordinated management, and a comprehensive strategy."[30] The commission linked cultural policy with national defence: "If we, as a nation, are concerned with the problem of defence, what, we may ask ourselves, are we defending? We are defending civilization, our share of it, our contribution to it … It would be paradoxical to defend something which we are unwilling to strengthen and enrich, and which we even allow to decline … Our military defences must be made secure; but our cultural defences equally demand attention; the two can not be separated."[31]

If Canada does not defend its culture, it is an "empty shell," an "absent nation." The linkage of culture to national survival is the primary justification for Canadian government intervention in the cultural sphere. Canadian cultural policy is rooted in "the security interests of the Canadian state."[32] Governments of every party stripe endorse this position, including that of Brian Mulroney, who said in 1985: "Cultural sovereignty is as vital to our national life as political sovereignty."[33]

Despite this declaration, the Mulroney government lacked a coherent cultural policy. It took money away from arts and cultural programs and later gave it back. It squeezed the CBC, while introducing a new act to renew and promote the mission of public broadcasting. It said that culture was not on the free-trade negotiating table, and then signed an agreement that allows for U.S. retaliation against Canadian actions in the cultural sphere. It posed as a defender of Canadian culture, while consenting to side deals harmful to the Canadian book-publishing and film industries. The confusion and incoherence stemmed from unresolved tensions in government policy. The Conservatives came into office in 1984 promising a "new direction for Canada" and "an agenda for economic renewal." This meant tackling the legacy of Trudeau government deficits and encouraging the spirit of private enterprise. Finance Minister Michael Wilson announced in November 1984:

> Government policies and programs must be changed to ensure that Canada's private sector can become the driving force of economic renewal in an increasingly competitive world marketplace. To foster growth in the private sector, Canadians must begin a process of change towards a new environment that encourages entrepreneurship and facilitates adaptation to new market realities. In some cases, this will mean less government regulation and intervention. In other cases, it will require reducing government subsidies and other expenditures which undermine the efficient allocation of our scarce resources. In yet others, it will be necessary to redirect or reinforce government activities which support growth and adjustment. This will be especially true in the case of R & D exports, and investment, and especially for small- and medium-sized business.[34]

This approach, while not in itself unreasonable, did not specify how the policy would work with respect to culture. The government wanted to encourage private-sector investment in and support of culture, while maintaining a role for government. The question demanding a clear answer was: Under the new regime, what was to be the role of government and what was the role of the private sector? There was a tendency for the Mulroney government to think in terms of "cultural industries" rather than culture per se. The former were often viewed as instruments of economic development and, as such, deserving of incentives and subsidies like other "small- and medium-sized businesses." This led to a dilemma in the free-trade negotiations with the United States. The United States demanded that cultural industries be included in the discussions; Canada refused, saying that culture was of vital national importance and could not be touched, all the while implementing policies premised on the belief that culture was an industry. No wonder the Americans were confused about where Canada stood. The contradictions were multiplied by the fact that at times the free market and cultural policy are unnatural partners. American-led globalization, of which the FTA was merely a sidebar, is driven by free-market capitalism and opposes cultural protectionism. When the Mulroney government tried to have it both ways – pro-free market and pro-Canadian culture – it became enmeshed in a mass of inconsistencies.

The failure of the government to clarify where it stood led to conflicts between communications ministers Marcel Masse and Flora MacDonald, on one side, and Finance Minister Michael Wilson on the other. Brian Mulroney, who was not deeply engaged in the Canadian arts and literary scene, generally sided with Wilson. Marcel Masse was a Quebec nationalist who, along with Lucien Bouchard, had been recruited to restore federal Conservative Party fortunes in that province. Masse had no qualms about using the power of the state to protect culture, a policy that was considered completely normal in both Quebec and France.

Although Flora MacDonald came at the issue from a different perspective, she ended up embracing the same policies as Masse. A Red Tory, a once-flourishing but now declining species of Canadian, she combined support for the liberal values of individual freedom, opportunity, and private enterprise with concern for the welfare of the community and respect for historical tradition. For her, the free market was not an absolute principle that trumped everything else, but rather a worthy goal that had to be situated in its proper cultural context. On one occasion Jack Valenti, the lobbyist for the Hollywood film industry, paid a visit to Flora MacDonald in Ottawa. He lectured her for twenty minutes, explaining that "U.S. culture was now global culture, and Canadians would just have to face up the reality." He "scoff[ed] at the notion of etching a national identity on celluloid. 'What you are doing is making a leap of faith' … 'Mr. Valenti,' MacDonald replied, 'What you don't understand is that from its beginning, Canada was a leap of faith. If the Fathers of Confederation took your dictates, we'd never have had a country.'"[35] She then gave Valenti a twenty-minute primer on Canadian history. Despite the bravado performance, MacDonald, while scoring modest victories for cultural nationalism, had to bow to the prevailing pro-market ideology of the Mulroney regime.

The trouble began in November 1984, when the government announced a cut of $85 million from the approximately $1.685-billion arts-and-culture budget. This included reductions of $75 million from the CBC, $3.5 million from the Canada Council, $1.5 million from the National Film Board, and lesser amounts from other cultural agencies. In addition, $10 million was taken from the CBC's capital budget.[36] The cuts were accompanied by the formation of a special task force "to propose initiatives to encourage the private sector to increase its support for the arts."[37] The group, chaired by Edmund C. Bovey, focused specifically on the performing, visual, and literary arts. Their report, which appeared in June 1986, repeated the usual homilies: "The arts lie at the heart of the cultural sovereignty battle. The spirit of a nation is expressed through the creative act, and the arts, by definition, are the focus of that activity." It went on to say that culture-related activities (the arts as defined in the task force report plus publishing, film, sound recordings, broadcasting, libraries, and related government expenditures) accounted in 1982 for between 2 and 3 per cent of Gross Domestic Product (GDP), a share that exceeded, "individually, those of the tobacco, rubber and plastic, textile, clothing, oil and coal products, and chemical industries; and [was] nearly equal to that of the mining and metals, the electrical energy and the oil and natural gas industries." [38] Viewed through the lens of economic-growth strategy, the report said, the arts were to the cultural industries what research and development were to industry as a whole: "There is little to be gained in protecting our cultural industries if our works of art are moribund, or if a weakened arts infrastructure cannot supply the necessary talent and creative product."[39]

In order to keep research and development for the cultural industries up to par, the task force recommended a 5 per cent annual increase in constant dollars for the performing, visual, and literary arts to the year 2000. The dollars required to meet this objective represented one-tenth of 1 per cent of GDP.[40] Apart from the overall increase, the report called for a reallocation of funding borne by the "arts funding partners – government, the private sector, consumers and the arts community."[41] The federal government share was to fall from 23 per cent in 1986 to 19 per cent in 2000, with the private sector making up the difference.[42] The entire report was predicated on the notion that arts organizations needed to become more business-like in their operations: "There is a general feeling in the business community that artists do not know how to sell their product," the report noted. "We can understand why artists hesitate to look on their works as 'products' when they are involved in making unique works of art that have little in common with the usual output of business and industry. Be that as it may, however, the business community will become more interested in the arts when artists learn to speak the language of business and to 'sell' themselves, their ideas and their work."[43]

To make this happen, the task force urged, among other things, that 'funding agencies should require, as a condition of their grants, that all organizations of a certain size retain on-staff marketing expertise"[44] and that "the Canadian Association of Art Administration Educators should develop, in conjunction with the Canada Council, a modular skills program, comprising business and marketing skills aimed at young artists currently in art colleges or other post-secondary institutions."[45]

Another study that impinged on the cultural sector was the Neilsen Task Force on Program Review, named after Deputy Prime Minister Erik Nielsen, who headed the exercise. Its sweeping mandate was to review all federal government programs with a view to improving their delivery, while reducing waste and duplication. As Tory cabinet minister John Crosbie conceded, the task force aroused a good deal of opposition and few of the recommendations were actually implemented,[46] but it reveals something of the context of public-policy discourse. The "study team" report on culture and communications suggested that the government "put more emphasis on marketing promotion, and that it provide less money for cultural lobby organizations."[47] Contradicting the position taken by Communications Minister Marcel Masse, who advocated supporting the performing arts on grounds that it generated a significant economic spin-off, the task force said that cultural spending was overrated as a catalyst for economic development. Such spending, the task force claimed, did have a large impact on employment but "only a modest impact on income, tax revenue, productivity and the balance of payments."[48]

The primary justification for cultural spending lay in "the intrinsic value of the arts, their contribution to the definition of national character, and their contribution to the quality of life."[49] For these objectives to be met, it was necessary to ensure that cultural activities were not confined to a small group: "The activities must infuse and permeate all regions and significant groups of the society."[50] The task force then undercut its own argument by recommending that "consumers of cultural products" pay a larger share of the cost of the benefits they were receiving.[51] It suggested that heritage institutions, such as the National Museums of Canada (encompassing the National Gallery of Canada, the National Museum of Man, the National Museum of Natural Sciences, and the National Museum of Science and Technology), the Public Archives, and the National Library "consider the implementation of a variety of revenue generation methods, including admission fees, voluntary contributions and sponsorships."[52] Admission fees were rejected because they would have restricted access to cultural institutions, but other forms of revenue generation, such as ancillary sales, were encouraged.

According to D. Paul Schafer and André Fortier, authors of a review of federal policies for the arts in Canada from 1944 to 1988, the appointment of a cultural-policy task force was a Conservative government strategy "designed to make people forget the $85 million budget cuts" announced in 1984.[53] If this was the plan, it did not succeed. About three hundred and fifty Toronto artists took to the streets in March 1985, carrying giant replicas of cameras, palettes, and brushes and chanting, "Tell the fat boys at the top, cultural cutbacks have got to stop." Signs attacked Marcel Masse with slogans such as "As Far as Artists Are Concerned, Masse Equals Wait," a reference to delays in receiving government grants.[54] Similar protests were held in Vancouver, Halifax, Moncton, Edmonton, and Winnipeg.[55] Not everybody sympathized with the artists' plight. A letter to the *Globe and Mail* advised: "These people are parasites and spongers: Let them sell chocolate bars for their money, as do the Boy Scouts and the Big Brothers."[56] The government, however, extended an olive branch and reinstated in the 1986 budget $75 million that had previously been cut.[57] The hero of the day was Marcel Masse, whom the cultural community credited for bringing about the partial reversal in government policy.[58]

The $75 million funded a number of cultural initiatives: $33 million to Telefilm Canada to support the production and distribution of Canadian feature films; $13 million for the Book Publishing Development Program; $5 million to assist the Canadian sound- recording industry; an additional $10 million for the Canada Council; $7 million for the Public Archives; $4 million "to develop means of electronic sharing of information contained in Canadian library data bases"; and $3 million for the Public Lending Rights Program, which compensated authors for the use of their works through public libraries.[59] The CBC received no share of the $75-million increase to the culture budget. Masse said this was because "before asking for any money, we have to review policy or create policies."[60] Presumably, once a broadcasting policy review had been completed, the money would begin to flow.

In the meantime, a crisis developed in the book-publishing industry. The American conglomerate Gulf and Western in December 1984 bought out the New Jersey-based Prentice Hall company. The takeover of Prentice Hall's Canadian subsidiary was subject to review by Investment Canada, the entity the Mulroney government had created in place of Trudeau's Foreign Investment Review Agency. As the Nielsen Task Force had observed, existing book-publishing policy was based on certain key assumptions: "The production and publication of Canadian-authored culturally significant titles is essential to maintain Canada's national and cultural identity; Canadian-owned publishers produce culturally significant titles to a much greater extent than foreign-owned publishers; and, therefore, Canada must have a Canadian-owned publishing industry."[61] On 6 July 1985, following a cabinet meeting held in Baie Comeau, Quebec, Marcel Masse took a strong stand.[62] He announced that U.S. companies acquiring

Canadian publishing companies through indirect takeovers would have to sell 51 per cent of the subsidiary's shares to a Canadian firm within two years. Gulf and Western's lawyers argued that it was unfair to apply the policy retroactively to the Prentice Hall purchase.[63] The amount of money involved was relatively small (Prentice-Hall had $30 million a year in Canadian sales), but Gulf and Western was afraid that the case would set a precedent for other countries to follow or that similar nationalistic policies would be implemented in other areas such as film and cable television.[64]

Allan Gotlieb, Canada's ambassador in Washington, wrote on 6 August 1985 to Regional Industrial Expansion Minister Sinclair Stevens stating that Canada's nationalistic book-publishing policy was "ill-timed, unclear and likely to damage the progress Ottawa ha[d] made recapturing the affections of U.S. investors."[65] Gotlieb conveyed a threat from Gulf and Western lobbyist and former Democratic Party chairman Robert Strauss to the effect that the conglomerate would adopt a "scorched earth response" if its acquisition of Prentice Hall Canada was blocked. The nature of the response was not specified, but it sounded ominous. The Gotlieb memo came under attack from Canadian publishers such as Mel Hurtig, who sharply commented: "I'm wondering if our ambassador remembers which country he's supposed to be working for."[66] Malcolm Lester, president of the Association of Canadian Publishers and of Lester and Orpen Dennys of Toronto, added that Gotlieb "seem[ed] to be arguing for the Gulf and Western position rather than presenting it."[67] The Canadian government caved in on 12 March 1986 with the announcement that Investment Canada had approved the takeover of Prentice Hall, which made Gulf and Western "the biggest presence in Canadian publishing."[68] Investment Canada also approved Gulf and Western's purchase of another Toronto textbook publisher, Ginn Canada, but in this case the government obtained a promise that in two years the conglomerate would have to sell 51 per cent of the shares to a Canadian firm. However, Ottawa had no legal means of enforcing this commitment.[69] In March 1988, when the two-year deadline was up, Gulf and Western informed the government that, having received no acceptable offers, it was going to keep 100 per cent of Ginn.[70]

At this point the dispute became entangled in the Canada-U.S. Free Trade Agreement, which contained a clause stipulating "if Ottawa required the forced divestiture of a U.S. business in the cultural sector as part of an indirect takeover, the government itself would have to offer to buy out the American owner 'at fair open market value.'"[71] Accordingly, the Canadian government offered to buy the controlling interest in Ginn from Gulf and Western. The negotiations dragged on for more than year before a deal was reached.[72] Gulf and Western insisted on inserting a clause in the sale agreement providing that, should the government's Baie Comeau policy be modified to eliminate the forced-divestiture provision and should Ginn still be in the Canadian government's hands, then Gulf and Western would automatically have the right to buy back the company for the same price it had received for it.[73] The government made the concession with one stipulation: the buy-back clause would not be put in writing. In January 1992 Perrin Beatty, the new communications minister, abolished the Baie Comeau's forced-divestiture rules that Masse had boldly proclaimed seven years earlier. Gulf and Western then activated the secret unwritten clause in the sale agreement, and in November 1992 the government quietly sold Ginn back to Gulf and Western for the same amount it had paid three years earlier.[74]

A similar pattern of "now-you-see-it, now-you-don't" cultural nationalism occurred in film-industry policy. Communications Minister Flora MacDonald announced on 14 February 1987 a new licensing policy for film distribution in Canada. The proposed legislation would prevent the major U.S. studios from distributing films and videos that they had not entirely financed or for which they had not purchased world rights. The government hoped that the new policy would raise the Canadian share of distribution fees from 10 per cent to 20 per cent of the total. For example, the British producers of *Chariots of Fire* sold its North American rights to Warner Brothers. Since Warner Brothers considered Canada part of its domestic market, the Canadian rights were included in the deal and no Canadian distributor could bid for them. MacDonald's bill would have given Canadians an opportunity to participate in this lucrative market. Sam Jephcott, executive director of the Canadian Film and Television Association, regarded the new policy as a "watershed in the development of the industry." "It's sensational," he said. "It's been something we've been waiting for seventy-five years."[75]

There were fears in the film community that the new bill was being used as a tactic in the free-trade negotiations. An unnamed senior official in the Ontario government was quoted as saying: "Our concern is that this is mainly a threat to get the Americans (the film companies) to negotiate. At the same time, it may be a bargaining chip, something that comes off the table or on the table, depending on the free trade talks."[76] The *Globe and Mail* reported in November 1987 that the introduction of the bill had been delayed because of heavy pressure from the U.S. film industry. Government sources indicated that the bill would not be presented until after the Free Trade Agreement had been presented to Congress in early 1988.[77] According to journalist Marci McDonald, Jack Valenti interceded with American Treasury Secretary James Baker to make sure the film bill did not see the light of day. In a memo to Baker that was leaked to a Washington trade newsletter after the free-trade negotiations had concluded, a U.S.

bureaucrat reported that Mulroney's government had "promised to solve Jack Valenti's problem on film distribution within the next two weeks." American negotiator Peter Murphy also acknowledged that Baker had worked out a secret deal with Valenti apart from the actual text of the free-trade agreement. A compromise bill on film legislation, a pale version of the original, was presented to the House of Commons in June 1988. A month later, Mulroney called an election and the bill died on the order paper, never to be revived.[78]

Marcel Masse returned to the Department of Communications in 1989 more determined than ever to "create a new cultural infrastructure for the country."[79] He wanted an omnibus cultural bill to put all foreign takeovers of cultural industries under the supervision of a new Cultural Investment Review Agency that would be run by the Canadian Radio-television and Telecommunications Commission (CRTC), the arms-length agency that regulated broadcasting ownership and content requirements. Finance Minister Michael Wilson damned the plan as "contentious and costly." He warned that it "could pose a continuing threat to our relations with the United States."[80] Masse struggled to move the omnibus culture bill forward but was unable even to get it on the cabinet agenda. He was transferred out of the communications portfolio and replaced by Perrin Beatty, who, as mentioned earlier, gutted the Baie Comeau publishing policy.[81]

It is not surprising that the Canadian cultural establishment did not, on the whole, regard the Mulroney government in high esteem. A number of luminaries contributed essays to *If You Love This Country,* a book published in 1987, which lambasted the Free Trade Agreement. Jack McClelland, the publisher who spurred the "Can Lit" boom in the 1960s and served as co-chairman of the Committee for an Independent Canada,[82] wrote a scathing denunciation:

> We have had our share of national heroes, and we have had more than our share of national rogues who for the worst sort of greeds would sell our heritage or even their own grandmothers to seek some advantage. The latest rogue may indeed become the most infamous in our history. We elected this smiling, genial man as our eighteenth Prime Minister. Without direction from us or any prior warning, he has done a two-step dance that may well destroy our heritage. The first step, called a Meech Lake Accord, was designed to weaken any central control in Canada. His second step was, in reality, a blank cheque to our American neighbors to turn Canada into an annex, a warehouse, a storehouse of riches that they could call on in the future. Kids, this is not the story about the wicked grandmother. I have dropped all that. But it is the story of a wicked Prime Minister who has sacrificed your heritage for reasons that I don't at the moment understand and I don't think I ever will understand.[83]

Mulroney countered with the argument that Canada must have a strong economy in order to support a distinctive cultural life, and the Free Trade Agreement, by promoting the former, enhanced the latter. He could also point to success stories in the cultural sector that were attributable, in part at least, to Conservative government policies. The U.S. music trade magazine *Billboard* ran a story in February 1994 headlined, "Oh Canada! One Nation under a Groove," highlighting the prominence of Canadian artists (Celine Dion, Crash Test Dummies, Barenaked Ladies, Blue Rodeo, and so on) in the global sound-recording industry. [84] The foundation for this development lay in 1971 when the federal government imposed Canadian-content regulations as a condition of granting licences to radio stations. A number of private companies and organizations (CHUM, Moffat Communications, Rogers Broadcasting, the Canadian Independent Record Producers Association, and the Canadian Music Publishers Association), which were concerned about the shortage of Canadian popular music suitable for radio broadcast, in 1982 established the Fund to Assist Canadian Talent on Record (FACTOR). A jury system was set up "to evaluate applications, and funding was given to produce demo tapes, organize promotional tours, make promotional clips and a variety of other activities."[85] When the Mulroney government put money into the sound-recording industry in 1986, it simply followed the FACTOR model, an outstanding example of effective collaboration between the private and public sectors.[86]

The results in the film industry, though less successful, were somewhat encouraging. The Trudeau government in 1968 had created the Canadian Film Development Corporation (CFDC) with an initial budget of $10 million to subsidize private-sector films. In 1983 the government began funding the production of television programming, and in 1984, reflecting the shift in priorities, the CFDC was renamed Telefilm Canada. The Tories boosted the Telefilm budget as part of its 1986 package of cultural initiatives. A 1991 review of the fund concluded that it "ha[d] been enormously successful in achieving its original objectives." In the period from 1986 to 1990, the fund helped finance "a total production volume of 2,275 hours of original television programming, of which more than 1,000 hours consisted of drama programs shown during peak viewing hours … For English television, viewing of Canadian programs during peak time went from 19.6 per cent in 1984–85, to 25.4 per cent in 1988–89, while viewing of drama programs went from 2.4 per cent in 1984–85 to 4.0 per cent in 1988–89."[87] The numbers for French television were, of course, significantly higher.

The government continued to fund feature-film production, but in this area the outcome was not as impressive. Through the 1980s and into the 1990s, screen time in Canadian movie theatres dedicated to Canadian films remained unchanged at about 3 per cent.[88] Hollywood's dream machine still prevailed. While government policies helped lure film and video production to Canada, creating a Hollywood North, the output was often not identifiably Canadian. As Ted Magder has written, "the net result of the policies and practices over the last generation has been an industry with two faces: one, tanned by the California sunshine, poised, eager and able to exploit the international marketplace with film, television and video (and multimedia) productions that, in many cases, seem to be Canadian only by virtue of the workers they employ; the other, hardened by the chill of the Canadian winter, resolute, eager and able to explore the dramatic diversity of everyday life in Canada."[89] Policies designed to develop Canadian cultural industries do not necessarily enrich Canadian culture, and Canadian ownership does not guarantee Canadian content, especially when the "product" is cloned to meet the expectations of the American market.[90] Economist Steven Globerman, writing for the Fraser Institute, pointedly asks: Why does the government subsidize Canadian cultural products when "the 'Canadian content' is ... at best, questionable?"[91]

From the nationalist perspective, no area of cultural policy is more important than broadcasting. More people watch a single television program in one evening than view the top-grossing Canadian films or attend live theatre productions in Canada over the course of an entire year. By the time Canadian children reach the age of twelve, they have spent more hours in front of the television set than in the schoolroom.[92] In 1994–95 fully one-third of the federal government's cultural and heritage dollars went to the CBC, making it the largest player in the government-supported cultural sector.[93] As mentioned above, one of the Tories' first moves in 1984 was to cut the CBC budget by 10 per cent. Marcel Masse then set up the Task Force on Broadcasting Policy, co-chaired by Gerald Caplan and Florian Sauvageau, to propose "an industrial and cultural strategy to govern the future evolution of the Canadian broadcasting system through the remainder of this century, recognizing the importance of broadcasting to Canadian life."[94] The task force, which reported in 1986, recommended that

> in both its organization and operation, the Canadian broadcasting system should serve the interests of all Canadians and their need to express themselves, in order to "safeguard, enrich and strengthen the cultural, political, social and economic fabric of Canada." The Canadian broadcasting system should play an active role in the developing an awareness of Canada, reflect the cultural diversity of Canadians and make available a wide range of programming that is Canadian in content and character and provides for a continuing expression of Canadian identity. It should serve the special needs of the geographic regions and actively contribute to the flow and exchange of information and expression among the regions of Canada.[95]

Caplan and Sauvageau criticized private broadcasters' over-reliance on American programs and urged that they be compelled to offer more

Canadian content during prime time. The report also said that the CBC, "the centerpiece of our broadcasting system,"[96] should receive more support for the production of Canadian drama and variety programs and for an all-news service channel.[97] The mandate of the public broadcaster was reaffirmed, except for one small change. Instead of contributing to "the development of national unity," it should confine itself to the less overtly political mission of developing "national consciousness"[98] and reflecting the country to itself. The new wording was included in the Broadcasting Act of 1991.

Despite the task force's endorsement of the role of the CBC, the budget cuts continued. Author-broadcaster Pierre Berton charged in 1986 that the Mulroney government was "slowly but surely killing the CBC and other cultural agencies that spawned a strong Canadian culture in the last 30 years." He said that, in his opinion, the Conservative caucus "wants to destroy the CBC. But they know they can't do that or sell it to their friend John Bassett [owner of Baton Broadcasting]. So they are doing it by attrition, by cutting the budget every year."[99] The *Globe and Mail* chimed in that "the Conservatives have it in for the CBC, largely because they think the CBC has it in for them. Senior ministers such as Don Mazankowski, Joe Clark and John Crosbie are among those highly critical of, and occasionally incensed by, what they perceive to be systematic anti-Conservative bias in the CBC."[100] This attitude, the *Globe* suggested, made it difficult for the government coolly and objectively to set policy for public broadcasting.

Outgoing CBC chairman and president Pierre Juneau declared in 1989 that the underfunding would make the corporation "unrecognizable," while Trina McQueen, head of CBC news and public affairs, warned that the network would become "a less relevant, less interesting, less worthwhile institution."[101] When Juneau stepped down, the chairmanship and presidency of the CBC were split into two positions. Mulroney appointed Patrick Watson, a journalist and staunch defender of the CBC, chairman, and Gerard Veilleux, former secretary of the Treasury Board, president. The Royal Canadian Air Farce, betraying the pervasive cynicism within the CBC concerning the government's intentions, joked that "Patrick Watson had been hired to restore excellence in programming and reaffirm the country's faith in public broadcasting. The other guy … was hired to make sure Watson doesn't have the money to do it."[102] The CBC in December 1990 closed down eleven television stations in different parts of the country and reduced non-national programming to two daily newscasts in each province.[103] All told, during nine years of Conservative rule, cumulative cuts reduced the CBC's base funding by $276 million. This led not only to reduced services and cancelled programs but also to increased reliance on advertising and the farming out of production to independent companies that received government grants.[104]

The tensions inherent in the Mulroney government's cultural policies came to a head in the Free Trade Agreement. Soon after Canada proposed to the United States that the two countries enter into negotiations on a comprehensive trade deal, External Affairs Minister Joe Clark headed to New York in November 1985 to give a speech stating that Canada's cultural subsidies were "not on the table." Yet, while appealing to Americans to be "sensitive to the seriousness" of Canada's concerns for the protection of its culture, he also acknowledged that "trade rules in the cultural sector, including immigration and border broadcasting, could be part of the talks."[105] The prime minister followed up with a speech in Chicago in December 1985 reaffirming that "our cultural sovereignty is not on the table. Our cultural identity is not on the table. It's not at risk in these discussions."[106] U.S. trade representative Clayton Yeutter responded almost immediately with the statement: "So far as I'm concerned, everything of economic consequence in the U.S.-Canada bilateral relationship is on the table." He said he would be "concerned if the term 'culture' is defined in such a way that it will have a major dampening effect on the overall negotiating process."[107]

Visiting Washington in March 1986, Prime Minister Mulroney reiterated to President Reagan the importance Canada attached to "cultural sovereignty."[108] The Americans, however, did not seem to get the message. Clayton Yeutter told a free-trade conference in Washington in February 1987 that he was prepared to put American culture on the table and "have it damaged by Canadian influence." "I hope Canada's prepared to run that risk, too," he said."[109] The comment sparked outrage in the House of Commons. New Democratic (NDP) MP Lynn McDonald urged Mulroney to explain to the Americans that "*Anne of Green Gables* is not a threat to American culture, that even if we beamed *Beachcomber* reruns to them non-stop that American culture would not be at risk."[110] Mulroney, for his part, blasted Yeutter, saying that his remarks displayed "a stunning ignorance of Canada." He added that the statements were "completely insensitive and totally unacceptable to the government and people of Canada." There would be no deal, he said, if Canada's "unique cultural identity" was not protected.[111] The *Globe and Mail* echoed Mulroney in an editorial that raked Yeutter over the coals: "Terrific. For fair and even-handed negotiations, there's nothing like a level playing field with a 10 to 1 gradient. The elephant will go into the ring against the mouse, provided they wear the same size boxing gloves. The eagle will risk being nibbled to death by the beaver."[112]

On 23 September 1987, after sixteen months of negotiations, Canada walked out of the free-trade talks. A key issue for Canada was U.S. trade remedy law (subsidies and countervailing duties, dumping and anti-dumping duties, and safeguard measures). The two countries could not agree on what constituted a subsidy, and the Americans refused to submit trade disputes to a bilateral panel for binding resolution.[113] They continued to object to Ottawa's support for cultural industries, insisting to the end that culture should be treated as an industry like any other.[114] As the 3 October deadline for fast-tracking the agreement through Congress approached, the United States agreed to the establishment of a binational panel to settle trade disputes. While this could be viewed as a major concession, the hitch was that the tribunal would base its decisions on the trade laws of the country where the complaint was filed. If the complaint originated in the United States, U.S. law would apply.[115] The *Globe and Mail* reported on 5 October 1987 that the agreement left "most of the cultural sector ... untouched."[116] The story in the New York *Times* was different. It stated accurately that "Canada has agreed that cultural measures it takes will not impair the benefits the U.S. would otherwise expect from the provisions of the agreement. In addition, Canada has agreed to alter a number of practices that discriminate against the U.S., including differential postal rates for U.S. periodicals and elimination of tariffs on printed material and recordings."[117]

Was culture in or was it out? Was the glass half full or half empty? NDP leader Ed Broadbent charged that Canada's freedom to protect cultural industries had been jeopardized.[118] Maude Barlow, co-president of the Pro-Canada Network, warned that extending national treatment to American firms in Canada "could mean the end of Canadian identity in areas such as publishing and communications."[119] Ontario Premier David Peterson stated that his previous concerns about the impact of free trade on cultural industries "[had] not abated."[120] The *Globe and Mail* reported that the cultural sector was "in turmoil, torn between hope and despair," as it contemplated the first news of the deal that had been signed. There was relief that cultural industries apparently had been exempted from the investment provisions of the agreement, but anger over the loss of the postal-rate subsidy that favoured Canadian periodicals over those published in the United States (Canadian publishers had paid 5.1 cents a copy to mail an average-sized magazine, compared with 42 cents a copy for U.S. publishers). Marcia George, executive director of the Association of Canadian Publishers, expressed satisfaction that the Baie Comeau policy on book publishing had survived. As we have seen, the policy required U.S. companies buying Canadian book publishers, even in indirect acquisitions from other U.S. companies, to sell 51 per cent ownership to Canadians within two years,[121] but it was abandoned in 1992.

Culture was not truly exempted from the Free Trade Agreement because the Canadian government conceded that the United States had the right to retaliate if it felt that it had suffered commercial damage from Canadian cultural policies. This grants a measure of credibility to American retaliation that did not exist before the agreement was signed.[122] At another level, culture, defined in the broad sense of "existentially significant meaning," was inevitably implicated in an arrangement that integrates Canada more closely with the U.S. economy. Culture, economics, and politics are not neatly defined categories; they intersect and overlap. It would have been impossible to keep culture out of an economic and political deal of the magnitude of the FTA. The discourse about "keeping culture of the table" was misleading. The Americans never understood it, and for good reason.

The Mulroney government's cultural policies lacked clarity and coherence. The government promoted policies to build up Canada's cultural industries as part of an economic-development strategy and then suggested that culture was somehow off-limits from trade negotiations. It said that the CBC was an important institution for the development of national consciousness, while not explaining how it was supposed to do that job with reduced funding. It dramatically cut funding to cultural agencies in the 1985 budget, calling on the private sector to pick up the slack, only to restore the funding substantially with targeted initiatives in the 1986 budget. It celebrated the renewal of free enterprise and market forces in Canadian society, without providing a clear plan for private-sector participation in developing and promoting Canadian culture. It was not enough to say to the private sector "spend more money on culture" or to say to artists "market your product more effectively." The private sector had to be engaged and mobilized in specific, concrete ways, as it had been in the music-recording industry with positive results. The same thing had to be done in the other cultural sectors.

British philosopher John Gray tells us that "the innermost contradiction encrypted within New Right thinking has always been between the free market as an engine of wealth-creation and its role as a destroyer of traditional institutions and cultural forms."[123] The free market dissolves cultural traditions when they clash with the ethos of individual freedom and when they do not "make sense" from the point of view of economic efficiency and rational cost-benefit analysis. To the extent that the Mulroney government embraced New Right thinking, it enabled free-market forces to undermine traditional cultural forms. Ironically, one of these "cultural forms" was the Progressive Conservative Party itself. It was a party that had never been a purely rational proposition because it expressed a distinctive set of policies, attitudes, and values that grew out of the Canadian historical experience. Just as Thatcherism destroyed the basis of traditional Toryism and left the Conservative Party in Britain in disarray and confused about its identity,[124] Mulroneyism ended up wiping out the old Progressive Conservative Party of Canada.

But from the ashes has arisen the new Conservative Party under the leadership of Stephen Harper, drawing support from some of the same old Tory sources that backed the Mulroney government. Canadian conservatism has shown an unexpected resilience. By analogy, we do not have to assume that free trade and the free market inevitably spell doom for Canadian culture. Of course, government has an important part to play in protecting and fostering culture, but we should not exaggerate its role. Canadians want to be Canadians; they do not need the government constantly preaching to them about the Canadian identity. But the government has to provide leadership, direction, and strategic financial support. It was not enough for the Mulroney government to cut back old programs and play around the edges with invocations to the private sector to pick up the slack. It needed to have a solid plan that the private sector could accept, and, unfortunately, it did not come up with one.

## NOTES

1 G. Bruce Doern and Brian W. Tomlin, *Faith and Fear: The Free Trade Story* (Toronto: Stoddart 1991), 97.

2 John Tomlinson, *Globalization and Culture* (Chicago: University of Chicago Press 1999), 18. For more discussion of the meaning of "culture," see R. Williams, *Culture* (London: Fontana 1981); J. Clifford *The Predicament of Culture* (Cambridge, Mass.: Harvard University Press 1988); J.B. Thompson, *Ideology and Modern Culture* (Cambridge, U.K.: Polity Press 1990); J. McGuigan, *Cultural Populism* (London: Routledge 1992).

3 Tomlinson, *Globalization and Culture,* 20.

4 Bernard Ostry, *The Cultural Connection: An Essay on Culture and Government Policy in Canada* (Toronto: McClelland and Stewart 1978), 1.

5 Tomlinson, *Globalization and Culture,* 19.

6 Ibid., 18.

7 Ibid.

8 Ibid.,19.

9 Ibid., 2.

10 Ibid., 20.

11 Ibid., 64.

12 Ibid., 71.

13 H.I. Schiller, "Transnational Media and National Development," in K. Nordenstreng and H.I. Schiller, eds., *National Sovereignty and International Communication* (Norwood, N.J.: Ablex 1979), 21–32.

14 Marci McDonald, *Yankee Doodle Dandy: Brian Mulroney and the American Agenda* (Toronto: Stoddart 1995), 165.

15 Richard J. Barnet and John Cavanagh, *Global Dreams: Imperial Corporations and the New World Order* (New York: Simon and Schuster 1994), 25.

16 Jose Joffe, "The Perils of Soft Power: Why America's Cultural Influence Makes Enemies, Too," *New York Times Magazine,* 14 May 2006, 15.

17 Ted Magder, "Film and Video Production," in Michael Dorland, ed., *The Cultural Industries in Canada: Problems, Policies and Prospects* (Toronto: James Lorimer 1996), 146.
18 Joyce Zemans, *Where Is Here? Canadian Culture in a Globalized World* (North York, Ont.: Robarts Centre for Canadian Studies 1997).
19 Canada, Department of Communications, *Vital Links: Canadian Cultural Industries* (Ottawa: Minister of Supply and Services 1987), cited in Zemans, *Where Is Here?*
20 McDonald, *Yankee Doodle Dandy*, 187.
21 Cited in Michael Hart, with Bill Dymond and Colin Robertson, *Decision at Midnight: Inside the Canada-US Free-Trade Negotiations* (Vancouver: University of British Columbia Press 1994), 264.
22 Victor Rabinovitch, "The Social and Economic Rationales for Domestic Cultural Policies," in Dennis Browne, ed., *The Culture/Trade Quandary: Canada's Policy Options* (Ottawa: Centre for Trade Policy and Law 1998), 31.
23 H.I. Schiller, "Electronic Information Flows: New Basis for Global Domination?" in P. Drummond and R. Paterson, eds., *Television in Transition* (London: BFI Publishing 1986).
24 Serge Latouche, *The Westernization of the World* (Cambridge, U.K. Polity Press 1996), xii, 3.
25 Tomlinson, *Globalization and Culture*, 89.
26 Ibid., 90.
27 Ibid., 100.
28 Anthony Smith, "Towards a Global Culture?" in M. Featherstone, ed., *Global Culture, Nationalism, Globalization and Modernity* (London: Sage 1990), 179.
29 William Christian, *George Grant: A Biography* (Toronto: University of Toronto Press 1993), 363.
30 Paul Litt, *The Muses, The Masses, and the Massey Commission* (Toronto: University of Toronto Press 1992), 248.
31 Royal Commission on National Development in the Arts, Letters and Sciences, *Report* (Ottawa, 1951), 274–5.
32 Kevin Dowler, "The Cultural Industries Policy Apparatus," in Dorland, ed., *The Cultural Industries in Canada*, 330.
33 Cited in Joel Smith, *Unwarranted Hopes and Unfulfilled Expectations: Canadian Media Policy and the* CBC (Orono, Me.: Canadian-American Centre 1999), 5.
34 Canada, Department of Finance, *A New Direction for Canada: An Agenda for Economic Renewal*, presented by the Hon. Michael H. Wilson, Minister of Finance, 8 November 1984, 25–6.
35 McDonald, *Yankee Doodle Dandy*, 188.
36 D. Paul Schafer and André Fortier, *Review of Federal Policies for the Arts in Canada, 1944–1988* (Ottawa: Canadian Conference of the Arts 1989), 50.
37 Department of Finance, Canada, Budget Papers, tabled in the House of Commons by the Hon. Michael H. Wilson, 23 May 1985, 58.
38 Ibid.

39 Canada, *Funding of the Arts in Canada to the Year 2000: The Report of the Task Force on Funding of the Arts* (Ottawa: Minister of Supply and Services 1986), 26.
40 Ibid., 7.
41 Ibid., 55.
42 Ibid., 87.
43 Ibid., 75.
44 Ibid., 63.
45 Ibid., 69.
46 John C. Crosbie (with Geoffrey Stevens), *No Holds Barred: My Life in Politics* (Toronto: McClelland and Stewart 1997), 252.
47 Hugh Winsor, "Team Disputes Effect of Cultural Spending," *Globe and Mail*, 12 March 1986.
48 Ibid.
49 Ibid.
50 *Culture and Communications: A Study Team Report to the Task Force on Program Review* (Ottawa: Minister of Supply and Services Canada 1986), 42.
51 Ibid., 16–17.
52 Ibid., 76.
53 Schafer and Fortier, *Review of Federal Policies for the Arts in Canada*, 57.
54 "Artists Stage Rally to Protest Cutbacks in Cultural Budget," *Globe and Mail*, 18 March 1985.
55 Letter to the editor from Jim Lotz, Toronto, *Globe and Mail*, 23 March 1985.
56 "Who Needs Artists," *Globe and Mail*, 23 March 1985.
57 "$75 Million for Arts Seen as Olive Branch after Last Year's Cuts," *Globe and Mail*, 27 February 1986.
58 Schafer and Fortier, *Review of Federal Policies for the Arts in Canada*, 50.
59 Department of Finance, Canada, Budget Papers, tabled in the House of Commons by the Hon. Michael H. Wilson, 26 February 1986, 23.
60 "'There Is Encouragement,' Film Producers Say of Fund," *Globe and Mail*, 27 February 1986.
61 *Culture and Communications*, 300.
62 McDonald, *Yankee Doodle Dandy*, 162.
63 Ibid., 163.
64 Ibid., 165.
65 John Partridge, "Publishing Policy Imperils U.S. Ties, Ambassador Says," *Globe and Mail*, 4 November 1985.
66 John Partridge and Christopher Waddell, "Nationalist Publishers Condemn Gotlieb," *Globe and Mail*, 5 November 1985.
67 Ibid.
68 McDonald, *Yankee Doodle Dandy*, 175.
69 Ibid., 176.
70 Ibid., 177.
71 Ibid.

72 Ibid.
73 Ibid., 178.
74 Ibid., 180.
75 Andrew Cohen, "Film Policy Stirs Trade Fears," *Financial Post*, 2 March 1987.
76 Ibid.
77 Hugh Winsor, "Liberal MP Leaks Delayed Film Legislation," *Globe and Mail*, 26 November 1987.
78 McDonald, *Yankee Doodle Dandy*, 190.
79 Ibid., 191.
80 Ibid., 192.
81 Ibid., 194.
82 James King, *Jack: A Life with Writers; the Story of Jack McClelland* (Toronto: Knopf 1999), 221.
83 Jack McClelland, "Once upon a Time There Was a Country Called Canada," in *If You Love This Country: Facts and Feelings on Free Trade Assembled by Laurier LaPierre* (Toronto: McClelland and Stewart 1987), 246.
84 Will Straw, "Sound Recording," in Dorland, ed. *The Cultural Industries in Canada*, 95.
85 Ibid., 106.
86 Ibid.
87 Magder, "Film and Video Production," 167.
88 Ibid., 150.
89 Ibid., 174.
90 Bernard Ostry, "Culture and Trade: One Policy/No Options," in Browne, ed., *The Culture/Trade Quandary*, 22.
91 Steven Globerman, *Culture, Governments and Markets: Public Policy and the Culture Industries* (Vancouver: Fraser Institute 1987), 32.
92 *Our Cultural Sovereignty: The Second Century of Canadian Broadcasting*, Report of the Standing Committee on Canadian Heritage (Ottawa: Communication Canada Publishing 2003), 17–18.
93 Raboy, "Public Television," in Dorland, ed. *The Cultural Industries in Canada*, 192. *Report of the Task Force on Broadcasting Policy* (Ottawa: Minister of Supply and Services Canada 1986), 703.
94 Ibid., 152.
95 Edward Greenspon, "CBC Growth Plan 'Extravagant,'" *Globe and Mail*, 23 September 1986.
96 Hugh Winsor, "Boost Canadian Content, Task Force Recommends," *Globe and Mail*, 23 September 1986.
97 *Report of the Task Force on Broadcasting Policy*, 285.
98 "Tories Slowly Killing CBC, Berton Claims," *Winnipeg Free Press*, 19 October 1986.
99 Jeffrey Simpson, "Broadcasting Limbo," *Globe and Mail*, 9 September 1987.
100 Hugh Winsor, "CBC to Become Unrecognizable in Wake of Cuts, Juneau Tells MPs," *Globe and Mail*, 25 May 1989.

101 Bronwyn Drani, "CBC Appointments Allow Scope for Hope and Fear," *Globe and Mail*, 14 October 1989.
102 Raboy, "Public Television," 189.
103 Ibid.
104 Jennifer Lewington, "Cultural Subsidies Safe from Talks, Clark Says," *Globe and Mail*, 19 November 1985.
105 Christopher Waddell, "U.S. Wants Discussions on Trade Wide Open," *Globe and Mail*, 19 December 1985.
106 Ibid.
107 William Johnson, Jennifer Lewington, and Hugh Winsor, "Mulroney, Reagan Agree on Program for Acid Rain," *Globe and Mail*, 19 March 1986.
108 Jane Taber, "U.S. Official's Trade Remarks Infuriate PM," *Ottawa Citizen*, 5 February 1987.
109 Ibid.
110 Ibid.
111 "Culturally Sensitive," *Globe and Mail*, 5 February 1987.
112 Hart, *Decision at Midnight*, 299.
113 "U.S. May Bend on Key Trade Issues," *Globe and Mail*, 2 October 1987.
114 "U.S. Reported to Accept Key Trade Demand," *Globe and Mail*, 3 October 1987.
115 "Continental Energy Market Part of Deal," *Globe and Mail*, 5 October 1987.
116 "Excerpts from U.S. Statement on the Accord," New York *Times*, 5 October 1987.
117 "Sovereignty Threatened, Critics Say," *Globe and Mail*, 5 October 1987.
118 Ibid.
119 Robert Sheppard, "Peterson Says He Needs 'A Lot of Persuading,'" *Globe and*
120 *Mail*, 6 October 1987.
121 John Partridge, "Cultural Sector in Turmoil, Torn between Hope and Despair," *Globe and Mail*, 6 October 1987.
122 Rick Salutin, "Keep Canadian Culture off the Table – Who's Kidding Who?" in *If You Love This Country*, 206.
123 John Gray, *Endgames: Questions in Late Modern Political Thought* (Cambridge, U.K.: Polity Press 1997), vii.
124 Ibid., viii.

# 15

# Brian Mulroney and the Environment

ELIZABETH MAY

When Brian Mulroney became prime minister of Canada, there was nothing in his background or campaign commitments that suggested a policy agenda which would later earn for him the title of "Canada's Greenest Prime Minister."[1] In fact, Mulroney's first choice to head the Department of Environment was disastrous and threatened to establish him as a prime minister completely lacking in environmental sensitivities. In hindsight, one might want to credit that first decision as the impetus that propelled him to build a great record in environmental policy. By 1993 and the end of a nine-year term of office, Mulroney had indeed achieved, both domestically and internationally, an impressive environmental record, one that surpasses that of any other prime minister. Even considering the environmental losses occasioned by the Free Trade Agreement (FTA), Mulroney's record is unquestionably outstanding.

Prime Minister Mulroney placed acid rain as his top bilateral issue when he was dealing with the United States. He also insisted on positive action at home, and, to this end, negotiated agreements with the seven eastern provinces to cut acid rain-causing emissions by 50 per cent. Ultimately, the United States agreed to the same binding target. Mulroney's government also negotiated in 1987 a binding international agreement to protect the ozone layer in the Montreal Protocol on Substances that Deplete the Ozone Layer (the "Montreal Protocol"), created eight new national parks (including South Moresby, for which Mulroney had to negotiate personally with British Columbia Premier William Vander Zalm), and took an early lead in demanding global action against the threat of climate change. He was the first international leader to sign the Rio Conventions to fight climate change and protect biodiversity. He also approved a $3-billion Green Plan for Canada, elevated the environment minister to the powerful Priorities and Planning (P&P) committee of cabinet, and made numerous

In 1991 Prime Minister Mulroney and U.S. President George Bush, Sr, signed the Canada-United States Air Quality Accord to reduce emissions of sulphur dioxide and nitrogen oxide, both of which contributed to acid rain. Photographer Bill McCarthy. Library and Archives Canada 91-C-9293-17A, negative number e006610657.

commitments to protect Great Lakes water, clean up the St Lawrence River, and preserve the Arctic National Wildlife Refuge.

No one other than Brian Mulroney can easily explain how his government developed such aggressive and trend-setting environmental policy. However, as an environmental activist and as a former senior policy adviser to Tom McMillan, one of Mulroney's environment ministers, I was able to observe some of the process. This chapter offers a highly personal and speculative reflection on how a champion of corporate Canada came to be lauded as an environmental prime minister.

## PHASE ONE: BLAIS-GRENIER

When Brian Mulroney came to be feted at an Earth Day Gala on 20 April 2006 at the Chateau Laurier Hotel in Ottawa, he delivered an impassioned address to a packed ballroom. Two of the best environment ministers in Canadian history were present that evening: Jean Charest, who was premier of Quebec at the time of the 2006 dinner, and Tom McMillan. Mulroney acknowledged and thanked them both, while also paying tribute to a third environment minister, Robert de Cotret, who had since passed away. In a spirit of great generosity and forgiveness, he thanked as well another superb former environment minister who was not present, his former friend Lucien Bouchard. Left un-thanked and unmentioned was Mulroney's first choice for the environment portfolio, Suzanne Blais-Grenier. In my opinion, the appointment of Blais-Grenier can be most likely attributed to Mulroney's penchant for advancing women within the civil service and his cabinet. It is, in my judgment, unlikely that he chose her in the belief that she would advocate mining and logging in national parks, which is what she did.

Blais-Grenier was a first-time MP in 1984 with an academic background in sociology and economics. Without any experience in environmental issues, she clearly hoped to gain a more important portfolio by pleasing her political masters through severe budget-cutting measures. The first sign that all was not well in Environment Canada came when reports surfaced in Ottawa that the new minister had crossed swords with her deputy minister. Jacques Gérin was widely respected in the non-governmental community and in the civil service. A civil servant with an engineering background, he was erudite, and one would have imagined that, as a francophone, he would have been the ideal deputy to a new francophone minister. Instead, it seemed that Blais-Grenier became convinced early on that every piece of advice proffered by her deputy was designed to undermine her. When Gérin warned her against cutting one-third of the wildlife biologists from the Canadian Wildlife Service (CWS) because such an action would arouse an angry, wildlife-loving public, she became even more certain that such cuts were essential. Like Briar Rabbit and the Tar Baby, she was sure that Gérin knew that cutting one-third of the CWS was brilliant and only wanted to stop her from making a move that would gain her great credit. The more he urged her not to cut the staff, the more determined she was to do so.

Although Blair-Grenier ignored her deputy's warnings and pushed ahead with the massive reductions, she faced an unprecedented barrage of criticism. Far from realizing her mistake, however, she became even more convinced of the duplicitous nature of her deputy. She was also prone to saying and doing inappropriate things. Her musings to the media that it seemed overly rigid to her to insist that one could never approve mining or logging inside national parks did not help her public image, nor did it help her keep her position at the cabinet table. Her final undoing resulted from the lavish use of limousines on a European trip, during which she commandeered a diplomatic car in Canada's mission to Finland and had the driver take her and her husband on a road tour from St Petersberg to Paris. People still talk about her indiscretion in embassy circles. She was removed from the cabinet in the late summer of 1985 for the "limo scandal." By then, Mulroney must have realized that he needed a true supporter of the environment to clean house. The real tragedy of Blais-Grenier's tenure was Jacques Gérin's decision to escape a nasty relationship by fleeing the department just days before her departure was announced. Regrettably, the clerk of the Privy Council did not try and convince Gérin to stay and work with the new minister.

## PHASE TWO: TOM McMILLAN

Tom McMillan had also been elected in the 1984 "Blue Tide." As a new MP from Charlottetown, Prince Edward Island, his first cabinet portfolio had been as minister of tourism. His brother Charlie was known as a brilliant strategist and was an insider in the Prime Minister's Office. Although younger brother Tom tended to be dismissed as a "pretty boy," he was smart and willing to roll up his sleeves and undo the damage of his predecessor. Tom McMillan would preside over one of the most productive and environmentally successful periods ever in the federal government. From 1985 to 1988, when he lost his seat in the general election, McMillan transformed a growing "brown" reputation for the Mulroney government into one that was genuinely green. As a member of his political staff from 1986 to 1988, I am clearly biased on this point. I was brought into the minister's office despite my lack of a membership card in any political party. Sadly, I left, not on the best terms, over a deal to trade dams in Saskatchewan for the Grant Devine government's agreement to translate its statutes into French. These admissions should go some way to balancing any perceived bias to exaggerate the record.

As environment minister, Tom McMillan had Mulroney's support and interest. Early in McMillan's tenure, Mulroney placed acid rain at the top of his bilateral agenda in dealings with the United States. His famous relationship with Ronald Reagan would be put to the test on this issue.

The 1970s were a decade when regulators believed that "dilution is the solution to pollution." At that time, factories in both Canada and the United States were required by government regulations to provide clean air in local areas. The immediate industrial response was to build taller smokestacks, and, as expected, the higher stacks emitted the pollution at such heights that it moved pollutants away from local communities and improved air quality in the immediate vicinity of industrial plants – and made things worse elsewhere. Acid rain from both Canadian and the American industry was moving cross-border, creating a regional North American problem of acidification which killed rivers, lakes, and streams and contributed to the destruction of forests across Canada. The country's lakes and rivers were acidifying and the reason was no secret. Acidic deposition from smelters and coal plants was killing them: sulphur from high smokestacks travelled thousands of kilometres and fell to earth as sulphuric acid. Quebec was experiencing "maple die-back," alarming both maple-syrup producers and the tourism industry. Acid rain was also recognized as a regional threat in northern Europe.

The Canadian government recognized the threat. The first environment minister to put his stamp on the issue was John Fraser, a member of the short-lived government of Joe Clark. Fraser insisted that the bureaucracy cease referring to Long Range Transport of Acidic Precipitation (LRTAP) and instead call it "acid rain." Later, in opposition, he approached the newly minted Liberal environment minister, John Roberts, to urge that the federal government provide critical financial support to the Canadian Coalition on Acid Rain (CCAR). It was the CCAR that took the story of dead Canadian lakes and rivers directly to our U.S. neighbours whose pollution was causing the damage. The organization lobbied effectively, building common cause with environmentally responsible members of the U.S. Congress, like Senator George Mitchell of Maine, whose state was also experiencing acidification.

The Mulroney government recognized that persuading the United States to accept a shared continental approach to acid rain would take more than hectoring. Canada decided to move with a "clean hands" policy. This meant getting our own house in order before approaching the United States for binding reductions in emissions of sulphur dioxide. The strategy worked. Over 1986 and 1987, the federal government achieved binding reduction commitments (of 50 per cent reductions of $SO_2$) from the seven eastern provinces. Then, and only then, did Mulroney turn to the United States. When he addressed a joint session of Congress in 1988, he was able to point to Canada's achievement and say: "We ask nothing more than this from you." He also asked this pointed question: "What would be said of a generation of Americans and Canadians who found a way to explore the stars, but allowed their lakes and forests and streams to languish and die?"

Mulroney himself has since given a glimpse of how he persuaded President Reagan to reach an agreement. The following excerpt from the former prime minister's speech at the 2006 Earth Day Gala is even more remarkable when one recalls that Reagan had initially said that acid rain was caused by ducks:

> Let me illustrate with the example of acid rain, which I raised with President Reagan on my first visit to the White House when I was still Leader of the Opposition in June 1984. In March 1985, at the Shamrock Summit, he agreed to the appointment of special envoys, Drew Lewis and Bill Davis, who reported directly to us. Frank Carlucci, President Reagan's National Security Advisor, describes how testy Reagan became when his officials continued to stall and stymie my government on issues ranging from acid rain to Arctic sovereignty to free trade. According

to a recent account published by Professor Jeffrey L. Chidester, Research Director for Presidential and Special Projects at the University of Virginia, before entering 24 Sussex, Reagan took Carlucci aside and said: "'I think we should do something for Brian.'" "I [Carlucci] said: 'Mr. President, we're doing well holding our positions on acid rain, the free trade agreement and the Northwest passage.' 'Oh, no, no, no,' said Reagan, 'we ought to do something.'

"After lunch, Carlucci continued to push for the American position. 'I said [to the President] no, no, we're holding to our positions. These are well established positions.'

"It was the only time [says Carlucci] I saw Ronald Reagan lose his temper. He turned to me and said: 'You do it.' Carlucci went right from the meeting and grabbed Derek Burney, Mulroney's Chief of Staff and asked: 'Derek would you reiterate your positions [on acid rain, trade and the Northwest passage?]' When Burney asked why, Carlucci said: 'Because they're our positions now.'

"Immediately after that exchange President Reagan sat with his cabinet officials and senior advisors behind closed doors in the living room at 24 Sussex and amended his speech to Parliament slated for that afternoon. He wrote that he 'agreed to consider' a bilateral agreement with Canada over acid rain and added a promise 'to inject new impetus' into talks regarding recognition of Canadian sovereignty over the Arctic." Professor Chidester concluded: "Personal diplomacy was the only way to break the bureaucratic inertia on these issues."[2]

The end result, said Mulroney, was that "in 1991, we signed the Acid Rain Accord with the first President Bush. Both President Reagan and President Bush rejected the advice of their officials on acid rain, because of the special relationship between the United States and Canada, and the personal rapport between President and Prime Minister."[3]

Meanwhile, the first major threat to the global atmosphere had been identified: ozone depletion. The Vienna Convention was the first multilateral treaty calling on nations to move towards global action to arrest this planetary threat. The saga of how Dupont, the world's largest manufacturer of ozone-depleting chlorofluorocarbons (CFCs), went from denying the problem to ridiculing it, accepting it, and, finally, supporting global action has been well documented by Paul Brodeur in a landmark series of articles in the *New Yorker*. Progress towards global action on ozone depletion had been in high-gear under President Jimmy Carter, but it was shelved in the early Reagan years, only to be advanced by stealth under the leadership of a truly heroic head of the U.S. Environmental Protection Agency, Lee Thomas. Thomas worked in the ongoing United Nations Environment Programme process within the Vienna Convention. By the time that U.S. Secretary of the Interior Don Hodell woke up to the reality that the United States was faced with a growing global diplomatic consensus that ozone-depleting substances would have to be banned, he was too late to do more than utter threats. Hodell memorably urged that no action should take place, expressing instead a preference for broad-brimmed hats and sunscreen.

The Canadian government and its scientists were in the lead on protecting the ozone layer. Canadian scientists led in the research area and were willing to act as advocates, and Canadian legal experts chaired the group drafting the text of what was to become the Montreal Protocol.[4] On 17 September 1987 representatives of nearly every country on earth gathered in Montreal and, after tense and often deadlocked negotiations, signed the most significant global treaty to protect life on earth since the 1962 Treaty to End Atmospheric Nuclear Weapons Testing. The Montreal Protocol committed industrialized nations to reducing emissions, while allowing developing countries to increase use by 10 per cent. The protocol included a mechanism to address global poverty and inequity, laying the ground for full elimination of ozone-depleting substances through subsequent action. Prime Minister Mulroney recalled the process of bringing industry on-side in his Earth Day Gala speech: "In 1987, when we signed the Montreal Protocol, we made it very clear to DuPont, the largest manufacturer of CFCs, that there was no turning back from our resolve to eliminate these dangerous ozone-depleting substances. DuPont responded to the challenge by creating innovative technologies that have only made the company more profitable, as well as a world leader in environmental responsibility."[5]

The next major global atmospheric challenge was the threat of climate change. Through my years in the office of the federal minister of the environment, government scientists expressed growing concerns about this issue. It was clear that the burning of fossil fuels was potentially threatening the stability of the entire planet's climate system. Millennia of climate stability, which had allowed the development of global civilization, was at immediate risk. With the acid rain issue in hand and the United Nations Convention and Montreal Protocol to protect the ozone layer concluded, the federal government turned its attention to the threat of climate change. In June 1988 Canada was, again, in the global lead in hosting the first-ever international scientific conference on climate change designed to give the issue a public face. The conference, which took place in the midst of a Toronto heatwave, was titled "Our Changing Atmosphere: Implications for Global Security" and was co-sponsored by the world Meteorological Organization and the United Nations Environment Programme.

Prime Minister Mulroney opened the conference, and the prime minister of Norway, Dr Gro Harlem Brundtland, was one of the keynote speakers. Mulroney spoke of the need for an international law of the atmosphere, citing Canada's work on acid rain and ozone as the first planks in this growing area of international environmental governance. The scientists gathered in Toronto told the world, in clear, unambiguous language, about the nature of the threat posed by climatic change. The consensus statement that emerged from the conference was dire in its warnings: "Humanity is conducting an unintended, uncontrolled, globally pervasive experiment, whose ultimate consequences are second only to global nuclear war." The threat of climate change was clearly on Canada's agenda by 1988.

Not all environmental challenges facing the Mulroney government were global, however. One of the most significant environmental issues in which the prime minister became personally involved was the fight to protect the southern third of the Queen Charlotte Islands, an area known as "South Moresby." The South Moresby area is an archipelago of hundreds of islands, large and small, and often described as the "Canadian Galapagos." It contains more species of rare plants and animals than anywhere else in Canada, and its ancient temperate forest holds trees that had been saplings when Jesus walked the earth. And it was under imminent threat as the chainsaws moved into the pristine watersheds.

By July 1987, the cause of saving South Morseby had been championed by every major conservation group in Canada, as well as by the royal families of the United Kingdom and the Netherlands. Canada's leading environmentalist, Dr David Suzuki, and the popular CBC television program he hosted, "The Nature of Things," took up the campaign. Faced with an intense public outcry, which grew especially furious when Haida elders were arrested on the logging roads at Lyell Island – the House of Commons passed an all-party resolution in support of saving the area. Tom McMillan worked in close alliance with the local New Democrat MP, Jim Fulton, and a number of key Liberals, including former environment minister Charles Caccia. The speaker of the House, John Fraser, referred to the struggle as the "conspiracy to save the planet." Then, despite all the public support, the government of British Columbia broke off negotiations with Ottawa to create a national park and proclaimed that there would be a provincial park instead. This provincial initiative provided for a much smaller park which would encompass the mostly rocky islands but offer little protection for the trees and other vegetation.

Ultimately, Prime Minister Mulroney personally intervened by calling British Columbia Premier Vander Zalm to revive the negotiations.[6] As the negotiations between British Columbia and Ottawa reached their endgame, a logging contractor sent his men into triple shifts, clear-cutting around the clock to log as much of South Morseby as possible. The logging reached the crest of a watershed called Windy Bay on Lyell Island, which conservationists had identified as the jewel in the emerald chain of islands. The chainsaws were heard in Windy Bay where a Haida encampment had planned a blockade and waited for a fresh conflict. But the blockades were never needed. The two governments reach an agreement and the logging was stopped. The saving of South Moresby remains one of Canada's great conservation achievements.

The McMillan years were amazingly productive. Canada played an important role in supporting and then welcoming the Report of the World Commission on Environment and Development (the "Brundtland Report"). Canada supported the Brundtland Commission's recommendation for a major United Nations Summit on the Environment for 1992. This eventually became the Rio Earth Summit, which led to positive results on a variety of fronts: the introduction of further measures to control acid rain and ozone depletion, the creation of five new national parks, the conclusion of a Great Lakes Water Quality Accord, the development of a plan to clean up the St Lawrence River, the passage of Canada's first (nearly) comprehensive toxic-chemical legislation, the beginning of efforts to make environmental-impact assessments a mandatory part of the federal policy-planning process, and the provision of greater support for small environmental groups across Canada. Observers might have had reason to fear for continued success when McMillan lost his seat in the 1988 election. Instead, the environmental performance of the Mulroney government just got better.

## THE BOUCHARD ERA

Ask any bureaucrat in the government of Canada to name the best minister of the environment in Canadian history, and it is uncanny how many will reply, without hesitation, Lucien Bouchard. They all tell the same story. When briefing Bouchard on any issue, he would ask a blunt question: "What is the right decision for the environment?" When told the officials' judgment of what the strongest course of action would be, he always replied, "Then that is my decision."

Mulroney had used his personal friendship with the moody and brilliant Bouchard to bring him into the Progressive Conservative and avowedly federalist fold, and Bouchard was reported to have asked to be made minister of the environment. He quickly became a "true believer" in the department's goals. The first significant strengthening of the department's clout in official Ottawa occurred when Mulroney named Bouchard to the P&P committee. Overnight, the minister of the environment moved from being a marginal to a powerful player in the cabinet. Bouchard soon decided that the department was badly under-resourced. He began working towards a $5-billion fund to be committed over five years to environmental projects, an initiative he dubbed the "Green Plan."[7] It was also under Bouchard that Canada committed in 1990 to the nation's first greenhouse-gas reduction target: freezing Canadian emissions at 1990 levels, so that by 2000 they would be no higher than they had been in 1990.

Yet, within days of making that commitment in Bergen, Norway, Bouchard abandoned the government, created the Bloc Québécois, and left a far less effective minister, Robert De Cotret, to pick up the pieces. It is worthy of note that Bouchard had made the greenhouse-gas commitment unilaterally, without prior cabinet approval. To the credit of the Conservative government and Mulroney, the cabinet approved Bouchard's targets after Bouchard had left its ranks.

De Cotret remained on P&P committee and continued the long-term process of moving Environment Canada towards a more significant role within the federal system. Unfortunately, de Cotret did not support his officials as his predecessor had. No Bouchard, de Cotret caved in to Grant Devine, once again on those same damnable dams over which I had resigned. By this time, the Federal Court had ruled that the original decision to permit the dams was illegal because a federal environmental assessment had not taken place. A federal panel, by court order, was then examining the second of the two dams. De Cotret promised Divine that the dam could go ahead. The entire environmental-assessment panel on the Alameda Dam quit in protest.

## CHAREST AND THE RIO EARTH SUMMIT

Brian Mulroney chose one of his youngest ministers to replace de Cotret. Jean Charest had been minister for youth, and he had, ironically, played a key role in the political firefight that prompted Bouchard's resignation over federal relations with the province of Quebec. Charest would have little time to adjust to his portfolio. The biggest files moving through his office concerned the 1992 Rio Earth summit, the world's largest-ever gathering of heads of government. Negotiations to achieve a binding convention in time for Rio were to span two years. To head Canada's efforts, Mulroney created a diplomatic post, the ambassador for environment and sustainable development, who was to work alongside the environment minister. He appointed one of his best friends from law school and articling days, Arthur Campeau, as the first ambassador. Campeau was a card-carrying Liberal when appointed, and, distrusted by official Ottawa, he had to earn his acceptance in the Environment Department and the ranks of the civil service in Foreign Affairs. As it turned out, he passed with flying colours. Canada took an early lead in the first preparatory meeting for the Earth Summit in August 1990 when Campeau refused to negotiate any issues until the participatory rights of civil-society and non-governmental organizations were settled.

When the Convention on Climate Change was under threat from U.S. opposition leading up to the Rio Earth Summit, the White House tried to have Campeau fired. Yet Mulroney not only stuck by Campeau but stood up to the first President George Bush on a key environmental issue. Though Bush announced that he would not sign the other major accomplishment of the Earth Summit, the Convention to Protect Biological Diversity, Campeau urged Mulroney to commit Canada to the treaty. Other G-7 nations were also waffling on the matter, and the protection of the species and spaces of the planet hung in the balance. Mulroney took Campeau's advice and, less than twenty-four hours after Bush had made his position known, Canada led the industrialized world in signing and supporting that important tool to protect vanishing nature on this beleaguered planet. Canada was the first industrialized country to sign and ratify both conventions.

Throughout this period, Mulroney also created new institutions to bring governmental decision making more closely in line with the concept of "sustainable development." He created the International Institute for Sustainable Development, based in Winnipeg, as well as the National Round Table on Environment and Economy. Both institutions are dedicated to the principle that the best economic decisions are the best ecological decisions, and their goal is to develop practical approaches that put that principle into effect.

## LOST GROUND

We have clearly lost ground on the priority given environmental policy under each prime minister since Brian Mulroney. Mulroney's speech on 20 April 2006 speech made it clear that he is still concerned about the large environmental issues. He warned those present that "if global warming is not arrested, climate change may be irreversible. In the fall of 2005, we witnessed the perfect storms of global warming – the hurricanes that slammed the Gulf Coast, incubated in the warm waters of the Gulf of Mexico and the Caribbean. The trends are clear – more Category 4 and 5 hurricanes, higher storm surges, serious loss of forests to pine beetles as in British Columbia, earlier spring, hotter summers and warmer winters."

This is not the kind of language that Prime Minister Stephen Harper uses (I have observed with great regret that, under Harper, the term "sustainable development" has been erased from approved "government-speak"). On the other hand, both of Harper's immediate predecessors, Paul Martin and Jean Chrétien, recognized the threat to the environment. To Martin's credit, his government actually developed an environmental strategy that was the best thing the environmental community had seen since Mulroney's Green Plan.

No assessment of Mulroney's environmental record can ignore the fact that the North American Free Trade Agreement (NAFTA) has seriously threatened Canada's ability to protect the environment and human health.

The investment provisions of NAFTA's Chapter 11 have led Canada, in response to legal challenges, to repeal laws it had passed in the public interest, and even to apologize and pay damages to U.S. corporations. This has had a huge chilling effect on regulators. Similarly, NAFTA's Energy Chapter, which commits Canada to preferential energy exports to the United States, is of serious concern. Canada's team in the NAFTA negotiations also refused to heed objections from McMillan's office that our right to protect Canadian water from bulk export was inadequately protected. This issue may still undermine Mulroney's green legacy. Even so, that legacy illustrates that progress on the environment can be made when a government sets a clear goal and remains committed to it in the face of recalcitrant industries, wavering provinces, and even a hostile United States.

## NOTES

1 "Corporate Knights" magazine contest, June 2005.

2 Notes for an Address by the Right Honourable Brian Mulroney Accepting the Award as the Greenest Prime Minister in Canadian History. Chateau Laurier Hotel, Ottawa, Ontario, April 20, 2006.

3 Ibid.

4 See http://archives.cbc.ca/400d.asp?id=1-75-316-1642-10&wm6=1 for a video clip of Tom McMillan, minister of the environment, and others, including Canada's recently appointed ambassador to Israel who chaired the drafting committee.

5 Notes for an Address by the Right Honourable Brian Mulroney Accepting the Award as the Greenest Prime Minister in Canadian History.

6 For a more complete account of the campaign to save South Moresby, see my *Paradise Won: The Struggle to Save South Moresby* (Toronto: McClelland and Stewart 1990).

7 The Green Plan was eventually released under minister Jean Charest and provided $3 billion over six years.

# 16

# Governing from the Centre: Reflections on the Mulroney Cabinet

JOHN C. CROSBIE

The Canadian system of parliamentary and cabinet government is modelled after that of Great Britain, but the system, including the role of the prime minister, has changed immensely, both in Great Britain and in Canada, since the latter part of the nineteenth century. There is no longer even any pretence that the prime minister is "the first among equals"' – he has become an imperial "potentate," similar to the president in the American system. When he has a majority in the House of Commons, the prime minister proposes and disposes. He invites MPs to join the cabinet, and, before he does so, he and his closest advisers make all decisions on the government structure and the system of reaching decisions. The minister, therefore, has to operate within the bounds of the government structure that he finds. Today, the prime minister is at the centre of power, and a minister who does not have a good relationship with the prime minister is not likely to accomplish much. As I said in my autobiography, *No Holds Barred – My Life in Politics*:

> Television, scientific polling, and modern communications have exalted him [the prime minister]. The Prime Minister is pre-eminent. He's at the centre of the spider's web of power. He has his own staff in the Prime Minister's Office (PMO) to provide him with political intelligence, the Privy Council Office (PCO) to oversee operations, and the Treasury Board staff to help him control government spending. The officials in the Department of Finance are at his beck and call for advice on all fiscal and economic matters. He has the power to delay or delete any item on the Cabinet agenda. If he has the energy, the will and the interest, he can control everything of any significance that happens in his administration. No mere Cabinet Minister can hope to compete with the influence of the Prime Minister.[1]

This was the case with the government of Prime Minister Brian Mulroney.

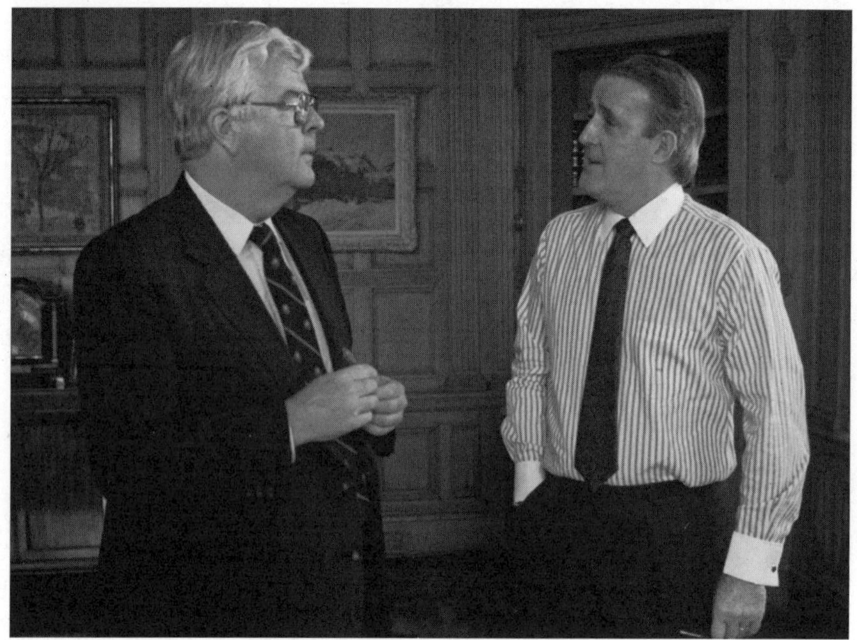

John Crosbie and Brian Mulroney in the Prime Minister's Office, March 1991. Crosbie held several portfolios in Mulroney's cabinet from 1984 to 1993. Photographer Bill McCarthy. Library and Archives Canada 91-C-09272-24, negative number e006610659.

As Donald J. Savoie explains in *The Politics of Public Spending in Canada,*[2] Prime Minister Mulroney carried on with much of the government machinery put in place by Pierre Trudeau. The priorities and planning committee (P&P) continued as the pre-eminent cabinet committee, chaired by the prime minister himself, with the membership usually limited to the minister of finance, the president of Treasury Board, the chairpersons of the other main cabinet committees, and a handful of senior ministers of whom I was fortunate to be one.[3] The cabinet as a whole numbered around forty members at one point, and usually included thirty-five to forty persons; such numbers meant, however, that the group could not function as an executive body. Then, as now, the cabinet was, in reality, a small caucus and sounding board, while the real power of directing or influencing the direction of the government lay with the P&P, which the prime minister usually attempted to limit to twelve or fourteen ministers. As Savoie points out, the "P&P sets the government's broad political agenda, deals with the major planning elements of government, such as the fiscal framework, 'politically manages' major issues for the government and, like full Cabinet, acts as a court of last resort for Ministers wishing to overturn or amend a Cabinet Committee decision. It also acts as a 'super' co-ordinating committee of Cabinet."[4]

The system was refined by Prime Minister Mulroney, who introduced another coordinating committee of cabinet called the "operations committee." Its first chairman was Deputy Prime Minister Don Mazankowski. Technically, this committee was not a decision-making body but reviewed issues and prepared proposals for the full cabinet or for P&P. It was meant to be a facilitating body. However, my experience was that, once a proposal or an issue and solution had received the blessings of the committee, the minister in charge of that issue was home free. This committee was very effective since its chair was one of Mulroney's most powerful and trusted ministers, and he relied on the committee for advice and looked to it to give "operational directions" to his government. The membership was restricted to the deputy prime minister, as chair, the minister of finance, the president of the Treasury Board, and the chairpersons of the cabinet committees on economic and regional development, social development, and foreign and defence policy, along with several other ministers of whom I was one.

Because of the importance Mulroney attached to controlling the escalating spending and the ever-increasing deficits left by the Trudeau administration, efforts to control spending in the departments was a major preoccupation for the government and its ministers. To deal with the financial problems, Mulroney created the expenditure review committee, which he chaired, with Mazankowski as vice-chair, to ensure that the government's expenditures were directed to its highest priorities and that expenditure control continued to contribute to deficit reduction.[5] As Herman Bakvis notes in his study of regional ministers and their power and influence in the Canadian cabinet, "it is in the Cabinet Committees, and in only certain committees at that, where the truly important bargaining takes place."[6] He concludes that, under Mulroney, the P&P and the economic and regional development committees remained important but "came to be superceded by the Operations and Expenditure Review Committees." It was within the "OPS Committee, whose existence was formalized only in January 1989, that proposals for presentation to P&P were screened and the government's future agenda largely determined. It is not without significance that those Ministers formally designated as a lead Minister for their province are also on these important committees."[7] There were several sectoral-policy committees, including the cabinet committee on economic and regional development (CCERD), the social development committee, the foreign and defence policy committee, the privatization and regulatory affairs committee, and the government operations committee. Each oversaw the spending "envelopes" and dealt with the majority of policy issues in their sectors.[8]

The central agencies included the Prime Minister's Office, the Privy Council Office, and the Federal-Provincial Relations Office (FRPO). The PMO is a partisan, politically oriented, but operationally sensitive central agency with a mandate to connect the political party in power with the bureaucracy and to bring partisan considerations to the attention of the prime minister when he considers proposals coming from departments or issues facing the government. The PMO also determines who has access to the prime minister. The PCO, on the other hand, is staffed by career public servants, and its clerk is also secretary to the cabinet and the most senior federal public servant who also advises the prime minister when he appoints deputy ministers. The PCO was organized to assist in the operation of the cabinet committee system. Moreover, hundreds of people in both the PCO and the PMO keep surveillance over all government departments and activities so that the prime minister will know about any politically important or sensitive issues, or decisions that are being made anywhere in government, so as not to be caught by surprise when some matter becomes politically controversial. The prime minister has an immense apparatus working on his behalf to keep him well advised on everything that is happening in the government and in each department and area where ministers exercise responsibility. He is thoroughly briefed by PMO, PCO, and FPRO officials before he attends any cabinet or cabinet committee meetings, and thus has two steady streams of advice, one about government operations from the PCO, and the other about federal-provincial relations from the FPRO.

There is no doubt that Mulroney favoured the American style of centralized executive government, as did his predecessors, and this was the style practised by his cohorts in the PMO. The nineteenth-century concept of the collegiality of the cabinet, with every member bearing a share of the collective responsibility for the decisions and actions of the government as a whole, is on the verge of vanishing. The PMO obviously believes that all power flows from the centre, from the prime minister and his office, and that the PMO can, and should, be involved in all activities of the government, with or without reference to the minister responsible. Certainly, for the most part, the Mulroney PMO in its early years acted as though it regarded cabinet ministers as impotent appendages. Cabinet ministers were deemed to be dispensable – and to be dispensed with – if, by so doing, the prime minister could be shielded from controversy or criticism. In fact, cabinet shuffles occurred at times when it was felt that ministers need to be realigned for greater effectiveness, or the prime minister and his government needed publicity or wanted to distract attention from some problem not yet disclosed.

When Brian Mulroney was elected as leader of the Progressive Conservative Party in June 1983, he benefited greatly in the policy field by appointing Erik Nielsen as his deputy leader. Nielsen had been house leader and in charge of the party caucus for Joe Clark, and he had worked with Clark after the 1980 election to develop and refine policy positions so as to have them ready for government whenever the next election was called. Clark had appointed Nielsen and Senator Arthur Tremblay, a Quebecer well respected for his intellect, as co-chairs of a policy group that included senior members of Clark's shadow cabinet and staff to provide leadership in developing policy options for the parliamentary caucus. This policy work, which had begun in early 1982, was well under way when Mulroney became leader in 1983.[9] After the leadership convention, Nielsen and Tremblay continued to develop a political and fiscal strategy for a new Conservative government, including the development of a fiscal framework for new policy proposals as well as non-expenditure policy priorities for each of the "fiscal envelopes." They also recommended the order in which things should be done when the Conservatives won power, and developed a detailed blueprint of the approach that should be taken to be the machinery of government once that day arrived.

Mulroney fully supported this process as well as the plan of having all members of the caucus, under the leadership of the official critics, carry out research and prepare advice on various policy options. Special caucuses on policy issues were also held from time to time, with everyone encouraged to put forward their views no matter what subject was under discussion or on what side of the issue they were. In fact, as the planning for the 1984 election began and after Mulroney won election in the District of Central Nova and became leader of the opposition on 6 September 1983, this work was accelerated, and all those who held the position of critics were asked to prepare research papers and policy recommendations. The Conservative caucus reviewed all of this policy work at a meeting in Montebello, Quebec, and Neilson provided Mulroney with four separate reports on policy, the fiscal framework, staffing and appointments, and the machinery of government in June 1984. The result of all this planning was that Mulroney and the party were well prepared to deal with not only policy issues but the machinery of government, staffing, and all relevant matters associated with the transition from opposition to government.

The first important initiative with respect to policy in the Mulroney administration, however, was the creation of the Nielsen Task Force. When the new Conservative cabinet was sworn in on 17 September 1984, Nielsen was appointed as deputy prime minister and president of the Privy Council, and Mulroney also gave him the job of chairing a ministerial task force to review all federal government programs in order to improve their delivery, make them more accessible, and reduce waste and duplication. The federal deficit for the year ending 31 March 1984 had reached a new record of $29.38 billion after a series of record deficits under the Trudeau administration, which held office from 1968 to 1979 and from 1980 to 1984. Finance Minister Michael Wilson, Treasury Board President Robert de Cotret, and I, as justice minister, were appointed to be members with Nielsen, who also insisted that the task force become a joint public and private-sector effort, with the private-sector advisers added on a no-pay basis but with reasonable expenses paid, of course.[10] Given the policy work that had been done when the Conservatives sat as the opposition, the party agreed that there was an urgent need in fiscal policy to control and reduce the level of expenditure that had occurred from 1980 to 1984. This view was reflected in the creation of the Nielsen Task Force, though the minister of finance, Michael Wilson, and his department had to develop the general direction of the government in financial and fiscal policy and that direction was outlined in our first and succeeding budgets. However, the members of caucus also played a role in policy initiation since they could – and did – indicate at the weekly caucus meetings privately where they felt new or revised policies were needed. A further major source of policy development was in the departments of the individual cabinet ministers, since many policy initiatives came forward from the departments and agencies and up through the system for consideration in the appropriate cabinet committees or the P&P committee.

When the task force was first set up, our ministerial colleagues and members of the caucus were quite understanding, supportive, and sympathetic of the need for the government's spending to be curbed and the deficit reduced, but, as the process proceeded and ministers became more involved and interested in their departments and in pursuing and expanding the programs in their own areas, that support lessened. The exercise was sensitive politically, since, whenever it was suggested that a program or service be eliminated, there was a chorus of opposition from all groups that benefited from that particular program or service. Nielsen did not help himself either when, for instance, he recommended the elimination of the Department of Indian Affairs without consulting or advising the minister, David Crombie, let alone the Aboriginal peoples. Such errors caused fierce opposition to the task force and prevented it from achieving its objectives. In fact, the ministers and top officials were almost completely excluded from the process, whereas it would have been better to call on the minister responsible to review the programs of his or her department and then place the results before the task force. The exercise was made even more difficult by Nielsen's insistence that the review be made public as we went along, with the inevitable result that the government came under siege whenever the task force threatened a program that was important to some particular pressure group. The task force also had to contend with the opposition Liberals' and New Democratic Party's vigorous opposition to any attempts by the Mulroney administration to restrain government spending and reduce the rate of spending increases. Because of the frenzied attacks of the opposition on every attempt to reduce spending and control the deficit, the task force soon became a symbol to the public of the Conservative government's "sinister hidden agenda."[11] Perhaps it was for this reason that the government did not act on many of the hundreds of recommendations contained in the task force's twenty-four volumes, which had reviewed 989 federal programs and services, involving annual federal expenditures of more than $92 billion (including tax expenditures in 1984–85). Moreover, as Donald Savioe has shown, the task force itself was consistently divided, with the chair, the minister of finance, and the president of the Treasury Board, on one side, supporting the findings of the various study teams, and the minister of justice, the lone representative from a spending department, on the other side, consistently opposing them. When the study group reports were tabled on 11 March 1986 – they called for expenditure and tax reductions of between $7 to $8 billion, including substantial reductions of subsidies in agriculture, fisheries, transportation, and business – the government chose not to act on many of the recommendations because of attacks by the opposition in the House and from public groups adversely affected by the cuts. Still, most members of the caucus and the cabinet agreed that the burgeoning deficit had to be controlled and spending reduced.

With general agreement on these objectives, it was easier to launch new initiatives or implement changes in policy that did not involve substantial new expenditures. This helped departments, like Justice, where there is always need for reform that usually does not involve large expenditures of money. As a result, the department produced legislation on some difficult and sensitive issues, including divorce, pornography, the sexual exploitation of children, prostitution and street soliciting, abortion, Aboriginal rights, the role of women in the armed forces, the legal protection of the mentally ill, the prosecution of war criminals, the rights of gays and lesbians, and even Senate reform. In the first two years of the Mulroney administration, nineteen bills from Justice were introduced to Parliament, and sixteen of them enacted. In the previous four and a half years, only eleven bills from the Department of Justice had been passed.

One immediate challenge at Justice when the Conservatives came to power was the fact that there were only seven months remaining until section 15, the equality-rights section of the Canadian Charter of Rights and Freedoms, was scheduled to come into force. All federal law had to be made to conform to section 15 by 17 April 1985. There had been little attention given to the matter, and we had to prepare and introduce legislation to amend fifty statutes. We also published a discussion paper on the subject of equality and the federal law which identified a number of significant economic and social issues that might be affected by section 15, including eligibility for unemployment-insurance benefits, mandatory retirement, and the treatment of the mentally challenged by the criminal justice system. The most controversial of these issues were referred to the equality rights subcommittee of the House of Commons justice and legal affairs committee, chaired with enthusiasm by Patrick Boyer of Toronto, whose subcommittee held public hearings and brought forth eighty-five recommendations. After months of explaining the issues to and cajoling cabinet ministers and caucus members, many of whom were not enthusiastic, I announced the government's response to the subcommittee report with a paper entitled "Towards Equality," which unveiled a policy that remains progressive even by today's standards. We recommended eliminating mandatory retirement at age sixty-five in areas under federal jurisdiction. We prohibited discrimination against homosexuals in employment in the federal sector, including in the RCMP and the Canadian Forces. We also expanded the role of women in the armed forces to include combat duty, while commanders retained the discretion to keep women out of the front lines if military effectiveness required it. Since those initiatives were all in areas of exclusive federal jurisdiction, we could act immediately.

New policy or changes to policy initiated by ministers and their departments are well illustrated by what occurred in the Department of Transport. In a June 1986 cabinet shuffle, Don Mazankowski moved from Transport to become deputy prime minister and house leader, and I replaced him as minister of transport. At that time, six ministers were removed, twenty-one were reassigned, and eight new faces were added. The transportation system was about to begin a period of deregulation and privatization, a process favoured by our caucus during its policy discussions and by the shadow cabinet before we formed the government. Mazankowski had proposed a new National Transportation Act, creating a new agency to replace the Canadian Transport Commission. Administrative changes included increased competition for business between different transportation modes; lower costs for air, truck, and rail users in densely populated areas; and the possibility of higher subsidies in more remote areas. The government was considering the sale of Air Canada to private investors and the introduction of user fees for the Coast Guard and other federal navigation services. A parliamentary committee was studying the future prospects of the St Lawrence Seaway and we had to reorganize the movement of western grain to our ports. Both Canadian National and Canadian Pacific had immense problems dealing with the cost of maintaining thousands of kilometres of unnecessary rail lines that previous governments simply would not allow the railways to abandon. Because many changes were needed in the transportation sector, it was an area that experienced intense policy activity.

The number of changes in transportation policy and the ease with which these were accepted by the cabinet and caucus was due to the fact that most of these changes were reviewed, discussed, and approved during the Nielson policy-review process before we became the government. They were popular with the members of our caucus, especially those from the west, and accepted because of the personal popularity of Mazankowski and the support he enjoyed in caucus. The detailed work necessary to prepare legislative amendments and implement the decisions reached was carried out by the personnel of the Department of Transport, and this area of policy innovation went smoothly for all the reasons mentioned.

At the time of the cabinet shuffle, the prime minister corrected a mistake he had made in not creating regional ministers or political ministers to represent each of the provinces in his first cabinet. Rather than following the previous practice of appointing regional ministers to be responsible for advising on patronage matters or for acting with respect to the interests of their provinces in the federal system, Nielsen had devised an elaborate system of provincial action committees to recommend who should get governor-in-council positions. What this did was to undercut the authority of the ministers from the provinces. It reflected the bias in the PMO to have the prime minister and the PMO control everything. The prime minister had to change that system two years into his mandate since, without a strong regional minister as the spokesman and defender of the government in each minister's province, the federal government was vulnerable to the incessant attacks of self-serving premiers only too happy to blame everything on Ottawa.

Obviously, a prime minister does not have the time or the knowledge to involve himself (or herself) in the local controversies that emerge regularly in one or more of the provinces. He needs a regional minister to represent the government in each province to answer allegations and to take the offensive against provincial challengers. In any event, Mulroney decided to make this change in policy and to designate, as the Liberals had done previously, a political minister for each province. In his excellent book, Herman Bakvis deals with regional ministers and their power and influence in the Canadian cabinet.[12] As he shows, a regional minister refers to an individual designated as the "lead" or "political" minister for a particular province. The status and power of regional ministers have evolved over the years, but these ministers have been responsible – and accountable – for the federal party organization in their province or sub-region within a province, and for assisting in the dispensing of patronage.

They have been involved, too, in influencing expenditures affecting their regions made by their own and other departments, while also being responsible for the injection of a regional dimension into delivery of departmental programs. They are the dominant figures within their provincial caucuses at Ottawa, with whom they meet from time to time. Aside from pressing regional concerns in departments and within cabinet, the regional ministers are also responsible for communicating the decisions or views of Ottawa to the regions, explaining the less palatable outcomes of deliberations in the nation's capital to provincial or local constituents, and helping to ensure that local support continues for the federal party. In July 1986 the prime minister announced the appointment of special "political ministers" for each province whose primary responsibilities were to improve the government's direct consultations with the ordinary voters and with the party and to bring to its attention in a political way those concerns that could be addressed most effectively at the federal level.[13]

While Mulroney was originally reluctant to use regional or political ministers – perhaps because he wanted to avoid the confrontations so characteristic of the Trudeau era and to build a consensus with the provinces on major goals – I believe that all experience to date indicates that it is not possible to avoid confrontations between the government of Canada and the provinces. The conflict often stems from the very nature of our federal structure, which makes it difficult to build a consensus with the provinces on major goals. My own experience leaves no doubt that it would have been impossible to deal with the political problems that arose between various provincial administrations in Newfoundland – whether Conservative or Liberal – and the Mulroney government without having the Newfoundland minister recognized as the regional minister for the province and in charge of the relationship between Ottawa and the province. In dealing with the media or the representatives of the province, and in responding to political crises involving both governments, it would not have been possible for the Newfoundland minister to be effective without recognition from the prime minister that he was delegating that minister to be in charge of the relationship. As Bakvis points out, regional ministers could also be used by provincial governments to influence the federal government, while distinct alliances often developed between regional ministers and their provincial governments, regardless of party affiliation.[14]

A further reason prompting Mulroney towards the regional-ministers model was that he learned that the previous administration had a legitimate complaint concerning the lack of credit given by the provinces to the federal government for the transfer and equalization payments they received. The government of Canada needed a direct link to citizens and to regions, and this new emphasis on "direct delivery" provided regional ministers with the opportunity to help shape the outcome of programs designed to recapture the hearts and minds of the Canadian people. The Mulroney government discovered that it was necessary for the government of Canada to battle provincial governments for prestige, authority, and recognition.

The financial policies of the Mulroney cabinet originated through the Department of Finance and its minister in close cooperation with the prime minister. The minister of finance obtained the general approval of the P&P committee shortly before a budget was brought down or a special financial announcement made. The most important challenge facing successive federal governments after 1979 was how to manage restraint and reduce the annual deficits. The government aimed to bring down its first budget in May 1985, and Michael Wilson had indicated in a firm statement in November 1984 that the government would "achieve net expenditure reductions of $15 billion in 1990–91." There had already been cuts in departmental spending, but his target could be achieved only through considerable reductions in the transfer of billions of dollars in cash annually to the provincial governments in support of a host of federal-provincial programs. Even with limiting the rate of growth of transfers to the provinces to provide savings of about $2 billion to the treasury by 1991, transfers were expected to grow by about 5 per cent per year. The only other major expenditure reductions of any significance that would allow the minister to reach his goal would have meant targeting universality in social programs and the indexation of selected programs designed to protect individuals against inflation. It was not felt possible to tamper with the principle of universality in social programs, but indexation might be a different matter. That is where the government turned its attention.

In his budget of 23 May 1985, Wilson announced that family allowances and old age security would increase in the future only to cover annual changes in the consumer price index (CPI) in excess of 3 per cent. This would save the government, faced with a projected deficit of $33.8 billion on spending of $105 billion, $2 billion by 1990–91. While, for several days, the budget seemed to be well received, a crescendo of protest soon spread across the country, particularly from those groups representing senior citizens. Wilson tried to show that the de-indexing would not apply to the Guaranteed Income Supplement paid to 1.3 million pensioners, but, all the same, it would expose basic old age security to inflation increases below 3 per cent. The 2.6 million old age pensioners of Canada stood to lose a total of $1,500 to $2,300 each over the following five years if inflation occurred at a rate in excess of 3 per cent each year.

It was clear that the indexation of tax (and social benefits) during the previous twelve years had been a major contributor to the national deficit and that, by cutting back on indexing, the government lessened the risk that inflation would return to the levels of the 1970s. However, the government was accused of favouring business and the rich at the expense of the poor, and the outrage generated in support of pensioners was especially difficult to handle. The cabinet's choice was to back off or alienate elderly Canadians, who even then accounted for more than 20 per cent of the electorate. Mulroney was under tremendous pressure, harassed and harangued by pensioners when he entered or left the Parliament Buildings, and all Tory caucus members felt the heat both in Ottawa and at home.

The P&P committee was divided on whether the proposals should be withdrawn. The question was whether the government would suffer greater damage by maintaining its position on indexing or reversing it. Believing that it would send the wrong signal while also weakening our determination and undermining future efforts to restrain spending, I argued against any change in the budget's proposals for de-indexing, as did Robert de Cotret, Marcel Masse, Erik Nielsen, and Sinclair Stevens. Joe Clark, Flora MacDonald, and others argued that we surrender on the issue and restore full indexing. Wilson failed to hang tough as minister of finance, and so the cautious won the day. The prime minister had concluded that his government could not defend the budget with respect to the elderly poor so we threw in the towel and restored indexing. This was damaging in the longer term since it became clear as a result that the government lacked the necessary will to slash spending and bring the annual deficits under control despite the consequences of not doing so. On 27 June 1985 the government backed down publicly, and Wilson restored full indexation of pensions.

The most important policy development of the Mulroney era was the decision to negotiate a free-trade agreement with the United States, which not only resulted in the historic Canada-U.S. Free Trade Agreement (FTA) but led the way for a wider North American Free Trade Agreement (NAFTA) with the United States and Mexico. The successful conclusion of the NAFTA negotiations and GATT's acceptance of a proposal for a New World Trade Organization based on the constitution put forward by Canada were great achievements in the field of trade for Mulroney. The negotiation of a free-trade agreement with the United States was a policy initiative of the prime minister himself and, so far as I can remember, he did not discuss it with his cabinet or the P&P committee until after he had publicly proposed taking such a step. I was particularly delighted with this initiative since I had called for just such a trade agreement in the leadership campaign, when Mulroney had opposed it. The prime minister named Simon Reisman as chief negotiator for the free-trade deal with the United States on 8 November 1985 and the agreement was concluded successfully in the fall of 1987.

Another important policy initiative during the second Mulroney term, but one that certainly did not win the government electoral support in

1993, was the introduction of the Goods and Services Tax (GST). This was an initiative of the minister of finance and his department and was debated for a considerable time in P&P because of its obvious political sensitivities. There was no question that the Manufacturers' Sales Tax, which it would replace, was an economically damaging tax since it applied to our exports. A GST, such as other countries had initiated, was necessary to gain the necessary revenues to continue meeting the expanding expenditures of the government of Canada and to balance taxation revenues more equitably between those who paid income taxes and those who paid taxes primarily when they purchased goods and services. After much debate and with the clear knowledge of the risks being taken – which we did not think could be avoided – the GST was introduced into Parliament, and pushed through, despite vigorous opposition both in the House of Commons and the Senate. This was a major and essential reform of the Canadian taxation system but, clearly, not one that was popular. The Liberals, with their usual cynicism, announced that they would oppose the GST and repeal it if elected but, as expected, once in power after 1993, they reversed their stand on the tax since they were not in any position to forego the huge revenues accruing from it in the face of their newfound determination to reduce or eliminate the annual deficit.

Constitutional change and reform was another important policy with which the Mulroney government had to deal. Again, this issue was made particularly difficult as a result of the constitutional changes the Trudeau government had forced through Parliament despite the absence of Quebec's support. When, in the fall of 1985, Robert Bourassa, at a meeting of the Quebec Liberals, set out five conditions as a basis for accepting the repatriated constitution and Charter of Rights, and was subsequently elected as premier, there was an opportunity to continue the constitutional negotiations. On 30 April 1987 Prime Minister Mulroney and the premiers, meeting in the Gatineau Hills, reached an agreement that became known as the Meech Lake Accord. A package of six constitutional amendments, including Bourassa's five conditions and a recognition of Quebec as a distinct society, was agreed upon. The accord was quickly approved by Parliament and the Quebec National Assembly, with the rest of the provinces having until 22 June 1990 to give their legislative assent. The events that followed are covered elsewhere in this book, including the failure of New Brunswick and Manitoba to ratify the accord and the decision of Newfoundland, led by Premier Clyde Wells, to rescind its earlier ratification. For the purposes of this chapter, it is sufficient to say that these constitutional issues were dealt with principally by the prime minister, the minister of justice, and other advisers to the prime minister, with the rest of the ministers giving what assistance they could in their respective provinces during the ensuing year. The other ministers closely involved in the process were Joe Clark and Senator Lowell Murray, both of whom played a pivotal role in attempting to change the constitution, an effort that ended with the defeat of the Charlottetown Accord in the referendum of 1992.[15]

A major innovation in government policy in the Mulroney era was the creation of three new development agencies to facilitate regional economic growth and the direct delivery of federal regional programs in Canada: the Atlantic Canada Opportunities Agency (ACOA), promised in the throne speech on 1 October 1986; the Northern Ontario Development Board (FED-NOR); and the Western Diversification Office (WDO). All were given a quasi-autonomous status, but ACOA had the most independence, since it was headed by a president and not a deputy minister. Each agency was assigned to a senior minister from the relevant region, however. Senator Lowell Murray was assigned to ACOA, and I reported for the agency to the House of Commons. ACOA was designed with a view to preserving, as far as possible, the integrity of the agency's means of evaluating individual applications for assistance, while meeting the needs of federal visibility and the electoral needs of ministers. The original suggestion that the delivery of programs be left to the provinces was not accepted. Delivery of programs and visibility were of paramount importance.

To help ensure that ACOA would not lapse into a slush fund, an ACOA advisory board was created, with board members selected in part by the four regional ministers in consultation with the provincial premiers. The initial board consisted of four provincial civil servants and fifteen business people. Only ten of the members were known Conservatives or Liberals and the rest were neutral. The board was valuable in discussing policy initiatives and in advising on individual cases so that the allocation process was originally non-partisan. Applications for less than $1 million were handled by the provincial ACOA office, those between $1 million and $5 million by ACOA headquarters in Moncton, and amounts over $5 million to a maximum of $20 million directly by the minister, but with the assessment and advice of the advisory board.

In fisheries policy, ministers in the Mulroney administration were involved in creating policy particularly to alleviate the effects on people's lives of the great crisis that resulted in 1992 with the closure of the cod fishery of Atlantic Canada. The problems of the fishery, principally the destruction of fish stocks, developed after the end of the Second World War as a result of the development of a world deep-sea fishing fleet consisting of factory freezer trawlers that could travel long distances finding, catching, freezing, and processing fish stocks. It is now possible, with modern technology, to find and catch every fish swimming in the oceans of the world if the necessary time and effort and investment are put into it.

The difficulties of managing the fishery occur primarily because the fishery itself continues to be a common property resource with all the problems of control and regulation that this involves for the people in charge of administering it. By the end of 1991, there had been a severe depletion of fish stocks, particularly in connection with the cod fishery and other fisheries off the east coast of Canada. For hundreds of years, the cod fish has been the most valuable food item in the history of international trade. In Newfoundland, the fishery in the early 1990s accounted for only 10 per cent of the gross provincial product but 25 per cent of all employment. It was also of great importance in the economies of the other three Atlantic provinces. In the years from 1988 to 1991, the quotas for the catching of northern cod and other cod species were reduced sharply, as were the quotas for other fish stocks. But, in the first four months of 1992, it became obvious that, for the cod species to survive, it was no longer just a question of reducing the total allowable catches (TAC) of cod and other species, but that the cod fishery itself would have to be closed completely for a considerable period of time. The difficulties of preventing over-fishing within Canada's 200-mile economic zone were great enough but it was impossible to stop over-fishing by foreign fishermen in the international waters on the nose and tail of the Grand Banks. The northern cod off the coast of Newfoundland and Labrador had been exploited by Europeans and other fishermen since 1481, and it had been the economic foundation for the settlement and growth of all coastal communities in Newfoundland, but particularly those along the east and northeast coast of Newfoundland and the coast of Labrador. Without those stocks of cod there would have been no Newfoundland as a British colony, a dominion, or a province of Canada. In the hundred years from 1850 to 1950, the cod fishery sustained an annual catch off Newfoundland averaging from 200,000 to 250,000 tonnes, without any obvious signs of decrease, but by the middle of the twentieth century new fishing technology had permitted the deep-sea fishery and the mid-shore fishery to increase the catch of fish tremendously, so that in 1968 a peak was reached of 800,000 tonnes of cod taken mostly by distant water fishermen from the Soviet Union, Germany, Spain, and Portugal.

The stocks could not sustain such intense fishing and it finally became obvious that no one really knew how many fish were out in the vast areas of ocean where fish were taken and that not even the marine scientists had more than a rudimentary notion of what proportion of the stock or biomass could be taken annually without causing the resource to go into decline and disappear. Space does not permit more detail here but both Canadian fishery scientists and the European scientists from the North Atlantic Fisheries Organization (NAFO) advised NAFO and the minister of fisheries of

Canada in April 1992 that the TAC for northern cod that year had to be reduced to 50,000 tonnes, which meant there could be no inshore cod fishery off the northeast coast of Newfoundland and Labrador. The survival of the species was at stake. As the minister of fisheries at the time, I had only until the end of June to devise a program to assist upwards of 20,000 fishermen and fish-plant workers in two to three hundred communities in Newfoundland and the Maritime provinces who would be left without work or income during the remainder of 1992 and for the indefinite future.

This was a time when the Canadian civil service was put to its greatest test in developing assistance policies to deal with the tide of human misery and economic deprivation that would ensue once the closure of the fishery was announced at the end of June. Deputy Minister Bruce Rawson and his chief aide, the associate deputy minister for policy, Mary Antonett Flumiam, went to work on an economic assistance plan with departmental officials and the help of the central agencies of the government. A special subcommittee of the cabinet was appointed by the prime minister under the sensitive chairmanship of Senator Lowell Murray to determine what kind of an assistance program could be devised to deal with the greatest crisis ever in the Atlantic fishing industry. For the first time in five hundred years, the northern cod fishery would be stopped, while haddock, pollock, and other stocks were at their lowest levels ever.

The special cabinet subcommittee met to devise a financial-support program that would be made public and put in place when I announced the closure of the northern cod fishery. This had to be done despite the continuing need to reduce the deficit. Despite several months of hard work, I was unable to convince my colleagues that the amount of assistance they were prepared to approve was woefully inadequate from either a political or a humanitarian point of view. On 2 July 1992 I announced a meagre assistance package and a moratorium on the Atlantic cod fishery at a press conference in St John's. Fishermen and fish-plant workers affected by the closure would receive $225 a week each for ten weeks until a longer-term and more comprehensive relief plan could be developed. It was obvious to me that $225 a week would be treated with contempt, and it was. Pandemonium broke out at the press conference in St John's, broadcast on CBC television across Canada.

The reaction in St John's and the TV coverage had a powerful effect on my cabinet colleagues and within two weeks I was authorized to return to Newfoundland to announce a revised northern cod adjustment and recovery program (NCARP), known to all as the "package." Under the package, the compensation ranged from a minimum of $225 a week to a maximum of $406. Applicants for assistance who did not wish to take any training at all received the minimum. Workers who opted for training inside or outside the fishery could receive up to the $406 maximum. Provision also was made later for payments for the retirement of licences of fishermen who left the fishery. Within eight months, 18,000 compensation forms had been processed, with 10,768 applicants choosing training inside the fishery, 2,045 choosing training outside the fishery, and 1,600 opting for early retirement. The traditional free entry into the fishery had to be changed and entry thereafter severely controlled.

The NCARP program, later called the Atlantic Groundfish Strategy (TAGS), fostered considerable change in the fishery; it provided training and assistance to tens of thousands of fishermen and fish-plant workers, and was a tremendous success. This was a complicated humanitarian-assistance program, which had had to be developed quickly over several months. It was a magnificent achievement on the part of the bureaucrats involved, from the deputy minister and associate deputy minister of the Department of Fisheries to the rest of the civil service. The policy was developed in emergency circumstances at my urging and with the support of the prime minister.

At the same time as these unprecedented difficulties were encountered in the Atlantic fishery, severe problems also developed in British Columbia, where the most valuable fishery on the Pacific Coast involves the five species of Pacific salmon. These fish have a two- to five-year cycle, from birth in the rivers, migration to the sea, and return to the same rivers to spawn and die, and, when they approach and concentrate off the river mouths, they are caught by large, modern fishing vessels, with the largest catches off the mouths of the Fraser and Skeena river systems. The salmon, either frozen or canned, are a valuable export for Canada. On the Pacific Coast, there is just one province to deal with, so there are fewer jurisdictional issues. But, even so, the picture is greatly complicated by the need for cooperation with the United States, since huge numbers of salmon returning from the Pacific each year swim first through American and then Canadian waters on their way to their home rivers. The fishery is also complicated by conflicts between the commercial fishermen who catch the salmon for processing and the recreational, or sports-fishing, industry, as well as by the question of Aboriginal fishing rights, which in recent years have been the subject of new and important decisions of the Supreme Court of Canada. (The court has recognized the Aboriginal fishery as having priority over all other fishing interests, though Aboriginal communities must observe conservation practices and regulations.) A new Aboriginal fisheries strategy was developed and approved by the cabinet in the late fall of 1991, resulting in a five-year, $135-million program.

During the first two years of the Mulroney government, the relationship between cabinet ministers and the prime minister and his office were not smooth or collegial. There was great tension between the staff of the PMO and ministers and their staffs. The attitude of PMO seemed to be that the prime minister's position and reputation had to be preserved and protected at all costs, and that the prime function of ministers was to serve that purpose since they were replaceable but the prime minister was not. Several years into his term, the prime minister reached beyond the ranks of early friends and supporters to bring Derek Burney from External Affairs to be his chief-of-staff. After that, the PMO began to function in a tight, organized, and disciplined way. Burney was a no-nonsense type of person who knew how to deal with persons to whom authority was delegated but who did not measure up. He brought to the PMO a firm hand, setting the agenda, delegating the workload, liaising with ministers, and creating an atmosphere where all could work towards common objectives. He obviously respected cabinet ministers and understood their importance in the system. He was a good man to work with, and the change in atmosphere continued when Stanley Hartt replaced him.

In January 1987 I had my own greatest clash with the PMO, one that became the most serious crisis of my political career. It all developed over a matter of policy in External Affairs in connection with our relationship with France. This subject was of great interest and concern to the prime minister and the PMO, particularly because of the separatist movement in Quebec and the rivalry that existed between Quebec and Ottawa for dominance in the relations between Canada and France. A new shining star in the Conservative universe, Lucien Bouchard, had been appointed by prime minister Mulroney as ambassador to France, with the goal of establishing good relations with that country and countering attempts by Quebec to gain French support for separation.

From my point of view and that of my province, the relationship with France was complicated by the fact that the two tiny French Islands of Saint-Pierre and Miquelon, off the south coast of Newfoundland, existed as part of metropolitan France, with the French, as a result, having certain fishing rights off the south coast of Newfoundland. France had had such rights for several hundred years since the Treaty of Paris ended the Seven Years' War in 1763. In rivalries and conflicts over fisheries and the right of France to catch various species off the south coast of Newfoundland, Newfoundlanders had always felt that, before Confederation in 1949, the government of the United Kingdom ignored their rights and interests, and so the relationship with France and its colony of Saint-Pierre and Miquelon with respect to fishing issues was a tremendously sensitive one in the province. This all became more tangled and complicated in 1977, when Canada, following the example of most of the international community, declared a 200-mile economic zone to protect our fisheries. France, for its part, claimed a 200-mile economic zone around Saint-Pierre and Miquelon, with the result that there was a large disputed area off the south coast of Newfoundland where it was unclear whether Canada or France had the right to control the fishery and determine total allowable catches or to explore for or exploit possible undersea mineral resources.

Negotiations regarding this matter were not made any easier by an agreement that the Trudeau administration had stupidly entered into with France in 1972 to govern fishing relations. That treaty gave the French metropolitan fishing fleet the right to send ten trawlers to fish in the Gulf of St Lawrence annually until the end of 1986 but did not specify any quotas for the French fishermen. If the two countries did not agree on the amount of quota the French could take, they had the right to go to international arbitration. The treaty, unbelievably, even gave French fishermen the right in perpetuity to take fish within Canada's 200-mile zone and to go to arbitration to have a quota determined if one could not be agreed on. This one-sided treaty had no termination date and would bind Canada forever unless the two countries agreed to terminate it. The Brian Peckford government in Newfoundland had already made it clear that the northern cod was a Newfoundland resource and the health of that stock was a top priority for the province. The provincial government did not want France to be allowed to take any northern cod regardless of treaty obligations. Canada wanted the boundary dispute referred to international arbitration, but France would not agree unless it received generous quotas for fish, including northern cod, within Canadian waters until the arbitration decision was reached. Since these negotiations were of immense interest to the Newfoundland fishing industry, to all of the fishermen and their union, to the provincial government, and to everyone living in Newfoundland, where the fishery dominates the culture and is the life blood of the rural economy, all were worried that Ottawa would "give away" too many Newfoundland fish at the expense of our local fishery in order to win an amicable settlement with France.

In view of this background, the various interested groups in Newfoundland had been fully consulted as the negotiations continued through 1986, with the fishing industry, the Fishermen's Union, and the provincial government supplying experts who attended the talks as advisers and observers. As the Newfoundland regional minister (I was also transport minister at the time), I was entitled to be fully consulted about these important negotiations with France, which were of the highest political priority in Newfoundland.

In mid-January 1987 the Canada-France negotiations broke down during meetings at Ottawa. The French negotiators returned to Paris but, unknown to me, External Affairs renewed contacts with them. It was suggested to the PMO that a deal could be made in which France would agree to arbitration if Canada agreed to "significantly increase" France's fishery quotas in Canadian waters after 1987. There was no way that I, or the government of Newfoundland, would have agreed to such a deal. External Affairs and the PMO were eager to send negotiators to Paris immediately, but they did not want to include anyone from the Newfoundland government or representatives of the Newfoundland fishing industry or fishermen. Nor did they want to send any officials from the federal Department of Fisheries and Oceans, since the French government had made it plain that their presence would not be welcome. I was not consulted about these proposals or the discussions regarding the trip to Paris. When I heard about the proposed trip, I contacted External Affairs Minister Joe Clark, who also knew nothing about it but said he would check for me. Later that day, he told me that the trip had been cancelled. On the following day, a Friday, I discovered through Department of Fisheries sources that the group had in fact gone to Paris.

The PMO official who was quarterbacking this operation was Fred Doucet. I spoke to him and expressed my alarm at what was happening but he assured me that the representatives of the province and the industry groups were not invited to Paris because it was only a technical meeting involving the drafting of language. He advised that the two Canadian negotiators were not empowered to sign any agreement binding on Canada and that the cabinet had to approve any agreement. On the following Monday morning, however, I learned with consternation that a binding agreement had been signed in Paris over the weekend under which Canada had given France an annual quota of northern cod during the arbitration period.

The anger and outrage in Newfoundland was horrendous. It was exactly the kind of ammunition Premier Brian Peckford needed to demolish the standing of the government of Canada in the province. The deceit, stupidity, and ham-handedness of the PMO and External Affairs had delivered me, as the regional political minister, into Peckford's hands. There was no one in Newfoundland who did not support Peckford in his opposition to the Paris agreement. I was ready to resign. The result of this blundering and duplicity was that I had to spend most of 1987 in a vicious civil war with the Peckford government. When Peckford went on province-wide television to attack the agreement and the Mulroney government, I had to go on TV to respond. When he sent a pamphlet to every household, I had to respond with a brochure explaining exactly what had happened, what was agreed at Paris, and how negotiations with France would be conducted in the future.

The measure of Mulroney as a leader and prime minister was that he understood immediately that this was a disastrous blunder by the PMO and External Affairs, causing untold political damage in Newfoundland in particular and in Atlantic Canada generally. I set out my complaints to him in a lengthy letter, stating that we owed the people of Newfoundland an apology (in fact, Deputy Prime Minister Mazankowski would later make a public apology on behalf of the federal government). I and the three other Tory MPs from Newfoundland met and were ready to resign if these actions were not repudiated. In a meeting with Mulroney, he agreed that I was to be fully involved with the External Affairs minister and the minister of fisheries and oceans in all further negotiations on these issues. He also agreed to state publicly that he particularly valued my advice in all matters affecting the Newfoundland fishery, as well as all other matters involving the people of Newfoundland and Labrador, and that no final agreement would be reached with France without my concurrence and without the support of the Newfoundland MPs in our caucus.

Mulroney shared my view that, if Newfoundlanders continued to have the impression that only Peckford and his provincial government truly represented their interests, we were finished as a political force in my province. I pointed out that our government could not properly govern or protect itself in Newfoundland unless I had the authority to deal with Peckford in the certain knowledge that the prime minister had delegated authority to me and would back me up. The prime minister subsequently sent me a very satisfactory, supportive letter, which was released to the press, affirming my role and authority. He made clear that "Canadian interests, not relations with France, are of primary consideration."[16] The prime minister knew I had been ready to resign and he gave me his support when I needed it most, and, as a result, my relationship with him grew more and more positive from that time on. He demonstrated his abilities as a leader when he reacted instantly in the right manner and admitted mistakes in his office and at External Affairs and made sure that France did not get its way. Later, the issue went to arbitration without pre-conditions and was decided basically in favour of Canada and Newfoundland.

This episode, when the PMO and the Department of External Affairs ignored the political minister representing Newfoundland and the united opinions of the provincial government, the provincial fishing industry, the fishermen's union, and just about every person resident in the province, illustrates, only too clearly, the greatly increased powers of the prime minister and the PMO in the modern governing of Canada. The power of the Canadian prime minister has grown as the Canadian political system has become more and more like that of the United States. Indeed, this is true even in the main area of government in Canada where the American example has not yet been imitated – Parliament. Unlike American congressmen and senators, who have considerable power and exercise great independence, Canadian MPs and senators can usually be ignored unless the government is in a minority position. The increase in party discipline and the influence of the prime minister and his main lieutenants has rendered Canadian parliamentarians virtually powerless.

Yet, despite the great increase in the powers of the prime minister and the PMO, the prime minister and his government – even with a strong majority – will suffer severely if his office does not know how to work with ministers and their staff and if its powers are not exercised wisely and with sensitivity and diplomacy. This was made clear by the number of ministerial resignations that occurred in the first two years of the first Mulroney government, as compared to later, when chiefs of staffs (first Derek Burney, then Stanley Hartt) with the necessary experience and skills were put in charge. The episode described above involving Canada-France relations demonstrates that Prime Minister Mulroney had empathy with his ministers and the ability to admit blunders in his own office and correct them when that became necessary. It also illustrates how the relationship between the PMO and ministers improved greatly after the first several years, when ministers were very vulnerable because of the way in which the PMO operated.

Another step taken by Mulroney that greatly improved the effectiveness of his cabinet and the relationship between ministers and the prime minister was his appointment of Don Mazankowski as the deputy prime minister. "Maz" was always unflappable, popular with all factions in the caucus, and a great help in resolving any crisis that arose. As I reflect on the Mulroney cabinets, particularly about its approach to policy generally, I realize how fortunate we were to have Maz as a sounding board and conciliator. I also realize – in fact, this had been clear to me since the leadership convention in 1983 – that Mulroney himself was the government's strongest asset. Through two mandates, Mulroney always listened to people, or at least appeared to be ready and willing to listen to them. He invariably gave the impression to his ministers and MPs that he was interested in their views in all aspects of government and politics. He was tireless on the telephone with all the members of his caucus or cabinet and also with those who organized and ran the party for him. In my own experience, whenever I needed to see the prime minister, I was able to do so, and whenever I needed assistance or support, he was forthcoming. He was a moderate conservative who believed, as I did, in the private sector's lead role in the creation of wealth in the country, and on social issues he was supportive of efforts to help those who could not help themselves.

And, as I think back on the Mulroney era, I am struck too by the prime minister's ability to attract to his side such first-class people as Joe Clark, Don Mazanskowki, Erik Nielson, Michael Wilson, Senator Lowell Murray, Jake Epp, and Harvie Andre – all very capable men and all highly regarded by their colleagues. Other strong performers in the cabinet were Robert de Cotret, Perrin Beatty, Barbara MacDougall, Jean Charest, Benoît Bouchard, Bill McKnight, Elmer MacKay, and Charlie Mayer. I found all of my caucus and cabinet colleagues to be motivated by a real interest in the process of government and by a sincere desire to improve life for the citizens of their country and for the regions from which they themselves came. An abler or more dedicated group of men and women could not be found than these colleagues with whom I worked, alongside the prime minister, for nine years.

## NOTES

1 John C. Crosbie, *No Holds Barred – My Life in Politics* (with Geoffrey Stevens) (Toronto: McClelland and Stewart 1997), 249.
2 Donald J. Savoie, *The Politics of Public Spending in Canada* (Toronto: University of Toronto Press 1990), 38.
3 I held the following portfolios over the course of the Mulroney government's two mandates: Justice (1984–86); Transport (1986–88); International Trade (1988–91); and Fisheries (1991–93).
4 Ibid., 39.
5 Ibid., 349.
6 Herman Bakvis, *Regional Ministers – Power and Influence in the Canadian Cabinet* (Toronto: University of Toronto Press 1991).
7 Ibid., 288.
8 The Treasury Board is the oldest and a very important cabinet committee with control over expenditures. Other committees included communications, legislation and house planning, security and intelligence, and public service, as well as a special committee of council that handled all routine issues requiring governor-in-council approval.
9 Erik Nielsen, *The House Is Not a Home* (Toronto: Macmillan of Canada 1989), 217–24.
10 An enormous amount of my time as well as that of the other members of the committee in the first two years of the Mulroney administration was taken up attending meetings of this task force. Since I was the only representative of spending departments rather than of central agencies, I often had a different viewpoint on the proposals made for reduction of spending.
11 The atmosphere was not at all comparable to that surrounding Paul Martin when he became minister of finance in 1993, since he reduced and slashed government spending with the support of the opposition parties, particularly the Reform Party.
12 See Bakvis, *Regional Ministers.*
13 The designated political ministers were Michael Wilson for Ontario and Marcel Masse for Quebec, each heading a committee of political ministers from their provinces because of their size, while in the other provinces the political ministers designated were Pat Carney (British Columbia), Donald Mazankowski (Alberta), William McKnight (Saskatchewan), Jake Epp (Manitoba), Gerald Merrithew (New Brunswick), Elmer MacKay (Nova Scotia), Thomas McMillan (P.E.I.), and John Crosbie (Newfoundland).

14 See Bakvis, *Regional Ministers,* especially chapter 10.

15 In that referendum, 63 per cent of Newfoundlanders voted in favour of the accord despite the failure of Premier Wells to support the "yes" side. But not enough Canadians in other provinces agreed, with the result that the referendum failed and the accord died.

16 See Crosbie, *No Holds Barred,* 265.

# 17

# The Complexity of Brian Mulroney: A Reflection

BOB RAE

When my bother David died in June 1989, the first call the following morning was from Brian Mulroney. I was then the opposition leader in Ontario, and he was prime minister of Canada. We had met a few times but did not really know each other well. The call had an impact then; it still does today. It was genuine, and sympathetic, as two men chatted briefly on loss and the hardness of life's turns. Later, when I was elected premier of Ontario in September 1990, his call was again the first the following morning, as it would be at the moment of our government's defeat in 1995. It is impossible to write about Brian Mulroney as prime minister without dealing with the extraordinary reach of his personal charm. Many would write it off as self-serving, but that would fail to understand his ability to break through formalities and touch both his supporters and his opponents. He made the telephone calls because he wanted to, because reaching out and talking was an essential part of his nature.

The complexity of the Brian Mulroney is that, in English at least, he was two people. In private he was funny, personal, and often profane. He loved to tell stories and listen to jokes. No one who sat next to him at dinner has ever come away thinking less of his charm and presence. At the same time, his public persona became increasingly formal, as if he was forced to be on his best behaviour. I was always struck by the vehemence of the opposition he aroused – there was no indifference. Indeed, there is no indifference to this day. That he has remained more popular in Quebec than in the rest of the country may be due at least in part to the simple fact that there was no such double act in French – his linguistic personality was consistently engaged and colloquial.

One of many ironies about his political career is that he started his tenure as Progressive Conservative leader by determinedly pulling the party to the ideological centre. While Liberal leader and Prime Minister John Turner hemmed and hawed on the language issue in Manitoba, for

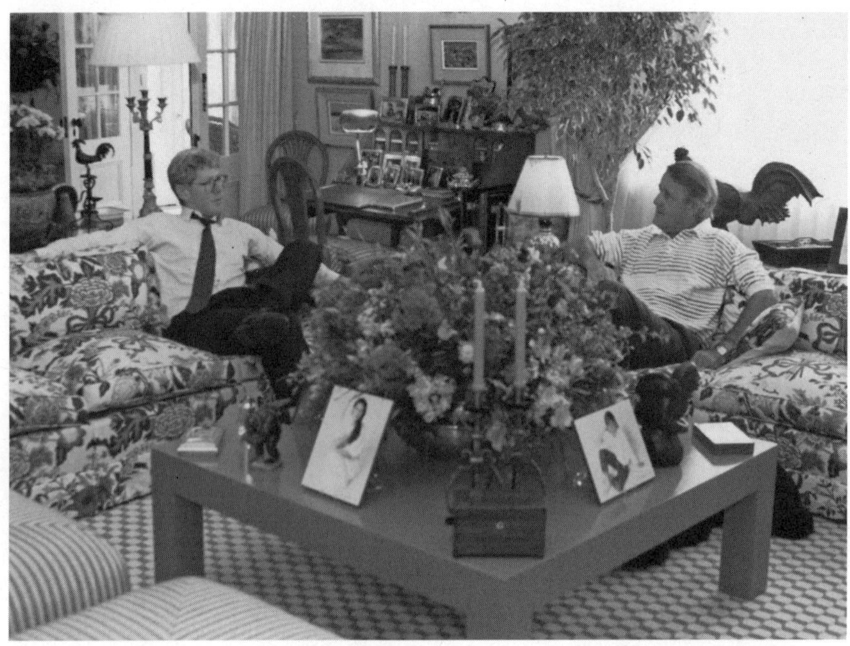

Brian Mulroney and Bob Rae at Harrington Lake, the prime minister's official summer home, discuss constitutional renewal in the aftermath of the failure of the Meech Lake Accord. Photographer Bill McCarthy. Library and Archives Canada 91-C-9991-7, negative number e007140473.

instance, Mulroney, with one eye on history and another firmly on Quebec, made it clear that he was four-square for bilingualism. He was not going to allow the Liberals to outflank him.

Mulroney presented himself to the country as a better successor to Pierre Trudeau than John Turner. Campaigning with Premier Bill Davis through Ontario in 1984, he let everyone know that social programs were safe, and that the enlightened capacity for reform and change that people associated with the Big Blue Machine would soon be in place in Ottawa. The campaign was not flawless, however. Dalton Camp's famous comment that Mulroney might be able to give up booze and cigarettes but couldn't shake hyperbole spoke to a trait that would later contribute mightily to the steady erosion in his public support – what seemed at first to be part of the blarney charm eventually gnawed away at his credibility. People didn't believe him.

But that was only a cloud on the horizon in 1984. Mulroney's mandate in that year was a tribute to his skill at presenting himself as a moderate of the centre. Just as John A. Macdonald had done in the middle of the nineteenth century, Mulroney taught the Conservatives the discipline of power. We would often joke with each other that it was not an easy task. There were many both in the New Democratic Party and among federal Tories who prefered the luxury of moral victories and the splendid warmth that comes from the comfort of correctness. But a party that fails to take power seriously will always be doomed to the margins of political life. Mulroney's whole being was about winning – he had no interest in leading a party that was incapable of grabbing, and then firmly holding on to, the prize of office.

The early negotiations with the premiers on constitutional change after 1984 spoke to his strengths as a mediator. He worked carefully with the team of the freshly reminted Liberal Premier Robert Bourassa to encourage Quebec to come forward with a limited number of constitutional changes. The premiers, meeting in Edmonton, agreed to a "Quebec Round" that would focus on these proposals and nothing else. What followed was a triumph of Mulroney's skills – the Meech Lake deal would not likely have been done without him – and a failure of ratification. The lengthy process in Manitoba reflected the second thoughts of the government of Howard Pawley and its social- democratic base. The elections of Liberals Frank McKenna in New Brunswick and Clyde Wells in Newfoundland and Labrador were even more problematic. McKenna wanted changes, but Wells's concerns were more root and branch.

The controversy over Meech led to the unravelling of the coalition Mulroney had crafted. While he won another mandate over the free-trade issue, his second term saw a collapse in his support as dramatic as Diefenbaker's twenty five years before. Preston Manning stole the populist underpinning right from under Mulroney's western support. Lucien Bouchard, whom the prime minister had wooed and nurtured to join him in Ottawa, repaid the kindness by putting a large shiv between the shoulder blades in 1990, an act of betrayal from which Mulroney never really recovered.

Donald Macdonald's Royal Commission on Canada's Economic Prospects – created by Prime Minister Pierre Trudeau – urged the government to take a leap of faith into a free-trade arrangement with the Americans. While Mulroney had expressed opposition to the idea in the Progressive Conservative leadership race and the subsequent election, he took the leap. Everything in his background drove him to it. He grew up in a community where the American-owned paper mill was the lifeblood of the town. He later took the job of shutting down an iron ore operation for an American company, and turned that task into a substantial political victory for him in Quebec. In his view, Trudeau had left Canada too isolated from the country that was our closest friend and the source of our economic life. Moreover, Ontario's economic nationalism left him cold. Just as his instinct to make a deal drove him to believe that he could persuade Quebec to accept the post-1982 constitution, he was convinced that, by establishing a uniquely close, integrated relationship with the Americans, Canada would get the best deal.

The detailed story of those negotiations on free trade has been told elsewhere in this book. What is clear is that it was Mulroney's personal determination to get a deal, and to go over the heads of the negotiators to do so, that in fact made it happen. All through the process, the central Canadian effort was to prevent Canada from being hit with unilateral decisions that would put our expanding access to the U.S. market in jeopardy. The Americans were equally determined that no foreign country be exempted from the application of U.S. sovereignty and U.S. law. What emerged at the end was substantially less than what we wanted: a dispute-resolution process that gave Mulroney some political cover but did not really go to the heart of the problem. Yet Mulroney had so committed himself to the objective that he could not possibly have walked away.

While trade with the United States has flourished, the free-trade deals – first with the United States alone (FTA), then with the United States and Mexico (NAFTA) – have not protected Canada from the excesses of American protectionism. We fared no better on softwood lumber under Mulroney than under Chrétien. Whether we're nice, stand-offish, or even churlish, it doesn't seem to matter: the Congress and the administration will put the interests of their farmers and producers ahead of those of anyone else, and that includes Canada. Yet, even so, the Canada-U.S. Free Trade Agreement itself, and subsequently NAFTA, has not had the permanently devastating effect that was predicted by its opponents. The border between Canada and the United States, contrary to that famous Liberal TV advertisement of the 1988 election campaign, has not disappeared, nor has the country's economy been laid waste. Ontario suffered a wrenching recession in the years after the agreement – we lost more than 300,000 jobs in a single year – but, with lower interest rates and a more realistically valued currency, we made a strong recovery in the years after 1993. The recovery was led by a significant increase in auto investment and exports to the United States. It is hard to gainsay the view of Canada's most famous economist, John Kenneth Galbraith, that freer trade around the world is part of the great trend of history.

The Liberals may have opposed the free-trade deal in 1988, but that did not lead them to change the broad direction of Mulroney's public policy on trade after 1993. On the contrary, they became great supporters of NAFTA and a free-trade deal for the Americas. Some would see this as a great betrayal. Others would call it growing up and accepting the prevailing realities of economic life.

David Peterson had set forth Ontario's free-trade concerns in the provincial elections of 1985 and 1987. He was Mulroney's ally on Meech

Lake. My own election in 1990 had much to do with the overvalued dollar, high interest rates, and dramatic job losses associated with branch-plant closures as a result of the free-trade deal. Apart from a jovial post-election call on 7 September 1990, my initial relationship with Mulroney was largely rhetorical. We had been promised a world-class training program to deal with the fallout from the trade deal. We got instead federal cuts directed at Ontario. This discrimination alone would cost us over ten billion dollars.

Ontario's inevitable budget deficit – in fact, the result of the curse of the recession, the high dollar, and inflated interest rates – was the subject of some Mulroney musings in Hong Kong. Demonstrations against the Goods and Services Tax (GST) gave rise to musings of my own. It was only in the summer of 1991 that I phoned Hugh Segal, one of Mulroney's advisers, at his cottage to discuss how things might be repaired. Many of my friends, advisers, and cabinet ministers might have wished that I had never done so.

But the depth of the constitutional impasse, and its consequences for the country, were too important to let partisan differences take over. Ontario did not set any conditions for our participation in the constitutional discussion which led to the Charlottetown Accord. Our view was that it had to be a broader discussion than that of the Meech Lake process, that the Aboriginal leadership had to be involved, and that it could not be a simple decentralization exercise. But we did not link the ending of financial discrimination against Ontario to being full partners in the constitutional process.

Once one enters the constitutional morass, it is impossible to emerge unscathed. That was certainly true for me, as it was for Mulroney. The Charlottetown process took a full year and a half, and was full of controversy and contention. But it was not until the referendum in the fall of 1992 that it became clear how far Mulroney had strayed from his western base. Charlottetown passed in Ontario, barely, failed in Quebec, and was trounced in the west. Its defeat was the last straw. Mulroney announced his departure early in 1993. His successor, Kim Campbell, led the party to an unprecedented defeat, two seats in the fall 1993 election that gave Jean Chrétien his first majority.

Pierre Trudeau often expressed the thought that Mulroney made the fatal error of opening a constitutional Pandora's box in 1985, that everything was fine after patriation, and that the Tories alone brought the country to the brink of disaster. This ignores certain inconvenient facts. No elected government in Quebec could let the issue lie after patriation. Mulroney did not "create" the resentment in Quebec. It was there, and had to be dealt with. The process was messy, and ultimately unsuccessful. But it had to be tried. And the end conclusions of the Charlottetown

Accord – an elected Senate, a clear constitutional direction for discussions with First Nations, some devolution, and a policy on the social union, as well as the key features of Meech on distinct society and the appointment of judges – amounted to the most comprehensive constitutional package ever agreed to by all the premiers and the Aboriginal leadership of the country. It was, ultimately, turned down by the people. The issues and challenges have not miraculously disappeared, however.

The Liberals did not repeal the GST. They did not end NAFTA. Continental integration on the economic side proceeded apace. An export-led recovery eventually allowed the Liberals to end years of deficit spending. The near disaster of the 1995 referendum forced a series of changes that have now given every part of the country an effective veto over constitutional change. The threat of secession is still with us. Chrétien's style, and substance, in the matter of U.S.-Canada relations was quite different. The same cannot be said of his early social and economic policies. They amounted to a confirmation of the direction set in the Mulroney years and the policies he followed.

Mulroney took great pride in being the first Conservative leader since Macdonald to lead his party in two successful elections. He did not lead the party into the third, and that turned into a rout which marginalized the party for a decade. The coalition he put together has yet to be reconstructed; however, the new Conservative Party – formed from a merger of the Canadian Alliance and the Progressive Conservatives – took a step in that direction when, under Stephen Harper's leadership, it won a minority victory in the 2006 general election, putting an end to the electorally disastrous split that had given the Liberals a free ride in three elections. Mulroney's legacy, and accomplishments, will always be hotly contested. He knew more than a little of the fickleness of public affection and support, how quickly the tide can turn. He never succeeded in making Canadians fully comfortable with the great directions of his policies. Free trade, more power to the provinces, closer ties to the United States – the "triple threat" in the eyes of many. It's almost as if Canadians are saying, "We know it has to happen, but let's not celebrate it."

When Richard Nixon left office, he quoted these words of Theodore Roosevelt: "It is not the critic who counts, not the one who points out how the strong man stumbled … The credit belongs to the man who is actually in the arena, whose face is marred with sweat and dust and blood; who strives valiantly … who, if he wins, knows the triumph of high achievement; and who, if he fails, at least fails while daring greatly." Brian Mulroney was certainly in the arena. He knew both triumph and defeat. And he touched both his friends and his opponents.

But how to assess his legacy? The controversies surrounding his life after leaving office have added another dimension to the mix. The process of separating fact from fiction is still not over. He was the subject of a lengthy RCMP investigation, which was followed by tempestuous publicity, a lawsuit for defamation brought by Mulroney, and a subsequent apology from the national police force. His reputation was hurt by the later revelation that he had accepted $300,000 in cash from Karl-Heinz Schreiber, as payment for advice about the pasta business in Canada. Schreiber was a lobbyist involved in both the Airbus transaction and the potential purchase by the Canadian government of helicopters. Mulroney was wounded, fought back, and was vindicated. But the fight has had its effect. Mulroney has successfully pursued a career as an adviser to the corporate world, and is a strong presence in the United States. He spoke at Ronald Reagan's funeral, which placed him high in the Conservative pantheon in North America. He remains close to the Bush family and continues to have great access to political leaders around the world.

And yet he is no Thatcherite. On South Africa, for example, Mulroney charted a course for Canada that followed Diefenbaker's leadership in expelling the apartheid regime from the Commonwealth. No political leader did more to bring the Commonwealth together in its efforts to change the politics of southern Africa. Together with Bob Hawkes of Australia, a labour leader with whom Mulroney established an immediate rapport, Canada firmly parted company with Margaret Thatcher and the United States, and continued to maintain sanctions and all the other steps that contributed to the release of Nelson Mandela from prison. It was a role that was completely genuine, deeply felt, and profoundly reciprocated by Mandela himself. It should not go unnoticed in any assessment of the legacy of this complex man.

# 18

# Prime Minister Brian Mulroney in Perspective

L. IAN MACDONALD

The election of a Conservative government on 4 September 1984, constitutes, in and of itself, a major piece of Brian Mulroney's service to Canada and his legacy as prime minister. Just getting himself elected was half the job. As with John Diefenbaker in 1957 and 1958, Mulroney broke the back of a Liberal dynasty and provided the political change so essential to Canadian democracy. Like Diefenbaker before him, he made Canadian politics competitive again by offering a credible mainstream alternative to the Liberals and thereby ending, or at least interrupting, their governance of Canada as a one-party state. In 1984, as in 1957, the Liberals had been in office for more than twenty years (interrupted only by the Clark interregnum in 1979), and their dynastic pretensions were a wonder to behold. Mulroney made electoral history again on 21 November 1988, when he became the only the second Conservative leader since Sir John A. Macdonald, and the only one other than Sir Robert Borden in the entire twentieth century, to win a second consecutive majority mandate. In the 1988 election, he secured the voters' approval to implement the Canada-U.S. Free Trade Agreement (FTA), the biggest achievement of his nine years in office.

Neither the degree of difficulty in winning either election nor their importance should be underestimated by historians, though Mulroney made winning both contests look easy. Relegated to near-permanent opposition status, riven by constant internal battles, marginalized by the narrowness of their base, the Progressive Conservatives were Canada's natural opposing party. They were – not to put too fine a point on it – a bunch of losers. Mulroney made them into winners in 1984 by taking them where they needed to go to win – to the centre of the political spectrum, into the cities, and into Quebec. A party of the far right, of rural Canada, of English Canada, and the west became a party of the centre right, of urban Canada, of French Canada, and the east, sweeping Ontario and Quebec.

This political cartoon, which appeared in Canadian newspapers at the beginning of discussions over the legacy of Prime Minister Jean Chrétien in 2002, shows how policies of the Mulroney government continued into the Chrétien period. Malcolm Mayes, 2002-11-20, image number MAY778, Artizans.

"My job is to get the party elected," he said after winning the Conservative leadership from Joe Clark in 1983. He saw his first task as uniting a caucus and a party that had been at war with itself since Diefenbaker's time. Then he sought to put a moderate face on the Progressive Conservative Party by supporting a Liberal resolution on French-language minority rights in Manitoba. An issue he knew by heart, from the heart, became his first test of party unity. "I'm sorry the caucus can't be unanimous on this," Dan McKenzie, a right-wing Manitoba MP told him. "My caucus will be unanimous," Mulroney icily replied. And it was.

Going into the campaign in the summer of 1984, Mulroney knew the underlying issue was change. But he chose to frame the ballot question differently. "The issue is competence," he said repeatedly. The voters could judge an opposition party's competence to govern only by the competence of its campaign. The discipline of Mulroney's campaign, from the leader's tour to the costing of his promises, presented a remarkable contrast to the

Turner campaign, which unravelled badly after Mulroney decisively won the French and English leaders' debates on 24 and 25 July. Mulroney was in Hamilton on 26 July when he took a call from his pollster, Allan Gregg, informing him there had been a "startling" overnight reversal of public opinion in his favour in Quebec. In August, polls that showed him winning Quebec helped him close the deal in Ontario, where voters prefer national parties with support in both English and French-speaking Canada. In the end, Mulroney won fifty-eight of seventy-five Quebec seats, including his own, Manicouagan, and his hometown of Baie Comeau on the North Shore. He had often spoken of Sir John A. Macdonald's "Grand Alliance, English and French, East and West." In 1984 he created his own, calling it "a new Conservative majority."

Repeating the feat in 1988 was no mere re-election of a government for a second term, but a watershed election that was transformed into a plebiscite on free trade. It was the last election in Canada about something that mattered. It was more, much more, than a question of economics or international trade. It was not just "a commercial agreement," as Mulroney himself rather disingenuously claimed in the leaders' debate with Liberal leader John Turner. "I believe you have sold us out," Turner said in that famous exchange. In that moment, it became a question of identity, of country, of Canadian sovereignty.

It was, as John Duffy would write in *Fights of Our Lives,* his fascinating book on landmark Canadian elections, "mano a mano" between Mulroney and Turner. Turner clearly tapped into something important – not just a normal fear of change, but a deep-seated insecurity of Canadians about the United States and a yearning to affirm Canada's independence. The timing of the debates, on 24 and 25 October, was no accident. "I wanted them early enough in the campaign that we would have time to recover in case we took a hit," Mulroney said many years later. Uniquely in the 1988 campaign, voters changed their minds twice, once when they moved away from free trade in October, and again when they moved back to it in November. Mulroney needed most of nearly four weeks between the debates and the election to turn his campaign around. Both leaders waged valiant campaigns, but it was Mulroney's vision that prevailed. In the end, he succeeded where Sir Wilfrid Laurier had failed in 1911 – he closed the sale with the voters on free trade between Canada and the United States.

I covered the 1984 campaign from the press section at the back of Mulroney's plane, and participated in the 1988 campaign from the staff section at the front. The perspectives were very different, but in both cases the outcomes were a result of Mulroney's formidable skills as a campaigner; he had the ability to make the case, stay on message, and close the deal. He also drove himself hard – in 1988 he made 110 speeches in 37 days on the road. Twenty years after his first victory, he said simply:

"You've got to want it bad." And he wanted it. He also had a gambler's instinct for living on the edge.

On 1 November 1988, as his Boeing 727 lifted off from Ottawa and headed for a crucial week of campaigning in the west, Mulroney said of Turner: "He's got the momentum – now we're going to find out what we're made of." Support for the Conservatives and free trade plummeted after the debate. Unless Mulroney made a strong case for free trade, he would lose. In Victoria a couple of days later, I was sitting on the PM's bus writing a speech for the next event, when our press secretary, Marc Lortie, came aboard.

"Do we have a copy of the Free Trade Agreement?" he asked.

"Sure," I replied. "Why?"

"Because Mulroney's going to debate a couple of hecklers," he explained. Actually, there were three of them, following Mulroney around and noisily disrupting his rallies.

"Over what?"

"Dispute settlement."

The dispute-settlement mechanism was at the heart of the agreement and had been Mulroney's deal breaker in the negotiations with the United States. On 1 October 1987, when the Americans wouldn't even consider it, the Canadian delegation flew home from Washington on Mulroney's orders. Back at the table in Washington on 3 October, they agreed to it only at the last minute, with the clock ticking towards a midnight expiration of President Reagan's congressional fast-track authority to negotiate free trade. Debating the hecklers was incredibly high-risk, a decision Mulroney made on the spot. He was putting three hecklers at the same table, and on the same footing, as the prime minister. There was also the risk that they would show him up.

"Does he know it that well?" I asked.

"We are," Lortie replied, "about to find out."

Asked about the incident in 2004, Mulroney replied: "Sure I knew it. I knew every nuance of it." Not only had he approved every step of the negotiations, he had been thoroughly briefed by officials on the contents of the FTA. He had even spent part of two weekends, before the campaign, reading the text at the PM's weekend residence at Harrington Lake. "I don't think it was known how hard I worked on this stuff," he said. As for spontaneous debate with the three hecklers, he said: "I knew it was high risk." Looking back on it sixteen years later, he agreed that "it was an important turning point in the campaign."

As it turned out, the sit-down with the hecklers was one of the defining moments of the campaign. Mulroney demonstrated a mastery of a complex file, and a strong conviction for the deal he was proposing. And three dissenting voices got to make their case, in a polite discussion with a prime minister. As Graham Fraser later wrote in *Playing for Keeps,* his definitive account of the 1988 campaign: "Mulroney seemed calm and sure of himself, while the critics of the deal appeared somewhat eccentric." It was a very civil, very Canadian moment. But make no mistake, it was an extraordinarily tough campaign, in which the momentous decisions were Mulroney's, and his alone, to make.

Twenty-four hours after the English leaders' debate, the Mulroney campaign was bedded down for the night in Toronto. In his suite at the Royal York Hotel, Mulroney watched on the news that his numbers had cratered overnight and decided that it was time to ditch his boy-in-the-bubble campaign and go on the attack. The next day, at a noon-hour speech in Toronto, he did, targeting the Liberal and New Democratic Party fear campaigns that free trade jeopardized old age pensions and universal public health care in Canada: "The tactics of Mr. Turner and Mr. Broadbent are shameful and dishonest," he said. "At the least, they are an attempt to hide the fact they offer no realistic alternatives, no plan of their own ... It is classic negative politics – if you shout long enough and loud enough about what you are against, perhaps people won't notice there is nothing you are for."

By the time Mulroney got to Victoria, he had sharpened the message and put the onus directly on Turner and Broadbent: "Mr. Turner, Mr. Broadbent," he asked, "where in the Free Trade Agreement is mention made of pensions or medicare? What article in the Free Trade Agreement allows you to say that pensions and medicare are affected? The opposition leaders are now bound to answer these simple, straightforward questions in a simple, straightforward way." Instead of making it about him, he managed, as do all successful campaigners, to make it about it them. He also had a leader's instincts, and an unfailing sense of occasion. When the prime minister's tour rolled into Kingston on 30 October, hundreds of protesters greeted his bus as it rolled up to the Holiday Inn. Advised that noisy demonstrators awaited the PM's arrival, the RCMP officer aboard his bus asked if they could detour and go in by the back door.

"No," Mulroney said, "we go in by the front door." When the bus pulled up, Mulroney was greeted by cries of "traitor" and "sell-out," and the crowd angrily jostled the prime minister, his wife, Mila, and their entourage, as they entered the hotel – by the front door. It was that kind of campaign – intense, impassioned, and important.

Mulroney and Diefenbaker were both exceptional campaigners, who successfully positioned the Progressive Conservative Party where the votes were – in the cities, among francophones and multicultural Canadians. Having attained their mandates, the question for historians to consider is what they did with them. Diefenbaker is widely regarded as having squandered his historic 1958 landslide, especially in terms of federal-provincial and Canada-U.S. relations, deemed by many to be the top two files on a prime minister's desk. Yet a revisionist case can be made in his favour – his 1960 Bill of Rights was a precursor to the 1982 Charter of Rights and Freedoms; his appointment of Emmett Hall as head of the Royal Commission on Health Care led to Medicare; his appointment of Vincent Bladen's commission on the auto industry led to the Auto Pact; he brought Canada into North American Air Defence (NORAD). Even viewed as a transitional figure, there is no doubt of his significance. Equally, there is no denying his importance among leaders who offered Canadians the fresh air of change after an era of dynastic stagnation.

In Mulroney's case, the question is what he did with two historic mandates – 211 seats out of 282 in 1984, and 169 seats out of 295 in 1988. His answer is simple. "We made history," he said in 2004, twenty years after his first election. "We made a lot of history." And did he ever. By the time he left office in 1993, there is no doubt that Canadians were happy to see the back of him. But, unlike Diefenbaker, Mulroney hadn't wasted any of his political capital with the voters, he had spent it. And then some. In modern times, only Prime Minister Pearson left a fuller legislative legacy. Like Pearson's achievements on domestic social policy, Mulroney's economic record should be appraised not for its parts but for the whole. Free trade, the Goods and Service Tax (GST), deregulation, and privatization of crown corporations were all part of an ambitious agenda to restructure the Canadian economy and improve Ottawa's fiscal framework. The GST, despised by Canadians as a consumption tax, has proven highly successful as a replacement tax, creating a competitive advantage for Canadian exporters. Unlike the hidden 13.5 per cent Manufacturers' Sales Tax it replaced, the visible GST does not apply to exports, and it has been a significant factor in the growth of Canada's trade with the United States, as well as a huge cash cow that helped the Chrétien government balance the books after 1993. As for free trade, exports of $100 billion to the United States in the last year before implementation in 1988 had grown to $350 billion in 2002. By 2003, fully 50 per cent of Ontario's output was in exports to the United States.

As for the fiscal framework, Mulroney managed to achieve an operating surplus, with Ottawa taking in more than it spent, and reduced the deficit as a percentage of GDP from 8.6 per cent when he took office to 5.9 per cent when he left. But he never successfully attacked the deficit and consequently was never able to pay down a penny of the national debt, which more than doubled on his watch, most of it compound interest on debt accumulated by Pierre Trudeau. When Trudeau took office in 1968, Canada's debt after a century of Confederation, and two world wars, was $18 billion; when he left in 1984, the debt exceeded $200 billion, an increase of 1,100 per cent. As Mulroney said during the transition in

September 1984, after getting his first look at the books: "I wish the Grits had left us some money." Instead, he left the Liberals money in the form of the GST as well as corporate and personal tax receipts from economic activity resulting from free trade. By the reckoning of Pierre Pettigrew, when he was the minister of international trade in the Chrétien government, exports accounted for four new Canadian jobs in five between 1993 and 2000 – and more than 85 per cent of Canada's exports went to the United States.

Foreign policy also needs to be viewed as a whole. While relations with the United States were critical, other initiatives included the creation of la Francophonie, Canada joining the Organization of American States (OAS), and a leadership role in maintaining economic sanctions against South Africa's apartheid regime. These policies proved to be a counterweight to the preponderant Canada-U.S. relationship. Far from being a stalking horse for the United States in the OAS, Canada was welcomed to the hemispheric club for both its influence in Washington and its ability to differ with the United States, as Mulroney did on Ronald Reagan's funding of the Contras against Daniel Ortega's left-wing regime in Nicaragua, for instance. On South Africa, Mulroney pursued sanctions on apartheid, notwithstanding an amiable disagreement with Reagan and a heated one with Margaret Thatcher. Even his own foreign minister, Joe Clark, spoke of "sanctions fatigue" before the Commonwealth Heads of Government summit in Vancouver in October 1987. At the time, the *Globe and Mail* published an interview with unnamed External Affairs sources complaining of the prime minister's "adventurism" in foreign policy. "Thanks a lot," Mulroney said sarcastically as he read the piece in his suite at Vancouver's Pan Pacific Hotel. "Here I am going downstairs to meet Thatcher in ten minutes, and my own officials are accusing me of 'adventurism' in our national newspaper." But he never wavered on apartheid sanctions, and when Nelson Mandela came to Canada in 1990, he went out of his way in his address to Parliament to thank Canada and its prime minister for the role they had played in securing his release from prison.

Canada's relationship with the United States, and Mulroney's with President Reagan and the first President George Bush, will undoubtedly be an important chapter in any assessment of the Mulroney years. It is a measure of how close they became that Mulroney delivered one of the eulogies at Reagan's funeral in Washington in June 2004 – the first foreign dignitary ever to speak at the state funeral of an American president. The very next day, in Houston, Mulroney was guest speaker at the eightieth birthday of former President Bush. While he was widely flayed in office for being too close to the United States, the passage of time allows a more balanced assessment. Mulroney did not hesitate to agree with the Americans, but he did not hesitate to disagree with them, either. In March 1985 he politely declined to join the United States in Reagan's cherished Strategic Defense Initiative, the so-called Star Wars plan, partly on the ground that it was not in compliance with the Anti-Ballistic Missile Treaty of 1972. What chance did the Americans have to sell the idea to their European allies, faced with the prospect of massive protests against it, when they couldn't even sell it to the Canadians?

Nor was Nicaragua his only hemispheric disagreement with the Reagan-Bush White House. He strongly opposed U.S. extraterritoriality over U.S.-owned Canadian firms doing business in Cuba. On acid rain, Mulroney famously gave Vice-President Bush "an earful" over an issue that was finally resolved in 1991. Yet Mulroney managed to persuade Reagan to accept Canada's claims of Arctic sovereignty. The suggestion that Canada played a subservient role to the United States is just that – a suggestion, unsupported by the facts. And where Canada strongly supported U.S. leadership, to stand fast in the North Atlantic Treaty Organization (NATO) against the Soviet Empire, Mulroney's policy was consistent with that of Louis St Laurent and Lester B. Pearson. At the same time, Mulroney reached out to the new man in the Kremlin, and wished Mikhail Gorbachev well in his pursuit of glasnost and perestroika. As he said in a 1988 address to a joint session of the U.S. Congress, "Mr. Gorbachev is a reformer, and in the Soviet system there is much in need of reforming."

Perhaps for these reasons and more, Brian Mulroney emerged as a clear second choice among a panel of thirty leading historians, political scientists, economists, former senior government officials, and a sprinkling of top editors, authors, and journalists, who were asked by *Policy Options Politiques* to rank the Canadian prime ministers of the last half-century, coinciding with the fiftieth anniversary of the coronation of Queen Elizabeth on 2 June 1953.[1] The respondents were sharply divided, usually between English- and French-speaking Canada, in their assessments of Mulroney's failed constitutional deals at Meech Lake and Charlottetown. They gave Mulroney full marks for what is unquestionably his biggest achievement – the Canada-U.S. Free Trade Agreement, and later NAFTA, including Mexico. Yet, as one panellist, Kim Nossal, head of the Department of Political Studies at Queen's University and a contributor to this volume, observed, Mulroney may be "over-appreciated" for free trade and "under-appreciated" for the GST. Mulroney also received high scores – second only to Pearson – for Canada's role in the world, and for restoring good relations with the United States during the presidencies of Ronald Reagan and the first George Bush. Besides the trade agreements, bilateral achievements included the Acid Rain Accord. Many panellists also noted that, like Pearson and St Laurent, Mulroney often differed with the White House on important issues – from Star Wars, in which Canada declined to participate, to sanctions against apartheid in South Africa and the Rio Earth Summit, where Mulroney signed the biodiversity accord but Bush did not.

The panel differed sharply over Mulroney's legacy on Canadian unity and managing the federation. There was a clear difference of views, largely though not exclusively along language lines, on the necessity and value of Mulroney's two doomed constitutional initiatives – the Meech Lake Accord, which died in June 1990 when the legislatures of Newfoundland and Manitoba failed to call a vote as promised by their premiers, and the Charlottetown Accord, soundly rejected by voters in a 1992 referendum. While some panellists from English-speaking Canada saw Meech as an unnecessary initiative whose failure plunged the country into a prolonged unity crisis, our Quebec-based panellists, both francophone and anglophone, saw it quite differently. "He tried to repair the bridges between Canadians," said Jean Paré, former publisher of *l'Actualité*, Quebec's leading magazine, "but without immediate success."

On the economy and the fiscal framework, most panellists agreed Mulroney inherited a mess from Trudeau – from deficits and debt to state interventions through such policies as the National Energy Program. While Mulroney receives high marks for deregulation, tax reform, and employment growth in his first mandate, there is general agreement that he did not do enough to attack the staggering deficits left behind by his predecessor. The Conservative government eventually achieved an operating surplus and reduced the deficit as a percentage of economic output from 8.6 to 5.9 per cent, but, as already noted, the deficits remained and the national debt more than doubled again during the Mulroney years.

Still, Mulroney finished a clear second in the overall rankings, pulled up by his strong leadership scores. The panel overwhelmingly regarded him, along with Pearson and Trudeau, as one of three transformational leaders of the last fifty years. Twenty years almost to the day from his election, Mulroney's wife, Mila, organized a surprise party on the anniversary at their Montreal home. Looking back at his two terms in office, he told the one hundred invited guests: "I don't know how we did it." The long and the short of it is that he did significantly change Canada. In his first term, he took the centre and held it. In the second, he set the agenda and dominated it. In both, he made history.

## NOTES

1 The remainder of this chapter is adapted from L. Ian MacDonald, "The Best Prime Minister of the Last 50 Years – Pearson, by a Landslide,"*Policy Options Politiques* 24(6) (2003). Respondents were asked to rate prime ministers on a scale

of 1 to 10 (low to high), in four critical policy areas: Canadian unity and the management of the federation; the economy and the fiscal framework; Canada's role in the world, as measured by foreign and defence policy and international trade; and social policy and the concerns of Canadians. Panellists were then asked to evaluate how each prime minister found the country and how he left it, and to assess the leadership of each as transformational, transitional, or transactional. Finally, taking all of those factors into account, the panel members were asked to rank each prime minister from first to sixth place. Panellists worked independently and the scores were tabulated by Daniel Schwanen, a senior economist with the Institute for Research on Public Policy, Montreal. The study can viewed and downloaded at www.irpp.org.

# Index